ALSO BY CLAUDIA RODEN

Coffee: A Connoisseur's Companion
Mediterranean Cookery
The Good Food of Italy — Region by Region
Everything Tastes Better Outdoors
A Book of Middle Eastern Food

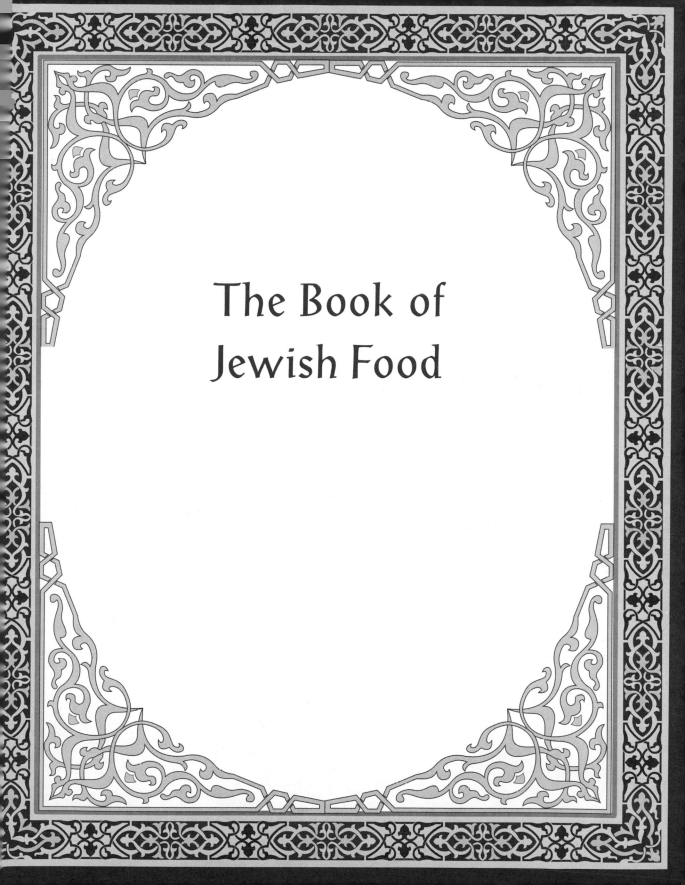

The Book of
Jewish Food

The Book of Jewish Food

AN ODYSSEY FROM

SAMARKAND TO NEW YORK

CLAUDIA RODEN

ALFRED A. KNOPF   *New York*   1996

THIS IS A BORZOI BOOK
PUBLISHED BY ALFRED A. KNOPF, INC.

Copyright 1996 by Claudia Roden

Grateful acknowledgment is made to the following for permission to
reprint previously published material:
CIS Publishers: Excerpts from *Pathway to Jerusalem: The Travel Letters of Rabbi
Obadiah of Bartenura*, translated by Yaakov Dovid Shulman, copyright © 1992
by CIS Publishers. Reprinted by permission of CIS Publishers.
Commentary and Allen Mandelbaum: The poem "From the Hungry, Praise"
by Immanuel ben Solomon of Rome, translated by Allen Mandelbaum
(New York: *Commentary*, 1951). All rights reserved. Reprinted by
permission of *Commentary* and Allen Mandelbaum.
International Universities Press, Inc.: Excerpts from *Life Is with People*
by E. Herzog and M. Zborowski (1952). Adapted by permission of
International Universities Press, Inc.

Library of Congress Cataloging-in-Publication Data
Roden, Claudia.
The book of Jewish food : an odyssey from Samarkand to New York /
by Claudia Roden.
p. cm.
Includes index.
ISBN 0-394-53258-9
I. Cookery, Jewish. I. Title.
TX724.R53 1996
641.5'676—dc2 96-28758
CIP

Manufactured in the United States of America
First Edition

*In memory of my parents, Nelly and Cesar Douek,
and my brother Zaki*

*For my children, Simon, Nadia, and Anna,
and my grandchildren, Cesar, Peter, and Sarah,
with love*

Contents

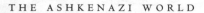

Acknowledgments

THE BEST PART of working on this book was meeting and getting to know people in many different countries. People gave me recipes, invited me to eat with them and to watch them cook, told me about their lives and those of their parents and grandparents, and about their trades. They sent me articles and other source material, lent me books and photographs, invited me to hear lectures and attend conferences, gave me all kinds of advice and information, and pointed me in the right directions. Having begun my research more than sixteen years ago, I am indebted to so many people that trying to acknowledge all those who have helped is impossible. But I would like them to know that their contributions have been precious and valued, that they have made the book what it is, and that they will always be remembered fondly and with enormous gratitude by me. Some will find their names in the text.

I would also like to thank my children, close friends, and other relatives who have encouraged me and sustained me with their enthusiasm for the project. Of these I have special thanks for my brother Ellis, my son-in-law, Clive Wolman, and my friends Ella Almagor and Sami Zubaida, all of whom read bits of first drafts, and for Danny Almagor, who found me poems and proverbs and references on Jewish law. I owe special thanks to my onetime neighbor Esra Kahn, librarian at Jews' College, London, who found me useful books and read and commented on my manuscript.

I have a special debt of gratitude to International Universities Press for allowing me to use material from *Life Is with People,* by Elizabeth Herzog and Mark Zborowski, and to Gerard

Sylvain for helping to choose photographs from his huge collection of Jewish postcards (he has more than fifty thousand) at the last moment, as we were going into print.

My warmest thanks are for my editor, Judith Jones, who encouraged me throughout the years, advised and guided me, and brought out the best in me, with sympathy and intelligence. I have fond memories of spending time with Judith and her wonderful husband, Evan: in New York, walking to their apartment from the office and meeting Evan halfway, stopping to pick up some goodies, standing in the kitchen while they cooked; at their home in Vermont, exploring the countryside, eating in grand style on the porch overlooking the lake after a swim; and in Paris, walking the streets with them and exploring the restaurants together. That was part of the pleasure of working on the book.

Introduction

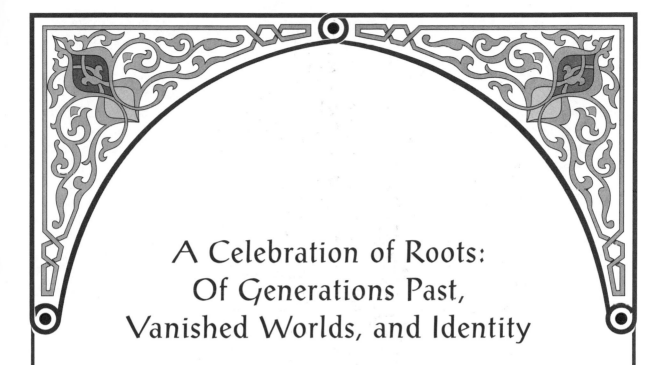

A Celebration of Roots:
Of Generations Past,
Vanished Worlds, and Identity

EVERY CUISINE tells a story. Jewish food tells the story of an uprooted, migrating people and their vanished worlds. It lives in people's minds and has been kept alive because of what it evokes and represents. My own world disappeared forty years ago, but it has remained powerful in my imagination. When you are cut off from your past, that past takes a stronger hold on your emotions. I was born in Zamalek, a district of Cairo with palm trees, pretty villas, and gardens with bougainvillea, scented jasmine, and brilliant red flowers we called "flamboyants." On the map it looks like a cocoon clinging to the banks of the Nile. For the first fifteen years of my life, it was the cocoon from which I never ventured unaccompanied. I lived in an apartment building with my parents; two brothers, Ellis and Zaki; and our Yugoslav-Italian nanny, Maria Koron. Awad, the cook, who came from

Lower Egypt, lived on the roof terrace, where servants had rooms. From the windows we could see the Nile and feluccas (sailing boats) gliding by. The sounds were the muezzin's call and the shouts of street vendors. It was a world full of people. It ended in 1956, after Suez, as a result of Egypt's war with Israel.

My father died last year at the age of ninety-four, a few months after my mother. They had spent the last years holding hands, switching from one radio station to another listening to the latest world events, and talking passionately about their life in Egypt. They lived near me in London, and I was the audience for their constant dramatized re-enactments of the stories of all the people they had known. These stories were capable of endless change as new interpretations were explored. At 16 Woodstock Road, it seemed that we had never left Cairo.

The smell of sizzling garlic and crushed coriander seeds in the kitchen, or of rose water in a pudding, and my mother's daily meals, reinforced the feeling.

When I look through the old notes and recipes given by relatives and friends soon after they left Egypt, it rekindles memories of our old life in a vivid way. They are written in French and interspersed with remarks about who gave the recipe long ago in Egypt, how much the dishes were appreciated by a certain person, and the occasion on which they were served. Each recipe has a name. There is "kobeba Latifa," "fromage blanc Adèle," "hamud Sophie," "pasteles Iris," "blehat Rahel," and so on. Most of the people are dead now. They were my parents' generation. But their recipes keep their memory very much alive, at least for me.

Our Cairo had been two cities that turned their backs on each other. One looked like Paris, because Khedive Ismail, who ruled in the middle of the nineteenth century, had wanted to pull Egypt into Europe and had brought in European architects to build it. The other had narrow meandering streets, mausoleums, and public baths; fountains with curvy iron grilles and windows screened by wooden lattices; Coptic churches and mosques with minarets rising into the sky like delicately embroidered candles. But our cooking was also from other cities. We made Istanbul pies, Aleppo cracked-wheat salads, Castilian almond-and-orange cakes, egg flans from Fez.

The Egypt I knew was a French-speaking, cosmopolitan Mediterranean country in which life for the better-off was a sort of continuation of the Belle Époque in an annex of Europe, with colonial-style clubs, opera and ballet, and entertaining on a grand scale. Egypt had been part of the Ottoman Empire and a British protectorate.

It was led by a foreign (Albanian) dynasty, a court made up of exiles from the Turkish aristocracy, and a royal council that spoke limited Arabic. The Jewish community had a happy and important place in the mosaic of minorities—which included Copts, Armenians, Syrian Christians, Maltese, Greeks, and Italians, as well as British and French expatriates—living among the Muslim majority.

Established mainly in Cairo and Alexandria but also in a number of small towns and villages, the Jewish community was itself a mosaic of people of different origins. The original community, which was as old as antiquity, had been joined by several waves of immigrants, and these had all kept up their different cultures and identities into the twentieth century. We gave ourselves the fictional name of "Basramite" to characterize our mixed backgrounds (no one knows where it came from). There were the Arabized inhabitants of the Haret el Yahoud—the Jewish quarter of Cairo, which we called the *hara* or simply *le quartier,* and which was built as early as 389—and of the equally ancient Souk el Samak (fish market) in Alexandria. Descendants of Jews from the Iberian Peninsula came in the sixteenth century and then again in the nineteenth from Salonika, Smyrna, Istanbul, the Balkans, and North Africa. They were called Espagnoli and Kekeres, the latter because of the way they asked "*Qué quieres?*" ("What do you want?"). Immigrants from Yemen and North Africa started coming in the Middle Ages. There were a few Ashkenazim. They were called Schlecht, meaning "bad" in Yiddish. They claimed this was the local deformation of the word "select," but nineteenth-century accounts reveal that they were so labeled because when they first arrived as escapees from pogroms in Russia and Eastern Europe they exclaimed in horror upon seeing the *hara: "Schlecht!*

Schlecht!" There were Italians who followed the old "Italki" rites, and Italians from Livorno, who followed Spanish rites, and people from Iraq and Syria. My own family was from Syria and from Turkey.

The community was polyglot. Our main language was French. We spoke it with an unorthodox grammar and special intonations, infected by all the jargons of the Levant and reinforced by gesticulations and facial expressions. We used many Italian words, such as *falso* and *avvocato.* We called our grandparents *nono* and *nona*, rag-and-bones was *roba vecchia* (old things), *taglio bianco* (white cut) was veal. We were great talkers, switching from one language to another. Every gathering was a fight to be heard. People shouted across the room and across conversations. Strangers thought we were quarreling. It was a closely knit community, and it felt as though we were all related. Our families were large and extended—almost tribal clans.

My two grandfathers, Elie Douek and Isaac Sassoon, had come from Aleppo at the end of the nineteenth century. My great-grandfather Haham Abraham ha Cohen Douek was the chief rabbi of that city when it was part of the Ottoman Empire. His portrait in turban and kaftan wearing medals given to him—"personally," my father said—by the Sultan Abdul Hamid II, still hangs in the synagogue in Aleppo. The same photograph looks down at me from my study wall, as it does from the walls of many of my relatives around the world. My family in Egypt always kept the key of the synagogue. When my great-uncle Jacques went to Aleppo on his honeymoon in the 1930s, he was able to open the door with it. His widow, Régine, who now lives near the Champs-Élysées, had thought Aleppo a bit of a disappointment after his buildup. She managed to get for Jacques a place in the Jewish

With my parents, Cesar and Nelly Douek, and my brother Ellis in 1939

cemetery of Versailles—a rare privilege, because it is full—and a red-carpet funeral treatment, by telling the Paris rabbis that he was the son of Haham Abraham.

Both my grandfathers left when Aleppo ceased to be the center of the camel-caravan trade because of the opening of the Suez Canal, and when the canal and the development of the cotton trade had turned Egypt into an "El Dorado of the Nile Valley." Both went to live in a newly built quarter of Cairo called Sakakini, in the Daher, where everyone was Jewish (my father insisted that I must distinguish it from the *hara*, where only the very poor were left by the time his family arrived). It was built on drained marshland by Sakakini Pasha. The streets converged like the spokes of a wheel towards a baroque rococo palace with turrets and carved angels where the Sakakini family lived. There were several synagogues, Jewish schools, ritual baths, and kosher butchers. When I asked my father what their everyday life had been like, he said, "We spent our time on the balcony talking to passersby. The men went to work, the women prepared the meals."

Their cooking was Aleppan. It was considered the pearl of the Arab kitchen—refined and delicate. It was labor-intensive, with a lot of pounding, hollowing, stuffing, wrapping, and rolling into tiny balls and fingers. The women prided themselves on their skills and—so my father said—were happy to spend hours in the kitchen. They cooked in company, and that was part of the fun. They filled chickens with meat and pine nuts, stuffed lamb with rice, rolled vine leaves, and filled pastries with mashed dates. Their crowning glory was kibbeh, which was a world in itself, with dozens of varieties. Basically, it had an outer shell of pounded wheat and meat, and a spicy meat-and-onion filling. The apartment resounded constantly with the ringing of the metal pestle and mortar with which they pounded the meat and wheat. It smelled of mint and spices and sizzling lamb, of tamarind and orange blossom.

My grandmother Sarah Hara did not read or write, although everyone from her large extended family sought her advice on every matter. She said the rabbis in Aleppo had forbidden her to learn because she was a girl. It had something to do with girls' becoming free and able to send notes to lovers. She had married a man much older than herself and was left a widow with many daughters to marry off. She wore a long brown dress called *habara*. With a little envy, she mocked the new generation's Frenchified ways.

My maternal grandmother, Eugénie Alphandary, was from Istanbul. She was a grande dame who spoke French like a Parisian, quoted Voltaire and Victor Hugo, and was fired by the

With my brothers, Zaki and Ellis, in 1943

ideals of "Liberté, Égalité, Fraternité." The private language she spoke with my mother when they did not want us children to understand was Judeo-Spanish. She called it Castilian to differentiate it from the Judeo-Spanish that she described as a "degraded Spanish mix" which some other people spoke. Hers was below French in her esteem, but to us it represented a mysterious lost paradise, a world of romance and courage and glorious chivalry which enmeshed us all in invisible threads of deep longing with its songs about lovers in Seville and proverbs about meat stews and almond cakes. That world was embodied by the little pies, sharp egg-and-lemon sauces, and meatballs incorporating vegetables that we ate at my grandparents' home. Her cold vegetable dishes had a faint sweetness about them, the pastries an orange flavor. When we bit into a pie, we found mashed eggplant or spinach. Everything had a Spanish name, and many things had an affectionate ending, like "pasteliko" and "borekita," which denoted that they were small.

The friends and relatives my grandmother entertained had names like Sol, Grazia, and Elvira, and family names like Pérez y Calderón, Santos, Abravanel, Rodrigues, and Toledano. But she had called her children Yvette, Marcelle, Nelly, Germaine, Giselle, and Joseph. Her father was a teacher at the Alliance Israélite Universelle in Istanbul. The Alliance was one of hundreds of Jewish schools, a charitable institution with headquarters in Paris, which brought French to all the Jewish communities of the Middle East. She had won a scholarship to their *école normale* (teachers' training school) in Paris and was sent to Egypt to teach at the Alliance school there. A few years ago, I found a book about the Jews of Egypt in the nineteenth century which contains letters by her father. He had been sent from Istanbul as a young man to assess the possibility of opening Alliance schools in Egypt and wrote back that the children spoke six languages but could not read or write and he doubted that they could ever be made to sit down. More than one school opened. My grandmother married as soon as she arrived. My grandfather Isaac, whose first wife had just died in childbirth, fell for her milky white skin and golden red hair.

Until the end of the nineteenth century, the indigenous Jews and those from other Arab countries had spoken Arabic and worn Arab clothes (they were Arab but different)— the women the *habara*, the men galabias and kaftans with turbans, skull caps, and tarbooshes (fezzes). The Europeanization and "emancipation" of the Jews began with the building of the Suez Canal and the modernization of the economy. A Jewish middle-class bourgeoisie, educated first in Jewish schools, then by Christian and secular missions, grew out of the developing cotton trade and the capitalist explosion of the country. Jewish men went into cotton, banking, the stock exchange, and industries like textiles, oil pressing, and sugar refining. Many stayed behind in the small trades and handicrafts. All my relatives were merchants in general commerce. They called themselves "import-export" but they were really "import-import," dealing with everything from towels and underwear to china, sugar, coffee, and tea. They were *khawaggat*, Europeanized men who wore suits and tarbooshes. Some toured the villages by train. Their offices and warehouses were in the bazaar area of the Hamzaoui.

My parents used to tell us how they pitied those of our relatives whose wives did not bother to give them proper breakfasts so they had to buy full medammes (Egyptian brown beans), taamia (the Cairo name for falafel), and lentil soup from vendors at the bazaar.

Later I heard from my relatives how they pitied my father because my mother did not let him eat out. It was a question of pride, not of religious orthodoxy. An account of a European Jewish traveler in Aleppo a hundred years before expresses the shock he felt at seeing Jews eating food prepared by non-Jews at the bazaar. Our community in Egypt on the whole was even more lax in its religious practice, but the synagogue was an important part of our lives. It was a joyous place to meet and socialize.

Every Friday evening and on high holidays, the Grand Temple was packed with people who came to hear Rabbi Nahum's famous speeches in French. By tradition, the prime minister of Egypt always came for the Kol Nidre prayer. We also attended a small synagogue on top of a garage in the garden of a private house in Zamalek. It was packed with men swaying from side to side (not backwards and forwards, as Eastern Europeans do). They sang plaintive nasal chants in Spanish modulations and tunes from Morocco, Syria, and Iraq, as well as some copied from the recitations of the Koran and the Egyptian national anthem. Every man started from the beginning of the prayer book, no matter when he arrived, so the result was a cacophony. The room glittered with chandeliers and velvet drapes embroidered with gold and silver thread. The women sat outside in the garden on golden chairs under a pergola. Dressed in colored silks, perfumed and bejeweled, they exchanged the latest gossip about matches, dowries, and infidelities, and visits to saintly tombs. Every so often, a face would appear at the window and shout *"Taisez-vous les dames!"* ("Shut up, ladies!"), and they would stop for a while and intone "Amen!"

Jewish holidays were important occasions.

They went on for days. Every member of the family was visited, the oldest first. There were always hundreds of people to kiss. The older relatives smelled of the rose water with which they washed. Depending on the time of day, sweetmeats and pastries or *mezze* (little salads and appetizers) were passed around. For the high-holiday dinners, tables were connected with planks. Huge quantities of food were prepared. Cooking went on for days. Housewives joined forces and brought their cooks. Itinerant cooks who specialized in certain dishes were also engaged.

Every family had its own special dishes for festive occasions. Although in my day the community had become relatively homogenized and many delicacies had become obligatory on every party table, those dishes which reflected the origins of families were also there, and you could trace the family's ancestry by looking at the spread on the table.

Part of the appeal for me of working on this book is that there is more to Jewish food than cooking and eating. Behind every recipe is a story of local traditions and daily life in far-off towns and villages. It is a romantic and nostalgic subject which has to do with recalling a world that has vanished. It is about ancestral memories and looking back and holding on to old cultures, and it is about identity. It has been like that since Biblical times. The Bible recalls in Exodus the wistful longings of the Jews for the foods they had left behind in Egypt.

At a gastronomic conference I attended in Jerusalem in September 1992 entitled "Couscous or Gefilte Fish?," I was down in the basement kitchen with cooks from Poland, Georgia, Morocco, Iraq, Kurdistan, and many other countries. We were preparing tastings and demonstrations of Jewish festive dishes from each of our communities while a black-bearded *mashgiah* (inspector) with a long black coat, black hat, and forelocks looked over our shoulders to make sure that we did not infringe the dietary laws. I was making kobeba hamda, a Syrian Passover dish of ground rice and meat dumplings in a lemony soup, and a Persian lamb stew with quince, and I watched others prepare Sabbath, Purim, Hanukah, and Rosh Hashanah specialties. The evening before, there had been a street festival with music and dancing, and the inhabitants of the street—Moroccans, Georgians, and others—had brought out unending trays of food for tasting. Following all these amazing displays of dishes, the first subject for discussion at the conference was "Is there such a thing as Jewish food?"

Cairo's Muski district, where Jewish men had their businesses

I am always asked that question. When I was taken out to dinner by a cousin recently and told him I was still researching Jewish food, he said emphatically, "There is no such thing!" A few friends keep telling me that. I have just put my hand on a paper I gave at the Oxford Symposium on Food in 1981 entitled "Cooking in Israel: A Changing Mosaic," in which I said, "There is really no such thing as Jewish food. What is familiar here as Jewish food is totally unknown to the Jews of Egypt, Morocco and India. Local regional food becomes Jewish when it travels with Jews to new homelands." Thirty years ago, when all that was known in the West of Jewish food was the cooking of the Ashkenazi Jews, whose ancestors came from Eastern Europe and Russia, no one wondered if there was such a thing. Since Jews began to pour out of the Middle East and exotic places like India and Georgia from the mid-1950s, such a bewildering range of "Jewish" dishes has come on the scene that the notion of a Jewish food culture has become questionable.

But because a culture is complex this does not mean it does not exist. The French historian Fernand Braudel, in his book *The Mediterranean*, wrote that there was undoubtedly a Jewish civilization, but that it was so individual that it was not always recognized as one. He described it as a scattering of countless islands in foreign waters, its matter dispersed like tiny drops of oil over the deep waters of other civilizations, never truly blending with them yet always dependent on them. The Jews, he said, adapted and adopted but never lost their cultural identity.

After years of researching the subject, I can say that each region or country has its own particular Jewish dishes and these are sometimes quite different from the local cuisine. Jews have adopted the foods of the countries they lived in, but in every country their cooking has had a special touch and taste and characteristic features and some entirely original dishes which have made it distinctive and recognizable. And in some countries their food was very different from that of the general population.

One reason for the differences was the adaptation of dishes to comply with the Jewish dietary laws. Because of the prohibition of combining meat and dairy foods, Jews used different cooking fats. In the Middle East, you could tell a Jewish home by the smell of oil, which was used instead of clarified butter. The substitution for forbidden foods like pork and seafood created such specialties as goose salami in Italy and Alsace, and white-fish soup in Livorno in Italy.

In Jewish families, cooking has always revolved around the Sabbath and religious festivals. All celebrations, whether they commemorate a religious holiday, an episode of Jewish history, or a moment in the cycle of life—a birth, a circumcision, a first tooth, a coming of age, a marriage, the inauguration of a new home, pregnancy, death—were once, and in some cases still are, ruled by tradition, and special foods were part of these traditions. The dishes chosen to celebrate these occasions became part of festive rituals and acquired embellishments as they acquired symbolic significance. They were glamorized to glorify the occasions, and that meant

coloring with saffron or turmeric, sprinkling with raisins and chopped nuts, stuffing, enclosing in pie crust, and pressing into a mold.

Some dishes changed because of the special dietary requirements of particular holidays. At Passover, for instance, when any leavening agents and indirectly flour and wheat are forbidden, ground almonds, potato flour, matzo meal, and matzos are used to make all kinds of cakes, pies, dumplings, pancakes, and fritters. The laws of the Sabbath, which prohibit any work, including lighting fires and cooking, from sunset on Friday to Saturday evening, have given rise to a very wide range of meals-in-a-pot to be prepared on Friday afternoon and left to cook overnight for Saturday lunch. These complex dishes comprise a variety of foods to be served as different courses, from the soup-and-meat course to side dishes and sometimes puddings, all in the same pot. There is also an extraordinary variety of original dishes that are to be eaten cold on Saturday. Another feature of Jewish cooking is the many substantial dairy and vegetable dishes which constitute meatless meals.

Apart from these differences, there was always, even centuries ago, a touch of otherness in Jewish cooking, a cosmopolitanism which broke even through ghetto walls. Jewish culinary interests were always wider than those of their immediate environment. Before the days of mass communication, Jews had their own network of communication. The vehicles of gastronomic knowledge were merchants and peddlers, traveling rabbis, preachers and teachers, students and cantors, professional letter carriers, beggars (who were legion), and pilgrims on their way to and from the Holy Land. They brought descriptions of exotic dishes in far-off lands, and sometimes even the exotic ingredients themselves, to the communities they stopped with, so that Jews, even in isolated places, became familiar with the foods of their foreign coreligionists.

For centuries Jews had been international merchants, for a time the only merchants in Europe and the Middle East. As early as the seventh century, they were the major channel of intercourse between East and West. As importers, middlemen, and wholesalers, they played a great part in the Byzantine commerce, which brought Eastern goods to Europe. The camel-caravan trade was concentrated in their hands. Jewish ships sailed the Mediterranean, and Jewish traders were said to be waiting at every port. As converted New Christians, they were among the earliest arrivals in South America with the Conquistadors, and they dealt with the New World produce. Foodstuffs were always a major part of their trade, and that had an impact on their cooking.

But the main influence on the development and shaping of their cuisine was their mobility—their propensity to move from one place to another. Jews moved to escape persecution or economic hardship, or for trade. Their history is one of migration and exile, of the disintegration and dispersion of communities and of the establishment of new ones. In their Diaspora, or dispersion, which began with the destruction of the Second Temple in the first century A.D., Jews brought dishes from past homelands to new ones. The way these dishes changed and adopted new forms in a new environment created hybrids that were particular to them. It is the cooking of a nation within a nation, of a culture within a culture, the result of the interweaving of two or more cultures. The almost complete dispersion of the old communities has radiated their styles of cooking in different parts of the world. Jewish history spans more than three millennia and has touched most parts of the globe, but each dish represents a unique historical experience in a particular geographic location.

Dishes are important because they are a link with the past, a celebration of roots, a symbol of continuity. They are that part of an immigrant culture which survives the longest, kept up even when clothing, music, language, and religious observance have been abandoned. Although cooking is fragile because it lives in human activity, it isn't easily destroyed. It is transmitted in every family like genes, and it has the capacity for change and for passing on new experience from one generation to another. It is possible, by examining family dishes, to define the identity and geographical origin of a family line.

The anthropologist Joelle Bahloul writes in her study of the Algerian Jewish table, *Le Culte de la Table Dressée*, that every family has its own culinary code, which gives it its bearings vis-à-vis its regional origin, its personal identity, and its position and prestige in the old country. The code attributes a menu, a dish, a flavor, and a ritual, with different table manners and different forms of conviviality, for every occasion, be it festive or ordinary and everyday. Every feast has its own rites and its own dishes and can be remembered by its tastes and its smells. In the selection of dishes—rejected or adopted, appreciated or depreciated and given mythical, ethical, or historical rationalization—there is a logic that combines mythological, historic, and moral significance to create a symbol.

This book was conceived as a grand comprehensive project. To finance visits to what was left of Jewish communities in various countries around the world, I took on other work and finished other books. But the more I researched and the more I discovered and the more I was fascinated, the more the project seemed impossible. I realized it could take me a lifetime and would fill several volumes. Scattered as the Jews have been over virtually the whole surface of the earth, residing in lands not their own for two thousand years, part of different cultures and traditions, it was impossible to attempt to cover all their cooking, from Babylon to New York.

Not only have there been Jews in every country, but the communities themselves were complex and subdivided into groups from different origins. When I visited the old Jewish Ghetto of Venice and met the ladies who cooked for the old people's home and for the holiday meals for tourists and Venetian returnees, they explained that Venice did not have one style of Jewish cooking but four. They pointed to the three synagogues standing in the piazza, which had followed different rites—Spanish, Levantine, and German—for hundreds of years. The cooking, they said, reflected those styles, and there was also an Italian cuisine, which was mainly southern Italian.

In Tunisia, there are two communities—the "Livornese," who came from Livorno in Italy, and the local "Tun," of Berber and Arab origins—which have separate synagogues, schools, and cemeteries. They do not intermarry, and there are differences in their cooking. Indian Jewry is the most complex, with at least three different communities that have always kept apart and whose histories and cooking are different. In many countries, including Italy, Morocco, Tunisia, Turkey, and Greece, Jewish cooking varied from one city to another. The cooking of Jews who originated in Eastern Europe and Russia is relatively standard, but it has changed according to whether emigrants settled in America, Canada, Britain, South Africa, or France.

Jewish cooking is in some ways archaic—some of the dishes have long been lost in the countries where they were adopted—but far from being fossilized; it is very much alive and full of movement. There are so many versions of a dish, so many regional variations, so many changes occurring when it was transported to different homelands, that collecting recipes is like looking through a kaleidoscope with bits moving all the time, or trying to hit a moving target, or, as a friend suggested, walking on quicksand. It is the extraordinary diversity and richness that so attracted me to the subject fifteen years ago, and it is its enormity and complexity that made me abandon it many times.

When I decided (as I did several times) to give up, my editor, Judith Jones, convinced me that the only way to deal with the subject was to make the book a "personal odyssey" and to forget about trying to be comprehensive. This was a very appealing idea, but I found that selecting is even more difficult than collecting. First there was the problem of what countries to represent. Could I leave out the West Indies or Mexico or Ethiopia? I started off intent on finding dishes from every possible community, from China, Libya, and Afghanistan to old Provence and Ferrara. I wanted to include many dishes from the lesser-known "exotic" communities, which have in the past been removed from the mainstream of Jewish life. In the end, I decided to concentrate more on those communities that have been in important Jewish centers and whose cooking is most widespread, and most particularly on those whose cooking is prestigious. Some of their cuisines are legendary, like those of the Moroccan and Syrian Jews, but many were a surprise to me, like the cooking of the Indian communities. The others are there too.

Another problem was to decide what dishes were representative of Jewish cooking. You cannot call everything that Jews have eaten Jewish. It is difficult to separate what is Jewish from the foods eaten by the general population, for many dishes are variations on a theme. Conversely, one of the difficulties is that people who came from Orthodox communities often assumed that they ate like everybody else, whereas many of their dishes were quite distinctive. They were not in a position to know, because they could eat only in Jewish homes. I did find a surprisingly large number of dishes that belong exclusively to various Jewish communities. Most are festive dishes. Nearly all the fish and chicken dishes in the book have been Friday-night specials somewhere, and most cold things were Saturday foods. But such a collection could still be unbalanced and unrepresentative, containing too many heavy bean and chickpea (Saturday) stews and too many biscuits and almond pastries. So I have included the everyday foods and some of the grand party dishes that Jews were most fond of, and which they brought to new homelands and passed on to their children.

In the wide repertoire to choose from, there are many similar dishes varying in flavorings or methods. There are hundreds of meatballs and fish balls, hundreds of stuffed vegetables, hundreds of cheese pies (why did they like all that rolling and stuffing and wrapping?), milk puddings, fritters in syrup, to name only a few. How did I decide? I would select a dish from France, for instance, in preference to similar ones in Britain or America, because the French make it better. It was not always easy to choose even when looking at one country, however. When I asked an Algerian for a Jewish couscous, the reply was: "From which town?" In every town it was different. In Morocco, there are Jewish specialties from Fez, Tangiers, Tétouan, Marrakesh, Ouezzane, Debdou, and Essaouira, and several Berber mountain villages have their own Jewish dishes.

There is also the question of authenticity. When communities emigrate, they start using what is available locally and what makes life easier—different cheeses, different rice, substitutes such as gelatine instead of calf's foot, yogurt instead of sour cream. In France, some North African "Pieds Noirs" use veal instead of mutton now, because under French influence they have been made to feel that mutton "is heavy and smells too strong." I had to decide if I should go back to the source in the country of origin or to go for the modern, lighter, more elegant version which most people have switched to; how much I should substitute oil for butter or chicken fat, and baking for frying. My decisions were, of course, influenced by a concern with health and with our modern taste for lighter foods, but not if that sacrificed the authenticity of a recipe. Luckily, there are still those who know how things were done in the old homelands and how to adapt them to our world; it is from them for the most part that I took my cue. Usually I offer the alternatives. Even when a community has not moved, recipes depend on the situation of the individuals who have given them. If they are poor, they can only use what they can afford. The communities that became impoverished use more bread or potatoes, for instance, to make their dishes go further. As an example, a Passover walnut cake in a privately published book, *Sefarad Yemekleri*, to raise money for a Jewish old people's home in Istanbul, calls for a large proportion of matzo meal, whereas the same cake, when it arrived in Cairo from Istanbul in the early nineteenth century, used only walnuts. It is not always easy to decide at what point in time and on what soil dishes were at their best.

There are dozens of Jewish recipes for head, feet, spleen, stuffed intestines, heart, lungs, testicles, even penis. Most of them are delicious, but who will be brave enough to cook them these days? Anyway, most offal is not available in Anglo-Saxon countries now, because of lack of demand and health risks (in Britain, because of "mad cow" disease).

I have been asked if I was going to offer dishes that people haven't cooked for a hundred years. The answer is that I may give them a mention, but the recipes I have included are all much alive in some corner of the world, although it may be in Sydney, Australia, instead of Bombay, India; and Afoula, Israel, instead of Djerba, Tunisia.

When I was in Israel, a woman whose family came from Iraq—an anthropologist who was also a brilliant cook—invited me to her home with a woman from India so that I could ask them both for recipes. I spent the afternoon taking detailed notes, and at the end the lovely anthropologist said, "Now, what we want from you is to go and get many other recipes for these same dishes and to find the very best version. That is what we want from you—to find the best." That night she brought me kishree, a dish of rice and red lentils, to taste, and it was wonderful. But I did get a better one from my friend Sami Zubaida in London, and I know I don't have to feel guilty about featuring it. After I had tried hundreds (perhaps thousands!) of recipes and many in their different versions, the selection made itself on gastronomic merits. Of course it reflects my tastes and my background, my travels, the people I have met who gave me

recipes, and also the degree of enthusiasm of the friends who came to dinner and tasted my trials.

It may seem to you, on looking at the book, that I have chosen a disproportionately large number of Sephardi recipes. But the Sephardi section includes many very different cultures and regional styles, from Italian to Indian, and they all needed representation. I started off thinking I would pick only a few recipes from each community, but as I tried one after the other and found them enchanting—like discovering raw diamonds—I had to include many.

Though I grew up in a Sephardi family and that tradition has always remained a part of my life, I have lived in the Ashkenazi world since the age of fifteen—first as a schoolgirl in Paris, then having married into a Russian Jewish family in England—so I have long been familiar with Eastern European Jewish food. But it was only when researching this book, and striving to find the best versions of dishes, that I realized just how many gems there were.

The criterion of selection throughout was to include only the most delicious.

The "testing" meals went on for years. There were tête-à-têtes when I made small quantities for two or three, and there were great noisy banquets for up to fifteen people—seated around my round hunting table while a dozen different dishes were passed around. The merits of the dishes and possibilities for improvement were discussed. I noted at the head of each recipe in my computer who had eaten the dish and how much they liked it. I dropped the dishes that did not meet with approval. Many of the friends who came to eat are cooks and chefs and food writers, and all are discriminating food-lovers, so it is reassuring for me to remember how much they enjoyed the dishes and how rapturously they received so many of them. Most of all, it is my family—my son, Simon, and his wife, Ros; my daughter Anna and her husband, Clive; and my daughter Nadia when she was over from New York—who went through the repertoire every week and made their comments.

History is important in the shaping of cooking traditions, and never more so than with Jewish food, which has no geographical base, no *terroir*, as the French call the native soil to which a gastronomy obeys stable and unvarying imperatives. Working on this book has been for me a voyage of discovery. To make sense of their dishes, I had to gain an insight into the culture and history of the Jews. It has been so fascinating that I have resisted recommendations that I should not burden readers with big chunks of history and have passed on what I found. It is good to be able to place a dish. The more delectable it is, the more I want to know something about it.

Two Cultures—Ashkenazi and Sephardi

Organizing the book to combine history and recipes with stories and personal anecdotes was very difficult. It was clear that I should divide it into parts representing the two main groupings and cultural branches of the Jewish people—Ashkenazi and Sephardi—mainly because Ashkenazi cooking is standard and the history which explains it needs to be told separately. The Sephardi grouping is arbitrary. In the strictest sense, the term "Sephardi" designates only those Jews whose ancestors lived in the Iberian Peninsula—"Sepharad" meaning "Spain" in Hebrew. But in the broad sense in which it is used today, it signifies those Jews whose roots are around the Mediterranean, in

the Middle East and in Asia. These days, in Israel, all Jews who are not Ashkenazi are classed as Sephardi, although many of the communities share little of the heritage of Spain or the Mediterranean and have never thought of themselves as Sephardi. The alternative—to call the Sephardi recipe section as belonging to "the *other* Jews"—would not do either. Although it represents the cooking of people from many different countries and cultures, there is a certain unity, which means that the great majority have enough in common to make their dishes go well together in a meal. For the sake of clarity and simplification, the Sephardi introduction allows the broad story that links the communities, makes sense of the recipes to be told, although it focuses on the Iberian story. It leaves out the stories of many unique and important communities, but these find a place throughout the recipe section.

From the tenth century, when they emerged, until the twentieth, when they came together for the first time, each group—Ashkenazi and Sephardi—developed its own separate culture in separate geographic areas. Broadly, the dividing line was the mountains that divide the North and South of Europe all the way from the Caucasus via the Alps to the Pyrenees. That the significant migrations in Jewish history have been between East and West, and not between North and South, encouraged the division between Sephardi and Ashkenazi.

The Ashkenazim are the Jews whose origin lies in Western and Eastern Europe and Russia. Their culture developed in a Christian world. It was born in the Middle Ages in Western Europe, and most particularly in Germany. "Ashkenaz" is the Hebrew name for Germany, and Yiddish, the Ashkenazi language, which is written in Hebrew characters, is a thirteenth-century South

German vernacular. About two out of three Jews in the world are Ashkenazi, although in Israel the Sephardim are slightly more numerous.

The Sephardi world stretched from the Atlantic to the Indian Ocean. With the exception of Christian Italy and Spain and parts of India, almost all the lands where the Sephardim lived before the seventeenth century were under Islamic rule. Judeo-Spanish, Judesmo, or Ladino was the language of the Iberian Sephardim.

There was a time when Sephardim and Ashkenazim did not marry each other's daughters. In my father's family, intermarriage was considered a *mésalliance* and a major catastrophe. In Egypt, Ashkenazim were thought of as lacking in refinement and their women as dangerously free and flighty. People were contemptuous and mocking about Ashkenazi cooking and would make guttural choking sounds when they pronounced words like "kreplach" and "knaidlach." The Ashkenazim no doubt felt the same about the Sephardim. And that was also the case centuries ago. There are dozens of written accounts of Ashkenazi travelers to the East who were so horrified to see their coreligionists sitting on the ground and eating with their hands that they could not bring themselves to eat their strange foods. One example is in the *Travel Letters* of Rabbi Obadiah of Bertinoro, written between 1488 and 1499 during a journey to the Holy Land (translated by Yaakov Dovid Shulman in a book published by CIS in 1992). In a letter to his father, Rabbi Obadiah describes a Sabbath meal at a feasting house in Alexandria when he was a guest of Rabbi Moshe Grasso, who was also the ambassador of Venice: "This is how the Jews in all the Muslim lands eat on Shabbos. They sit in a circle on mats. There is no table. Instead a small tablecloth is spread out on

a mat, on which are placed many varieties of local fruits." In Elkan Nathan Adler's *Jewish Travellers in the Middle Ages* (New York: Dover Publications, 1987), a certain Rabbi Menachem, who was granted lavish hospitality in a Jewish household in Jerusalem, recounts that he "could not eat and enjoy their dishes, for they are different to our peoples and strange to a healthy man."

Until recently, each group knew little about the cuisine of the other. When my parents first came to London after Suez in 1956, Jewish neighbors knocked at the door to welcome us. My mother invited them to tea, and when they saw the sesame bracelets, little cheese pies and nut-filled pastries, they asked, "Are you sure you are Jewish?" When I married an Ashkenazi of Russian origin, my then mother-in-law announced at once that she was sorry but she would not eat my fancy food.

The differences in the two styles of cooking have to do with climate and soil and local produce. The Ashkenazi world is a cold world. It is a world of chicken fat, onion and garlic, cabbage, carrots and potatoes, freshwater fish, especially carp, and salt herring. The Sephardi world is a warm one of peppers and eggplant, zucchini and tomatoes, rice and cracked wheat, saltwater fish and olive oil. The Ashkenazi culture is Northern European and Slavic, the Sephardi predominantly Mediterranean and Middle Eastern. Whereas Jews in Christendom were mainly provincial, Jews in Islam were mostly urban, concentrated in ports and main cities. The Ashkenazim were more cut off than the Sephardim from the non-Jewish world, confined as they often were to ghettos and restricted areas. Their history since the late twelfth century is full of persecutions and expulsions. Whereas they were more concerned with spiritual and intellectual values, the Sephardim were more preoccupied with secular pursuits and more interested in the senses. Ashkenazi women in Eastern Europe generally worked outside the home; Sephardi women stayed at home and spent hours in the kitchen.

There were few cases where the two worlds overlapped geographically, and when they did it was a matter of one culinary culture's taking over the other—there was no fusion of styles, no Ashkenazi-Sephardi hybrids, and no unifying element. In Venice, cooking styles remained separate and distinct from the sixteenth until the twentieth century. In the Balkans, the Ashkenazim were swamped in numbers by the Iberian Jews in the sixteenth century and adopted the Judeo-Spanish language as well as the cooking styles (Skinazi, Polako, and Tedeschi are old Sephardi names). In Amsterdam, there is little sign now in the kitchen of the enormous migration from Spain and Portugal in the late sixteenth century—Jewish cooking in Holland is Ashkenazi. In South America, no foods are associated with the Spanish and Portuguese Jews who came in the sixteenth century. The two styles that have predominated there since the nineteenth century are Syrian and Ashkenazi. The first Jewish cookbook published in English, in 1846, *The Jewish Manual* edited by "A Lady," contains a large number of Spanish and Portuguese recipes with a few German and Eastern European as well as familiar English and French ones, but Iberian dishes have disappeared entirely from Britain as Ashkenazi cooking became the sole Jewish style. A few dishes said to have been adopted by the Ashkenazim from the Sephardim are macaroons and almond cakes, sponge cake (which is like the Sephardi "pan d'Espanya"), and the English fried fish in batter, which was a Portuguese import.

The two worlds have now come together in the same countries and through intermarriage.

The Jewish Dietary Laws
of Kashrut

THROUGHOUT THE HISTORY of the Jews, observance created a spiritual atmosphere around food and gave it special importance. The dietary laws of kashrut have been one of the most significant factors that influenced Jewish styles of cooking. Until the late eighteenth century, they were kept by all Jews universally. All Ashkenazi Jews observed them until the ghetto walls in Europe were broken and they were "emancipated" and moved towards the big cities. The movement that spread modern European culture among Jews, called the "Haskalah," meaning "Enlightenment," freed them from religious constraints. The Reform movement, which started in Germany and spread to America in the nineteenth century, declared that a Jew could be a Jew and not practice kashrut. In Oriental lands, Jews remained wholly observant until the end of the nineteenth century, and

practiced kashrut while they remained in their closely knit communities into the twentieth century.

The practical intricacies involved in keeping the laws of kashrut, the way they acted as a barrier to free intermingling with non-Jews, fostered exclusiveness and separateness and ensured the perpetuation of an identity and a way of life. This resulted in a tendency to preserve archaic styles of cooking. Because Jews could not eat in a non-Jewish home, they did not always become aware of new culinary trends.

According to tradition, the basis of the dietary laws was revealed by God to Moses on Mount Sinai as commandments. The divine commandments, which form part of the Torah, the first five books of the Bible (Genesis, Exodus, Leviticus, Numbers, and Deuteronomy), are seen as absolute, eternal, immutable, and universal. They were interpreted, elaborated, and expanded by Jewish sages and rabbinic commentators whose remarks are recorded in the Talmud, the Book of Law and Tradition. The most important collection of Jewish codes of law—compiled by Joseph Caro, who was born in Toledo in 1488 and went on to live in Constantinople and Safed—is entitled "Shulhan Arukh" or "The Prepared Table." One section, entitled "Yoreh Deah," is concerned with food. It became the universal Talmudic legal reference for the Jewish people and was accepted by the Ashkenazim when Rabbi Moses Isserlis adapted it to Ashkenazi custom by adding the Mapah or "Tablecloth."

The laws of kashrut deal with what is permitted or *kasher* (kosher-fit) and what is *terefah* (forbidden); with the preparation of meat to avoid the consumption of blood and the separation of meat from milk products.

All fruit and vegetables are permitted in accordance with the Biblical statement "I give you all plants that bear seed everywhere on earth, and every tree bearing fruit which yield seed."

Animals that both "chew the cud" (meaning herbivores that eat grass and leaves) and have cloven hooves are considered clean and permitted. (The cloven hooves mean that they cannot hold prey and cannot be carnivores.) All others—including pig, rabbit, horse, and beasts of prey—are considered unclean and forbidden. All birds of prey or carrion, and certain birds such as owls, storks, and ostriches, are forbidden, as are creatures that have died of natural causes or of disease. Because of the obligation of ritual slaughter, game that has been hunted and killed by gunshot may not be eaten.

From the sea only fish that have both fins and scales can be eaten. Since the advent of the microscope has made it possible to see tiny scales which could not be seen with the naked eye, the status of some fish is controversial. Forbidden fish and seafood include sturgeon (whose status is uncertain, because the tiny scales on its tail do not overlap like normal scales), swordfish (because certain types of fish with a sword do not have scales), monkfish, ray, rockfish, skate, turbot, shark, eel, all shellfish and crustaceans, sea urchins, octopus, and squid. Reptiles, turtles, snails, frogs, and insects are also prohibited.

Blood is forbidden. Following the Biblical injunctions "Thou must not eat flesh with its life-blood in it" and "Thou shalt not eat the blood for the soul resides in the blood," animals must be slaughtered in the ritual manner called *shehitah* by cutting the throat to let as much blood as possible drain. Large animals must be killed by a skilled professional slaughterer (*shohet*) with a razor-sharp knife in a single slash, which must sever both the trachea and the jugular vein so as to cause the least possible pain. The *shohet* says: "Blessed art thou, O Lord our God, King of the Universe, who has sanctified us with his commandments and commanded us the *shehitah* [slaughtering]." A searcher (*bodek*) or an inspector (*mashgiah*) or the *shohet* himself must examine the carcass for any trace of disease, which renders meat non-kosher. The sciatic nerve, or the hindquarters where the nerve has not been removed, is forbidden. This injunction is in remembrance of Jacob's struggle with a mysterious stranger who came suddenly out of the night, when Jacob's thigh was injured and he was left with a limp. Unless a butcher can remove the nerve and sinews very carefully, the entire hindquarters of an animal cannot be eaten. Fat from below the abdomen must not be eaten, because in early times it was sacrificed on the altar.

In a few countries, including Israel, hindquarter meat that has been porged—that is, where nerves, tendons, and blood vessels have been removed—is used. In the Middle East, porging was practiced and sheep's-tail fat (from below the abdomen) is eaten. In Victorian times in England, the Chief Rabbinate permitted the porging of hindquarter meat. But now that part of the animal is forbidden.

For the meat to be kosher, all traces of blood must be removed by soaking in cold water for half an hour, then sprinkling the meat on all sides with coarse salt and allowing it to drain for one hour before washing it again in cold water three times. An alternate method of withdrawing the blood, which is used for liver, is by preliminary grilling. In that case, the meat does not need to be koshered by salting.

The Biblical command "thou shall not seethe the kid in its mother's milk" has been interpreted by the rabbis and sages who compiled the Talmud between the second and fifth centuries to mean the complete separation of meat and milk. Foods containing the one may not be eaten at the same meal with foods containing the other. Nor may such foods be cooked together; they must be kept completely apart at all stages, from storage and cooking to eating and washing up. In observant homes, there are two separate sets of utensils, crockery and cutlery, napkins and tea towels for the two types of meals. Milk may not be eaten after meat before an interval of several hours, the precise time varying according to local custom. For Eastern Europeans it is six hours, for Germans it is three, and for Dutch Jews it is one hour. But meat can be eaten soon after milk if the mouth is rinsed and bread is

Postcard depicting ritual slaughter in a part of the Paris meat market reserved for shehitah, *c. 1903*

eaten in between. Neutral foods, called *pareve*, such as fish, eggs, grain, vegetables, and fruit, can be eaten with either meat or milk products.

No reasons for the prohibitions are given either in the Bible or in later rabbinic sacred books. Rabbinic literature has advanced various explanations for the dietary laws, including moral, philosophical, mystical, and metaphysical ones. A popular traditional interpretation is that, by mastering their sensual urges and subordinating their sensual nature to the will of God, human beings rise from their animal to their human nature, attaining sanctification and moral freedom. Modern attempts to rationalize the laws speculate that they were created by the ancient rabbis for health reasons as a precaution against disease.

The Ashkenazim have been much stricter in their practice of kashrut, whereas the Sephardim, even when deeply religious, are known to have been more tolerant and easygoing. The Yiddish proverb "If you ask permission the answer will be 'It's forbidden!' " refers to the once widespread custom of asking a rabbi if a pot or a chicken is kosher. Since the anwer was more likely to be "It's forbidden," you were better off acting without asking. The concept of separating *milshig* (dairy) and *fleyshig* (meat) in different parts of the kitchen emerged in Europe in the Middle Ages, when public bakehouses in the ghettos were di-

vided into two parts. In the shtetl, those whose ways of observance were different were scorned and considered as kinsmen who had assimilative tendencies and wandered from the fold. The Sephardim usually managed a synthesis between religious consciousness and the world around them and had little time for hairsplitting pilpulistic arguments about the law. European travelers to Egypt and Syria in medieval times were shocked to see local Jews buying cooked food such as harissa, a meat-and-wheat porridge, as well as pastries and sweetmeats, from non-Jews in the bazaar for their evening meals. In the late fifteenth century, the Italian Obadiah of Bertinoro wrote in letters to his father from Egypt that "the Jews in Cairo only cook at home for the Sabbath."

Jewish tradition always attached great importance to the local customs of a community. These local customs, although not based in the written law, and varying from one community to another, were regarded as binding. Most Sephardi communities allowed the eating of rice during Passover and still do, whereas Ashkenazim do not. They also ate sheep's-tail fat, from below the abdomen. Some Ethiopians mixed meat and milk but were careful not to cook the meat of an animal in its actual mother's milk. Some Yemenites will not eat geese because they are both "land and water" and do not fit in any precise category.

A Hassid goes into a Jewish restaurant and asks if it is super-kosher. The waiter shows him the portrait of a rabbi hanging on the wall and says, "You can trust us with him hanging there," and the Hassid replies, "I could trust you if he was standing in your place and you were hanging up there."

The Food of the Ancient Hebrews— in the Bible and the Talmud

DISCOVERING SIMILARITIES between the cooking of Israelis from Middle Eastern and "primitive" countries like Yemen and Ethiopia and that of their Biblical ancestors—such as flatbreads and cracked wheat—and finding plants mentioned in the Bible growing wild are subjects of fascination in Israel. Cooking columns are full of pieces making connections. It is an expression of romantic nationalism—a way of establishing roots and proving the unbroken Jewish presence and the right to the land through culinary roots. When I was there after Sadat's historic visit, a newspaper ran a big story with pharaonic illustrations about the likelihood of Jews' eating falafel when they were slaves in ancient Egypt. When I talked to my Hebrew publisher, the food writer Ruth Sirkis, about quails landing exhausted on the beaches in Alexandria, only to be caught in nets and plucked and grilled at once,

her eyes lit up and she cried: "The quails falling from the sky for Moses when the Jews were hungry in the wilderness!" As I walked in Tel Aviv with the food editor and writer Dalia Lamdani, she noticed a dusty plant growing between stones on a derelict site and picked it up with great tenderness, explaining that it was an herb mentioned in the Bible. Of course it is enthralling to find the same produce growing wild on the land after more than three thousand years.

The food of the ancient Hebrews has always been important to Jews, a wandering people who have used their ancient history and the continuity of their culture to define themselves. What was eaten in Biblical times—seen as the era of glory, when the Jews had political independence in their own land—has always been more significant than what was eaten in the long era of dispersion and exile which started after the destruction of the Second Temple in the first century A.D.

Some of the foods mentioned in the Bible have continued to be used as symbols in rituals of religious festivals. Wine, which had a sacramental place and was used in libations, is used for the Kiddush (ceremonial blessing), recited on the Sabbath and holidays. Bread, which was the most important staple and had a sacred character, is an important part of the Sabbath celebration, during which a blessing is said over two loaves. Salt, which symbolized the making of a covenant and the offering of a sacrifice, is sprinkled on bread over which grace is said before meals.

At Rosh Hashanah (the New Year), a piece of apple or bread is dipped in honey so that the year will be sweet. Honey also recalls the "land flowing with milk and honey." Bee-keeping is not mentioned in the Bible, and it is believed that every mention of honey in the Pentateuch refers to date honey—a thick syrup obtained by reducing the juice of boiled dates. Today, date syrup, called halech, made by soaking and boiling dates in water, then reducing the liquor, is a ritual food of Passover. However, the Book of Judges relates that Samson ate honey from a hive of bees made in the skull of a lion.

Olive oil, which was used for ceremonial purposes in temple offerings and for anointing and in temple lamps, is used for deep-frying morsels during Hanukah to commemorate the miraculous oil in the story of the victory of Judah Maccabeus. Other foods that have a role in rituals are etrog (citron), on the Feast of Tabernacles; pomegranates, which symbolize fecundity and renewal, on the New Year; "bitter herbs," such as chicory, to commemorate the bitter lives of the Jews oppressed by the Pharaohs; paschal lamb, which represents the sacrificial an-

imal; and matzah (or matzos), which represent the unleavened bread. Dairy delicacies are eaten at Shavuot to commemorate the day when the Torah was given and the Hebrews found their milk had curdled after they spent the day on Mount Sinai.

Manna, a sweet food found by the Hebrews in the desert, appeared every morning except the Sabbath. Today a confection called "manna from heaven" is made with the sweet, sticky substance secreted by the tamarisk tree. It is first dissolved in hot water and strained, to rid it of twigs and leaves, then cooked to a thick paste and mixed with chopped almonds. A pudding made with the manna cooked to a soft cream is eaten with thick buffalo cream.

The diet in Biblical times was the early Mediterranean one of grain, legumes, wild plants, and meat from animals mostly raised by nomads. Wheat and barley, lentils and fava beans were cultivated (lentils feature in the story of Esau). Melons and cucumbers, leeks, onions, and garlic grew wild. Grapes and figs are constantly mentioned. They were eaten fresh and dry. Dates too make an appearance. Adam and Eve's apple tree is thought to have been a fig tree, and to have become an apple tree in later literature. Meat—mainly mutton and goat—was eaten on festive occasions. Beef and veal were very scarce and highly prized; they feature only in accounts of sumptuous banquets. Game, ducks, and geese as well as fish and birds' eggs are also mentioned. Milk was important and was used to make butter and cheese and sour milk.

Different wines—sweet, sparkling, and spiced—were made with grapes or raisins, and wine was also made from fermented dates, figs, and pomegranates. Wine vinegar was used as a dressing and for pickling. Olives were preserved. Walnuts, almonds, and pistachios were considered delicacies. Herbs and spices were used as flavoring and for medicinal purposes. There was cumin, fenugreek, dill, sesame seeds, and fennel.

What the Jews ate in Palestine in the early centuries of the Christian era is known through the Palestinian Talmud, which is a compilation of academic discussions and recorded judicial administration by rabbinic scholars and jurists between 200 and 400 A.D. To the vegetables mentioned in the Bible we can add cabbages, beets, celery, turnips, colocasia, radishes, chickpeas, and lupines. New fruits named include carobs, apricots and peaches, quinces and pears, apples, mulberries, and medlars. Among the herbs and spices used for flavoring and medicinal purposes are mustard seed, hyssop, fenugreek, fennel and aniseed, mint, sage, marjoram, and bay leaf. Saffron was used for coloring. Caraway, coriander, and cumin were important—cumin was used to stop bleeding caused by circumcision. Spices were used for religious purposes too, especially as incense, and their scent was inhaled after a meal.

The Talmud concerns itself very much with food and cooking—mainly what is permitted and what is not—with extreme minutiae. But there is general advice, such admonitions as "Eat a third, drink a third, and leave a third of your stomach empty so that if you get angry you'll have your fill," "A change of diet is the beginning of bowel trouble," "Who eats in the street acts like a dog," and such proverbs as "Better is a dinner of herbs where love is than a fatted ox and hatred with it."

The following ruling is astonishing: "A man once gave his slave to his friend so that he will teach him 1,000 recipes, and he taught him only 800. He sued and brought him in front of the Rabbi. Said the Rabbi: 'our forefathers said: we saw the good things. But we have not even seen them with our own eyes'" (Talmud, Nedarim 50). I am not sure that I understand what the rabbi meant by his reply, but are we to believe that in the days of the Mishnah, before the fifth century, during the bad times, under Roman rule, there were Jewish homes that kept slaves who knew a thousand recipes—even if "one thousand" in the Talmud may just mean "a great number"?

The Sabbath and Festivals—
the Jewish Calendar

IN THE OLD DAYS, cooking revolved around the Sabbath and festivals. A characteristic of traditional Jewish life was the contrast between the sobriety of weekday food and the opulence of Sabbath and holiday food. According to Biblical prescription, the Sabbath should be a day of joy and beauty, when the best possible food must be prepared. This is also set out in the Talmud, by rabbinical decree. The pattern was to eat very meager cheap food all the week, but come the Sabbath the choicest foods were on the table. During the week, the food depended on the day's position with regard to the Sabbath. On Thursday night and Friday lunch, you ate light, usually dairy, meals in preparation for the onslaught on the stomach of the Sabbath. On Sunday and thereafter, you made do with the leftovers.

Feasting and fasting are major elements in the holidays, and food plays a symbolic role in the rituals and celebrations. In her book about Algerian Jewish traditions, *Le Culte de la Table Dressée: Rites et Traditions de la Table Juive Algérienne* (The Cult of the Set Table: Rites and Traditions of the Algerian Jewish Table), social anthropologist Joelle Bahloul describes the festive table as a place of cult, and the unfolding of the meal as a liturgical re-enactment of what goes on in the temple. She explains that the ritualization of gastronomic acts transforms the kitchen into a sanctuary; the dining room into a miniature temple; the table into an altar; the convivial gatherings into a commune of the faithful; and the wife-cook into a high priestess. The lighting of candles by the woman of the house; the ritual washing of hands; the reciting of Kiddush (the prayer of sanctification of the day) over wine by the head of the family; the breaking of bread and passing around of pieces with a sprinkling of salt—all these actions, accompanied by blessings, hymns, and special prayers, contribute to giving the meal a sacred character.

If you look at photographs of a table laid out for the Sabbath or a holiday in any corner of the world, you will see it impeccably set with embroidered white tablecloth and napkins and richly ornamented dishes, silver goblets, and candlesticks. This is a reflection of the importance of the table, and of the solemnity of festive occasions in Jewish life.

Friday-night gatherings and festive occasions have always been one of the highlights of the Jewish experience and one of the great bonds of Jewish family and community life. And it is through such occasions that traditional dishes are kept up. There are high holidays, which are Biblical and set out in the Torah; rabbinical holidays, established by the sages to remind the Jews of the miracles performed for them by God; and holidays that commemorate historical events and are a reminder of the fate of the Jewish people. Each holiday is marked by its own special foods.

Though Ashkenazi dishes associated with particular festivals are the same whatever the country of origin, festive dishes from the rest of the Jewish world vary from one country and even from one city to another. In Cairo, there were no ritual or traditional holiday dishes common to the community as a whole; they belonged to extended families and depended on where the family came from. For Orthodox Jews, the gastronomic calendar is linked to the spiritual and religious life; for others, it represents a celebration of roots and of generations past. What often happens is that when parents die their children apply themselves to reproduce the tra-

ditional family dishes as faithfully as they can.

The following are the main important festivals which are widely celebrated.

THE SABBATH

AT THE END of the fifteenth century, a certain Rabbi Obadiah of Bertinoro wrote to his father from Egypt: "The Jews in the Muslim lands welcome Sabbath in the following manner: On Sabbath eve, the men go to the bathhouse. When they return home their wives give them wine and they drink liberally. Afterwards while it is still daylight, they eat the food that was cooked for the evening meal, until darkness falls. Then they go to the synagogue wearing clean, freshly-pressed clothing and chant songs and praises to God, stretching out the evening prayers for two hours into the night. Then they return home, make Kiddush, eat a minimal portion of bread and conclude with grace" (*Travel Letters*, translated by Yaakov Dovid Shulman).

My father described the Sabbath in Egypt when he was a little boy in exactly the same terms, adding that my grandfather brought my grandmother a bunch of flowers when he came back from the bathhouse. It was in response to my question about whether my grandfather loved my grandmother. For my father, the bouquet and the happiness of the day represented love in the family.

I have since discovered that the custom of putting scented herbs or flowers in the dining room was meant to enhance the beauty of the Sabbath and to give "a foretaste of heaven." According to rabbinic sources, paradise was formed on the third day of Creation. When the just man appeared at the gates, eight fragrant myrtles were put into his hands, and he was directed to a place where there were many rivers and eight hundred kinds of roses and myrtles.

The Sabbath is the day of rest and the focal point of Jewish life. The fourth commandment calls upon the Jews to keep it holy and free of all work: "Six days shalt thou labour and do all the work, but the seventh day is a Sabbath unto the Lord thy God, in it thou shalt not do any manner of work."

The Sabbath begins on Friday, eighteen minutes before sunset, and ends the following evening, after dark, when three stars can be seen in the sky. During that time, lighting fires, cooking, and baking, which are among thirty-nine forms of activity considered "work," are prohibited. In the past, in many Jewish quarters, a crier would rush around making shops close on time and warning housewives that their preparations should be over.

There have always been ways of getting around the problem of lighting fires. It was common in the Oriental world for Muslims to go around the houses kindling fires and doing little jobs for the Jews. Israel Zangwill gives us an insight into turn-of-the-century London in his 1892 novel, *Children of the Ghetto,* where he writes, "The Rabbis had modified the Biblical prohibition against lighting any fire whatever, and allowed it to be kindled by non-Jews. Poor women, frequently Irish, known as *Shabbos-goyas* or fire-*goyas,* acted as stokers to the Ghetto at

Kiddush, the Friday-night prayer over wine, in Poland

twopence a hearth. No Jew ever touched a match or a candle, or burnt a piece of paper, or even opened a letter. The *Goyah*, which is literally 'heathen female', did everything required on the Sabbath." Zangwill tells that, when the reb's fire sank and he could not give direct orders to the shiksa (non-Jewish woman) to replenish it, he would rub his hands and remark casually (in her hearing), "Ah, how cold it is!"

In observant families, all preparations for two rich festive meals, for Friday evening and Saturday lunch, and for a third, simpler meal to be served before sunset on Saturday, have to be completed before the Sabbath begins. In the old days, without ovens and modern facilities, most Saturday dishes were eaten cold, except for one hot meal which was left to cook through the night, often in a communal oven. Nowadays, of course, modern technology makes it possible to arrange for heat to go on and off by itself at prearranged times, but the old-style Sabbath dishes, which are usually very old and unique, remain.

The whole Ashkenazi world has a common standard menu for the Sabbath, most of which dates back to the Middle Ages (for more information about this, see page 42). On Friday night in medieval Germany, they ate hallah—a braided bread—salt herring, and stuffed freshwater fish, broth with noodles, followed by meat pies, boiled pickled beef or roast goose, stuffed neck, and noodle pudding. Today meat pies have gone and roast goose has been replaced by roast chicken. And there are other alternatives: sweet-and-sour fish, fish in egg-and-lemon sauce, and fish with walnuts; braised beef; carrot tzimmes or prune-and-potato tzimmes; potato salad; stewed parsnips; and potato kugel.

For Saturday lunch, cholent, the meal-in-the-pot left to cook overnight, is accompanied by stuffed kishke, potato kugel, chaleth (apple-and-bread pudding), compote, and sponge cake. On Saturday afternoon, cold fish, chopped liver, and calf's-foot jelly are eaten with pickles followed by sweet lockshen kugel with apples, nuts, and raisins. On Saturday evening, smoked salmon and bagels, pickled herring and potato salad, chopped eggs, sliced cucumbers with sour cream, and cheesecake are laid out.

The Sephardi world has as many traditional Sabbath dishes as there are communities. Indeed, you will find that most of the Sephardi recipes in the book are Friday and Saturday dishes. One chapter in the Sephardi part of the book is devoted to dafina and other, variously named dishes that are left to cook overnight for the Saturday lunch.

ROSH HASHANAH— THE NEW YEAR

On the 1st of Tishri, which usually falls in late September or early October

THE JEWISH NEW YEAR begins at sunset and is celebrated for two days. They are solemn as well as happy, joyous days. The shrill sound of the shofar (ram's horn) blown in the synagogue with sobbing and wailing notes followed by a long piercing sound recalling Abraham's offering of his son Isaac as a sacrifice to God, reflects the solemn, dramatic character of the holiday.

It is a widespread custom to eat a piece of apple dipped in honey while a prayer is said asking God for a sweet year. Some Sephardim, including ourselves in Egypt, dipped the apple slices in sugar, having dropped them first in water with a little lemon juice and orange-blossom water so that they did not brown.

Traditional Ashkenazi New Year foods include a round hallah with raisins, which looks like a crown and symbolizes continuity and the hope that the year will be rounded like a circle. The same bread is baked in the shape of a ladder—representing life's ladder, which is in the hands of God—and also in the shape of a bird, following the words in Isaiah: "As hovering birds, so will the Lord protect Jerusalem." Chicken soup is eaten with round pasta—farfel or mandlen. A fish, symbol of fertility, is cooked with the head on, to express the hope of being at the head. In Yiddish folklore, carrots are associated with gold coins, and carrot tzimmes is eaten as a symbol of prosperity and good fortune, or, according to another interpretation, to increase merits over shortcomings. Honey cake and teiglach (honey pastries) and apple strudel are New Year pastries. A new fruit of the season is eaten—usually pomegranate, because of its regular appearance in the Torah as a fruit of the Land of Israel, and because it is said to have 613 seeds, the same number as the commandments.

The Sephardim eat a sheep's head baked in the oven so "that they may always be at the head and not at the tail and hold their heads up high." This very ancient tradition, which appears in writings in the early Middle Ages, also recalls the sacrifice of Isaac by his father, Abraham. God, who had demanded it, stopped it in time. At that moment, Abraham and Isaac saw a ram and sacrificed it to God. The ram's or sheep's head is generally baked in the oven and is delicious, but it is commonly substituted for by brains—cooked as fritters or in an egg-and-lemon or tomato sauce, or baked with eggs (as in the North African minima)—or by boiled tongue, both of which are parts of the head, or

by a fish with the head left on. Many different foods are eaten to bring all that one hopes for in the New Year.

In Egypt, we ate fresh or dried black-eyed peas as a symbol of abundance and fecundity. Other communities eat chickpeas, rice, and couscous and sesame seeds for the same reason. All kinds of dishes, including pilafs, omelettes, almodrotes (gratins), salads, stuffed vegetables, vegetable fritters and pies, are made with green vegetables, such as chard, spinach, fava or broad beans, green peas, green beans, zucchini, and okra, to symbolize a new beginning. In North Africa they served green (not black) olives and drank mint tea, and when the New Year fell on the Sabbath there was t'fina pkaila with beans and spinach. Round foods, such as meatballs, green peas, chickpeas, and round or ring-shaped breads and pastries, embody the aspiration that the year is full and rounded. Because the number seven is believed to bring good luck, couscous is prepared "aux sept légumes" (with seven vegetables).

The New Year is a time for sweet things. In some countries, even meat, chicken, and vegetable dishes are sweet. Potatoes are replaced by sweet potatoes, onions are caramelized, and meats are cooked with quince, prunes, dates, and raisins, and sometimes also with sugar or honey.

Zette Guineaudeau in her book *Les Secrets des Cuisines en Terre Marocaine* lists various vegetables sweetened with sugar eaten by Jews on the New Year in different parts of Morocco. On the Mediterranean coast, it was chickpeas, beans, little onions, turnips, zucchini, and pumpkin cooked with oil, sugar, and cinnamon. On the Atlantic coast, green vegetables such as spinach and Swiss chard were cooked long and slow—sometimes with pieces of meat from a sheep's head—until the vegetables acquired a soft, jammy taste.

In *La Cuisine Juive Marocaine*, Viviane and Nina Moryoussef describe a dish of seven vegetables and meat from a lamb's head, symbolizing achievement and good luck. Carrots, turnips, leeks, potatoes, quinces, pumpkin, and beets (seven is a lucky number) are put in a large pan and cooked with oil and water, a little sugar, cinnamon, and saffron.

Oriental New Year meals end with fresh dates, figs, and above all pomegranates—all of which are mentioned in the Bible—as the new fruits of the season. In Egypt, we thought pomegranates would cause our family to bear many children. We ate the seeds sprinkled with orange-blossom water and sugar. Pastries were made with sesame or aniseed, which also symbolized fecundity, or were stuffed with nuts or dates and soaked in syrup. Jams were made with quince, figs, dates, and apples. White things—such as milk puddings, coconut jam, and the sharope blanco (an almost all-sugar jam)—evoke purity, whereas golden-pumpkin jam, like all saffron-colored foods, evokes joy and happiness.

Nothing sharp or bitter is served—there is no vinegar or lemon or tamarind—and nothing black—no eggplants or chocolate. Green, not black olives are eaten, and mint or green tea is drunk instead of black coffee.

Yom Kippur— the Day of Atonement

Comes ten days after Rosh Hashanah, on the 10th of Tishri

THE DAY OF ATONEMENT is a day of fasting and praying. It is a time for making up with people, for paying emotional and other debts and giving money to charity; for remembering deceased relatives and lighting candles for them. Men and women wear white clothes at the synagogue as a symbol of purity, and shoes made out of cloth, not leather. For Sephardim, it is a time for top hats and tails and finery. For the Ashkenazim, it is a time for solemn dress. The evening service is dramatic and emotive, with the chanting of the Kol Nidre accompanied by heart-rending sad melodies and the Viduim, or "confessions," when sins are enumerated while the heart is beaten with the right hand and the shofar is blown.

The meal before the fast—eaten in the afternoon, before sunset, on the eve of Yom Kippur—must be filling but simple and bland. It must not be salty or spicy, so as not to induce thirst. It is traditional for the Ashkenazim to eat chicken soup with stuffed matzo balls or kreplach filled with chicken, "so that kindness will cover (as the dough does the filling) any strict judgment of misdeeds." For breaking the fast, the usual meal, served with lemon tea, is chopped herring, chicken soup with mandlen, roast chicken with stuffing (in Alsace they serve poule-au-pot), carrot tzimmes, fruit compote, sponge cake, teiglach, and fresh fruit.

In the Sephardi world, the pre-fast meal is simple and plain with no sweets at the end. It also starts with chicken soup, of which there are many versions (in Egypt it was an egg-and-lemon soup), followed by a plain chicken dish (with us it is boiled chicken with rice). The fast is broken with a cold drink—lemonade or apricot juice, almond milk, orange or sour cherry syrup—followed by little savory and sweet pastries—borekas, cigars, cookies, pastries stuffed with nuts, buns with raisins and walnuts, sweet anise-flavored breads—served with tea. In many communities the meal is a dairy meal. My mother made sambousak with cheese, spinach fila, kahk, taramasalata, a cream-cheese dip, an eggplant cream, salads, and various pastries. That was enough for us in London, but back in Egypt we waited until it was possible to eat meat and had another full meal with chicken—usually stuffed with rice, ground meat, raisins, and pine nuts.

The custom of the second meal is widespread. Mouths are rinsed and a piece of bread is eaten in between. Chicken is the traditional Yom Kippur food in all communities, because of the custom of *kapparoth* (atonement) by which a chicken is killed for every member of the family (see the chapter on Sephardi poultry). Dishes are prepared that can be cooked the day before and simply reheated. In North Africa there are, among many dishes, chicken couscous, chicken stew with chickpeas, chicken fried with eggplant or with quince, and especially the rich soup full of vegetables and legumes called harira, which the Muslims eat at Ramadan.

SUKKOT

Beginning on the 15th of Tishri, it lasts eight days (seven in Israel) and usually falls in early October

SUKKOT, also known as the Feast of Tabernacles or booths, is the festival when Jews spend their time in a *sukkah*—a booth or hut built with plants and branches, which represents the temporary huts the Jews lived in during their time in the wilderness and symbolizes God's protection. In the Talmud it was laid down that "branches of fig trees on which there are figs, vines with grapes, palm branches with dates, and wheat with ears" should be used for the *sukkah*, and that

pomegranates and phials of wine should decorate the table.

In *Les Secrets des Cuisines en Terre Marocaine*, Zette Guineaudeau remembers it in Fez, when hundreds of bundles of reeds and long grasses were sold, lined against the walls of Bab Smarine and Bab Maghzen. People carried them away on their backs, the ends sweeping the ground. Huts were built on rooftop terraces and lined with cloth, then filled inside with rugs, mattresses covered with brocades, and silk shawls and embroidered cushions. Strings of electric bulbs lit them up. At night you could hear the men singing prayers at the top of their voices, calling from one rooftop to another and toasting each other with wine and mahia (a liquor that the Jews specialized in making).

Four symbolic plants enumerated in the Torah are part of the rituals of Sukkot. They are the etrog (citron), which looks like but is larger than a lemon and has a magnificent fragrance; the young shoot of a palm tree; the branch of a myrtle bush; and the branch of a willow. Blessings are recited while these are held together and gently swayed as a symbol that Jews should complement each other and stick together in harmony.

Sukkot is one of the most beautiful and enjoyable of festivals, and one of the most noticeable to outsiders because of the huts. There are many accounts by travelers and writers commenting on the huts built on terraces, rooftops, and balconies. In North Africa, it was the custom to burn the branches in a bonfire around which the family would make a ring.

Sukkot is also a harvest festival, which celebrates farming and nature and the gathering in of fruit. There are no special foods for Sukkot, but vegetables and fruit are the theme of the meals that are eaten in the *sukkah*. Soups, rice

Mazagan während des Laubhüttenfestes.

Postcard of Sukkot huts on rooftops in Mazagan, Morocco

dishes, and couscous are made with vegetables. Fruit salads and compotes are embellished with pomegranate seeds, and all kinds of fruit pies and puddings, cakes and strudels, jams and preserves are presented. A traditional Ashkenazi dish on the last day of the feast is chicken soup with kreplach, a kind of ravioli, the dough folded into a triangle over the ground meat or chicken filling. This soup symbolizes the covering up of God's stringency with loving kindness. Madame Guineaudeau writes that, in Morocco, on the first day of Sukkot a couscous was eaten. On the sixth day some families ate fresh fava-bean soup. During the week they ate maakouda with chicken, and on the last day of the feast caramelized almonds were distributed by the synagogue.

HANUKAH— THE FESTIVAL OF LIGHTS

Beginning on the 25th of Kislev and lasting eight days, it usually falls at the end of December

HANUKAH COMMEMORATES a victory and the rededication of the desecrated Temple to the God of Israel. The victory is that of a small band of Jews led by Judah Maccabeus in their battle against the Syrian Hellenists and the oppressive reign of King Antiochus Epiphanes in 165 B.C. The Maccabean uprising is significant because it was the first time that the Jews resorted to arms in order to preserve their faith and religious liberties. The victorious Judah returned to Jerusalem to find a sacked and burned

Temple which had been desecrated by pagan rituals. All the oil vessels had been polluted by substances repugnant to the Jewish faith, except for one cruse, which contained the pure, consecrated olive oil and still had the High Priest's seal. But it contained only enough oil to burn for one day. The Jews lit it, and it lasted eight days, allowing the priests to cleanse the Temple precincts while they prepared new supplies of holy oil.

The miracle of the oil is symbolized in Jewish homes by the kindling of eight lights. Starting with one light, each night one more is lit until the eighth day, when eight are lit. Years ago in Egypt, we had wicks floating in oil in little glass cups, but a nine-branched candlestick or menorah, called a *hanukiah,* is generally used today. The ninth candle, in the middle, serves to light the eight others. The miracle of the oil is remembered in the kitchen with the abundant quantities used to deep-fry the traditional Hanukah treats. The Ashkenazim eat potato latkes (grated potato fritters). In Israel they make soufganioth or ponchkes (jam-filled doughnuts). The Sephardim eat fritters in syrup variously called zalabia, loukoumades, sfenj, and yoyos. Italians eat chicken pieces dipped in batter and deep-fried. Moroccans eat couscous with chicken that has been deep-fried rather than boiled.

A "flaming-tea" ceremony, which celebrates the burning light, is an old Hanukah custom of Russian Jews. Everybody puts a lump of sugar in a spoon, pours brandy over it, then sets it alight and drops it in a glass of tea.

Another Hanukah custom practiced since the Middle Ages is to eat dairy foods. This is in tribute to Judith, who saved her besieged city—Bethulia, in Judea—from the enemy Holofernes. According to the story, he was in love with her. One night she served him a salty cheese, which made him thirsty, so that he drank a lot of wine. When he fell into a drunken stupor, she cut his head off with a sword. To commemorate her action, Ashkenazim eat foods with curd cheese and sour cream, such as cheese blintzes and cheesecake, and Sephardim eat cheese bemuelos. In Morocco, couscous au beurre is accompanied by milk.

Once upon a time, Jews ate goose for the festive Hanukah dinner—a habit adopted from the Christians, who ate goose at Christmas, which falls a few days from Hanukah. The custom continues in Alsace, but elsewhere the main dish is now roast turkey, duck, or chicken. In Alsace it is also usual to eat choucroute at Hanukah. I wonder if the cabbage is symbolic, because soupe aux choux (cabbage soup) is eaten in North Africa.

PURIM

On the 14th of Adar, which usually falls in March

PURIM IS a day of jubilation and a time to exchange edible gifts. It is a historical feast commemorating the outwitting by Esther—a Jewess who was married to the king of Persia—of the Persian Haman, who had decreed a sentence of death for all Jews; and commemorating by extension all the times that Jews escaped persecution. It is celebrated with street parades and little plays performed in fancy dress representing Queen Esther, King Ahasuerus, and the odious Haman, who ended up hanged.

The festive meal, which takes place in the late afternoon, is the only holiday meal where heavy drinking is encouraged as a way of showing elation. Families send trays of mixed pastries to each other. The symbolic foods of Purim are connected with Haman and Esther. The Ashkenazim have hamantashen, a three-cornered pastry like the three-cornered hats worn during the Babylonian exile in Haman's time, which can be stuffed with various fillings, including plum jam and poppy seeds. The poppy seeds are in memory of Queen Esther's three-day fast, during which she subsisted only on seeds when she broke her fast at night while she prayed to God to repeal the decree. Poppy-seed biscuits and poppy-seed cakes are also eaten. Another Purim specialty is the triangular kreplach filled with cheese.

The main meal is vegetarian and dairy, because Queen Esther lived in the palace on a vegetarian diet so as not to infringe the dietary laws. Beans, peas, and chickpeas are eaten. In North Africa, berkokch (large-grained couscous) was served with fava beans and butter and milk poured over it, or the grain was eaten with raisins, sugar, and cinnamon (page 505). A fish was served as a symbol of fertility. It was cooked with saffron—the yellow representing joy. And to add to the merry atmosphere, cake was soaked with brandy and liquor was poured over fruit compotes.

In Sephardi communities, pastries shaped like Haman's ears—orejas de Aman—baked or deep-fried, then dipped in syrup, were traditional. Families prepared mountains of little delicacies—sweetmeats stuffed with marzipan, pastries stuffed with almonds, walnuts, or dates—and sent them around in trays to relatives and friends.

PESAH—PASSOVER

Beginning on the 14th of Nisan and lasting eight days (seven in Israel), it usually falls in April

PASSOVER CELEBRATES one of the most important events in Jewish history: the Exodus from Egypt, which led to the birth of the Jewish nation. In memory of the Jews who fled in such a hurry that their dough did not have time to rise, and following the injunction in the Torah that "Seven days shall there be no leaven found in your home," foods considered leaven (*hametz*) are forbidden. Fermenting agents such as yeast are forbidden, as is the fermentation of five types of grain—wheat, barley, rye, oats, and spelt—which are named in the Torah and can ferment. Bread, cakes, biscuits—all foods that contain ingredients made from these grains—are *hametz.*

The Ashkenazim also forbid rice and dried corn, dried beans, peas, and lentils, because of their similarity to the grains mentioned and because of their capacity to ferment, but the Sephardim allow them. Fermentation per se is not forbidden (Passover wine is fermented), and the grains are forbidden only when there is a possibility that they may ferment. Indeed, matzos—the unleavened bread of Passover, called "matzah" in Israel and by the Sephardim, is made with flour. Flour that has been milled with new millstones from wheat that has been guarded from the time of growing to the time of cutting, through storage, so that it could not get wet, is allowed.

The rituals of ridding the home of *hametz* involve weeks of cleaning extensively, and "selling" forbidden *hametz* to non-Jewish neighbors and buying it back when the feast is over. In Orthodox homes, only after total cleansing can the special Passover silverware, dishes, and utensils be taken out of storage and the "kosher for Pesah" provisions, including matzos, be brought into the home. Part of my father's happy childhood memories was the "search for *hametz*" the night before Pesah, when, armed with a candle, a feather, a wooden spoon, and a paper bag, he looked with his older sisters for pieces of bread hidden by his father, and the whole thing was burned.

The most important event of Passover is the Seder meal, which can occur twice, over two nights, at the beginning of the festival. Food plays an all-important part in the rituals by in-

carnating, with its symbolism, episodes of the Exodus epic. Every year at the Seder table, Jews retell the story of the Israelites' fantastic and miraculous escape from slavery in Egypt more than three thousand years ago. It is told in great detail, and the unfolding events are relived with great passion and ceremony.

In Egypt, with our extended family, we celebrated our ancestors' flight from Egypt, but we were still there. As children bunched together at the end of the table, we found this a matter of hilarity. For the Muslim cooks sitting in the kitchen, it was also a laughing matter, even when my father poured the wine enumerating the ten plagues on the Egyptians. (They could vaguely understand, because the Hebrew

Seder in Tbilisi, Georgia, 1924. All over the world, in every Jewish community, the Seder meal of Passover, which recalls the story of the Exodus from Egypt, brings extended families together.

for Egyptians—al Mitzraim—and many other words are similar to the Arabic.) But after the first war against the new State of Israel, the celebration of Passover in Egypt became tense.

The large Seder tray was one of the few things my parents brought with them to England. Every year we placed it in front of my father on a pile of telephone books and covered it with a small embroidered tablecloth. On it were placed six little dishes, containing three matzos under a napkin, to remind us of the Jews who had no time to let their dough rise when they fled, and five symbolic foods.

In Europe, a decorative ceramic Seder plate, which is divided into sections, carries the ritual foods: karpas, a green vegetable such as parsley or little Bibb lettuce, representing new growth, which is dipped in salt water, symbolizing the tears of the slaves; maror, bitter herbs, which can be chicory, cress, or grated horseradish, to remind us of the bitter times of slavery; betza, a roasted egg, representing the sacrificial offering of a roasted animal to God in the Temple on each holiday (in my family we had one hamine egg for every member of the family); zeroah, a lamb-shank bone, representing the lamb sacrificed by the slaves on the eve of the Exodus and the sacrificial paschal offering in the Temple (in my family we had a boiled shoulder, which we ate); haroset, a fruit-and-nut paste recalling the color of the mortar made with Nile silt that the Jews used when they built the pyramids for the Pharaohs.

Reading from the Haggadah—the book that recounts the story of the liberation and gives the order of procedure—my father chanted in the old Egyptian style, and broke up and passed around the symbolic foods and the wine. He broke off half of the middle matzos and rolled it in a cloth so that it could be hidden away as the afikomen. His voice became exalted when he got to the crossing of the Red Sea, the manna from heaven, the giving of the Torah to Moses on Mount Sinai, and the ten plagues. We averted our eyes as he poured the wine symbolizing the plagues from a glass into a bowl held by my youngest niece. As he grew older and more tired, he shortened the readings, muttering, "Wa casa, casa, casa" (etc., etc., etc.). We always left the door open for Elijah's expected visit and set a chair and a glass of wine for him.

The demands of cooking without grain or leaven have produced a whole range of distinctive Jewish variants of dishes making use of ground almonds, potato flour, ground rice, matzo meal, and sheets of matzos to make all kinds of cakes, pancakes, pies, dumplings, and fritters. For instance, in the Arab world, kibbeh, usually made with cracked wheat and lamb, was prepared with ground rice. In Eastern Europe, matzo-ball or egg-drop soup replaced vermicelli. Stuffed neck was filled with mashed potato instead of the flour-based filling; sponge cake was made with ground almonds or potato starch. One of the gastronomic highlights was the splendid cakes made with ground almonds, hazelnuts, or walnuts. One of the most affectionately remembered is matzo-meal fritters.

In Morocco at Passover, it was the tradition to barbecue foods, because when the Hebrews left Egypt they ate in a hurry and grilled their foods on a wood fire. One of the Passover specialties is a fresh fava-bean soup, because fava beans were eaten by the Hebrew slaves in Egypt.

Shavuot—the Giving of the Torah

On the 6th of Sivan, usually falls in late May or June

SHAVUOT CELEBRATES the giving of the Torah, the book that holds the Ten Commandments, by God to the Jews at Mount Sinai, and their becoming a nation by accepting his commandments and pledging to be "a kingdom of priests and a holy nation." By ancient tradition, a dairy meal is eaten on the first day. It is attributed to the Biblical quotation "And He gave us this land flowing with milk and honey," and to the legend that Jews did not have time to slaughter animals and kosher the meat after leaving Sinai. The specialties of Shavuot are all the usual things in their cheese or dairy versions. For the Ashkenazim, they are cheese blintzes and strudel, cheese kreplach, lokshen pudding with cream cheese, borscht with sour cream, cheesecake, and paschko. For the Sephardim, they are filas and sambousak with cheese, milk puddings like sutlach, and pastries like ataif, stuffed with cheese. Shavuot is also regarded as a harvest festival of fruit, and all kinds of fruit puddings and cakes are eaten.

The Ashkenazi World

The Development of an
Ashkenazi Style of Cooking

WHAT WAS first known in the West as "Jewish food"—gefilte fish, chopped liver, pickled cucumber, chopped herring, and potato latkes—was the cooking of the Russian, Polish, and Eastern European Jews, who immigrated to America and Western Europe in waves; this started as a trickle in the mid-seventeenth century and turned into a great flood by the late nineteenth and early twentieth. Theirs was the greatest mass movement of Jews ever to take place. It had an enormous impact on the Jewish communities they joined in America and Canada, Palestine, Britain, France, Belgium, and Holland, as well as in South Africa and South America, and it radiated the styles of cooking of the countries they came from throughout the world. Through these migrations the world first became acquainted with the cheesecakes of

Eastern Europe, the borscht of Russia, and the strudels of Hungary.

The immigrants came from a vast territory, but their foods—like their language, Yiddish, and their culture—were similar, because they shared the same roots and history, and also because the countries they came from had similar foods. In their countries of origin there had been two parallel systems of cooking—peasant food and an aristocratic cuisine influenced by France and Italy. The basis of the "Jewish food" that we know is the peasant food of the shtetl—the provincial townlets and villages that represented the Jewish experience in Eastern Europe during the past three centuries. It was the "poor food" of people whose life was a perpetual struggle between crushing poverty and insecurity, for the history of the Ashkenazi communities from the twelfth century—the time of the Crusades—was one of flight and destruction, with a succession of restrictions, expulsions, and massacres. Some of the dishes represent a grander life-style, and the legacies stretch beyond the shtetl deep into the past.

In the early Middle Ages, there were large communities of Jews in Western Europe—mainly in France and Italy, and in Germany, where they were most numerous. They began to move east to escape persecution at the time of the Crusades (the first Crusade was at the very end of the eleventh century, and the last in 1320), but the great exodus was in the sixteenth and seventeenth centuries. In the same way that Yiddish, a thirteenth-century German dialect that became the Jewish lingua franca, absorbed new vernaculars in the different environments and combined Hebrew elements and a spicing of old French, old Italian, and Slavic, the culinary repertoire of the Jews grew from a medieval German base with old French and Italian influences and eventually drew in dishes from many parts of Eastern Europe, especially Poland, Lithuania, the Ukraine, Hungary, Bohemia, Slovakia, Bulgaria, and Romania. It reflects the movement of the Jews in the area, and variations of certain dishes have been shown to coincide with the different Yiddish dialects in geographic belts which follow the movements of particular communities. For instance, sweet versions of the famous gefilte fish follow the areas where Hassidic communities, who originated in Polish Galicia, spread through the Ukraine and all over Eastern Europe.

German Beginnings

MANY JEWISH DISHES originate in Germany, where Jews had lived since very early times, dispersed in small towns and villages, and where, in the tenth century, an important Jewish culture was born. Religion was central to everything, and everything was directed by the Torah and the Talmud.

In medieval Europe, Jews had congregated in separate parts of towns for protection and so as to be able to practice their religion, and Jewish quarters grew up around synagogues. In Germany, the Judengasse (Jewish quarters) had their own cemeteries, schools, laundries, public baths, law courts, slaughterhouses, and bakehouses. Housewives brought their food to be cooked in the communal oven and did their cooking at the bakehouse. Few had cooking facilities at home. One part of the bakehouse was reserved for meat, another for dairy. The oven and cooking utensils, including huge copper cauldrons used for wedding feasts, were provided free by the congregation. A *shohet*, or slaughterer, was available. There were banqueting rooms and dancing halls for weddings and festivals, and for getting together on the Sabbath, and there were guest houses for travelers. A community fund provided those who could not pay with three days' free board and lodging.

The religious dietary laws were abided by with strict tenacity, and this had the effect of involving Jews in food trades. Because wine manufactured by a gentile could not be consumed and food cooked by an unsupervised gentile could not be eaten, Jews were encouraged to produce and sell wine and food themselves. At one time they controlled the market in wine and grain, dealing in oil as a side line. In Southern Europe they owned flour mills and vineyards. Jewish orchards were renowned in France. In France and in Germany, where Jews had had vineyards along the Rhine as early as the fourth century, they produced wine. In Germany they reared geese.

Throughout Europe, Jews were much in evidence at city markets and country fairs, selling pickles, preserves, and pastries. Jewish bakeries were common.

There was a strong ascetic streak in German Jews, and their lives were inclined to spirituality rather than sensual expression. Ethical writings from medieval times are full of encouragement towards frugality and self-restraint in eating— "the most animal of instincts." Rabbis expressed distaste at the way their French, Italian, and Spanish coreligionists enjoyed their meals and their glass of wine. In *Eat and Be Satisfied*, John Cooper quotes a thirteenth-century letter reprimanding the French Jews for "studying the Talmud with their stomachs full of meat, vegetables and wine" and another warning that "gross overeating is as dangerous to the body as a sword, besides that it bars one from occupation with the law of God and the reverence due to him." But despite all the protestations they were hearty eaters like the Germans. They ate like the Germans—substantial foods, warming soups thick with oats, barley, groats, and dumplings; heavy rye and dark breads; pickled and boiled meats and sausages; freshwater fish and salt herring, cabbage and carrots. They had a penchant for strong flavors, such as horseradish, sour pickles, and sauerkraut, and for sweet-and-sour and savory-sweet combinations like cabbage and apple. And like the Germans, they stuffed goose necks, chopped goose liver, and chopped and stuffed fish.

But there were also foreign elements in their cooking, adopted through their contacts with their European coreligionists. Noodles came from Italy. Pasta had been introduced there by the Arabs in Sicily when the island had a substantial Jewish community. The Jews called it "grimseli" and "vermisellish," after the Italian vermicelli. Their mercantile activities brought the Jews of Europe into contact with exotic ingredients and Oriental culinary styles. Since the early Middle Ages, they had been involved in international trade, trafficking by raft and craft down the valleys of the Rhone, the Danube, and the Rhine, and going far afield. For their own ritual requirements, they imported myrtle from France and citrons from the coasts of the Mediterranean. They dealt in sugar, spices, dried fruit, and nuts, and all kinds of foodstuffs from the East. Their role in introducing such comestibles to Northern Europe produced an enlightened spirit in their own cooking. They became known for their immoderate use of garlic and onion, and for their taste for spices, fruits, and nuts (they were famous for using almond marzipan in their pastries).

Until the thirteenth century, Jews had been only partly isolated, by the practice of their religion and through the needs of their communal organization, from the people they lived among. In many ways their lives had been interwoven and symbiotic with the lives of the German people, which meant they were familiar with regional foods from all over the country. But when the Church's efforts to proselytize turned into animosity, contacts with Christians became minimal. The Jews were expelled from one town to another; they were obliged to wear badges and forbidden to socialize. They were gradually denied the right to trade. Excluded from handicrafts (they had been silk dyers, jewelers, glassblowers, metalworkers, spinners, weavers, and bookbinders), barred from many trades, and not allowed to own land, they were pushed into moneylending and peddling secondhand goods—the only trades left open to them. The Crusades, which destroyed many communities; the Black Death in 1349; and the turmoil that followed the Protestant Reformation in the sixteenth century, left the Jewish communities much reduced and desperately poor. As their material horizons narrowed and they were denied a free and open public life, they turned in on themselves to find solace in religion and in their home life.

In their closed-in world, the celebration of religious festivals, weddings, bar mitzvahs, and circumcisions made it possible to remain indifferent to the world outside. Feasting and fasting became all-important. Indeed, so luxurious and ostentatious did banqueting become that communal authorities enacted sumptuary laws to curb the excesses. The laws and guidelines were designed to prevent envy from the outside towards the community, and as an egalitarian measure to protect poorer Jews from humiliation.

Only get-togethers of a religious or semi-religious nature were allowed, such as a circumcision, *pidyon ha-ben* (the redemption of a firstborn son), betrothal, wedding, bar mitzvah, or banquet in honor of a visiting scholar or rabbi. Communal rules regulated the number of guests (how many men, how many women and children, how distant the relatives) and the variety and quantity of food that was offered. A hospitality tax was levied for each extra guest, and anyone who infringed the laws was liable to pay a fine to the synagogue. The synagogue authorities were invited to all festivities and were able to gauge the extent to which the sumptuary limitations were exceeded.

The only entertaining permitted without bounds was that offered to the poor. Meals provided for the poor were considered offerings to God. Hospitality had become a necessity to protect the class of traveling preachers and teachers and itinerant beggar-students that resulted from the persecution and destruction of communities. No restrictions were placed on the number of poor students a rabbi might entertain, and some had dozens permanently at their tables. Poor wayfarers who wandered from place to place had become a part of Jewish life, and looking after them was a necessary branch of communal organization. Guests were distributed among households in the town at which they stopped. Sometimes, on Friday night, they waited at the gate to be chosen. Although a stigma was attached to any man in the community who was observed too often at other men's tables (he was labeled a "diner out"), it was considered not merely permissible but praiseworthy to attend certain hospitable gatherings of a semi-religious kind.

By the time Jews became segregated in their ghettos, by edict, in the sixteenth century, they had developed a unique and powerful internal social culture. As the French historian Fernand Braudel commented, the ghetto became their prison but was also the citadel into which they withdrew to defend their faith and the continuity of their culture. It was at that time that ritual took an increasing hold on Jewish life. A code of kitchen and table manners was formalized, and particular dishes were adopted to celebrate the Sabbath and festivals. The men, who often devoted themselves entirely to studying Jewish Law and left their wives and daughters to earn the family living, took a particular interest in the kitchen. They became involved with the minutiae of the dietary laws and rituals concerning food. On Thursdays and Fridays they would be seen bargaining for Sabbath delicacies at the market, and on Fridays they helped with cleansing the dishes and saucepans and setting the table.

It is in the cooped-up world within the

ghetto walls, in the tall houses that met at the top and obscured the sunlight from the narrow streets, that a set of dishes became associated with holidays and were marked forever with a Jewish stamp. Everyday food could be desperately poor, but the best German burgher dishes were reserved for Sabbath and religious festivals. Braided white hallah bread, sweet-and-sour fish, stuffed fish, chopped goose liver, broth with noodles, meat pies, boiled pickled beef, roast goose, and kugel—a sweet pudding made with noodles or bread—were eaten on Friday evening. Cholent was left to cook overnight in the communal oven for Saturday. This dish—one of the most representative of Jewish cooking—in a version cooked today combines different meats, sometimes including goose and sausage, with barley or buckwheat and beans, and is cooked slowly in plenty of goose fat. It is believed to be related to the French cassoulet, and its name to be a combination of the medieval French words *chauld* (hot) and *lent* (slow). This interpretation is given weight by the fact that Jews in the region of the Languedoc, where cassoulet originated, were expelled in 1394 and headed for Germany. In *Eat and Be Satisfied*, John Cooper notes that the first reference to cholent was by Rabbi Isaac of Vienna (c.1180–c.1250), who reported that he had seen it in his teacher's home in France at the end of the twelfth century. White haricot beans, which came to Europe from the New World, were a late addition to the dish. They may have arrived through connections with the secret Jews from Portugal, who were very familiar with the beans and who settled in cities in southwestern France in the sixteenth century. In Spain, today, large white beans are called judías, meaning "Jewish." I wonder if there is a link.

IN POLAND AND RUSSIA

FROM THE thirteenth century, Jews in flight from France, Italy, and Germany were moving into Poland, which already had some Jewish communities, mainly from Byzantium. By the sixteenth and seventeenth centuries they moved in great masses at the invitation of the king of Poland. At first they lived under the king's protection in the royal cities of Cracow, Poznan, and Lemberg. But by the end of the seventeenth century, faced with the hostility of the townspeople and of the Church, they moved to the provinces of Galicia, Lithuania, and the Ukraine, where the Polish nobility (Jews called them Poretz) invited them to manage their agricultural lands and to settle in the shtetl—the new towns built on their demesnes. The nobles leased the Jews flour mills, dairy-processing plants, and taverns, and gave them exclusive rights to brew vodka and schnapps. They allowed them to farm fish in ponds, especially pike and carp, which became associated with Jewish foods. But the masses remained very poor, on the verge of starvation, limited by restrictions and prohibitions, and in constant fear of attacks by the peasantry and Cossacks.

When Poland was partitioned three times at the end of the eighteenth century and its territories were annexed by Russia, Prussia, and Austria, the Jews in these territories became subjects of three different crowns. It was in this way, and also with the heavy migrations of Jews from Poland into neighboring countries, that the foods of the shtetl—including those that originated in Germany, such as hallah bread, gefilte fish, chopped liver, cholent, and lock-

Street scene in Vilkomir. Lithuania was a Jewish center of major cultural importance.

shen pudding—were transported all over Eastern Europe, together with the social structures (large families, men devoted to religious studies, women earning the family living) and the culture based on the Yiddish vernacular and German rabbinic traditions.

In 1772, when the Polish territories of the Ukraine, Lithuania, Courland (now in Latvia), and Belorussia were annexed by Russia, the great Jewish masses living in those territories became Russian subjects under the rule of the tsars (before that, Jews had not been allowed to live in Russia). In this way, Russian Jewry was a continuation of Polish Jewry. It came to represent the largest Jewish community in the world, and was the stronghold of the Ashkenazi culture.

In the beginning in Russia, as in Poland, the Jews had represented a kind of middle class between landowning aristocracy and peasantry. Many earned their living from leasing flour mills, inns, and taverns and managing estates and forests. They were also craftsmen, shopkeepers, and hawkers, and their shoestring enterprises included making and selling soda water and shoe wax, syrup, pretzels, goose fat, and pickles. But their position deteriorated. They were confined, by Catherine the Great, to restricted areas in the Pale of Settlement (former Polish territories) and lived in a state of disenfranchisement and poverty under the constant threat of pogroms. Permission to live outside the confines of the Pale was granted only to certain groups, such as professionals and wealthy businessmen.

By the middle of the nineteenth century, Jewish society in Eastern Europe and Russia was transformed. With the growth of capitalism and the modernization of society, a Jewish proletariat and bourgeoisie had emerged in the cities. There were Jews of great wealth in St. Petersburg, Moscow, Kiev, and Odessa, and in Cracow and Warsaw. Some went into the sugar and flour industries, into soda-water and beer brewing, and into the salted-and-pickled-herring trade, importing their fish from Scotland, England, Norway, and Holland. Jewish dairies produced sour milk and curd cheese. Almost the entire grain trade of the northwestern provinces was in Jewish hands. Fortunes were made in banking, shipping, and the railroads. A rich and vital new Jewish secular culture emerged. Literature, poetry, music, and painting blossomed. There were Jewish art collectors and patrons, lawyers, and doctors. A Russian and Polish Jewish intelligentsia played an important role in the cultural and political life of their countries. Jews became eligible for officer ranks in the Russian armed forces and could be elevated to the status of gentry. But the great majority of Jews in Russia and Poland were hopelessly poor, and suffered all kinds of restrictions, legalized discrimination, and the ever-present threat of pogroms. A large number lived in the shtetl in total ignorance of the world beyond. The Russian Revolution shattered the whole traditional Jewish social structure in Russia, and the Holocaust ended the world of the shtetl.

The Culinary Baggage from Poland and Russia

The cooking traditions adopted in the different provinces of Poland and Russia were not all that different from each other, because most of the regions shared the same in-gredients and predilections, notably a taste for carp and salt herring, sausages and sauerkraut. They all had heavy dark and rye bread, they all made cucumber pickles, chicken soup, thick bean and lentil soups, pancakes and dumplings, and also sweet noodle puddings. They all used sour cream, dill, caraway, and poppy seed. The severe winter climate had enforced a reliance on grains such as barley, millet, and buckwheat, and on root vegetables and cabbage. The abundance of fruits—there were apples, pears, plums, cherries, gooseberries, currants, and raspberries—meant that they were used in everything from soups and sauces to pancakes, compotes, cakes, and pastries, and also as accompaniments to meat and poultry. Potatoes from the New World, which were rejected at first by the famished peasantry, became the best-loved staple in the late eighteenth century. In the nineteenth century, many impoverished communities survived on bread, onions, and potatoes. But each region did have its specialties and its special touches.

In Poland, Jews acquired a taste for sweetish foods. They used sugar with pickled herring and with vegetables such as carrots, turnips, and cabbage. It was there that they developed some of their most famous dishes, including fish with raisin sauce and the sweet version of gefilte fish with chrain—a red sauce made with grated horseradish and beet juice that counterbalances the sweetness of the fish. The Polish heritage includes cabbage leaves stuffed with rice; bagels, the famous ring breads that are first boiled, then baked; and the bialy, a bread roll covered with onion, which is named after the city of Białystok; slivovitz (plum brandy) and the habit of drinking wine with brandy and honey.

Lithuanian Jews, like their coreligionists in northern Poland, put very little sugar in their food and used a lot of pepper. Sour foods, such as iced beet soup, sorrel soup with lemon and sour cream, and fermented pickled cabbage, were most common in Lithuania, as was meat cooked with prunes. The areas near the Baltic Sea were famous for curing and pickling fish in the Scandinavian style. The Ukraine and Russia generally were strong on beet soups, on grain—especially kasha (buckwheat)—on curd cheese and sour cream. Blini (buckwheat pancakes) and knishes (potato-and-buckwheat pies), pirogi, piroshki, and baranki (sour-cream-dough cakes with poppy seed) were staples. The grander days of the Jewish elites in Eastern European communities brought the zakuski—spreads of small cold and hot dishes with which Russians and Poles began formal meals. They occasionally appear today in Jewish entertaining on blini as canapés.

THE HERITAGE FROM EAST CENTRAL EUROPE AND THE HAPSBURGIAN EMPIRE

THE ASHKENAZI DIASPORA also gradually spread westward and southward. During the Thirty Years' War (1618–1648), Germany began to readmit Jews, who supplied the armies. By the eighteenth century, the numerous German courts offered opportunities to financiers and "court Jews"—as those who served as financial advisers and agents to rulers in Europe were known—some of whom became extremely wealthy and powerful. The old Jewish communities in the lands that were to become Romania, Hungary, and Czechoslovakia grew large with

Походная жизнь. Закупка кавалеристами фуража у еврея.

Jewish grain merchants, Russia

Jews from the annexed Polish territories and immigrants from Poland and Russia.

In the nineteenth century, the Jews of Europe achieved emancipation. The process had begun when Napoleon's revolutionary armies carried their ideals of the Rights of Man and equality into the countries they conquered, ending the age of the ghetto. The spirit of Enlightenment spread through a Europe that was shedding feudalism and industrializing and helped all the Jewish communities to achieve economic and social integration. Jews flocked to large cities like Prague, Budapest, Vienna, and Bucharest.

A small minority attained wealth and prominence in banking and commerce, the liberal professions, and various industries, but the majority who flooded in from Russia and Poland remained a poor, uprooted working class. While Jews in the villages remained steeped in religious orthodoxy and tradition, speaking Yiddish—their Polish roots much in evidence—the Haskalah (Hebrew for "Enlightenment") spread modernization, acculturation, and integration in the cities. Although there was a certain replication of Polish Jewish culture, there was also a gradual assimilation of the varied local and ruling cultures (the lands were part of the German, Russian, and Austro-Hungarian empires and were ethnically diverse). Several essentially different Jewish communities developed. Hungarian became the language of the Jewish elite, German that of the business communities, and Czech, Romanian, and other languages were spoken regionally.

For the wealthy city elites who integrated the new European societies, the hold of the past and of tradition loosened. Many turned their back on their Jewish heritage and opened themselves to the new experiences of the modern, non-Jewish world. It was through this middle-class society who lived well that many of the more refined dishes entered the Jewish repertoire. At that time, the term *fressfroemingkeit,* or "culinary Jew," was used to describe assimilated Jews whose devoutness found expression only in eating traditional dishes on Jewish holidays.

Romania, which comprised the territories of Moldavia, Wallachia, and part of Dobrogea, became the second-largest country of East Central Europe in 1918, when it annexed neighboring Bukowina, Bessarabia, Dobrogea, and Transylvania. It had an important and mixed Jewish community, including a small but influential group of Sephardi families in Bucharest who dominated the commercial life of the country, and Hassidic Polish communities in Moldavia.

Czechoslovakia, which encompassed Bohemia, Moravia, Slovakia, and Sub-Carpathia, also had an agglomeration of different Jewries. It was greatly industrialized by the beginning of the twentieth century, with considerable help from the Jews who constituted a well-to-do middle class. Prague was, over many centuries, one of the most important Jewish centers in the world, its Judenstadt (Jewish quarter) a city within a city.

The Austro-Hungarian Empire had the largest Jewish population in Europe. Many assimilated into the Vienna and Budapest bourgeoisie, and "court Jews" were prominent, especially in Vienna. In Hungary, Jews became more politically and culturally assimilated than in any other country. They were agents and lessees of the Magyar landed, nobility who welcomed them into their midst, and they also constituted the industrial and commercial bourgeoisie.

The glittering epoch in East Central Europe left a rich culinary heritage with the Jews, especially those of the dual Austro-Hungarian

Jewish-owned shops in Budapest, 1890. In the late nineteenth century the Jewish population of Hungary had become centered in Budapest and constituted an industrial and commercial bourgeoisie.

monarchy. There, a rich and refined cosmopolitan cuisine, which was shared by the two countries, evolved through Viennese, French, Ottoman, and Magyar influences. (Viennese court food was Austro-French, and Hungary had been ruled by the Ottoman Turks.) A magnificent range of pastries and luscious flourless tortes, which you can see in Jewish patisseries around the world, is part of that grand tradition.

Peasant food was also part of the heritage. It is represented most remarkably by the incredible variety of dumplings, often interchangeably served sweet or savory, that are still part of the peasant diet in all of Central Europe.

The German, Austrian, and Czech legacy includes goose, cured meats, sausages, and salamis, sauerkraut, sweet and savory dumplings, potato salads, and a general passion for the potato. Veal

schnitzel and the jam-filled doughnuts that have become the ritual foods of Hanukah are from Vienna. Goulash, the famous paprika stew, and chicken paprikash were adopted in Hungary, as were cherry soups, blintzes (stuffed pancakes), and strudel. The paper-thin strudel dough was a legacy of the Turks, as were Hungarian stuffed peppers and tomatoes, which had never been accepted before in the Ashkenazi world. It seems that Jews had been afraid that tomatoes might not be kosher: the red juice looked like blood, which is forbidden. In Hungary the Jews learned to cook with wine, garlic and onion, and herbs and spices, and to put paprika, the sweetish red pepper powder, in almost everything. The cooking of Romania and the Balkans, which had much more in common with Turkey, brought grilled meats, roasted peppers, and eggplant puree, as well as the cornmeal mush known as mamaliga and the lavish use of yogurt and garlic.

When the Jews left in great waves for America and elsewhere to avoid conscription, escape pogroms, and earn a living, and later to flee Nazism, they took with them the old cooking traditions of their various regions of origin. The foods that recall the old communities have been passed on from one generation of immigrants to another, in every corner of the world. It seems, sometimes, as if martyrdom and nostalgia have invested them with almost holy qualities.

THE WORLD OF THE SHTETL

BY THE NINETEENTH CENTURY, the great majority of East European Jews were living in cities, but it was the world of the shtetl—in the countryside, with its wooden huts and muddy streets, which were often exclusively Jewish—that was the center of Ashkenazi life within the area stretching from the eastern borders of Germany to the western regions of tsarist Russia, for more than three centuries. Shtetl life shaped the Jewish cooking that we know, and memories of the great warmth and vitality of these closely knit communities inspire the sentiment around the food.

Through the first third of the twentieth century, the core of Jewish life remained in the shtetl. You cannot fully appreciate Ashkenazi food without an understanding of the setting in which it developed. An insight into life in the Jewish townlet and the particular culture that stretched across Eastern Europe in the period between the wars is provided by a remarkable book by Mark Zborowski and Elizabeth Herzog, *Life Is with People* (International Universities

Seder in an Austro-Hungarian home, with portraits of Archduke Franz Ferdinand and Emperor Franz Josef on the wall and the Prophet Elijah at the door

A shtetl in Poland

Press, 1952; Schocken, 1962). This anthropological study, based on interviews, is an analysis and presentation of the work of a research group at Columbia University in 1949. It is the best primary source on the subject, a general portrait that pieces together the memories of people and deals with every aspect of a world that no longer exists. It is extraordinary in that it sparkles with warmth and life. What follows about shtetl life, through page 57, is drawn from this brilliant work. In my adaptation and summary, I have tried to retain the words of the authors and the voices of the people.

In the small houses, which consisted of one or two rooms with wooden or earth floors, everything went on in the kitchen, including tailoring and making shoes. Sometimes a corner of the kitchen was rented out to a neighbor to carry on his own business. Geese and chickens were also kept in the whitewashed kitchen, which smelled of goose fat. People walked in and out from the street at all times to borrow an onion, to have a drink of tea from the simmering samovar, and to pass on the latest gossip. The door was always left open, except at night. Nobody knocked before coming in. Everyone was always busy, but never too busy to welcome a guest. At night everybody sat around the table for the light, to a variegated hum of activity—the mother picking feathers with the girls, the boys studying, the father chanting. Sometimes the children or grandchildren slept on top of the oven or on the wooden table.

Faced with a hostile and brutal outside world, the Jews developed otherworldly values, became obsessed with their mythical past, and waited for a redeeming future. Religious study offered men an escape from the reality of persecution and from the difficulty of earning a living, and became for them the most prestigious as well as the most cherished recreation. The minutiae of ritual were a prime source of satisfaction, and the rituals connected with food, such as the precise way in which a chicken should be slaughtered and the kinds of food to serve on Friday evenings, were an expression of the Jewish ethos and came to symbolize the eternal unity of Jewish life. The observance of religious dietary laws was a mixture of ritual prescribed in the sacred writings and folk custom interwoven with the written law. In that world, where people talked intimately with God, where the spiritual was exalted over the physical, and the ideal man was a pale emaciated scholar aflame with inner light, food was the link between the holy and the profane.

In the shadows of lawless disorder and the cramping boundaries of the shtetl, the Jews developed a powerful internal order and a highly formalized society which was dominated by rabbis. The men's area was the shul, or synagogue, where they spent most of their time, while the women ruled at home. The women were usually the breadwinners, with a store or stall at the market. The marketplace was the heart of the shtetl. It was a large earthen space surrounded by stores all run by women selling ironware and odds and ends—textiles, leather goods, shoes and hats, furs and pelts, pharmaceuticals, flour, pickles, spices, fruit, and meat. There was always a small hand-mill where you could take your grain to be ground, and a tavern serving liquor and tea from a big samovar. On Wednesday the market came alive, filled with high peasant wagons that arrived early in the morning packed with produce and livestock—horses, cows, and chickens, grain and fruit, vegetables and eggs. The peasants haggled and bantered until the deal was clinched with a clap of hands.

Jewish women did not have a sheltered life.

They moved around in carts from one town to another—as did the uneducated or *prost* men—selling dried fish and pickled herring, pickled cucumber and sweet preserves, as well as needles, threads, soap, and headscarves. They had contact with Christian peasants and merchants, and although most could hardly read they could speak Polish, Russian, and Hungarian, which the studious men in their ivory tower could barely do.

The women were responsible for the observance of the dietary laws and for maintaining and implementing domestic ritual. Even when her husband performed the ceremony, it was the wife's duty to have in readiness a cup of wine, a loaf of bread, the knife, and the napkin. The mother was the key link in the family constellation, providing the setting in which each member performed his or her part. A man was always "a child" with regard to physical needs and domestic arrangements and depended on his mother, sister, or wife. The ideal Jewish woman was a good wife and mother—clean, patient, hardworking, silent, and submissive. In reality, not many were silent and submissive, but they were all devoted to their families. Their own well-being was unimportant, and if they complained of the burden of it all, it was to boast. A mother's concern was mainly in the physical well-being of the family—that the children did not hurt themselves or get into a draft or get chilled and, above all, that they should eat enough. Because of its scarcity, food represented a mother's love—and that was one thing the Jews did not lack. The *yiddisheh mammeh* manifested her unbreakable and unconditional love by constant and solicitous overfeeding. No matter what you did, she always loved you and she never stopped feeding, hovering, trying to arouse the appetite, and asking, "Have you had enough to eat? Take a little more." Whereas Jewish girls were meant to be pink and plump, Jewish boys were pale, bent scholars and never saw the sun. Their mothers pressed them to eat but were proud of the studious, hungry appearance of their sons. In the shtetl, with its veneration for the power of the mind, respect was for the head of a person and diminished for the lower parts of the body towards the stomach until it evaporated as the feet were reached.

Every family event was marked by communal celebrations, which always included food. Bar mitzvahs were followed by a Kiddush with brandy and cakes at the synagogue and a simple reception at home. The birth of a baby was an occasion for boundless excitement and festivities, with a constant stream of visitors bringing food. The first Friday evening after a boy was born, the happy family kept open house with brandy, cakes, and cold boiled chickpeas. Everyone was invited to attend a *bris* (circumcision), during which a piece of cotton was dipped in liquor and put between the baby's lips while the *mohel* performed the operation, then honey cakes and brandy were passed around amid hearty "mazel tov"s (congratulations) and cries of "May you have pleasure in your children, and in your children's children and in their children." After a death, guests would bring food to fill the house of the bereaved. Hard-boiled eggs, bagels, and other round foods, such as peas and lentils, symbolized mourning.

In the shtetl, the week was lived from Sabbath to Sabbath, and the year from religious holiday to religious holiday. Wednesday and Thursday you did the shopping (usually the men went to look for delicacies at the market). You bought the fish live and you kept it in the bathtub. On Thursday chickens and geese were plucked and singed and the streets smelled of burning feathers. In the evening, hallah dough for the Sabbath loaves was mixed and kneaded so that it could be left to rise overnight. Friday you did the cooking. Sunday, Monday, and Tuesday you ate the leftovers. You could tell by the smell in the street what day it was—on Thursday it was burning feathers, on Friday smells of fish wafted from the windows, on Saturday night and Sunday the odors were those of dishwater thrown out to moisten the dust.

Friday was the busiest day, when the house and the kitchen were transformed and life became steeped in another world, which was in the past, with different clothes and different foods. It was a breathless rush that started very early in the morning so that everything would be entirely ready by sundown. Every housewife would put on her oldest dress and apron, tie a handkerchief around her head, and rush through the day sanding floors, sweeping, scrubbing, polishing, and ironing. When everything shone with cleanliness, she would start cooking. She cleaned the chicken and chopped and seasoned the fish. She kneaded the dough for the noodles, rolled it out on a floured sheet, rolled it up, sliced it into thin ribbons, and spread them out to dry. She chopped the liver with chicken fat, and she made gingerbread. She braided the bread dough and glazed it with egg to prepare it for the baker's oven. Before she put it on the hot stones of the wood oven, she threw a bit of dough in the fire and said a blessing. A beggar usually came around, and she would have a pile of coins and some food waiting for him.

The men and boys went straight to the bathhouse from work or school. They would wash and slap themselves with sticks and be purified by three ceremonial immersions in a pool.

Market day in Krzemieniec, Poland, 1925

They returned home dressed in their special silk kaftans and velvet skull caps, went off to the synagogue, and returned before sunset. The women made their ablutions at home with the little ones and put on their finery—a black silk dress and pearls and their *shaytl* or wig—and set the table in the best room: the kitchen, or a bedroom that doubled as study and dining room. The table, with its brilliant white linen cloth, best dishes and silverware, silver candlesticks and wine goblet, and the two Sabbath loaves under a richly embroidered napkin, gave the room an air of enchantment.

The most glorious memories of the shtetl were of Sabbath eve. When all the family sat around the Sabbath-eve table, they stepped into a world so beautiful that it represented "a fore-taste of the world to come." The men and boys sat on one side in their silk kaftans, on the other the women in their black silk and pearls, and the girls beside them; the father sat at the head, the mother on his right. There was always a guest—a traveler collecting alms, a rabbinical student, or a peddler who could not get back to his community in time. When the mother lit the candles, weeping with emotion as she said the prayer, moving her arms over the candles in a gesture of embrace; when the father held the silver goblet filled to the brim with wine and chanted the Kiddush (the prayer consecrating the Sabbath)—these were moments of ecstatic happiness. After the blessing of the hallah bread, the father ceremoniously lifted both loaves and set them down again. He passed the knife over one and cut the other in half, giving each person a slice; then everyone broke off a piece and dipped it in salt, making the blessing for bread. The prayers were in Hebrew, and no Yiddish was spoken until the ritual was over.

Then the meal began. It was always the same—chopped liver and gefilte fish, followed by chicken broth with noodles and boiled beef, chicken or pigeon, goose or turkey, accompanied by sweetened carrots. For dessert there was kugel (a sweet made of noodles baked with raisins and cinnamon), pancakes, or gingerbread. Although every woman had her turn of hand and her secret touch, they all cooked in the same way, which they learned by watching their mothers and other women at the bakehouse. The meal was slow and long-drawn-out, so that the men could have plenty of time for learned conversation. When it was over, the mother received her weekly recompense of praise meted out in ritual fashion. Then everyone broke into song. On Friday every Jewish woman felt like a queen and every Jewish man like a king. It was a time of ecstasy, when it was good to be a Jew and you felt pity for those who had been denied this foretaste of heaven.

The morning of Saturday was spent in prayer at the synagogue, and the midday meal was eaten quickly so that rest, "the delight of Sabbath," should be as long as possible. The cholent, the Saturday meal-in-the-pot, was taken from the oven where it had been left the day before—a heavy dish that contained a variety of ingredients including potatoes and groats. It was said that you had to go to the synagogue on Sunday and pray for your stomach to recover. This dish was eaten with the cold remains of the previous night's meal and with drafts of vodka and brandy for the men. After the meal, everyone slept. They all forgot their worries and their grief, and they felt at peace. They woke up to a reviving glass of tea from a kettle that had been kept hot since the day before and spent the rest of the day at home. Neighbors, relatives, and friends dropped in to talk and were offered sweet tea or a glass of almond milk, a biscuit and a piece of cake, or some dried fruit and nuts, such as prunes, dates, raisins, and almonds. Before sundown, another light meal was eaten—for there had to be three—after a short service at the synagogue, and the meal was followed by an evening service. Then the father said a prayer over a goblet of wine, holding a silver box filled with aromatic spices, and the Sabbath was over.

Pesah (Passover) was the most important holiday. A week before the feast, every family started a dramatic and frenzied cleaning of the house to purge it of any food that was *chometz*—tainted in any way by leaven. All the furniture, everything in the house, was taken outside to be scrubbed with boiling water, then sanded. The stove was burned out. Walls were whitewashed. Dishes and silver were koshered by being cleaned with sand and coarse salt, then ritually dipped in boiling water at the public bath. A special bakery was put up to make matzos for the whole shtetl. Charitable societies collected matzos, potatoes, and wine for the poor. All the family—grandparents, grandchildren, and all—got together for the first night of the Seder. Everyone was in his or her best clothes, wearing something new. The master of the house—in a white robe, girdled at the waist with silk cord—distributed the ritual foods. The meal featured chicken soup with matzo balls and matzo-meal pancakes.

Apart from on the Sabbath, holidays, and special occasions, there were few fixed meals.

During the week, meals were hurried and irregular, snatched in solitude at different times. The women and children ate when they were hungry (women never seemed to eat, they tasted while they cooked), the men when they returned home. They mostly nibbled and snatched at bits while they drank a glass of tea. Food was always there, never locked away, ready to be served at once if somebody dropped in. It was pickled herring and cucumber, boiled potatoes and bread, bean or barley soup, sour milk, and potato pancakes, or mashed potato made to taste "like fish" with fried onion. Mother's special cupboard always held a supply of raspberry preserve and cherry juice. No one sat down at the table, and women hardly sat at all. If they did, it was always on the edge of the chair, not on the whole seat.

The cycle of domestic life was marked by the preparation of seasonal foods and holidays. At the end of summer, there was a bustle of preserving and pickling fruit and vegetables. In winter, there were plums, apples, and cabbages to preserve. Gluts of fruit were strung up and left to dry around the stove. For the lucky ones there were geese to feed and to fatten and then to kill. The fat was melted down into soft creamy schmaltz.

Food in the shtetl was always chopped, mashed, kneaded, rolled, long-simmered—never left alone. It was mostly hot, soft, and very tender. Fat was much prized for its flavor and as a sign of opulence. It was spread on toast and used in cooking. There was little taste for raw vegetables other than radishes, cucumbers, and onions. Apart from carrots, cabbage, and potatoes, fresh vegetables were not appreciated. Beets

Jewish family beside a stone oven

were used in borscht, and dried legumes, such as peas, beans, and lentils, were used in soups. Food was accompanied by strong-flavored relishes, like horseradish, and by pickles, such as cucumbers and green tomatoes. There was an abundance of starchy foods, like noodles, potatoes, and above all bread. Most of the food was nondescript in color and unappealing to the eye. There was little effort at presentation. The main thing was that it should be very hot.

Appetizers and Salads

FORMAL DINNERS in well-to-do homes in Poland and Russia started with a spread of cold and hot appetizers (*zakaski* in Polish, *zakuski* in Russian) served with vodka and arranged on a separate little table before sitting down to the meal, but this was not a habit adopted by the Jews, partly because they were not drinkers. Like their family meals, their formal ones started with soup. In Jewish restaurants it was different. In the 1920s, the Polish-French gastronome Édouard de Pomiane wrote that as you entered a Jewish restaurant in Poland you saw a range of cold hors d'oeuvres at the counter to be eaten with a glass of liquor before you went on to the meal in the dining room. He added that the Jews were sober people who rarely drank hard liquor. Only those who originated in Russia had kept the habit of drinking vodka.

The practice of serving appetizers—*forspeizen*

in Yiddish—was taken up by the delicatessen trade in the new countries (North America, Canada, France, and Britain in particular), and they became favorite Jewish foods. Indeed, the preferred Jewish meal for many people is a selection of appetizers. They also represent the usual traditional cold Saturday fare.

Serve them as a first course, or choose an assortment and make up a snack meal. You will find gefilte fish—the most important appetizer—in the fish chapter.

Gribenes
Goose or Chicken Cracklings

The bits of fried goose or chicken skin with onion, the side products of fat rendering, are a much-prized delicacy. They are eaten as an appetizer, on toast or with boiled potatoes, and are used to garnish and flavor mashed potatoes, soups, farfel, kasha (buckwheat), and millet.

Remove the skin and fat from a goose or a chicken and cut it into small pieces. Melt down the fat on very low heat in a heavy-bottomed frying pan, add a thinly sliced onion, the pieces of skin, salt, and pepper, and cook very gently until the skin is crisp and brown. Let the fat cool a little before straining it into a jar. You may pour the gribenes into the jar too and heat them up again when you need them.

Chrain
Cold Horseradish Sauce

The powerful, piquant taste of horseradish and its penetrating smell make a perfect balance as an accompaniment to some of the bland or slightly sweet savory dishes, such as gefilte fish and boiled beef and chicken. Commercial sauces do not generally have the intense, unadulterated quality of the real thing, but recently, while judging supermarket foods, I found one that is the pure fresh grated root alone. Roots are hard to come by. They make an appearance at greengrocers in Jewish areas at Passover time, when horseradish has a place

SCHMALTZ

Rendered Goose or Chicken Fat

ONCE UPON A TIME, the smell of rendered goose fat permeated every Jewish home, clinging to the walls and furniture. The Jews in Eastern Europe and the Rhineland provinces bred geese, and their fat was the cooking medium that replaced the gentile's pork fat. It was dropped in favor of chicken fat in the new countries, and that too was more recently abandoned, for simulated chicken fat—a pure vegetable product—or margarine or oil, when people became concerned with their weight and their health. I wonder if goose fat will come back

into fashion now that the goose-rearing areas of France have been found to have the lowest incidence of heart disease and its chemical analysis has revealed properties akin to those of olive oil. A few New York delis offer it on the table in syrup-dispensing decanters for people to pour over their food. It certainly has a very agreeable nutty flavor.

To make schmaltz, take the fat from a goose or boiling fowl. Cut it into small pieces and melt it slowly over low heat in a heavy-bottomed frying pan. It is common to add a thinly sliced onion, and to let the fat sizzle until the onion is golden, then strain the fat into a jar while it is warm. The onion imparts a delicious flavor. Keep it in a cool place.

on the Seder tray, symbolizing the bitter lives of the Jews in captivity in Egypt.

Three Ways to Make Chrain

1. Wash, peel, and grate a piece of horseradish root (it is long and brown outside and white inside) and add to taste salt, sugar (optional), and a little vinegar or lemon juice.

2. Peel and grate a piece of horseradish and add salt, a pinch of sugar, a squeeze of lemon, and a few tablespoons of sour cream. This may be used with fish and vegetables.

3. Add grated cooked beet, which softens the flavor and gives a bright-red color to sauce 1. The amount of beet added varies from very little (1 beet only) to 3 times the weight of horseradish.

PICKLED VEGETABLES

VEGETABLE PICKLES, especially cabbage, beet, and cucumber, were staples in the diet of Jews in Poland, Lithuania, the Ukraine, and Russia. Developed as a method of food preservation, they had strong flavors that brought a welcome sharpness to the bland tastes of the bread-and-potato diet of these areas. Housewives would prepare stocks as winter provisions, leaving them to ferment in cellars and outhouses. To the country markets, where peasants brought their farm produce, Jewish housewives brought their pickles in barrels for sale.

Pickled Cucumbers in Brine

Pickling cucumbers is so simple, but it is difficult to find the definitive recipe because there are so many and because you are supposed to develop a "hand" for it and to "taste" for saltiness. This one makes a delicious pickle.

2 lbs (1 kg) small cucumbers or ridge cucumbers
6 cups (1½ liters) water
3 tablespoons coarse salt
1 tablespoon white-wine vinegar
A bunch of fresh dill
4 peeled garlic cloves
1 teaspoon black peppercorns or 2 small dried red chilies

Scrub and rinse the cucumbers thoroughly. Bring the water to boil with the salt and vinegar and let it cool. Pack the cucumbers tightly in a 2-quart (2-liter) jar with the dill, garlic, and peppercorns or chilies and pour the salted water over them. It should cover the cucumbers entirely. Put the lid on and store in a cool place. The pickles may be ready to eat in 4–6 days, and they keep several weeks in the refrigerator.

VARIATIONS

• Sprigs of thyme, bay leaves, parsley, fennel, or celery leaves are alternative aromatics which can be used, as are pickling spices (1 teaspoon), a small piece of cinnamon bark, or a few cloves. A tiny piece of horseradish or gingerroot is sometimes put in. One teaspoon of citric acid may be used instead of vinegar. Some people like to add a tablespoon of sugar.

• For mezrie, a Polish sweet-and-sour alternative, peel and slice a large cucumber and pack it into a jar. Pour over it a boiled mixture of I cup (250 ml) white-wine vinegar, 1½ cups (350 ml) water, 2–3 tablespoons sugar, and I tablespoon salt.

PICKLED CUCUMBERS IN BRINE

PICKLED CUCUMBERS—"saure igerkiss" in Yiddish—known as "sour," "half-sour" (depending on the amount of vinegar), "new green" (when just made and still crisp and green), and "dill pickle" (when that herb is in the brine), and also "*haimishe*" (homemade)—are so representative of Jewish food that they have come to symbolize it.

In a piece about the New York deli, American food columnist Ed Levine explained that "a deli must have both sour and half sour pickles in a bowl on the table when you sit down. If you have to ask for pickles or if they don't arrive until your sandwich does, it is not the real McCoy." He tells the story of a woman's first experience of a deli. She sits down and orders a pastrami sandwich on rye. When the sandwich arrives, she asks the waiter if a green vegetable comes with it. The waiter points to the bowl of pickles on the table and asks, "What color are the pickles, blue?"

Beet Salad with Sour Cream

SERVES 4

I am not very fond of beet salad, but, prepared in this way, with sour cream, I find it very nice.

6 cooked and peeled beets, about ¾ lb
(375 g), diced
1 mild onion, chopped
Salt
Juice of ½ lemon or 2 tablespoons vinegar
1 tablespoon sugar
5–6 tablespoons sour cream

Put the beets in a serving bowl with the onion. Dress with salt, lemon or vinegar, and sugar. Then stir in the sour cream.

Cucumber Salad with Sour Cream

SERVES 4

This refreshing salad has a Polish touch with a delicate sweet-and-sour flavor.

1 cucumber, peeled and thinly sliced
Salt
2 tablespoons vinegar
1 tablespoon superfine sugar (optional)
4 tablespoons sour cream

Sprinkle the cucumber with plenty of salt and leave to drain in a colander for at least

½ hour, until it softens and loses its juices. Then rinse in cold water and drain. Mix the vinegar with the sugar and sour cream and pour over the cucumber slices. Mix well.

Radish Salad

SERVES 4

This Russian salad is usually made with the large, strong-tasting black or violet winter radishes, but other radishes will do very well. It is an easy and unusual way of serving them.

> *12 oz (350 g) radishes*
> *1 small mild onion, grated*
> *3 tablespoons light extra-virgin olive oil*
> *A little salt and pepper*

Trim and grate or slice the radishes thinly. Mix with the onion and dress with oil, salt, and pepper.

VARIATION

• Dress with 1¼ cups (300 ml) sour cream and a little salt.

Coleslaw

SERVES 6

This shredded-cabbage salad can be tangy or slightly sweet. It is usually smothered in mayonnaise, but it is most pleasing simply dressed with oil and vinegar.

> *1 white cabbage, about 2 lbs (1 kg)*
> *1 large carrot*
> *1 green pepper, stem and seeds removed (optional)*
> *1 mild onion*
> *1–2 tablespoons sugar*
> *4–6 tablespoons white-wine vinegar*
> *6 tablespoons sunflower or extra-virgin olive oil*
> *1 teaspoon prepared mustard*
> *Salt and white pepper*

Cut the cabbage into quarters, remove the hard cores, and shred. Coarsely grate the carrot, the pepper, and the onion. Mix the sugar, vinegar, oil, mustard, salt, and pepper and stir into the shredded vegetables. Mix thoroughly and leave in a cool place for at least 1 hour before serving.

VARIATION

• Use ⅔ cup (150 ml) mayonnaise instead of the oil. Add it just before serving.

CREAM CHEESE

THERE WERE many small Jewish dairies in the little rural towns of Eastern Europe. The only dairy foods they produced were butter, buttermilk, sour cream, and cream cheese. These were sold in the open markets from large earthen-ware pots, or wrapped in leaves. Some families owned a cow. According to John Cooper (*Eat and Be Satisfied*), in Lithuania goats were also kept in Jewish households, to provide milk and cream cheese (they were called the national Jewish cattle). A variety of cream-cheese appetizers are sold by delicatessens. The ones below are classics.

Potato Salad

SERVES 6

I was given dozens of recipes for potato salads. This simple one is excellent.

2 lbs (1 kg) waxy new potatoes
Salt
6 tablespoons extra-virgin olive oil
2 tablespoons wine or cider vinegar
Pepper
1 large mild onion or 8 scallions, finely chopped
3 tablespoons finely chopped parsley

Boil the potatoes in salted water until tender, then peel and slice them. Dress while still warm with a mixture of oil, vinegar, salt, and pepper. Add the onion and parsley and mix well.

VARIATION

• Beat into the dressing 1 teaspoon dried mustard and add 2 chopped pickled cucumbers and 3 quartered hard-boiled eggs.

Cream Cheese with Chives

Blend 1 lb (500 g) cream cheese with 4–5 tablespoons finely chopped chives, adding a little salt to taste. You may lighten the cheese by mixing in a few tablespoons of sour cream.

Cream Cheese with Paprika

Blend 1 lb (500 g) cream cheese with 2 tablespoons paprika, a good pinch of cayenne or chili powder, and a little salt. Add a few tablespoons of sour cream for a lighter consistency.

Cream Cheese with Gherkins and Caraway

Mash 1 lb (500 g) cream cheese with salt and pepper and 2 teaspoons of caraway seeds, and add 4 or 5 large chopped pickled gherkins.

Chopped Eggs with Onion

SERVES 6

This popular appetizer is common fare in the deli trade.

6 hard-boiled eggs
8 scallions or 1 mild Spanish onion, finely chopped
A little salt and white pepper
3 tablespoons softened chicken fat, butter, or light vegetable oil

Chop the eggs coarsely, add the rest of the ingredients, and mix well. Serve with slices of bread.

Scrambled Egg and Onion

SERVES 4

This simple Polish way of cooking eggs makes a nice breakfast dish as well as a homely appetizer.

1 large onion, coarsely chopped
3 tablespoons melted chicken fat, butter, or light vegetable oil
4 eggs, lightly beaten
Salt and white pepper
2 tablespoons finely chopped chives

In a frying pan, cook the onion in the fat on very low heat till soft and golden. Add the eggs, salt, pepper, and chives and stir until the eggs have set but are still soft.

Potato Latkes

Potato Fritters

SERVES 6

This is one of the most famous of Jewish foods and a specialty of Hanukah (see page 32). The latkes are served as an appetizer, as a side dish, and even for tea with a sprinkling of confectioners' sugar. They can be marvelous if properly prepared, just before eating.

2 lbs (1 kg) potatoes
2 large eggs
Salt
Oil for frying

Peel and finely grate the potatoes. Put them straight into cold water, then drain and squeeze them as dry as you can by pressing them with your hands in a colander. This is to remove the starchy liquid, which could make the latkes soggy.

Beat the eggs lightly with salt, add to the potatoes, and stir well. Film the bottom of a frying pan with oil and heat. Take serving-spoonfuls, or as much as ¼ cup (50 ml), of the mixture, and drop into the hot oil. Flatten a little, and lower the heat so that the fritters cook through evenly. When one side is brown, turn over and brown the other. Lift out and serve very hot.

VARIATION

• You may add black pepper, chopped parsley, and finely chopped onion to the egg and potato mixture.

• Adding 4 tablespoons of potato flour binds the fritters into firmer, more compact cakes, easier to handle but not quite as lovely to eat.

Tarte aux Oignons d'Alsace

Creamy Onion Tart

SERVES 6

At a Jewish library in Paris, a reader asked me what I was researching. When I told him, he said proudly that he was from Alsace, the home of the best Jewish food in France, and that he was a great cook. We went out to eat together and he gave me several recipes. You must try this luscious, creamy onion tart, which is one of my favorites.

For the pastry

> *4½ oz (125 g) unsalted butter*
> *1⅔ cups (250 g) all-purpose flour*
> *¼ teaspoon salt*
> *1 egg, lightly beaten*
> *1–2 tablespoons milk (if required)*

For the filling

> *3 large onions, about 1½ lbs (750 g)*
> *2 oz (50 g) butter*
> *2 tablespoons sunflower or light vegetable oil*
> *Salt*
> *2 tablespoons flour*
> *1¼ cups (300 ml) heavy cream*
> *2 eggs, lightly beaten*
> *White pepper*

For the pastry, cut the butter into small pieces and rub it into the flour and salt with your hands. Add the egg, mix well, and work very briefly with your hand until bound into a soft dough, adding a little milk if necessary. Cover in plastic wrap and leave in a cool place for 1 hour.

For the filling, cut the onions in half, then into thick slices. Heat the butter with the oil in a large pan and cook the onions over very low heat and with the lid on for about 1 hour, until very soft and lightly colored, stirring occasionally and adding a little salt. Now add the flour and stir well.

Beat the cream into the eggs. Let the onions cool a little before stirring in the cream mixture. Taste before adding a tiny bit of salt if necessary and pepper. This should not be a salty tart.

Line a greased 10-inch (25-cm) tart pan or flan mold with the dough by pressing it in with the palm of your hands (easier to do with this soft dough than to roll it out) and pressing it up the sides. Pour in the filling mixture and bake in a preheated 300°F (150°C) oven for 1 hour, or until set and golden. Serve hot or cold. It is nicer hot.

SCHMALTZ HERRING AND MATJES HERRING

Salt Herring

IN EASTERN EUROPE, herring was the cheapest fish. It arrived presalted in barrels from Norway, Holland, England, and Scotland. Jews were prominent in the herring trade, importing and transporting the fish by rail to Germany, Poland, and Russia and selling it in stores and from pushcarts. This poor man's food—turned rich man's delicacy—was an all-important part of the diet of the Jews. In the 1920s, the Polish-French gastronome Édouard de Pomiane wrote that the Jews of Poland ate a herring a day. According to the British columnist Chaim Bermant, in England it was much the same story. He reminisced in one of his articles, "On Sunday one had a pickled herring, on Monday soused herring, on Wednesday baked herring, on Thursday herring fried in oatmeal, and on Friday herring with sour cream."

Herring remains one of the great Jewish favorites. Fishmongers, delis, and supermarkets in my area of London offer a variety of pickled and marinated herrings and the salt-cured fish, which needs to be soaked and desalted before it can be prepared.

Schmaltz herring is cured by being covered with coarse salt and left with a weight on top for up to four days. Before it can be used, it needs to be soaked for as long as one or two days in a few changes of cold water to remove the salt. Matjes herring is preserved in brine and is relatively fresh, so it usually needs no more than one hour's soaking. My fishmonger gets matjes from Holland and skins and fillets them for me. They are my favorite, and particularly delicious when they have been soaked in milk instead of water.

Once filleted, skinned, and soaked, herrings can be eaten as they are, raw, simply dressed with oil and a squeeze of lemon, or smothered in sour cream or crème fraîche with a little lemon or a touch of sugar, accompanied by bread or a hot boiled potato. Salt herrings are usually eaten with onion rings. The onions' strong flavor can be muted by sprinkling with plenty of salt and letting the juices drain for one hour, or by pouring boiling water over them and adding a little lemon juice or vinegar. I can understand that you might easily become addicted to herring. You can keep desalted herrings in a jar covered with olive oil. Cut them diagonally into two-inch (five-centimeter) pieces, or leave them whole.

Marinated Herring

SERVES 6–8

When you buy salt herring, find out from the merchant how much soaking it needs. Matjes need only 1 hour.

> *4 salt herrings, filleted and soaked as*
>   *required*
> *1 large mild onion, sliced*
> *1½ cups (350 ml) white-wine or cider*
>   *vinegar*
> *8 black peppercorns*
> *3 cloves (optional)*
> *2 tablespoons sugar*
> *2 bay leaves*

Soak the herrings as necessary in cold water or milk and drain on a few layers of paper towels. Cut into 2-inch (5-cm) pieces and arrange in a ceramic dish or glass jar, alternating with layers of onion. Boil the vinegar with the peppercorns, cloves, sugar, and bay leaves for 5 minutes. Let it cool, and pour over the herring. Refrigerate for 2 days before eating. It keeps for 2 weeks.

VARIATIONS

• For a sweet-and-sour Polish version, add 8 oz (250 g) sugar to the vinegar. You may also add 8 juniper berries or a few thin slices of ginger.

• For a Lithuanian sour-cream dressing, add 1 cup (250 ml) sour cream to the cooled vinegar.

Chopped Herring

SERVES 14

There are many ways of making chopped herring, with all kinds of additions, from onion, chopped egg, and apple to bread and gingersnaps, vinegar, and lemon juice, which are usually combined to taste. One Russian way is simply to chop the (desalted) herring fillets finely and dress with oil and vinegar. The following is very good, both with and without the optional "trimmings"—hard-boiled egg and apple.

> *4 fat herrings, filleted, skinned, and soaked in*
>   *cold water or milk as required (see box*
>   *opposite)*
> *1 large mild onion*
> *4 thin slices brown bread, crusts removed*
> *4 tablespoons wine or cider vinegar or the juice*
>   *of 1 lemon*
> *2 tablespoons sunflower oil*
> *4 hard-boiled eggs (optional)*
> *2 tart apples (optional)*
> *Juice of ½ lemon (optional)*

Drain the herring fillets on paper towels. Chop them and all the ingredients together by hand, or use the food processor. If you use the processor, you must chop the ingredients separately and briefly, being careful not to turn them into a paste or a mush: Chop the onion and drop it into a bowl. Crumb the bread and add to the onion. Stir in the vinegar and oil. Chop the herrings and mix all together. If you like, add the chopped boiled eggs and the apple, chopped with the lemon juice to keep it from discoloring. Serve with additional slices of bread.

VARIATIONS

• For a Polish version, add 4 teaspoons superfine sugar and, instead of the bread, 6 small crumbled gingersnaps.

• For a Ukrainian specialty, add I cup (250 ml) sour cream.

• In South Africa they used Marie (plain) biscuits instead of bread crumbs.

Potato Salad with Herrings and Apples

SERVES 6

I was served this salad at the home of a day student when I was at boarding school in Paris. It made quite an impression. I have tried to reproduce it from memory.

> *1 lb (500 g) new potatoes*
> *2 tart apples*
> *Juice of 1 lemon*
> *3 salt-herring fillets (skinned and desalted)*
>   *or pickled or marinated fillets, cut into*
>   *2-inch (5-cm) pieces diagonally*
> *2 celery stalks, thinly sliced*
> *1 mild onion, finely chopped*
> *1¼ cups (300 ml) sour cream*

Boil the potatoes in salted water until tender, then peel and cut them in thick slices. Peel and cut the apples into small pieces and toss

with the lemon juice. Mix all the ingredients together.

VARIATIONS

• Add to the sour cream I tablespoon Dijon-type mustard and/or I tablespoon sugar.

• For a herring-and-horseradish salad, omit the apples and add 3 tablespoons of grated horseradish.

• For a herring-and-apple salad without potatoes: Cut 3 desalted, or marinated herrings diagonally into pieces. Mix with 2 coarsely grated tart apples and dress with I cup (250 ml) sour cream, and a little grated horseradish to taste.

Fish Roe Caviar

Carp-, herring-, and pike-roe caviar are Eastern European delicacies. Remove the membranes and put the fish eggs in a bowl. Sprinkle with plenty of salt and leave for 12–24 hours, then rinse and drain. Beat in a light vegetable or olive oil and a little lemon juice to the consistency of mayonnaise. You may also mix in a little grated onion.

A man goes into a delicatessen and asks, "What makes you Jews so clever?" The owner replies, "It's because we eat so much pickled herring." The man comes back every day and buys pickled herring. Then, one day, he comes in looking angry and says, "For four months now you've been charging me twice as much as they charge next door." "You see," the owner says triumphantly, "it's working already!"

SMOKED SALMON

SMOKED SALMON became the prime Jewish delicacy in Britain and America at the turn of the century, long before it became generally established as the most prestigious appetizer, comparable to caviar, in these countries. In Eastern Europe, Jews dried, smoked, salted, and pickled fish to preserve it, because of the constant fear of scarcity. Preserved fish was an important part of the Jewish grocery trade, because, according to tradition, it is not "cooked" and is therefore kosher even if it is prepared by non-Jews, which makes it an easy commodity. Although salmon was too much of a luxury to have been part of their general diet in Eastern Europe, it was immigrants from Russia who brought the smoking techniques to London and New York, where Jewish smokehouses became famous.

Different styles of curing developed. The original, old-style Brooklyn smoked salmon, called "lox" after the Yiddish word *lachs* for salmon, was pickled in brine in the days before refrigeration, then desalted and lightly smoked. It remained very salty and was partnered with cream cheese to mitigate the saltiness. The grandest and favorite American breakfast food is now smoked salmon with cream cheese and bagels, sometimes accompanied by finely chopped mild onion, chopped hard-boiled eggs, and capers. The newer-style "Novy," so named because it was once imported through Nova Scotia, is cured in salt and brown sugar, then washed and cold-smoked over smoldering hardwood. It is silky-soft and mild-tasting and is more likely to be eaten on thinly sliced buttered rye or pumpernickel bread or on blini.

Smoked salmon was eaten by Jews in the East End of London long before the English middle classes discovered it. Jo and Morris Barnet, whose grandfather smoked salmon back in 1879, and whose smokehouse in Frying Pan Alley was one of the first, remember the days when their product was a great luxury, bought in very small quantities for the Sabbath and special occasions. Foreman & Son—one of the city's original five smokehouses, founded in 1905 by the present owner's great-grandfather Aaron (Harris) Foreman, who came from Russia—produces a delicious, mild, delicate cure known as the "London cure"; the salmon is dry-salted for a day, rinsed in cold running water, then dried and cold-smoked over smoldering oak-and-juniper sawdust. Their finest product is the Scottish wild salmon, which has a rich, gamy flavor and a firm texture. It is best served with thin slices of brown bread and nothing else, except perhaps a squeeze of lemon and a sprinkling of black pepper.

Since the advent of cheaper, farmed salmon, smoked salmon has become mass-produced and widely consumed.

CHOPPED LIVER

LIVER CHOPPED to a paste is one of the two best-known Jewish foods (the other is gefilte fish) and one of the high points of Jewish cookery. It is obligatory on the Sabbath table. The French pâté de foie gras is said to be of Jewish origin. The practice of fattening duck and goose livers is very ancient. The Romans used various methods to cause the livers to swell, but in the seventeenth century, Jews in the Rhineland community of Alsace developed a special way of breeding and fattening geese by force-feeding them, which became their trade. Their way of chopping the cooked livers into a paste was adopted by the French for what became the supreme gastronomic product of the region. The finest foies gras still come from the livers of fattened geese reared in Alsace and southwestern France, but Jews everywhere—outside Alsace—have now replaced goose and duck livers with chicken livers. In Britain, calf's liver was used until the 1940s, when it became too scarce and expensive.

Chopped liver is made with liver, onions, and eggs, and only salt and pepper as flavoring. The ingredients have never changed, but the taste and texture have. Once the onion was used raw; now people divide between traditionalists, who fry it until it is soft but not colored, and new-stylers, who fry it until it is golden and sweet. Whereas tradtionalists may chop the ingredients by hand or put them through a meat grinder using the medium cutter, now most use the food processor, which produces a soft paste. And though goose or chicken fat is the traditional fat in which to fry the onions and to pour over the finished product when serving, oil is now also widely used. Because liver has too much blood a special koshering process is required. Salting alone is not enough. The livers must be thoroughly washed then salted all over immediately before broiling over an open fire or under the grill.

Hyme always ate at the same restaurant for years and years. Then, one day, they saw him go into the restaurant across the road. When he came back the next week, they asked, "Hyme, what's the matter, why did you go across the road?" And Hyme replied, "What could I do? I went to the dentist and he told me to eat on the other side!"

Chopped Liver

SERVES 4

Although proportions of liver, onions, and eggs vary, the following are classic.

½–¾ lb (250–350 g) onion (1 large
    onion), chopped
3 tablespoons chicken fat or vegetable oil
½ lb (250 g) chicken livers
Salt
1 or 2 hard-boiled eggs
Pepper

Fry the onion in chicken fat or oil on low heat in a large frying pan with the lid on, until very soft and golden, stirring occasionally. Let cool.

Rinse the livers and sprinkle with salt. Put them on aluminum foil under the grill and cook briefly, turning over once, until they change color. Let them cool.

Cut the hard-boiled eggs in half and chop them finely in the food processor, then put them in the serving bowl. Chop the onions and liver in the food processor very briefly, so that the paste is a little coarse. Take out 2–3 tablespoons of chopped egg to use as a garnish. Mix the liver and onions with the rest of the chopped eggs by hand. Season with salt and pepper and mix well. Smooth the surface flat and sprinkle with chopped egg. Serve with slices of hallah or rye bread.

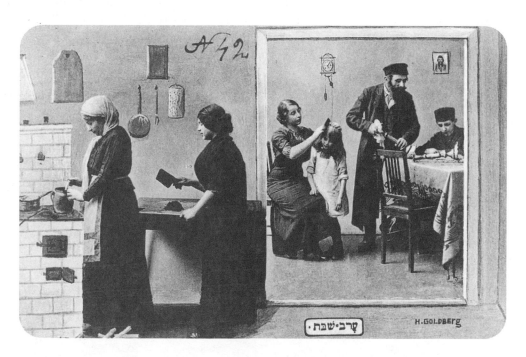

Postcard depicting cooking, preparing chopped liver, and getting ready for the Sabbath

Fried Chicken Liver with Onions

SERVES 2–4

1 lb (500 g) onions (2 large)
3 tablespoons rendered chicken fat or
    4 tablespoons sunflower oil
½ lb (250 g) chicken livers
Salt and pepper
1–2 teaspoons paprika (optional)

Cut the onions in half and slice them. In a large frying pan, fry them in the chicken fat or oil on low heat for a long time, stirring occasionally, until soft and brown. Grill the chicken livers briefly to kosher them, as described in preceding recipe. Add them to the onions just before serving, season with pepper and paprika, and cook for half a minute, stirring constantly.

Petchah

Calf's Foot Jelly

SERVES 6–8

Here is a delicacy that has gone out of favor. Hardly anyone makes it now, and you would have trouble finding a calf's foot, but it was once one of the great delicacies and it still has its devotees. Other names for it are "galeh" and "footsnoga."

2 calf's feet (have the butcher cut each of them
    into 3 or 4 pieces)
1 onion
4 garlic cloves
3 bay leaves
1 teaspoon peppercorns
1–1½ teaspoons salt
3 hard-boiled eggs
2 lemons cut into wedges or a bottle of wine
    vinegar, to serve with

Wash and blanch the calf's feet—cover with cold water, bring to the boil, simmer 5–10 minutes, and when the scum collects, pour out the water.

Cover the feet again with fresh water. Add the onion, 2 garlic cloves, the bay leaves, peppercorns, and salt. Simmer for 3–4 hours, adding water if necessary, until the meat and cartilage are very soft and come away from the bone. Strain and reserve the broth (it will form the jelly).

Remove the bones and chop up the meat and cartilage. Add the remaining 2 garlic cloves, crushed or minced, and arrange at the bottom of a serving dish. Cover with a layer of hard-boiled eggs and ladle the strained broth over them. Chill overnight, or until jellied and firm. Serve cut into squares or slices accompanied by lemon wedges or with a bottle of vinegar for everyone to sprinkle on a few drops.

KNISHES—PIROSHKI

Russian Pies

AMERICAN FOOD WRITER Suzanne Hamlin sent me a piece she wrote about the knish, which she calls New York's favorite nosh. She says: "If you've never eaten a knish you can't call yourself a New Yorker. If you've only eaten one you probably didn't get the right one. They were sold from pushcarts at the turn of the century. Now there are knisheries, knish nosh establishments, and knish kings, but they are still sold on the street. In Russia and Eastern Europe they were small. In New York they have become huge, like big oversized buns the size of a squashed tennis ball with a thin crisp crust. You also find them as dainty little canapés, sometimes made with strudel dough, and just about everything is used as filling, from liver, chicken, mushrooms, and nuts to spinach and rice. But the favorites are still the old traditional onion and mashed potatoes and kasha [buckwheat groats]."

In France the pies are known by their Russian name, "piroshki," and also as "beiglach." Pies are legendary in Russian folklore and fairy tales. They are usually served as *zakuski,* and sometimes to accompany soup. *Pir* means "feast" in Russian, and they are indeed special-occasion foods. For the Jews they were the ideal bites to pass around at events such as a circumcision; a Shalem Zachor, the first Friday evening after the birth of a boy to welcome him into the family; a *pidyon ha-ben,* or "redemption" of a firstborn boy, a month after his birth; and of course betrothals, bar mitzvahs, and the like.

Various doughs are used to make these pies. In New York the pastry is made with egg or potato-based. In France they use puff, shortcrust, and a yeast dough. Traditional fillings are meat, chicken liver, mashed potatoes, kasha, mushroom, curd cheese, cabbage, sauerkraut, salmon, and a sweet rice cooked in milk. Having spent many days trying out dozens of little pies with so many different pastries, different fillings, and different shapes, I became worried that, what with the Sephardi varieties, pies would take over the entire book. However, I decided that little pies are not what people are willing to spend their time on today, and that they have now come into the realm of mass-produced fast foods, so I decided to feature only a few favorites.

Toast with Beef Marrow

Rub toasted bread with garlic and spread with hot, cooked bone marrow.

Pastry Dough for Knishes and Piroshki

MAKES 24

This is the classic New York pastry, which bakes into a thin crisp crust. For a filling, see the recipes that follow.

> 2 eggs
> ½ teaspoon salt
> 1 teaspoon baking powder
> 2 tablespoons vegetable oil
> Not quite 1⅔ cups (250 g) all-purpose flour
> 1 egg yolk mixed with 1 teaspoon of water, for glazing

Beat the eggs with the salt, baking powder, and oil. Gradually add the flour—just enough to make a soft dough that is no longer sticky—mixing it in with a fork to begin with, then working it in with your hand. Knead for about 10 minutes, until very smooth and elastic, sprinkling in a little flour if necessary. Coat with oil by pouring a little into the bowl and turning the dough around in it. Cover the bowl with plastic wrap and leave for an hour. Knead again for a moment and roll out as thin as you can. Cut into rounds 3 inches (7½ cm) in diameter. Because the dough is elastic and springs back, pull it a lit-

tle to stretch it again. Place 1 tablespoon of filling in the center of each round, then fold over and pinch the edges together firmly to seal them. Place on greased baking sheets, brush with the egg yolk, and bake in a preheated 350°F (180°C) oven for 20–25 minutes, or until golden. Serve hot.

Cream Cheese Filling

MAKES ENOUGH TO
FILL 24 PIROSHKI

> 10 oz (300 g) curd or cream cheese (drained)
> 4 tablespoons sour cream
> Salt and white pepper
> 4 tablespoons chopped chives or dill
> 1 egg, lightly beaten

Mix all the ingredients together.

Meat Filling

MAKES ENOUGH TO
FILL 24 PIROSHKI

> 1 onion, chopped
> 2 tablespoons oil
> ½ pound (250 g) lean ground beef
> Salt and pepper
> 2 tablespoons chopped parsley

Fry the onion in the oil till golden. Add the meat and cook, stirring and crushing it with a fork, for about 8 minutes, until it changes color. Season with salt and pepper and stir in parsley. Let it cool before using.

Potato Filling

MAKES ENOUGH TO
FILL 24 PIROSHKI

In the shtetl, where they sometimes ate potatoes three times a day, this filling would be a leftover.

> 2 medium onions, chopped
> 3 tablespoons chicken or goose fat or
>   vegetable oil
> 1 lb (500 g) potatoes
> Salt and pepper

Fry the onions in the fat or oil until soft and golden. Boil the potatoes in their jackets, then peel and mash them. Season with plenty of salt and pepper and mix in the onions.

Smoked Salmon Filling

Patrick Goldenberg, who owns the restaurant Goldenberg, at the Avenue Wagram in Paris, calls his pies "pirojki au saumon" and uses 1 lb (500 g) store-bought puff pastry. Whereas the potato filling above evokes the world of the shtetl, this one evokes the grand world of Moscow. I used smoked-salmon trimmings, which are sold cheap at the supermarket.

> 1 onion, chopped
> 2 tablespoons vegetable oil
> ½ lb (250 g) smoked salmon, coarsely
>   chopped

Fry the onion in oil till golden and mix with the smoked salmon. Cut the pastry in rounds, fill, and bake following directions on page 74.

Large Knishes and Piroshki Made with Potato Dough

MAKES ABOUT 40

This dough is used to make long rolls, which are baked and cut into slices. For the filling, use the meat, potato, or cream-cheese filling above, doubling the quantity.

> 1 cup (250 g) mashed potato
> ¾ teaspoon salt
> 3 eggs, lightly beaten
> 3 cups (450 g) flour
> 1 egg yolk for glazing

You can start in a food processor. Blend the potatoes, salt, and eggs, then add enough flour to make a firm dough. Knead, adding a little flour if necessary, until the dough is very smooth and elastic.

Divide the dough in 3. Roll out 1 piece into a rectangle 12 inches (30 cm) long and about 9 inches (23 cm) wide. Spread a third of the filling over the surface of the rectangle to within about ½ inch (1¼ cm) from the edges. Roll up the dough lengthwise with the filling inside. Place the roll on a greased baking sheet, seam side down, and tuck the edges underneath.

Do the same with the other 2 pieces of dough and the filling. Brush the tops with the egg yolk mixed with I teaspoon of water, and bake in a preheated 350°F (180°C) oven for about 40 minutes, or until golden brown. With a fine-serrated knife, cut into I-inch (2½-cm) slices. Serve hot.

Matzo Brei

SERVES 2

During Passover, dozens of little goodies are made with matzos and matzo meal. Matzo brei is an old classic, eaten for breakfast or tea and as a snack.

2 eggs
Salt and pepper
2 whole matzos, broken into small pieces
2 tablespoons unsalted butter or vegetable oil
  for frying

Lightly beat the eggs with salt and pepper. Soak the matzos in cold water for I–2 minutes, until it softens, then drain and gently squeeze the excess water out. Drop it into the beaten eggs and mix well.

In a frying pan, heat the oil or butter until it sizzles and pour in the mixture. Cook on low heat for about 2 minutes, until the bottom sets, then turn and brown the other side, or put under the grill to brown the top. Serve hot.

Accompany if you like with sour cream. At breakfast or teatime, sprinkle with a little sugar and cinnamon or serve with jam or honey, a fruit preserve or compote.

THE AMERICAN STORY

BY ITS NUMBERS, by its wealth and influence, by its ability to assist Israel and Jewish communities all over the world, American Jewry has attained a stature unequaled in any part of the Diaspora over two millennia.

The story of American Jewry is the story of a modern Golden Age of Jewish life—of full integration in the economy, of involvement in the process of government and participation in scientific and artistic endeavors. It is also a story of loss of culture, of assimilation and acculturation, and of rediscovery and renaissance of a heritage.

The adoption of bagels as a national bread—and lox and bagels as the grandest American breakfast—and of cheesecake as the all-American cake symbolizes the integration of Jews in American life, and their part in shaping the ethos and character of the country and its largest city.

The immigration of Jews to all the new countries—such as Canada, South Africa, Brazil, Britain, France, and Australia—created changes in the cooking brought over from the old countries, but nowhere did it change so much as in America, and nowhere is there so much enthusiasm today for the old dishes, which represent the old life. America has taken the role of heir to the Jewish culinary heritage. Latkes, kasha, kugel, and knishes have become fashionable. Restaurants in New York specialize in Roman Jewish dishes, whereas many Jews in Italy cannot name one single Jewish Italian dish apart from carciofi alla giudea. A Yemeni chili relish called "zhoug" is sold in street markets in San Francisco. What is "in" in the United States soon becomes fashionable in the rest of the world. It is through its reflection in American eyes that the Jewish food of Eastern Europe has become fashionable in Israel.

The success story of American Jewry happened over the last 50 years, but the Jewish presence in America dates back almost 350 years. The earliest Jewish settlements, in the late seventeenth century, were mostly Iberian Sephardim of Marrano stock, fleeing the Inquisition in South America or coming via Holland. The first arrivals, in 1654, were a group from Recife in Brazil, seeking refuge in Dutch-ruled New Amsterdam. They settled along the Atlantic coast, in New York, Newport, Philadelphia, Charleston, and Savannah. The sprinkling of Ashkenazim, who immigrated from Amsterdam and London, grew, but they joined the Sephardi congregations and followed Iberian synagogal rites. There is little trace today in the cooking of American Jews of the original Iberian Sephardi period, even among the descendants of the early settlers. But the early Sephardim had a culinary impact on the

The ghetto on market day, Chicago

country as a whole. They were among the first to bring the New World foods from South America to North. Many people of Jewish birth accompanied Christopher Columbus on his first voyage of discovery, and in the sixteenth century Portuguese New Christians began to settle throughout Central and South America, where their Jewish antecedents were not generally known and they felt safer from the Inquisition. The Sephardim had become familiar with tomatoes, potatoes, beans, chocolate, and vanilla in South America, and it was through their New Christian brethren who remained there that they imported the produce. In *Jewish Pioneers in America, 1492–1848* (New York: Brentano, 1931), Anita Libman Lebeson mentions a physician in early-eighteenth-century Virginia named Dr. Siccary, who is believed to have been a Portuguese Jew. Credited with the introduction of the tomato (then known as the love apple) and the advocacy of its consumption in large quantities, he believed "that a person who should eat a sufficient abundance of these apples would never die." Jews were also involved in the Jamaican sugar trade and brought coffee and spices from the East Indies and almonds and olive oil from the Mediterranean. Most of their trading was with Marranos settled in various parts of the world.

By the second quarter of the nineteenth century, Jews had begun to arrive in a steady stream from Germany—at the same time as non-Jews. They moved inland and westwards, so that by the middle of the century there was hardly a town of size that did not have a Jewish shopkeeper or tailor shop or a modest German-speaking congregation. Many German Jews were peddlers, carrying their wares across the country and stopping for the Sabbath with these congregations. The Gold Rush of 1849 brought them to California and the Pacific. It is among them that Reform Judaism, the modernizing movement that had begun in Germany in response to the Napoleonic Emancipation, took root, through the efforts of Isaac Mayer Wise. It advocated that practices that separated the Jew from his neighbor, such as covering the head at worship and the dietary laws, were anachronistic and should be abandoned. Cincinnati, where many Jews prospered in the garment trade, was its main center.

The influence of the German period of immigration is with us today through the impact of the huge number of early, predominantly German, community fund-raising cookbooks, and through the delicatessen trade. The first kosher cookbook published in the United States, called *Jewish Cookery Book*, printed in Philadelphia in 1871, is full of German foods like sauerkraut, wosht (wurst) and rice, frimsel (noodle) soup, dumpfnudeln, and kouglauff. The author, a Mrs. Esther Levy, née Jacobs, was probably from England and of German extraction. She gives many Victorian recipes, like mulligatawny soup, Yorkshire and Cumberland pudding, and chicken curry, and a few Sephardi recipes popular in the Jewish community in England at the time, like bola, a yeast cake with citron peel, almonds, cinnamon, and nutmeg, dipped in syrup, and a baked almond pudding with plenty of eggs. Scores of community books followed, giving instructions for cooking goose and pickled beef, fish balls and noodle pudding, German sauces, breads, and cookies. The most famous—*The "Settlement" Cook Book: The Way to a Man's Heart*, published in 1903 to help new immigrants settle, was all-American in its choice of recipes and not at all kosher. It featured lobster, shrimps, and oysters, but it gave a large number of German Jewish recipes, including gefilte fish, matzo balls, potato pancakes (latkes), kugel, schnecken, Berliner pfann kuchen, and apple strudel. It was to become one of the great American classics, and it is still going strong. Continually revised and updated, its different editions reflect the changing culinary fashions, the breaking away from Orthodoxy, and the Americanization of the Jewish communities. Perhaps the greatest culinary contribution to America by German Jews was the introduction of the beef sausage—the hot dog—in a soft bun.

But it was the great mass immigration from Eastern Europe that definitively shaped the character of Jewish life and cooking in America. It began in the 1880s, when pogroms broke out in Russia after the assassination of Tsar Alexander II. By 1920, more than 2.3 million Russian Jews had arrived. They passed through Ellis island and stopped in New York and a cluster of cities on the East Coast. Entire shtetls came together and stayed together with their rabbis. They arrived full of socialist revolutionary ideals, imbued with Jewish nationalism and spiritual orthodoxy and dreaming of a better life. But life turned out to be a struggle for existence, often of slave labor in sweatshops. That era, when New York was the heart and stronghold of Yiddish culture, was immortalized in Yiddish literature and American fiction.

A memoir by B. Weinstein describes a sweatshop: "The sweatshop is both a factory and a dwelling. It is the home of the owner and his family. The front room and the kitchen serve as the workshop. The family itself sleeps in the dark bedroom. In the front room there are sewing machines worked by 'operators.' Chairs set out along the walls are intended for the 'basters.' The middle of the room, filthy and dusty, is piled with bundles of materials. These bundles are used as seats by the 'finishers,' who put the final touches to coats, skirts, pants and other articles of clothing. They in turn transmit the garments to the pressers, who are usually old men. The pressers heat their irons and press the ready garments on boards in the light of a gas lamp. The employer often spreads kerosene over the tables used by the 'finishers' to prevent them from keeping food there." Weinstein goes on to tell about the torments and humiliations the employers constantly invented for their workers. Most of the eating was in the workplace. It was usually a herring with a pickle or a knish bought from a pushcart, or a sandwich—a new experience, for eating without dirtying the hands—from a deli.

The inhabitants of the Lower East Side of New York and the Jewish areas of cities like Chicago, Philadelphia, Boston, and Baltimore, where the largest concentrations of new immigrants were to be found, spent their leisure hours in the street, because there was no room indoors. In a piece entitled "Russian Jews in the United States," M. Osherovich (in *Russian Jewry 1860–1917*, an anthology published by Thomas Yoseloff in 1966) writes how every inch of space in apartments was used for "practical purposes" and every corner of a dwelling was rented. At night the entire space was filled with folding beds and mattresses on the floor for "tenants." Filth and disorder reigned, and there was hardly any light or air. Everyone escaped outdoors. Women and old men sat on stairs for "fresh air." Children spent their lives in the street, and the sidewalks teemed with people. There was always a feverish hubbub mingled with the melodies of Russian hurdy-gurdies and the cries of peddlers with pushcarts selling pickled cucumbers and herrings, bagels and knishes.

Those times, when Jews stood at the crossroads between Eastern Europe and America, between the shtetl and the tenement, are long past, but they are the times that American Jewish cooking evokes and celebrates.

The street food and the deli food of that time formed the standard menu known today as Jewish food. The Jewish deli started when lone male immigrants were forced to buy kosher meals from Jewish neighbors. Soon there were hundreds of small neighborhood kosher delis catering to workers and families in which the women also worked. They offered homely foods from the shtetl and specialized in the pickled, cured, and smoked foods that housewives did not make at home. A deli could be a store that sold cooked foods or a restaurant. It specialized either in meats or in cheese and fish, never in both. It served corned beef (which the British call salt beef), tongue, and pastrami. One of the great inventions of the American deli was pastrami.

It is said to be of Romanian origin, but it is entirely different from the cured meats with a similar-sounding name that you find in Turkey, Romania, and the Balkans. Pastrami is brisket of beef cured in a mixture of salt with spices, garlic, and pepper, then smoked, and eventually steamed. The old-style Romanian pastrama is mutton, salted and hung up to dry. Traditionally it is made in September and October to be eaten—fried or grilled— with the new wine. Recently, in Romania, with modern food-processing methods, and styles copied from Northern Europe, they have started making pastrama of cured and smoked fillet of beef or pork flavored with garlic and spices. The famous Turkish pastirma, which is made in Kaiseri, is cured beef. The whole fillet is rubbed with garlic, herbs, spices, and plenty of salt, then pressed with a heavy weight for several days and hung up to dry. It is sold cut very thin, like prosciutto, into small oval slices, by machine.

Besides smoked meats, the delis offered wurst, frankfurters, knishes, and pickles. Their great trade was sandwiches. They used rye bread with mustard. Those who offered cheese and pickled fish—smoked salmon and various kinds of salted and pickled herring—were called "dairy" and "appetizing" stores. Delis were geared to a very fast pace, and now, even though they may be busy only on weekends, there is still an atmosphere of hurry and bustle in the few dozen traditional old-style ones left.

The Russian Jews came to play a vital role in the country in fields such as journalism, literature, theater, and the film industry, in the clothing and building trades, as well as in trade unions, politics, and the sciences. At first, the new immigrants formed a separate community from the well-established "native" German Jews, who looked down on them, but by the 1940s, when a second generation began to prosper, and they found themselves thrown into the same melting pot, the two assimilated, and their Americanization began. For the most part, the second generation rejected their Jewish heritage. For many of the third generation, the Eastern European heritage became irrelevant, for it was no longer even a memory. It had become an echo of the distant past, without meaning, while the merger of different cultures in the country created a new symbiosis and a vital and dynamic new society of which the Jews, like everybody else, craved to be part.

As New York became by far the greatest Jewish center the world had ever known, it was also the most cosmopolitan city in the world, embracing African Americans, Puerto Ricans, Italians, Chinese. American Jews absorbed at great speed all that was happening in the country—the new technology, the labor-saving devices in the kitchen, the cans, the jars, the frozen foods, the Jell-O, the changing culinary fashions. Processed, mass-produced foods revolutionized the American kitchen. Food companies (many of which were Jewish-owned) with an eye on the Jewish market employed *mashgiahs* and obtained kosher certificates. Heinz brought out vegetarian (without pork) kosher baked beans. Jewish women discovered canned tuna, salmon, and tomatoes. Vegetable shortening transformed their cooking and their lives. Their community books became full of apple pies and turkey, Hawaiian chickens, pecan pies, and dishes from all over the world. Like all American women, Jewish women did not wish to spend all their time in the kitchen. Their galley kitchens were small, and anyway it was not the American way of life.

After the Second World War, a wave of refugees arrived from Europe, and since the fifties the country has absorbed Jews from every corner of the world, including Iran, Iraq, Egypt, India, Georgia, Bukhara, Yugoslavia, Russia, and also Israel. The few Sephardi communities, notably the New Orleans one of Marrano stock that came from Jamaica in the 1860s, and the Syrian and Salonikan ones that were founded at the turn of the century and had kept themselves to themselves, found their congregations hugely enlarged.

Though American Jewry has become one entity—integrated and acculturated in American life—and though most Jews know little about the legacies they have inherited, there have been stirrings of interest—a kind of Jewish cultural renaissance. It has to do with the new generation's nostalgia and yearning for roots, a need for identification to fill a cultural vacuum. Whereas some look for anchorage in religious orthodoxy, others rediscover the cultural heritage in the kitchen. There are all kinds—Yiddish gourmets, purists, followers of kosher "nouvelle," and eclectic creators. Latkes and knishes have become chic. So have kasha and kugels.

Another trend is the discovery of the "exotic" brethren from around the Mediterranean and the Middle and Far East. For about fifteen years, American colleagues have been sending me recipes and articles about "exotic" Jewish cuisines which appeared in *The New York Times* and other papers around Passover and Jewish holidays. Their foods fit in with contemporary notions about healthy eating—full of grains and vegetables, low in cholesterol, and cooked with oil—and they reflect what is fashionable in the eclectic American kitchen today—lots of herbs and spices, chilies and aromatics, such as tamarind and pomegranate molasses. Bene Israel Indian chutneys sell on Long Island, Syrian lahma bi ajeen (meat pizzas) are popular in Los Angeles. All the flowers of Jewish gastronomy have blossomed here, albeit transformed into something a little different. No one, it seems, can resist doing his or her own thing in this country where anything goes and where creativity and originality are valued above everything. Dishes that hardly changed in centuries have been transformed to fit in with the latest fashion and the chef's creative urges.

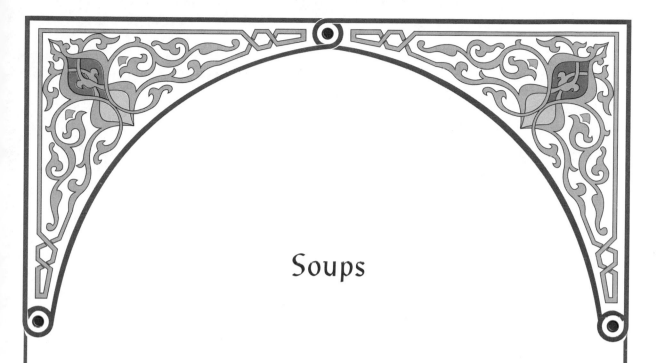

Soups

AN OLD JEWISH JOKE my brother Zaki used to tell when we were schoolchildren in Paris is still around: A man calls a waiter in a restaurant and says, "I'm not happy." The waiter asks, "What's the matter?" The man replies, "You tell me!" The waiter asks, "Is the soup cold?" The man replies, "No!" The waiter asks, "Would you like some salt and pepper?" The man replies, "No!" The waiter says, "You always have this soup and it's always the same?" The man says, "Taste it." The waiter asks, "Where's the spoon?" The man says, "Aha!"

It is often said that no traditional Jewish meal is complete without soup, and indeed many a thick, hearty soup is a meal in itself. The most famous is chicken soup, which has a variety of accompaniments.

Chicken Soup

GOLDENE YOICH

Chicken Soup

THIS ALL-TIME FAVORITE is the basis of Sabbath and holiday meals. Friday night is not the same without it. It is also the traditional wedding-party soup. In the old days it was called the "golden broth," because it was "like amber with golden globules of fat floating on top." These days the fat is often skimmed off as unhealthy, and the color is sometimes accentuated with a pinch of saffron. The soup has long been considered a cure-all, the "Jewish penicillin," and the idea that it has medicinal properties has recently been backed by scientific research and commercial enterprise.

The broth is traditionally made with a fat boiling chicken. The chicken is served as a second course, with horseradish sauce and pickled cucumbers to lift the blandness. But many people now use chicken carcasses or packages of giblets (including chicken feet, which are available at Jewish butcher shops) to make the soup, and serve roast chicken as a main dish.

Recipes for additions and accompaniments that are commonly part of the soup follow.

> 1 stewing chicken weighing about 5 lb
>   (2.5 kg), or 1 chicken carcass and
>   2 packages of giblets weighing
>   1 lb (500 g)
> 1 large onion, quartered
> 2 carrots cut into fat pieces
> 1 leek
> 1 turnip, quartered
> 2 celery stalks and leaves, cut into large
>   slices
> 2 sprigs of parsley (optional)
> Salt and white pepper
> Additions: see end of recipe; recipes follow
>   for knaidlach, mandlen, egg and flour
>   dumplings, kreplach

Put the chicken, or the carcass and giblets, in a large pan with 9 cups (2 liters) of water. Bring to a boil and remove any scum. Then add the vegetables, the parsley stems (keep the leaves for garnish), salt, and white pepper. Simmer, covered, on very low heat, for 2½ hours, adding water as necessary.

If you are using a whole chicken lift it out after 1 hour, remove the meat so as not to overcook it, and keep it moistened with a little broth, for a second course. Return the carcass and bones to the pot and continue cooking for another hour or so.

Strain the broth. If you want to remove the fat floating at the top, you can mop it up with paper towels or make the soup a day ahead and keep it covered in the refrigerator, then skim off the congealed fat with a spoon.

A few minutes before serving, add a handful of fine lokshen (vermicelli), broken into small pieces in your hand, or other additions, and simmer until tender. Serve very hot, sprinkled, if you like, with a little finely chopped parsley.

Lokshen are the usual addition, but others may be substituted, including pasta shapes such as plaetschen (little squares), shpaetzlen (bow ties), and farfel (grated or chopped pasta), pastry croutons called mandlen, and egg and flour dumplings. Kreplach (meat ravioli) are for holidays and special occasions; knaidlach (matzo balls) are for Passover, but people make them anytime. Recipes for these follow the variations.

VARIATIONS

• A chicken soup with a wonderful intense flavor that I enjoyed at the home of my daughter's mother-in-law, Estelle Boyers, adds half a small rutabaga and a squashed tomato, also a speck of sugar, and occasionally a touch of saffron at the start of the cooking.

• The French add 2 bay leaves and a sprig of thyme.

• Put in a good pinch of powdered saffron towards the end.

• Tiny unborn eggs, available from Jewish butchers, can be added at the end and simmered for 1–2 minutes.

• For chicken soup and barley (made famous as the title of Arnold Wesker's play), add 2 chopped leeks and 4 oz (100 g) of pearl barley and simmer 1 hour, or until the barley is tender.

Knaidlach
Matzo Balls

MAKES ABOUT 16

The Yiddish word *knaidl* is derived from the German *Knödel*, meaning "dumpling." Since the early Middle Ages, dumplings of all kinds have been popular in German, Czech, and Austrian cooking, and came into the Jewish diet. All over Eastern Europe, they epitomize the robust peasant-and-poor-man's food. The basis of many—both savory and sweet, in soups or served with meat and gravy—is egg combined with bread crumbs. The Jewish version, with matzos, was born as a Passover specialty, but it is so liked that it appears throughout the year. There are very many versions, with chicken fat or oil, and including beef marrow, ground almonds, grated onion, chopped parsley, and powdered ginger. Most, including the old traditional one—beat 1 egg, then add 1 heaping tablespoon of melted chicken fat, 2 tablespoons of warm water, salt, white pepper, and ½ cup (75 g) matzo meal— are heavy and stodgy. This one is beautifully light and fluffy.

2 eggs, separated
½ cup (75 g) medium matzo meal
Salt

Beat the egg whites stiff. Fold in the lightly beaten yolks, then the matzo meal and salt, and continue to mix gently until amalgamated. Chill, covered, for 30 minutes. Then roll into ¾-inch (2-cm) balls and drop into plenty of boiling salted water. Simmer for about 20 minutes. Just before serving, heat them up, then lift them out and drop them into the boiling soup broth. It is usual to cook knaidlach in boiling water rather than right in the broth, because they soak up so much liquid that unless you have made a very large quantity you will end up with very little broth.

VARIATIONS

• Add 2 tablespoons very finely chopped parsley or a pinch of powdered ginger.

Mandlen

Pastry Croutons

SERVES 4–6

In Eastern Europe, housewives made large quantities at a time and kept them in jars. The name "mandlen," Yiddish for "almonds," refers to their shape.

1 large egg
2 teaspoons light vegetable oil
½ teaspoon salt
¾–1 cup (75–125 g) flour

In a bowl, beat the egg with the oil and salt, then beat in as much flour as you need to make a soft dough that just holds together and is not sticky. Knead 10 minutes and allow to rest 20 minutes. Divide the dough into 2 pieces and press, roll, and pull each into a long rope shape about ½ inch (1¼ cm) wide. Cut this into pieces ½ inch (1¼ cm) long. Put them on an oiled bak-

ing sheet and bake in a preheated 375°F (190°C) oven for 35–45 minutes, or until lightly golden.

Alternatively, deep-fry them in medium-hot oil till lightly browned, lift out with a slotted spoon, and drain on paper towels.

Egg and Flour Dumplings

SERVES 4–6

These make a pleasant addition to a chicken soup. Do not expect them to be round: they come out in irregular ameboid shapes.

2 large eggs
½ teaspoon salt
½ cup (65 g) flour

Beat the eggs with the salt. Add the flour and beat vigorously until smooth and creamy. Drop the batter by the teaspoonful into simmering broth and simmer 10 minutes. It will sink to the bottom of the pan, and rise when it is almost cooked.

Kreplach

Pasta Stuffed with Meat or Chicken

SERVES 6 (MAKES 22)

These dumplings of stuffed pasta in chicken soup—they are likened to Chinese wonton, Turkish manti, and Italian cappelletti—have a prestigious place in the Jewish menu and are usually prepared for such important meals as the New Year, the eve of Yom Kippur, and the Seventh Day of Sukkot. They are sometimes served as a pasta first course with meat gravy from a roast.

There are many alternative fillings. The chicken-liver and mushroom ones that follow in the variations are particularly good.

Pasta dough (see page 152) made with 1 egg, a pinch of salt, and about 1 cup (150 g) flour

For the filling

1 small onion, finely chopped
2 tablespoons oil
6 oz (175 g) lean ground beef
Salt and pepper
1 egg
2 tablespoons finely chopped parsley

Knead the dough well until smooth and elastic, adding a little flour if sticky or a drop of water if necessary. Wrap in plastic wrap and allow to rest 20 minutes.

Fry the onion in oil till soft. Add the meat, season with salt and pepper, and cook, stirring and crushing the meat with a fork, until it changes color. Let it cool a little, then put it in the food processor with the egg and parsley and blend to a paste.

Roll out the dough as thin as possible on a lightly floured surface and cut it into 2½-inch (6½-cm) squares. The Jewish way to do it (as opposed to the Italian) is to fold the sheet of dough over and over into a flattened scroll, and to cut across into pieces 2½ inches (6½ cm)

wide. Then unroll the strips, put them in a pile, and cut them into squares. Scraps can be rolled into a ball, rolled out again, and cut into squares.

Put a teaspoon of filling in the middle of each square and fold over diagonally, bringing one point to meet the opposite point to make a triangle. Pinch the edges together firmly to seal tightly. Now make a ring by bringing the two longer points of the triangle together and pressing them firmly to stick them. Leave to stand 15 minutes.

Drop the kreplach in plenty of boiling salted water and cook over medium heat for about 20 minutes. Start with a fast, hard boil to prevent them from sticking to the bottom, and when they float to the top, continue cooking on medium heat. Remove the cooked dumplings with a slotted spoon. When you are ready to serve, drop them into the chicken broth. (You can cook them in the broth, but they give it a cloudy appearance.)

VARIATIONS

• You can make kreplach with leftover cooked beef or chicken mashed to a paste in the food processor with parsley and seasonings.

• For kreplach with a chicken-liver filling (also called "varenikes"): Fry 1 small chopped onion in 2 tablespoons of oil until soft. Sprinkle 6 oz (175 g) chicken livers with salt and sear on both sides under the grill to kosher them. Blend lightly in the food processor with 1 small egg and a little pepper. A wonderful Hungarian version is made with goose liver.

• For a mushroom filling: Fry 1 small chopped onion in 2 tablespoons of oil, then add 6 oz (175 g) mushrooms (preferably shiitake) that have been finely chopped in the food

Kreplach (cont.)

processor. Sauté gently, adding salt and pepper and a little water, until thoroughly cooked and the liquid is absorbed. Add 2 tablespoons finely chopped parsley. Bind with a beaten egg added in at the end. There are those who mix in a little mashed potato to bind the hash into a paste, making it easier to use.

Krupnik

Mushroom and Barley Soup

SERVES 10

It looks very unappealing, but it is heartwarming in winter, and the dried cèpes with which it is traditionally made give it a unique musty flavor. Krupnik is important because it was a mainstay in Poland, Lithuania, and the Ukraine, and it has been kept up. There is even a dried soup mix produced in Israel. In Eastern Europe, people went out to pick cèpes in season and dried them on top of the stove. They kept them in jars and built up stocks to last the year. The soup can be very simple, with only onions, barley, and mushrooms, or it can have several vegetables. It can also be made with chicken stock or with a meat bone.

1–1½ oz (25–40 g) dried cèpes
13 cups (3 liters) or more water or stock
2 small carrots
2 small turnips
2 small onions
2 medium potatoes
2 celery stalks and celery leaves
¾ cup (125 g) pearl barley

Soak the cèpes in a little water for 15 minutes, until they soften. Chop all the vegetables finely in 2 batches in the food processor and put them in a pan with the barley and all the water, including the mushroom-soaking water. Chop the softened mushrooms in the food processor, and add them too. Bring to the boil, remove the scum, season with plenty of salt and pepper, and simmer for 1 hour, or until the barley is very soft and bloated. It gives a jellylike quality to the soup. Add water, if necessary, to thin it.

Serve with sour cream if you like if you have used water.

Borscht

Cold Beet Soup

SERVES 6

This cool sweet-and-sour soup, which was particularly popular in Lithuania, has become one of the great Jewish standbys of the restaurant trade. It is one of my favorites.

2 lbs (1 kg) raw beets
A little salt and pepper
Juice of 1 lemon
2 tablespoons sugar or to taste
6 peeled boiled potatoes (optional)
1 cup (250 ml) sour cream to pass around

Peel the beets and dice them. If they are young, that is easy to do. If they are old and too hard to dice, simply cut them in half and, when they have softened with boiling, lift them out, cut them up, and put them back in the pan. Put the beets in a pan with 9 cups (2 liters) of water and salt and pepper and simmer for 1½ hours. Let the soup cool, then chill, covered, in the refrigerator. Add the lemon and sugar to taste before serving (these could be added when the soup is hot, but it is more difficult to determine the intensity of the flavoring). Remove some of the beet pieces with a slotted spoon if they seem too much and keep them for a salad.

Serve, if you like, with a boiled potato, putting one in each plate. Pass around the sour cream for all to help themselves.

VARIATIONS

• When the soup is served with meat to follow, and the sour cream cannot be added, it is usual to thicken it with 2 egg yolks. Beat them in a bowl, add a little of the boiling soup, beat well, and pour into the pan, beating all the time.

Take off the heat at once, before the soup curdles.

• There are dozens of different Russian and Ukrainian borschts. These are rich hot soups made with a number of ingredients, including meat, cabbage and potatoes, carrots, onions, celery and parsnips, sometimes spinach or sorrel, tomatoes or mushrooms, leeks, dried beans, apples, and dried fruit. The common ingredient, which gives them their name and their color, is beets.

Hyme is eating at Bloom's when a shnorer comes in on his knees, imploring, "I haven't eaten for three days." And Hyme says, "So, force yourself."

Jewish vendor of cooking pots, Lida, Belorussia, 1916. Photographed by a German soldier during World War I

Yellow Split Pea Soup with Frankfurters

SERVES 10

This makes a rich and appetizing winter soup. The old way was to cook the yellow peas in a stock made with beef and marrow bones, and you may like to do that. The same soup can be made with dry white haricot or butter beans, and also with lentils. Red and yellow lentils do not need soaking.

> 1 large onion, chopped
> 2 carrots, sliced
> 3 tablespoons light vegetable oil
> 1 lb (500 g) yellow split peas, soaked
>   overnight
> 13 cups (3 liters) chicken or beef stock
>   (you may use 2 bouillon cubes)
> A bunch of celery leaves, chopped
> Salt and pepper
> 2 bay leaves
> ¾ lb (350 g) skinless frankfurters or wurst
>   sausages, sliced
> Juice of ½ lemon or more to taste

In a large pan, gently fry the onion and carrots in the oil till they soften. Add the drained yellow peas and about two-thirds of the stock and bring to the boil. Remove the scum, add the celery leaves, and simmer, covered, on very low heat for about 1 hour, or until the peas are soft.

Liquefy the soup in a blender or food processor and return it to the pan. Add salt and pepper, the bay leaves, and the rest of the stock—the amount depends on the consistency that you prefer. (The reason for adding it at this stage is to make blending easier with less liquid.) Cook ½ hour longer. Add the sausages and lemon juice, and a little water if necessary, and cook a few minutes more. Serve very hot.

Goulash Soup

SERVES 4–6

Jews adopted this meat-and-paprika soup from the Austro-Hungarian world and turned it into a stew, but my favorite version is the original light soupy Hungarian one without frills. It is most appetizing. In Hungary there are various types of paprika, from mild and sweet to very hot. The kind we find in Britain is mild. You may add a pinch of chili powder if you like it hot. I prefer not to. Use meat that provides good meat jelly, such as blade or neck.

> 1 large onion, chopped
> 2 tablespoons light vegetable oil
> 1 tablespoon sweet paprika
> 1¼ lbs (600 g) beef, cut in ½–¾-inch
>   (1½–2-cm) cubes
> Salt
> 2 lbs (1 kg) potatoes, cubed or quartered
> 2 tomatoes, peeled and cubed
> A good pinch of cayenne or red chili powder
>   (optional)

Fry the onion in the oil till golden. Then stir in the paprika and add the meat. Sprinkle with salt and sauté for a few minutes, turning the meat over. Then add a little water and braise with the lid on for 1½ hours. Add the potatoes and tomatoes and enough water to make a soup rather than a stew—altogether, with the water at the start, about 9 cups (2 liters). Simmer gently for 1 hour or longer. The meat should be extremely tender. Add a little cayenne or red chili powder if you like.

VARIATIONS

• A Viennese version is to add 2 crushed cloves of garlic and ½ teaspoon caraway with the meat.

• Add 1 diced green or red pepper with the potatoes.

• Kidney beans, sauerkraut, cabbage, and pasta may also be added.

Kartoffel mit Prash Zup

Leek and Potato Soup with Milk

SERVES 6

There are many potato soups in the Yiddish-speaking world. This one with a good proportion of leeks has a delicate flavor and lovely creamy consistency. It is like a vichyssoise and can be served hot or cold.

1 lb (500 g) potatoes
1 lb (500 g) leeks
4½ cups (1 liter) water
2¼ cups (½ liter) milk
Salt and white pepper
1 cup (¼ liter) sour cream or crème fraîche
4 tablespoons finely chopped chives to garnish

Peel and cube the potatoes. Trim the leeks and chop them very finely—almost to a pulp—in a food processor. Put them both in a pan with the water and milk. Add salt and pepper and simmer gently for 1 hour. Mash the potatoes with a potato masher. Serve hot or cold. Beat in the sour cream, or let people help themselves to it. Serve sprinkled with chives.

COLD FRUIT SOUPS

FRUIT SOUPS served as a starter to sharpen the appetite—an old tradition all over Eastern Europe, especially in Germany, Poland, and Hungary—have become very popular in Israel. All kinds of fruit—in particular apples, plums, gooseberries, apricots, blackberries, and rhubarb—are stewed in water or a mixture of water and a fruity white wine or, occasionally, water and milk, with a little lemon and sugar and a flavoring such as cinnamon, lemon peel, or vanilla. The fruit is cooked till soft and left as it is, or blended to a light puree. The soup is sometimes thickened with flour, cornstarch, or potato flour, or with beaten egg yolk added in at the end (to me these are unnecessary). It can be served hot but is most commonly chilled. When the rest of the meal does not include meat, the soup is served with sour cream. Sometimes boiled potatoes are added.

Cold Cherry Soup

SERVES 6

Cold cherry soup—a Hungarian specialty—is the most famous and popular of the fruit soups. It is tasty and refreshing and looks beautiful, ideal for a summer meal. Morello cherries are the best kind to use but are not readily available. If you do use them, do not add lemon juice, for they are very sharp. I managed to get them when we had a family reunion of seventeen, but it meant I had to spend hours pitting them the day before. Still, it was a great start to the banquet.

> 2 lbs (1 kg) black cherries or sour morello
>   cherries
> 2½ cups (600 ml) light fruity red or white
>   wine
> 3–4 tablespoons sugar, or to taste
> ½ teaspoon cinnamon (optional)
> Juice of 2 lemons (none if using morellos)
> Zest of 1 lemon (optional)
> 6 tablespoons brandy
> 1 cup (¼ liter) sour cream

Remove the stems and pits and put the cherries in a pan with the wine, sugar, cinnamon, lemon juice, and zest. (Because the flavoring depends very much on the taste of the cherries and the wine, use less sugar and lemon to start with and add more if necessary towards the end.) Simmer for 15–20 minutes, until the cherries are soft. Add the brandy and chill. Beat in the sour cream before serving or, better still, pass the sour cream for all to help themselves.

Note

If there is meat to follow, the soup can be made without sour cream.

Plum Soup

SERVES 6

This Eastern European soup can be sharp or sweet. Add the sugar to taste, starting with 1 or 2 tablespoons. Apricots, gooseberries, and apples can also be used in the same way.

> 2 lbs (1 kg) plums, pitted
> 9 cups (2 liters) water or ½-and-½ mixture
>   of water and fruity white wine
> Juice of 1 lemon
> Grated zest of 1 lemon
> 1 cinnamon stick
> Sugar to taste, from 2 tablespoons to ¾ cup
>   (150 g)
> 6 boiled potatoes (optional)
> 1 cup (¼ liter) sour cream

Wash the plums and remove the stones. Put them in a pan with the water or a mixture of wine and water. Add the lemon juice and zest, cinnamon, and 1–2 tablespoons sugar, and simmer 15 minutes, or till soft. Remove the lemon peel and cinnamon. Taste before adding more sugar. Serve hot with potatoes or cold with sour cream. Beat in the sour cream before serving, or pass it around for all to help themselves.

VARIATIONS

• Blend to a puree and serve hot with boiled potatoes or cold with sour cream.

Pumpkin Soup

There is a version of this soup with water instead of milk, but it is not half as good as this delicious creamy one. Because the taste of pumpkin varies so, it is important to get the right balance of salt and sugar. Start with a little and taste and add more, if necessary, later.

3½ lbs (1½ kg) orange pumpkin (weighed with the seeds and fibers scraped away)
2 lbs (1 kg) potatoes, peeled and cubed
11 cups (2½ liters) milk
Salt and white pepper
2 tablespoons sugar or to taste
1 cup (250 ml) sour cream (optional)

Peel the pumpkin and cut it into cubes. Put them in a large pan with the potatoes and milk, a little salt, pepper, and sugar. Bring to the boil, then simmer, covered, on low heat, for about 30 minutes, until the potatoes and pumpkin are very soft. Mash them with a potato masher, adjust the seasoning, cook a few minutes more, and serve very hot. I prefer it without sour cream but some like it with, so pass it around for those who want it to help themselves to a dollop.

Schav Borscht

Cold Sorrel Soup or Green Borscht

Sour flavors were much favored by Jews in Eastern Europe. Sharp sorrel soup was a favorite in Poland, Hungary, Transylvania, and especially Lithuania. It is one of my favorites too. Although it grows like a weed, sorrel is rarely available in the shops. But this situation may be changing, because I have recently seen it a few times at my supermarket.

1 lb (500 g) old mealy potatoes
9 cups (2 liters) stock
7 oz (200 g) sorrel leaves, chopped
Salt
1 teaspoon sugar or to taste (optional)
2 eggs

Wash the sorrel leaves and cut off only tough stalks (keep thin soft ones). Boil the potatoes in the water or stock until they begin to fall apart, and mash them lightly with a fork or potato masher. Add the sorrel, salt, and sugar and simmer 5 minutes.

Beat the eggs with a little of the hot soup, then pour into the pan. Beat until the soup thickens, but do not let it boil or it will curdle. Turn off the heat quickly. Serve hot or cold.

VARIATION

• Another version, with water instead of stock, has 1 cup (250 ml) sour cream stirred in at the end.

Jerusalem Artichoke Soup

This knobbly potatolike tuber, which came to Europe from North America at the beginning of the seventeenth century, is popular in Jerusalem, where it features regularly on menus, because of its name, although the name has nothing to do with the Holy City. It is a seventeenth-century English distortion of the old Italian name, *girasole* (sunflower) *articiocco*, acquired because it tastes like an artichoke and produces a flower that turns with the sun.

The following is adapted from a soup eaten at the Eucalyptus Inn in Jerusalem. I was being filmed there stirring the soup in a huge cauldron, together with the owner-chef, for Israeli TV.

1 large onion, chopped
2 tablespoons light vegetable oil
2 garlic cloves, chopped
3 tomatoes, peeled and chopped
1 lb (500 g) Jerusalem artichokes, peeled
5¾ cups (1¼ liters) chicken stock or water
Salt and pepper
Juice of ½ lemon

In a large pan, fry the onion in the oil until very soft. Add the garlic and fry till the aroma rises. Add the tomatoes and cook, stirring, for 5 minutes. Add the artichokes and pour in the stock or water, season with salt and pepper, and simmer for 30–40 minutes, or until the Jerusalem artichokes are very soft. Mash them roughly with a potato masher and add the lemon juice.

Mushroom Soup

There are many versions of mushroom soup from Eastern Europe, often with fried onions and thickened with flour or with egg yolk. This one, with potato, is my favorite. It has a beautiful pure flavor, and the parsley enlivens the color.

2 potatoes, weighing about 1 lb (500 g)
6¼ cups (1½ liters) water or stock (you may use a bouillon cube)
½ lb (250 g) mushrooms, preferably shiitake
4 tablespoons light vegetable oil
Salt and pepper
A large bunch of parsley (about ¾ cup), finely chopped

Peel the potatoes and cut them into pieces. Put them in a pan with the water or stock and simmer until soft, then crush them with a potato masher.

Finely chop the mushrooms in the food processor. Sauté for 5 minutes in the oil in a frying pan, stirring all the time. Then pour into the pan with the potatoes, add salt and pepper, and simmer a few minutes. Just before serving, add the parsley and heat through. Serve as it is, accompanied by lemon wedges, and if you like by sour cream.

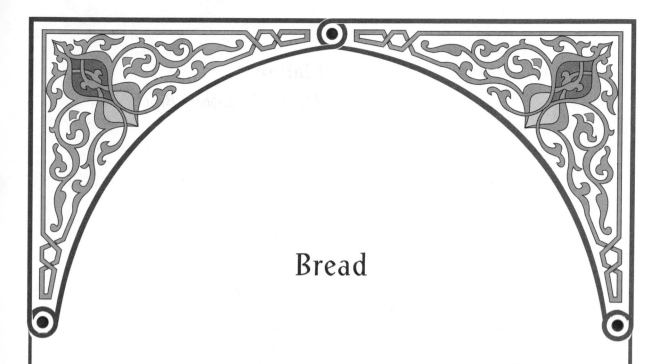

Bread

JEWS ADOPTED many different types of bread in Eastern Europe—from a potato bread with caraway seeds in Galicia, a sourdough white bread in Austria, and the round flat roll called "bialy" after the Polish city of Białystok, to the dark, strong-tasting, slightly sour pumpernickel and the hard, dry flat pletzel with onions and poppy seeds. A rye bread made with plenty of caraway seeds is one of the most widespread and popular, but the two great breads of the Ashkenazi world, which are bound up with Yiddish culture and identity, are the hallah and the bagel. The first is the bread of celebration, the second represents the everyday.

ABOUT FLOUR

ALMOST ALL THE PEOPLE who gave me recipes did not specify what kind of flour to use, but simply said "flour"—white flour always being assumed. Many also gave no quantities, saying "as much flour as it takes" or "as much water as the flour absorbs." That is how recipes are passed on in traditional societies. When I started trying the recipes and measuring and weighing flours, I became alarmed by the disparities. For instance, 500 grams of all-purpose flour varied between 3½ and 4 cups; 500 grams of bread flour ranged from 3¼ to 3½ cups. The amounts of egg or water that different batches of flour absorbed also varied. This was the case not only with flours from different sources but with those from the same. I have been making pizza dough for many years, with both all-purpose and bread flours. When I tried new recipes for my Italian book, I found that the amount of water I had recorded in my Mediterranean book was not right, and I phoned the British flour board. They explained that flour from wheat grown even in the same field varies from year to year in its capacity to absorb liquid, and that indeed the difference was marked between the two periods I mentioned. So I can only say, as my informants did: When using flour, be prepared to add a little more flour or a little more water as necessary.

Hallah

The Braided Sabbath Bread

MAKES 4 LOAVES

It is made with eggs and comes out so beautiful that you do not resent the labor.

2 tablespoons dry yeast
2¼ cups (500 ml) lukewarm water
½ cup (100 g) sugar
4 eggs, beaten, plus 2 yolks or 1 whole egg
*   for glazing*
1 tablespoon salt
½ cup (125 ml) vegetable oil
About 9¼ cups (1⅓ kg) flour
Poppy or sesame seeds (optional)

Dissolve the yeast in the water with 1 teaspoon of the sugar. Beat well and leave 10 minutes, until it froths.

In a very large bowl, lightly beat the eggs. Then add the salt, sugar, and oil and beat again. Add the frothy yeast mixture and beat well. Now add the flour gradually, and just enough to make a soft dough that holds together, mixing well, first with a large spoon, then working it in with your hands. Knead vigorously for about 15 minutes, until it is very smooth and elastic, adding flour if the dough is too sticky. Pour a little oil in the bowl and turn the dough, so that it is greased all over. Cover the bowl with plastic wrap and put it in a warm place to rise for 2–3 hours, or until it has doubled in bulk. Punch the dough down and knead again, then divide into four pieces to make 4 loaves.

To make round hallah: Take 1 piece of dough, roll it between your palms, and pull it out into a long fat rope about 18 inches (46 cm) long and 2 inches (5 cm) thick—a little fatter at one end. Take the fatter end and put it in the middle of an oiled baking sheet, then coil the rest of the rope around it like a snail. Continue with the remaining 3 pieces.

To make braided hallah with 3 strands: Divide 1 piece of the dough into 3. Roll each piece between your palms and pull into long thin ropes about 18 inches (46 cm) long and 1¼ inches (3 cm) wide. Pinch 1 end of all the strands together and plait them: bring the rope on the right over the middle one, then bring the one on the left over it and continue to the end. Pinch the ends together and tuck them under the loaf. You may find it easier to begin plaiting in the middle of the 3 strands and plait towards the 2 ends. Continue with the remaining 3 pieces.

Place the 4 loaves on well-oiled baking sheets, leaving plenty of room for them to expand, then leave to rise for 1 hour, or until doubled in bulk. Now brush gently with the beaten egg yolks, or, if you want to sprinkle with poppy or sesame seeds, brush first with the whole beaten egg (the seeds stick better if the white is there too). Bake in a preheated 350° F (180°C) oven for 30–40 minutes, or until the loaves are beautifully golden brown. They are done if they sound hollow when you tap the bottoms.

VARIATIONS FOR SWEET HALLAHS

• Add ½ cup (125 ml) honey to the beaten eggs.
• Add ¾ cup (100 g) raisins and knead them into the dough after it has risen and been punched down.

HALLAH

THE BRAIDED HALLAH, which is made with eggs, is the Jewish Sabbath-and-holiday bread. It is surrounded by folklore and tradition and loaded with symbolism. On festive occasions a blessing is said over two loaves, symbolizing the two portions of the manna that was distributed on Fridays to the children of Israel during their Exodus from Egypt. The breads are covered on the table by a white napkin, which represents the dew that collected on the manna in the morning. Poppy and sesame seeds sprinkled on the bread also symbolize the manna that fell from heaven. Hallah is made in various sizes and shapes, all of which have a meaning. Braided ones, which may have three, four, or six strands, are the most common, and because they look like arms intertwined, symbolize love. Three braids symbolize truth, peace, and justice. Twelve humps from two small or one large braided bread recall the miracle of the twelve loaves for the twelve tribes of Israel. Round loaves, "where there is no beginning and no end," are baked for Rosh Hashanah to symbolize continuity. Ladder and hand shapes are served

at the meal before the fast of Yom Kippur—
the ladder signifying that we should ascend to
great heights, the hand that we may be inscribed for a good year. On Purim, small triangular loaves symbolize Haman's ears; at
Shavuot, two oblongs side by side represent
the Tablets of the Law. The bulkah is a seg-
mented rectangular hallah. Sweet hallahs with
honey or raisins are baked during the festive
season to bring joy and happiness.

The name "hallah" is derived from the
Hebrew word used for "portion" in the Biblical commandment "of the first of your
dough you shall give unto the Lord a portion
for a gift throughout your generations." Jews
were biblically commanded to separate from
their doughs one twenty-fourth and give it to
the *kohanim* (priests) every Sabbath. In post-
Temple times, the rabbis ordained that a *hallah*
(portion), which had to be at least the size of
an olive, must be separated from the dough
and burned. It is still a tradition for Jewish
bakers and observant houswives to tear a tiny
lump of risen dough from any type of bread
and to "burn" it (usually wrapped in foil)
in the oven or fire while making a blessing.

The name "hallah" was given to a bread in
South Germany in the Middle Ages, when it
was adopted by Jews for the Sabbath. It was the
traditional local Sunday loaf, and its various
shapes and designs were in the local tradition
of decorative breads. John Cooper (*Eat and Be
Satisfied*) notes that the first mention of the
bread was in the fifteenth century and that the
term was coined in Austria. Before that the
bread was called "berches," a name that is still

Hassid eating a hallah

used by Jews in some parts today. The bread
became the Jewish ritual bread in Germany,
Austria, and Bohemia and was taken to Poland,
Eastern Europe, and Russia when the Jews migrated east. Housewives kneaded the dough on
Thursday, let it rise overnight, and got up early
on Friday to bake it. They often baked all the
bread for the week at the same time, so as not
to waste fuel. The distinctive smell which emanates from the oven and fills the house
when it is baked is the Sabbath aroma
that pervades the memories of the old
Yiddish-speaking world.

Alsatian Kugelhopf

Serves 10

This famous sweet yeast bread, traditionally baked in a high fluted mold with a funneled center, is usually eaten for breakfast in Alsace, but it can also serve as a dessert, moistened with kirsch or rum and accompanied by whipped cream.

> 1 tablespoon active dry yeast
> 1 cup (250 ml) warm milk
> ⅔ cup (125 g) sugar
> 3⅓ cups (500 g) flour
> 1 teaspoon salt
> 2 teaspoons oil to grease the dough
> ⅓ cup (50 g) raisins
> 6 tablespoons kirsch or rum
> 4½ oz (125 g) butter, softened
> 3 eggs
> Grated zest of 1 orange
> ¼ cup (50 g) blanched almonds
> Confectioners' sugar to garnish

In a large bowl, dissolve the yeast in ½ cup (125 ml) of the warm milk with 1 teaspoon of the sugar and leave for 10 minutes, until the mixture froths.

Add the flour, salt, and remaining sugar and warm milk, mixing first with a large spoon, then working with your hand until a soft dough is formed that holds together in a ball. Add a little more flour if it is too sticky, or a little more milk if it is too dry. Knead for about 15 minutes, until smooth and elastic. Pour the oil into the bowl and roll the dough around to grease it all over. Cover the bowl with plastic wrap and leave the dough to rise in a warm place for 1 hour, or until doubled in bulk.

Soak the raisins in the kirsch or rum for an hour.

In a food processor, blend the butter with the eggs and the grated orange zest. Punch the dough down and put it in the food processor with the butter-and-egg mixture. Blend to a homogenous creamy paste. Add the drained raisins and blend very briefly—just enough to work them into the dough.

Grease a preferably nonstick kugelhopf mold—about 9 inches (23 cm) in diameter and 4½ inches (11 cm) high—generously with butter. Sprinkle the blanched almonds on the bottom and pour the dough over them. The mold should be only half full.

Leave the dough to rise again in the mold for about 1 hour, or until doubled in bulk. Bake in a preheated 350°F (180°C) oven for 45 minutes. If the top is already brown after 30 minutes, cover it with foil. After removing the bread from the oven, leave it in the pan for about 5 minutes before turning it out upside down. Let it cool, then dust it with confectioners' sugar.

BAGEL

The Bread with the Hole

THE CRUSTY ring-shaped bagel—the word means "bracelet" in German—which was the everyday bread of the Jews in Eastern Europe, has become the most famous Jewish food in America and a standard American bread. Like hallah, it is of South German origin, but it came into its own and took its definitive form in the Polish shtetl. It was sold on the street by vendors with baskets or hanging on long sticks. Hawkers had to have a license. Illegal selling of bagels by children was common and viewed as respectable, especially by orphans helping their widowed mothers, but if they were caught by a policeman they would be beaten and their baskets, bagels, and linen cover would be taken away.

Because of their shape—with no beginning and no end—bagels symbolize the eternal cycle of life. In the old days, they were supposed to be a protection against demons and evil spirits, warding off the evil eye and bringing good luck. For these reasons, they were served at circumcisions and when a woman was in labor and also at funerals, along with hard-boiled eggs. When the Jews left Eastern Europe in great masses for America, Canada, and Europe, many sold bagels from pushcarts on the Lower East Side of Manhattan and in the East End of London. When my great-uncle Jacques immigrated to New York from Syria at the turn of the century, the only jobs he could get were peddling door to door and selling bagels from a pushcart. He found this so demeaning that he migrated back to Egypt, where a large part of his family had settled. A month ago in Paris, his widow, Régine, told me of his difficulties in communicating in either English or Yiddish, and of his surprise when he first encountered bagels.

Although so many new varieties of bagels have now appeared in New York, purists will have only the original plain water bagels, which are made by throwing rings of risen dough into violently boiling water for a few seconds, then draining, cooling, and baking quickly till golden, shiny, and crisp. They are wonderful when very, very fresh and still spongy inside but quickly become tough and leathery, in which case the best thing is to cut them open and toast them. New York is said to make the best, supposedly because of the mineral content of their water.

A bagel is a doughnut with rigor mortis."

Bagels

MAKES 11

When I phoned around for tips to improve my bagels, I found that most people now use an egg in the dough, which makes the bread lighter, softer, and less chewy than the traditional version, which calls for only flour and water. I made the egg version with the "fast action" dried yeast, which is mixed straight into the flour, and it was perfect.

3½ cups (500 g) bread flour
1 envelope "fast action" dried yeast
1½ teaspoons salt
1½–2 tablespoons sugar
1 egg, lightly beaten
1½ tablespoons vegetable oil, plus a drop more
  to grease the dough
About ½ cup lukewarm water
1 egg white, to glaze

In a large bowl, mix the flour, yeast, salt, and sugar well. Then mix in the egg and the oil and add the water gradually, working it in with your hand—enough to make a soft dough that holds together in a ball. Add more water if necessary, or more flour if it is too sticky.

Turn the dough out and knead on a floured board for 10–15 minutes, until it is very smooth and elastic. Grease the dough all over by putting a drop of oil in the bowl and rolling the dough around in it. Cover the bowl with plastic wrap and leave to rise in a warm place for 1½ hours, or until doubled in bulk.

Punch the dough down and knead again briefly.

A bagel peddler, Kishinev

An easy way of shaping the bagels into rings is to roll out the dough to a rectangle about 1 inch (2½ cm) thick, and cut it into 11 equal strips with a pointed knife. Roll each strip between your palms into a rope about 7 inches (18 cm) long and ½ inch (1½ cm) thick and bring the ends together, pinching them to seal and form a bracelet. Place the rings on an oiled surface, and let them rise for about 1 hour, or until doubled in bulk.

Bring plenty of water to a boil in a wide

pan, then lower the heat to medium. Slip in 4 bagels at a time. Boil them for 1–2 minutes, turning them over once as they rise to the top. Then lift them out quickly with a slotted spoon and place them on a cloth to dry. Do the same with the rest of the bagels. Arrange on oiled baking sheets, brush with egg white, and bake in a preheated 375°F (190°C) oven for 15–20 minutes, until nicely browned.

VARIATIONS

• Sprinkle the bagels lightly with poppy or sesame seeds, fried onion, or coarse salt before baking.

• Another way of shaping the bread is to roll it into small balls, make a hole in the middle, and widen it by pulling the ring from the center.

• If you want to make the bagels in the old way, without the egg, you will simply need to add a little more warm water to bind the flour.

Rye Bread

MAKES 2 LOAVES

This bread, made with beer, is denser than the usual rye bread sold in a bakery, which contains a smaller proportion of rye flour, but it fills the house with an intoxicating smell and is more like traditional bread used to be. Letting it rise overnight gives a slight sourdough flavor.

1½ tablespoons active dry yeast
1 tablespoon honey
½ cup (125 ml) lukewarm water
3½ cups (500 g) rye flour
3½ cups (500 g) white bread flour
1 tablespoon sea salt
1 tablespoon sugar
3–4 tablespoons caraway seeds
2 tablespoons vegetable oil
About 1½ cups (350 ml) lukewarm
*   beer (you may use lager)*
1 small egg, lightly beaten

Prepare the dough the night before. Dissolve the yeast and honey in the warm water, and leave in a warm place for about 15 minutes, until it froths. In a large bowl, mix the flours, salt, sugar, 2–3 tablespoons caraway seeds, the oil, and the yeast and honey mixture. Then gradually add the beer, mixing it in with your hand and adding just enough to make a dough that holds together.

Knead the dough on a floured surface or in the bowl for 10–15 minutes, adding a little flour if it becomes too sticky. (Do not add too much, as this dough is a little sticky compared with white bread dough.) Pour a little oil in the bowl and roll the dough around to grease it all over. Cover the bowl with plastic wrap and leave to rise in a warm place overnight.

Punch down the dough and knead for 5 minutes. Divide in half and press into two greased 9 × 5 × 3-inch (23 × 13 × 7½-cm) loaf pans, or shape into round or oblong loaves and place them on a greased baking sheet, a little distance apart. Using a sharp knife dusted with flour, make diagonal cuts on the top about ¼ inch (5 mm) deep, at 1-inch (2½-cm) intervals. Cover with a damp cloth or greased plastic wrap and let the dough rise again for 1½ hours, or until doubled in bulk. Brush the top of the loaves with beaten egg and sprinkle with the remaining caraway seeds (the yolk gives a shine and the whites make the seeds stick better). Bake in a preheated 375°F (190°C) oven for 50–55 minutes. Placing a pan of water in the bottom of the oven to create steam improves the texture. Turn out and cool on racks.

Pumpernickel Bread

MAKES 2 LOAVES

A sourdough starter and dark molasses give this moist, dark, dense German bread its characteristic intense flavor. The starter, a mixture of yeast, flour, and water left to ferment, should be made 24 hours in advance. The bread keeps very well in a tin box or airtight bag in the refrigerator. It is best cut very thin.

For the starter

> 1 tablespoon active dry yeast
> 1 cup (250 ml) lukewarm water
> ¼ cup (4 tablespoons) white bread flour
> ¼ cup (4 tablespoons) rye flour

For the dough

> 1 tablespoon active dry yeast
> 2 tablespoons honey
> About 1⅔ cup (375 ml) lukewarm water

> 3⅓ cups (400 g) rye flour
> 2 cups (300 g) whole wheat bread flour
> 2 cups (300 g) white bread flour
> 1 tablespoon salt
> 2 tablespoons caraway seeds (optional)
> 4 tablespoons vegetable oil
> 4 tablespoons dark molasses
> 1 egg, lightly beaten, to glaze

To make the starter, mix the yeast with the water and both flours in a bowl. Cover with plastic wrap and leave at room temperature for 24 hours. The starter will rise, then drop and ferment.

The following day, make the dough. Dissolve the yeast and 1 tablespoon of honey in ½ cup of the lukewarm water and leave for 15 minutes, until it froths, then stir it. In a large bowl, mix the three flours. Add the salt, caraway seeds (if using), oil, molasses, the remaining tablespoon of honey, the starter, and the frothy yeast-honey-and-water mixture. Mix well and gradually add the remaining water, mixing it in with your hand and using just enough to make a dough that holds together. Turn it out on a floured surface and knead for about 15 minutes. This dough is a little sticky, but if it is too sticky, add a little more white flour.

Grease the dough by putting a drop of oil in the bowl and rolling the dough in it. Cover with plastic wrap and leave in a warm place for about 2 hours, or until doubled in bulk.

Punch the dough down and knead for 5 minutes. Divide in half and press into greased 9 × 5 × 3-inch (23 × 13 × 7½-cm) loaf pans. With a sharp, floured knife slash

Pumpernickel Bread (cont.)

diagonal cuts about I inch (2½ cm) apart on the top. Cover with a damp cloth or greased plastic wrap, and let rise until doubled in bulk—about 45 minutes.

Brush the top of the loaves with lightly beaten egg and bake in a preheated 350°F (180°C) oven for I hour. Placing a pan of water in the bottom of the oven to create steam improves the texture. Remove the loaves and cool on a rack.

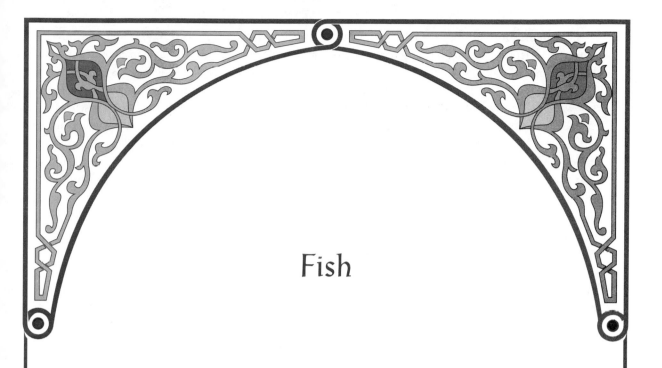

Fish

IN A PIECE entitled "Culinary Aspects of Anglo-Jewry" (in *Studies in the Cultural Life of the Jews in England* [Jerusalem: Magnum Press, 1975]) John Shaftesley quotes an eminent British surgeon, Sir Henry Thompson, writing in 1883: "If evidence were needed of the fact that such a dietary [as fish] is consistent with a high degree, both of bodily and mental vigour, it may be found in the Jewish race, whose ritual requirements have impelled them to be, both in this and other countries, large consumers of fish." Mr. Shaftesley also notes a query in the *Folklore Journal* from 1888: "What is the connection between Jews and halibut? The Dublin fishmongers say that when they have one for sale the Jews rush to buy pieces of it; but all try to get the head if possible." This story illustrates the Jewish love not only for fish but for quality fish, because halibut is one of the choicest and most expensive.

My mother-in-law, Fanny Nadel, came from Russia as a girl. Her father had gone ahead and set up as a fishmonger in the East End of London before the family joined him. He was a "scholar," with not too much interest in the trade, and Fanny, the eldest, helped in the shop. The East End was a great stronghold of the fish trade, which was entirely in Jewish hands. Now the suburbs of North West London are full of Jewish fishmongers with great queues on Thursday, Friday, and Sunday mornings. They provide the favorite fish for Jewish cooking, and also finely chopped fish and onions for preparing gefilte fish.

Fanny was no great cook, but she made a marvelous fried fish and excellent halibut in egg-and-lemon sauce, and she had very high standards in the quality of the product. She called many perfectly good fish "cat food" and had contempt for some of the Mediterranean fish we Oriental Jews ate, refusing to consider them "Jewish."

Eastern European Jews acquired a liking for freshwater fish from the hundreds of rivers which crossed the mainly landlocked areas they inhabited. Édouard de Pomiane, the French gastronome of Polish origin who wrote about the cooking of the Jews of Poland, remarked that "every observant Jew eats river fish. The wealthy buy carp and pike. The poor content themselves with a miserable roach or sometimes a piece of salt herring."

Carp, pike, perch, sterlet, and trout were all grand fish. The poor ate what de Pomiane observed as well as tench and chub. Carp was associated with Jews because Jewish traders on the silk route were involved in introducing carp from China to Central and Eastern Europe in the seventeenth century, and it was Jews who first farmed carp in Poland. They managed fish ponds and also bred fish from the Black, Azov, and Caspian seas and from the river Don. It was the carp, which traveled easily live in tanks, that they adopted as their fish. Whereas carp became a symbol of the Sabbath, salt herring, which Jewish merchants also traded in, and which was a lot cheaper than fresh fish, was the symbol of the weekday and marked the contrast between the two.

Many of the old recipes for freshwater fish and herring are now used for saltwater fish like halibut, haddock, cod, plaice, sole, hake, flounder, and salmon. Salmon has become the great Jewish party dish, ever-present at weddings and bar mitzvahs. At my local fishmonger, Corney's, which specializes in salmon, both wild and farmed, there are always long queues of people waiting to have theirs filleted or cut into steaks for the Sabbath.

According to the Jewish dietary laws, all fish with scales and with fins may be eaten. Shark, swordfish, monkfish, rockfish, skate, and eel are among the fish that are not kosher. Some confusion exists as to certain fish, such as sturgeon, which has tiny scales that do not overlap on its tail. Otherwise, fish is an easy option because it is *pareve* and can be eaten in a meal with either meat or dairy foods. (It may be eaten at the same meal as meat, but not on the same plate or cooked in the same dish, and in between one and the other something hard like bread must be eaten and a drink must be drunk.) And fish does not need to be ritually slaughtered or salted like meat.

Fish is prominent on the holiday table, especially on the New Year and Shavuot. In Jewish lore it is a symbol of fertility, because Jacob gave his children a blessing that they should multiply like fish in the sea. It is also associated with the coming of the Messiah. According to a legend, the Messiah will come in the form of a great fish from the sea.

Since earliest times, it was the custom among Jews to have fish on Friday night. There are references to that in the Talmud. The rabbis who codified the oral law, known as the Mishnah, ruled that it was meritorious to eat fish at each of the three Sabbath meals. "Without fish," the saying goes, "there is no Sabbath." The smell of fish cooking is associated with the Sabbath. In a Yiddish story that I came across, a rebbe was certain that he smelled the odor from paradise every time his wife, the rebbetsin, cooked fish for the Sabbath.

In the shtetl, fish was bought live on Thursday. It was swimming in tubs at the market and was kept swimming in the bath till Friday, with several changes of water to get rid of the muddy taste, and it was killed on Friday morning with a knife or a hammer blow. There was always great competition between Jews and Christians to buy fish on Friday; prices would go up, and the acquisition of a Sabbath fish was always fraught with suspense and excitement.

Today fish is still the first course and one of the highlights of the Friday-evening meal, and it is also eaten on Saturday. Because it was always cooked in advance for the Sabbath, fish was usually eaten cold. That is why many fish dishes described as "Jewish style" are cold—often in their jelly. Those that originate in Poland are sweet. Édouard de Pomiane complained in 1929 that the Jews cooked a lot of fish but prepared it in their own way, which was not appealing to Western tastes. "This is primarily because of their frequent use of sugar and also large amounts of onion." He was forced, he said, to add grated horseradish to mask the flavor. The sweet fish dishes of Polish Jewry are the butt of many Sephardi jokes in Israel. It may seem odd to put a lot of sugar with fish, but this is the kind of thing that you acquire a taste for.

GEFILTE FISH

THE MOST FAMOUS and most representative of Jewish dishes is the historic first course of Sabbath and holiday meals. When I say that I am working on a Jewish book, a common response is "Is there anything besides gefilte fish?" It is the most popular cold appetizer in the deli trade, and it is also mass-produced and sold in jars and cans in supermarkets.

The dish has changed since its medieval forebear. *Gefilte* means "stuffed." Originally a fish forcemeat made from chopped freshwater fish was used to stuff pike or carp skin, which had been pulled off from head to tail down from the neck. Nowadays gefilte fish generally means the forcemeat alone, made into balls and poached in fish stock. In Britain, the traditional carp and pike have been replaced by a mixture of saltwater fish.

Gefilte fish evolved as a Sabbath dish because stuffing gave it glamour and because certain versions eliminate the need to remove bones, which could be considered a forbidden activity on the Sabbath. There are mentions of Jewish housewives chopping fish and stuffing fish in Germany in the early Middle Ages. The fish used then was pike. Carp was adopted in Poland, Lithuania, and the Ukraine.

In every region the dish was the same except for the taste. In Poland it was markedly sweet. In Lithuania it was peppery. In his book *The Yiddish Language in Northern Poland: Its Geography and History*, Marvin Herzog shows how variants in gefilte fish, with or without sugar, followed the same boundaries as did the Polish and Lithuanian Yiddish dialects and that there was a geographical belt of sweet gefilte fish wherever Hassidic communities settled.

Today Jews of Russian and Lithuanian background prefer their fish unsweetened, and those of Polish ancestry like it sweet. The sweet commercial version called "Old Vienna" is so named in reference to the large number of Jews who immigrated to that city in the nineteenth century from Poland.

Gefilte Fish

Cold Poached Fish Balls

MAKES 16 FISH BALLS

Hardly anybody today stuffs the chopped fish back into its skin, and although some people still chop it by hand, most now use the food processor. In America, whitefish is often used, as are other fish (it varies in different parts of the country). In Britain, two or three types of fish are used, most commonly cod, haddock, whiting, bream, or hake. Jewish fishmongers have their special ready-chopped fish mixture. In France, they still use pike and carp. For the fish stock in which to poach the fish balls, you need fish heads or bones to produce the jelly that forms when it is cold. What is always the same everywhere is the slice of carrot topping each fish ball. My daughter laughed when she saw my carrot garnish and told me this one: "How do you recognize a Jewish fish? When there is a carrot on top."

For the stock

> 2 carrots, sliced (you need at least 16 slices, as these are to be used as garnish)
> 1 onion, sliced
> 1 or 2 fish heads (not oily)
> 2 teaspoons salt
> 1–3 teaspoons sugar
> ¼–½ teaspoon white pepper or 6 peppercorns

For the fish balls

> 1 medium onion
> 2 eggs
> 2 teaspoons or more salt
> 2 teaspoons or more sugar
> White pepper
> ½ cup (75 g) medium matzo meal
> 2 lbs (1 kg) fish fillets, skinned (choose 2 or 3 from cod, haddock, bream, whiting, and hake)

Put all the stock ingredients in a saucepan, add about 11 cups (2½ liters) water—enough to cover the fish heads—and bring to the boil. Remove the scum and simmer for 30 minutes. For the fish balls: Put the onion, quartered, in the food processor with the eggs, salt, sugar, and pepper, and blend to a cream. Pour into a mixing bowl and stir in the matzo meal. Now cut the fish into pieces and process for about 5 seconds only, until it is finely chopped. Be careful not to turn it into a paste. This is important. Add the fish to the onion and matzo meal and mix very well. Leave covered in the refrigerator for ½ hour.

Wet your hands and shape the mixture into balls the size of a tangerine or into oval patties. Lower them into the fish stock and simmer, covered, on low heat for 30 minutes. Cool, then lift out the fish balls and fish heads (they are considered a delicacy) and arrange them in one layer on a deep serving dish. Ladle a little of the stock over the fish and reduce the rest by boiling it down, then strain it over the fish. Retrieve the carrot slices and decorate each ball with a slice of carrot placed on top. Leave to cool overnight in the refrigerator, by which time a firm aspic will have formed.

Serve with chrain (see page 59).

- One common fish mix in America is I lb (500 g) carp, ½ lb (250 g) pike, and ½ lb (250 g) whitefish. Americans also include celery in the stock. If using carp, cook for 1½–2 hours.
- For a Polish gefilte fish, sweeten the minced fish with 3 tablespoons of sugar and add an extra teaspoon of sugar to the stock. And do not add any pepper.
- Grate a carrot with the onion for the fish balls.
- Use ground almonds instead of the matzo meal.
- In South Africa they used crushed Marie (plain) biscuits instead of matzo meal—about 6 biscuits for 2 lbs (I kg) of fish—and flavor it with ⅔ teaspoon of powdered ginger.

A matchmaker is asked to find a husband quickly for a young girl who is pregnant. To convince another matchmaker acting for a young man, he says, "She is very, very beautiful. Between you and me, I hear that in bed she moves like a fish." A few months later, they bump into each other, and the matchmaker acting for the young man says, "Between you and me, the Litvik bride was a gefilte fish."

My cousin Donald Sassoon's story

Fried Gefilte Fish

Fried Fish Balls

The fried version of gefilte fish was born in London, and you can find it only in Britain. It was the result of the influence of the Jews of Portuguese origin on the cooking of immigrants from Eastern Europe.

Make fish balls as in the recipe above, but make them smaller—the size of a large egg. Roll them in medium matzo meal or fine dry bread crumbs to coat them all over, and deep-fry a few at a time over medium heat for about 6 minutes, or until crisp and brown, turning them over once. Drain on paper towels. They are usually served cold but are also very good hot.

Stuffed Carp Slices

SERVES 8

This type of gefilte fish—in which forcemeat fills the hollow in the center of a slice of carp—is still popular. I find it in the kosher takeout establishments that have proliferated in Golders Green in North West London. To make it, you need complete slices, surrounded entirely by skin. Ask the fishmonger to draw the carp from the neck so that the belly is not cut. Let him cut off the fins and tail and cut the fish in I-inch (2½ cm) slices. Keep the roe, which is a delicacy, and the head, which will help to form the aspic.

> 1 carp weighing about 3¼ lbs (1½ kg), cut into 1-inch (2½-cm) slices
> 2 teaspoons salt
> 1 onion, cut in half
> 2 carrots, sliced (to be used for stock and to garnish)
> 2 teaspoons sugar
> ¼ teaspoon white pepper
> ½ recipe fish-ball forcemeat (gefilte fish, page 108)

Sprinkle the carp slices lightly with salt, cover, and refrigerate. Put the head in a pan with the onion, carrot, salt, sugar, and pepper. Cover with water and simmer for 20 minutes.

Make a forcemeat following the recipe for gefilte fish balls but using only half the quantity. Use the flesh from the carp tail in the mince. Take lumps the size of a large egg and press into the hollow in the center of each fish slice. The forcemeat will expand in cooking and will bulge and hold its place.

Put these stuffed slices in the pan with the fish stock and simmer for 1½–2 hours. Uncover towards the end to reduce the liquid a little. Allow to cool, then lift out the slices and arrange them on a serving dish with the head too. Decorate with carrot slices retrieved from the stock. Remove the onion and pour the reduced stock over the fish. Refrigerate, covered, overnight. Serve with chrain (page 59) and pickled cucumbers.

VARIATIONS

• For a Polish version, add 2 more tablespoons of sugar and if you like put in 4 tablespoons of chopped almonds and 4 tablespoons of golden raisins at the start, at the same time as the fish slices.

• Add 2–3 tablespoons of vinegar for a sweet-and-sour flavor.

• For another Polish version, add 2 gingersnaps to the stock. They will disintegrate and contribute a ginger flavor.

Carpe à la Juive– Polish Style

Jellied Carp

SERVES 6

A Polish version in Paris today.

> 1 carp weighing about 3¼ lbs (1½ kg)
> 2 onions, cut in half and sliced
> 3 carrots, sliced
> 2 bay leaves
> Salt
> Ground white pepper or 6 peppercorns
> 1–3 tablespoons sugar
> Wine vinegar to pour over when serving

Have the fishmonger clean the carp and cut it into ¾-inch (2-cm) slices. Reserve the head. Put the onions and carrots on the bottom of a large pan. Put the fish steaks and the head on top. Add the rest of the ingredients and cover with water. Bring to the boil, remove the scum, then simmer with the lid on as gently as possible, on the lowest possible heat, for 1½–2 hours, until the fish is tender. It seems an excessively long time, but that is the traditional time, and also what fishmongers recommend, because carp has very tough flesh. It also allows the bones to produce a very rich jelly, which is part of the appeal of the dish. But the cooking must be very gentle.

Lift out the slices without breaking them and arrange them in a serving dish with the head at the end. Reduce the liquid, if necessary, by simmering, uncovered, then pour it over the slices. Cool and refrigerate, covered with plastic wrap. Serve cold, in its jelly, accompanied by vinegar to pour over and chrain (page 59).

VARIATIONS

• Add 2 tablespoons of chopped almonds and 2 tablespoons of raisins at the start.

• Some people like to set some of the jelly in a separate bowl and serve it chopped up with the fish.

A man orders a five-course meal at Soli's. He stuffs himself, and everyone wonders how much else he can eat. When the bill comes, he says he has no money at all and can't pay. Soli is furious; he wants to call the police. Then he says, "I will let you go if you do one thing—if you go tomorrow and do the same thing across the road at Sam's Deli." The man replies, "I already ate there yesterday and they told me to come here today."

"CARPE À LA JUIVE"

Jellied Carp

POACHED CARP served cold in its own jelly is one of the classics of Jewish cooking. It features in Russian and Polish cookbooks as "in the Jewish Style." In 1929, Édouard de Pomiane described a version with plenty of sugar, plenty of onions, and a few sultanas and chopped almonds, which, he said, appeared on all the Sabbath luncheon tables in Cracow. "The Jews are so proud of their recipe," he wrote, "that they call it 'à la Juive' in Jewish restaurants. If one had to sum up all of Jewish cooking in a single dish, this is the one that would epitomise it." He found the dish excessively bland and always asked for grated horseradish to sharpen it. He preferred the recipe given to him by a rabbi in Paris, which had evolved there in émigré circles. It was without sugar, almonds, or sultanas, and was flavored instead with garlic, thyme, bay leaf, and parsley. But when he described it to the rabbi in Cracow, that rabbi found it far from traditional. The rabbi in Paris must have come from Lithuania or the Ukraine, where it was not the custom to add sugar.

Carpe à la Juive–
Russian Style

Jellied Carp in White Wine

SERVES 6

In the nineteenth century, the wealthy Jews in tsarist Russia adopted the style of cooking fish with white wine, introduced by the French chefs employed by the upper classes. This is how my Paris friends make it.

> *1 carp weighing about 3¼ lbs (1½ kg)*
> *2 medium onions, cut in half and sliced*
> *2½ cups (600 ml) medium-dry white*
>   *wine*
> *Thinly pared peel of 1 lemon*
> *2 bay leaves*
> *1 sprig of thyme*
> *A few parsley stalks*
> *Salt and pepper*

Have the carp cleaned and cut in slices, reserving the head. Put the onions on the bottom of a pan. Place the fish steaks and head on top. Pour in the wine, then add the same amount of water and the rest of the ingredients. Bring to the boil, remove the scum, then simmer very gently, covered, on the lowest possible heat, for 1½–2 hours, until the fish is tender. Lift the slices and the head out, and arrange in a serving dish. Reduce the stock if necessary by simmering, uncovered, and strain over the fish. Cool and refrigerate, covered with plastic wrap. A rich, firm jelly will form.

VARIATIONS

• Garlic, allspice, and bouquet garni can be part of the aromatics.

• Garnish, if you like, with chopped pickled cucumbers.

Cold Fried Fish

You may use halibut, haddock, cod, flounder, hake, plaice, or sole—steaks or fillets. Cut the fillets into serving pieces but leave steaks whole. Sprinkle lightly with salt and leave for an hour, covered, in the refrigerator. Drain off the water that has been drawn out.

Dip each piece in flour, then in lightly beaten egg, then fine bread crumbs or matzo meal, turning them so that they are well coated all over.

Deep-fry in about 1 inch (2½ cm) light vegetable oil. The oil must be sizzling but only medium hot, or the coating will burn before the fish is cooked. Put the fish pieces in carefully and fry, turning them over once, until brown on both sides. Drain on paper towels. Serve cold with lemon wedges.

VARIATION

• For a batter that is used in France, just before frying, beat 4 egg whites stiff, then lightly beat in the 4 yolks and not quite 1 cup (100 g) of fine matzo meal. The fried fish is as good hot as it is cold.

COLD FRIED FISH IN THE JEWISH STYLE

I N *Children of the Ghetto* (1892), Israel Zangwill writes of a young man in the East End of London who held a Christian girl he fancied to be cold of heart and unsprightly of temperament. "Perhaps," he wrote, "though he was scarcely conscious of it, at the bottom of his revulsion was the certainty that the Christian girl could not fry fish. She might be delightful for a flirtation of all degrees, but had not been formed to make him permanently happy."

The Jews in London had a very particular way of frying fish in batter and eating it cold which has become a classic of Jewish cooking in Britain. It was a legacy of the Portuguese Marranos (crypto-Jews) who came to England in the sixteenth century, many of them via Holland. Manuel Brudo, a Portuguese Marrano, wrote in 1544 that the favorite diet of Marrano refugees in England was fried fish. They sprinkled it with flour and dipped it in egg and in bread crumbs. Lady Judith Montefiore, the anonymous editor-author of the first Jewish cookbook in English, published in 1846, referred to the frying oil as "Florence oil," which meant olive oil. At that time an important community of Marranos in Livorno (where her husband came from) exported olive oil to England.

Thomas Jefferson, the third President of the United States and a famous epicurean, discovered "fried fish in the Jewish fashion" when he came to England. When his granddaughter Virginia put together a collection of his favorite recipes, she included a recipe for fried fish in the Jewish manner to be eaten cold from Alexis Soyer's *A Shilling Cookery Book for the People*, which was published in 1855. Soyer, who was the chef at the Reform Club, explained that the fish was simply salted and either dipped in a flour-and-water batter or, as in some Jewish families, dipped first in flour, then in egg, and fried in oil. He added that frying in oil was superior to frying in fat or dripping, but more expensive.

Cold fried fish in the Jewish style was much praised by gourmets and featured in early English cookbooks. Hannah Glasse was the first to include a recipe in her *The Art of Cookery Made Plain and Easy* in 1781. Eliza Acton gave one in *Modern Cookery for Private Families* in 1845.

In a piece on the "Culinary Aspects of Anglo-Jewry" (see p. 105), John Shaftesley notes that in 1968 the National Federation of Fish Friers presented a commemorative plaque to Malin's of Bow in the East End as the oldest enterprise to sell fish and chips together in Britain. Joseph Malin, a Jewish immigrant newly arrived from Eastern Europe, founded a fish business in Bow in 1860 and began selling chips with fried fish. It was a combination of Ashkenazi, Sephardi, and Irish ways in an East End which was a mix of Eastern European and Irish immigrants (this was after the potato famine) with some long-established Sephardi families. Dozens of fish-and-chip shops opened in the East End, and all around the country the Jewish fried-fish trade joined up with the Irish potato shop.

Whereas fish and chips became the English national dish, cold fried fish became the most popular method of cooking fish for Jews in Britain. My mother-in-law told me that when her family had the fish shop in the East End, they used to fry fish every Friday and distribute it to relatives.

Pickled Fried Fish

SERVES 6

This marinated fried fish has a rich, spicy, sweet-and-sour flavor. It will do very well as a cold snack.

> 1½ lbs (750 g) fish fillet, cut into 6 serving
>   pieces and fried as in the preceding
>   recipe
> 1 cup (250 ml) cider vinegar
> 2 tablespoons sugar
> 2 bay leaves
> 3 garlic cloves, sliced
> ¼ teaspoon ground ginger
> 5 peppercorns
> ½ teaspoon whole coriander seeds
> A pinch of mace

Arrange the fried fish in a dish. Put the vinegar in a pan with the sugar, 2 bay leaves, garlic, ginger, peppercorns, coriander, and mace. Simmer for 5 minutes and let it cool. Pour over the fish and leave to marinate for 48 hours in the refrigerator. It keeps very well for at least a week.

Halibut with Egg and Lemon Sauce

SERVES 4

In this Anglo-Jewish dish—a legacy of the early Sephardi community—the delicate taste of halibut is enhanced by the sharp flavor of the sauce. Other fish, such as pike, salmon, flounder, haddock, hake, and cod, can be treated in the same way.

> 1 onion, sliced
> 1 carrot, sliced
> 2 celery stalks, sliced
> 2 bay leaves
> Salt and white pepper
> 4 halibut steaks
> 2 teaspoons cornstarch
> 2 eggs
> Juice of 1½ lemons
> 1–1½ tablespoons sugar (optional)

Put the onion, carrot, celery, and bay leaves in a wide shallow pan. Pour in about 3 cups (750 ml) of water, or enough to cover the fish eventually, add salt and pepper, and simmer 10 minutes. Put in the fish steaks and barely simmer for 10 minutes.

To make the sauce, ladle off and strain into a smaller pan about 1¾ cups (400 ml) of the stock. Add the cornstarch, diluted in a little cold water, and bring to the boil, stirring. In a bowl, beat the eggs lightly, then beat in the lemon and sugar. Add a ladleful of hot stock, beat well, then pour the egg-and-lemon mixture into the simmering stock, stirring vigorously. Continue to stir until the sauce thickens, but do not let it boil, or the sauce will curdle. Lift the fish carefully out of the pan and serve with the sauce poured over. It is good both hot or cold.

Note:

A very similar recipe called "plaice solpado" is a Danish Jewish recipe of Portuguese origin. It was sent to me by Birgit Siesby, who with her sister Hanne Goldschmidt has written a book about the Jewish kitchen in Denmark around 1900. Solpado means "hidden" or "covered" and refers to the fish's being covered by the sauce.

Fish in Sour Cream

SERVES 4

This recipe was for pike or perch and also for salt herring, but white saltwater fish like halibut, haddock, and cod are used today.

4 fish steaks or pieces of fillet
2 tablespoons butter
2 tablespoons light vegetable oil
Salt and pepper

Juice of ½ lemon
1 cup (250 ml) sour cream

Fry the fish very briefly in a sizzling mixture of butter and oil for 2 minutes on either side, turning the pieces over once. Season with salt and pepper and arrange in a baking dish. Pour the lemon juice and sour cream over them and bake for 15 minutes in a preheated 400°F (200°C) oven.

SALMON HAS REPLACED CARP AS THE JEWISH FISH

WHEN I first came to England, in the fifties, many Jewish delicacies were made with canned salmon. There were fritters and rissoles and pies that combined the flaked fish with mashed potatoes. Nowadays, especially since the advent of salmon farming, salmon has become the common fish. Caterers find it the cheapest fish and the easiest to deal with in serving large numbers. Cold salmon is the king of the buffet table, and it has also become an everyday fish. People are always on the lookout for new recipes, marinades, and sauces. I include some that find their inspiration in old traditional Jewish themes.

Cured Salmon

SERVES 10–12

Fish cured in salt has long been a Jewish custom. In the old Sephardi communities they cured bonito, a kind of tuna, to make the famous lakerda, and mackerel to make garato. Now salmon is the universal candidate of choice for this kind of treatment. The following recipe is for a very lightly cured salmon (with a shorter time in salt than gravadlax and without sugar). I tasted it at my sculptress friend Ruth Adler's in Paris and found it enchanting. When I asked her for the recipe, she faxed me reams of drawings and information. The recipe came from Geneviève Lehmann, her fishmonger in Sens, in northern Burgundy. Sens was once an important Jewish center, and although there is no connection with the salmon recipe it was interesting to read the pages from the guidebook sent by Ruth recounting the trials of the old community and describing the Rue de la Grande Juiverie, la Petite Juiverie, and the Rue de la Synagogue. Madame Lehmann says her way of preparing the fish is a result of recipes she receives from clients. The important thing is to get very fresh fish.

Ask the fishmonger to fillet a salmon but to leave the skin on.

2 fillets weighing about 2 lbs (1 kg)
4 tablespoons coarse sea salt

Carefully remove any small bones from the fillets (tweezers will help). Sprinkle the fillets with the salt, on the skin side as well as inside, and put them together to re-form the fish. Cover with plastic wrap and leave in the refrigerator for 12 hours, turning the salmon over when juices start to collect.

Before serving, scrape off the salt and wipe with a paper towel, then rinse in cold water under the tap. Taste a piece. If it is too salty, the saltiness can be removed by soaking in fresh water for as long as necessary. Cut thin slices at an angle.

I served it with salsa verde per pesce (page 327), which was great, but Madame Lehmann's sauce follows.

VARIATION

• One hour before serving, scrape off the salt, sprinkle inside with a good bunch of dill or mixed chervil and chives, finely chopped (about ½ cup), put together again, and refrigerate, covered with plastic wrap.

Madame Lehmann's Sauce for Cured Salmon

SERVES 6

1 cup (250 ml) whipping cream
Salt and pepper
A good bunch of herbs—dill, chervil, or
*   chives, or a mixture of these—finely*
*   chopped (½ cup)*

Whip the cream and add salt and pepper and herbs.

Grilled Salmon Fillets

Ask the fishmonger to fillet the fish and to leave the skin on. It is most important, as always when cooking salmon, not to overcook, and best to undercook slightly. Brush with olive oil and season with salt. If you have a plancha (a grill that goes over the burner) or a very large frying pan, and the salmon is not too large—say about 2 lbs (1 kg), which is enough for 4—a good way is to brush the plancha or pan with oil, put the fillets in, cut side down, and cook over medium heat for 5 minutes, then put under a preheated grill for 4 minutes, until the skin is crisp and brown.

Alternatively, cook the fish entirely under the grill, turning it over carefully.

Salmon Poached in White Wine

In the nineteenth century, the wealthy Jews in tsarist Russia, who were allowed to live outside the Pale of Settlement in cities like Moscow and St. Petersburg, had access to a cuisine inspired by French chefs in the service of the upper classes. One of the refinements, according to Lesley Chamberlain in *The Food and Cooking of Russia,* was to poach salmon and other fish in white wine, such as Chablis. This way of cooking fish, such as fillets of Dover sole, baby halibut, and in particular salmon, is now very popular in Jewish homes.

To poach a whole salmon, put it in a fish kettle and cover with a half-and-half mixture of cold water and dry white wine. Add salt, cover, and bring slowly to the boil. Turn off the heat and let the fish go cold in the broth. It will cook as it cools. It should be a little underdone, for that is the best way to eat it. Serve with one of the sauces on page 118, salsa verde per pesce (page 327), or Madame Lehmann's sauce (page 116).

Whole Salmon Baked in Foil

SERVES 6–8

This is the easiest way of cooking a large whole salmon. The fish cooks in its own juice, which preserves the moistness and flavor. Have the fishmonger clean and scale it but keep the head on, or, for easier serving, have him fillet it and put the fillets together in the foil.

A 5-lb (2.25 kg) salmon
3 tablespoons light vegetable oil
Salt
⅓ cup (90 ml) white wine or the juice of
*   ½ lemon*

Cut a sheet of heavy foil large enough to hold the fish entirely and brush it with oil. Place the fish (or the fillets together) in the center. Brush lightly with oil, season with salt inside and out, and sprinkle with white wine or lemon juice. Wrap the tail end with more foil to prevent it from cooking faster and drying out. Bring up the edges of the foil over the fish and fold together to enclose it in a loose parcel.

Bake in a preheated 375°F (190°C) oven for 30–45 minutes. Open the foil and test for doneness with the point of a knife. It is better slightly undercooked than overcooked—only just opaque and beginning to flake. Serve hot or cold. If serving cold, let it cool in the foil, then chill. Serve with one of the following sauces.

VARIATION

- Bake sea bass in foil in the same way.

Wine and Cream Dill Sauce

SERVES 6

1 cup (250 ml) dry white wine
1 cup (250 ml) heavy cream or sour cream
*   or a ½-and-½ mixture of the two*
Salt
3 tablespoons finely chopped dill or fennel

Simmer the wine until reduced by half. Add the cream and sour cream and a little salt and simmer till thick. Then add the herbs. Can be hot or cold.

Horseradish Cream Sauce

SERVES 6

1 cup (250 ml) heavy cream
2 tablespoons freshly grated horseradish
*   or from a jar*
1 tablespoon white-wine vinegar or
*   lemon juice*
Salt

Beat the cream till stiff, then beat in the rest of the ingredients.

Sorrel Sauce

SERVES 6

Sorrel is not easy to find in markets, but it is simple to grow. When you do have some, this very easy recipe is one you must try, for the sharp taste of sorrel, the delicate flavor of wine, and the creamy richness.

2½ oz (65 g) sorrel, washed and shredded
1 cup (250 ml) dry white wine
2 garlic cloves, crushed in a press
1 cup (250 ml) heavy cream
A little salt

Remove only tough sorrel stems—you can keep the very thin ones. Put the wine and garlic in a pan and simmer for about 10 minutes to reduce. Then stir in the sorrel and the cream and cook on very low heat for about 8 minutes more. Season with salt. It is good both hot and cold.

VARIATION

- For a sour-cream version with onions, fry 1 small finely chopped onion in 2 tablespoons of butter until soft. Add the wine and reduce, then add the sorrel and sour cream instead of the cream. Before the sauce has time to heat through, beat in 3 egg yolks, and continue stirring until it thickens.

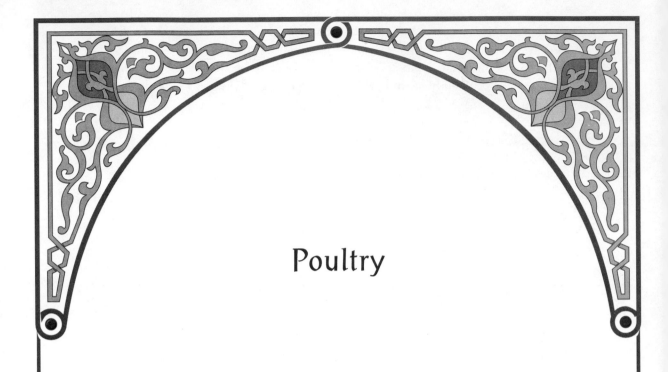

Poultry

Since the early Middle Ages, European Jews have eaten a variety of poultry, including goose, duck, pigeon, and chicken, and these, as well as turkey, are still important in Jewish cooking. One reason is that, without a *shohet* (professional slaughterer) around, it was easy for people to slaughter the birds themselves according to kosher laws—something they could not do with large animals. Another reason is that rearing geese and poultry was a traditional Jewish occupation in Germany and in Eastern Europe (in Germany, from as early as the fifteenth century).

In the shtetl world, birds were always bought live and taken to a *shohet* to be slaughtered. If some defect was found, the bird would be taken to the rabbi to decide if it was kosher. In *Life Is with the People*, Mark Zborowski and Elizabeth Herzog describe the anxiety of a housewife inspecting a chicken for any forbidden flecks of blood, blisters on the gizzard, or other calamity that would raise doubts as to whether her chicken was ritually fit to eat. If it did happen, someone would have to hurry to the rabbi and wait in painful suspense until the rabbi, after studying the chicken and the relevant laws, declared it kosher. If it was not, it would be sold at a loss to someone outside the community.

There are dozens of stories about rabbis' having to decide about chickens. In Israel Zangwill's *Children of the Ghetto*, a rabbi recounts: "A woman brought me a fowl in the morning and said that in the cutting open the gizzard she had found a rusty pin which the fowl must have swallowed. She wanted to know whether the fowl might be eaten. It was a very difficult point, for how could you tell whether the pin had in any way contributed to the fowl's death? I searched the Shass and a heap of Shaaloth-u-Teshuvoth. I went and consulted the *Maggid* and Sugarman the *Shadchen* and Mr. Kalkammer and at last we decided that the fowl was *tripha* and could not be eaten. So the same evening I sent for the woman, and when I told her of our decision, she burst into tears and wrung her hands. 'Do not grieve so,' I said, taking compassion upon her; 'I will buy thee another fowl.' But she wept on uncomforted. 'Oh woe! Woe!' she cried. 'We ate it up yesterday.' "

Although chicken is no longer a luxury,

the quarter portion is still the inevitable standby at all big Jewish celebratory affairs, including weddings and bar mitzvahs. Considering its importance, it is a wonder that there is not a great deal of variety in the way it is treated, but tradition has focused on a few dishes only. The classic Friday-night menu has chicken soup followed by boiled or roast chicken. Jennie Grossinger writes in *The Art of Jewish Cooking,* "To serve anything else might almost border on the sacrilegious in the minds of many who have had no other Friday night dinner during their life-time."

Raising geese, Trnava, Czechoslovakia

Poule-au-Bouillon

SERVES 4–6

Boiled chicken is much maligned these days in Anglo-Saxon countries, because it used to be cooked more for the soup than for the chicken, and the chicken was done to death. But French Jews do not despise it at all and make it very well with plenty of vegetables. Here is their poule-au-bouillon or poule-au-pot, a heart-warming and delicious Sabbath meal-in-a-pot, which provides a first and a second course.

1 fat boiling chicken or roaster, if possible
    with its feet, neck, and giblets
4 carrots
4 small leeks
2 medium onions
2 celery stalks with leaves
2 turnips or parsnips, quartered
4 cloves
2 bay leaves
Sprig of thyme
A few sprigs of parsley
Salt and pepper

In a large pan, put the chicken and giblets and cover with 13 cups (3 liters) of water. Bring to the boil and remove the scum. Add the vegetables whole—washed, trimmed, and/or peeled—and the cloves, herbs, and seasonings, and simmer gently (the water should barely tremble) for at least an hour, or until the juices run clear when you pierce the thickest part of the thigh with a pointed knife. Older birds can take up to 2 hours.

Strain 8 cups (2 liters) of stock and use it to make chicken soup with vermicelli, egg dumplings, knaidlach, or kreplach (see pages 84–86).

Serve the chicken, cut in pieces, with a little stock poured over, surrounded by the vegetables and accompanied, if you like, by boiled potatoes. It is also very good served cold on Saturday with pickled gherkins and chrain (see page 59).

VARIATION

• Some people add knaidlach (matzo balls, page 85) to the pot towards the end of the cooking and serve them together with the chicken.

*C*hickens were always part of the shtetl world. In The Adventures of Hershel Summerwind *by Itzik Manger, Hershel tells how "in the house a rooster roamed about, behaving as if he owned the place, doing whatever he wanted and dirtying up wherever he liked. No one asked him any questions." He complains that his stepmother, who treated him like a dog when he was a small boy, cuddled the rooster as if it were a pigeon.*

Hungarian Chicken Paprikash

SERVES 4

This chicken, rich with the flavors of onion, tomato, and paprika, was adopted in Hungary and Czechoslovakia as a Sabbath dish. It was popular in Romania and Transylvania, where it was eaten with mamaliga (page 159); otherwise it is served with rice.

> 1 chicken, quartered (or buy 4 chicken
>   quarters)
> 3 tablespoons chicken fat or oil
> 1 large onion, coarsely chopped
> 1 red or green pepper, sliced
> 3 tomatoes, peeled and chopped
> 1 teaspoon sugar
> Salt
> 1–2 teaspoons paprika
> A pinch of cayenne or red chili powder

In a large frying pan, brown the chicken quarters, turning them over once, in the fat or oil, and put them aside. Now sauté the onion and pepper in the same fat or oil until soft. Add the tomatoes and stir in the sugar, salt, paprika, and cayenne or chili powder. Return the chicken pieces to the pan and simmer for about 30 minutes, or until tender, adding a little water if it becomes too dry. Serve hot with rice.

Potravka

Chicken with Wild Mushrooms

SERVES 4

Mushroom hunting was a favorite pastime in Russia. This simple and delicious dish is one of the legacies.

> 1 chicken, quartered, or 2 Cornish hens cut
>   in pieces
> 4 tablespoons light vegetable oil
> 1 lb (500 g) wild mushrooms or shiitake,
>   sliced or quartered
> 1¼ cups (300 ml) white wine
> Salt and pepper
> 3 tablespoons finely chopped parsley

In a large casserole, brown the chicken or Cornish hens all over in the oil and remove the pieces. Then sauté the mushrooms briefly in the same oil. Add the wine, salt, and pepper and return the chicken or Cornish hens to the pan. Simmer for about 30 minutes, or until tender, adding a little water if necessary. Serve hot, sprinkled with parsley.

Stuffed Roast Pigeons, Squabs, or Poussins with Chicken Liver Stuffing

SERVES 4–8

Stuffing gives a dish an air of celebration. The traditional Jewish stuffing for all kinds of birds, which is used throughout Eastern Europe, is mashed potato or matzo meal with onions fried in goose fat, sometimes flavored with a touch of ginger or paprika, garlic or parsley, and embellished with the livers or with sliced mushrooms. The sumptuous chicken-liver stuffing used in this recipe is from Alsace. It is so delicious that it makes the effort of stuffing worthwhile, which other stuffings frankly do not. In Alsace, foie gras, which originated in the Jewish community, is often used instead of chicken livers, and truffles are sometimes added.

Use only the Mediterranean-type baby pigeonneaux; otherwise use squabs or poussins. My guests cannot usually manage a whole poussin if it is part of a 3-course meal, so I cut the poussins in half when serving.

For the stuffing

> ½ lb (250 g) chicken livers, fresh or frozen, defrosted slowly
> 2 small slices of hallah bread, crusts removed
> 3 egg yolks
> 4 tablespoons cognac

> 2 tablespoons oil or chicken fat
> Salt and pepper

> 4 pigeonneaux, squabs, or poussins
> 4 tablespoons oil
> Juice of 1 lemon
> Salt and pepper

First prepare the stuffing. To kosher chicken livers, sear them briefly under the grill on both sides until the color changes. Soak the bread in water to cover, then squeeze dry. Put it in the food processor with the livers, egg yolks, cognac, oil or fat, and salt and pepper and blend to a cream (don't worry, it will firm up when it is baked).

Now rub the birds with oil, lemon, salt, and pepper. Using a pointed dessert spoon, fill the cavities through the tail opening with the stuffing. Then close the opening with a toothpick or sew it up with a needle and thread.

Roast in a preheated 425°F (220°C) oven for 30–45 minutes, or until they are browned and the juices no longer run pink when you cut into the thigh with a pointed knife. If serving halves, cut down through the breast bone on one side of its keel with a large, very sharp carving knife, using a strong, steady pressure.

VARIATION

- I love the stuffing as it is, with a pronounced taste of cognac, but an alternative flavoring is a pinch of nutmeg and 2 tablespoons of very finely chopped parsley.

Turkey Schnitzel

Breaded Turkey Cutlets

SERVES 4

Ask anyone in Israel to name a wholly Israeli dish and the answer will be turkey schnitzel.

> *4 large slices of turkey breast, less than ½ inch*
>   *(about 1 cm) thick*
> *Salt and pepper*
> *Flour*
> *2 eggs lightly beaten with a tablespoon of*
>   *water*
> *Fine bread crumbs or matzo meal*
> *Oil for frying*
> *1 lemon, quartered*

If the turkey slices are not thin enough, flatten them between 2 pieces of greaseproof or wax paper. Put a board on top and hammer it. Season the slices with salt and pepper. Dip in flour, then in the beaten eggs, and finally dredge in the bread crumbs or matzo meal. Fry in sizzling medium-hot oil, about ⅓ inch (1 cm) deep, for about 4–5 minutes on either side, until lightly browned. Drain on paper towels and serve with lemon quarters.

Roast Goose with Apples

SERVES 6

Roast goose was a St. Martin's Day and Christmas dish in Germany and Eastern Europe. It was also a festive dish for the Jews, who cooked it with a stuffing of mashed potato. In Alsace, where some geese are bred for their meat and are found on the market before Christmas, when they are around 3–4 months old and still tender, Jews still make roast goose for Hanukah, but with apples and with red cabbage and chestnuts. It is common to prepare the stuffing separately and to serve it as a side dish.

> *A young goose weighing about 8 lbs*
>   *(3½ kg)*
> *Salt and pepper*
> *1 onion, quartered*
> *1 apple, quartered*

For the sautéed apples

> *8 apples, tart or sweet*
> *Light vegetable oil or goose fat for frying*
> *6 tablespoons cognac or Calvados or*
>   *to taste*
> *2 teaspoons cinnamon*

Prick the skin of the goose in several places with a pointed knife to allow the fat to run out during roasting, then pour boiling water all over it. Rub the goose inside and out with salt and pepper and put the onion and apple inside. Place the goose on its back on a rack in a deep roasting pan.

Roast in a preheated 450°F (230°C) oven for 20 minutes, then reduce the temperature to 350°F (180°C), turn the goose over on its breast, and roast for another 1½–2 hours, or until the juices no longer run pink when you cut into the thigh with a pointed knife, basting occasionally with the pan juices. Pour the fat out of the pan at least once.

Peel and cut the apples into slices when you are ready to fry them in batches (they tarnish if they hang around). Use a large frying pan, and sauté only one layer of apple slices at a time. Fry gently in sizzling goose fat or oil until lightly browned, turning them over once. Lift them out carefully with a slotted spoon and arrange in a baking dish. Continue with the rest of the apples. When they are all done, sprinkle with cognac or Calvados and cinnamon; reheat in the oven when you are ready to serve.

Allow the goose to rest 15 minutes out of the oven before serving. Drain off the goose fat from the pan and put the pan over a burner. Pour in a little water and boil vigorously for 1 minute or so, scraping the pan juices to make a sauce.

VARIATIONS

• You could use a little white wine—about ⅔ cup (150 ml)—instead of water to make the gravy with the juices at the bottom of the pan.

• You may add a teaspoon of cinnamon and a handful of currants or raisins, black or golden, to the apples.

• Duckling is often used these days instead of goose, with the same apple stuffing or side dish. Sprinkle the duckling inside and out with salt and lemon juice. Put an onion inside. Roast breast side down in a 400°F (200°C) oven for ½ hour. Then take it out, turn it over, prick the skin all over with a fork to allow the melting fat to escape, and roast ½ hour longer. Now pour out all the fat from the pan, sprinkle with cognac or Calvados, and return to the oven until it is done and the juices run clear when you cut into the thickest part of the thigh.

GOOSE

GOOSE IS not my favorite bird. It has too much fat and too little flesh for the price, and the meat is tough unless it is a very young bird. But it is considered glamorous, and it is a very important part of Jewish culture. For centuries it was the traditional Sabbath meal and favorite festive dish. Since the Middle Ages, the rearing of geese has been a Jewish occupation. All the memories of Jewish life in Central and Eastern Europe are suffused with the smell and taste of goose fat and have goose feathers in the background. Geese provided feathers for the bedding which was part of a bride's dowry. Little girls were expected to "pluck for their wedding" as soon as they were able to.

CONFIT D'OIE

Preserved Goose

THE RHINELAND REGION of Alsace was part of Germany until the seventeenth century, when it came under French rule. It was annexed again by Germany between 1871 and 1918. After the French Revolution, when Jews were given full civic rights, the Alsace community became the backbone of French Jewry. It was a large community scattered in numerous villages (against the usual trend of Jews' congregating in towns). Part of the community is still dispersed in some forty villages, but the majority lives in the city of Strasbourg. Their cooking, which represents a dual French and German culture, is considered the best of French Jewry. The Jews of Alsace specialized long ago in the breeding of geese and had developed a way of fattening them for their livers, which is the method used today to produce foie gras. They, more than any community, have kept their old culinary traditions, because these are rooted in their *terroir* (region). In Alsace, geese are primarily bred to provide foie gras. The meat of such large birds is tough, and the best use for it is as confit.

For confit d'oie, pieces of goose are rubbed with garlic and left covered in coarse salt for four hours, then cooked with onions in goose fat on very low heat for three hours and packed, with fat poured over them, in stoneware pots or glass jars. You can buy jars of confit in the Jewish charcuteries to make cholent (see page 149) and choucroute garnie.

In Jewish tradition, the gizzard, heart, and stuffed neck are also preserved, and the fat is used for cooking (see pages 59 and 130).

A woman goes to the butcher and asks for a Canterbury duck. The butcher says, "Certainly, madam," goes behind the shop, fetches a duck from the refrigerator, and puts it on the counter. The woman puts her fingers in the duck's bottom and says, "This isn't a Canterbury duck, this is a Yorkshire duck!" The butcher apologizes and fetches another. The woman puts her fingers up its bottom and says angrily, "This isn't a Canterbury duck, this is an Aylesbury duck!" The butcher goes back and after some time comes back looking fed up. The woman puts her fingers up its bottom and says, "That's fine! Wrap it up." Before she goes she asks, "I can't quite make out your accent. What part of England are you from?" The butcher pulls down his trousers, bends down, and says, "You tell me."

Story told by Marcel Knobil

A goose-seller in one of the Jewish markets in Warsaw, 1899

GIBLETS

WHEN POULTRY REARING was their trade in Eastern Europe, housewives would sell the birds and keep the giblets for the family. That explains the saying "If a Jewish farmer eats chicken, one of them is sick," and accounts for the special fondness for giblets. Jewish housewives used them for soup and to make mixed fries and stews with onion and garlic. Goose and chicken feet were a special delicacy. The housewives would plunge them by the dozen in boiling water to skin them, then cook them for hours in salted water with as many garlic cloves. They boned them, chopped the meat with the garlic, and chilled it with the broth, which turned into a firm jelly.

One of Jerusalem's most profitable street foods, the Jerusalem grill, is a mix of chicken giblets cooked on a metal sheet. London kosher butchers have a big trade in chicken giblets. They sell packets of gizzards, necks, feet, livers, and combinations of these.

Bolbess

Mashed Potato Stuffing for Goose and Other Birds

ENOUGH FOR AN 8-LB
(3½-KG) GOOSE

This is the most traditional Eastern European stuffing, which you can also serve as a side dish.

> 2 large onions, coarsely chopped
> 3 tablespoons goose fat or light vegetable oil
> Salt
> 3 lbs (1½ kg) potatoes
> 2 eggs, lightly beaten
> Pepper
> ½ cup parsley, finely chopped

Fry the onions in the goose fat with a little salt until golden brown. Peel and boil the potatoes in salted water till soft, then drain. Mash and beat in the eggs while very hot. Add salt if necessary, pepper, parsley, and the onions, and mix very well. If using it as a side dish, serve with a little of the sizzling fat poured over.

A man had a peacock presented to him, and since this is such a rare bird, he went to the rov *to ask if it was kosher. The rabbi said no and confiscated the peacock. Later on the man heard that the rabbi had given a banquet, at which his peacock was the crowning glory. He went to the rabbi and reproached him. "I may eat it," replied the rabbi, "because my father considers it permitted, and we may always go by what some eminent Son of the Law decides. But you, unfortunately, came to me for an opinion, and the permissibility of peacock is a point on which I have always disagreed with my father."*

From Children of the Ghetto
by Israel Zangwill

Question: What is the Jewish sequel to the film Deep Throat? *Answer:* Stuffed Neck.

GEFILTE HELZEL

Stuffed Goose Neck

THIS IS one of the dishes that Ashkenazi Jews regard with special affection. It is made with goose, chicken, duck, or turkey necks—or, rather, with their skins used as a sausage casing. It is part of folklore.

The skin is pulled off the neck and tied at one end, then filled loosely (so that it does not tear) with a variety of fillings. The other end of the neck is sewn up, and the neck is then simmered in stock or dropped in a stew or soup or a cholent. It is sometimes further baked or roasted in the oven. The cooking time is very long—2 or 3 hours—and the filling acquires a wonderful meltingly soft texture. There should be one neck per person. As necks are very hard to come by, some people resort to using the skin of a whole chicken.

FILLINGS INCLUDE:

- Chopped onion and garlic fried in goose or chicken fat mixed with flour, seasoned with salt, and sometimes flavored with ground ginger or paprika.
- Chopped onions fried in goose fat mixed with grated potatoes, raw eggs, salt, and pepper.
- Mashed boiled potatoes and fried onion.
- Bread or matzos soaked in water and squeezed dry, mixed with eggs, salt, pepper, and garlic.
- Minced veal mixed with eggs, bread crumbs, salt, pepper, and garlic.
- Chopped goose or chicken liver mixed with bread or matzo meal.
- Chopped cooked chicken breast with matzo meal and egg.

FRANCE—A MIX OF ALSATIAN "VIEILLE FRANCE," EASTERN EUROPE, AND NORTH AFRICA

IN THE EIGHTH CENTURY, Jewish merchants were encouraged to settle in the Rhone Valley and the Champagne by Charlemagne. Until the ninth century, their activities were mainly in the south of France, but by the eleventh, the Jewish communities of northern France had become the most densely settled and also the most important culturally in Europe. The influential rabbinical scholar Rashi lived in Troyes, where he started a famous rabbinical school.

But the condition of the Jews deteriorated until finally they were expelled in 1306. Most took refuge in Alsace, and some remained in southern France, which was not incorporated in the French kingdom. Marseilles, which had been called "la Juive" in the sixth century by the Abbé Grégoire of Tours, became an important center of Talmudic studies. In the sixteenth century, after an edict of expulsion of the Jews from France, the Jews of Marseilles and Provence, which had become part of France, were driven out. They were received in Savoy (now Piedmont), and many found refuge in the enclaves under papal rule, in Avignon and in the Comtat Venaissin, in cities like Avignon, Carpentras, and Cavaillon, which had large communities and Jewish quarters. The "Juifs du Pape," as they became known, stayed on until after the French Revolution, when the Declaration of the Rights of Man granted Jews equal rights and full emancipation in 1791. Most left for Paris, and especially for Marseilles and its environs, where they integrated and where they enjoyed a kind of *âge d'or* until the Vichy regime.

Another kind of Jewish settlement was of the outwardly Christian Marranos, who arrived in the sixteenth century and settled in Rouen, Nantes, Bordeaux, and Bayonne, the natural stopping places for Portuguese Marranos traveling to Antwerp and Amsterdam, and in the Auvergne (the Protestant village of Chambon is noted for its Jews), as well as in Toulouse, Montpelier, and Marseilles in the south. The communities of Bayonne and Bordeaux became so important that they were known as the "Portuguese Nations" of the southwest. Alsace and Lorraine, which had very large Jewish populations, passed from German to French rule in the seventeenth century, and their communities came to represent the bulk of French Jewry. After the emancipation of the Jews, the communities of Alsace and Lorraine spread across France and settled in all the main cities.

The Jewish population of France was increased enormously at the turn of the twentieth century by a wave of immigrants from Eastern Europe, who quickly became the majority. They remained "foreigners" in the margins of the old community, but the former,

The Rue des Rosiers, the Jewish quarter and center of Jewish life in Paris

predominantly Alsatian, character of French Jewry was transformed, and Eastern European culture, including the cooking, became the dominant one.

A wave of Sephardim from Turkey and the Balkans arrived in the early part of this century, and now, since Algerian, Tunisian, and Moroccan Jews have flooded in, the community, which is the fourth largest—after the U.S., Israel, and the old Soviet Union—is dominated by the Jews from North Africa, who make up the large majority. Almost all of Algeria's Jews went to France when Algeria gained its independence, and so did the Jewish middle classes from Tunisia and Morocco. The discreet and self-effacing low profile long held by the French Ashkenazim has been replaced by the colorful traditional Judaism and ebullient assertiveness of the Sephardim.

Except for the long-established Alsace community, modern French Jewry had been concentrated in the major cities, such as Marseilles, Lyons, Bordeaux, Toulouse, and, overwhelmingly, in Paris, but many of the new Sephardim have settled in smaller, provincial communities where you find North African kosher restaurants and Jewish butchers who sell kosher meat, merguez, and the offal, which is used in North African Jewish cooking. The food stores and restaurants in the famous Rue des Rosiers, Rue Cadet, Rue Richier, and Faubourg Poisonière of Paris offer North African specialties next to Eastern European ones. Many of the Jewish weddings that you hear of have *henna* nights with pastilla, couscous, and cornes de gazelle. I was invited to two this year and could make neither, but I received a description of the party menu.

The only "Vieille France" Jewish cuisine is Alsatian. Whereas the Portuguese Marranos assimilated and lost their special culture, the old Jewish cooking of the south of France, which had an Iberian character, became indistinguishable by integration into the local Provençal cuisine and passed to the Piedmont and cities of northern Italy. I have spent weeks trying to trace, unsuccessfully, old dishes of the Juifs du Pape. I found their descendants. They are very proud of their ancestry and attach great importance to a legend according to which, after the destruction of Jerusalem in the year 70 A.D. by the Roman general Titus, some of the most important families of the House of David and of the tribe of Judah were exiled in southern Gaul. They were governed for centuries by dynasties of Nassis (hereditary Jewish kings descended from King David) and in the Middle Ages many were reputedly knights and nobles and troubadours. I wonder if some of the almond pastries, like the calissons d'Aix, are a Jewish legacy, because for centuries Jews were the sole importers of almonds. I wonder too if the papeton d'aubergines is related to the Judeo-Spanish almodrote (see page 521), because the resemblance is uncanny.

The Jewish quarter in Alsace Riquewihr

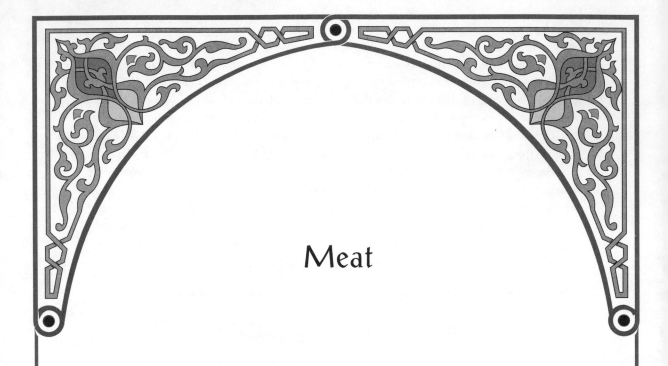

Meat

A WOMAN RUNS to a neighbor to borrow a pot for meat. The neighbor embraces her warmly and proceeds with an enthusiastic monologue: 'Mazel tov! When is the wedding? How do I know? You must be cooking a lot of meat. You only cook meat on Shabbes or holidays and this is the middle of the week, so you must have something to celebrate. Your husband is sick and your two sons are out of work. But you have a daughter, may the evil eye not fall on her. That must be it, may she live in good health with her bridegroom, and may you have much joy from them and many fine grandchildren.' " (From a story in *Life Is with the People: The Shtetl Book* by Mark Zborowski and Elizabeth Herzog.)

Jews have always had a passion for meat, and it has always been the most highly prized food. If they could afford to eat plenty of it, they did, and they cooked it in huge cauldrons. But in the shtetl world people could usually afford meat only once a week. In the nineteenth century, a tax on kosher meat was imposed in Russia and in several countries in Eastern Europe, the proceeds of which went to the state treasury. There were also communal taxes on kosher meat to raise funds for the community and for charities to help the poorer brethren. So kosher meat was twice as expensive. It was seldom eaten and was reserved for the Sabbath, holidays, and special occasions. The poor hardly ever ate it. The cheaper offals—feet, spleen, lungs, brains, liver, and intestines—were widely used and became popular. These form a characteristic part of Jewish cooking which has largely been abandoned in the new countries of immigration—especially the Anglo-Saxon countries, which have long been squeamish about organ meat.

Because the dietary laws allow only the

tougher, more muscly forequarters of the animal to be eaten, and require that meat be koshered within seventy-two hours of slaughter, which is not enough time for it to hang and tenderize, kosher meat is usually tough. (A good hanging time for nonkosher beef is two weeks.) This means that the best way to treat kosher beef is to stew it gently for a long time or to chop it. Long slow cooking, which is also typical of peasant cooking and cooking for large families everywhere, characterizes Jewish meat cookery. The two main cultural influences are the German, typified by the use of fruit, and the Polish, evident in sweet-and-sour flavorings.

The need to preserve meat gave rise to a range of Jewish charcuterie that includes corned beef and tongue, pastrami, frankfurters, and wurst—a pink German sausage. Some centers became famous for it. Alsace in particular is known for its Jewish specialties, which include soft pink pickled tongues, smoked beef "pickelfleisch" veined with yellow fat, confits d'oie, rillons d'oie, splendid foie gras, and varieties of beef salami and sausages. You can see all these in the Jewish charcuterie-patisseries, which also sell pickled cucumbers, choucroute (sauerkraut), and salt herring as well as apple tarts.

Wurst and Egg

SERVES 4

The spicy pink German salami makes a delicious combination with scrambled eggs for a light snack meal.

12 oz (350 g) frying wurst, sliced
2 tablespoons vegetable oil
4 eggs
Salt and pepper

Heat the slices of wurst in the oil in a large frying pan, and turn over when they begin to curl. Lightly beat the eggs with salt and pepper and pour over the wurst. Cook, stirring, until the eggs are set to your taste. Serve at once.

To Cure Beef for Salt Beef or Corned Beef

Most people these days buy the meat already cured, but if you want to do that yourself, here is the way.

For a 4½-lb (2-kg) piece of brisket, prepare a pickling mixture. Mix 2–4 garlic cloves crushed in a garlic press or chopped and mashed, 3 teaspoons mixed pickling spice, 2 crumbled bay leaves, 1 teaspoon crushed peppercorns, ⅓ cup (75 g) Demerara sugar, ¾ cup (175 g) coarse salt, 2 teaspoons saltpeter (this is sodium nitrate, which gives the meat its distinctive pink color). Pierce the meat all over with a fork. Rub the mixture all over the meat and put the meat in a clean earthenware, glass, or enamel crock. Add enough cold water to cover the meat entirely, and keep it submerged by placing a clean plate and a weight on top. Cover with a cloth and keep in the refrigerator or a cold larder. The longer you leave the meat in the brine, the more salt will penetrate. The minimum time is 4 days, the maximum 10.

On the day you want to cook the meat, remove it from the brine (it will feel slippery), rinse it well, and soak it in cold water. If it has been salted for 3–4 days, it will need a few hours in several changes of cold water. If it has been salting for longer, it will need to be soaked overnight.

To Cook Salt Beef or Corned Beef

You can buy brisket already salted and soaked and ready to cook, or at least requiring little soaking, from Jewish butchers and also from many supermarkets. It is very easy to cook, and the result is really magnificent. A 4½–5½-lb (2–3-kg) piece of brisket is enough for 8–10 people.

Place the meat in a large pan with plenty of cold water to cover. Add 2 onions, 2 carrots, 2 bay leaves, and (optionally) 10 juniper berries. Bring to the boil, remove the scum, and simmer very gently, covered, for 4 hours, or until you can pierce the meat easily with a pointed knife. The cooking must be so gentle that the surface barely trembles.

Carve generous slices and serve hot with boiled potatoes and carrots, cabbage, or sauerkraut, accompanied by chrain (page 59), English mustard, pickled cucumber (page 60), and rye bread.

For cold salt beef, wrap it in greaseproof or wax paper and press it by putting a plate and a weight on top, then refrigerate.

SALT, PICKLED, OR CORNED BEEF

BEEF PRESERVED in salt—in Yiddish pickelfleisch, known as "salt beef" in London, "pickled beef" in the north of England and provinces, and "corned beef" in America (because it is preserved with "corns" or kernel-sized granules of dry salt)—is one of the great strong points of Jewish meat cookery. It can be superlative, deliciously soft and moist with a distinctive delicate flavor.

It evolved in the days before refrigeration as a way of preserving meat and killing bacteria with a coating of dry salt or by soaking in salt brine. This method of curing and maturing brisket—a cut that comes from the lower shoulder with a natural interlarding of fat—imparts delicious taste and results in a particularly tender texture.

Salt beef became the mainstay of the deli trade on both sides of the Atlantic just before the middle of the twentieth century. In England, hot salt-beef sandwiches were first sold at standup counters in the East End and spread rapidly to the West End snack bars around the rag-trade area. In New York, food columnist Ed Levine wrote, "By definition a deli must serve pastrami, corned beef brisket and turkey sandwiches too thick to eat, meaning they must be six inches high minimum."

Boiled Salt or Pickled Tongue

SERVES 8

Ox tongue is sold pickled in brine (usually vacuum-packed) at kosher butcher shops and many supermarkets. If you want to pickle fresh tongue yourself, use the same pickling solution and method as for salt beef.

1 ox tongue pickled in brine
2 onions
1 carrot
2 garlic cloves
5 peppercorns
2 bay leaves

Wash and soak the tongue in cold water for 24 hours or according to instructions (it depends on the degree of salting), changing the water once. Drain and put in a pan with cold water to cover. Bring to the boil, and when scum appears pour out the water. Cover with fresh water, bring to the boil again, and add the rest of the ingredients. Simmer 3 hours, until very tender. (Test with a fork at the root end.) Plunge in cold water before peeling the skin off. Trim away the root and bones.

If serving hot, return the tongue to the broth and reheat before serving cut into slices. For serving cold, coil the skinned tongue in a round dish and cover with broth. Lay a sheet of foil on top and put a plate and a weight on top to press it down. (That gives an elegant shape.) Chill and slice just before serving. Serve with mustard or the following sweet-and-sour sauce, and a little of the jelly that has formed.

VARIATION

• Suzanne Roukhomovski (*Gastronomie Juive*) gives an Alsace way: cook the tongue as above, peel off the skin, then return the tongue to the pot with the strained cooking liquid, ½ glass of white wine, and plenty of sliced mushrooms, and simmer another ½ hour.

Sweet-and-Sour Raisin Sauce for Tongue

MAKES ENOUGH FOR
1 OX TONGUE

1 onion, chopped
2 tablespoons chicken fat or light vegetable oil
2 tablespoons flour
2 cups (500 ml) tongue stock
2–3 tablespoons white- or red-wine vinegar
2 tablespoons honey or sugar, or to taste
Salt if necessary
½ teaspoon powdered cinnamon or ginger
4 tablespoons raisins
1 lemon, cut into thin slices

Fry the onion in the fat or oil till golden. Stir in the flour and cook, stirring over low heat, until it browns. Add the stock gradually, a little only to begin with, stirring constantly, and bring to the boil. Add the vinegar, honey or sugar, and salt if necessary (bearing in mind the saltiness of the stock), the cinnamon or ginger, raisins, and lemon slices. Simmer for 10 minutes.

VARIATION

• A Hungarian version omits the flour and thickens the sauce with a mashed parsnip and carrot (both boiled with the tongue) and 4 tablespoons ground almonds.

——THE NEW YORK DELI——

NOT LONG AGO the Jewish deli was the main New York eating experience. The New York deli was the first place ever where Jewish food was visible outside the home, and it came to represent that food in the eyes of the world. Nowadays the corner deli is likely to be run by Koreans. A handful of "appetizing" stores—such as Flaum (in Williamsburg, Brooklyn), Russ and Daughters (Lower East Side), and Murray's Sturgeon Shop (Upper West Side)—which sell smoked and pickled fish, pickles, dried fruit, and nuts, and the pickle specialist, Essex Street Pickles (formerly known as Guss Pickles), are all that is left of a trade that once served every neighborhood. Zabar's, on upper Broadway, is an international food emporium selling two hundred different types of cheeses, all kinds of salamis and smoked fish, and a huge array of prepared foods from all over the world, as well as the old traditional Jewish foods. It looks like an Oriental bazaar, with chilies and pots and pans hanging from the ceiling and the smell of coffee mingling with those of cheese and garlic.

Traditional deli restaurants—there are little more than a dozen—attract tourists and nostalgic Jews who come for the occasional fix of sentimentality. Most have kept their seedy '40s and '50s diner-type decor intact, with Formica tables, plastic-covered chairs, bright neon or art deco lighting, and the old show-business photographs from their glamorous golden age. At Katz's, the famous self-service deli on the Lower East Side, the decor doesn't seem to have changed since the turn of the century. They still have World War II rhyming slogans such as "Send a salami to your son in the army." Delis are no longer meeting places for regulars, but they are still homey and convivial. Waiters—who now may be Pakistani or Chinese—tell you brusquely what to eat and offer you a paper bag to take home what you can't finish.

The relationship between patron and tyrannical waiter has been the subject of many Jewish jokes, such as this one: "Mrs. Rosenberg orders prune tzimmes and Mr. Rosenberg orders fried fish. The waiter brings the prune tzimmes, but instead of the fried fish he puts meatballs in front of Mr. Rosenberg and says: 'Eat it! It will do you more good than the fish. There's no fish.' Mrs. Rosenberg tastes her tzimmes and says, 'Mory, order a tzimmes—it's really good.' He tastes it and asks the waiter why he didn't give him tzimmes instead of meatballs. The waiter looks at him with contempt. 'Because you ordered fried fish. If you had ordered gefilte fish, you would have gotten tzimmes.' 'But my wife ordered tzimmes and that's what she got.' The waiter replies sarcastically, 'We were out of gefilte fish.' "

The ritual deli meal starts with a bowl of pickled cucumbers and green tomatoes on the table. The regular menu of mushroom and barley soup, chicken soup with kreplach, chopped liver, potato salad and coleslaw, kishke, petchah, stuffed cabbage, meatballs, and flanken has become enshrined. At "dairy" delis like Ratners—the most famous of them, on the Lower East Side—there are borscht and gefilte fish, blintzes and cheesecake. I did the rounds with my daughter Nadia, who lives in SoHo. On a Sunday at the Second Avenue Deli, in the East Village, we had cholent. A waitress brought out a tray of chopped liver and chopped egg sandwiches to stave off the hunger of the people waiting in line. The Triplets, in SoHo, had entertainers ("so bad," a food guide said, "that they are good"). With the menu were printed wedding and bar mitzvah songs—"Hava Nagila," "Tzena Tzena," "New York, New York" ("I want to wake up in the city that doesn't sleep to find I'm king of the hill, top of the heap")—so that everyone could join in. At Sammy's Famous Roumanian Restaurant, on the Lower East Side, they had Israeli singers and musicians who played "like they're at a wedding" (as it said on a handout). On one Passover night, a rabbi sang and told jokes and offered his tapes for sale.

Bernstein-on-Essex-Street (now out of business), which catered to the Orthodox and called itself the "pastrami king," was packed with men in black hats and side curls eating Chinese food. In the kitchen all the cooks were Chinese. An inspector watched to see that everything was properly kosher. They had an old smokehouse, and the cooks cured, pickled, and smoked pastrami and prepared some of the old favorites from the Hassidic communities of Poland and Russia. The restaurant once sponsored a writing competition for sayings to put into the fortune cookies. Among the winners were: "If wishes were knishes, every shnorer would be fat," "Better a loving fat wife than a skinny cross one," and "The wurst is still to come." A fax machine received orders to be delivered: two wonton, one moo goo gai pan, one chow gai kow, two rugelach.

Apart from bagels and lox, the sumptuous deli sandwiches of corned beef and pastrami on rye are the greatest New York contribution to the international Jewish culinary repertoire. We enjoyed them at the Carnegie Deli and the Stage Deli, two legendary "kosher style" (meaning *not* kosher) delicatessens on Seventh Avenue near the Broadway Theater District. They are famous for their huge double- and triple-decker sandwiches, named after film stars and other celebrities and packed with turkey, ham, and cheese, coleslaw and mayonnaise. There was always a free table for comics at these Broadway delis, and that is one reason for the important place Jewish food has in the New York comedy repertoire. Another is that all the old vaudevillians and stand-up comedians got their start at the Jewish resorts of the Catskill Mountains, where Brooklyn families spent their summers. The hotels in this "borscht belt" served gigantic quantities, and the talk all day was about food.

Prune Tzimmes

Meat and Potato Stew with Prunes

SERVES 8 OR MORE

Tzimmes is a general term for a sweet vegetable or meat dish. Just as Oriental Sephardi Jews inherited a taste for meat with fruit from tenth-century Baghdad, Ashkenazi Jews acquired similar tastes in medieval Germany. This meat-and-prune tzimmes is the most popular. South African Jews of Lithuanian origin seem the most fond of it. It is traditionally served for Sukkot, the harvest festival, which celebrates farming and nature and fruit picking, when fruit is the theme of meals taken in the festive booths. I wondered about adding sugar when I cooked it, but the result was very good.

2 lbs (1 kg) slightly fat beef brisket, flank, or rolled rib
3 tablespoons chicken fat or oil
1½ large onions, coarsely chopped
Salt and pepper
1 teaspoon cinnamon
½ teaspoon allspice
A good pinch of nutmeg
2 lbs (1 kg) new potatoes
1 lb (500 g) pitted prunes
2 tablespoons sugar or to taste

In a heavy pan over medium heat, turn the meat in the fat or oil to brown it all over. Then remove it and fry the onions gently till soft. Return the meat to the pan and cover with water. Season with salt and pepper, add cinnamon, allspice, and nutmeg, and simmer for 1½ hours.

Add the potatoes and prunes and the sugar and more water to cover, and simmer ¾ hour longer. You may want to have plenty of black pepper to balance the sweetness. There should be a lot of liquid. Serve hot.

VARIATIONS

• 4 large carrots cut into pieces may be added.
• In America, sweet potatoes, cut into cubes, are used as an alternative to potatoes.
• Add ½ teaspoon ground ginger.
• Sweeten with 2 tablespoons of honey instead of sugar.
• Some red wine could be added to the water.

Pot Roast

SERVES 8

The Jewish pot-au-feu of boiled beef and vegetables, a Friday-night alternative to chicken soup and roast chicken, makes a deliciously heartwarming meal. Adding marrow bone gives a wonderful gelatinous quality to the broth. The vegetables are there for the flavor and to make a good broth, which is served first as a soup with lokshen (vermicelli). The meat is served with other vegetables, which are cooked separately, and it is accompanied by pickled gherkins, and chrain (page 59).

1 beef marrow bone (optional)
3 lbs (1½ kg) beef—brisket, breast, or flank
Salt and pepper
1 small celery root, peeled and cut in 4

1 parsnip
1 turnip
2 small leeks
2 small onions
2 carrots
2 celery stalks with leaves
3 bay leaves

In a large pot, blanch the marrow bone (if using) in boiling water for a few minutes. Throw out the water. Bring plenty of fresh water to the boil in the pot. Put in the bone and the meat, whole, on top. Bring to the boil again, remove the scum, and add the rest of the ingredients, also whole. Barely simmer for at least 3½ hours, keeping the meat covered with water. Remove as much of the fat as possible from the surface with a spoon, and mop up what is left by trailing a rolled-up paper towel over the surface.

SERVING SUGGESTIONS

• If you like, make a soup with the broth. Strain it into another pot, add vermicelli broken into bits with your hand, and simmer till they are done. Serve as a first course.

• Serve the meat with extra vegetables cooked separately in boiling salted water. Use potatoes and any (or a combination) of the following: carrots, parsnips, turnips, leeks, cabbage, and celery hearts.

• Accompany with a sauce made by mixing about 6 tablespoons of grated horseradish (you can buy it in bottles now in supermarkets) with 1½ tablespoons of vinegar, 1–2 teaspoons of sugar, salt and pepper, and a little of the broth.

Beef Stew with White Beans

SERVES 8

In this long-simmered stew where the beans turn a delicate shade of brown and the meat is cooked to melting tenderness, fatty meat that does not go stringy is best used. The melted fat can be skimmed off the top at the end.

8 small onions, peeled
3 tablespoons sunflower oil
4 garlic cloves, chopped
2 lbs (1 kg) beef—breast, brisket, or flank
1 lb (500 g) dried butter beans or large haricot beans, soaked for 2 hours or overnight
Salt and pepper
1 lb (500 g) potatoes, cubed
½ lb (250 g) cèpes or shiitake mushrooms, sliced (optional)

In a large pot, gently fry the onions in the oil, shaking the pan and stirring occasionally, until lightly colored. Add the garlic and the meat and turn to brown the meat all over. Cover with water and bring to the boil. Remove the scum and add the drained beans. Then simmer, covered, for 2½ hours, adding salt and pepper when the beans have begun to soften, adding more water if necessary. Add the potatoes and mushrooms and cook ½ hour longer.

Wiener Schnitzel

Bread-Crumbed Veal Escalopes

SERVES 4

This famous Viennese dish was adopted by Jews all over Central Europe. On Sundays, when gentiles had roast pork, Jews had Wiener schnitzel.

4 veal shoulder steaks or cutlets about ⅓ inch
    (1 cm) thick
Salt and pepper
Flour
1 egg lightly beaten with a tablespoon of
    cold water
Fine bread crumbs or matzo meal
Light vegetable oil for frying
1 lemon, quartered

Trim the pieces of veal. Put them between 2 sheets of greaseproof or wax paper and flatten slightly with a mallet. Cut the edges at intervals to prevent the meat from curling up while it cooks, and sprinkle with salt and pepper. Dip the veal first in the flour, then in the beaten egg, and finally in the bread crumbs, making sure that the coating is thick and even and pressing the bread crumbs firmly on with the palm of your hand. Fry in plenty of hot oil for 3–5 minutes, turning them over once, until golden on both sides. Drain on paper towels and serve very hot with lemon wedges.

VARIATION

• Jews in Italy simmer the fried escalopes in Marsala.

Klops

Meat Loaf

SERVES 6–8

This kind of meat loaf is common the world over, but to the Jews it has been a standby. Slightly fatty meat will give a moist, easier-to-cut loaf.

1½ lbs (750 g) ground beef
1 onion, finely grated
2 tablespoons tomato paste (optional)
¼ cup (30 g) bread crumbs or matzo meal
Salt and pepper
1 egg, lightly beaten
A bunch of parsley, finely chopped (½ cup)
3 hard-boiled eggs, peeled

For the optional sauce

1½ lbs (750 g) tomatoes (if fresh tomatoes
    not at their best, use canned)
1–2 teaspoons sugar
Salt and pepper

Mix all the meat-loaf ingredients except the hard-boiled eggs and work well with your hands to a soft paste that holds together. (You may also blend in a food processor.) Form into a fat sausage-shaped loaf and place in an oiled loaf pan or baking dish. Make three depressions along the top, press a hard-boiled egg into each, and pat the meat over them so that they are well covered. Bake at 375°F (190°C) for 1 hour, until browned.

At the same time, make the sauce. Liquefy

the tomatoes (unpeeled) in the food processor, then simmer in a saucepan with sugar and a little salt and pepper 20 minutes to reduce the sauce.

Serve the meat loaf hot or cold, cut into slices with the hot or cold tomato sauce poured over.

VARIATION

• Meat patties using the same ground-meat mix, shaped like little hamburgers, and sautéed in a frying pan greased with oil or baked in the oven, are also *klops*.

Sweet-and-Sour Meatballs

SERVES 6

There are dozens of recipes for meatballs to be dropped in sauces or stews in the Ashkenazi repertoire. They are made with ground beef bound with eggs and with bread crumbs or matzo meal or bread soaked in water and squeezed dry, seasoned with chopped onions or garlic and flavorings such as paprika, mace, and ginger. These have a strong and delicious intriguing flavor. They can be served hot with a potato kugel (page 161), kasha (page 156), or mamaliga (page 159), or as a cold appetizer.

1 large onion, sliced
4 tablespoons sunflower oil
3 garlic cloves, crushed
2 lbs (1 kg) tomatoes, liquefied in the blender, or a 28-oz (800-g) can of peeled tomatoes
Salt and pepper

4 tablespoons vinegar or the juice of 1 lemon
3 tablespoons brown sugar
4 gingersnaps
2 lbs (1 kg) ground beef
1 medium onion, grated

Make a tomato sauce. Fry the sliced onion in oil till golden, then add the garlic and stir till slightly colored. Add the liquefied tomatoes, the salt, pepper, vinegar or lemon, sugar, and gingersnaps, and simmer for about 15 minutes.

Mix the meat with the grated onion, salt, and pepper and work to a paste with your hands. Roll into 1-inch (2½-cm) balls. Drop them into the sauce and cook on very low heat for 1 hour, turning the meatballs so that they cook all over, and adding a little water if necessary.

VARIATION

• Add 3 tablespoons of raisins and a pinch of ground cloves to the sauce.

Blintzes (Pancakes) Stuffed with Meat

SERVES 8

This is one of the grand refined dishes inherited from the Austro-Hungarian world. It is easier than it seems, and it is worth the effort.

For the pancakes

> 4 eggs
> 2 cups (300 g) all-purpose flour
> 2 cups (500 ml) carbonated or soda water
> A pinch of salt
> Oil to grease the pan

For the filling

> 1 large onion, chopped
> 3 tablespoons light vegetable oil
> 1½ lbs (750 g) lean ground beef
> Salt and pepper
> 3 tomatoes, peeled and chopped
> Zest of 1 lemon
> 1 teaspoon paprika
> A good pinch of cayenne or red chili powder,
>   to taste

For the tomato sauce

> 1½ lbs (750 g) tomatoes or ¾ of a 28-oz
>   (800-g) can of peeled tomatoes
> 2 tablespoons tomato paste
> 2 tablespoons oil
> Salt and pepper
> 1–2 teaspoons sugar
> ½ cup (125 ml) water

Prepare the pancake batter first. Beat the eggs lightly, and gradually add the flour, beating vigorously. Then beat in the carbonated or soda water and add salt. (Using an electric beater will help to eliminate any lumps very quickly.) Leave to rest while you prepare the filling.

In a large frying pan, fry the onion in the oil till golden. Add the meat and cook, turning it over and crushing it with a fork until it changes color. Add salt and pepper, the tomatoes, lemon zest, paprika, and cayenne or red chili powder and about ½ cup (125 ml) water. Stir and cook, uncovered, for 10 minutes, or until the water is absorbed. The filling should be moist and juicy but not runny.

Now make the pancakes. Cook only one side, and fill each one as it is ready. Grease a non-stick frying pan with a bottom at least 8 inches (20 cm) wide. Do that by dipping a folded paper towel in a bowl of oil and gently brushing the bottom of the pan. Put the pan over medium heat. Pour in half a ladleful of batter (about ¼ cup) and tilt and move the pan so that the batter runs all over the bottom. As soon as the pancake sets and is easily detached, slip it onto a plate, cooked side down. Put a generous line of filling—about 2 tablespoons—at one end and roll up the pancake, tucking in the sides as you start rolling. Continue with the rest of the batter (you should end up with 16 pancakes), and arrange all the rolls side by side in an oiled oven dish.

For the sauce, liquefy the tomatoes in the food processor (you do not need to peel them). Put all the ingredients together in a pan and simmer for about 15 minutes. Pour over the stuffed pancakes and bake in a preheated 425°F (220°C) oven for 10–15 minutes.

Leber mit Tzibbeles

Calf's Liver and Onions

SERVES 4

This reminds me very much of the Venetian dish. Could it have been the *"tedeschi"* from Germany who came to live in the ghetto who introduced it to the lagoon city?

1½ lbs (750 g) calf's liver
Salt
2 large onions, cut in half and thinly sliced
5 tablespoons light vegetable oil or a mixture of oil and chicken fat
3 tablespoons finely chopped parsley

To kosher the liver, sprinkle with salt and briefly sear both sides under the grill until it changes color.

Cook the onions in the oil with a little salt in a large frying pan on very low heat with a lid on, stirring occasionally, for about 1 hour, until very soft and creamy. Now cut the liver into thin strips and add it to the pan. Raise the heat and fry quickly, stirring constantly, until just cooked through. Serve sprinkled with parsley.

VARIATIONS

• As with everything in Ashkenazi cooking, liver too has a Polish sweet-and-sour version. Add 4 tablespoons lemon juice and 1 tablespoon sugar before you put the liver in.
• For a Hungarian version, add 1–2 teaspoons paprika.

Choucroute Garnie à l'Alsacienne

Sauerkraut with Boiled Meats

SERVES 10–12

The Jewish version of this famous Alsatian dish has smoked or corned beef, boiled tongue, beef sausages, sometimes goose confit, and boiled potatoes, all on a bed of steaming-hot sauerkraut. Choucroute makes a spectacular party dish. Buy the sauerkraut ready-made from a barrel or in jars or cans. Cook the meats separately (see pages 136 and 137) and serve them arranged on the sauerkraut. You can make a simpler meal using only boiled frankfurters.

2 28-oz (800-g) cans of sauerkraut
1 large onion, finely chopped
5 tablespoons vegetable oil or goose fat
4 garlic cloves, crushed
8 juniper berries
6 cloves
2 bay leaves
2 cups (500 ml) fruity white wine, such as Sylvaner or Riesling
A very little salt (if any) and pepper

Drain the sauerkraut and soak it in cold water for about 25 minutes, changing the water twice. Drain and squeeze the water out.

In a large saucepan, fry the onion in the oil or fat until golden. Add the garlic and stir well. Then add the well-drained sauerkraut and the rest of the ingredients. Mix well and cook on very low heat, with the lid on, for about 30 minutes, until the sauerkraut is very tender.

CHOLENT

The Sabbath Stew

THE TRADITIONAL stew for the Sabbath midday meal and the only hot dish of the day, which is prepared on Friday and left to cook overnight, is the most characteristic Jewish dish. In an ironic parody on Schiller's "Hymn to Joy" entitled "Princess Sabbath" (1850), about assimilated Jews in nineteenth-century Germany who frequented the Berlin salons while holding on to their Jewishness, the German poet Heinrich Heine rhapsodized about cholent, which "alone unites them still in their old covenant."

> Cholent, ray of light immortal!
> Cholent, daughter of Elysium!
> So had Schiller's song resounded,
> Had he ever tasted Cholent,
> For this Cholent is the very
> Food of heaven, which on Sinai,
> God Himself instructed Moses
> In the secret of preparing.

Cholent has deep emotional significance. The smell exhaled when the lid is lifted is the one that filled the wooden houses in the shtetl. In the old days in Central and Eastern Europe, the pot was hermetically sealed with a flour-and-water paste and taken to the baker's oven, and the men and children fetched it on their way home from the synagogue. Jewish bakeries in the East End of London continued the tradition, and on Saturdays their ovens were full of copper pots brought over from Russia and Poland. They would give metal tags with numbers for people to retrieve the pots and used a paddle to pull them out. Children were usually sent to fetch the cholent from the communal bakery when school ended. It is this custom that led to the popular belief in England that the name "cholent" is derived from the words *"shule"* (Yiddish for "synagogue") and "end."

Cholent is currently enjoying a renaissance. In my area in London, people buy it ready-cooked, chilled or frozen, in foil containers. In Israel, young people, including Sephardim, now flock to fashionable eateries that advertise "Jewish Cooking" to eat it on the weekend. In New York, a restaurant advertises, "The French have cassoulet, we have cholent." (Cassoulet combines different meats, including goose and sausage, with beans slowly cooked in plenty of goose fat.) The likeness is not pure coincidence.

The name "cholent" (there are various pronunciations) is generally believed to come from the medieval French *chault* (hot) and *lent* (slow) in reference to the long slow cooking. There were Jews in the region of the Languedoc, where cassoulet originated, since earliest times. Many lived off the land. Toulouse, Narbonne, Nîmes, Lunel, Béziers, and especially Montpellier were centers of Talmudic studies. Then there was a massacre during the Albigensian Crusade in the thirteenth century and measures were taken against them. When they

Housewives in Bialystok taking their cholent pots to the bakery

were finally expelled in 1394, many headed for Germany. That may well be how a kind of cholent (there were no white beans at that time—they came from the New World) and the name were introduced to the Yiddish-speaking world. The German rabbis were stricter than the French rabbis, who allowed their servants to rekindle the Sabbath fire and reheat the pots. And in Germany the rabbis decreed that the public ovens be sealed with clay on the Friday. In medieval Germany the dish took on the various additions that we know today.

The tradition of cooking a meal in a pot overnight is of course much older than the fourteenth century and has to do with the interdiction against lighting fires or cooking on the Sabbath (see pages 27–28). It was often referred to in Talmudic days and dates back to the ancient Hebrews. It is only the combination of ingredients that can be traced back to southwestern France and medieval Germany.

There are many versions now, including meatballs, tongue, sausages, meat loaf, chicken or lamb, and a variety of beans. In the old days families who could not afford meat had cholent composed only of beans

Selling cholent pots

and grain. Nowadays it is vegetarians who make meatless cholent.

The basic traditional cholent is meat, potatoes, barley, and beans. The traditional accompaniments, which are cooked in the same pot, are of German origin. They include kishke (a sausage filled with a flour-and-onion stuffing, page 150) and various knaidlach (see accompaniments at the end of the recipe)—all part of the dumpling family of foods. There is good reason for the saying that cholent is so heavy with stodge that "people have to go to the synagogue on Sunday to pray for their stomach to recover."

A test of "who is a Jew" is supposed to be whether you like cholent. One of my Israeli friends found himself eating it with friends in Jerusalem. When he complained that it was not very good, one of his companions replied, "It's not supposed to be." Of course, it depends on the cook.

Cholent

I had watched Shmulik and his wife Carmela, owners of the restaurant Shmulik on Herzl Street in Tel Aviv, demonstrate cholent and kishke at the Jerusalem Gastronomic Congress in 1992, and I enjoyed the two dishes at a party at their restaurant. The following is based on their recipe.

2 lbs (1 kg) fatty beef—brisket, breast, or rib
3 tablespoons light vegetable oil
2 large onions, sliced
3–5 garlic cloves, peeled and left whole
2 marrow bones (optional)
2 lbs (1 kg) potatoes, peeled, whole if small,
  quartered if medium
½ lb (250 g) dried white haricot or butter
  beans, soaked for an hour
½ cup (100 g) pearl barley (optional)
Salt and pepper

In a large heavy pot or casserole with a tightly fitting lid, brown the meat in the oil. Remove it, and fry the onions till soft. Add the garlic and fry till the aroma rises. Return the meat to the pot, add the marrow bones, and arrange the potatoes, beans, and barley around it, sprinkling each layer with salt and pepper.

Cover with water and bring to the boil. Remove the scum, then put the lid on and leave in the lowest oven (225°F; 110°C) overnight. Remove the lid at the table, so that everyone can get the first whiff of the appetizing smell which emanates.

VARIATIONS

• Two marrow bones (ask the butcher to slice them for you) add a wonderful rich flavor and texture.

• Use 1¼ cups (250 g) kasha instead of the beans and barley.

• Some people put onion skins on top of the stew to give a more pronounced brown color.

• Flavor with 1 teaspoon paprika and 1 teaspoon ground ginger.

• Hungarians and Alsatians add smoked or preserved goose.

ACCOMPANIMENTS TO CHOLENT WHICH ARE PLACED IN THE STEW POT BEFORE COOKING

• For a cholent knaidlach (dumpling) also referred to as "cholent kugel" (pudding), work 4 tablespoons finely chopped chicken fat into 1 cup (150 g) flour with your hands, add 1 egg, 2 tablespoons grated onion, salt and pepper, and if you like 1 tablespoon finely chopped parsley or 1 teaspoon paprika. Add a little water if the dough is too dry, or a little flour if it is too sticky. Roll into a fat oval loaf or ball and place on top of the other ingredients in the stew. When serving, cut in slices.

• For a matzo knaidlach, beat 2 eggs with salt, pepper, and 3 tablespoons rendered chicken fat and mix in 1⅓ cups (175 g) medium matzo meal. Form into a ball and put on top of the other ingredients in the pot. When serving, cut in slices.

• Other knaidlach are made with hallah bread, semolina, or grated potatoes.

In Eastern Europe there was always a poor man at the Sabbath table. The meal could not start without a shnorer. Israel Zangwill's shnorer in the East End of London felt no shame, regarding himself as the Jacob's ladder by which the rich man mounted to paradise, but he did not look for gratitude. He felt that virtue was its own reward.

Kishke–Stuffed Derma

Flour and Onion Sausage for the Cholent

SERVES 6

Israelis were once contemptuous of this kind of food, but it is now back in fashion, along with the nostalgia for roots. Restaurants advertising "Jewish" food have them on the menu. The word "kishke" means "intestine," and the sausage casing is a piece of cow's intestine. In Israel it can be bought frozen, cleaned and ready to use, and it is probably being exported. You can buy fresh ones from kosher butchers, but it is an effort to clean them. They have to be turned inside out and scrubbed well. Kishke is served as a first course or as a side dish with meat, and it is also part of cholent (preceding recipe). This too is Shmulik and Carmela's recipe.

1 large onion, grated
4 tablespoons raw chicken fat, grated or finely chopped
Salt and pepper
¾ cup (75 g) flour
2 tablespoons matzo meal
For the sausage casing: large beef intestine cut into 3 8-inch (20-cm) lengths

Mix all the ingredients except the casings. Tie the intestine pieces at one end, stuff them loosely with the mixture, and tie the other end tightly. Prick them with a fork to prevent them from bursting during cooking. Boil the sausages in salted water for 10 minutes, then drain. Simmer with meat in a stew, or cook in boiling salted water for 1 hour, or bake in a dish with a little water and surrounded by potatoes for 1½ hours at 350°F (180°C), or until browned. If part of a cholent, lay on top of the other ingredients before cooking. Serve cut in slices.

VARIATION

• Add 1 teaspoon of paprika or ½ teaspoon of allspice.

Stuffed Breast of Veal with Kasha and Mushroom Filling

SERVES 6

This version, with a kasha and mushroom filling, is Ukrainian. More common Polish ones, with potato stuffing, are given as variations. Have the butcher bone the veal breast and cut a long pocket in it.

For the kasha (buckwheat) stuffing

> 1 large onion, chopped
> 6 tablespoons vegetable oil
> ¼ lb (125 g) mushrooms, cut into smallish
>   pieces
> Salt and pepper
> 1¼ cups (250 g) kasha (buckwheat)
> 2½ cups (600 ml) chicken or beef bouillon
>
> 1 prepared breast of veal
> Salt and pepper
> 2 tablespoons vegetable oil
> 1 onion, chopped
> 2 carrots, chopped
> 2 garlic cloves, chopped
> 1 cup (250 ml) meat or chicken bouillon

Make the stuffing first. Fry the onion in a saucepan in 4 tablespoons of the oil until soft and beginning to color. Add the mushrooms, salt, and pepper, and cook, stirring, for 5–10 minutes. Fry the kasha in a frying pan in the remaining 2 tablespoons of oil, stirring, for about 7 minutes, until browned, then add it to the onion and mushrooms. Pour in the hot bouillon, stir well, and cook, covered, for about 15 minutes, until the grain is tender and the water absorbed. Let cool.

Sprinkle the veal breast all over with salt and pepper and fill the pocket with the cooled stuffing. Sew up or skewer the opening and rub the breast with oil.

Spread the onion, carrots, and garlic on the bottom of a roasting pan and sprinkle lightly with salt and pepper. Lay the breast on top and pour in the bouillon. Cover with foil and roast in a preheated 350°F (180°C) oven for about 2½–3 hours, or until the meat feels very soft when you press on it, basting with the juices oc-

casionally and removing the foil for the last ½ hour to let the meat brown.

Serve cut into large slices, accompanied by the vegetables and reduced juices from the pan.

VARIATIONS

• For a Polish potato stuffing: Mix 1½ lb (750 g) potatoes—grated, drained, and their juices pressed out in a sieve—1 medium onion, grated, 4 tablespoons potato flour, 1 egg, salt, pepper, and 1 teaspoon paprika.

• For a stuffing with mashed potatoes: Peel, boil, and mash 1½ lb (750 g) baking potatoes. Add 1 large onion, chopped and fried until golden in 2 tablespoons chicken fat or oil, salt and pepper, 2 lightly beaten eggs, and 4 tablespoons chopped parsley.

A woman goes to the butcher and says, "I want you to cut me exactly two pounds of this meat." He cuts it and it weighs just two ounces more. She says, "Cut a little bit off, I want exactly two pounds." He cuts a little bit more and it is still not exact. She asks him to cut a tiny bit more. Then he cuts too much and now it is a little bit less than two pounds. So she asks him to add a tiny bit more. When at last it is two pounds exactly the woman says, "I wanted to see what two pounds of meat looked like, because I was told next door that I only had to lose two pounds to fit into the dress in the window."

Noodles, Kugels, and Grains

To Make Pasta Dough

MAKES ABOUT 1 LB (500 G)
DOUGH (ENOUGH FOR 6)

Pasta in the old Ashkenazi as in the Sephardi world used to be a combination of flour and eggs with water. Nowadays as in Italy, it is simply flour and eggs. Because different flours have different weights (see page 96) and because the amount of flour the eggs absorb varies depending not only on the provenance and type of wheat but also on the weather and harvest, it makes sense and works better to start with the eggs and to add the flour gradually—as much as it takes to have a soft dough. In that way you cannot go wrong.

One large egg absorbs about 4 oz (100 g).

3 large eggs
Pinch of salt
About 2 cups (300 g) all-purpose
    flour

If making the dough by hand, lightly beat the eggs with salt and add the flour gradually, working it in first with a fork and then with your hands, until the ingredients are well mixed and the mass holds well together. You may use a food processor to blend the ingredients, but do not add all of the flour from the start, in case you need less.

Knead for 10–15 minutes, until the dough is smooth and elastic, adding a little more flour if it is too sticky or a drop of water if it is too dry. Wrap in plastic wrap and leave to rest for 15–30 minutes at room temperature.

Divide the dough into 2 balls for easier handling. Roll out each ball as thin as possible into a rectangle on a floured surface with a floured rolling pin. With experience you should be able to roll it out evenly, almost paper-thin, without breaking it.

If making ravioli, use right away; if making noodles, leave the sheets to dry for 15 minutes. Then roll up loosely—or, rather, fold over and over—into a flattened scroll 3 inches (7½ cm) wide and slice with a sharp pointed knife. For noodles to be used in puddings, cut ¼ inch (½ cm) wide. For vermicelli (used in soup), cut as thin as possible. Unroll and leave to dry a few minutes before using.

VARIATIONS

• Other traditional shapes are plaetschen — little squares, about ½ inch (1¼ cm)—and shpaetzlen—bow ties. For the latter, pinch 1-inch (2½-cm) squares in the middle.

• Farfel, also called "egg-barley" pasta because the dough is formed into tiny barley-sized lumps, is made by grating it through the thick holes of a grater, or chopping the dough, or rolling tiny bits between the fingers. This pasta is now mass-produced commercially in Israel. It is boiled, fried, or baked and served as a garnish for fried and roast meats, as well as in soups. For farfel and mushrooms, see page 165.

LOKSHEN AND OTHER PASTA

JEWS WERE making pasta in the ghettos of Germany, through contact with their brethren in Italy, with whom they had trade and rabbinical connections, long before it reached Germany in the sixteenth century. In the early fourteenth century, a famous Jewish scholar, Kalonymus ben Kalonymus, who had moved from Rome to the Rhineland, was known to eat strips of boiled dough with honey, over which he recited the blessing for cakes on Friday night.

The early names for pasta, variously called "grimseli," "frimzeli," or "vermisellish," derive from the Italian "vermicelli" (noodles are still called "frimsel" by the Jews of Alsace), but the Yiddish word "lokshen" comes from the Polish "lokszyn." Pasta came to Poland as a result of Italian presence at the royal courts and also by way of Central Asia. That may be why the cheese kreplach, sauced with sour cream, owes more to the Turkish-Mongolian manti with yogurt poured over than to Italian ravioli or cappelletti.

Hardly anyone today makes lokshen at home, because we can buy it, but it was once the cornerstone of feminine dexterity. It was part of the two main Sabbath meals, and Friday preparations in the shtetl involved the making of noodles for chicken soup as well as for the kugel (pudding), which could be savory or sweet. Every housewife owned a large wooden pastry board and a long thin rolling pin like a broomstick to make it. Although there is a certain mystique attached to the process, it is really very easy—the way they make fresh pasta in Bologna.

Preparing lokshen for Friday night in Alsace.
Turn-of-the-century drawing by Alphonse Levy

Simple Jewish Ways with Lokshen

In Alsace, where lokshen is called "frimsel," noodles are simply boiled in salted water or milk and served with butter. Sometimes a few pieces are set aside to be fried in melted butter until brown, and sprinkled over the dish. Another simple snack is boiled noodles with scrambled eggs cooked in butter or fat.

Lokshen Kugel
Savory Noodle Pudding

SERVES 6

This noodle pudding can be savory or sweet. It is traditionally served hot on Friday night and cold on Saturday.

½ lb (250 g) medium egg noodles or
    vermicelli
Salt
1 large onion, chopped
4 tablespoons chicken fat or vegetable oil
3 eggs, lightly beaten

Boil the noodles in salted water until just tender and drain. Fry the onion in 3 tablespoons of fat or oil until soft. Cool a little, then mix with the eggs and noodles. Add a little salt. Line a loaf pan or mold with greaseproof or wax paper or foil and grease well with the remaining fat. Pour in the noodle-and-egg mixture and bake in a preheated 350°F (180°C) oven for about 45–60 minutes, or until firm and lightly brown on top. Turn out, peel off the foil, and serve hot cut in slices.

VARIATION

• For a sweet and peppery Israeli version add to the above ingredients ½ cup (100 g) sugar, 4 tablespoons raisins, and 1½ teaspoons black pepper.

Lokshen Kugel with Cheese

SERVES 6

This deliciously creamy noodle dish is a specialty of Shavuot. It can be savory or sweet.

> 10 oz (300 g) medium egg noodles
> 4 tablespoons butter
> Salt
> 2 eggs
> ½ lb (250 g) curd or cream cheese
> 2 cups (500 ml) sour cream
> A good pinch of nutmeg (optional)

Cook the noodles in boiling salted water till tender, then drain, and mix with the butter.

At the same time, in a large bowl, with a fork, beat the eggs with the curd or cream cheese, then beat in the sour cream. Add salt and nutmeg, if using, and mix in the cooked pasta. Pour into a baking dish and bake at 350°F (180°C) for 30 minutes, or until set.

VARIATIONS

- Use vermicelli instead of flat noodles.
- This kugel can also be a sweet dessert. In this case, do not add salt or nutmeg to the cheese mixture. Add instead ½ cup (125 g) sugar, the grated zest of an orange or a lemon and ¾ cup (100 g) raisins, black or golden, or dried pitted cherries.

Cheese Kreplach
Stuffed Pasta with Cheese Filling

SERVES 4–6

Stuffed pasta, shaped like giant cappelletti or tortellini, came to the Jews of Germany through Venice in the early fourteenth century. A variety of traditional fillings developed. The most famous are meat kreplach, which go into chicken soup, and cheese kreplach, which are served as a starter or main dish in dairy meals. These are a specialty of Shavuot and most delicious, despite their surprising sweetness. To make them, follow the instructions for making pasta (page 152) and for making kreplach (page 86), but with the following filling.

> 1 recipe pasta dough, page 152

Cheese filling

> 5 oz (150 g) curd or cream cheese
> 1–2 tablespoons sugar
> 2 tablespoons fine bread crumbs or matzo
>   meal
> 1 small egg, lightly beaten
> Grated rind of ½ lemon
> 1 tablespoon raisins soaked in boiling water
>   for 10 minutes and squeezed dry
> 1¼ cups (300 ml) sour cream or 4 oz
>   (75 g) butter to accompany
> Cinnamon to sprinkle on (optional)

Mix the filling ingredients and make the kreplach as described on page 86. Boil in salted water and drain. Serve hot with sour cream poured over (pass the pot around) or with plenty of melted butter, and a sprinkling of cinnamon.

Fruit Varenikes
Plum and Apricot Ravioli

MAKES 20 LARGE VARENIKES

Plums and apricots are sharp enough to serve as a first or main dish. These Russian ravioli are best in a dairy meal, so that they can be served with sour cream or butter. They are intriguing and very appealing to those who like fruit as part of a savory meal. Use one fruit or the other or both. To serve as a sweet see the variations.

> *2 eggs*
> *A pinch of salt*
> *About 1⅓ cups (200 g) flour*
> *10 apricots or plums or 5 of each, pitted and cut in half*

Make a pasta dough as in the recipe on page 152, cover in plastic wrap, and leave to rest at room temperature for 20 minutes. Then divide the dough into 2 for easier handling. Roll each piece out as thin as possible. With a pastry cutter, cut into rounds about 3½ inches (9 cm) in diameter. Roll scraps into a ball, and roll out again as thin as you can to use up all the dough.

Place half a plum or apricot in each round, a little to one side, and fold the dough over it. Pinch the edges firmly all around to seal them,

trying not to trap any air inside (it expands in cooking and could puff up and tear the ravioli). The dough should stick very well, but if you have any trouble, moistening the edge with a drop of water or a little egg yolk helps to stick it.

Cook a few ravioli at a time in plenty of boiling salted water. Boil fast until they float to the surface, then reduce the heat to medium and cook for about 10–12 minutes. Lift out with a slotted spoon and serve hot with sour cream or melted butter.

VARIATIONS

• To serve as a sweet, put the half fruit cut side up, and fill with ½–1 teaspoon of sugar and a pinch of cinnamon. Serve with sour cream and sprinkle with more sugar and cinnamon if you like.

• Cherries are an alternative fruit.

To Cook Kasha (Buckwheat)

To cook enough for 3–4, bring 2 cups (500 ml) of water to the boil with a little salt, and add 1 cup (200 g) roasted buckwheat. Stir well and simmer on very low heat with the lid on for about 15 minutes, until the grain is tender and the water is absorbed. Stir in 2 tablespoons vegetable oil, chicken fat, or butter and let it melt in before serving.

Note:

You may substitute stock for water. If it is part of a dairy meal, you can serve kasha with sour cream poured over.

KASHA

Buckwheat

JOYCE TOOMRE, in her translation of Elena Molokhovets' *Classic Russian Cooking*, in writing about kasha, one of Russia's oldest and most traditional dishes, states that any grain—buckwheat, cornmeal, barley, millet, rice, semolina—that is cooked with water, milk, or broth is called "kasha" in Russia. To the Jews in Russia, Lithuania, and the Ukraine, for whom buckwheat was the second staple after barley, kasha meant buckwheat.

Buckwheat groats or kernels are very easy to cook and have a wonderful nutty flavor.

They can be served as a side dish with meat or as part of a dairy meal. Two traditional ways of preparing kasha are with mushrooms or with pasta "bow ties." You find buckwheat in health-food shops and specialist and ethnic grocers. It is best roasted before being cooked. Fortunately, these days it is mostly sold already roasted. Otherwise, it should be heated in the oven or in a frying pan until it browns a little. An old traditional Jewish way has it coated first with egg to keep the grounds separate when they cook. For this, beat a raw egg, stir in the kasha, then cook, stirring, over low heat to set the egg. In France they fry the grain in oil or butter before cooking.

VARIATIONS

• For kasha with mushrooms (a lovely combination), fry 1 large sliced onion in 3–4 tablespoons of sunflower oil until soft and golden. Add ½ lb (250 g) sliced or quartered mushrooms—preferably shiitake or wild mushrooms such as boletus or chanterelles—season with salt and pepper, and cook, stirring, until tender. Mix with the cooked kasha and heat through.

• For kasha varnishkes, a famous dish, boil in salted water and drain about 6 oz (175 g) of bow-tie noodles (farfel). Stir in 2 tablespoons oil, butter, or chicken fat and mix with the cooked kasha. You can also mix in a sliced fried onion.

Barley

SERVES 3 OR 4

Barley was the main staple in Eastern Europe until the potato took its place in the nineteenth century. It makes a very good side dish.

3¾ cups (900 ml) water
Salt
1¼ cups (250 g) pearl barley
2 tablespoons melted chicken fat, butter,
*   sour cream, or vegetable oil*

Bring the water to a boil in a large pot and add the salt. Throw the barley in the boiling water. Simmer, covered, on very low heat for 30–40 minutes, or until the barley is tender and the water is absorbed. Stir in the melted chicken fat, butter, sour cream, or oil. My own preference is for oil.

VARIATIONS

• Add a large sliced fried onion.
• For pentchak, add a large sliced fried onion and ½ lb (250 g) cooked white haricot beans.
• For mushrooms with barley, fry 1 large chopped onion in 4 tablespoons of vegetable oil till golden, add ½ lb (250 g) mushrooms and sauté briefly, then mix with the barley.

Millet

Millet these days is an unusual grain. It has a distinctive flavor and quality worth exploring.

To serve 3 or 4, pour 1 cup (250 g) millet in 3 cups (750 ml) boiling salted water with 3 tablespoons of oil. Simmer, covered, on very low heat for about 30 minutes, or until tender, adding a little water if necessary.

You may stir in 1 large sliced onion fried in 2 tablespoons of oil till soft and golden.

Millet can also be served as breakfast porridge with a knob of butter, a tablespoon or two of jam or honey, and hot milk poured over.

MAMALIGA

Cornmeal Porridge—Polenta

CORN CAME to Europe from the New World, after the discovery of the Americas, in the sixteenth century. Having arrived first in Venice, where it was used to make the porridge polenta, it was eventually grown in Eastern Europe, where it became known as "Turkish wheat." But it is only in Romania and Georgia in the Caucasus that it became a staple. Romania became addicted to the porridge they called "mamaliga," made by pouring the meal into boiling water. Peasants ate it for breakfast, lunch, and supper.

Mamaliga

Cornmeal Porridge

SERVES 6

This famous Romanian-style polenta makes a heartwarming winter dish.

> *2 cups (350 g) yellow cornmeal, fine*
> *or coarse*
> *6 cups (1½ liters) cold milk*
> *4 oz (100 g) butter, cut in pieces*
> *1 lb (500 g) curd or cream cheese*
> *Salt*

Mix the cornmeal with about half the amount of cold milk very thoroughly to avoid any lumps. Bring the rest of the milk to the boil and pour in the cornmeal-and-milk mixture, stirring vigorously. Continue to stir with a wooden spoon over very low heat for a few minutes, until all the water is absorbed and the thick paste comes away from the sides of the pan and is almost too thick to stir.

Remove from the heat and add the butter and cheese. Mash them in and mix well, adding salt to taste. Pour into a greased baking dish and bake in a preheated 350°F (180°C) oven for 30–40 minutes. Serve very hot.

VARIATIONS

• You may pour sour cream over it when serving.

• Mamaliga can also be made plain—with water only, and no butter or cheese—to be served with meat.

Reizflomesa

Rice with Prunes and Raisins

SERVES 4

This is a Friday-night dish in Alsace. It is for those who like a taste of sweet with their meat and chicken.

> *1 large onion, coarsely chopped*
> *3 tablespoons light vegetable oil*
> *1¼ cups (250 g) long-grain rice*
> *¾ cup (100 g) raisins*
> *½ cup (100 g) pitted prunes,*
> *cut in half*
> *2 teaspoons cinnamon*
> *Salt and pepper*
> *3 cups (750 ml) water*

Fry the onion in the oil till golden. Add the rice, and stir until it is well coated with oil. Add the raisins, prunes, cinnamon, salt, and pepper. Stir well and pour in the water. Bring to the boil, stir again, then simmer, covered, on very low heat for 25 minutes, or until the rice is very tender and the water has been absorbed.

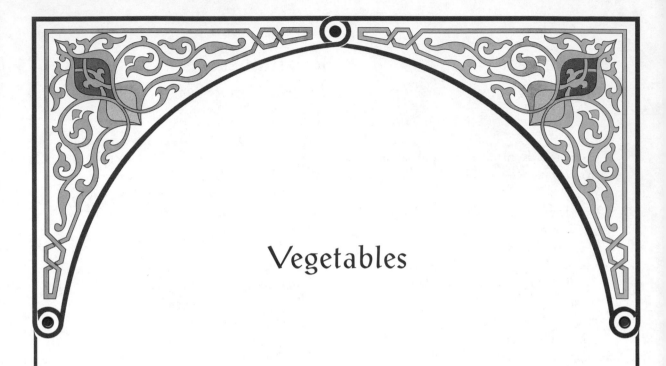

Vegetables

THE COLD COUNTRIES of Eastern Europe were very poor in vegetables. That is why, apart from potatoes, carrots, and cabbage, vegetables have not been important in Ashkenazi kitchens, except among Jews from Hungary and the Balkans, where the impact of the Ottoman occupation was strong. In Romania and Bulgaria, large numbers of Sephardi settlers introduced the tastes of the Iberian Peninsula. I have put their vegetable dishes in the Sephardi section, because they belong to that tradition. Otherwise, grains, legumes, fruit, and chestnuts took the place of fresh vegetables.

Until the nineteenth century, grains, primarily barley and also buckwheat, were the staples. The potato was very late in coming to Eastern Europe, but when it did, in the middle of the nineteenth century, its cultivation spread so quickly and became so intensive that it became the main staple, eaten every day—sometimes three times a day, at every meal. It is what the poor Jews survived on. They kept tons of potatoes in the cellar for the winter. They ate them simply boiled, with raw onions, or mashed and mixed with onions fried in goose or chicken fat, or with sour cream. Potatoes went into everything, including breads and pies. Potato dumplings were dropped into soups and stews, potato kugel was the grand Sabbath dish, like a cake or pudding, and latkes (see page 64), or potato fritters, were for special occasions.

Potato Kugel

Potato Pudding

In 1825, the German poet Heinrich Heine wrote in a letter to the editor of a Jewish magazine, "Kugel, this holy national dish, has done more for the preservation of Judaism than all three issues of the magazine." The dish is still very popular. It is sold by all the kosher stores selling takeout foods. It can be served as a first course or a side dish to accompany meat. It is often made with mashed potato and fried onions, but the traditional way, with grated potatoes, has a better texture and flavor. There are various ways of making it—with eggs or with flour or with both, and sometimes matzo meal is used. I prefer this simple version with eggs only and oil rather than chicken fat.

> 4 eggs
> Salt and pepper
> 5–6 tablespoons chicken fat or light
>   vegetable oil
> 1 large mild onion, grated
> 3 lbs (1½ kg) potatoes

In a bowl, lightly beat the eggs with the salt and pepper, the oil, and the onion.

Peel and grate the potatoes (you may use a food processor) and stir them quickly into the egg mixture (if you don't do it quickly, they will tarnish). Pour into a wide, shallow baking dish brushed with oil—kugel is usually made in a loaf pan, but a wide, shallow dish allows for more of the brown crispy crust. Bake at 350°F (180°C) for about 1 hour. Then turn the heat to 450°F (230°C) for 5–10 minutes, or until browned. Serve hot.

VARIATIONS

• The cooking of the Dutch community is Eastern European. One of the few local characteristics is the great use of cheese and also of cabbage.

• For a potato kugel with cheese, use oil or butter instead of chicken fat, and mix in ½ lb (250 g) grated cheese such as Edam or Gouda.

• For a potato kugel with cabbage, mix in ¾ lb (350 g) cabbage, cut into ribbons, and boiled in salted water until only just tender.

• A firmer, denser kugel is made by adding 4 tablespoons of potato flour (farina) to the mixture.

CABBAGE

CABBAGE IS the historic Ashkenazi vegetable. Before the potato, it was the only vegetable, apart from carrots. Every shtetl smelled intensely of cabbage. It was cooked in various ways, usually boiled or braised, often with onion. A common flavoring was caraway; sometimes a little white wine was added; often vinegar and sugar gave a sweet-and-sour flavor. It was partnered with apples and sometimes with potatoes, mushrooms, or chestnuts, and it was used in soups and as a filling for strudel and blintzes.

Sweet-and-Sour Red Cabbage with Apple

SERVES 6

This famous German combination with an exciting flavor accompanies roast poultry and meat.

> 1 red cabbage weighing less than 2 lbs (1 kg)
> 2 tart apples, such as Granny Smith
> Juice of ½ lemon
> Salt and pepper
> 4 tablespoons wine or cider vinegar
> 1½ tablespoons sugar
> 2 tablespoons vegetable oil
> ½ cup water

Remove the outer leaves and cut the cabbage in 4 through the core. Cut away the core and shred the cabbage. Grate the apple and mix with the lemon juice. Put the cabbage and apple in a pan with a tight-fitting lid. Add salt and pepper, vinegar and sugar, oil and water, and mix well. Steam with the lid on, on very low heat, for 20 minutes, or until the cabbage is very soft. Serve hot or cold.

VARIATIONS

• Add the juice of 1 lemon and omit the vinegar.
• Use red wine instead of water.
• Fry 1 chopped onion in 2 tablespoons of oil to start with, then add the rest.
• You may add 4 tablespoons or so of raisins.

White Cabbage with Sour Cream

SERVES 6

This traditional way of treating cabbage gives the vegetable a delicate, elegant touch.

> 1 small white cabbage, about 1½ lbs (750 g)
> 4 tablespoons light vegetable oil
> Salt and white pepper
> Juice of ½ lemon
> 1 egg
> 1 cup (250 ml) sour cream

Remove the outer leaves and cut the cabbage in 4 through the stem end, then cut out the cores and cut the cabbage into thin ribbons. Put it in a pan with a tight-fitting lid, with the oil, 4 tablespoons of water, salt, and pepper. Cook, with the lid on and no extra water, for about 20 minutes, or until the cabbage is very soft. Add the lemon juice.

Beat the egg with the sour cream and pour over the cabbage. Stir over low heat for 6–8 minutes, until the cream thickens a little, but do not let it boil.

VARIATIONS

• Add 2 teaspoons of caraway seeds at the beginning.
• You may use 2 tablespoons of vinegar instead of lemon juice.
• You may make it sweet-and-sour by adding 2 tablespoons of sugar.

SAUERKRAUT

Sour Cabbage

ALL JEWISH FAMILIES HAD at least two barrels in their cellars—one for gherkins and one for sauerkraut. They ate it throughout the year, cold as an hors d'oeuvre with black bread, hot as a vegetable side dish, and even as a dessert with sugar or honey.

I don't expect you to make sauerkraut, but here is the information, for your interest. Remove outer leaves, hard inner core, and thick veins of a head of cabbage, and shred the leaves finely. Mix well with sea salt or rock salt—for every 2 lbs (1 kg) of cabbage, use 1 oz (30 g) of salt—and pack into large glass jars. Put a big cabbage leaf on top and weigh down with a heavy object. Cover the jar with a cloth and leave to ferment in a cool, dark place. If the cabbage does not give out enough juice to cover itself, add a little slightly salted, boiled and cooled water. Skim the foam that forms at the top as the cabbage ferments, and stir once in a while. The sauerkraut will be ready in 3–4 weeks. You can leave it another 4 weeks to mature further. Then close the jar with a lid. Wash thoroughly in cold water before using. Juniper berries, caraway seeds, and bay leaves, and also apple slices, are sometimes added among the layers of cabbage.

In Eastern and Central Europe and in France, you can buy sauerkraut from barrels. We have to rely on what is sold in jars and cans, and it too needs to be washed in 2 or 3 changes of cold water and soaked for ½ hour, because the flavor is too strong. The Jews of Alsace are especially fond of its sour, fermented flavor. For the Alsatian choucroute garnie, see page 145.

TZIMMES

A TZIMMES CAN be a vegetable or a meat dish (see page 140) sweetened with sugar or honey. The combination of sweet with savory, common throughout Eastern Europe, was never more so than in Poland. Because of its appeal and prestigious festive image, the word "tzimmes" has come to mean in common language "a big fuss." To most Jews, "tzimmes" means "glazed carrots." But dried fruit, in particular prunes, which were often used to replace vegetables, are also broadly referred to as "tzimmes." Tzimmes can be served as a first or main course or as a side dish. Occasionally it is served as a dessert.

Carrot Tzimmes

Honeyed Carrots

SERVES 6

In Yiddish lore, sliced carrots are associated with gold coins, and carrot tzimmes are eaten at Rosh Hashanah (the New Year) as a symbol of prosperity and good fortune. The honey symbolizes the hope that the year should be sweet. This tzimmes has become one of the dishes most commonly associated with Jews. It is prepared for the Sabbath, and offered in Israeli hotel buffets and kosher takeout places. The following basic version with orange juice and ginger is very popular.

> 1½ lbs (750 g) carrots, sliced
> 3 tablespoons goose fat, butter, or light
>   vegetable oil
> Salt
> Juice of 1 orange
> ¼ teaspoon powdered ginger
> 2 tablespoons honey

In a large wide pan, sauté the carrots in the fat, stirring and turning them over. Add the rest of the ingredients and water to cover. Simmer gently, covered, for ½ hour, or until the carrots are tender. Remove the lid towards the end to reduce the liquid to a shiny glaze.

VARIATIONS

• Omit the ginger and orange, flavor with a pinch of nutmeg or a teaspoon of cinnamon, and add 2 tablespoons of currants or raisins halfway during the cooking.

• For an apple-and-carrot tzimmes, which can be served as a dessert, add 1 diced apple and 1 teaspoon of cinnamon towards the end and cook until tender.

Pumpkin Tzimmes

SERVES 6

This pumpkin cream has an intriguing and delightful savory-sweet flavor and glorious color. It is important to taste as you add salt and sugar, because the balance makes all the difference and the taste of pumpkins varies.

> An orange pumpkin weighing about 2½ lbs
>   (1¼ kg)
> A little salt
> 2 teaspoons sugar
> 2 tablespoons butter
> ½ cup (125 ml) sour cream

Cut the pumpkin up, scrape out the seeds and stringy bits, peel it, and cut it into cubes. Put it in a pan with a tight-fitting lid with about 5 tablespoons of water. Put the lid on and steam on very low heat for about 20 minutes, or until the pumpkin is soft. Mash it with a potato masher or a fork. If it is a bit wet, cook uncovered for a minute or so, to dry it out. Add the salt, sugar, butter, and sour cream and mix very well. Cook, stirring, for 1–2 minutes more.

Oignons aux Marrons

Chestnuts with Onions

SERVES 6

Chestnuts are served as a vegetable in Alsace. Suzanne Roukhomovski gives this recipe in her book *Gastronomie Juive*. The dish is delightful.

1 lb (500 g) chestnuts
1 large onion, sliced
3 tablespoons light vegetable oil, butter, or
    goose fat
Salt and pepper

To peel the chestnuts and remove their skins, make a slit on one side with a sharp-pointed knife and put them under the broiler, for a few minutes only, turning them over once, until they are lightly browned. Alternatively, you may roast them in the oven. Do not cook them to the point of browning them inside, only just enough to peel them. Peel them while still hot. Fry the onion in the butter, goose fat, or oil until golden. Add the chestnuts and season with salt and pepper. Cover with water and simmer for ½ hour. The sauce should be much reduced.

Wild Mushrooms with Sour Cream

SERVES 6

Mushroom-picking was one of the few events that brought Jewish men involved in the study of the Talmud out into nature. Boletus (cèpes) and chanterelles were the most popular wild mushrooms, because of their delicious taste and because they were easy to identify without the risk of poisoning. The most common way to deal with them was to cook them simply with chopped onions. White wine was an extravagance. The following is one of my special favorites. These days mushrooms are so expensive that I often make it with shiitake and other commercially grown mushrooms.

1 lb (500 g) boletus, chanterelles, or
    shiitake mushrooms
1 large onion, chopped
4 tablespoons goose fat or, preferably, light
    vegetable oil
Salt and pepper
1 cup (250 ml) fruity white wine
1¼ cups (300 ml) or more sour cream to
    pass around

Wash the mushrooms and cut them in half or in quarters. Fry the onion in the fat till soft. Add the mushrooms, salt, and pepper and cook, stirring, for a minute or two. Add wine and simmer until the mushrooms are tender. Serve with sour cream.

VARIATIONS

• For farfel and mushrooms, boil ½ lb (250 g) of the pasta called "farfel" (see page 153) until done *al dente*. Drain and stir into the cooked mushrooms. Cook a few minutes longer, so that the pasta absorbs the wine and mushroom flavors.

• For a hot Hungarian version, season with 1 teaspoon paprika and a pinch of cayenne. Add sour cream at the end and let it bubble for ½ minute.

Mushrooms Hungarian Style

In Romania this was served with mamaliga.

1 lb (500 g) boletus, chanterelles, or
*   shiitake mushrooms*
1 large onion, chopped
4 tablespoons light vegetable oil
4 garlic cloves, crushed
½–1 teaspoon paprika
1 lb (500 g) tomatoes, peeled and
*   chopped*
1 teaspoon sugar or to taste
Salt
Juice of ½ lemon
¾ cup (175 ml) red wine
1 small chili pepper, cut open and seeds
*   removed*

Wash the mushrooms and leave them whole. In a large pan, fry the onion in the oil till soft. Add the garlic and paprika and the drained mushrooms and stir for a minute or so. Then add the tomatoes, sugar, salt, and lemon juice and simmer for 10 minutes. Add the wine and chili pepper and cook for 20 minutes, or until the mushrooms are tender and the sauce is reduced.

Apples

SERVES 4

Pureed or sautéed apples often take the place of vegetables. They can be tart or sweet.

1 lb (500 g) apples
Juice of ½ lemon
1–2 tablespoons sugar
½ teaspoon cinnamon

Peel and core the apples and put them in a pan with the lemon juice and a drop of water. Put the lid on and steam them on very low heat for about 10 minutes, or until they fall apart. Then mash them with sugar and cinnamon. Serve hot.

VARIATION

• For a dairy meal, sauté 1 lb (500 g) peeled and sliced tart or sweet apples in 3 tablespoons of butter and 1 tablespoon of vegetable oil until tender. Sprinkle with 1 teaspoon of cinnamon and 1–2 tablespoons of sugar. Add sour cream and heat through.

Holishkes
Stuffed Cabbage Leaves

SERVES 6

Stuffed cabbage leaves were eaten in every Central and Eastern European country. Other Yiddish names for them are "galooptchy" and

166   THE BOOK OF JEWISH FOOD

"prakkes." There are many versions and different flavorings. The following is common.

> 12 large leaves cut from a white Dutch
>   or Savoy cabbage
> Salt
> 1 medium onion, finely chopped
> 2 tablespoons oil
> 1 lb (500 g) ground beef
> ½ cup (100 g) raw rice
> Pepper
> Small or torn leaves to line the bottom of
>   the pan

For the sauce

> 2 lbs (1 kg) tomatoes, peeled, or a 28-oz
>   (800-g) can of peeled tomatoes, liquefied
>   in the food processor
> Salt and pepper
> Juice of 1 lemon
> 4 tablespoons sugar or to taste

To detach cabbage leaves, cut a deep cone into the core at the stem end with a sharp-pointed knife and plunge the whole cabbage into boiling salted water. This will soften and loosen one or two layers of leaves. Detach these and plunge again into boiling water to detach more leaves, and continue until you have at least 12 large leaves. Shave off the thickest part of the hard rib if necessary with a knife.

For the filling, fry the onion in oil till soft, then add the meat and stir till it changes color. Add the rice and season with salt and pepper.

Lay the cabbage leaves on a plate, one at a time. Put 2 heaping tablespoons of filling on each leaf near the stem end, and roll up loosely, tucking in both sides so as to trap the filling. The parcel must be loose, not tight, to leave room for the rice to expand without tearing the leaves. Line the bottom of the pan with reject leaves so that the cabbage rolls do not stick. Pack the stuffed rolls, seam side down, close together on top. You can have more than one layer.

Mix the sauce ingredients and pour over the cabbage rolls. Add enough water to cover, and put a small plate on top to keep them from unfolding. Simmer on very low heat for about 2 hours, being careful to add water so that the rolls do not dry out and burn. You may, alternatively, cook the cabbage rolls, covered, in a slow oven for 3 hours.

VARIATION

• For a Polish version, which spread to Hassidic strongholds of the Baltic States, add to the sauce a pinch of powdered ginger, 1 tart apple chopped or grated, 4 tablespoons seedless raisins, and 1 or more tablespoons of honey.

NAHIT—ARBIS

Sweet Chickpeas

THIS IS traditionally served hot or cold to guests on the first Friday night after the birth of a baby son. Soak the chickpeas for at least an hour, then drain and simmer in fresh water for 1½ hours, adding a little salt as they begin to soften. Serve with sugar or honey.

Gefilte Feffers

Stuffed Peppers Hungarian Style

SERVES 8

Peppers came to Hungary via the Turks, but this is the only pepper dish that was adopted generally by the Ashkenazi world.

> ½ cup (100 g) rice
> Salt
> 1 onion, chopped
> 3 tablespoons oil
> 1 lb (500 g) ground beef
> Pepper
> 4 tablespoons chopped parsley
> 1 egg, lightly beaten
> 8 green bell peppers

For the sauce

> 1 onion, chopped
> 2 tablespoons oil
> 2 lbs (500 g) tomatoes, peeled and chopped,
>   or a 28-oz (800-g) can of peeled
>   tomatoes
> Salt
> 1–2 teaspoons paprika
> A good pinch of cayenne or chili powder,
>   to taste
> 2–3 teaspoons sugar

For the filling: Boil the rice in plenty of salted water for about 10 minutes until half cooked, then drain. Fry the onion in the oil till soft. Add the ground meat and stir, crushing it with a fork and turning it over, until it changes color. Remove from the heat, add the drained rice, salt, pepper, parsley, and egg.

For the sauce: Fry the onion in oil till golden. Add the tomatoes, salt, paprika, cayenne or chili powder, and sugar, and simmer for 10 minutes.

To stuff the peppers, cut a circle around the stalk ends and reserve as caps (with the stems). Remove the cores and seeds with a pointed spoon and fill loosely and not quite to the top (to give the rice room to expand) with the meat-and-rice stuffing. Replace the caps. Arrange side by side standing up in a baking dish and pour the tomato sauce around them.

Cover with foil and bake in a preheated 375°F (190°C) oven for 1–1½ hours, or until the peppers are soft. Be careful that they do not fall apart and remove them from the oven if they start to. Serve hot.

SPLIT PEAS

Zorica Herbst-Kraus writes, in a little book entitled *Old Jewish Dishes* published in Hungary, that to celebrate a circumcision it was traditional to serve boiled split peas seasoned only with salt and pepper.

Desserts and Pastries

THERE IS no great emphasis on desserts and puddings in Ashkenazi cooking—on the Sabbath, meals end with a simple preparation like lokshen (noodle) or apple pudding or fruit compote—but cake-making and baking for the Sabbath and festivals is an all-important institution. A holiday without cakes and kichelach (cookies) is unthinkable. Until not so long ago, nearly every Jewish housewife had several special tins for cakes and pastries which were refilled every week for the Sabbath, and every feast had its special ritual pastries. In Israel, on kibbutzim, baking is the one culinary activity that women continue by themselves, despite the facilities of the communal kitchen. And when magazines there ask readers for cake recipes, they are inundated with letters.

Jews are known for their fondness for sweet things. It has been said that their involvement in the sugar trade—they were in sugar refining in a big way in Poland and Russia and in sugar plantations in the West Indies—may have had an influence, but I am not sure that it has. Everybody likes sweet things—they are the obvious comfort food—but for Jews they have a symbolic significance too. They represent joy and happiness and have to be present at festive and happy occasions.

Cakes and pastries were adopted from various countries—honey and ginger cakes and butter biscuits from Germany, cheesecakes from Poland and Russia, strudel from Hungary, yeast cakes and flourless nut cakes from Austria. Sponge cake and marzipan biscuits, of Iberian origin, were introduced into Germany through Venice, and into England with the early Marrano settlers. But most of the cakes popularized by Jewish "continental" patisseries in the West were in the grand tradition of the court of Maria Theresa and Franz Josef, when Vienna was the capital of the Austro-Hungarian Empire. The Jews had become accustomed to them in the coffeehouses of Vienna and Budapest.

Vienna has been full of coffeehouses since the mid-eighteenth century. Everyone went—the gentry, the middle classes, the intelligentsia, and the poor. The city was crowded with immigrants from all over the empire, a great many of them Jews, who went to coffeehouses to keep warm. By the turn of the century, coffeehouses had adopted a luxurious decor and become the center of social life, where you went to meet your friends and read the newspaper, to play chess or cards and billiards and hear music or poetry. There were two very distinct types, the *Kaffeehaus,* where you could drink beer and wine as well as coffee, which was frequented mostly by men, and the *Café Konditorei,* frequented mostly by women, which sported the opulent Biedermeier salon look, with soft furnishings and rococo moldings and painted glass, and which offered a greater range of cakes and pastries.

Ashkenazi Jews of various origins adopted the pastry-making traditions of those who came from Vienna and Budapest. Some pastries, like the famous chocolate Sacher torte and the berry-jam Linzer torte, remained in the domain of the professional patissier, but many, like cheesecakes and strudel, became part of the familiar home-baking repertoire.

Lemon Water Ice or Sorbet

There is a very old tradition of serving water ices or sorbets at weddings, bar mitzvahs, and Jewish public banquets. They are served between courses or at the end of a meal that includes meat or poultry. They remain popular for their refreshing lightness and their capacity to reopen the appetite.

1¼ cups (250 g) sugar
2 cups (500 ml) water
⅔ cup (150 ml) lemon or lime juice

Boil the sugar and water for 5 minutes, until the sugar has dissolved, and let it cool, then stir in the lemon or lime juice. Pour into ice-cube trays and freeze, covered with plastic wrap, until the mixture sets hard. Drop the frozen cubes into a food processor and blend to a very fine slush. Pour into a serving bowl and return to the freezer, covered with wrap. Remove from the freezer 15 minutes before serving.

VARIATION

● To make a sorbet, which has a softer texture, after the frozen cubes have been turned to a fine sludge, fold in 2 stiffly beaten egg whites and return to the freezer.

Fruit Compotes

Fresh or dried fruit poached in sugar syrup is one of the classics of Ashkenazi cooking. Compotes are a simple and easy dessert and because of their lightness make an ideal end to a heavy meal. They can be quite enchanting. Almost any type of fruit can be used, alone or in combination. I love to accompany them with rice pudding.

For the fruit: Favorites for winter compotes are apples and pears; for summer, peaches, plums, apricots, gooseberries, cherries, and grapes. There are also summer and winter berry compotes, and dried-fruit compotes with prunes and raisins, dried apricots, apples, and pears. The sweetness (or thickness) of the syrup is a matter of taste and of how tart the particular fruit is. Although a variety of flavorings can be added, simply using water and sugar alone gives perfect results.

For the syrup: For 2 lbs (1 kg) fruit to serve 6 people, bring to the boil 2¼ cups (½ liter) water and ½–1¼ cups (100–250 g) sugar. Start by using the lesser amount of sugar and add more during the cooking of the fruit, after tasting.

As special flavoring you may add: lemon juice, the peel of a lemon or an orange, a vanilla bean, a stick of cinnamon, a few cloves, or a few tablespoons of kirsch, cognac, or Cointreau. Instead of water, you may use a mixture of wine—red or white—and water.

To make the compote: Wash the fruit and peel, halve, and stone if necessary. Apples and pears should be peeled, cored, and sliced. To prevent their discoloring, drop the fruits in a bowl of water acidulated with the juice of half a lemon, and drain.

Drop the fruit in the boiling syrup. Each fruit needs a different cooking time, which also depends on their degree of ripeness. Ripe fresh fruit should be poached very briefly. Currants, cherries, gooseberries, and grapes need only 1–3 minutes, apricots require 5 minutes, peaches 10 minutes, apple slices 10–15 minutes, clementines with their peels (cut in half) and plums may need 25 minutes, and pears—if they are unripe and hard—more than 40 minutes. For mixed compotes, it is best to poach the various fruits separately or add them at different times, so that none is overcooked.

Serve warm or chilled.

Berries in Syrup

Berries—such as strawberries, raspberries, blackberries, and blueberries and red and black currants—macerated in a sugar syrup, make a luscious sweet. Briefly wash, stem, and hull the fruits. Cut large strawberries in half. For 2 lbs (1 kg) mixed berries, make a syrup by bringing to the boil ½ cup (100 g) of sugar with about 6 tablespoons of water or white wine and boiling until the sugar is dissolved. Let it cool before pouring over the berries and leave for at least 1 hour, gently turning the berries over once. Much of their juice will be drawn out, and they will be sweet and soft. Serve cold.

A French way is to use wine instead of water for the syrup and to stir a few tablespoons of pureed raspberries in at the end.

Baked Apples

Apples—the main fruit of Central and Eastern Europe—were a traditional standby used in cakes, puddings, and fritters. They were often simply baked as they were, with nothing else, or cored and filled with sugar, or, for a meatless meal, with butter and sugar. You can use tart apples or sweet ones.

> *6 medium large tart or sweet apples*
> *3 tablespoons unsalted butter or margarine*
> *1½ teaspoons cinnamon*
> *6 tablespoons sugar*

Wash the apples and core them, trying not to pierce the bottoms. Prick the skins with the point of a knife in 1 or 2 places, so that they do not burst. Put the apples side by side, open side up, in an oven dish.

Fill each with a piece of butter or margarine, a sprinkling of cinnamon, and a tablespoon of sugar. Pour half a finger of water in the dish to prevent them from sticking and bake at 350°F (180°C) for 45 minutes–1½ hours (the time depends on the size and type of apple), until they are soft right through. Watch them so that they do not fall apart and take them out of the oven before they do. Serve hot, with or without cream.

VARIATION

• Another popular version is with raisins and walnuts. Make the cavities a little wider with the apple corer and fill with the sugar and butter or margarine mixed with ⅓ cup (50 g) coarsely chopped walnuts, ⅓ cup (50 g) raisins, and 1½ teaspoons cinnamon or the zest of half a lemon.

Apple Latkes

This is a specialty of Hanukah. Of several fritters that I have tried, this one is the most scrumptious, because the apples are macerated in brandy, which gives them a most wonderful flavor, and the batter is very light.

> *4 tart or sweet apples*
> *2–3 tablespoons sugar*
> *3 tablespoons brandy, dark rum, or fruit*
>   *liqueur*
> *2 eggs, separated*
> *2 tablespoons light vegetable oil*
> *A good pinch of salt*
> *1 cup (150 g) flour*
> *⅞ cup (200 ml) water*
> *Vegetable oil for frying, preferably sunflower*
> *Superfine sugar for sprinkling on after*
>   *serving*

Core and peel the apples and cut each into 4 thick slices. Put them in a shallow dish with the sugar and brandy, rum, or liqueur, and turn them so that they are well coated. Leave for at least 1 hour, turning the slices over occasionally so that they absorb the spirit.

For the batter, beat the yolks with the oil and salt, then stir in the flour and mix well. Now beat in the water gradually and vigorously, squashing any lumps. Leave for an hour, then fold in the stiffly beaten egg whites.

Heat at least ¾ inch (2 cm) of oil in a large frying pan. Dip the apple slices in the batter—about 5 at a time—making sure that they are well covered with batter. Lift each one out carefully and lower into the hot oil. The oil must be sizzling but not too hot, or the fritters will brown before the apple is soft inside. Fry in batches, and turn the slices over to brown both sides. Lift out with a slotted spatula and drain on kitchen paper before serving. Pass the superfine sugar for everyone to sprinkle on.

VARIATIONS

• You may use beer or milk instead of water for the batter.

• Pass powdered cinnamon and sugar around for people to sprinkle on.

Shalet

Apple Pudding

SERVES 6

Apple pudding is the time-honored Sabbath pudding. The name is used interchangeably with the word "cholent" for the Sabbath stew (see page 149). In the old days, it was covered with a dough crust and left to bake overnight with the stew. In France they have kept up the tradition of apple pudding. There are several versions. I love this one for its light soufflé texture and pure, sharp flavor.

2 lbs (1 kg) tart apples
¾ cup (100 g) currants or raisins, black or golden
½ cup (125 ml) white wine
¾ cup (175 g) sugar
6 eggs, separated

Peel and core the apples and cut them in half. Put them in a pan with a tight-fitting lid with the raisins and sultanas and the wine. Put the lid on and steam on very low heat for about 15 minutes, or until the apples fall apart. Mash them with a fork and stir in the sugar. Cook, with the lid off, for 1 or 2 minutes.

Add the egg yolks when the apples have cooled a little and stir well. Beat the egg whites stiff and fold them into the applesauce. Pour into a well-oiled wide, flat baking dish and bake in a preheated 350°F (180°C) oven for about 50 minutes, by which time the top will be browned. It is great both hot and cold.

VARIATIONS

• You may add ¾ cup (100 g) chopped walnuts.

• You may flavor with the zest of 1 lemon or with 1 teaspoon of cinnamon.

• For a shalet with bread, pour the apple-and-egg mixture over 6 slices of hallah (5 oz—150 g), crusts removed, cut into cubes, previously soaked in water and squeezed dry in your hand.

• For a Passover shalet with matzos, break 3 matzos into small pieces, moisten with water, and squeeze dry.

• Sometimes the apples are chopped or cut into slices and mixed raw with the egg yolks and beaten egg whites.

• For a French-style shalet, soak 5 oz (150 g) crustless hallah bread in water, squeeze dry, and blend in a food processor with 4 egg yolks, ½ cup (100 ml) rum, ⅔ cup (125 g) sugar, the grated rind of 1 lemon, and ½ teaspoon cinnamon. Beat the 4 egg whites stiff, fold them into the mix-

Apple Pudding (cont.)

ture, and pour into an oven dish. Mix in 2 lbs (1 kg) apples cut into small pieces, and bake at 350°F (180°C) for 1½ hours.

Bread and Apple Shalet with Milk

SERVES 8

You may use tart apples or sweet ones. When the apples are tart, there is an appealing contrast between their acidity and the sweetness of the cream-soaked bread. On Rosh Hashanah it is usual to add 2 tablespoons of honey.

> 2 lbs (1 kg) tart or sweet apples, peeled and
>   sliced
> Juice of ½ lemon
> 4 eggs
> 2½ cups (600 ml) milk
> ¾ cup (150 g) sugar or to taste
> Zest of 1 lemon
> 4 tablespoons rum
> ¼ teaspoon nutmeg or 1 teaspoon cinnamon
> 6 slices hallah bread (150 g),
>   crusts removed, cut into cubes
> ⅓ cup (50 g) currants or raisins, black
>   or golden (optional)
> 2 tablespoons melted unsalted butter

Drop the apple slices as you peel them in water acidulated with the lemon juice, so that they do not brown. Beat the eggs lightly, then beat in the milk. Add sugar (keep 2 tablespoons to sprinkle on the top), lemon zest, rum, and

nutmeg or cinnamon and mix well. Drain the apple slices, mix with the bread and the raisins, and spread on the bottom of a large shallow baking dish. Pour the egg-and-milk mixture over them and bake in a preheated 350°F (180°C) oven for 1 hour. Brush the top with the melted butter and sprinkle with the remaining 2 tablespoons of sugar, then bake for ½ hour more, until golden.

VARIATION

• A Rosh Hashanah (New Year) version from Alsace has 2 tablespoons of rum and 1–2 tablespoons of honey beaten into the egg and milk.

Lokshen Kugel mit Eppel
Noodle Pudding with Apple

SERVES 6

This traditional Sabbath pudding has been made by Jews in Germany since the Middle Ages. It came from their Italian brethren before Germany adopted noodles. In the Polish and Russian shtetls it was made the year round, and when fresh apples were not available, apple rings hung on strings around the oven to dry were used. I prefer it with wide or medium-wide noodles, but vermicelli are also used.

> ¾ cup (100 g) currants or raisins, black
>   or golden
> 4 tablespoons rum

½ lb (250 g) medium egg noodles
Salt
3 eggs
⅔ cup (125 g) sugar
¾ cup (75 g) walnuts or almonds, coarsely
    chopped
Zest of 1 orange or 1 lemon
4 tart apples, such as Granny Smiths
Juice of ½ lemon

Soak the raisins in the rum. Boil the noodles
in lightly salted water until well done—rather
soft.

At the same time, beat the eggs lightly with
the sugar. Add the walnuts or almonds and the
soaked currants or raisins together with the rum
and the lemon or orange zest. Drain the noodles
when they are done and stir them in.

Peel, core, and coarsely grate or chop the
apples and mix with the lemon juice, then add to
the egg-and-noodle mixture. Mix very well and
pour into a loaf pan lined with greaseproof or
wax paper brushed with oil. Alternatively, pour
into an oiled baking dish and cover with foil.
Bake in a preheated 350°F (180°C) oven for
about 50 minutes, or until lightly browned on
top and turn out.

VARIATIONS

• Omit the orange or lemon zest and flavor
with 2 teaspoons cinnamon, ¼ teaspoon nutmeg, and a pinch of ground cloves.
• Some people add ¾ cup (100 g) chopped
candied fruit or citrus peel; some add jam.
• This can be served as a side dish to
accompany meat. In that case use very little
sugar.

Hungarian Lokshen Kugel

SERVES 4

This simple pasta with walnuts and poppy
seeds makes a quick dessert.

½ lb (250 g) egg noodles
Salt
4 tablespoons unsalted butter or light
    vegetable oil
1 teaspoon cinnamon
4 tablespoons sugar
1 cup (100 g) coarsely chopped
    walnuts
2 tablespoons poppy seeds (optional)

Cook the noodles in salted water till just
done. Drain and toss in butter or oil, then stir in
the rest of the ingredients. Serve hot.

Blintzes

Cream Cheese Pancakes

MAKES 12

Blintzes are of Hungarian origin. Pancakes of every kind with various fillings, called "pala-csinta," are common in Hungary. This one was adopted as a specialty of Shavuot, when it is customary to eat dairy dishes. It is a magnificent sweet and one of my favorites.

For the pancakes

> 1 cup (150 g) flour
> 1¼ cups (300 ml) milk
> ⅔ cup (150 ml) water
> 1 egg
> ½ teaspoon salt
> 1 tablespoon oil plus more for greasing the pan

For the filling

> 1 lb (500 g) curd cheese
> ½ lb (250 g) cream cheese
> ½ cup (100 g) or more sugar, to taste
> Zest of 1½ lemons
> 3 egg yolks
> A few drops of vanilla extract (optional)
> ¾ cup (100 g) currants or raisins soaked
>   in a little rum for ½ hour (optional)
>
> 2–3 tablespoons melted unsalted butter
> Confectioners' sugar to sprinkle on (optional)
> 2 teaspoons cinnamon to sprinkle on
>   (optional)
> Sour cream to pass around

Add the milk and water to the flour gradually, beating vigorously. Add the egg, salt, and oil and beat the batter until smooth. Leave to rest for 1–2 hours.

Heat a preferably nonstick frying pan—with a bottom not wider than 8 inches (20 cm)—and grease very slightly with oil. Pour about half a ladleful of batter into the frying pan and move the pan around until its entire surface is covered with batter. The batter and the resulting pancake should be thin. As soon as the pancake is slightly browned and detached, turn it over with a spatula and cook a moment only on the other side. Continue until all the batter is used and put the pancakes in a pile.

For the filling, blend the curd and cream cheese with the sugar, lemon zest, egg yolks, and vanilla, if you like, in a food processor. Then stir in the raisins, if using.

Take each pancake, 1 at a time, put 2 heaping tablespoons of filling on the bottom half, fold the edge of the pancake over the filling, tuck in the sides so that it is trapped, and roll up into a slim roll. Place the rolls side by side in a greased oven dish. Sprinkle with butter and bake in a preheated 375°F (190°C) oven for 20 minutes.

Serve hot, dusted with confectioners' sugar and cinnamon, if you like, and pass the sour cream for people to help themselves if they want to.

VARIATIONS

• For an apple filling: Peel and core 2 lbs (1 kg) apples. Steam in a pan with the lid on and only a drop of water. Then puree and sweeten with sugar to taste, and add 1 teaspoon cinnamon and a few gratings of nutmeg.

• For a cherry filling: Pit 2 lbs (1 kg) cherries and steam them in a pan with the lid on. Some mix this with ½ cup (75 g) ground almonds and 2 or 3 drops of almond extract.

Palacsinken Torte

Layered Pancake Cake with
Apricot Jam and Meringue Topping

SERVES 4

There are versions of this Hungarian cake with 2 or more different fillings, but I like this one with apricot jam. It makes an elegant, though time-consuming, after-dinner dessert.

> *1 cup (125 g) flour*
> *1 cup (250 ml) soda or carbonated water*
> *2 eggs*
> *Pinch of salt*
> *1½ tablespoons sugar*
> *10 oz (300 g) apricot jam*
> *4 tablespoons rum or cognac*
> *2 small egg whites*

Add the soda to the flour gradually, beating vigorously. Add the eggs, salt, and 1 teaspoon of the sugar, and beat the batter until smooth. Then leave to rest for 1 hour.

Heat a preferably nonstick frying pan with a bottom about 8 inches (20 cm) wide over medium heat and grease very lightly with oil. Pour about half a ladleful of batter into the frying pan and move it around until the pan's entire surface is covered with a thin layer of batter. As soon as the pancake is slightly colored and detached, lift it up with your fingers or a spatula and turn it over. Cook a moment only on the other side. Continue until all the batter is used

and put the pancakes in a pile. The recipe makes about 9 8-inch (20-cm) pancakes.

For the filling, beat the apricot jam with the rum. Layer the pancakes 1 on top of another on an ovenproof platter on which the cake can be served, spreading each thinly with apricot jam. Keep 1 tablespoon of jam for the meringue topping.

For the topping, beat the egg whites until stiff. Add the remaining sugar and the tablespoon of jam and beat a moment more—enough to fold them in gently. Spoon the meringue on top of the pancakes and bake in a preheated 350°F (180°C) oven for 15 minutes, or until golden brown. Serve at once. Cut into wedges with a sharp knife.

VARIATIONS

• Spread the pancakes with alternating fillings of: 5 oz (150 g) apricot jam with 2 tablespoons of rum or cognac; 1 cup (150 g) ground walnuts mixed with 4 tablespoons of sugar.

Paschka

Cream Cheese Mold

SERVES 8

This rich and luscious sweet was adopted in Russia, where it was the traditional Easter sweet, drained and pressed into a muslin-lined wooden mold in the shape of a pyramid with holes in the form of a cross. There are several versions, cooked and uncooked. I like this very simple uncooked version made with curd or cream cheese or what is now often called "soft cheese," which is slightly sour. It is very rich, and people can eat only a small slice of it.

> 1¼ lbs (600 g) curd or cream cheese
> 3½ oz (90 g) unsalted butter, softened
> 4 tablespoons sour cream
> 2 egg yolks
> ½ cup (4 oz—100 g) superfine sugar or
>   to taste
> Zest of 1–1½ lemons
> A few drops of vanilla extract
> ¼ cup (40 g) coarsely chopped almonds
> ¼ cup (1½ oz—40 g) mixed raisins
>   and/or chopped crystallized fruit and
>   citrus peel

Put all the ingredients except the almonds, raisins, and crystallized fruit in the food processor and blend to a very smooth cream. Taste to adjust the amount of sugar and flavorings. Add the almonds, raisins, and crystallized fruit and blend briefly so that they are well mixed.

Pour into a small bowl lined with plastic wrap and cover with another piece of wrap. (This makes it easier to unmold.) Leave in the refrigerator overnight. Unmold and serve in thin slices.

VARIATIONS

• You can freeze the paschka and turn it into an ice cream. Take it out of the freezer ½ hour before serving.

• You can make paschka plain—without fruit or almonds.

• The Jews of Alsace blend cream cheese with a custard made with egg yolks and cream, and mix in those wonderful "fruits confits" that really taste of the fruit.

Reiz Kugel
Rice Pudding

SERVES 4–6

There are many versions of this simple and very appealing comfort food. Do look at the variations for the additions that can be made. You can serve it with fresh berries, a fruit compote, applesauce, or jam, but it is very good plain, as it is.

> ¾ cup (125 g) Italian round risotto rice
>   (such as Arborio)
> Salt
> 3¼ cups (800 ml) milk
> ⅔ cup (125 g) sugar or to taste
> 2 or 3 drops of vanilla extract
> 3 egg yolks

Boil the rice for about 5 minutes in plenty of slightly salted water, then drain. Bring the milk to the boil, add the rice, and simmer on very low heat, stirring occasionally, for 30 minutes. Add the sugar and the vanilla and continue to cook for another 5 minutes, or until the rice is tender and there is still a good bit of unabsorbed milk. Remove from the heat.

Beat the yolks with a little of the milky rice, then pour this into the pot, stirring vigorously. Stir over low heat until the milk thickens to a custardy texture, but do not let it boil or the yolks will curdle. Serve hot or cold. When it is hot it has a light, creamy texture and the grains of rice keep their shape. When it is cold it sets into a firm cakey texture.

VARIATIONS

• Mix the yolks into the slightly cooled milky rice, pour into a baking dish, and bake in a preheated 350°F (180°C) oven for 15–20 minutes. Sprinkle the top with 2–3 tablespoons of sugar, then put under the grill for a minute or two until caramelized.

• With this baked version you can also fold in 3 stiffly beaten egg whites, which gives a souf-flélike texture.

• Add ½ cup (75 g) pitted dried cherries—sweet or sour. This version is my own favorite, particularly with the pitted sour cherries from California.

• Add ½ cup (75 g) currants or raisins soaked in rum.

• Stir in a good pinch of nutmeg at the start and sprinkle with cinnamon when it comes out of the oven.

• Flavor with the grated rind of 1 lemon instead of vanilla.

• Add ⅓ cup (50 g) chopped candied fruit instead of raisins.

• Alternate layers of sliced apple and rice pudding, then bake.

Cheesecake

SERVES 10–12

Cheesecakes are among the foods that Jews adopted in Central and Eastern Europe and spread throughout America, Britain, and Western Europe, where they acquired a life of their own and a Jewish identity. They are a specialty of Shavuot—the festival that celebrates the giving of the Torah to the Jews on Mount Sinai—on the first day of which a dairy meal is eaten to symbolize the Biblical saying "And He gave us this land flowing with milk and honey."

In the old days in Eastern Europe, housewives made their soft cheese at home, and Jewish dairy plants specialized in it and in sour cream. Among Western innovations are toppings of jelly, jam, fresh soft fruits like strawberries, raspberries, and blackberries, fruits in syrup, and also whipped cream. Some cheesecakes are thickened with flour, cornstarch, semolina, or ground almonds, and variously flavored with grated lemon rind, orange juice, vanilla, cinnamon, kirsch, or rum, while bases vary from crumbed zwieback biscuits and thin sponge slices to shortcrust. Everyone has a favorite soft-cheese mixture combining low- and medium-fat curd (or farmer's) cheese with cream cheese, sour cream, and eggs in varying proportions. But the pure and simple traditional classic, with a sweet shortcrust base and a curd-cheese filling, is unbeatable.

When I was an art student living with my brothers in a flat in London, our landlady, Janey Trenner (everyone called her Auntie Janey), would bring us constant gifts of food, which made us feel at home and happy. When my parents were forced to come in a hurry after the Suez crisis, the Trenners told us that we could all stay without paying rent as long as we needed to. Even now when I visit her, and although she is ninety-six, she forces a hundred goodies on me, even if I tell her that I have just eaten. She has always kept an open house and still makes sure that all those who call are well fed. One of her specialties is a beautiful cheesecake.

For the pastry base

> 1⅓ cups (200 g) flour
> Pinch of salt
> ⅓ cup (75 g) sugar
> 4 oz (100 g) unsalted butter, cut in
>   pieces
> 1 medium egg, lightly beaten

For the filling

> 1 lb (500 g) curd cheese
> ⅔ cup (150 ml) sour cream or fromage
>   frais
> 5 eggs, separated
> ⅞ cup (175 g) superfine sugar
> Zest of 1 lemon
> Juice of ½ lemon
> A few drops of vanilla extract

For the pastry base, mix the flour, salt, and sugar in a bowl and rub the butter in with your hands. Mix in the egg and work very briefly until bound into a soft dough, adding a little flour if it is too sticky. Wrap in plastic wrap and leave for ½ hour.

Line a greased 10½-inch (26-cm) spring-form pan or flan mold with the pastry by pressing it all over the bottom and a little up the sides with your hand (it is difficult to roll out). Bake it blind in a preheated 350°F (180°C) oven for 30 minutes. Let it cool before you cover it with the filling, or it will break up.

For the filling, mix the curd cheese with the rest of the filling ingredients except the egg whites and beat until smooth. Beat the egg whites to stiff snowy peaks and fold into the cheese mixture. Pour into the pan or flan mold over the pastry shell. Bake in a preheated 300°F (150°C) oven for 1½ hours. Let it cool slowly in the oven with the door open.

VARIATIONS

- Stir ½ cup (75 g) black or golden raisins soaked in water, rum, or kirsch into the cheese mixture after the egg whites have been folded in.
- Pour 1 cup (250 ml) sour cream over the top after baking.

Apple Strudel

MAKES 4 STRUDEL ROLLS, SERVING UP TO 16

This makes a great after-dinner dessert or tea-time pastry which can be served warm, just out of the oven, or cold. There are 2 ways of making it. The more common is to spread the filling all over the top sheet of pastry, then roll it up. But the one I prefer is to put a line of filling at one end. Using ground almonds rather than the usual bread crumbs to soak up the juices during the cooking gives a richer flavor and very pleasant texture.

> 20 sheets of filo (preferably a thick quality
>   of sheets; see page 297)
> 6 oz (175 g) melted unsalted butter or
>   vegetable oil
> Confectioners' sugar to sprinkle on

STRUDEL

JEWISH HOUSEWIVES in Budapest and Vienna made their own paper-thin dough. It was considered an art and the real test of the perfect cook. Some households had a special white tablecloth set aside for it. Years ago, a performance of Arnold Wesker's play *Four Seasons* at the Golders Green Hippodrome featured four protagonists stretching strudel dough over a table dredged with flour. The audience gasped as the actors, moving around the table, pulled the dough gently in all directions, with their hands underneath it, pulling, lifting, and waving the edges till the dough hung down over the sides, as thin and transparent as tissue paper and without a single hole or tear. As people left the theater, they talked of nothing else.

Making strudel dough is a very painstaking operation which requires much skill, and now that you can buy frozen filo pastry in all the supermarkets—although this is not as good as the homemade dough—there is not much reason to make it yourself. There are many versions of the dough but here, for the record, is a classic way: Mix 2 cups (300 g) flour (it is best to use one with a high gluten content, which is most elastic), ½ teaspoon salt, the yolk of an egg, ¾ oz (20 g) of fat, a few drops of vinegar, and just enough warm water to make a fairly soft dough. Knead till smooth and elastic and not at all sticky. Put a drop of oil in a bowl and turn the dough in it to grease it all over. Cover with plastic wrap and leave to rest for about 25 minutes. Then roll out and stretch as thin as possible.

Commercial frozen filo varies in weight per package and in thinness of sheets (for more detailed information see page 297).

For the filling

> 2 lbs (1 kg) tart apples, such as Granny
>   Smiths
> Juice of 1 lemon
> 4 tablespoons sugar or to taste
> ¾ cup (100 g) walnuts, coarsely chopped
> ¼ cup (40 g) golden raisins
> 1 teaspoon cinnamon
> ¾ cup (75 g) dry fine bread crumbs
>   or ground almonds

Prepare the filling. Peel and core the apples. Squeeze the lemon juice in a bowl and turn the apples around in it so that they do not brown. Then coarsely chop or finely dice them. Return the apples to the bowl and mix with the rest of the filling ingredients. (The bread crumbs or ground almonds are there to absorb the juices so that the pastry does not become too soggy.)

Open the package of filo just before using. Open out the sheets and leave them in a pile. Brush the top one lightly with melted butter and put it on one side. Brush 4 more with melted butter and put them on top. Put a quarter of the filling in a line along one long edge, about 2½ inches (6 cm) from the edge and 1 inch (2½ cm) from the sides. Lift the edge up over the filling and roll up like a fat, baggy sausage, tucking in the sides halfway so that the filling does not fall out. Then

Apple Strudel (cont.)

lift up the roll carefully and place on a greased baking dish or tray, seam side down.

Do the same with the rest of the filling and all the sheets of filo, making 4 flat rolls, and arrange them side by side. Bake in a preheated 350°F (180°C) oven for 30–40 minutes, until crisp and golden and puffed up. Serve warm or cold, sprinkled with confectioners' sugar.

OTHER FILLINGS

• Sour-cherry filling (one of my favorites): Mix 2½ lbs (1¼ kg) pitted sour morello cherries (it is not very good with sweet ones), ½ cup (100 g) sugar or more to taste, 1¼ cups (175 g) ground almonds, and 1 teaspoon cinnamon. This fills 3 rolls, for each of which you need 5 sheets of filo and serves 12.

• Curd-cheese filling: Mix 2 lbs (1 kg) curd cheese, 4 eggs lightly beaten, ¾ cup (150 g) sugar, the grated rind of 1–2 lemons, 5 tablespoons raisins or sultanas.

• Apricot filling: Pit 3 lbs (1½ kg) fresh apricots and steam them in a pan with 4 tablespoons of water, with the lid on, for about 15 minutes, or until they collapse. Mash them with a fork, add ¾ cup sugar or to taste, and cook for another 5 minutes with the lid off to dry out the paste. Stir in 5 lightly beaten eggs, and cook, stirring, over very low heat until the mixture sets to a thick cream.

• Walnut filling for 2 rolls to serve 8: Put 2½ cups (300 g) walnut halves in the food processor with 4 eggs, 1½ cups (300 g) sugar, and the grated rind of 1 large orange. Process just enough to chop the walnuts a little coarsely. Add 1 cup (150 g) of ground almonds and blend together.

The Singer family of Budapest, 1900. The Jews in Hungary before World War I had become very well integrated, and the ruling Magyar gentry welcomed them in their midst. Many adopted a grand style of living.

ANGLO-JEWRY

ANGLO-JEWISH COOKING is basically Russian and Polish. It was not always so. The first Jews to settle in England came from northern France following the Norman Conquest in 1066. They formed colonies in London, York, and Lincoln. Old Jewry in Cheapside, Jewry Street (near the Tower of London), and Jewin Crescent in Aldersgate are reminders of their presence.

If I had discovered the French connection earlier, I would have been able to help my son-in-law Clive to plan the menu of his and my daughter Anna's betrothal lunch. Ever since he visited Lincoln as a child, Clive had been fascinated by Jew's Court, the oldest surviving synagogue building in Britain (now home to the local historical society), which stands on the steep cobbled street below Lincoln Cathedral, and by the story of Belassez, a beautiful Jewish woman and the betrothal of her daughter Judith in that building in 1271. Clive staged a re-enactment of the ceremony that had taken place 721 years before. Family and friends played their parts according to the records, and read from the original contract, in the presence of a *minyan* (ten Jewish men), which constituted itself as a Beth Din—a rabbinic court of law. Clive had hoped to arrange a period lunch in the restaurant in the building next door, which is known as "the Jew's House," and which had been the home of Belassez. But after some research into thirteenth-century English food, we abandoned the idea. I had not yet found out that in those days, according to the historian Cecil Roth, the Jews in England ate much as the French ate. He mentions roast poultry, fruit tarts and pies, meat cakes and rissoles. As it happened, the restaurant was French, so at least there was a connection with the origin of the community.

Belassez was hanged soon after her daughter's betrothal for an offense relating to dealings in coins. In 1290, Edward I expelled all Jews from England. The first to come to this country after the expulsion were secret Jews from Spain and Portugal, who settled in London in the sixteenth century. They were so discreet about their faith that they remained undiscovered.

Jews professing their faith openly were readmitted to England for the first time in 1656 by Oliver Cromwell, who invited the Amsterdam rabbi Menasseh ben Israel to negotiate their readmission. The first to arrive were from Holland, of Iberian descent. They were followed by Marranos from Spain and Portugal and by Ashkenazim from Germany and Holland. Between 1881 and 1933, there was a massive influx of emigrants from the Russian Empire and Poland. They became the overwhelming majority, and their culture and character came to represent Anglo-Jewry. But until the late nineteenth century, it was the well-established Sephardim, part of a Jewish upper class in Victorian England, who dominated the cultural life of the community.

A cookbook published in 1846 called *The Jewish Manual* and subtitled *Practical Informa-*

tion and Modern Cookery with a Collection of Valuable Hints Relating to the Toilette provides an insight into the tastes and life of the wealthy and influential Jewish elite, a rising bourgeoisie of merchants, financiers, and manufacturers, which had penetrated high society and even the aristocracy. Edited anonymously by "A Lady," it was addressed to "women of refinement" with cooks in their employ—women who traveled, read, painted, hunted, and played music and cards. It claims to offer dishes "in common use at refined English tables" as well as those "handed down from one generation to another of the Jewish nation." The collection includes English dishes like oxtail and mock-turtle soup, Cumberland and Grosvenor pudding; exotic dishes like curried chicken and East Indian cassereet and French ones like soupe Cressy, Maintenon cutlets, and blanquette of veal. The Jewish dishes are mainly from Spain and Portugal, with names like "almondegos soup," "impanada," "escobeche," and "bola Toliedo." There are a few German specialties and a sprinkling of Italian and North African dishes, but the dishes known as Jewish in Britain today, like gefilte fish, pickled herring, cheesecake, and chopped liver, are missing. The anonymous editor-author is presumed to be Lady Judith, wife of the famous benefactor Sir Moses Montefiore. Lady Judith's family came from Holland and was of German descent, and Sir Moses' was of Portuguese Marrano origin, from Livorno in Italy.

A later book, *The Economical Jewish Cook,* by May Henry and Edith Cohen, published in London in 1897, is a collection of almost entirely English recipes, such as sausage rolls, roly poly, and suet pudding, adapted in accordance with the Jewish dietary laws. Apart from Passover recipes with matzo meal, there is little that can be identified as Jewish. The book came out at the time when the Russian and Polish immigrants had begun to pour in. The East End of London was their main point of arrival. Their numbers were soon so enormous, and their conditions became so wretched in the ever more crowded tenement houses, that the Anglicized community took fright and tried to send them back to Eastern Europe or on to America and the colonies. But the influx continued, and by the 1930s the new immigrants had swamped the existing community.

The flavor of the East End at the turn of the century was captured by Israel Zangwill in his 1892 novel *Children of the Ghetto.* He describes it as a "swarming place for the poor and ignorant huddling together for social warmth in their self-made ghetto, few as well-to-do as the Jew of the Proverb, but all rich in their cheerfulness, their industry and their cleverness." Social life focused around "The Lane," as Petticoat Lane, the great marketplace, was affectionately called. Every insalubrious street and alley abutting on it was covered with mud and the overflowings of its trade, but it was full of laughter and bustle. Peddlers went around with baskets of bagels. Salt herrings, sauerkraut, and pickled cucumbers were sold from barrels. Most of the East End population earned their living by tailoring and dressmaking, working at home or in sweatshops. There were also cabinetmakers, and shoemakers.

Nearly all the Jews have moved away now from the East End, mainly to the North London suburbs (other big centers are Manchester and Glasgow). Indians and Pakistanis have

Sunday morning on Middlesex Street, Petticoat Lane, London

replaced them and the Huguenots and Irish who came before them. All that remains is a bagel bakery, which is kept open all night for taxi drivers. Bloom's in Whitechapel, where a mural photograph depicted the market when the restaurant first opened on Brick Lane, and where the menu was the same as it had been seventy-five years ago, closed down as the proofs of this book arrived.

The East End is no longer Jewish, but it holds the memories of the once warm and vibrant environment and Jewish village atmosphere which Anglo-Jewish cooking evokes. People can afford now to be nostalgic about the times when families lived in one or two rooms with outside toilets, no hot water, and no bath, when Mother cooked for a family of eleven from a tiny kitchen measuring just a few square feet, and Father woke up in the middle of the night to finish a suit.

There is little trace now of Lady Montefiore's Spanish and Portuguese dishes in Britain. The famous fried fish in batter, which the Jews eat cold, and which has become the English national dish (the chef Alexis Soyer and other nineteenth-century writers describe it as a Jewish way of cooking fish), is a Portuguese import; the all-purpose sponge cake called "plava" is probably the Sephardi "pan d'Espanya" (in North Africa it is called "palebe") and the little almond biscuits are Iberian too. As the Montefiores and the old Sephardi families have become entirely Anglicized and have abandoned their Iberian dishes, chopped liver and salt herring, gefilte-fish balls and latkes have become the Jewish foods of Britain. My first taste of them was in Soho, where the immigrants who made quality crafted suits for Savile Row made their home and where I went to art school, and at Isow's Restaurant in Brewer Street, where my onetime husband Paul courted me. The famous restaurant was frequented by actors and members of the boxing and racing fraternities, and the chairs had celebrity names on them. We always sat at the table marked with the boxing promoter Jack Solomons' name. By then the Second World War refugees had added the cakes and pastries of the Austro-Hungarian Empire to the Jewish repertoire, and in the last few years Middle Eastern specialties have made their mark on the deli trade in Golders Green and Stamford Hill and other Jewish strongholds.

Lekach
Honey Cake

Honey cake and the related ginger cake have been favorite Jewish cakes since the early Middle Ages in Germany. Although the earliest recorded German recipe for Lebkuchen (honey-sweetened gingerbread) is from the sixteenth century, there are much earlier mentions in Jewish records—some as early as the twelfth century, when it was the custom for young boys attending *heder* (Jewish school) to bring a piece of honey cake on the first day. In Eastern Europe they became Jewish festive cakes and were eaten at all joyful celebrations, such as betrothals and weddings. Honey cake is the traditional cake of Rosh Hashanah, symbolizing the hope that the New Year will be sweet, and also of Purim. This one is moist and delicious with a great richness of flavor. It should be made at least 3 days before you want to eat it, and it keeps a long time.

2 eggs
1 cup (200 g) sugar
½ cup (125 ml) light vegetable oil
Scant 1 cup (250 g) dark liquid honey

2 tablespoons rum or brandy
½ cup (125 ml) warm strong black coffee
2 teaspoons baking powder
½ teaspoon baking soda
A pinch of salt
1 teaspoon cinnamon
¼ teaspoon powdered cloves
Grated zest of 1 orange
2 cups (300 g) flour, plus extra to dust the dried fruit and nuts
½ cup (50 g) coarsely chopped walnuts or slivered almonds
⅓ cup (40 g) golden raisins

Beat the eggs with the sugar till pale and creamy. Then beat in the oil, honey, brandy, and coffee.

Mix the baking powder, baking soda, salt, cinnamon, cloves, and orange zest with the flour. Add gradually to the egg-and-honey mixture, beating vigorously to a smooth batter.

Dust the golden raisins and the walnuts or almonds with flour to prevent them from dropping to the bottom of the cake, and stir them into the batter.

Line a 9-inch (24-cm) pan with greaseproof paper or with foil, brushed with oil and dusted with flour, and pour in the batter. Or divide between 2 9-by-5-inch (24-by-13-cm) loaf pans. Bake the large cake in a preheated 350°F (180°C) oven for 1¼ hours, or longer, until firm and brown on top, and the smaller ones for 1 hour.

Ginger Cake

When my daughter goes to stay with her mother-in-law, Estelle Boyers, in Sheffield, she tells me of the good things that await her and Clive. Then I telephone Estelle and ask her for the recipes. This ginger cake is one of them. It is rich and moist and quite delicious, with a strong taste of ginger. Like the honey cake, it is best made 3 days before you want to eat it, and it keeps a long time.

> 2 eggs
> 1¼ cups (250 g) sugar
> 1 cup (250 ml) light vegetable oil
> 1 cup (250 ml) golden syrup
> 1–2 teaspoons powdered ginger (I like it
>   with the larger amount)
> 1 teaspoon cinnamon
> ¼ teaspoon baking powder
> ½ teaspoon baking soda
> 2 cups (300 g) self-rising flour
> 1 cup (250 ml) warm water
> 1–2 tablespoons ginger marmalade
>   (optional)

Beat the eggs with the sugar until pale and creamy. Then beat in the oil and the golden syrup (using the oily measuring cup for the syrup prevents it from sticking to the cup).

Mix the ginger, cinnamon, baking powder, and baking soda into the flour. Then pour into the egg-and-syrup mixture gradually, alternating with the warm water, and beat vigorously to a smooth batter. If you like, beat in the ginger marmalade at the end.

Line two 10-by-3-by-3-inch (25-by-8-by-8-cm) loaf pans with greaseproof paper or foil brushed with oil and pour in the cake mixture. Bake in a preheated 325°F (160°C) oven for 1 hour, or until firm and brown on top.

Sponge Cake

A sponge cake without butter or any other fat is the all-purpose Jewish cake, made every week to be eaten for tea or after supper with fruit salad or compote. So many people have told me of their mothers' biscuit tin from which the wonderfully ever-so-light cake (it is called "plava" in Britain) came out, and how you could never stop eating. It is thought that the origin of the cake is the Sephardi "pan d'Espanya."

> 5 eggs, separated
> 1¼ cups (250 g) superfine sugar
> Grated zest of 1 lemon
> A pinch of salt
> 1 cup (175 g) all-purpose flour

Beat the egg yolks with about half the sugar, till thick and very pale, then stir in the lemon zest.

Beat the egg whites stiff with the salt. Add the remaining sugar and beat to a very stiff, shiny meringue. Then fold in the yolk mixture. Sprinkle the flour on top and very gently fold in as lightly as possible.

Turn into a deep, oiled, nonstick spring-form cake pan about 9 inches (23 cm) in diameter and bake at 350°F (180°C) for about 1 hour, until browned on top.

VARIATION

- You may add 2 or 3 drops of vanilla extract to the yolk mixture.

Hazelnut Cake

There are flourless Passover cakes made with almonds and walnuts, but this one with hazelnuts is deliciously light and scrumptious. When I was an unexpected guest at an impromptu meal at Sheila Moses', her husband went out for fish and chips and we finished the dinner with this lovely cake, which she served with an apricot compote and whipped cream.

4 large eggs, separated
1 cup (200 g) superfine sugar
A few drops of vanilla extract (optional)
1½ cups (200 g) ground hazelnuts

Beat the egg yolks with the sugar until pale and creamy, then beat in the vanilla if using. Beat the whites into soft peaks and fold into the yolks. Then fold in the hazelnuts.

Pour the mixture into a greased, preferably nonstick 9-inch (23-cm) pan, or one lined with greaseproof or parchment paper. Bake in a preheated 350°F (180°C) oven for 45 minutes.

Apple Cake

Apple cake is one of the standbys of Jewish baking. This version is light and scrumptious.

6 apples, tart or sweet
Juice of 1½ lemons
4 eggs, separated
¾ cup (150 g) sugar
1 cup (140 g) flour
2 tablespoons unsalted butter, melted,
*   or vegetable oil*
½–1 teaspoon cinnamon to sprinkle on top

Peel, core, and slice the apples and drop them in a bowl of water acidulated with a third of the lemon juice (this prevents them from going brown), then drain.

Beat the egg yolks with the sugar (reserve 1 tablespoon to sprinkle on top). Add the remaining lemon juice, then the flour, gradually, beating vigorously. Beat the egg whites stiff and fold them in.

Pour half the cake mixture into a greased and floured 9–10-inch (23–25-cm) springform pan. Spread half the apple slices in a layer on top and pour the rest of the cake mixture over them. Arrange the rest of the apple slices in circles on top. Brush with melted butter or oil and sprinkle with cinnamon and 1 tablespoon of sugar.

Bake in a preheated 350°F (180°C) oven for 1 hour. You can put the cake under the broiler for a minute at the end to caramelize the top.

The Warburgs, a big banking family in Germany

Turn-of-the-Century Danish Apple Macaroon for Pesah

SERVES 6

This wonderfully fresh and creamy apple pie with a macaroon topping is slightly adapted from a recipe sent to me by Birgit Siesby of Denmark. She and her sister Hanne Goldschmidt have written a book about middle-class Jewish life in Copenhagen around the turn of the century as seen from the kitchen. At the time, the majority of the Jews had come from Germany—as did this pastry. There was also an old Sephardi community, and Russian Polish Jews, who arrived poor and took a gen-eration to join the middle classes. Jews were well integrated into Danish society, and this showed in the mutual adoption of dishes. A Danish bread sprinkled with poppy seeds is called "birkes," which means "blessing" in He-brew, and "Jew biscuits" with sugar and cinna-mon are baked at Chrismas.

> *4 apples*
> *1 cup (200 g) sugar*
> *3 tablespoons matzo meal*
> *5 eggs*
> *1 cup (150 g) blanched almonds*
> *3 drops almond extract*

Make an applesauce. Peel, cut in half, and core the apples, and steam them at once, before they brown. Put them in a shallow pan with a tight-fitting lid and about 4 tablespoons of water, and cook on very low heat for about 20 minutes, until they fall apart. Mash them to a puree with a fork, and cook further with the lid off if too watery. Beat in ½ cup (100 g) of sugar, the matzo meal, and 4 of the eggs, and pour into a pie plate.

For the crust, grind the almonds in a food processor with the remaining ½ cup (100 g) of sugar, then add the remaining egg and the almond extract (this is an addition I have made to give a more pronounced almond flavor), and blend to a stiff marzipan paste. Oiling your hands so that the paste does not stick, take lumps, press thin between your palms, and lay like patchwork on top of the apple puree so that it covers the entire surface of the apple mixture. It does not matter if the apple shows in between the marzipan pieces.

Bake in a preheated 350°F (180°C) oven for about 25 minutes, or until the top is golden. It is best to eat it warm.

Mrs. Cohen, who is having lunch with Mrs. Marks, says, "Do you know Debra Joseph is having an affair?" Mrs. Marks asks, "Who's doing the catering?"

Swetschkenkuchen
Plum Tart

This popular German tart is traditionally made with the sweet black *zwetschken* plums, baked in large square trays, and served cut into squares. I have tried it with other kinds of plums and it was also very good. Of course, the quality and flavor of the fruit matter. It is very simple and easy to make, with pure fresh flavors and a marvelous biscuit base. You must try it. We all love it.

> ⅔ cup (125 g) superfine sugar
> 1¼ cups (175 g) self-rising flour
>   (or all-purpose flour plus ½ teaspoon
>   baking powder)
> 3 oz (75 g) unsalted butter or margarine,
>   cold
> 1 small egg, lightly beaten
> 1 tablespoon cognac
> 1½ lbs (750 g) plums, pitted and cut in
>   half
> Confectioners' sugar

Mix half of the sugar with the flour. Cut the cold butter in pieces and rub it into the flour and sugar. Then mix in the egg (remove half the white if you only have a large egg) and the cognac and work very briefly with your hand—just enough to bind the pastry together—adding a little flour if it is too sticky. Take lumps of pastry and press into a 10-inch (25-cm) baking tray or tart pan.

Arrange the fruit, tightly packed, cut side up on top of the pastry, and sprinkle the remaining sugar on the plums. Bake in a preheated 375°F (190°C) oven for 50 minutes, or until the pastry is golden and the plums are very soft. The sugar draws out the plum juices, which run into the pastry and make it rise up between the plums so that these are embedded in the light pastry. Serve hot or cold, sprinkled with confectioners' sugar.

VARIATIONS

- Apricots could be used instead of plums in the same way.
- The fruit is sometimes topped with a layer of streusel (crumble): mix ½ cup (50 g) flour with 4 tablespoons superfine sugar and rub in 2 oz (50 g) butter to a crumbly texture. But I prefer it without.

Mohn Torte
Poppy-Seed Cake

Also called kindli, this is a rich poppy-seed filling sandwiched in a biscuity pastry.

For the pastry

> 2 cups (250 g) flour
> 1–2 tablespoons sugar
> 6 oz (175 g) unsalted butter
> 1 egg, lightly beaten
> 1–2 tablespoons milk, if necessary
> 1 egg yolk, to glaze
> Confectioners' sugar, to sprinkle on
>   (optional)

For the filling

> 1 cup (150 g) poppy seeds
> ¾ cup (175 ml) milk
> ½ cup (150 g) honey
> ⅓ cup (60 g) ground almonds
> ½ cup (75 g) raisins
> 1 egg, lightly beaten

For the pastry, mix the flour and sugar and rub in the butter with your hands. Mix in the egg; if this is not enough to bind the pastry into a soft dough that holds together, add a little milk, a tablespoonful at a time. Cover with plastic wrap and let rest for 30 minutes.

For the filling, put the poppy seeds in a pan with the milk and bring to the boil. Leave to soak for 30 minutes, then stir in the rest of the ingredients.

Divide the pastry dough into 2 balls. On a well-floured surface, roll the first ball out and line a greased 9–10-inch (23–26-cm) pie pan. Pinch the edges of the pastry up to make a very slight rim and spread the filling over the surface. Roll out the remaining dough and place it carefully on top of the filling. Gently press down the edges to touch the bottom pastry. Brush with egg yolk mixed with a teaspoon of water and bake in a preheated 350°F (180°C) oven for about 35 minutes, until nicely golden.

Hamantashen

MAKES ABOUT 20

At Purim (see page 33), to celebrate the demise of the hated Haman, the Sephardim make pastries in the shape of his ears and the Ashkenazim make pastries in the shape of his 3-cornered hat. There are different types of dough, including a yeast dough. This bicuity one is meltingly delicious. There are various fillings. The most traditional and most popular is a poppy-seed one. Another is with prunes.

For the dough

> 1¾ cups (250 g) flour
> A pinch of salt
> 2 tablespoons sugar
> 2 or 3 drops vanilla extract
> 5 oz (150 g) unsalted butter
> 1 egg yolk
> 2–3 teaspoons milk, if necessary
> 1 egg, lightly beaten, to glaze

For the mohn (poppy-seed) filling

> 1 cup (150 g) poppy seeds
> ¾ cup (175 ml) milk
> 2 tablespoons honey
> 4 tablespoons sugar
> 4 tablespoons raisins
> Grated zest of 1 lemon
> 1 tablespoon lemon juice
> 1½ tablespoons unsalted butter

In a bowl, mix the flour with the salt, sugar, and vanilla extract. Cut the butter in pieces and rub it into the flour. Mix in the egg yolk and press into a soft ball. Work very briefly, adding a little milk if necessary to bind it. Wrap in plastic wrap and cool in the refrigerator.

For the filling, put the poppy seeds in a pan with the milk and simmer for about 15 minutes, or until thick. Add the honey, sugar, raisins, and butter and cook 5 minutes more. Add the lemon zest and juice and the butter and mix well. Let it cool.

Divide the dough into 4 for easier handling. Roll out each piece on a floured surface with a floured rolling pin until it is ⅛ inch (3 mm) thick. Cut into 3-inch (7½-cm) rounds with a pastry cutter. Take the scraps, roll out again, and cut into rounds. (Another way is to take a lump of dough a bit bigger than a walnut and to flatten the dough by pressing it in the palm of your hand.) Put a heaping teaspoon of filling in the center of each round. Lift up the edges on 3 sides and fold over the filling to form a triangular pyramid, pinching the sides together to seal them but leaving the top open. Arrange on a greased tray and brush with beaten egg. Bake in a preheated 375°F (190°C) oven for 15–20 minutes, or until golden. Do not try to remove the pastries from the tray while they are hot, or they will crumble. Let them cool and lift them very carefully off with a spatula, because they are fragile.

VARIATIONS

• It is easier to cut the dough into 3-inch (7½-cm) squares. Place a tablespoon of filling on each, a little closer to one corner, and fold the dough over into a triangle, sealing the edges. Though not as evocative as the other shape, this too can represent a 3-cornered hat.

• For the prune filling: Blend ½ lb (250 g) of moist pitted prunes in a food processor with

½ cup (90 ml) of orange juice or enough to make a thick paste. Add 2 tablespoons of honey and, if you like, a few chopped walnuts.

Rugelach

Little Nut and Raisin Crescents

MAKES 24

These miniature crescents, which are a specialty of Hanukah and Shavuot, are very popular in America, but you do not see them much in Britain or in France. A pity, because they have a unique quality, the pastry made with curd cheese and sour cream.

For the dough

> 4 oz (100 g) unsalted butter, cold
> 4 oz (100 g) curd or cream cheese
> ½ cup (125 ml) sour cream, plus a little
>   more if necessary
> A pinch of salt
> 1¾ cups (250 g) flour
> 1 egg yolk to glaze

For the filling

> ¼ cup (50 g) superfine sugar
> 2 teaspoons ground cinnamon
> 4 tablespoons raisins, finely chopped
> ¾ cup (100 g) finely chopped walnuts

Using an electric beater or a food processor, beat the cold butter (it must be cold) to a cream. Add the curd cheese, sour cream, and pinch of salt and blend well. Add the flour—just enough

so that the dough holds together in a soft ball—and combine briefly in the processor. If necessary, add a tablespoon or more extra sour cream, or a little more flour. Do not work the dough any further. Wrap it in plastic wrap and leave it in the refrigerator for at least 4 hours.

Divide the dough into 4. With floured hands, roll each piece into a ball. On a floured surface and with a floured rolling pin, roll each ball out into a large round as thin as possible. You will need to keep dusting the sheet of dough with flour and to turn it over, because it is very sticky.

With a pointed knife, cut each round like a cake, into 6 triangular wedges. Sprinkle each wedge evenly with a mixture of the filling ingredients. Roll up each triangle tightly with the filling inside, beginning from the wider, curved end, and finishing with the point in the middle. Curve the rolls slightly into little crescents and place them, point side down, on well-greased baking trays, a little apart from each other.

Brush with egg yolk and bake in a preheated 350°F (180°C) oven for 20–25 minutes, until slightly colored. Let them cool.

Teiglach

Pastry Nuggets Cooked in Honey

Teiglach is very popular with Jews of Lithuanian origin who have kept up the tradition in South Africa. When I ask people from there if they had any foods that are different from Jewish foods elsewhere, many say they don't often find teiglach and sound very nostalgic. Honey makes it a specialty of Rosh Hashanah and celebrates the "land of milk and honey." It is

Teiglach (cont.)

very sweet and the kind you can only eat a little at a time.

For the dough

> 3 eggs
> 1 tablespoon oil
> A pinch of salt
> 1 teaspoon baking powder
> 2 cups (300 g) flour

For the syrup

> 2 cups (500 g) fragrant honey
> Grated zest of 1 lemon
> 1 teaspoon ginger

> ½ cup (50 g) chopped walnuts to garnish

Beat the eggs with the oil, salt, and baking powder. Add just enough flour to make a soft dough that holds together, mixing it in with a fork, then working it in with your hand. Knead for 10 minutes, until smooth and elastic, adding a little flour if the dough is sticky. Then wrap in plastic wrap and leave in the refrigerator for ½ hour.

With floured hands, roll the dough between your palms into pencil-thin ropes about ½ inch (1¼ cm) thick. Lay them on a floured board, and with a sharp knife cut them into ½-inch (1¼-cm) pieces.

Bring the honey to the boil in a pan and add the lemon zest and ginger. Put in the teiglach, a few at a time, so that they do not stick together, and simmer for about 15 minutes, until they are a rich brown color. If the honey becomes too thick and sticky, add a little water to thin it. Pour into an oiled dish (to prevent it from sticking) and sprinkle with walnuts.

VARIATION

• Another way is to bake the nuggets of dough in the oven for 5–10 minutes before cooking them in the honey, but that tends to harden them more.

Kichelach
Cookies—Biscuits

Offering a biscuit with a glass of wine or schnapps is one of the enduring traditions of Ashkenazi hospitality. All kinds of biscuits have joined the Sabbath repertoire, but South African Jews, more than anyone, have kept to the ones from their old Lithuanian homeland—oil-based, so that they can be offered after a meat or a dairy meal. Kichelach is what most often comes to their mind when I ask if they have anything different from the usual Ashkenazi foods. Gillian Hoffmann, a lovely woman I met at a party who works for Amnesty International, brought me more than a dozen recipes for the original classic, all of them entirely simple, varying only in the proportions of ingredients and the baking time and temperature.

> 3 eggs
> 3 tablespoons light vegetable oil
> A pinch of salt
> 2 tablespoons sugar
> About 2 cups (300 g) flour, or more

Preheat the oven to a maximum 525°F (275°C) with baking sheets lined with grease-proof or wax paper inside.

Beat the eggs with the oil, salt, and 2 teaspoons of the sugar. Gradually mix in the flour—first with a fork, then working it in with your hand—just enough to make a very soft dough that can be rolled out without sticking. Divide into 2 balls and roll out with a floured rolling pin onto a floured surface to about ¼ inch (½ cm). Sprinkle the top with the rest of the sugar and gently roll the rolling pin over the dough to press in the sugar. With a pointed knife, cut into 2-inch (5-cm) squares. Place the squares on the hot baking sheets lined with greaseproof paper and bake 1 sheet at a time for 8–10 minutes only, until the biscuits are puffed up and golden. They keep well in a tin box.

VARIATION

• A modern way is to beat 3 eggs with 2 tablespoons sugar, ½ cup (125 ml) vegetable oil, and 1 cup (150 g) self-rising flour and to drop it by the tablespoon on greaseproof paper and bake in a preheated 350°F (180°C) oven for 20–25 minutes.

Mandelbrot
Toasted Almond Slices

The name means "almond bread." Although it is not made with bread dough, the cake is sliced like bread and the slices are toasted. They are less hard and more cakey than biscotti, the Italian biscuits they resemble, and they too are traditionally served with sweet wine.

> 3 eggs
> ¾ cup (175 g) sugar
> 1 cup (250 ml) vegetable oil
> Grated zest of 1 lemon
> Grated zest of 1 orange
> A few drops of vanilla extract
> A pinch of salt
> 1 tablespoon baking powder
> 3¾ cups (500 g) flour
> ½–1 cup (100–200 g) whole blanched
>   almonds
> 1 egg yolk to glaze

Beat the eggs with the sugar to a pale, thick cream. Add the oil, lemon and orange zest, vanilla extract, salt, and baking powder and beat to a light emulsion. Now blend in the flour and work in the blanched almonds. Oiling your hands so that they do not stick, shape the dough into 2 or 3 long slim logs about 3 inches (7½ cm) wide, on a well-oiled baking sheet. Leave a good space in between because they spread. Brush with egg yolk and bake in a preheated 350°F (180°C) oven for 30 minutes, or until lightly browned.

Let the cakes cool, then cut into diagonal slices about ½ inch (1¼ cm) thick. Arrange the slices, cut side up, on baking sheets and bake in a preheated 400°F (200°C) oven for about 10 minutes, or until lightly browned. They keep for a long time in a tin box.

Joodse Boterkoeke

Jewish Butter Cake in Holland

SERVES 10

At the end of the sixteenth century, after the Dutch revolt against Spanish rule, Amsterdam became a transit center for Marranos from Spain and Portugal who went on to cities like London, Hamburg, Frankfurt, Antwerp, Bayonne, Bordeaux, and Livorno. In the Netherlands they were allowed to return openly to Judaism, and their history in the seventeenth and eighteenth centuries is one of the glories of the Diaspora. Many became leading figures in the newly created companies trading in luxury goods from the East Indies with centers in Northern Europe, where Marranos opened trading and finance houses, and around the Mediterranean seaports, where they had connections.

Despite the thriving Marrano community—and unlike other centers, such as Livorno and Tunis, where there is a strong legacy of Iberian cooking—no trace of it remains in the Dutch community, which is dominated entirely by Eastern European culture. This is also the case in other historic Marrano centers in Northern Europe, and I wonder if it has to do with the easy cultural assimilation which was possible in these countries for communities that had been Christian for 100 years. A few dishes, seen as Jewish but presenting a distinctive Dutch character, reflect the rich dairy pastures of Holland. This ever-so-buttery shortbread pastry is one of them.

2 cups (300 g) flour
1 cup (200 g) superfine sugar
A pinch of salt
6 oz (175 g) butter
1 egg, lightly beaten

Mix the flour, sugar, and salt, and rub the butter in with your hands. (You may process until this stage in the food processor.) Add only half the beaten egg and work very briefly with your hand into a soft ball. Press with the palm of your hand into a 9-inch (23-cm) pie plate lined with greaseproof or wax paper, and brush the top with the remaining egg.

Bake for 30–40 minutes in a preheated 350°F (180°C) oven until golden. It will seem much too soft, but it will firm when it cools. Turn out when cool. It will still be deliciously soft inside. Cut into small squares: it is exceedingly rich. It cuts easily, even the next day.

VARIATIONS

• Mix in ½ cup (75 g) finely chopped candied ginger or coarsely chopped almonds.
• Flavor if you like with 2 or 3 drops of vanilla extract.

Soufganioth (also called ponchkes)

Hanukah Jam Doughnuts

MAKES 12

A few nights before Christmas, I heard singing coming from the Golders Green bus station. I thought it was carols and ran to see. There was no Christmas tree but a giant *hanukiya* (candlestick). A crane had lifted a Hassid so that he could light the first candle. Men with black coats and hats were dancing and chanting in the empty bus station. Women were handing out soufganioth to passersby from the back of a van. This Austro-Hungarian peasant carnival doughnut, which became a "royal" delicacy at the French court of Marie Antoinette, has been adopted in Israel to celebrate Hanukah (see page 32) because it is fried in oil.

1 teaspoon dried yeast
¼ cup (50 ml) lukewarm milk or water
2 tablespoons sugar
1 whole egg
1 egg yolk
3 tablespoons sour cream or vegetable oil
A pinch of salt
2 or 3 drops of vanilla extract
1⅔ cups (250 g) flour, plus a little more
 if necessary
Oil for deep-frying
Apricot, red-currant, or raspberry jam
Confectioners' sugar to sprinkle on

Dissolve the yeast in the warm milk or water with 1 teaspoon of sugar and leave for 10 minutes, until it froths.

Beat the rest of the sugar with the egg and the yolk. Add the sour cream or oil, the salt, vanilla, and yeast mixture, and beat very well. Fold in the flour gradually, and continue beating until you have a soft, smooth, and elastic dough, adding more flour if necessary. Then knead for 5 minutes, sprinkling with a little flour if it is too sticky. Coat the dough with oil by pouring a drop in the bowl and turning the dough in it.

JAMS

IN EASTERN EUROPE, families kept stocks of homemade jams—usually plums, greengages, sweet or sour cherries, and berries. The fruits were washed and pitted and put to cook in a pot with the same volume of sugar and very little water for ½–1 hour, over very low heat. A few chopped bitter almonds were sometimes added.

Cover the bowl with plastic wrap and leave in a warm place to rise for about 2 hours, or until doubled in bulk.

Knead the dough again for a few minutes, then roll out on a floured surface with a floured rolling pin to ¼-inch (½-cm) thickness. With a pastry cutter, cut into 2-inch (5-cm) rounds. Make a ball out of the scraps so as not to waste them, roll out, and cut into rounds. Put a teaspoon of jam in the center of a round of dough, brush the rim with a little water to make it sticky, and cover with another round. Press the edges together to seal. Continue with the rest of the rounds and arrange them on a floured tray. Leave them to rise for about 30 minutes.

Heat 1½ inches of oil in a saucepan to medium hot. Drop in the doughnuts, a few at a time. Fry in medium-hot oil for 3–4 minutes with the lid on until brown, then turn and fry the other side for 1 minute more. Drain on paper towels. Serve sprinkled with confectioners' sugar. They are at their best when still warm and fresh.

VARIATION

• An easier way is to fry a thicker round of dough—about ½ inch (1¼ cm) thick—and when it is cool enough to handle, cut a slit with a pointed, serrated knife and put in a teaspoonful of jam.

Chremslach
Matzo Meal Pancakes

MAKES 12–14

This is the rich Alsatian version of the little Passover pancakes (also called "bubeleh"), which usually consist of only eggs and matzo meal.

> *2 eggs*
> *⅔ cup (150 ml) water*
> *1 tablespoon brandy*
> *Pinch of salt*
> *2 tablespoons sugar*
> *½ teaspoon cinnamon*
> *½ cup (75 g) fine matzo meal*
> *3 tablespoons coarsely chopped almonds*
> *4 tablespoons raisins*
> *Oil for frying*

In a bowl, put the eggs, water, brandy, salt, sugar, and cinnamon and beat well. Add the matzo meal and beat to a thick, smooth batter, adding a little more water if it seems too thick. Stir in the almonds and raisins.

Grease a preferably nonstick frying pan generously with oil and put it over medium-low heat. To cook the pancakes, first dip a tablespoon in oil so that the batter does not stick, then scoop up batter and pour by the tablespoon a little distance apart, so that the pancakes do not touch. Turn over when the batter has set and you can see a brown line around the edges. Cook until browned on both sides. Keep greasing the pan and continue with the rest of the batter. Serve hot.

VARIATION

• For a bread version of the pancakes: Soak crustless slices of white bread weighing 1 lb (500 g) in water for an hour and squeeze dry. Put it in a bowl with 5 eggs, ½ cup (100 g) sugar, a pinch of salt, a pinch of cinnamon, 1 tablespoon cognac, ⅓ cup (50 g) raisins, ⅔ cup (100 g) chopped almonds. Mix well (if too liquid, add a little matzo meal). Fry in hot oil by the tablespoon.

Ashkenazi Haroset

On the Passover Seder plate, haroset symbolizes the mortar used by the slaves in Egypt. These are the classic Eastern European ingredients. Only the proportions vary. For the Passover ritual, see page 34.

> *2 medium-sized tart apples*
> *½ cup (50 g) walnuts, chopped*
> *½–1 teaspoon cinnamon*
> *2–3 tablespoons sweet red wine*
> *1 tablespoon sugar or honey or to taste*

Peel, core, and finely chop or grate the apples. Mix with the rest of the ingredients.

Cherries in Brandy

Wash and dry 2 lbs (1 kg) cherries and prick each with a needle in a few places. Put them in a jar, sprinkling each layer abundantly with sugar—about 1¼ cups (250 g) total. Leave un-covered for a day. The following day, cover with brandy, seal the jar hermetically, and leave to macerate for 8 weeks at least. The preserve lasts for months.

Other fruit that can be preserved in the same way include plums, greengages, and muscat grapes. They must be of good quality and ripe.

The Schwab family of Libau, Latvia, c. 1908

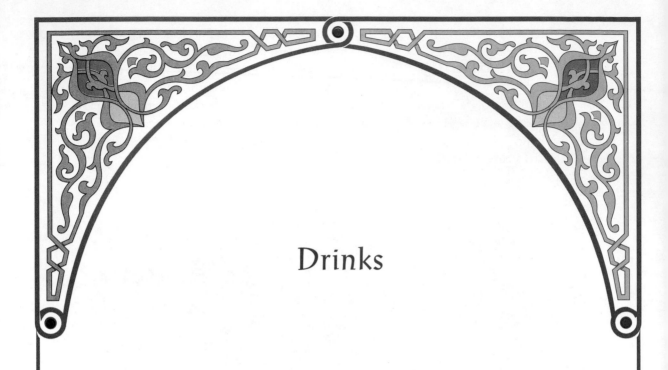

Drinks

AT JEWISH EVENTS in Eastern Europe and Russia, the men drank liquor before and during the meal. There was vodka in Poland and Russia, plum brandy (Tzuica) and mastic-flavored mastica in Romania and the Balkans, schnapps and (plum) slivovitz throughout the area. After the meal, fruit brandies and liqueurs were served. They did not drink wine, with a few exceptions, such as spritz, a mixture of dry white wine and carbonated mineral water, which was the fashionable drink at Jewish eating places on the Danube.

Tea was drunk black, or weak and with lemon, from the samovar and sipped from a glass through a small lump of sugar between the teeth. It was often served with a fruit preserve, a spoonful of which might be stirred into the tea. In the shtetl, "coming in for a glass of tea" meant finding out how your neighbor lived. Raspberry syrup was the miracle drug of the shtetl, given to the sick.

The production of carbonated water was a Jewish industry in Russia which was carried over to America as seltzer, the drink that became famous in its blue-and-green glass siphon bottles. The classic New York Jewish "egg cream" (no egg and no cream) is a mixture of milk and chocolate syrup with seltzer spritzed in. I discovered it when Raymond Sokolov invited me to dinner at Sammy's on Chrystie Street, off Delancey Street, in New York. Here are Raymond's instructions for one serving from the book he wrote with Susan Friedland, *The Jewish American Kitchen:* pour three ounces of milk into a glass and spritz in eight ounces of seltzer, spoon in two ounces of chocolate

*Delivering liquor, Jurbarkas,
Lithuania, 1913*

Selling seltzer, Proskurov

syrup, and combine with vigorous wrist action.

Coffee-drinking was adopted in Vienna and Budapest, where Jewish intellectuals, writers, artists, and musicians formed the bulk of café society at the time of the Hapsburg Empire and up to the Second World War. It was Jewish émigrés who transported the model of the Viennese coffeehouse all over the world, with the bentwood chairs and marble tables, rococo moldings, great mirrors and chandeliers, old prints and posters, as well as the black-and-white waitress's uniform and the doughnuts and pastries. I have just heard that an Israeli company opening a chain of coffeehouses, in imitation of the Starbucks company which swept America, could not bring themselves to emulate the ultramodern minimalist style, because in Israel coffee is associated with old Vienna or Italy.

ISRAEL–FORGING A NATIONAL STYLE
WITH GEFILTE FISH
AND COUSCOUS

W HEN I FIRST went to Israel, more than twenty years ago, to see my relatives and to find out what was happening in the kitchen, people would say, "Please don't write anything bad," or "Why don't you write a sexy novel instead?" Visitors then always complained about the food and had praise only for Arab restaurants, most of which were mere kiosks at the back of gas stations. They would ask, "What happened to all the foods from all those different countries?" This year, friends were keen to take me to wonderful new restaurants, to make me try new products and to talk about cooking. But when I asked about trends I was told, "It's for you to find out and to tell us," as though an outsider was better able to discern.

Since the establishment of the state, everything has changed constantly, as we should expect from a new land of immigrants from more than seventy countries where each new wave of settlers has brought something new. Culinary trends are sometimes contradictory. They have to do with the economic and political situation, with the direction the food industries take, the fruits the kibbutzim decide to grow, the fish that are farmed. Trends also depend on the mix of population, on who works in the kitchens of the land, who sells food in the street, and who is in the business of catering for weddings and bar mitzvahs. Moreover, ideology is involved. In the early days of the state, the Diaspora and its food was something to be forgotten, but now it is back in a big way.

What you can see is a longing for a national cuisine so that, as Israelis say, "we can feel at ease at each other's tables." Thirty years ago, an Israeli writer expressed the view that: "We will be near to becoming one nation when we can sit at each other's tables without feeling unease or strangeness. Liking each other's foods is a big step towards liking each other." It is part of the need for cohesion in this ethnically mixed society, where cooking in the home is a mosaic acquired in the four corners of the world—where Eastern European food is considered "Jewish" and the rest "ethnic," and where Arab street food such as falafel, hummus, babaghanouzh, shakshouka, and Moroccan cigars is considered Israeli. Only turkey schnitzel, which is the main food eaten regularly by everybody, and not shared with neighboring Arab countries, is identified as purely Israeli.

Trendy chefs and food writers try to create a new Israeli cuisine using Biblical ingredients such as honey, figs, and pomegranates; indigenous foods, like prickly pears and chickpeas; and Israeli produce, like avocado, citrus, mango, and cream cheese, which the national fruit and dairy boards are promoting. They use French, Italian, and Chinese techniques, and flavors from the ethnic communities. They do so with an eye on *The New York Times'* food pages and *Gourmet* magazine and the latest fads in California. America's appeal is powerful, and it is easier for Israelis to identify with a young country of emigration. They call what they are doing "melting-pot" cooking and "fusion cuisine."

There is another kind of "fusion cuisine" which develops by itself and has nothing to do with fads and fashions. One example is the falafel in pita now offered by vendors with a choice of salads and pickles and peppery relishes such as the Yemeni zhoug and Moroccan harissa. A new hybrid, which I found at an Ethiopian snack bar near the old Tel Aviv bus station, is the "Jerusalem mix"—a chopped-up mixture of fried chicken giblets and offal—flavored with the fiery-hot spices of Ethiopia. One could say that much of the food produced in the army, hospitals, schools, and institutional cafeterias can be classed as "fusion cuisine." A disgruntled hotel food-and-beverages manager called what has developed in the kitchens of the land "a horrible mishmash of what cooks learn from each other, usually when they are in the army."

The mishmash is a far cry from the cooking of one of the first established Jewish communities in Palestine, which was made up of families from Syria, Lebanon, and Turkey, who came to be known as the "Jerusalem aristocracy." They were highly sophisticated about food and possessed a wide repertoire of delicacies on which they lavished much time, starting sometimes to prepare on Sunday for the following Sabbath. Their dishes—pies like sambousak, pasteles, and borekas, vegetable gratins and stuffed vegetables, rice and bulghur pilafs, delicately flavored with herbs and spices and aromatics like tamarind, sour pomegranate syrup, and flower waters—are now considered Jerusalem classics.

Apart from these Oriental Jews, established long before the creation of the state of Israel, there were those who came to Palestine to die, and ultrareligious Ashkenazi communities who came for a pious life. The Zionist *halutzim* (pioneers), who migrated from Russia and Poland at the beginning of the century to start the first kibbutzim, or cooperative settlements, brought with them a deep sense of mission and socialist ideology, and they founded Israel as a puritanical society with the ideals of the simple life. The bread, olives, cheese, and raw vegetables which they ate at 9 a.m., after they had been working for four hours in the fields, was the basis of the famous kibbutz breakfast, which in its more opulent form is standard fare in all hotels in Israel today. The self-service consists of many types of cheese, soft and hard; pickled and smoked herring; yogurt, leben, and sour cream; olives and hard-boiled eggs, served up with a variety of breads and accompanied by fresh orange juice and coffee. Tomatoes, cucumbers, and scallions are served whole for everyone to create his or her own salad. There are also a variety of prepared salads including grated carrot, peppers, and cole slaw, and omelettes, eggplant purees, hummus, and pickles, followed by compotes of figs and plums and fresh fruit. These "kibbutz foods" have become a national institution and have been adopted by Israelis for their light everyday evening meals as well as for breakfast. The puritanical legacy is expressed today as a profound distaste for the Israeli enthusiasm for food, seen as "conspicuous consumption" and "oral fixation."

The early pioneers and the first immigrants from Europe to the newly established state were happy to abandon the "Yiddish" foods of Russia and Poland as a revolt against a past identity and an old life. Zionism's early desire had been to leave the shtetl behind and to break with everything it stood for. The new state lived by a vision of the future and looked with distaste at the foods that represented exile and martyrdom. There was no place in the Promised Land for food that smelled of persecution and anti-Semitism. Anyway, it was not suitable in the hot Mediterranean climate.

The new Hebrew type, the antithesis of the old passive Jew, looked for his identity in the Bible, and it was assumed that the Yemenites and Oriental Sephardim were closest to the early Jews of Biblical times. The European immigrants learned from the old, established Sephardim how to use the local produce, especially vegetables such as zucchini, peppers, eggplant, and artichokes, which were new to them. The food of the local fellahin (villagers) and Bedouin Arabs had a strong appeal for the early Zionists. They were shepherds and dressed like the Biblical figures depicted by nineteenth-century painters, and represented their forefathers in appearance and way of life. Arab and Oriental food like hummus and falafel, both of which are based on the indigenous chickpea, exerted a powerful pull on the young. It was very tasty and cheap, and it was offered by street vendors, at a time when eating a cheap snack on the go was becoming a way of life.

The first ten or more years after the establishment of the state in 1948, when the country was isolated and at war with all her neighbors, have left their mark in the kitchen. Many refugees lived in absorption camps; apartments were small and sometimes had three families sharing. People cooked on tiny oil stoves in pots called "sirpella" (we called them *casseroles palestiniennes*), which are still used today to save on fuel. There were no refrigerators, only iceboxes, and at mealtime dining tables had to be dragged from under school books and sewing. The Tzena period, as it is called, was a time of rationing, of making do from nothing, from what you got with coupons. And close memories of the Holocaust were not conducive to inspired cooking. A legacy of those times of scarcity and austerity is a repertoire of mock or simulated foods which are the popular butt of humorists. They were ingenious ways of making something out of something else—chopped liver from eggplant,

Halutzim—early pioneers—harvesting in an agricultural collective in Palestine

applesauce from zucchini, radish jam as a substitute for cherry jam, semolina pudding instead of whipped cream, and turkey as a substitute for veal schnitzel or for lamb in kebabs. Restaurants at the time also served an ubiquitous fish "fillet"—an unidentifiable compressed fish mixture imported from Norway—nondescript "white" cheese, yogurt and salad, bean-and-vegetable soup, mushy pasta with a little goulash. You only went to the restaurant if your mother was sick and there was nothing to eat in the house. Pioneers and volunteers never went; by their standards, only decadent people spent time in restaurants.

Part of the normalization process in the late 1970s—explained as the euphoria of finally emerging from the trauma of deprivation and austerity and the constant threat of war into a new affluence with greater travel facilities and the peace with Egypt—was an explosion of interest in food, from French cuisine and the exotic dishes of China, Hawaii, and Bali, to cooking with wine and herbs and healthy vegetarianism. Eating out in restaurants became a popular recreation.

At home today, people still on the whole eat according to their background. In street markets, as in the frozen and chilled food sections in the supermarket, you see a variety of foods of different origins. You find Bulgarian yogurt-and-cucumber salad and Bulgarian palamida (marinated bonito), Iraqi kubba and Syrian kibbeh, Turkish borek, Yemeni flaky and spongy breads and hot peppery zhoug, Moroccan cigars, Polish lokshen pudding, Russian piroshki, Hungarian blintzes, and Viennese tortes. Every group of immigrants has made an impact, and the repertoire of foods at people's disposal is forever growing.

The greatest impact has come from the large Sephardi migration, and most particularly from Morocco, which forms the largest single ethnic group. The Sephardim are seen as knowing and caring more about food. A young Moroccan cook explained: "The Ashkenazim are more concerned with getting on, studying and going to university. We want to enjoy our life. We like to keep the family together round the table with friends chatting and joking. The mother cooks so that the children come back on Shabbath, even when they are married."

For years, the kitchens of the land—from the army, schools, and hospitals to restaurants and hotels—have recruited their staff from the working-class population of Oriental Jews, from countries like Morocco, Tunisia, Turkey, Iraq, Kurdistan, and Yemen, and Israeli Arabs. Caterers too are from the Middle East. But despite its predominance, North African and Oriental food is seen as low-class, poor food. As Israelis often complain, it is the poor Sephardim who settled in Israel, while the rich and educated have gone elsewhere.

When I express my appreciation of Moroccan dishes to some of my Israeli friends, they look surprised, to say the least. The truth is that the cooking standards of Moroccan immigrants have deteriorated in Israel more than in other countries. One catering manager explained it in this way: "The cooks have rejected their mothers' cooking, because they see it as part of a humiliating backward culture. Yet, after learning the basics at the army catering school, they fall back on what they vaguely remember from home." In the early days of their massive immigration, the Sephardim were labeled backward and primitive. It was believed that the way to transform them into modern Israelis was to make them forget their backward Oriental past and assimilate them into the dominant Ashkenazi culture. The "melting-pot" policy was at the expense of Sephardi cultural pride and identity. It has a lot to answer for in the state of the kitchens.

Things have changed now. Intensive attempts are made to restore the lost pride of all the ethnic communities by reviving and disseminating their rich cultural heritage. The media make much of ethnic foods. Women's magazines and radio announcers ask people to send in recipes from their old hometowns and children are encouraged to bring their mothers' special dishes to share at school. Although it is still not fashionable for trendy restaurants to admit to Arab and Oriental influences, "Mediterranean" styles are in and young chefs visit their parents' old homelands to rediscover the more refined dishes.

The Diaspora has become fashionable, with a revival of interest in roots in old homelands and a strong nostalgia for the past. While Israelis are struggling to define themselves, confronted daily by the questions of their rights to the land and of who is a Jew, they have felt the need for an older cultural heritage to fall back on. Young people are rediscovering their roots through the Jewish writers of America and a revival of Yiddish music, theater, and food. Gefilte fish, cholent, kishke, tzimmes, and lokshen pudding are "in," imbued with the charm of nostalgia and sentimentality. Once you found these dishes in the big hotels catering for American tourists; now the trendy cafés that offer "Jewish food" are places where the young congregate.

Like other aspects of cultural heritage, the food is being decided by the new generation. People look at each other's food when they get together on Friday nights and when they eat at weddings and bar mitzvahs. As one caterer told me, they have to offer an enormous selection, because their clients choose an enormous list so that "everybody will be satisfied." There has to be everything—from gefilte fish and latkes to Moroccan cigars and stuffed vine leaves.

Israelis love food and, judging by how busy the vendors are all day, they eat all the time. National insecurity is given as one reason for the constant noshing or grazing. Another is the traditional Eastern European idea of good mothering by constant feeding, immortalized in the old joke about the Jewish mother who presses food on her offspring to induce guilt, and in the refrain of a seventies song that translates, "Danile, Danile, eat your bananile!" Who knows? Things change so fast, by the time this book comes out, Israel might be on the gastronomic tourist map.

The Sephardi World

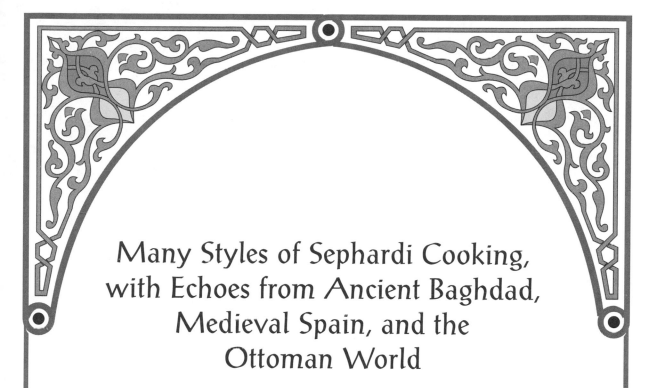

Many Styles of Sephardi Cooking, with Echoes from Ancient Baghdad, Medieval Spain, and the Ottoman World

WHAT WE CALL Sephardi cooking today is the cooking of Mediterranean and Oriental Jews. There are four broad styles. Judeo-Spanish, which is Turkish and Balkan, is the cooking of the Jews of Iberian ancestry who went on to live in the Ottoman heartlands. North African or Maghrebi Jewish cuisine includes Moroccan, Tunisian, Algerian, and Libyan. Then there is Judeo-Arab cooking, which is at its best in Syria and Lebanon, and the Jewish cooking of Iraq and Iran. But the cooking of the Jews in this part of the world is so immensely varied, eclectic, and regional—different in every country and sometimes in every city—that it defies definition. Its main characteristic is its diversity. It sometimes varies even within a city. A long tradition among the Sephardim allowed Jews leaving one area to establish their own unique congregation in their

new community. These separate congregations persisted for centuries, and in the same spirit different styles of cooking were also maintained. Dishes from Italian, Indian, and other communities that have unique styles are included in the section.

Because the Sephardim have left their old—mostly Arab—homelands only in the last forty years, and they have not had two or three generations of integration like the Ashkenazim, their cooking has not yet become standardized. They are still attached to the dishes of their hometowns, while the need to preserve family identity and the memory of an old life is strong and the generation that cooked in the old homelands is still around.

A friend who came to dinner asked, "Is anybody ever going to be able to taste these dishes anywhere? Could we ever walk into a restaurant and ask for them? Could they become fashionable, like Italian or Mediterranean food?" In the last year in Golders Green, which is near where I live in London, several kosher restaurants and takeout caterers have opened, specializing in Oriental foods. They serve Moroccan cigars and spiced fish, Turkish borek, Syrian kibbeh, Yemeni breads and peppery relishes. In France, where the community has taken on a North African character since Algerian, Tunisian, and Moroccan Jews flooded in, there are dozens of Sephardi butchers and North African kosher restaurants. In Israel, from time to time, you find a restaurant that specializes in one particular type of food, such as Iraqi Kurdish, Syrian, Bukharan, "Tripolitanian" (Libyan), or Yemeni. But the most refined Sephardi dishes are to be found in the Diaspora—and only in the home. They represent some of the "secret" cuisines of the world. No doubt the opportunities for tasting them in public places will grow, but they will still be only a minute proportion of the great repertoire that exists in Jewish homes. Twenty years ago, Sephardi dishes were entirely unknown. It is only in the last few years that books have started to come out featuring the cooking of individual communities. As for being popular, the cooking includes that of the entire Mediterranean world, which is currently the most fashionable cuisine because it is seen as healthy and full of flavor.

Sephardi cooking is sensual, aromatic, and colorful. It makes use of anything that gives flavor—seeds, bits of bark, resins, pods, petals, pistils, and flower waters. The Sephardim had a sunny, hedonistic nature. They were less concerned with the inner, spiritual life than the Ashkenazim, more sensitive to beauty and pleasure; and good eating has always been part

of their traditional Jewish life. Their cooking is of a kind that lifts the spirits. The warm and sunny world they lived in had something to do with this, as had their way of life and historical experience.

Hospitality had an all-important place in their culture. They entertained warmly, graciously, and constantly. To honor a guest, especially on a Jewish holiday or family celebration, was the ultimate joy. Festivities went on forever. In Morocco, for instance, there were seven days of celebration for a birth or circumcision, seven days for a bar mitzvah, two weeks for a wedding—the day of showing the trousseau; the henna day; the day of the mikvah (ritual bath); the day of the presents; the day of the fish, when the bride stepped over a fish to ensure fecundity. And after the week of celebrations, when the newlyweds returned from their honeymoon, for an entire week they went around visiting relatives. The year was a constant succession of events, and food was always part of it.

In the recent past, Jews in Islamic lands were economically and culturally depressed, and indeed their culture is still considered backward and primitive in Israel. For what has been happening in Israel, see page 202. But the Sephardi heritage is beginning to be recognized in Israel, and Oriental Jews are beginning to assert their ways and customs. Their food is one part of their culture that has become dominant although it is still not valued.

The repertoire of Sephardi dishes, which can be simple, crude, and primitive but is often refined and sophisticated, even in the poorer communities—with elaborate procedures, delicate flavorings, and appealing presentation—is a clue to a once rich and dynamic civilization. Many of the grand dishes and refinements were acquired during the great periods in the

Sephardi experience—from the eighth to the twelfth century in Baghdad, from the mid-tenth to the mid-twelfth in Spain, from the late fifteenth to the late seventeenth in the Ottoman world. They represent times of synthesis between Jewish and other civilizations, and periods when Jewish elites were in an elevated environment, as they were when they were part of a royal court. Though there is a great deal of poor food, a part of Sephardi cooking was shaped by an aristocratic elite and is a legacy of court traditions.

The world of the Sephardim was located within Islamic civilization. With the exception of Christian Italy and Christian Spain, all the lands where the Sephardim lived before the seventeenth century were under Islamic rule. Even the Jews of Spain came, for the most part, with the Arabs, mainly from North Africa, and when they were expelled in 1492, they returned, for the most part, to the Islamic world. Whereas Ashkenazi cooking on the whole was the cooking of a people closed in on itself with little contact with the non-Jewish population and the outside world, Sephardi cooking developed in communities whose people had an intimate contact with and were deeply influenced by the world they lived in. Sephardi life was characterized by an openness which was the result of generations of living at ease with their neighbors. Sephardi Jews lived close to each other, in quarters, by choice. They were never forced to, except for one period in Morocco when they were confined to their mellah, supposedly for their own protection. Officially, in Muslim lands, Jews, like Christians, were considered *dhimmis*—protected subjects. This meant that they were granted security of life, property, and worship and allowed a great measure of internal communal autonomy, but they had to accept an inferior status

with certain legal and social disabilities, in particular a liability to special taxes. In practice, the official limitations were usually disregarded. Jews were not subject to occupational restrictions such as existed in Europe, and they were rarely excluded from taking part in the intellectual, cultural, and political activities and the commercial and economic life of the country. In times of stress and instability the Islamic social system could become harsh and restrictive, but it rarely made close personal relations between Jews and Arabs impossible.

The Sephardim were never isolationist. What has been called the special symbiosis of the Jews with the Islamic world and the complex environment of ethnic and religious groups that existed within it produced an enhanced quality of Jewish life with an emphasis on style and taste. It also meant that Jews had access to various regional styles of cooking.

Despite the diversity, there is a certain unity in the cooking of the Sephardim, and you find echoes of dishes from one community to another. It is because the countries they inhabited once shared the same occupiers and influences, and also because the Jewish communities had links of their own.

The French historian Fernand Braudel explains in *The Mediterranean* that the extent and immensity of intermingling of Mediterranean cultures is all the more rich in consequences since, in this zone of exchanges, cultural groups were so numerous from the start. In one region they might remain distinctive, elsewhere they merged to produce the extraordinary charivari suggestive of Eastern ports as described by romantic poets: a rendezvous for every race, every religion, every kind of man, for every hairstyle, fashion, food, and manner to be found in the Mediterranean. He quotes Théophile Gautier's descriptions in *Voyage à Constantinople* of the overwhelming carnival of a spectacle at every port of call, everywhere the same Greeks, the same Armenians, the same Albanians, Levantines, Jews, Turks, and Italians. Braudel adds that cultural entanglement is to be found in all the cosmopolitan ports, from Barcelona, Genoa, Venice, Livorno, and Marseilles to Salonika, Alexandria, and Istanbul.

All the old civilizations—Greek, Roman, Arab, Ottoman, and others—that spread over the area have left their lasting marks as much in the produce and the way of cooking as in everything else. And the Jews were everywhere. As Braudel puts it, "As one prince persecuted, another protected them; as one economy ruined them, another made their fortune; as one city closed its doors, another opened them; as one civilization expelled them, another received them with open arms." They became the heirs of various civilizations, whose gifts they passed on to others.

The early history of the Jews was played out in the Middle East. The Bible claims that the early Semites who became the Jews are descended from Abraham, who was born in Ur in Mesopotamia (now Iraq) in 1800 B.C. He had a vision of the one true God and traveled westwards with his followers and flocks to Canaan (now Israel) to settle his people as a distinctive nation. The Sephardi story begins twenty-six hundred years ago, when the Babylonian King Nebuchadnezzar destroyed Jerusalem and its temple and carried most of its inhabitants back to Babylon (near present Baghdad). When the Persian King Cyrus conquered Babylon fifty years later, he allowed the Jews to return to their Holy Land and rebuild their Temple, but many chose to stay. When Roman Palestine declined as a center of religious learning in the third century

A.D., the leadership of world Jewry was transferred to the Babylon community, which had thrived under the Sassanian Persian Empire, and Babylonian Jewry remained the leading community of the Jewish dispersion until the eleventh century. It was the center of learned Jewish academies, where the Babylonian Talmud, the great book of oral Jewish Law, was compiled, and where the square Hebrew script originated. And it was here that the foundations of Sephardi culture were laid.

When Babylonia became part of the Persian Empire, the Jews prospered and flourished. A Jewish nobility emerged, which was close to the Sassanian courts and took its styles and manners and culinary practices from the local aristocracy. Various Persian dishes, such as sweet-and-sour dishes and combinations of meat and fruit, entered the Jewish repertoire. They are one of the recurring characteristics of Sephardi cooking today. Jews show a greater fondness for sweet-and-sour flavors—obtained by mixing sour pomegranate juice, tamarind, sour grapes, lemon, or vinegar with sugar or honey—and also for meat with fruit, than Muslims do. Even in modern Baghdad, Jewish specialties mysteriously show a stronger Persian influence than those of the Muslim population.

Before the advent of Islam, there were Jews in Arabia and large communities in Southwest Asia and North Africa; there were Aramaic-speaking Jews in the Fertile Crescent (Syria and Palestine) and Hellenized Jews in Alexandria; there were Romaniot Jews of the Roman and later the Byzantine Empire; Jews in the Visigoth kingdom of Spain; and Jews of the Persian Empire, which ruled over Iran and Iraq. In the seventh and eighth centuries, when the Arabs spread across the Middle East and the Mediterranean in great conquering waves, joining one country after another under a vast Islamic caliphate stretching from the Iberian Peninsula and the shores of the Atlantic to the borders of India and China, the numerous Jewish communities dotted across the area found themselves subjects of the one Islamic state. That state, which was eventually divided into different states—Abbassid, Andalusian, Umayyad, and Fatimid—was centered first in Damascus, then in Baghdad, for a time in North Africa, and later in Spain. The whole region, a mosaic of different cultures, was homogenized to a degree by religion and language and by a culture that absorbed the various elements that had made up the area. In the Islamic world, the Jews were usually one of several religious and ethnic minorities. They integrated the society in which they lived, adopted the Arabic language, and to a large extent shared the same culture and way of life.

The empire created commercial opportunities and cultural intercommunication between its far-flung regions. It spread the cultivation of various new products, such as rice and eggplants from India, spinach fron Nepal, melons from Egypt, figs from Constantinople, pomegranates from Persia, watermelons from Africa. New vegetables, like artichokes, asparagus, and colocasia, and new fruits, including oranges, lemons, quinces and pomegranates, apricots and peaches, almonds and pistachios, were grown across the whole region. Jews were involved in the trade that brought olive and sesame oil, dried and salted fish, dried fruit and nuts, honey, and cheese from one part of the empire to another and from outside it. They brought spices and pepper from the Far East and India by ship to the Persian Gulf, transferred them to camel caravans, and took them across the desert to Cairo and Aleppo, where they controlled the markets.

The entire caravan trade was concentrated in their hands. They traveled from one end of the empire to another and made contact with their brethren everywhere. Regular and intense communications were established between Jews in countries as far apart as Iran, Morocco, Spain, and Yemen, with exchanges of rabbis, correspondence on points of Jewish Law and political matters, and trade. Migration was made easy. All this had a unifying effect on the cooking.

Baghdad became the seat of the Abbassid Caliphate in 762. The city that was built by the Abbassids remained the cultural and political capital of the Islamic Empire until the eleventh century. It was a magnificent city, the hub of international trade and the center of science and the arts, attracting people from all over the empire—including Jews, who flooded in. A prosperous and leisured Jewish elite of courtiers and merchants, physicians, mathematicians and philosophers, poets and musicians emerged, aspiring to the good life.

Cooking in the imperial capital reached magnificent heights. The culinary tradition, which was a synthesis of regional styles with Greek and Indian influences and dishes from the old Sassanian Persian courts, is one of the aspects of the Abbassid society that endured, its influence extending to other great centers of the empire, most particularly to North Africa and Spain, where it is still evident in the cooking of Morocco and Tunisia, Andalusia, Valencia, and Catalonia.

During the reign of Harun al-Rashid (786–809), cooking became a high art. Courtiers, poets, and physicians wrote recipes and poems extolling dishes. Jewish physicians were involved with food through dietetics, which was a branch of medicine. In writings of the period they are depicted sitting at the table with the caliphs advising them on what food was good for the body and the spirit. Medical books contained sections on the defects and attributes of each food and also on how to cook them. The rich culinary literature, which blossomed at the time, did not survive, except for one manuscript written by Abu Muhammad al-Muzzafar ibn Nasr ibn Sayyar al-Warraq in the tenth century. It was edited only recently by Kaj Ohrnberg and Sahban Mroueh in Helsinki. But a later, thirteenth-century cookery manuscript gives a good idea of the grand medieval Arab tradition. It is an object of fascination to gourmet scholars and has been the source of many a modern banquet in the style of the Abbassids. Called the *Kitab al Tabikh* and written by Muhammad ibn al-Hassan ibn Muhammad ibn al-Karim al Katib al-Baghdadi, it was first translated by Professor A. J. Arberry in 1939. I saw the translation more than thirty years ago, when I was researching my *Book of Middle Eastern Food.* I had been collecting hundreds of recipes from the region, and I was struck by the similarities of cooking today in North Africa. Now, in researching Jewish food, I am fascinated by the extent to which elements of the old Abbassid cuisine have been inherited by Jews who live in many different countries.

Al-Baghdadi's collection features fish dishes, rice dishes, stuffed vegetables, savory pastries, and sweets. A main theme is cubed meat or chicken or meatballs combined with chickpeas or lentils and such vegetables as spinach, turnips, leeks, and eggplants, or with fruit. There is meat cooked with apricots, quinces, peaches and dates, apples and pears. Garlic and onions are much used. Aromatics include cinnamon, cumin, coriander, ginger, turmeric, mastic, saffron, and sumac. There are caraway and sesame, mint, rocket, and rue. Souring agents such as sour grape juice, tamarind, and pomegranate, are called for. Orange-blossom water and rose water are used in sweets. Ground almonds and ground rice are used as thickeners; raisins and pine nuts, blanched almonds, and pistachios as garnishes.

This kind of cuisine is familiar throughout the Middle East today, but it is also part of the common threads that characterize Sephardi cooking, even in communities where it is not part of the local cuisine. Of course, the Jews could have picked up their tastes and culinary practices anywhere at any time, but it is not too wild a conjecture to believe that what was assimilated in medieval Baghdad and passed on became the basis of their "haute cuisine." After all, Babylonian and Baghdadi Jews were the leaders of world Jewry for more than ten centuries. They traveled backwards and forwards in the Islamic world, spreading their religious traditions and also setting the tone in matters of taste for their coreligionists. Think of the attraction of the hamburgers and Coca-Cola spread by our superpower today. The haute cuisine of Baghdad was a legacy of Iran. It was exported by the Arabs especially to North Africa and Spain, but the Jews passed it on along the same route through their own channels.

In Muslim Spain

WHEN THE ARAB MUSLIMS invaded Spain in 711, the Jews—who had lived there since the destruction of the Temple but had suffered a hundred years of persecution at the hands of the last Visigoth kings—fought on the Arab side. As the Arabs marched north and took one city after another, the Jews held the garrisons and helped take control of the cities. When virtually all of Spain came under Muslim rule, the Jews became administrators and intermediaries between the new rulers and the

Christian population and helped set up a new order.

Jewish communities flourished in Muslim Spain, which lasted in the south until 1492, when the last bastion, Granada, was defeated. Muslim Spain was a strong military power and a very wealthy state. It attracted a mass immigration of Jews from around the Mediterranean, and especially from North Africa. Large Jewish communities came into existence in the major cities in southern Spain—which was given the name Al-Andalus. Toledo, Córdoba, Granada, and Seville became important Jewish centers. Jews established themselves in every sector of the economy, and by the tenth century were deeply rooted in the local society, alongside the Arabs, Berbers, and Mozarab Christians. They spoke Arabic and wore Arab clothes. They acquired land and developed estates. They owned fields and vineyards. A Jewish peasantry came into being, which earned its living from agriculture—working the soil, growing grain, tending fruit, olive trees, and vineyards. Andalusia had fruit trees in profusion. The methods of irrigation developed by the Arabs produced crops three times a year. Jews were artisans and merchants and also government administrators, statesmen, soldiers, and financiers. Jewish scholarship in philosophy and poetry, arts and sciences went through a glorious period. The Jews participated in the flowering of an extraordinarily rich new civilization, which became known as the "Golden Age of Spain." They played a role in the symbiosis of Muslim and Spanish Christian culture. The Muslim culture was a combination of Syrian (the first Umayyad Caliphate was based in Damascus, and the first Andalusian Caliphate was also Umayyad); North African Berber, represented by the soldiers who made up the army and settled; and the various different groups—Iraqis, Yemenites, and from the Hedjaz—who constituted the retinues of Arabs brought by the caliphs. A major influence was from Baghdad through the Abbassid Caliphate.

As Spanish cities filled with beautiful palaces and mosques, public baths and caravanerais, orchards and running water, harems with concubines and courtesans were established in the royal courts in the manner of Damascus and Baghdad. The Abbassids from Baghdad revived in the royal courts ceremonies and celebrations after the manner of the former kings of Persia. An Iraqi Kurdish musician called Ziryab, a refugee from the court of Harun al-Rashid in Baghdad, who was introduced to the court of Córdoba by a Jewish musician, Abu an Nasser Mansur, is credited with revolutionizing "the art of living" in Andalusia. He set the pattern of social life and the etiquette of manners. He showed the nobles in the capital how to dress in silk and to wear white in summer, how to cut their hair short and how to dye their beards, how to play the lute and how to eat. He introduced grand and refined dishes, ways to set the table, how to proceed with a succession of courses and to behave at table. Many Jews were part of the upper strata of Andalusian society and reached high office at the royal court, and many were already familiar with Ziryab's ideas of gracious living and eating through their contacts with Babylonian Jewry, and helped to promote them.

From the beginning of the Arab conquest, the indigenous Jews of Spain, who had been isolated from their brethren, established contact with the Jewish authorities in Baghdad and turned to them for guidance and inspiration on religious and legal matters. The rabbis of North Africa were the intermediaries between the Babylonian academies and the Jews of Spain. Missives about questions of Jewish

Jewish barrio, Hervás, Spain

depend on Spanish Jewry for financial help. The Jewish community of Muslim Spain took over their mantle, assumed the leadership of the Jewish world, and became the most influential community in Europe. Jewish life in Spain at that time was at its most noble, gracious, and joyful. Walking around the old Jewish quarters of Spanish cities today, you can imagine just how attractive the life must have been. The well-to-do inhabitants would sit in their marble or tiled courtyards under a cool trellis of climbing vines and scented jasmine, shaded by a fig tree and an orange tree with the sound of water running from a fountain and the notes of a lute floating from a neighboring house. A stew would simmer slowly in the ashes of the clay oven in the corner. Large glazed pots filled with preserves, olive oil, honey, dried fruit, nuts, grains, legumes would be stacked under the staircase. The houses had blind, windowless walls to protect the intimacy of the family. (The balconies we see today were added on centuries later.) Living rooms, which opened onto the courtyards, were furnished with divans covered by opulent materials and embroidered cushions, with small low tables and velvet and silk hangings. Brasiers with burning coal heated the rooms in the winter. Candles in decorative candlesticks lit them at night. The bedrooms were on a floor above, giving onto a gallery that overlooked the courtyard.

In 1992, invited by the American organization Oldways Preservation and Exchange Trust to a conference in Seville, I stole some time by myself to wander around the old Jewish quarter of Seville, intoxicated by the smell of orange trees, by the thrilling sight of courtyards through ornate wrought-iron gates, and by the narrow winding streets which bore the names of relatives and friends of mine. I found myself pitying the poor Sevillian Jews who arrived in

Law were sent by the Spanish communities to Kairouan, near Tunis, where official representatives of the academies were located, and then by way of Fostat, Palestine, and Syria to Baghdad. The Jews of Spain followed Babylonian Jewry in the practice of religion and in the pronunciation of Hebrew. Culturally, they were in a sense a colony of Babylonian Jewry. This meant that in matters of life-style they were directly connected with and absorbed the special civilization that had flowered in Baghdad.

By the eleventh century, when Judeo-Spanish culture was in full flower, Baghdad was in decline, and the impoverished Babylonian Jews had to the Jewish quarter of Cairo in the fifteenth century, and feeling that if I were given the choice of a place and time in history to dwell in I would choose Spain in its "Golden Age."

Despite wars, the chemistry of the three cultures and three religions that constituted Muslim Spain produced a tolerant, convivial civilization which loved music, song, and dance and story-telling; where everything that exalted life, that could make it more agreeable and beautiful, was cultivated and encouraged; and where the company of others was prized above all. That experience had a great impact in shaping the Sephardi character.

The epicureanism and the exuberant food that that period produced are reflected in cookbooks and books on dietetics and medicine that a few scholars have recently translated. In *La Cuisine Andalouse: Un Art de Vivre, XIe–XIIIe Siècle*, Lucie Bolens has translated three hundred medieval Andalusian recipes into French and explains the place of gastronomy in that exceptional society. The majority of the recipes are from an anonymous thirteenth-century Arabic cookery manual first edited and translated into Spanish by Ambrosio Huici Miranda entitled *Kitab al Tabikh fil Maghrib wal Andalus* (*Cookbook of the Maghreb and Andalusia*). The book has also been translated into English and richly annotated by Charles Perry in *A Collection of Medieval and Renaissance Cookbooks*, edited by David Friedman and Betty Cook, volume 2 (fifth edition, 1992, University of Chicago Press). Many recipes are very like those in Al-Baghdadi's cookbook, with meats cooked with fruit, and sweet-and-sour flavors, and names of dishes ending in "-ak" and "-aj" denoting a still-powerful Persian influence. But there are many different ones too. Some depict North African Berber foods, such as couscous, and paper-thin pancakes, semolina sweets

with dates, and very many dishes with eggs.

The book contains five recipes described as Jewish. They are incredibly elaborate and rich in aromatics, with a variety of ingredients. A "Jewish Partridge" is stuffed with almonds, pine nuts, coriander, and eggs—some of the stuffing going under the skin. It is then stewed in a sauce with cinnamon, mint and citron leaves, vinegar, sugar, and murri (which Charles Perry describes as "rotted" barley), and garnished with pistachios, almonds, pine nuts, and hard-boiled egg yolks. In those days, game birds were hunted with falcons, which immobilized them but did not kill them so that they could be ritually slaughtered and fit to eat. In "A Jewish Dish of Chicken" a sauce is made with the giblets and a long list of aromatics, including onion juice, coriander, pine nuts, vinegar, oil, citron leaves, and fennel stalks, and thickened with eggs, flour, bread crumbs, and the crushed chicken liver. The chicken is roasted, then left to marinate in a mixture of murri, vinegar, rose water, onion juice, and various spices and flavorings. It is served with the sauce and garnished with almonds and eggs.

Bolens mentions harissa as another Jewish Saturday dish which was sold ready to eat by vendors at the market. It was and still is in the Arab world a wheat-and-meat porridge enriched with melted fat and cinnamon (nothing to do with the peppery-hot Tunisian paste of the same name today). I have had it described to me as a Sabbath breakfast dish in Samarkand and also in Aden. Another Andalusian Saturday dish, which is left to cook on Friday afternoon in a sealed clay pot and cracked open for Saturday lunch, is called a "Stuffed Buried Jewish Dish." Meatballs flavored with cumin and other spices, rose water, and onion juice are cooked in the pot between two layers of cinnamon-flavored omelette and covered by a third omelette of egg combined with pounded meat, salt, pepper, cinnamon, and rose water. The dish is served garnished with pistachios, pine nuts, mint leaves, and a sprinkling of spices. The name "adafina," used in medieval Spain for the Saturday dish cooked overnight, means "to hide" and "to bury" in Arabic. There is a curious echo in a modern Tunisian Sabbath dish, "t'fina nikitouches," which includes a molded omelette called "dabbahia" made with chopped-up chicken breast. A great many of the other recipes featured by Charles Perry and Lucie Bolens, which represent an amalgam from various cultures—mainly Arab, Persian, Berber, Spanish, and Greek—find an echo in Sephardi dishes today, especially in those of North Africa and of the old Ottoman lands.

The recipes show a great concern with flavor, texture, and visual appeal and include information on dietetics, such as what is good for the liver and the stomach or for depression. Jewish physicians were much in evidence in Spain. They followed the traditions, inherited from antiquity and pursued by Avicenna and Razi, which linked eating with health and humors. They passed on to their communities the philosophy of happy, convivial eating and the importance of good food—that you "became what you ate." Isaac Israelicus, an ophthalmologist from Kairouan who died in 932, is famous for his treatise on dietetics—the *Kitab al-Agdiya* (*Book of Foods*)—which was translated into Latin and printed in Padua in 1487. The book, entitled *Liber Dietetarium Universalium,* was still used in the seventeenth century in the medical schools of Salerno. Israelicus preached that food had to be really delectable if the body and the mood were to benefit.

Maimonides (Moses ben Maimon) developed the theme of the psyche and its capacity to change the body, the importance of serenity and of tasty, appetizing food for the mood and the spirit. He advocated that a shared convivial meal was a way of conquering anxiety and tension and also suspicion between ethnic groups. He was born in Córdoba in 1135, and although he left at the age of twelve, he remained part of the Andalusian civilization. He was famous as the physician to the sultan of Egypt, the son of Saladin.

In the old Jewish quarter of Cairo is the little synagogue of Maimonides. We called him Rambam. One of my aunts used to spend the night there when one of her family was ill or in trouble, bringing a bit of the sick person's hair, to ask Maimonides' protection. I visited the synagogue a few years ago for the first time. It looked so small and had become derelict, flooded with water. Later, when I voiced my surprise that people could sleep there at a lecture I gave in London that was attended by Jews from Egypt, three women volunteered that they had slept on a kind of high platform, because there was water then too. Some of Maimonides' teachings filtered down to my family. My father's elderly brother-in-law, a cabbalist, whom I always saw in a white galabia (robe) and skull cap, would often quote his aphorisms on food and eating.

In Christian Spain

THE RECONQUISTA, as the reconquering of Muslim Spain in the south by the Christian states in the north was called, began in the eleventh century, and by the beginning of the thirteenth, the Christian rulers had conquered all of the south except for Granada. But from the ninth century, which was a period of civil war between Arab factions, Jews had begun to trickle into the Christian principalities in the north. And when two fanatically religious Islamic sects from North Africa—the Almoravids and later the Almohads—conquered Andalusia in the twelfth century, creating a Berber empire which extended over the whole of North Africa, they tried to force the Jews to convert to Islam, and the Jews fled to the north.

By the thirteenth century, the major concentration of Jewish life had moved to the Christian areas of the Iberian Peninsula, within the various states into which Christian Spain was divided, some of which are now Portugal. In all, the Jews remained in post-Muslim Christian Spain for almost three hundred years. They were treated well for the first two hundred years, enjoying royal protection and rising to high positions of state as diplomats, ministers of finance, and royal advisers, as well as doctors and scholars. A Jewish middle class earned its living from the land, and from commerce and manufacture, while craftsmen and artisans were involved in all kinds of trades. There were many wealthy "court Jews" who lived in the courts of the Catholic kings and princes; they acquired land and houses and imitated the ways of the nobility to the point of having their own coats of arms.

This second golden age for the Jews finally ended in 1391, when Christian mobs, furious at their privileged position, destroyed the Jewish quarters of Seville, Castile, Aragon, Barcelona, Córdoba, and Toledo. There were massacres and persecutions and forced conversions to Christianity throughout Spain. Thousands died as martyrs at the stake. Many fled and the majority were converted, some begging for baptism outside churches. They were made to eat pork publicly to prove their allegiance to the new faith. "Marrano," which means "pork" in Spanish, came to stand for these converted "New Christians" or *conversos,* who were suspected of keeping their old faith in secret.

For a few decades, being a "New Christian" was an advantage. The converts had everything open to them as Christians. They entered the government, the army, law, even the Church. They married into the best families of Spain. But they aroused jealousy and were suspected of remaining Jews in their hearts and of carrying out a Jewish plot to infiltrate Christian society from the inside. Cardinals complained about the crimes against *limpieza de la sangre* (purity of the blood) committed in the very highest society. The Inquisition was established in 1480 by King Ferdinand and Queen Isabella to root out and destroy the New Christians who continued to practice Judaism in secret, in the privacy of their homes. Under the direction of the Inquisitor, General Tomás de Torquemada, people were arrested and given up to forty days to confess so as to get a lighter sentence. Those who would not seek forgiveness and reconciliation, as well as second offenders, would be burned at the stake.

Thousands were brought to the tribunals, and witnesses were called who had noticed strange behavior that could be a sign of reverting to the old faith. Many women went in front of the inquisitors and were put to the stake because they were discovered cooking their Saturday dish adafina on Friday, before the Sabbath. Inquisitors would walk the streets on Fridays and Saturdays to catch the cooking smells, or lack of them, that emanated from beneath the doors, which would be a sign of converts' still adhering to their old religious traditions. Many Jews gave themselves away by not lighting the fires in their houses on Saturdays. Fernand Braudel quotes a story told by Ibn Verga in 1500 about an inquisitor who said to the governor of Seville: "My Lord if you wish to see how the *conversos* keep the Sabbath, come up the tower with me." When they reached the top he said, "See how you can tell the houses of the *conversos:* however cold it is, you will never see smoke coming from their fires on a Saturday."

Cynthia Levine, an American researcher, studied the testimonies against 111 women in Toledo from records of the Inquisitorial Court, seventy-one of whom were condemned—of them, fifty-six were burned at the stake, the remainder imprisoned or exiled. The testimonies were usually given by former servants or neighbors whose identities were never revealed to the accused. The charges most often made were that the women lighted candles and wore clean clothes on the Sabbath; that they did not eat pork or seafood and did not mix milk and meat; that they salted their meat and cooked on Friday for the Saturday; that they made matzos at Passover and fasted on Yom Kippur; and that they prepared special meals for the Sabbath and holidays. Specific clandestine dishes mentioned were adafina, a lamb stew with onions and chickpeas, and a dish eaten cold on Saturday made with eggs, cheese, and eggplants. It came as an extraordinary revelation for me to find that the most popular dish of the Jews in Istanbul today, called "almodrote de berenjena," is mashed eggplants baked with eggs and cheese.

Andrés Bernaldez, the chaplain to the Inquisitor and historiographer of the Catholic kings, wrote that the *conversos* "never lost the habit of eating in the Jewish manner, preparing their meat dishes with onions and garlic and frying them in oil which they used instead of pork fat." Today this is how everyone cooks in Spain. But in the past Christians used pork fat for cooking, and its displacement by oil was a legacy of the Jews. Arabs used clarified butter. What became known in Spain as the "Jewish manner" of cooking was really Muslim styles adopted by the Jews in Muslim Spain. But when they left the country they also took with them the new culinary baggage from Catholic Spain.

On March 30, 1492, Ferdinand and Isabella signed the decree expelling all Jews who had not converted; the Inquisition continued to seek out Marranos until the end of the eighteenth century. It was also instituted in all colonies of Spain, including southern Italy, Sicily, Sardinia, Provence, and the New World of South America (namely, Mexico and Brazil). Today Spain celebrates the Jewish contribution to its culture, and it is fashionable there now to claim Jewish blood. Many families believe that some of their practices, such as hanging a joint of ham outside the house, lighting candles in the cellar, and cleaning on Friday morning, reveal Jewish ancestry. Family names that are city names, like Sevilla and Burgos, are also supposed to be a sign of Jewish ancestry. In Majorca there is a Christian sect called Chueta, a word derived from Chuya, meaning "pork eater," who are known descendants of converted Jews. They live in Palma and are mainly in the jewelry-and-silver trade, and locals call them *judíos* or *hebreos.* Two hundred inhabitants of a medieval hilltop village in Portugal called Belmonte have officially reverted to Judaism with the help of rabbis from Israel. They claim that their parents' grandparents and great-grandparents had maintained their faith in secret.

Spanish gastronomes, too, are fascinated by the Jewish legacy. The famous Spanish meat stew "cocido," the only dish to be found in every region of Spain (in different versions), is said to be derived from the old Sabbath adafina. Pork was added by the *conversos* to prove the sincerity of their conversion. Another dish, called "olla podrida," is similar to adafinas of today—with meat, chicken, chickpeas, a large sausage, cabbage, garlic, saffron, and cumin—except that it uses pork fat and the sausage is pork. As with adafina, the stock is eaten first as a soup and the meat is presented separately.

When I visited El Molino, the center of gastronomic research outside Granada, some years ago and asked what the influences on Spanish cooking were, I was told "Arab and Jewish." And when I asked what the Jewish heritage was the reply was: "There is a special way of doing suckling pig and a few pork dishes. When the Marranos cooked pork they cooked it in a different way—the way they cooked lamb—and that came into our traditions." Certain dishes that are Arab in origin, like those with eggplants or with marzipan, are considered Jewish because they were introduced to the north by the Jews.

The expulsion from Spain in 1492 was the end of the greatest and most culturally assimilated Jewish community of Europe in the Middle Ages, and it had a gigantic impact on the entire Jewish people. The effect on the gastronomy was powerful too. You can see it especially in the cooking of the Jews of Turkey and the Balkans, who call their style "Judeo-Spanish," and in the cooking of North African Jews. But it can even be detected in dishes from far-flung places such as Egypt and India, Jamaica and Surinam, where there were once families with names like Toledano, Sevilla, Carmona, Mallorca, León, and Burgos. Some of the dishes are very like dishes cooked in the Iberian Peninsula today.

Many of the banished exiles found refuge in Portugal, only to be forced to convert there five years later without being given the chance to leave. The discovery of the Americas coincided with the expulsion from Spain. When Christopher Columbus set sail in 1492, many conversos—they included Christopher Colombus' translator

and doctor—managed to get on the boats with the Conquistadors. Many thousands of the settlers who went in the next century were conversos, because life was difficult for them in the Iberian Peninsula, and also because repentant Judaizers were sent to the colony from Portugal. Some of these conversos were strict Christians, some were secret Jews. Mexico and Brazil were soon filled with secret Jews. But the Inquisition pursued them there too. It was set up in Mexico in 1571. Many fled to Peru. It is difficult to distinguish any Jewish trait in Latin American cooking today, although I hear there is some research being done on the subject.

Some of the exiles found refuge in Italian cities that were independent city-states. In Rome and Ancona, the cardinals were glad to have Jewish doctors, because there were so many cases of poisoning by rivals. They were accepted by the Medicis in Florence, and by the Este family in Ferrara. They went to Pisa, Mantua, Genoa, and Venice. They traveled by sea, and captains of ships would sometimes sell them off as slaves and seize their belongings, or Tunisian pirates would be lying in wait for them. The slaves would be bought back by Jewish communities, who sent emissaries to Tunis, and they sometimes found themselves in strange places.

Larger numbers fled to North Africa. There had been a strong Jewish presence in the Maghrebi countries of Morocco, Algeria, Tunisia, and Libya, which dated back centuries before the advent of Islam, and there had always been very close ties with the communities of the Iberian Peninsula. The new immigrants settled in the coastal towns and cities, where they took on the role of intermediaries between their Muslim neighbors and foreign traders and consuls—a role that lasted until the European takeover. Until the eighteenth century, many served as diplomatic

Main street of the mellah (Jewish quarter) in Fez, Morocco.
It was the first Jewish quarter, established in the fifteenth century.

people remembered nostalgically the meals they had had at their now departed friends' homes and described them in detail.

Above all, the Jewish exiles from Spain headed for the lands of the Ottoman Empire. The Sultan Beyazit II welcomed them, famously remarking that the Catholic monarchs' loss was his gain. He needed them to populate and to help administer the war-depleted empire of Byzantium that the Ottoman armies had destroyed. The Jews settled in Anatolia (Turkey) and the Balkans—Greece, Yugoslavia, Bulgaria, Romania—and in Cyprus and Crete. They were moved and relocated by imperial decree from one part of the empire to another. They were joined by Jews banished from southern Italy and Provence. Many went on to centers of the Islamic world such as Aleppo, Damascus, Alexandria, Jerusalem, and Baghdad, which were dominated by Ottoman dynasties. The Ottoman Empire became the center of the Sephardi world.

representatives to European governments on behalf of the sultans of Morocco. By the early twentieth century, the largest Sephardi community in the world was that of North Africa, half of it in Morocco. It is in Morocco that one of the most prestigious styles of Jewish cooking developed. It has a strong Andalusian character, and it is still recognized in Morocco and cited as one of the four great national styles, even now, when only a few Jews remain. When I traveled in Morocco to research the regional cooking, the "Jewish" style was so often mentioned that I began to wonder if my identity was obvious and that they were trying to please me. But many

The emigration of thousands of Marranos from Spain and Portugal continued until the end of the sixteenth century. These later waves of immigrants had been wealthier and more educated than those who left in 1492. They were the ones who had stayed behind and converted because they had more to lose by leaving. As Christians, they had intermarried more often into the aristocracy than with the humbler classes. In their gestures, manners, looks, language, occupations, and aspirations they differed from their brethren who had left in 1492. A century of life as Marranos had transformed them. Their appearance changed because of intermarriage; many were blond and blue-eyed. Their language was pure. They had developed a secretive double personality and psychology which prepared them to adapt easily to Western culture.

Many settled in Atlantic ports like Amsterdam, Rotterdam, Antwerp, and Hamburg, where they established trading and finance houses. In 1593, Ferdinand II, grand duke of Tuscany, invited New Christians to settle in great numbers in Pisa and Livorno and allowed them to reconvert to Judaism. At the same time, France opened its doors to New Christians, who settled in Bayonne, Toulouse, Bordeaux, Marseilles, Avignon, Carpentras, and Cavaillon, which became important Marrano centers. They ended up scattered everywhere, even in the East Indies, India, America, and England, where they remained secretly as Portuguese Christians until Cromwell allowed Jews in officially in 1656 (they had been banished since 1290).

Many Marranos followed their Sephardi brethren to North Africa and the Ottoman lands. Most but not all reconverted to the Mosaic faith. Even though most may have been of Spanish origin, they had had one or two generations in Portugal, and they were seen as Portuguese. Their cooking too was Portuguese, and one of its characteristics is that it made use of all of the products of the New World before anybody else in the wider Mediterranean. Based in ports around the Mediterranean, and as the main maritime merchants dealing with the produce of Spain and Portugal, they were largely responsible for introducing New World vegetables like tomatoes, chili peppers, potatoes, corn, beans, and pumpkin, which had been brought back to Spain and Portugal by the Conquistadors. It is through them that chocolate cakes and vanilla flavoring, tomato sauces and pumpkin and bean dishes spread throughout the Jewish world.

Very little remains of the Marrano culinary culture in Northern Europe. A few things have passed into the Ashkenazi style in Britain, such as fish fried in batter, fish in egg-and-lemon sauce, sponge cake, and macaroons. I was sent a Danish recipe called "plaice solpada" by food writer Birgit Siesby, *solpado* being a Portuguese word meaning "hidden" or "covered"; in this case the fish was "covered" with an egg-and-lemon sauce. But Portuguese-type dishes are evident in the Mediterranean in centers like Livorno and Tunis. Perhaps if we look closely in France we should find something in Bayonne and Bordeaux, where the Marranos were once so important that the communities were known as Portuguese "Nations" of the Southwest.

Being widely scattered, the Iberian Sephardim were in a position to form a commercial network and an organization of mutual confidence and cooperation throughout the world, for they had relations and representatives everywhere. Great Jewish banking and merchant families emerged, with interests in the sugar trade and the grain and spice trades. Some possessed enough capital to lend money to kings. Many were of Marrano origin.

THE OTTOMAN WORLD

IN THE BALKANS and Anatolia, where they settled in vast numbers, the Sephardim very quickly became the leading social and economic force within the mostly Greek-speaking Byzantine and Romaniot communities. By their numbers, not to speak of their cultural superiority, the Iberians overwhelmed the Balkanic communities. They had all the skills, know-how, and sophistication. They were proud, strong, resolute, refined in manners. To their Oriental coreligionists they represented what was great and noble—a Jewish aristocracy. In the Ottoman world they came to constitute the bourgeoisie and merchant class. Some of what they had been and seen and done rubbed off on their coreligionists. The Sephardim, as the exiles were called after the Hebrew word "Sepharad" for Spain, were to have an important impact on the indigenous Oriental Jewish communities, many of which took on an Iberian character. Spanish styles and customs were absorbed in varying degrees, depending on their numbers, relations of the Jews of Iberian ancestry with the indigenous communities, whether they tended to be isolationist or assimilationist, and whether there was tension and conflict. Where they became more influential and their culture was seen as prestigious, their language, music, and also their cooking were adopted.

Some Turkish and Balkan cities became bastions of Jewish life. Salonika (now Thessaloniki), Smyrna (now Izmir), and the island of Rhodes, where Jews became the majority of the population, were like diminutive Jewish republics. Salonika had the largest Jewish community and became the most important Sephardi city that ever was. Spanish was the language of the land. You could hardly hear anything else. Even non-Jews spoke it. Istanbul had the second-largest Jewish community in the Ottoman Empire. Being at the administrative core of the empire, it acquired considerable authority over the Jewish communities in the provinces of the empire. It dispensed spiritual inspiration and material support and set the standard for all aspects of community life. Istanbul and Salonika delicacies became fashionable in the far-flung communities of the Eastern Mediterranean.

The sultans allowed the Jews internal autonomy. Within their quarters they lived according to their own administration and managed their communal affairs in a style adopted from Spain. They had no central organization. Each city, each community had its own rabbi and self-appointed dignitaries. The communities were divided into groups according to regional origin called *cales*. In many big towns there were dozens of these *cales*, each with its own synagogue, rabbi, school, and charitable organizations. In Salonika in the early seventeenth century there were forty-four of these *cales*, including an Apulian, Sicilian, Neapolitan, Calabrese, Catalan, Aragonese, Majorcan, North African, Greek, Provençal, Lisbon, and one Ashkenazi. They were like little self-governing mini-states within a Jewish mini-state.

In the Ottoman world, Jews were in every stratum of society and had all kinds of professions—doctor, printer, bookbinder, actor, interpreter. In Spain, Jews had spoken Spanish and Arabic; in Turkey, they spoke four or five languages. They controlled the wholesale trade and were engaged in overseas commerce, with a network of agents around the world, including Spain. They were the successors in the Levant of the rich Italian merchant bourgeoisie which once controlled the entire Mediterranean. They served as middlemen or local representatives for European merchants, who are often quoted as finding "a Jew in every port." Jews had a monopoly in the trade of luxury goods, from precious stones, pearls, silk, and wool to coffee, spices, dried fruit, and nuts. They dealt with the business affairs of pashas who were sent out to the outposts of the empire. Many prominent Jews reached high-level positions in the Ottoman courts and central administration, as advisers to the sultan, court physicians, local governors, and

Une Villa de Salonique.

Postcard depicting the villa of Elia Benouzilio, president of the Jewish community in 1930–32, Salonika

diplomats. They minted coins, manufactured arms and gunpowder for the Turkish armies, and provided the uniforms for the Janissaries. They were employed in government office and were in charge of customs. There was also a large Jewish working class of craftsmen in silk dyeing and embroidery, jewelry and metalwork; Jewish masons, carpenters, porters, and peddlers selling haberdashery and pastries. In Salonika they were famously porters and dockers. It was said by Greeks that there was nothing they would not do.

As an effort at unification, the Sephardi (Iberian) synagogue ritual, the prayers and music, were adopted by Jewish communities all over the Mediterranean, the Balkans, and the Middle East, with some exceptions. That is why the label "Sephardi" extends to all these communities.

The Iberian Jews had come from various regions in Spain and Portugal and spoke different languages and dialects, but the majority were from Castile, and when they were still in Spain, Castilian—the language of the court—had already been imposed on the whole of Spain. In exile, Castilian was adopted as the unifying language of the Hispanic Jews, and in Turkey and the Balkans it became the Jewish language. The Judeo-Spanish language, which was written in Hebrew Rashi script and was used to teach the Talmud and for liturgical purposes, was called Ladino. It remained basically the archaic Castilian of before the exile. The spoken vernacular called Judesmo contained Hebrew elements and Portuguese, Catalan and other regionalisms. It was infiltrated, over the centuries, by foreign languages—first Italian, then French, Turkish, and Arabic. Bastardized forms varied from town to town. Judesmo was replaced by French as a home language and as the official language of the rabbinate in the late nineteenth century, but it is still spoken today by older people. In North Africa, Judeo-Spanish was dropped for Arabic, and later in the nineteenth century Arabic was dropped for French, but in Spanish-dominated Mediterranean areas like Tangiers and Tétouan in Morocco, a Judeo-Spanish dialect mixed with Berber and Arabic called *haquetia* was kept up. Italian was adopted in Libya when it was conquered by Italy. All this information may help to explain the inconsistency of names of the Sephardi dishes featured in this book, which are variously in Spanish and Italian, French and Arabic. It will also give an idea of how dishes changed in a way that reflected language variations.

The Iberian Sephardim never forgot Spain. Their cooking became unified and gradually adopted new styles, including Italian and most particularly Ottoman. At one time I imagine you could tell that dishes were clearly from Aragon, Castile, Catalonia, or Naples. In some cases you still can, but by now it is difficult to unravel what is Iberian from what is Turkish, Greek, Balkan, or Arab, because, of course, Spanish cooking was influenced by Arab styles. You cannot always tell by the names, because Judeo-Spanish speakers gave everything a Judeo-Spanish name, but very many dishes have obvious Iberian roots, like the fish pies called "empanadas," the garlicky mayonaise-type sauce called "ajada," orange-and-almond cakes, and little egg-and-almond pastries such as marunchinos and almendrada. Sometimes a little touch like flavoring with orange zest is a clue to an old Spanish ancestry.

Jews in Salonika wearing Jewish costumes

The flowering of the Jews of the Ottoman world did not last forever. The communities began to decline in the eighteenth century. They suffered earthquakes and fires. They had built wooden houses, and whole quarters regularly burned down. Competition from Greek and Armenian merchants, with whom the European traders preferred to do business as fellow Christians, affected them deeply. When the Ottoman Empire and the Islamic world declined, the Jewish communities declined even faster, both economically and educationally. They suffered poverty, segregation, and persecution. There was less intellectual life, because of lack of contact with Europe. Education was limited to rabbinic schools for boys. There was also the destabilizing phenomenon of a false messiah called Shabbetai Zvi (1626–76), who attracted thousands of believers, then converted to Islam, splitting the communities as many of his followers in Salonika converted and moved to Muslim quarters. I have got in my cupboard a manuscript cookbook written by a *deunmeh* (meaning "convert" in Turkish), as the descendants of the Sabbatians are called (they are also referred to as Salonikis). The author is a Turkish actress, Esin Eden, whom I met in Istanbul. Her recipes are very like those of the Jews from Salonika and Istanbul.

The end of the eighteenth century to the second half of the nineteenth was the lowest point in the existence of Jews in Muslim lands. Travelers found them in a state of degradation compared with the Jews in Western Europe, who were beginning to enjoy the fruits of emancipation. In North Africa they were described as "miserable, helpless, pitiful social pariahs." In Morocco, for the first time in Islamic lands, they were exposed to active hostility—violence, pillaging, expulsions, even massacres.

The end of the nineteenth century saw a substantial emigration from Muslim lands to North and South America and to Egypt. But at the same time, Balkan and Ottoman Jewry underwent a kind of renaissance through the intervention of the Jews of France and the financial assistance of mentors like the Rothschilds. In 1860, the Alliance Israélite Universelle was established in Paris for the emancipation and "moral progress" of the Ottoman Jews, who were seen, according to Alliance reports, as living in grinding poverty, ignorance, and insecurity. The historian Bernard Lewis writes that the occupations most frequently listed in Alliance records for students' parents are hawker, ragman, tinker, bootblack, match vendor, and water carrier. A few were clothiers, jewelers, butchers, and tavernkeepers.

Secular Alliance schools that taught children French and also trades opened in all the major and some minor cities in the far corners of the Ottoman world and produced a generation of French-educated Jews. French became the common language of the Sephardim. It brought closer ties between the dispersed Oriental communities and meant exposure of these communities to French ways—in gastronomic terms, also a certain refinement. The Italian government opened Italian schools which were mostly filled with Jewish chidren. The Jews of Salonika and Alexandria in particular spoke Italian fluently.

By the end of the nineteenth century, the Iberian and Oriental Sephardim were well rooted in contemporary Ottoman culture, and their life-styles and tastes reflected the prevalent ones in the empire. The Jews were generally part of the urban populations and their cooking was in the urban styles, modeled in part on the cooking at the sultan's court and in the houses of the

The Alliance girls' school in Baghdad, 1900

nobility in Istanbul. The style, which spread through the main cities of the empire and includes kebabs, pilafs, stuffed vegetables, various pies, milk puddings, baclawa, and kadaif, is one of the unifying elements of Sephardi culinary culture today.

The Sephardi world suffered with the dismantling of the empire, with the nationalist movements in the Balkans and the re-Christianization of newly independent regions. The Young Turk Revolution of 1908, which turned Turkey into a secular republic, gave equal rights but brought insecurity to the previously protected minorities, and the Jews lost their internal autonomy. They could also be called up in the army. The result was a massive emigration towards Palestine, Egypt, France, and North and South America. In 1912 the Greek army occupied Salonika, and in 1917 it was filled with Greek refugees from Anatolia. The city declined in importance as an outpost of the Greek kingdom, and the Jews never had a symbiosis with the Greeks. Fires burned down their quarters, and the community decayed.

European colonialization followed the dismantling of the empire in the nineteenth and twentieth centuries. Russians annexed Muslim lands around the Black Sea and in Transcaucasia and Central Asia; the British took Egypt and Aden; the French took Algeria, Tunisia, and for a short time Morocco; Italians took Libya. The Jews were the first and largest elements of the native population in every country to seek the benefits of Western education, adopt Western ways, and take on foreign passports.

In World War II, the Balkan communities were destroyed by the Nazis. Ninety percent of the Jews who were left in Salonika, Rhodes, and Corfu were exterminated. The independence movements within the Arab states, the clash of Jewish and Arab nationalism, the establishment of the State of Israel undermined their position in Arab countries. After 1948, their emigration started, and it continued until the 1970s.

The French novelist Edgar Morin writes in *Vidal et Les Siens,* the story of his Salonika family, that the kernel of every culture is gastronomic, and that in the case of Salonika pastellicos (little pies) lie in the kernel of the kernel. This centuries-old chapter of Jewish life has come to an end, but we will always have traces of it on the table, for cooking is the part of culture that lasts.

Spices
and Flavorings

SEPHARDI COMMUNITIES are known for the wide range of aromatic herbs, seeds, bark, roots, pods, pistils, petals, flower waters, and oils they use. Every community has its favorites. Where one uses saffron another uses turmeric. Cumin and coriander are favorites of Egyptian Jews, allspice and cinnamon are much used by Turks, and cardamom is popular with Iraqis and Indians. Tamarind goes into sweet-and-sour foods of families originating in Syria, Persia, Iraq, and India, and sour pomegranate syrup has the same role with people from Persia and Syria. Where North African Jews use orange-blossom water, Turkish and Balkan Jews use rose water. Grated orange zest, chocolate, and vanilla are a sign of Iberian ancestry. The sharp red berries of the sumac tree; mastikah (mastic), the resin of the acacia tree; and sahlab,

the ground bulb of a type of orchid, are a sign of roots in the Arab world. Each community used all the aromatics of its locality, but in a slightly different way from the general population, so that the food tasted a little different.

Herbs and spices were also valued for their therapeutic and medicinal qualities, as aphrodisiacs, and for magic purposes. People knew which were good for digestion, which calmed the nerves and helped circulation, which killed bacteria, increased the appetite, and acted as sexual stimulants. Garlic was supposed to protect from the evil eye and evil spirits. In Turkey, once, when Jews were in the habit of hanging a head of garlic outside the door, during a cholera epidemic when no one died in the community Muslims said it was the stench of garlic that had kept the bacteria away.

Salt

IN BIBLICAL TIMES, salt was used as an offering to God. "With all thy offerings thou shalt offer salt" is a directive in Leviticus, and as the table represents the altar, it means that there should always be salt on it. Bread dipped in salt is a symbol of hospitality. Kings and lowly strangers have always been welcomed with it in Jewish lore. Salt also has various symbolic meanings in Jewish folklore. In Egypt, at Passover, we dipped lettuce in salted water, which represented the tears of the Hebrew slaves of the Pharaohs. Moroccans sprinkle salt at the birth of a child to ward off the evil eye.

I do not generally give precise quantities of salt in my recipes, because I believe salting is so much a matter of personal taste and it is the one flavoring that people know how to use and have an "eye" for even before tasting. And the need for it varies, depending on climate and medical conditions. In recent years, after the link between high levels of salt consumption and high blood pressure was made, people started to use much less salt and their tastes have changed. On the other hand, in hot countries, including parts of America, where people sweat a lot and lose salt, they need more salt and experience fainting weakness if they lack it. Another reason for preferring not to give quantities is that salt varies in strength and intensity of flavor, depending on where it originates. English sea salt, for instance, is saltier than French, which has a delicate flavor, and salt from the earth, extracted from underground deposits, is far less salty.

I recommend fine-ground sea salt for most cooking, but coarse salt is necessary for curing

Jewish spice merchant, Sefrou, Morocco

and dry salting and for koshering meat and chicken, because fine salt melts and can be drawn into the fish or meat instead of drawing out the juices or blood.

Pepper

AS WITH SALT, I have not normally given quantities of pepper. We have got used to putting it in most of our dishes, and we know how much we want. In restaurants we have become used to waiters coming around with the pepper mill because we differ in our tastes for it.

Oils

OLIVE OIL WAS much used by Sephardi cooks everywhere, and exclusively in a few communities, such as those of Greece, Turkey, and Tunisia, until a few decades ago. Elsewhere it was used for cold dishes and to dress salads. For general all-purpose cooking, sesame and corn oil were used in Egypt, peanut oil in North Africa and India, sesame oil in Syria, Iraq, and India. These days sunflower oil has been generally adopted throughout the Mediterranean for cooked dishes. People say this is because it is light and flavorless, but it also has to do with European Union subsidies. Nut oils such as almond, walnut, hazelnut, and pistachio were used very occasionally. A very rare and famous oil, much prized in Morocco, is the argan oil, from the argan tree, which grows around Essaouira, once the very Jewish city of Mogador.

Spice Mixtures

SPICE MIXTURES suitable for certain kinds of dishes were common. Ready made ones were sold at the bazaar, but Jews made their own, in case tiny insects had invaded a batch, or because of something that was not kosher—such as the golden beetle in the ras el hanout mixture of North Africa. They bought fresh whole spices and roasted and pounded them themselves. Nowadays in many homes you still find two or three jars of ground mixed spices in the larder.

In Egypt we used a combination of cin-namon, nutmeg, cloves, and allspice which we called quatre épices (four spices). Zahtar, a mixture of wild thyme, roasted sesame seeds, the ground sour red berries of the sumac tree, and salt, has become very popular in Israel, where it is eaten with bread dipped in olive oil. Kama is a Moroccon blend of black pepper, turmeric, ginger, cumin, and nutmeg used for stews and soups. Hawaij, a Yemeni ground spice mixture famous in Israel and used in meat dishes and soups, is made up of black pepper, cardamom, saffron, and turmeric. The Aden version has coriander, cumin, cardamom, and black pepper. Adenis also have a mixture of ground cinnamon, cloves, and cardamom for their tea, which they drink without milk, and a mixture of ginger, cardamom, cloves, and cinnamon for their black coffee.

Mai Ward—Mai Qedda

Rose Water and Orange Blossom Water

THE OLD PEOPLE in my family smelled of roses because they washed with rose water. That is why we enjoyed kissing them. Houses too smelled of flowers, because petals—rose and jasmine especially—were left in bowls and were sometimes scattered on the floor. Distilled rose and orange-blossom waters were used to flavor puddings and pastries. When we went to bed, we had a drink of water with a drop of rose water in it. It was said to have a digestive and calming effect, to be good for the heart, and to affect the mood and give a rosy view of life. Our parents made "café blanc" (white coffee) by adding a few drops of orange blossom to a cup of boiling water, and drank it with or without sugar.

My aunt Latifa had a still in the cellar for

COCONUT MILK

Coconut milk, which goes into the cooking of the Jews of India, is made by soaking the grated flesh in very hot water to extract its juice (the liquid that runs out of a coconut when you crack it open is not coconut milk). Two perfectly good alternatives that can be used are:

- *Unsweetened canned coconut milk or cream* (which is thicker than the milk)
- *Creamed coconut* sold in hard blocks of 7 oz (200 g). This needs to be melted in boiling water. To obtain 1¼ cups (300 ml) of coconut cream, cut into pieces 4 oz (100 g) creamed coconut and boil in 1 cup (250 ml) water, stirring until it has melted. For coconut milk, dilute further with an additional 1 cup (250 ml) water. Creamed coconut can also be used by slipping pieces into a stew or soup and letting them melt.

To extract the milk (Indian Jews call it "juice") from a fresh coconut, crack the coconut open with a hammer, pry the flesh out of the shell, and peel off the brown skin. Then break the flesh into pieces and grate or finely chop it in a food processor. Pour the grated coconut into a measuring jug, measure the volume, and pour it back into the food processor. Add about three-quarters of the volume of not-quite-boiling water and blend thoroughly. Leave to stand for 10 minutes, then pour into a colander lined with a thin layer of cheese-cloth. The strained liquid is the coconut milk. Bring the edges of the cloth together in a bundle and squeeze out as much liquid as possible from the coconut. One coconut should give you about 4 cups of grated coconut and about 1½ cups (350 ml) thick coconut milk.

You can buy shredded frozen coconut, which can be used like the fresh.

---

making the waters. Vendors would come to the door with huge basketfuls of petals during the season. She bought mountains, by the kilo, and made enough perfumed waters to last the year. The petals were covered with water in a large copper pot with a thin neck and a lid and put to boil on a fire. A small pipe connected to a long tube was placed through a hole in the lid, which was sealed. The tube passed through a basin of icewater, which caused the vapor to condense and drip into glass bottles. The first bottles had the strongest flavor. A finger of rose oil collected at the top. The smell of roses or orange blossom filled the house and made you dizzy.

The distilled waters you can buy in this country are usually diluted and not as strong as the concentrated ones you find in Middle Eastern markets. The quantities I give in the recipes relate to this diluted form. But because the strength varies, and some concentrated qualities are now available here, you should taste and adjust the amount according to your taste.

Tamarhendi

Tamarind

Jews are particularly fond of the sharp taste of tamarind and use it in many sweet-and-sour dishes—it is prominent in Syrian, Iraqi, Indian, and also in Georgian dishes. Tamarind pods are sold in dry compact blocks containing hard seeds and fibrous broken pods. They need to be soaked in water overnight; then the water is strained through a fine cloth. Unless you make a large quantity and keep it in a jar, it is not worth the trouble of making. A tamarind syrup that I find in Italy is perfect for cooking. One that is sold in London, which is made in Lebanon, is much too sickly sweet and not good at all for cooking. The best alternative is tamarind concentrate—a dark, shiny paste that is widely available in Indian and Oriental stores, both in England and in the United States. You can simply dissolve a tablespoon or two straight into a stew.

Pomegranate Concentrate

The thick dark-brown, almost black, syrup—also referred to as molasses—made from sour pomegranates is used by families from Syria, Iran, and Iraq for sweet-and-sour dishes in the same way as tamarind. You can easily find it now in bottles in Iranian and Oriental stores.

Dried Limes

Iraqis call dried limes "noomi Basra," Persians call them "limoo Omani." They are used to flavor soups and stews and also to make an infusion to drink. The usual way is to pierce the limes with the point of a knife in a few places or to crack them open with a hammer or pulverize them in a food processor. In that case the seeds must be removed first. You can buy the dried limes whole or pulverized in Indian and Oriental stores. You can also make them yourself very easily. Simply leave limes to dry out, preferably out in the sun or, as I do, on radiators, until they are brown and very light and sound hollow when you tap them.

Agresto—Aceto Ebraico

Sour Grape Juice

Sour grape juice or verjuice was much used in the old days by Italian Jews and was referred to as "Jewish vinegar." You can make it from unripened grapes. Crush them, collect the juice, and boil it down to one-third, then let it cool before bottling. Use it instead of lemon or vinegar in sweet-and-sour dishes.

Pickles, Relishes, and Chutneys

Macédoine de Légumes Confits

Mixed Vegetable Pickle

This pickle is made with brine alone for quick use (less than a week) or with added vinegar. After only 2–3 days, the vegetables are still crisp but have acquired a special mellow quality which makes them different from ordinary crudités.

Have an exciting selection of vegetables. Choose from the following: carrots, cauliflower, turnips, fennel, snow peas, green beans, bell peppers, baby corn, and cabbage.

Wash the vegetables and cut them into bite-sized pieces or leave them whole if very small. About 2 lbs (1 kg) will fit into a 2-quart (2-liter) jar. Pack them very tightly in the jar with about 3 sliced garlic cloves, a few celery leaves, and 2 bay leaves.

For a brine alone, in a pan put 4½ cups (1 liter) of water. Add 3 tablespoons of salt, 1 tablespoon of black peppercorns, and 1 tablespoon of coriander seeds. Bring to the boil and simmer 3–4 minutes, then pour immediately over the vegetables in the jar. Wait until they cool before closing the jar. Keep in a cool place.

For a brine with vinegar, the traditional mix is 3 cups (750 ml) water and 1 cup (250 ml) white-wine vinegar. I use only about 4 tablespoons.

VARIATIONS

• A North African version has 2 chilies or a good pinch of cayenne or chili pepper.

• The Baghdadi Jews of India use an all-vinegar liquid flavored with a 1¼-inch (3-cm piece of ginger cut into thin slices, 4 sliced garlic cloves, 2–6 green chilies, ½ teaspoon turmeric, and 2 tablespoons sugar. They call it "chakla bakla."

Macédoine de Légumes Marinés

Marinated Vegetables

This instant pickle, which can be ready on the same day, is a particularly wonderful way of serving crudités. The vegetables, first salted to draw the juices out, then marinated in oil and lemon juice, acquire an exquisite flavor and softness.

In a colander, put 2 lbs (1 kg) of the following: cauliflower cut into florets, sliced carrots, quartered artichoke hearts, little asparagus, sugar snaps, and small green beans. Each layer should be sprinkled generously with plenty of salt. Leave for 3–4 hours to draw out the juices. Serve dressed with extra-virgin olive oil and lemon juice, or pack tightly into glass jars, pressing them down hard, and cover with extra-virgin olive oil (or a mixture with a light vegetable oil) beaten with the juice of 3 lemons. They keep for a week.

VARIATION

• Add a chili and 3 garlic cloves to the jar. There are those who add ¼ teaspoon powdered ginger.

PICKLES

PICKLES AND MARINATED vegetables had an important place in the old Sephardi world. They were brought out as appetizers with drinks and again as side dishes during the meal. Originally a way of preserving seasonal vegetables, they became delicacies to be eaten as soon as they were ready.

For long storage (up to a year), the pickling liquid was a half-and-half mixture of brine and vinegar. For quick use, it varied between three-quarters brine and one-quarter vinegar to hardly any vinegar at all. Since we are now so well provided with every kind of vegetable all year round and there is no need to put them away for long periods, my own preference is for the less vinegary type of pickle.

The important thing with all pickles is to have them entirely covered with the pickling liquid or oil, for any little part that rises above it becomes moldy. One way to do this is to weigh the vegetables down with a small plate or a well-scrubbed stone.

Torshi Left

Pink Turnip Pickle

This is the most popular pickle among families from Egypt, Syria, and Lebanon. A beet gives it shades of pink. People can never wait for it to be ready, and eat the turnips while they are still crisp and underdone. My parents made it all the time. My father liked a drink of whisky every evening, and these were part of the *mezze* my mother brought out for him.

2 lbs (1 kg) turnips
1 beet, raw or cooked, peeled and cut in slices
3 or 4 garlic cloves, cut into slices
3¾ cups (850 ml) water
3–4 tablespoons red or white wine vinegar
2½ tablespoons salt

Peel the turnips, cut in half or quarters, and put them in a jar interspersed with the slices of beet and garlic. In a pan bring the water, vinegar, and salt to the boil, stirring to dissolve the salt. Then pour over the turnips. Let cool before closing the jar.

VARIATION

- You may also add a chili pepper.

Citrons Confits (or Marinés)

North African Preserved Lemons

The skins of lemons preserved in salt, also referred to as "pickled," lend a curious and wonderfully intense flavor to North African dishes.

6 lemons (choose them with thick skins)
6 tablespoons coarse or fine sea salt
Juice of 3 lemons or more

Wash and scrub the lemons. The classic Moroccan way is to cut each lemon in quarters but not right through, so that the pieces are still attached at the stem end, and to stuff each with plenty of salt. Put them in a glass jar, pressing them down so that they are squashed together, and close the jar. It is best if they pack the jar tightly. Leave for 3–4 days, by which time the juice will have been drawn out of the lemons and the skins will have softened. Press them down as much as you can (it is usual to put a clean stone or heavy object on top to keep them down) and add fresh lemon juice to cover them entirely. Close the jar and leave in a cool place for at least a month, at which point they should be ready. The longer they are left, the better the flavor.

Before using, wash well to get rid of the salt.

VARIATIONS

- Salted water is sometimes poured in instead of the extra lemon juice.

• Some people pour a little oil on top as a protective film.

• Another Moroccan way is to slice 2 lbs (1 kg) lemons, sprinkle with 3 tablespoons of salt, and put them in a jar. After about 3 days, when the juice has been drawn out, add more lemon juice to cover and about ¼ cup of peanut or olive oil, which acts as a protection.

Poivrons Marinés
Marinated Bell Peppers

As everyone knows, roast peppers are magnificent. Roast and peel green, red, or yellow peppers (see page 253) or a mixture of these. Put them in a jar and cover them with extra-virgin olive oil. If well covered with oil, they keep for months.

A North African version is to marinate in equal quantities of wine vinegar and olive oil with a little salt and chopped garlic and a touch of cayenne pepper.

Brinjal Kasaundi
Eggplant Pickle

This sensational pickle is a specialty of the Bene Israel, one of the Jewish communities of India. It is a real find.

> 2 lbs (1 kg) eggplants, cut into ½-inch
>   (1½-cm) slices

Salt
¾–1 fresh chili
2-inch (5-cm) piece ginger
7 or 8 cloves garlic
1 tablespoon ground cumin
1 cup (250 ml) wine vinegar
1 cup (250 ml) sesame oil (I used toasted
   sesame oil)
1 tablespoon mustard seeds
1 teaspoon fenugreek seeds
6 curry leaves (optional)
1 teaspoon turmeric
½ cup (100 g) sugar

Soak the eggplant slices in salted water for about an hour to extract the bitter juices, then rinse and dry.

In a food processor, blend the chili, ginger, garlic, and cumin to a fine paste, using a little vinegar to moisten.

In a large saucepan, heat 2–3 tablespoons of the oil. Add the mustard and fenugreek seeds, and when these crack add the curry leaves and the chili-and-ginger paste. Fry, stirring, until the oil separates out and the mixture becomes a rich golden color. Now add the turmeric, vinegar, and sugar and stir well. Put in the eggplant, bring to the boil, and simmer gently for about 30 minutes, or until the eggplant is tender. Cool before pouring the whole thing in a jar. Cover with the remaining oil.

Green Coriander Chutney

This is one of many magnificent relishes made by the Indian Bene Israel. It is used as a stuffing or sauce for fish, and it can be served with cold meats. It is so good that you want to eat it by itself with bread. There are many versions. This is Sophie Jhirad's. Make it a few hours before you need it. In India freshly grated coconut is used.

> 1 large bunch of coriander, including stems, weighing about 4 oz (100 g)
> 3 or 4 sprigs of mint
> 1–5 green chilies (to my taste, 2), slit open and seeded
> 1 inch (2½ cm) fresh gingerroot
> 2–6 garlic cloves
> 3 oz (75 g) creamed coconut (see page 235), cut into pieces
> 4–6 tablespoons wine vinegar
> ½ teaspoon salt
> 1 teaspoon sugar or more to taste (optional)

Cut off the roots and coarse ends of the coriander and mint, then wash and cut into pieces. Put the chilies, gingerroot, garlic, and creamed coconut in the food processor and blend to a paste. Then add the coriander, mint, vinegar, salt, and sugar and blend thoroughly. Pour into a jar. In about an hour the mixture will firm up into a paste. It keeps a month in the refrigerator and months in the freezer.

Note

• When the chutney is used with meat or fish, no sugar is added.

• Instead of creamed coconut, you can use 3 tablespoons unsweetened dried coconut moistened with a little water.

Mango Chutney

I have fallen for all the Bene Israel Indian chutneys that I have tried. They are really great gastronomy, with their gentle combination of sweet and sour and peppery spiciness, and good to serve with almost anything from stews to cold dishes and vegetable omelettes. This delectable fruity one is worth making and keeping in the refrigerator.

> 3 fleshy mangoes, about 2 lbs (1 kg), cut into small cubes
> 3 oz (75 g) fresh ginger, peeled and finely chopped or grated
> 2 garlic cloves, minced or crushed in a press
> ½ teaspoon salt
> ¼–½ teaspoon cayenne or chili powder
> 1 cup (250 ml) white-wine vinegar
> ¾ cup (150 g) jaggery or muscovado (unrefined) sugar
> ¼ cup (50 g) slivered almonds
> ¼ cup (50 g) raisins

Put all the ingredients together in a pan and simmer over very low heat for about 15–20 minutes. Cool before putting in a jar.

VARIATION

• Instead of mangoes, use 2 lbs (1 kg) cooking apples or pineapple, chopped or cubed.

Coconut and Date Chutney

This is another really delicious Bene Israel Indian relish that I can't stop eating when it is in the house.

4½ oz (125 g) dried coconut
A large bunch (about 1 cup) coriander
    leaves
8–10 pitted dates
Juice of 2 limes or lemons
1 tablespoon tamarind paste dissolved in
    2 tablespoons boiling water
2 garlic cloves, minced or crushed in a garlic
    press
½ teaspoon salt
¼ teaspoon cayenne or chili powder,
    or to taste

Moisten the dried coconut with ⅔ cup (150 ml) water and leave for 15–20 minutes, until the water is absorbed. Chop the coriander in the food processor, then add the rest of the ingredients and blend to a paste. Add 1–2 tablespoons of water if necessary to make a soft creamy paste.

Hot and Spicy Tomato Sauce

Jewish families in India make this sumptuous sauce, which is always kept in the house. It lasts for months in the refrigerator.

3 lbs (1½ kg) plum tomatoes
⅔ cup (150 ml) wine vinegar
2 oz (50 g) fresh ginger
6–8 garlic cloves, crushed in a press
½ teaspoon chili pepper
1½ tablespoons tamarind paste
⅓ cup (75 g) sugar
2 teaspoons salt

Wash and dry the tomatoes but do not peel them. Cut them into quarters and turn them to a cream in the food processor. Pour into a saucepan, add the rest of the ingredients, and simmer for about ¾ hour, until the sauce is thick. Cool before pouring into a jar. It keeps for weeks in the refrigerator.

Harissa
North African Chili and Garlic Sauce

This fiery North African condiment is all-pervading in Tunisian Jewish dishes, from hors d'oeuvres and salads to fish, chicken, and couscous. Harissa can be bought in cans and tubes, but it does not have the quality of a freshly made one. This recipe is from Edmond Zeitoun's *250 Recettes Classiques de Cuisine Tunisienne*, the culinary bible of Tunisian Jews in Paris.

½ lb (250 g) dried hot red peppers
1 head garlic, peeled
1 tablespoon ground coriander seeds
1 tablespoon ground caraway seeds
1 tablespoon salt
Extra-virgin olive oil to seal the
    paste

Using rubber gloves, open out the peppers and remove stems and seeds. Soak in water for ½ hour, until soft. Drain and finely chop, together with the garlic and the rest of the ingredients, in a food processor, adding 2–4 tablespoons of water if necessary to obtain a thick coarse paste. Put into pots and pour in a little olive oil to seal the paste. It keeps refrigerated for a few weeks.

Note

The usual substitute for a teaspoon of harissa is a combination of 1 teaspoon of paprika and ¼ teaspoon of cayenne or chili pepper.

Green Zhoug

Yemeni Chili Relish

This hot chili salsa is eaten with bread as an appetizer. A Jewish specialty in Yemen, it is commonplace in Israel. It is really quite addictive and makes a good accompaniment to various foods, including fish and grilled and boiled meats and chicken. It is usually served with bread and with pureed fresh tomatoes (you can put these in the blender without peeling). A medium-hot variety of chili, 6–8 inches (15–20 cm) long, is used.

> 2 cups fresh coriander, or 1 cup each of
>   coriander and parsley
> ½ lb (250 g) fresh medium-hot chilies
> 6 garlic cloves, crushed or minced
> 1 teaspoon caraway seeds
> Seeds of 4 cardamom pods
> ½ teaspoon salt
> ½ teaspoon black pepper
> 5 tablespoons cold water or sunflower oil

Cut off the coriander roots but keep the stems. Wash well and squeeze the water out with your hands. Remove the parsley stems. Blend all the ingredients together to a rough paste in a food processor and press into a jar. I use sunflower oil instead of water—I prefer the texture, and that way it keeps for many weeks. Store in the refrigerator.

VARIATIONS

• You can make this relish successfully with very hot chilies. In that case use only 3–4 chilies.
• For a red zhoug blend red chilies with 6 medium tomatoes (you do not need to peel them) and add salt to taste.

Calcutta Hilbeh

I first had a taste of this hilbeh at a memorable Friday-night dinner at the home of Bernard and Philomène Jacobs. It is also served with the Saturday dish hameen. It is strange and extraordinary.

> 2 tablespoons ground fenugreek
> 1 large bunch of flat-leafed parsley, including
>   stems (about 1 cup)
> 1 large bunch of coriander, including stems
>   (about 1 cup)
> 1 hot green chili, seeded
> Juice of 1 inch (2½ cm) fresh ginger,
>   crushed in a garlic press
> Juice of 1 lemon or to taste
> Salt and pepper to taste

Soak 2 tablespoons ground fenugreek (see box on next page). Blend the rest of the ingredients in the food processor (the flat-leafed parsley and coriander must be well washed and have all the water squeezed out), then add the drained fenugreek jelly and process to a soft, slightly frothy paste. It keeps for at least a week, covered in the refrigerator.

Yemeni Hilbeh

The Yemeni hilbeh is a mixture of the fenugreek jelly (see box) with zhoug (see green and red zhoug, page 243). The following is if you do not have a tablespoon of zhoug to mix in.

>*2 tablespoons ground fenugreek*
>*4 garlic cloves, crushed in the garlic press*
>*2 large tomatoes, peeled and quartered*
>*1 tablespoon tomato paste*
>*Salt and black pepper*
>*¼ teaspoon caraway seed*
>*½ teaspoon powdered cardamom*
>*½ teaspoon chili pepper or more to taste*

Blend the rest of the ingredients in the food processor, then add the drained fenugreek jelly (see box) and process to a soft, slightly frothy paste. It keeps for at least a week, covered in the refrigerator.

Aden Hilbeh

Soak 2 tablespoons of ground fenugreek (see box) and beat till it froths. Add salt, ½–1 teaspoon of chili powder, and plenty of lemon juice to taste.

HILBEH
Fenugreek Jelly

THIS UNUSUAL JELLY is used to make a relish which is eaten with bread as a dip and is much loved by the Jews of Yemen and Aden, and in a different version by the "Baghdadis" of Calcutta. The relish is present at most meals, and especially on Friday night and at Saturday lunch. Its slightly bitter flavor and gelatinous texture derive from fenugreek seeds. The flat square yellow-brown seeds need to be crushed or ground, so it is best to buy the fenugreek in powder form. It needs to be soaked to remove some of the bitterness and to develop the gelatinous texture.

TO PREPARE the fenugreek jelly: Pour plenty of boiling water over the ground fenugreek (2 tablespoons absorbs a large quantity of water and gives you a large amount of jelly), stir well, then let rest for at least 2 hours but preferably overnight, by which time a gelatinous mass will have settled at the bottom, leaving a clear liquid on top. Drain all the liquid off without disturbing the gelatinous substance. Now beat in about ½ cup (125 ml) of water, drop by drop, until the mixture is light and foamy (the beating is traditionally done with the hand and can take 10 minutes).

Cold Vegetables,
Salads, and Appetizers

In the old Sephardi world, Saturday was a day for dropping in on relatives and friends. Since cooking, or even warming up food, was forbidden in religious households, little cold things and casual foods that did not spoil were always there for any eventuality. Depending on the time of day, they were offered with a glass of arak or mahia (the North African eau-de-vie), whiskey, beer, Coca-Cola, or other soft drinks.

The Friday-night meal started with an array of appetizers, and these were also important on weekdays. In the Oriental manner of serving, they were put on the table at the beginning of the meal and stayed on as side dishes. Raw vegetables—crudités—were always present, as were cold vegetables and salads. Some of the appetizers were complex, like pies, which you will find in the chapter on savory pastries, and stuffed vegetables, which are in the vegetable chapter.

One reason for their appeal is that appetizers are generally more richly flavored and aromatic than main meals, because they are supposed to open the appetite. In North Africa, cumin is a dominating flavor; in the Judeo-Spanish world, it is the sweet-and-sour combination of lemon or vinegar with a touch of sugar. They have gone down well in Israel, which is said to be a nation of snack eaters and grazers. North African Jews call them *kemia*. Otherwise they are generally called *mezze*.

UEVOS HAMINADOS—
BEID HAMINE

Long-Cooked Hard-Boiled Eggs

EGGS COOKED for hours or overnight, acquiring creamy buttery yolks and light-brown whites, epitomize Sephardi food. In Israel, they are sold by vendors in the street as "hamine"—which is what Oriental Jews call them. They are eaten on the Sabbath; at births and deaths and at all important moments of the cycle of life; at the end of Yom Kippur; at Passover; and to commemorate the destruction of the Temple. The egg in its shell is a symbol of procreation and of the continuation of Jewish life. More mundanely, hamine are taken on picnics and served as appetizers.

The eggs are cooked in many traditional ways—boiled in a pan; or gently baked in the ashes of a dying fire; or stewed in a Saturday pot with other ingredients, or on top of the lid. In Egypt, we boiled them for at least four hours in a pan lined and packed with onion skins and with a tablespoon of coffee grounds, which we thought made the whites browner. The onion skins stopped the shells from breaking and gave a slight flavor. The water was salted, and we added a few tablespoons of oil to prevent its evaporating. In Iraq eggs were placed on the lid of the Saturday pot, as it cooked in the ashes of a fire, covered by a blanket, and were eaten for breakfast on Saturday. They call them "beid al tabeet," "tabeet" being the Iraqi Sabbath dish of chicken and rice. I have seen Yemeni and Aden Jews simply putting them in the oven on a tray. According to tradition in Turkey, two people should not share one egg or they may come to hate each other. But in my family we often shared them and there was no obvious change in our relationships.

Vinegared Raw Vegetable Salad

SERVES 10

This is a way of making a quick and delicious pickle with a variety of raw vegetables. It is a good alternative to crudités for a party.

½ head of cauliflower, cut into small florets
2 carrots, cut into slices or thin sticks
2 turnips, ¼-inch (½-cm) slices or thin sticks
2 celery stalks, ¼-inch (½-cm) slices or thin sticks
2 zucchini, ¼-inch (½-cm) slices or thin sticks
Plenty of salt
½ cup (100 ml) wine vinegar
A dribble of extra-virgin olive oil (optional)

Put all the vegetables in a bowl, sprinkle very liberally with salt, and leave for 1 hour. Then add the vinegar, mix well, and leave for another hour. Drain well (the salt will go with the juices and vinegar) and serve with or without a dribble of olive oil.

Ajada

Garlic Mayonnaise

This popular Judeo-Spanish sauce is served as a dip for raw vegetables, or with fried or poached fish, boiled potatoes, or hard-boiled eggs.

4 or 5 garlic cloves, crushed
1 egg yolk, at room temperature
Salt and pepper
1 cup (250 ml) light extra-virgin olive oil
   or, preferably, a mixture with sunflower
   or light vegetable oil
Juice of ½ lemon

In a warmed bowl, beat the garlic with the egg yolk till pale and creamy. Add 1 teaspoon of water, and a little salt and pepper, then add the oil gradually—first drop by drop, then in a thin stream—beating vigorously all the time. As the oil becomes absorbed, the sauce will thicken into a heavy, thick consistency. Finally, beat in the lemon juice.

Agristada

Cold Egg-and-Lemon Sauce

SERVES 6

This sharp, refreshing sauce is one of the cornerstones of Sephardi cooking. It is generally known as Greek and Turkish, but it also appears in old Judeo-Spanish and Portuguese recipes. It is served with fish or brains or with boiled or steamed vegetables. I like it with an assortment of cooked green vegetables such as cauliflower, green beans, and asparagus. The addition of cornstarch is optional but it ensures a firm consistency.

1 tablespoon cornstarch
2 cups (500 ml) stock or water
3 eggs, lightly beaten
Juice of 2 lemons
Salt
1–2 teaspoons sugar (optional)

In a pan, mix the cornstarch with a few tablespoons of the stock or water into a smooth paste. Add the rest of the stock or water and stir well. Bring to the boil, stirring constantly so that no lumps form, then simmer for 10 minutes, until the sauce thickens slightly.

In a small bowl or cup, beat the eggs with the lemon juice, a little salt, and the sugar. Beat in a few tablespoons of the hot stock or water from the pan, then pour this mixture into the pan, stirring constantly on very low heat until the sauce thickens. Do not cook any further or it will curdle. Let it cool.

Mixed Israeli Salad

SERVES 8

This salad, born as part the famous kibbutz breakfast—eaten when the members had already spent several hours working in the fields and orchards—has become an Israeli classic. It is always mentioned as one of the wholly Israeli foods, although every Sephardi community has a version. In the kibbutzim the ingredients are laid out for members to make up for themselves, and everyone takes pride in peeling, chopping, and dressing the salad in a way that is considered an art.

1 cos or 2 Bibb lettuces
2 firm ripe tomatoes
1 peeled cucumber
1 green pepper, seeds removed (optional)
A few small or 1 long radish (optional)
1½ mild red onions or 9 scallions, chopped
3 tablespoons chopped flat-leafed parsley
5 tablespoons extra-virgin olive oil
Juice of 1 lemon
Salt and pepper

Cut all the vegetables into very small dice or pieces and put them in a bowl with the onions and flat-leafed parsley. Just before serving, dress with olive oil, lemon juice, and salt and pepper to taste.

VARIATIONS

• The Baghdadi Jews of India add to the dressing about ¾ inch (2 cm) ginger, chopped very finely or grated, and 2–3 seeded and finely chopped fresh green chilies.

• In North Africa they may add preserved lemon peel—washed and chopped—and sometimes a pinch of cayenne in the dressing.

• Bukharan Jews chop the vegetables really very small and dress only with salt, pepper, and vinegar—never with oil.

Salade de Carottes Rapées

Moroccan Grated Carrot Salad

SERVES 4–6

This sharp and refreshing salad is ubiquitous in Israel.

1 lb (500 g) carrots, finely grated
Juice of 1 lemon or more
Salt and pepper
4 tablespoons extra-virgin olive oil (in
  Morocco they used the delicate argan oil)
3 tablespoons chopped flat-leafed parsley
  or coriander

Dress the carrots with lemon juice, salt, pepper, and olive oil and mix in the flat-leafed parsley or coriander.

VARIATION

• You may add 2 crushed garlic cloves, the juice of 1 orange, or 1 tablespoon sugar.

Salade d'Oranges aux Olives

Orange Salad with Olives

SERVES 6

This famous Moroccan salad is best made with slightly sour or bitter oranges—though sweet ones will do—and with the rare argan oil. Argan oil, which the Jews of Essaouira traditionally use, gives the oranges a distinctive taste.

> *4 oranges*
> *Juice of ½–1 lemon or 2–3 tablespoons wine vinegar*
> *3 tablespoons argan oil or light extra-virgin olive oil*
> *3 garlic cloves, crushed in a press or finely chopped*
> *Salt*
> *A handful of black olives*
> *1 teaspoon cumin (optional)*
> *1 teaspoon paprika*
> *Pinch of cayenne or chili pepper (optional)*

Peel the oranges, removing the pith. Cut them into slices and then into pieces. Dress with a mixture of lemon juice, oil, garlic, and salt and add the olives. Serve sprinkled with cumin (if using), paprika, and cayenne pepper.

VARIATION

• For an orange-and-radish salad, mix with a bunch of sliced radishes and dress as above.

Apiu Ilado

Celeriac and Carrots in a Lemon Sauce

SERVES 4–6

This simple Judeo-Spanish dish of Turkey and the Balkans is most appealing, with its pure flavors and very slight sweet-and-sour touch.

> *3 largish carrots cut into ¾-inch (2-cm) slices*
> *1 celeriac weighing about 1 lb 11 oz (800 g), peeled and cut into 1-inch (½-cm) cubes*
> *Juice of 2 lemons*
> *2 teaspoons sugar*
> *Salt and pepper*
> *4 tablespoons mild-tasting extra-virgin olive oil or vegetable oil*
> *2 tablespoons chopped flat-leafed parsley*

Put the carrots and celeriac in a pan with just enough water to cover. Add lemon, sugar, and a little salt and pepper, and simmer 25–30 minutes, or until very tender, covering with the lid only part of the time, to reduce the liquid to a sauce. Serve cold, dressed with oil and sprinkled with parsley.

Céleris Raves et Fenouils au Citron

Celeriac and Fennel Salad

SERVES 6

This refreshing cold dish that we made in Egypt has a very lovely slightly anise flavor.

  5 garlic cloves, chopped
  3 tablespoons peanut or light vegetable oil
  *1 celeriac weighing about 1 lb 11 oz
      (800 g), peeled and cut into ¾-inch
      (2-cm) cubes*
  *1 large or 2 small fennel heads, cut in half,
      then in thick slices*
  Juice of 2 lemons
  2 teaspoons sugar or to taste
  Salt and white pepper
  *2 tablespoons chopped flat-leafed
      parsley*

In a large pan, fry the garlic in the oil till lightly colored. Add the celeriac and fennel and barely cover with water. Add the lemon juice, sugar, and a little salt and pepper, and simmer with the lid on, stirring occasionally, for ½ hour. Then take the lid off and reduce the liquid to a thick sauce. Serve cold mixed with chopped flat-leafed parsley.

VARIATION

• In Egypt we sometimes added ¼ teaspoon of turmeric to the water, which gave the vegetables a pale-yellow tinge.

Salade de Pommes de Terre aux Olives

Moroccan Potato Salad with Olives

SERVES 6

The strong flavors of the preserved lemons and the olives make an intriguing combination with potatoes.

  1 lb (500 g) new potatoes
  Salt
  4 tablespoons extra-virgin olive oil
  Pepper
  ½–1 preserved lemon (see page 239), optional
  *About 2 dozen olives (black or green),
      chopped*
  *2 tablespoons capers, soaked in water and
      squeezed to remove the excess salt*
  6 scallions, sliced

Boil the potatoes in salted water till tender. Peel and slice them or, depending on their size, cut them in half or in quarters. Dress with olive oil, salt, and pepper. Add the lemon, rinsed well in cold water, and the chopped olives, capers, and scallions, and mix very well.

VARIATION

• For an everyday Tunisian potato salad, dress boiled potatoes with the juice of 1 lemon, salt, 4 tablespoons olive oil, ½ teaspoon harissa (see page 242), and 1 teaspoon ground cumin and mix well. Add, if you like, 2 quartered raw artichoke hearts that have been left to marinate in lemon juice.

Carottes au Carvi

Sliced Boiled Carrot Salad with Caraway Seeds

SERVES 6

This specialty of the Jews of Meknes in Morocco is now common in Israel.

1½ lbs (750 g) carrots
Juice of 1–1½ lemons
4 tablespoons extra-virgin olive oil
Salt and pepper
2 cloves garlic, crushed
1 teaspoon caraway seeds

Boil the carrots until they are tender. Drain and slice them thickly. Dress with a mixture of lemon juice and oil, salt and pepper to taste, garlic, and caraway. Leave for at least an hour before serving.

VARIATION

• In Fez and Tangiers they used cumin instead of caraway, and also a little paprika.

Apyo

Celery Cooked in Oil

SERVES 6

This simple way of treating celery is from Turkey and the Balkans and makes a special dish out of a very ordinary vegetable.

1 lb (500 g) celery, a large head with leaves or 3 hearts, sliced
4 tablespoons sunflower or extra-virgin light olive oil or a mixture
Juice of 1 lemon
1 tablespoon sugar
A little salt

Put all the ingredients together in a pan, stir well, and simmer over gentle heat with the lid on for ½–¾ hour, or until the celery is very limp.

Salade de Carottes et Pommes de Terre

Boiled Carrot and Potato Salad

SERVES 6

This North African salad is usually made with carrots alone, but the mixture with potatoes is particularly good. It has long been a favorite in my family.

¾ lb (350 g) carrots
¾ lb (350 g) potatoes
Salt
Juice of ½ lemon or more
4–5 tablespoons extra-virgin olive oil
½ teaspoon cumin
1 teaspoon paprika
Pinch of cayenne
3 garlic cloves, crushed in a press or finely chopped

Trim and scrape or peel the carrots. Peel the potatoes. Cut both into large pieces and boil in slightly salted water for about 20 minutes, or until they are very tender. Drain, then cut up the vegetables, and mash them with a fork or potato masher. Beat the lemon juice and olive oil with salt, cumin, paprika, cayenne, and garlic and mix well with the carrots and potatoes.

Salade du Shabbat

Boiled Vegetable Salad

SERVES 6

This is a Tunisian Friday-night special.

> *2 carrots*
> *2 turnips*
> *½ cauliflower*
> *2 celery stalks*
> *2 waxy potatoes*
> *Salt*
> *4–5 tablespoons extra-virgin olive oil*
> *Juice of 1 lemon*
> *1 teaspoon harissa (page 242) or*
> > *1 teaspoon paprika and a good pinch*
> > *of cayenne*
> *1 teaspoon ground caraway*
> *½ teaspoon ground coriander*

Slice or cut the vegetables into ¾-inch (2-cm) pieces. Boil in salted water for about 25 minutes and drain. In a serving bowl, mix the olive oil with the lemon juice, harissa, caraway, and ground coriander. Add the vegetables and mix well.

Salade d'Oignons

Onion Salad with Capers

One way of cooking onions is to roast them very gently in the oven. Once upon a time it was in the ashes of the fire. Put medium-sized onions on a sheet of foil on a baking sheet and roast in a 350°F (180°C) oven for 1–1½ hours, or until they feel soft when you press them. Peel off the outer skin and any inner skin that seems dry, then cut them into quarters and dress with olive oil alone or a mixture with vinegar or lemon juice in a ratio of 3 tablespoons of oil to 1 of vinegar or lemon. Serve cold, sprinkled if you like with a few capers.

Oignons Caramélisés

Sweet-and-Sour Caramel Onions

SERVES 6

These little onions have an intense sweet-and-sour burnt-sugar flavor which makes them a good accompaniment to bland foods. The only bother is the peeling. But blanching makes it easier, and it is the kind of thing that you can do in front of the television.

> *1½ lbs (750 g) shallots or baby pickling*
> > *onions in their skins*
> *3 tablespoons extra-virgin olive oil*
> *3 tablespoons sugar*
> *Juice of 1½ lemons*
> *A little salt*

Drop the shallots or baby onions in their skins in a pan of boiling water and simmer for about 5 minutes (this is to make peeling easy). Drain and, when cool enough to handle, remove the skins. They should come off very easily. Put the oil and the sugar in a wide pan in which the onions could fit in 1 layer. Heat until the sugar turns brown. Toss in the onions and stir. Add the lemon juice and a little salt and cover with water—about 1 cup (250 ml). Simmer for about ½ hour—put the lid on for the first ¼ hour, then cook uncovered to reduce the liquid to a thick, rich sauce.

TO ROAST AND PEEL BELL PEPPERS

CHOOSE FLESHY PEPPERS. Put them on a baking sheet under the broiler, about 3½ inches (9 cm) from the heat (or grill them on the barbecue). Turn them until their skins are black and blistered all over. Alternatively, roast them in the hottest oven for ½ hour, or until they are soft and their skins begin to blister and blacken—they need to be turned only once. To loosen the skins further, put them in a pan with a tight-fitting lid or in a strong polyethylene or brown paper bag and twist it closed. Leave for 10–15 minutes. This helps to loosen the skins. When the peppers are cool enough to handle, peel them and remove the stems and seeds. Keep the juice that comes out and strain it to remove the seeds, for it can be used as part of the dressing.

Salade de Poivrons Grillés
Grilled Pepper Salad

Choose fleshy red, yellow, or green bell peppers or use mixed colors. Roast and peel them and remove the seeds (see box), and cut them into wide ribbons. I like them dressed with only a tiny bit of salt and extra-virgin olive oil and their own juices. But it is usual to add a squeeze of lemon or a little vinegar.

VARIATIONS

• You may roast a head of garlic at the same time—but take it out before, because it cooks more quickly than peppers, in about 10–15 minutes. Peel the cloves and add them to the peppers.

• Tunisians roast a few hot chilies at the same time too and chop them up in the dressing.

Salade de Tomates et Poivrons Grillés
Grilled Tomato and Pepper Salad

SERVES 6

3 red or green bell peppers
3 tomatoes
4 tablespoons extra-virgin olive oil
1–2 tablespoons wine vinegar
Salt and pepper

Broil or roast the peppers and tomatoes (see box). Take the tomatoes out after about 10 minutes, when the skin is loosened and they are only a little soft. Peel the peppers and tomatoes and cut them into pieces. Dress with oil, vinegar, salt, and pepper.

VARIATIONS

• For a flavorsome Moroccan version, add 2–3 chopped garlic cloves, I teaspoon cumin, the chopped peel of I preserved lemon (see page 239), and I–2 hot chili peppers, seeded and finely chopped. If you have an opportunity to buy the rare argan oil, it is wonderful with this, as well as with most salads.

• You may grill or roast a head of garlic at the same time, then peel the cloves. Garlic needs 10 minutes in the oven to become soft.

after 10 minutes, when their skins come off easily and they are only slightly softened. Peel them and cut them into quarters. Follow instructions "to roast and peel bell peppers" on page 253, and cut them into ribbons.

On a serving platter or individual plates, arrange the elements of the salad—the peppers, tomatoes, flaked tuna, and eggs—in a decorative way. Mix the oil, lemon, salt, and pepper and dribble on top.

VARIATIONS

• Garnish if you like with I chopped preserved lemon (see page 239) and I–2 tablespoons capers, squeezed to rid them of some of the vinegar.

• Add 6 or 7 cloves of garlic, grilled in their skins until soft, then peeled and served whole.

Mechouia

"Grilled" Salad

SERVES 4

This most popular Tunisian salad is usually served as a first course but can be a meal in itself.

> 2 green or red bell peppers
> 3 medium tomatoes
> A 7-oz (200-g) can of tuna in brine, drained
> 2 hard-boiled eggs, quartered
> 4–5 tablespoons extra-virgin olive oil
> Juice of 1 lemon
> Salt and pepper

Turn the peppers and tomatoes on a baking sheet under the broiler. Take the tomatoes out

Marmouma

Tunisian Fried Pepper Salad

SERVES 8

In this salad, which also goes by the name of "chouka," the peppers have a different flavor from when they are grilled.

> 4 red bell peppers
> 3–4 tablespoons extra-virgin olive oil
> 4 garlic cloves, finely chopped
> 1½ lbs (750 g) tomatoes, peeled and cut into pieces
> Salt and pepper
> 1–2 teaspoons sugar
> 1 lemon, cut in 6 wedges

Cut the peppers in half lengthwise and remove the stems and seeds, then cut them into ¾-inch (2-cm) pieces. Fry them in the oil on very low heat, turning them over until they are soft. Add the garlic and cook till the peppers are slightly browned. Then add the tomatoes, salt, pepper, and sugar and simmer, uncovered, for about 25 minutes, until the tomatoes are reduced to a thick, jammy consistency. Serve on slices of bread accompanied by lemon wedges.

VARIATION

• One teaspoon of caraway seeds could be added, and a good pinch of hot red pepper.

EGGPLANTS— A JEWISH CONNECTION

ALTHOUGH EGGPLANTS were brought by the Arabs to Spain and Italy, Jews have been credited for introducing them because they took them to the north of these countries when they fled from the Almohades and Almoravides in southern Spain and when the Inquisition banished them from southern Italy. They remained forever associated with the vegetable and were exceedingly fond of it.

Fried Eggplant Slices

It is a very old Jewish tradition in many countries to serve fried eggplant slices cold on Saturday.

To serve 6 people, cut 2 lbs (1 kg) eggplants into ⅓-inch (⅘-cm) slices. Sprinkle with salt and leave to draw out their juices for 1 hour. Then rinse in cold water and drain. Spread them on a tea towel or paper towels, cover with another cloth or more paper towels, and gently pat dry. Fry in a bland olive oil or a light vegetable oil, turning to brown them lightly all over. The oil must be sizzling but not too hot or they will brown too quickly before they are cooked inside. Lift out with a slotted spatula, slice, and drain on paper towels.

VARIATIONS

They are very good as they are, but you might like to try some traditional dressings. Sprinkle on one of the following:

• The juice of one lemon, or 3 tablespoons wine vinegar, and chopped flat-leafed parsley.

• For a Tunisian flavor, bring to the boil about 6 tablespoons water with ½ teaspoon harissa (see page 242; or 1 teaspoon paprika and ¼ teaspoon cayenne) and add 3 crushed garlic cloves. Stir well and add the fried eggplant, turning the pieces over very gently. Simmer for a minute or two so that they absorb the dressing.

• A Moroccan way is to sprinkle with cumin and to serve cut into pieces and mixed with diced preserved lemon skin (see page 239).

• Another Moroccan way is to mix the eggplant with fresh lemons pared to the flesh, sliced, then cut into little pieces.

• A Turkish way for a dairy meal is to spread the eggplant slices with thickened yogurt.

• A Syrian way is to pour 2 tablespoons of pomegranate concentrate diluted in 2 tablespoons of water over the fried slices.

Eggplant Fritters

A Judeo-Spanish way of dealing with fried eggplant—"berengena frita"—so that it does not absorb too much oil is to dip it in beaten egg before frying, in which case you do not need to salt them to draw out the juices first. Trim and cut the eggplants into ⅓-inch (1-cm) slices lengthwise or across, in rounds, dip in beaten egg, and deep-fry in sizzling but not too hot oil, turning over once. Lift out and drain on paper towels. Sprinkle with salt and serve hot or cold.

Caviare d'Aubergines
Mashed Eggplant Salad with Oil and Lemon

This is the famous eggplant puree popular all over the Mediterranean, the Balkans, and the Middle East.

Grill 1 lb (500 g) eggplants (see box).

TO ROAST AND MASH EGGPLANTS

PRICK THE EGGPLANTS in a few places with a fork or a pointed knife and turn them over or under a grill or broiler, or roast them in the hottest oven, turning them once, for 45 minutes, or until the flesh feels very soft when you press and the skin is blistered and black. When they are cool enough to handle, peel or scoop out the flesh into a colander. Drain and press out the juices, then chop the flesh with 2 sharp knives and mash it with a fork, still in the colander, or puree in a food processor when all the juices have been pressed out.

Chop and mash the flesh or turn to a puree. Beat in 3 tablespoons of extra-virgin olive oil, the juice of 1 lemon, and a little salt.

VARIATIONS

• In Syria they may add 2 crushed garlic cloves and 1 tablespoon of dried mint.

• A Moroccan version has 1 teaspoon of ground cumin and a pinch of cayenne.

• In Israel they stir in 3–4 tablespoons of flat-leafed parsley, a little diced green pepper, tomato, and scallion, and finely chopped chilies.

• Bukharan Jews make this salad with only garlic and salt—and nothing else. It is the first course of their Friday-night meal.

Salade d'Aubergines et Poivrons Épicée

Spicy Eggplant and Pepper Salad

SERVES 6–8

Many Moroccan salads are highly spiced to develop an appetite for the meal, and cumin is a ubiquitous part of the aromatics.

> *2 eggplants, weighing about 1½ lb*
> *(750 g)*
> *2 red bell peppers*
> *1 teaspoon cumin*
> *1 teaspoon paprika*
> *A good pinch of cayenne or chili pepper*
> *2 or 3 garlic cloves, crushed*
> *4 tablespoons extra-virgin olive oil or*
> *light vegetable oil*
> *Juice of 1 lemon*
> *Salt*

Roast the eggplants and peppers (see pages 256 and 253). Take the peppers out after ½ hour. Leave the eggplants for about ¼ hour more if necessary. Peel the peppers and cut into ¾-inch (2-cm) squares. Peel the eggplants and cut into ¾-inch (2-cm) cubes.

In a pan put the cumin, paprika, cayenne, garlic, and oil and stir over low heat until the aroma rises. Take off the heat for a minute to cool and add ½ cup (125 ml) water, the lemon juice, and salt. Put in the eggplants and peppers and cook for 10–15 minutes, stirring occasionally, until the liquid is absorbed. Serve cold.

VARIATION

• For a very different sweet-and-sour Moroccan flavor: Fry 7 chopped garlic cloves in 3 tablespoons of oil till golden. Take off the heat for a minute and add ½ cup (125 ml) of wine vinegar, 1½ tablespoons of honey, salt and ¼ teaspoon (or to taste) of cayenne pepper. Stir well and bring to the boil. Put in the cubed eggplants and peppers and simmer, stirring occasionally, for about 10 minutes. Serve cold.

Salade d'Aubergines Frites et de Poivrons

Fried Eggplant and Pepper Salad

SERVES 6–8

This salad, in which the vegetables are fried, has a very different flavor from the one above, in which they are roasted.

> *2 eggplants weighing about 1½ lbs*
> *(750 g)*
> *Salt*
> *Olive oil for frying*
> *2 tablespoons wine vinegar*
> *5 cloves garlic, sliced*
> *3 red or green bell peppers*

Trim and slice the eggplants into rounds ⅓ inch (1 cm) thick. Sprinkle with salt and leave 1 hour in a colander. Then rinse and dry on a tea towel or paper towel. Fry in hot oil (not so hot that they brown too quickly), turning the slices once to brown them all over. Lift them out and drain on paper towels. Arrange in a layer on a serving dish and sprinkle with vinegar.

Fry the garlic in 2 tablespoons of oil, stirring, until lightly colored. Lift out of the oil and sprinkle over the eggplants. Fry the peppers whole, turning them so that they are soft and browned all over. Cut them in ribbons, remove the seeds, and spread over the eggplants.

VARIATION

• A Moroccan way is to add 2 preserved lemons (see page 239), rinsed and chopped.

Boil the eggplants in water to cover with the garlic and a little salt for about 25 minutes, or until they are very soft. Drain and, when cool enough, press them in a colander so as to squeeze all the water out. Chop the eggplants and garlic and mash them with a fork, then add the rest of the ingredients and mix very well.

VARIATION

• For a Tunisian ajlouk, boil the eggplants in salted water and mash them with ½ teaspoon harissa, the juice of ½ lemon, I garlic clove crushed in a press or finely chopped, I teaspoon ground caraway or coriander seeds, and 2 tablespoons olive oil.

Zaalouk d'Aubergines

Spicy Boiled Eggplant Salad

SERVES 4–6

This Moroccan salad has the advantage of not having all the oil that comes from frying. Boiled eggplant is usually rather unpleasant, but the flavoring used here makes it delightful. There is a lot of garlic, but since it is boiled it loses all its strength. It is best made several hours in advance.

> *2 lbs (1 kg) eggplants, peeled and cubed*
> *8 cloves garlic, peeled*
> *Salt*
> *4 tablespoons extra-virgin olive oil*
> *2 tablespoons vinegar*
> *½ teaspoon paprika*
> *A good pinch of cayenne, or to taste*
> *½–1 teaspoon cumin*

Caponata alla Giudea

Italian Eggplant Salad

SERVES 6

Caponata is a popular Saturday dish in Italy, served cold to accompany meat or fish. This eggplant salad with olives and capers and a slight sweet-and-sour flavor is Sicilian, and now famous, but for centuries, in the rest of Italy, it was associated with Jews. Large colonies of Jews had lived in Sicily since Roman times. They were among those of the Diaspora who had the richest culture and traditions. When the Inquisition banished them from the island, which was under Spanish rule at the beginning of the sixteenth century, it is said that over thirty-five thousand Jews left Sicily. The foods they took with them when they fled to central- and northern-Italian cities are still labeled "alla giudea" or "all'ebraica." Eggplants, unknown and at first rejected in the rest of Italy, remained Jewish favorites.

2 lbs (1 kg) eggplants, peeled and cubed
Salt
1 large onion, chopped
Olive oil
2 or 3 garlic cloves, finely chopped
1½ lbs (750 g) tomatoes, peeled and
*   chopped*
3 celery stalks with leaves, cut into ½-inch
*   (1-cm) slices*
4–6 tablespoons wine vinegar
1½–3 tablespoons sugar
Pepper
4 oz (100 g) green olives, pitted and cut
*   in half*
2 tablespoons capers

Cut the eggplants into ¾-inch (2-cm) cubes. Sprinkle with salt and leave to drain in a colander for an hour.

Fry the onion in 4 tablespoons oil until golden. Then add the garlic and when the aroma rises add the tomatoes, celery, vinegar, and sugar (for the latter two, start with the lesser quantities and add more at the end, to taste), salt and pepper, olives, and capers, and simmer about 15–20 minutes, until the tomatoes have cooked down to a thick sauce.

Rinse the eggplants, then dry them gently on a tea towel or paper towels. Fry them quickly, in batches, in plenty of hot oil, turning to brown them all over. Drain on paper towels and add to the tomato sauce. Stir and simmer another 5–10 minutes. Serve cold, garnished if you like with quartered hard-boiled eggs.

Kamfounata

Moroccan Ratatouille

SERVES 6

Notice the name's similarity to "caponata." Variants of the famous ratatouille of Nice are cooked by Sephardi communities around the Mediterranean. This version from Morocco, in which the vegetables are fried separately and then put together in a fresh tomato sauce, is delightful.

2 eggplants, cut in ½-inch (1-cm) cubes
2 zucchini, cut in ½-inch (1-cm) slices
Olive oil
2 bell peppers, cut in half, seeded, and cut
*   into thin slices*
1 large onion, cut in half and sliced
5 cloves of garlic, finely chopped
1½ lbs (750 g) tomatoes, peeled and
*   chopped*
Salt and pepper
2 teaspoons sugar
A good bunch of flat-leafed parsley or
*   coriander, chopped (½ cup)*

Sprinkle the eggplants with salt and leave for 1 hour to draw out their juices, then rinse and dry them. Very briefly shallow-fry the eggplants and zucchini separately in hot oil until lightly browned, then drain on paper towels. Fry the onion and pepper over gentle heat in 3 tablespoons of oil till the onion is golden and the pepper is soft.

Make a tomato sauce: fry the garlic in 2 tablespoons of oil till golden. Add the tomatoes, salt, pepper, and sugar and simmer about 20 minutes, until reduced to a thick sauce. Stir in the fried vegetables and the flat-leafed parsley and take off the heat. This can be eaten hot or cold.

VARIATION

• When it is to be eaten cold, it is sometimes made with a few sprigs of fresh mint (chopped) or I tablespoon dried mint, and some black olives may be added.

Concia di Zucchine

Marinated Zucchini

SERVES 6

This too is a Sicilian specialty that was brought to northern cities by Jews fleeing the Inquisition. It is still a Jewish favorite. In the Veneto dialect it is "zucchete in aseo." We had made it for a Jewish event at the Italian Cultural Institute in London, and the kosher caterer had not fried the zucchini enough, so they appeared steamed. Tulia Zevi, the head of the Jewish community in Italy, who arrived from Rome, remarked at once that they should be brown.

1½ lbs (750 g) zucchini
Olive oil
2 or 3 garlic cloves, finely chopped
A few sprigs of fresh basil or mint, finely chopped
4 tablespoons wine vinegar
Salt and pepper

Trim the ends of the zucchini and cut in thin slices diagonally. Fry quickly in batches in hot olive oil, turning them over once, until browned all over. Lift out and drain on paper towels.

Fry the garlic or leave it raw. Lay the zucchini slices in layers, sprinkling each layer with the drained garlic, the basil or mint, the vinegar, salt, and pepper. Leave to marinate a few hours before serving cold. It keeps very well for days.

VARIATIONS

• For a peppery version, put a small chili pepper in the oil at the start and discard it after frying the zucchini, or mix a pinch of cayenne with the vinegar.

• A sweet-and-sour ("agrodolce") version mixes I tablespoon of sugar with I–2 tablespoons of vinegar.

• For "concia di melanzane," do the same with sliced eggplants.

Ajlouk de Courgettes

Mashed Zucchini Salad

SERVES 6

This Tunisian salad is proof that boiled zucchini do not have to be dull.

1½ lbs (750 g) zucchini
Salt
Juice of ½ lemon
2 tablespoons extra-virgin olive oil
3 garlic cloves, crushed in a press

1 teaspoon ground coriander
8 black olives

Trim and wash the zucchini, then boil them in salted water till soft. Drain and press gently to squeeze out the excess water, then chop with a pointed knife and mash with a fork. Add the rest of the ingredients and mix well. Serve cold.

Ajlouk de Potiron

Spicy Pumpkin Puree

SERVES 4

This North African dip to eat with bread is only as good as the pumpkin, and they do vary.

> 1 lb (500 g) orange pumpkin, peeled and
>   cut into pieces
> Salt
> Juice of ½–1 lemon
> 2 garlic cloves, crushed in a press
> ¼–½ teaspoon harissa (see page 242),
>   or ½ teaspoon paprika and a good pinch
>   of chili pepper
> 1 teaspoon caraway seeds
> ½ teaspoon ground coriander
> 2 tablespoons extra-virgin olive oil

Steam or boil the pumpkin in salted water for about 15 minutes, till tender. Drain in a colander and press out the water. Mash with a fork in a bowl. Add the rest of the ingredients and mix well.

Mushrooms with Cumin Moroccan Style

SERVES 6–8

> 1 lb (500 g) mushrooms
> 4 tablespoons extra-virgin olive oil
> 3 or 4 garlic cloves, crushed
> Salt
> 2 teaspoons cumin
> A good pinch of chili pepper
> Juice of ½ lemon
> 3 tablespoons finely chopped coriander

Wash the mushrooms. Cut them in half or quarters, or leave whole if very small. Fry quickly in the oil with the garlic. Add salt, cumin, chili pepper, and lemon juice and cook on very low heat, stirring occasionally, for about 10 minutes. Add coriander towards the end. Serve cold.

Ispanakhi Salati

Spinach Salad with Walnuts and Pomegranate Seeds

SERVES 4–6

I came by this recipe for a Georgian salad at the Museum of the Diaspora in Tel Aviv. It was given to me by Lily Macal, a Georgian who helped to organize an exhibition on Georgian life that was on there at the time.

> 1 lb (500 g) spinach
> Salt
> 1 tablespoon vinegar
> 2 tablespoons extra-virgin olive oil
> 1 garlic clove, crushed in a garlic
>   press
> ¼ teaspoon cayenne pepper or to taste
> 2 scallions, chopped
> A few sprigs of coriander, chopped
> A small handful of pomegranate seeds
> 5 walnut halves, broken up into
>   pieces

Wash the spinach leaves and remove only hard stems (keep thin ones). Drain and squeeze the excess water out with your hands. Put in a large pan, sprinkle with a very little salt, and steam with the lid on until the leaves collapse into a soft mass. Then drain.

Mix the vinegar and oil with the garlic and cayenne and dress the spinach. Arrange on a large flat plate, pulling the spinach apart, and garnish with sprinklings of scallions, coriander, pomegranate seeds, and walnut pieces.

VARIATION

• A simple salad of steamed spinach with oil and lemon is common throughout the Middle Eastern communities.

Piyaziko

Dried White Haricot Bean Salad

SERVES 4–6

This is a very important salad for Balkan and Turkish Jews. It can be a meal in itself. It is perfectly good to use canned beans.

> ½ lb (250 g) small dried white haricot
>   beans, soaked overnight, or 1 lb (500 g)
>   canned beans
> 4 tablespoons extra-virgin olive oil
> 2 tablespoons white-wine vinegar
> Salt and pepper
> 1 mild onion, finely chopped
> 3 tablespoons chopped flat-leafed parsley
> 8 black olives
> 2 tomatoes, cut into wedges
> 2 hard-boiled eggs, cut into wedges

Drain the soaked dried beans and boil in fresh water for 1–1½ hours, or until tender, or drain the canned beans. Dress with oil, vinegar, salt, and pepper and mix with chopped onion and flat-leafed parsley. Serve garnished with black olives, tomatoes, and hard-boiled eggs.

VARIATION

• For "fassoulia bi zeit," an Egyptian version: Blanch and drain the soaked beans. Fry 1 large chopped onion and 2 chopped garlic cloves in 2 tablespoons of olive oil until golden. Add the beans and 2 tablespoons of tomato paste. Cover with water and boil, covered, for 1–1½ hours, until tender, adding water if necessary and letting it reduce when they are done. Add 2 tablespoons of olive oil.

Chickpea Salad

SERVES 6–8

This Oriental salad is best made a few hours before it is to be eaten.

> 1 lb (500 g) chickpeas, soaked for 1 hour
>   or overnight
> Salt
> ⅓ cup (80 ml) extra-virgin olive oil
> Juice of 1 lemon
> 1 teaspoon cumin
> ¼–½ teaspoon cayenne or chili pepper
>   (optional)
> 3 garlic cloves, crushed in a press
>   (optional)
> 4 tablespoons chopped flat-leafed
>   parsley

Drain the chickpeas and boil in fresh water for 1½ hours, or until tender, adding salt when they have softened. Drain, then add the rest of the ingredients and mix well.

Loubia
Black-Eyed Pea Salad

SERVES 6–8

In Egypt we served this salad for Rosh Hashanah, the New Year. It represented new life and fecundity.

> 1 lb (500 g) black-eyed peas, soaked for
>   1 hour
> Salt
> 1 mild red onion, chopped, or 2 garlic cloves,
>   minced or crushed in a press
> 4 tablespoons chopped flat-leafed parsley
> Black pepper
> ½ teaspoon cumin (optional)
> 5 tablespoons extra-virgin olive oil
> Juice of 1 lemon

Boil the drained peas for about 20 minutes, or until tender, adding salt towards the end. Drain, then add the rest of the ingredients and mix well.

VARIATION

• A similar salad is made using brown or green lentils.

GEORGIAN FEASTS

THE ORIGINS of the Jews of Georgia, in the Caucasus, are shrouded in romantic legends. One such is that they belong to one of the Lost Tribes. Another is that they are descended from the Khazars—a Turkish tribe settled in the Volga Delta, on the Caspian Sea, whose king and nobility converted to Judaism in the eighth century—who disappeared after the Tartar invasion in 1237. It is a very old community with long-standing ties to neighboring communities in Turkey and Persia. Until the twelfth century, it was under the religious authority of the Babylonian exilarch in Baghdad. When Russia annexed Georgia in the nineteenth century, some Eastern European Jews settled there. Although Jews shared the language, beliefs, and customs, and had the same dress, music, and song and the same cooking as the rest of the population, they maintained their identity and communal organization—even throughout the Soviet communist regime.

Waves of immigration to Israel and America started in the 1970s. In Israel, the part of their culture that they have kept up, and which has made a strong impact, is their music and dance, and especially their legendary feasting. Georgians entertain in an extraordinary way. They have always been known for their conviviality and warmth, for their joy of living and extreme hospitality, and still today, whether in Tbilisi or Ashkelon, every opportunity is taken to "set out a table," be it a spontaneous affair or a banquet planned months ahead. I have not had the good luck to attend one of their legendary banquets, but friends have told me wondrous stories of meals going on for hours with wine flowing like water and dishes brought in a continuous stream piled on top of each other, with music, singing, and dancing, and constant toasting. The toasts—which are gracious speeches that go on throughout the entire meal—are the object of the greatest fascination. They are recited or chanted with flowery passion and humor in honor of the hosts, the celebrants, their relatives, the deceased, the guests and notables present, and to peace, love, and friendship, beauty, motherhood, women, the Divine Presence, the state, and so on.

A paper by my friend the anthropologist Gerald Mars and Yochanan Altman entitled "Alternative Mechanism of Distribution in a Soviet Economy" (in *Constructive Drinking: Perspectives on Drink from Anthropologists,* edited by Mary Douglas) gives an insight on the feasting rituals of Georgians. Every feast has an appointed head of table—the *tamada,* or master of ceremony, who orders the proceedings, offers the toasts, then passes the right to reply and to toast to others, dictates the themes of speeches they make, and controls the flow of wine. Wine, in Georgian tradition, is associated with manhood and male friendship, and drinking is competitive and carried out with bravado and bonhomie. The men actually make the wine, and they are largely the sole consumers of their product. They drink it in one gulp, and the more they can drink, the greater their standing. The women, who sit at one end of the table or at separate tables, normally drink only one glass—when they accept the thanks from the men for the feast's preparation, which is carried out cooperatively by relatives and neighbors.

I visited the Museum of the Diaspora (Beth Hatfutzoth) in Tel Aviv when they had an exhibition of Georgian life. The curator, Rahel Arbal, described her visit to Georgia and arranged for Lily Macal, a Georgian who helped with the exhibition and had traveled with her, to give me recipes that she translated from Hebrew. Rahel Arbal recounted her experiences and gave me a copy of the proofs of the book on Jewish life in Georgia which they wrote for the exhibition.

Much of the old Jewish life, which had its roots in the countryside, disappeared during the communist regime. Jews had in the past been engaged in commerce, agriculture, and crafts, but their main occupation was petty trade, peddling and touring villages with perfumes, clothes, confectionery, pots, and utensils, strapped to their shoulders or packed in sacks on horseback. Many left their families for months, returning only for the holy days. By the end of the nineteenth century, when railway tracks had been laid and the Black Sea ports were developed, some began to trade with Europe and Russia and became prosperous. After the 1917 revolution, when the communist regime was established in the early 1920s most lost their source of livelihood and moved to Tbilisi and other big towns. They became artisans—hatmakers, shoemakers, soapmakers, porters, shoeshines, and photographers. In the last fifty years, many of the young have gone to university and become doctors, chemists, and civil engineers.

By the 1960s, most had moved away from the crowded Jewish quarters, where they had lived as extended families in homes built around a courtyard, and into government housing projects or houses they built for themselves. In the villages, they continued to live in the old houses built of stone, river pebbles, or wood with fenced yards, fruit trees, vines, vegetable plots, chicken runs, cowsheds, and stables. Round clay ovens were built outside for baking bread and cooking the Sabbath dishes.

The old traditional Georgian house had one large room, with sofas around the walls for sleeping on and rugs hanging on the walls. A large copper cooking pot, the *shwatzetzkhli*, hung over a fire on a heavy chain from the ceiling in the center of the room. Water was boiled in a samovar. Wine, pickles, and jams were stored in cellars. Fruit and vegetables were dried on rooftops and verandas. Men made the wine, gathering in the grapes and treading them in wooden vats. The dregs were fermented to make arak, which was flavored with roses, mint, and cherries.

Because of the mild climate and fertile soil, fruit and vegetables were always plentiful. They were those of the Mediterranean, plus exotic fruits like sour plums and pomegranates. Georgian cooking is deliciously rich in strong flavors. Sharp ones are obtained from sour plums, fresh pomegranate juice, vinegar, and tamarind (in Turkey, sauces with sour plums are considered uniquely Jewish, and that may have something to do with Georgian Jews' joining the Turkish communities). Garlic is much used, and raw onion, and also herbs like coriander, dill, mint, and basil, and hot red chili pepper. The most ubiquitous ingredient is ground walnuts, which go into sauces for fish, chicken, and also vegetables. The most popular dishes are khachapuri, cheese pies; sateni, fish with a walnut-and-tamarind sauce; satzivi, chicken with nut sauce; gomi, a thick corn porridge like polenta; and salads made of vegetables mixed with nuts and pomegranate seeds.

Jewish dishes are the same as those of the general population, but with little differences, like the use of tamarind paste in some instances instead of pomegranate juice, and they have even more echoes of the cooking of neighboring countries, which bears witness to the ties that, despite their isolation, they maintained with their brethren in Turkey, Kurdistan, and Persia.

Lobio Tkemali

Small Red Kidney Beans with Sour Plum Sauce

SERVES 10 OR MORE

This is one of the favorites at Georgian feasts. The bland, slightly sweet-tasting beans combine with the sharp fresh flavor of the herby plum sauce in an intriguing and delicious creation. The plums used in Georgia are of a sour yellow or red variety. Sour plums make a brief appearance in Iranian stores in London in the early summer (they will surely soon find their way to the United States), but slightly unripe red plums with added lemon juice give very good results. The same tkemali (plum sauce) can be served to accompany Georgian cheese pies (page 295) and also the shashlik (lamb kebabs, page 385).

1 lb (500 g) dried red kidney beans, soaked in cold water for 5 hours
Salt

For the tkemali (sour-plum sauce)

> *1 lb (500 g) plums*
> *A good bunch of coriander (½ cup)*
> *3 sprigs of fresh mint*
> *A little salt*
> *¼–½ teaspoon cayenne or chili powder*
> *Juice of ½ lemon or to taste*
> *3 garlic cloves, crushed*

Drain the beans and put them in a pan with fresh cold water. Boil hard for about 10 minutes, then lower the heat and simmer for 1–1½ hours, adding salt towards the end, when they are already very tender.

In the meantime, prepare the sauce. Put the plums in a pan with about 4 tablespoons of water, cover on, and let them steam for about 15 minutes, till they are very soft. Let them cool and remove the pits. Finely chop the coriander and mint in the food processor. Add the plums, salt, cayenne or chili powder, lemon, and garlic, and blend to a light cream. Pour over the beans and mix well.

Accompany, if you like, with bowls of sliced red onion and black olives.

Insalata di Riso

Rice Salad

SERVES 8–10

This is a Sabbath dish in Italy.

> 1 lb (500 g) long-grain rice
> Salt
> 6 tablespoons extra-virgin olive oil
> 4 tablespoons white-wine vinegar
> Pepper
> 12 black olives
> 3 tablespoons capers, rinsed and
>   squeezed
> 6 artichoke hearts preserved in oil,
>   quartered
> ½ lb (250 g) canned tuna, drained and
>   flaked
> 4 oz (100 g) canned anchovy fillets,
>   chopped
> 12 small cherry tomatoes, cut in half

Pour the rice into plenty of boiling salted water and cook for about 20 minutes, until tender, then drain. While it is still hot, dress with a mixture of oil, vinegar, salt, and pepper. Add the rest of the ingredients and mix well.

Muhammara

Walnut and Roast Pepper Paste

SERVES 8–10

There are many different versions of this marvelous paste. This delicious Syrian one is Dalia Carmel's. She is the angel of American food writers, because she makes her gigantic library of cookbooks available to all who ask.

> 4 large red bell peppers
> 1 hot chili pepper
> 2 slices whole-wheat bread, crusts
>   removed
> 1½ cups (175 g) shelled walnuts
> 1 garlic clove, crushed in a press
> 3 tablespoons pomegranate concentrate
>   (molasses)
> Juice of 1 lemon
> 1 teaspoon sugar
> ½–1 teaspoon salt
> 1 teaspoon cumin (optional)
> ½ cup (125 ml) extra-virgin olive oil,
>   or more if necessary
> 3 or 4 sprigs of flat-leafed parsley, finely
>   chopped, to garnish

Roast and peel the peppers following the method given on page 253. Put all the ingredients except the parsley in a food processor and blend to a thick creamy paste. Serve sprinkled with the parsley.

Tabbouleh

Cracked Wheat Salad with Parsley and Tomatoes

SERVES 4

The tabbouleh that was made a hundred years ago in Aleppo and Damascus—the way Jews preserved the recipe when they left for Egypt and the Americas at the turn of the century—is more substantial and wheaty than the very green salads you find in Lebanese restaurants, which have only specks of wheat.

> *1 cup (175 g) fine bulgur (cracked wheat)*
> *1 lb (500 g) firm ripe tomatoes, diced small (¼ inch—5 mm)*
> *Salt and pepper*
> *Juice of 1 lemon or more to taste*
> *4 scallions, thinly sliced*
> *A very large bunch of flat-leafed parsley, finely chopped, preferably by hand (1 cup)*
> *A bunch of mint, finely chopped (¼ cup)*
> *6 tablespoons extra-virgin olive oil*
> *4 Bibb lettuces for serving with*

Soak the cracked wheat in plenty of cold water for 10 minutes. Rinse in a colander and put in a bowl with the tomatoes. Leave for 30 minutes to absorb the tomato juices. Mix gently with the rest of the ingredients.

A traditional way of eating tabbouleh is to scoop it up with small Bibb lettuce leaves or very young vine leaves.

Bazargan

Cracked Wheat and Nut Salad

SERVES 6–8

This is an old Syrian dish that was taken abroad by immigrants and seems to have disappeared in Syria itself, or perhaps it never existed outside the Jewish community. The name, meaning "of the bazaar," implies, I suppose, that all the ingredients can be bought at the bazaar. Sour pomegranate concentrate (molasses) and tamarind give the grain (bulgur) a delicious sharp sweet-and-sour flavor and lovely brown color. Use a coarsely ground cracked wheat if you can, but a fine-ground one will do. Make it at least 4 hours before serving, so that the wheat can properly absorb the dressing.

> *2¾ cups (350 g) bulgur (cracked wheat)*
> *Salt*
> *6–8 tablespoons extra-virgin olive oil*
> *3 tablespoons sour pomegranate concentrate (molasses), or 2 tablespoons tamarind paste dissolved in 4 tablespoons boiling water*
> *Juice of 1 lemon or to taste*
> *5 tablespoons tomato paste*
> *1 teaspoon ground cumin*
> *1 teaspoon ground coriander*
> *½ teaspoon ground allspice*
> *½ teaspoon cayenne or chili pepper, or more to taste*
> *1¼ cups (150 g) very coarsely chopped walnuts*
> *1 cup (100 g) very coarsely chopped hazelnuts*

¼ cup (50 g) pine nuts, lightly toasted
A large bunch of flat-leafed parsley, finely chopped (1 cup)

Put the cracked wheat in a large bowl and cover with plenty of cold, slightly salted water. Leave to soak for ½–¾ hour, or until it is tender (the coarsely ground one takes much longer). Drain in a colander with small holes and press the excess water out.

In a serving bowl, beat the olive oil with the pomegranate concentrate or dissolved tamarind paste. Add the lemon juice, tomato paste, cumin, coriander, allspice, and cayenne pepper and beat well. Pour over the cracked wheat and mix very well. Taste before you add more salt if necessary. Add the nuts and flat-leafed parsley and mix well.

VARIATION

• Another particularly tasty version includes 2 large choppped onions fried in oil.

Note

Without the flat-leafed parsley, this keeps very well for several days and also freezes.

To Make Yogurt and Labne (a Cheese)

Bring to the boil 4 cups (2 liters) whole milk, simmer 1–2 minutes, and turn off the heat. Cool to 106–109°F (41–43°C) (the way we gauged the right temperature was if we could leave our little finger in while we counted till ten—but it had to sting). In a large bowl, put

YOGURT

YOGURT IS to the Sephardim what sour cream is to the Ashkenazim. It was always part of the meatless meals, usually in the evenings. It was used like a sauce—poured over hot rice or cracked wheat or lentils and spread on slices of fried eggplant, or served as a bed for poached eggs or as an accompaniment to vegetable omelettes. It was also served with fresh dates, fruit compotes, or jams, and it was eaten with honey. In Iraq they sweetened it with dates or date syrup. Milk from cows, sheep, goats, and buffalo was used. Buffalo milk gave a fabulous thick, creamy yogurt. Yogurt was also strained to make a kind of cream cheese (called "labne" in the Arab world) that was eaten as an appetizer.

4 tablespoons yogurt with a little of the hot milk and beat very thoroughly, then beat in the rest of the milk. Cover the bowl with plastic wrap and leave in a warm place to set overnight. Then refrigerate.

To make labne: Pour the chilled yogurt into a colander lined with thin muslin or cheesecloth, and let it drain for 24–36 hours in a cool place with a bowl underneath to collect the whey. Or—in the old, traditional way—tie the corners of the cloth together and suspend over a bowl or the sink. The result will be a very creamy soft cheese.

Serve it with bread, lightly salted to taste,

with a dribbling of olive oil and chopped fresh herbs such as mint, dill, or marjoram, with crushed or minced garlic if you like, and a sprinkling of paprika.

Khiar bi Laban
Yogurt and Cucumber Salad

SERVES 6

This is a regular accompaniment of meatless meals in Sephardi homes. Unless the salad is going to be eaten as soon as it is made, it is important to salt the cucumber and let the juices drain before mixing it with the yogurt; otherwise the salad will be very watery.

> *1 cucumber*
> *Salt*
> *2½ cups (500 g) natural or thick "strained" yogurt*
> *2–4 cloves of garlic, crushed (optional)*
> *White pepper*
> *1–2 tablespoons dried crushed mint*

Peel the cucumber, cut in half lengthwise, then into not too thin half-moon slices. Sprinkle with plenty of salt and leave for more than an hour in a colander for the juices to drain.

Beat the yogurt in the serving bowl with the garlic (if using) and pepper. (Add salt later if necessary, since the cucumber is salty.) Rinse the cucumber of excess salt and let drain, then mix into the yogurt. Serve sprinkled with crushed dried mint.

VARIATION

• Leave out the mint. Beat 3 tablespoons olive oil, 1 tablespoon vinegar, and 3 tablespoons chopped dill into the yogurt.

Raita
Indian Yogurt and Cucumber Salad

SERVES 8–10

This is the Bene Israel (Indian) version of the preceding recipe, with added onion and cayenne. The grated onion gives a very pleasant texture. You can make it mild or hot.

> *2 cucumbers*
> *1 large mild onion*
> *Salt*
> *3¾ cups (750 g) natural or thick "strained" yogurt*
> *Cayenne or chili pepper to taste*

Peel and finely chop or grate the cucumbers and onion. You can do it in the food processor. Put them together in a colander, sprinkle with plenty of salt, and mix well. Leave for about 2 hours to let the juices drain. The salt reduces the powerful onion flavor, and most of it disappears with the juices. Rinse and drain well.

Beat the yogurt with the cayenne pepper. Then stir in the cucumber and onion.

VARIATION

• Add 1–2 tablespoons of raisins soaked in water.

ABOUT CHEESE

IN THE OLD SEPHARDI WORLD, cheeses were eaten as appetizers with olives, and not at the end of the meal. Those commonly used in Sephardi cooking are the Greek and Turkish ones, usually made with goat or sheep's milk. They are feta, the sharp, salty, white, crumbly cheese preserved in brine; the slightly chewy and salty semi-hard halumi; kefalotyri, the strongly flavored, pungent hard cheese that is used for grating and is very like Parmesan; kaser or kasseri, a mild-flavored firm cheese with the texture of a Gouda which the Jews in Turkey call "kasher"; and kashkaval, a yellow cured cheese with an herby flavor. They are mashed or grated and used—often a mixture of two cheeses—in omelettes, gratins, or pies, and to stuff vegetables.

Very religious Jews in North Africa did not eat cheese or dairy products, because it was too difficult to have two sinks or bowls and two sets of dishes and silverware.

Gebna Beida–Keso Blanco

White Cheese

Most families in the Oriental world made a soft white cheese on a regular basis. It was eaten for breakfast or as an appetizer with olives, and in the evening with watermelon. It was also used, unsalted, as a filling for pastries with syrup poured over. When my parents first came to England, my mother made it every week. In Egypt, animal rennet was used to coagulate the milk—it was considered kosher to use, although it is extracted from the lining of a calf's stomach, because it is an enzyme—but lately I have used vegetable rennet because I have not been able to find the animal kind. The problem now is that rennet does not work and cheese cannot be made with pasteurized milk or milk that has been boiled, and since 1983 all milk has to be pasteurized in Britain. So you have to add a starter. I use cultured buttermilk, which works very well. The cheese is quite different from anything that you can buy, with a soft junkety texture.

Into a large pan pour 10 cups (2¼ liters) of milk. Add ½–1 teaspoon of salt or to taste. Heat the milk to lukewarm only. You should be able to hold your little finger in without feeling any sting. In a little bowl, beat 1 tablespoon of buttermilk with a little of the warm milk, then pour into the pan and stir well. Leave for 1½ hours in a warm place, such as an airing cupboard, covered by a cloth.

Count 20 drops of vegetable rennet and dilute it in 10 times its volume of water that has been boiled and cooled—that is what it says on the bottle (or use animal rennet and follow the instructions on the bottle). Stir this into the warm milk and let stand again for 1 hour in the same warm place, until it sets. Cut the curd with a spatula. It will separate into curds and whey. After 30 minutes, tip it into a colander lined with a thin cloth and let it drain for at least 1 hour. Then turn the soft cheese out of the cloth straight into the colander and leave to drain over a bowl in the refrigerator for 12–24 hours.

It is lovely to eat as a cream cheese, slightly more salted to taste, with a dribble of extra virgin olive oil and a sprinkling of pepper. After 2–3 days, the cheese becomes firm enough to broil (on a piece of foil) or fry—a treatment that turns it into a creamy, chewy affair—something like a soft mozzarella.

VARIATION

• If you want a more salty cheese, after it is made you can soak it in salted water.
• The Jews of India pour boiling water over the cheese, cut it into large pieces, and leave it to soak for ½ hour. It acquires a rubbery texture like that of fresh mozzarella. It is called "panir," and they pull it into long strands and plait it, then soak it in salted water. I have not been able to plait it successfully, but it is very good worked into balls.
• The same cheese, unsalted, is used as a filling for konafa (page 580) and for ataif (page 590).

Keso Assado
Grilled Cheese

Kashkaval and the slightly rubbery, salty halumi cheese are most commonly used. Cut cheese into ½-inch (1-cm) slices. Place on a piece of foil under the broiler and cook until it begins to blister and brown on the outside. Turn over once and serve on toasted bread, sprinkled if you like with pepper.

Another way is to spear a cube of cheese on a fork and hold it over an open flame.

Kashkaval Pané
Cheese Fritters

Cut the cheese into ½-inch (1-cm) slices. Dip in lightly beaten egg, then in fine bread crumbs or matzo meal, and deep-fry in medium-hot oil, turning over once.

Uevos kon Keso
Egg and Cheese

SERVES 2

This is a simple snack common throughout Oriental Jewry.

2 thick slices of halumi or kashkaval cheese

FALAFEL

I WAS TOLD this story in Israel when fashionable restaurants started opening—and closing just as quickly. A man goes into a fashionable French restaurant in Tel Aviv, sits down, looks at the menu, and asks, "Have you got frogs' legs?" The waiter replies, "We do." The man says, "Then hop around the corner and fetch me a falafel."

Falafel is considered the national food of Israel. I was there soon after Sadat's historic visit, and the papers were full of articles about falafel's origin in ancient Egypt. There were drawings of tomb paintings depicting its making, musings about whether the Jews would have eaten it when they were slaves of the Pharaohs, and recipes for the way Egyptians make it, with fava beans rather than chickpeas.

Yemenites who arrived in the Holy Land before 1948 were the first Jews to sell falafel. They made them in the local Palestinian way, with chickpeas, but spiced them more fiercely. They sold them in the streets and brought them to the settlements. Then Romanians joined the Yemenites but made their falafel less peppery. Falafel became the most popular street food. Now that they are mostly made with a dehydrated powder, they are far less appetizing. But the way they are served—in pita bread with pickles and a fiery Yemeni relish tucked between them, and with a topping of mixed salad and tahini—makes them a cheap, tasty and nourishing meal in the hand.

---

2 tablespoons sunflower oil
2 eggs
Salt and pepper

Fry the cheese lightly in the oil for a few minutes, until it softens. Break the eggs on top, sprinkle with salt and pepper, and cook for about 5 minutes, until they have set.

VARIATION

• Soften 2 chopped tomatoes in the oil before you put in the cheese.

Falafel
Fava Bean Fritters

SERVES 12

These falafel are so much better than anything you can buy—very herby, spicy, and garlicky, crisp outside and very soft inside. And they are far better made with the large variety of dried fava beans than with chickpeas, which are generally used in Israel. Buy the beans already skinned, in Oriental and Indian stores. The secret to keeping the falafel from falling apart in the frying oil is to towel-dry the soaked and drained beans so that the paste is not watery, and to blend them long in the food processor.

> 1 lb (500 g) large skinless dried fava beans
> A large bunch of flat-leafed parsley or
>   coriander or a mixture of the two,
>   finely chopped (1 cup)
> 8 scallions, finely chopped
> Salt
> ¼ teaspoon or more cayenne or chili pepper
> 2 teaspoons ground cumin
> 2 teaspoons ground coriander
> 6 garlic cloves or to taste, crushed in a press
> 1 teaspoon baking powder
> Vegetable oil for frying

Soak the beans for 24 hours. Drain, rinse, and drain well. Dry them a bit on a tea towel or paper towels.

Chop the flat-leafed parsley (it should be dry) and scallions in the food processor, then put them aside. Put the beans in the food processor and blend to a smooth, soft paste. The longer you process the better. Add salt, cayenne pepper, cumin, coriander, garlic, and baking powder and continue to process until the paste is very soft and holds well together. Add the flat-leafed parsley and scallions and blend very briefly—just enough to mix them in. Allow the paste to rest for 1 hour.

Heat about 1 inch (2½ cm) of oil in a pan to medium hot. Take small, walnut-sized lumps and make round flat cakes about 1½ inches (4 cm) in diameter, and deep-fry a few at a time. It is easier if you put the little cakes on a plate and push them in at the same time with a flexible spatula (they are too soft to be picked up). (There is a contraption that you can buy in Egypt and Israel which you can use to make them. You press some paste into a small cup and push it out.) The oil should be hot enough to start with so that it sizzles as the falafel go in; then reduce the heat to low. Fry until golden brown, turning over once. Lift out with a slotted spatula and drain on paper towels. Serve with an Israeli salad and hot pita bread.

VARIATIONS

• Before frying, sprinkle sesame seeds on the plate and lay the uncooked falafel on them, then sprinkle the tops with more sesame seeds.

• Use chickpeas instead of fava beans for the more common Israeli version.

Tehina

SERVES 8

This sauce has become ubiquitous in Israel as a dip and as a dressing for falafel. Sesame paste is an oily paste sold in jars, mostly with the Greek spelling "tahini."

> 1 cup (250 ml) tahini (sesame paste)
> Juice of 1–2 lemons
> 2 or 3 cloves of garlic, crushed
> Salt
> ½ teaspoon paprika
> 2 tablespoons finely chopped flat-leafed parsley

Pour the tahini into a bowl and very gradually beat in the juice of 1–2 lemons and enough water—about ¾ cup (175 ml) to make a pale, thick cream. Keep beating. It will thicken into grainy lumps at first, before it blends into a thin-nish cream. Add garlic and salt.

To use as a dip, garnish with paprika and flat-leafed parsley.

To use as a dressing, beat in more water until it reaches the consistency of a light cream.

Hummus bi Tehina

Chickpea and Tahini Dip

SERVES 6–8

Simply called "hummus," which means "chickpeas," this lemony, garlicky, pale, creamy paste has become ubiquitous in Israel, and indeed all over the Western world. You must add the ingredients as you blend, a little at a time, to taste, for you may prefer it more or less sharp and more or less garlicky.

1¼ cups (250 g) chickpeas, soaked overnight
Salt
Juice of 2–3 lemons
2 or 3 garlic cloves, minced or crushed
6 tablespoons tahini
4 tablespoons extra-virgin olive oil
1 teaspoon paprika (optional)
2 tablespoons finely chopped flat-leafed parsley

Boil the drained chickpeas in fresh water for 2 hours, until very soft, adding salt when they begin to soften, then drain and reserve the cooking water. Blend or process the chickpeas with a little of their cooking water—enough to make a smooth paste. Add the lemon juice, garlic, tahini, 2 tablespoons of oil, and more salt if necessary, and blend or process, adding a little more of the cooking water to obtain a soft creamy texture.

To serve, spread the paste on a plate and sprinkle with the remaining oil, the paprika, if you like, and the parsley.

VARIATIONS

• Some people add 1–1½ teaspoons cumin to the paste.
• Yemenites garnish with hot red pepper or zhoug.

Babaghanouzh or Moutabal

Eggplant and Tahini Puree

SERVES 6

A dip to serve with bread, it makes a good accompaniment to falafel.

1 large eggplant
3 tablespoons tahini (sesame paste)
Juice of 1 lemon
Salt
1–2 garlic cloves, crushed in a press
2 tablespoons finely chopped flat-leafed parsley

Prick the eggplant with a pointed knife and turn under the broiler or over a flame till it is very soft inside and the skin is blackened. Peel, chop finely, and mash in a colander, letting the juices run out. Beat the tahini with a tablespoon of water and the lemon juice, then beat into the eggplant puree in a bowl. Add salt and garlic and garnish with chopped flat-leafed parsley.

Tarama

Fish Roe Cream

SERVES 6

Gray-mullet roe was once used but smoked cod's roe has replaced it. The Jews of Turkey today prefer using the blander sunflower oil, rather than olive oil, so that the delicate flavor of the roe is dominant. I like to have a mixture with only a little olive oil.

> *5 oz (150 g) smoked-cod roe*
> *2 slices white bread, crusts removed, and soaked in water*
> *Juice of 1½–2 lemons or to taste*
> *¾ cup (175 ml) sunflower oil or a mixture with a little extra-virgin olive oil*

Skin the smoked-cod roe and put it through the food processor with the bread, squeezed dry, and the lemon juice. Gradually add the oil in a thin trickle while the blades are running and blend to the consistency of mayonnaise. Chill, covered with plastic wrap. If it is too liquid, do not worry, it will become thick and firm after an hour or so in the refrigerator.

Cured Fish–Lakerda and Garato

Fish cured in salt was always popular. Garato was made with cured mackerel, lakerda with bonito—a species of tuna. The fish, filleted but with the skin left on, was salted inside and out, and the fillets put together again. It was left in the refrigerator 4–5 days with a plate and a weight on top, covered hermetically. Then the fish would be rinsed and cut into thin slices. It was served with mild chopped onions and lemon wedges. Nowadays salmon has replaced these fish. (For cured salmon, see page 69.)

Butarga

Drying salted or smoked fish roe is a very old Jewish tradition right across the Mediterranean. All kinds of roes are used, depending on what is available, including those of sea bass, gray mullet, and cod.

My own way with smoked cod's roe, which works very well, is simply to let it dry on a plate in the refrigerator for a week, turning it over a few times to air each side as it becomes moist. I do not add salt at all, for it is already very salty. It gradually hardens and becomes a dark orange brown. Some like it very dry and hard and strong-tasting, but I prefer it a little soft and milder.

Serve thinly sliced on bread with a sprinkling of extra-virgin olive oil.

Feuilles de Vigne– Yalandji Dolma– Yaprak–Warak Einab

Cold Stuffed Vine Leaves

MAKES ABOUT 40

While Muslims preferred their vine leaves hot and stuffed with ground meat, Jews had them cold with rice. This family version is a combination of Syrian and Turkish styles. The pine nuts and raisins are the Turkish legacy.

- 8 oz (250 g) vine leaves preserved in brine
- 1 cup (200 g) long-grain rice
- 2 medium tomatoes, finely chopped
- 1 medium onion or 4 scallions, finely chopped
- 2 tablespoons chopped mint leaves
- 2 tablespoons chopped flat-leafed parsley
- 2 tablespoons chopped dill or fennel leaves
- ½ teaspoon cinnamon
- ¼ teaspoon allspice
- Salt and black pepper
- 2 tablespoons pine nuts (optional)
- 1½ tablespoons raisins or currants (optional)
- Lettuce leaves or sliced potatoes to line the saucepan
- 3 or 4 garlic cloves, slivered
- ⅔ cup (150 ml) olive oil
- 1 teaspoon sugar
- Juice of 1 lemon
- 1 lemon cut in wedges

To remove the salt from the vine leaves, pour boiling water over them and soak for 20 minutes, then drain and rinse in cold water.

For the stuffing, mix the rice with the tomatoes, onion or scallions, mint, parsley, and dill or fennel leaves. Add the cinnamon, allspice, salt and pepper, and, if using, pine nuts and raisins, and mix well.

Line a heavy-bottomed saucepan with lettuce leaves or sliced potatoes to prevent the stuffed vine leaves from burning. Place a vine leaf on a plate, vein side up and stem end towards you. Put 1 heaped teaspoonful of the filling in the center, near the stem end. Fold this edge up over the filling, then fold both sides towards the middle and roll up loosely like a tiny cigar. Squeeze gently. The rolls must not be tight—allow some room for the rice to expand in them, or the leaves may tear. Stuff all the leaves in the same way and pack them in the saucepan side by side in tight layers on top of the lettuce leaves, with the points of the vine leaves towards the bottom of the pan. Slip a piece of garlic between them here and there.

Mix the olive oil with ⅔ cup (150 ml) water, the sugar, and the lemon juice, and pour over the stuffed leaves. Put a small plate on top to prevent them from unrolling. Simmer over very low heat with the lid on for about 1 hour, adding a little water occasionally as the liquid is absorbed. Cool in the pan before turning out. Serve cold with the lemon wedges.

Note:

If you have fresh vine leaves, all you need to do is plunge them in boiling water until they become limp (they do so in seconds), then drain.

Savory Pies

MANY YEARS AGO, I went to Istanbul to research Turkish food with a few telephone numbers of Jewish families in my pocket. One evening, after a day of eating in kebab houses, I visited an address in Teshvekieh that had once been a Jewish quarter in the center of town. Three elderly ladies—Louise Pardo-Rokes, Nelly Kahia, and Yetty Treves—were waiting for me, each holding a plate with several different little pies which they had made especially for me. They spoke Ladino to each other and French to me. I said I would die if I ate any more, because I had already filled myself with kebabs, and asked if I could take the little pies to my hotel and eat them the next day. No, they insisted, I had to eat the pies in front of them and tell them what I thought.

Little pies are the pride and joy and the trademark of the Sephardi table. There is an enormous variety, with different fillings and doughs, from the borekitas of Turkey and the pasteles of Salonika, to the sambousak and filas of the Arab world, the cigares of North Africa, and the sumoosaks of India. The ending "-ak" of sambousak—the Arab version in the shape of a small half-moon pasty or turnover—denotes a Persian origin. These Persian pies were brought by the Arabs to Spain and Portugal, where new versions with the same shape but different fillings were developed. Some of the old Iberian fillings are still with the Judeo-Spanish communities of Turkey and the Balkans.

Pies are considered festive foods of celebration, because they require skill and time. They are made for weddings and bar mitzvahs, for holidays and the Sabbath. They were already part of the Sabbath meal in the sixteenth century, as noted by Joseph Caro (1488–1575), who wrote the Shulhan Aruch, a codification of Jewish Law. In the modern Iberian Sephardi communities, they still make meat borekas and pasteles for Friday night and a variety of savory pies for *desayuno* (which means "breakfast" in Spanish) for Saturday morning. Among these are the affectionately named "three B's"—borekas, bulemas, and boyos. On Saturday the pies were reheated on a metal sheet—a practice permitted by Jewish law if foods have already been cooked and all their constituents are dry (if they are liquid, a change of state might take place). The pies can be put in the vicinity of a fire (not directly over it), just long enough to heat them up.

Recently, as I was testing recipes and feeling lonely and very sorry for myself for spending hours rolling, shaping, folding, and pinching, I remembered pastry-making in Egypt. Friends would always come to help, and the house would be full of gossip and laughter. Women had all the time in the world then. I wondered if anybody would be prepared to spend hours making little pies nowadays, except for very special occasions, and if some enterprising food-processing company would mass-produce them one day. When they became impoverished refugees, several women of my mother's generation made such labor-intensive delicacies to sell privately. One even sent consignments of frozen sambousak, fila, and kibbeh by plane to Geneva every week.

Every community has its own special pies with different fillings, different doughs, and different traditional shapes. There are cigars, triangles, rectangular bundles, fingers, half-moon turnovers with festooned edges, crescents, cornets, circles, balls, and tiny raised pies. The most common traditional fillings are cheese, spinach, or meat, but there are some unique to one particular community, like the eggplant fillings of the Jews of Turkey, the mashed chickpea and chicken of Iraqi Jews, and the pumpkin filling of Bukharan Jews. Italian Jews have the greatest variety for their buricche. I find that people always give recipes for dough in a kind of chant, as though the quantities have been learned by heart. The dough used for pies containing meat is with oil; the one used for pies with cheese usually has butter. And there are yeast doughs (these are favored by Iraqi Jews) and various types of paper-thin and puff pastry that are famous. Many people now use store-bought puff pastry, and there is no reason why you should not. Of the many recipes I have tried, I give those that are the most common and which work best.

BOREKAS—BOREKITAS

BOREKAS ARE the culinary representatives of Turkish, Greek, and Balkan Jewry. The name comes from the Turkish word *boerek* for "pie," but they are quite different from the numerous Turkish varieties in size, shape, type of pastry, and filling. They are closer to the Spanish and Portuguese empanadas. Some fillings are unique. In Istanbul, certain varieties—in particular one with an eggplant-and-cheese puree—made by Jewish caterers have started appearing on restaurant menus as borekitas. A woman who was selling jewelry at my hotel in Istanbul said she was making them for a restaurant in the evenings, while watching television.

Basic Pie Dough 1

For Pies Containing Meat or Cheese—for Pasteles, Borekas, Sambousak, and Buricche

MAKES ABOUT 20 TURNOVERS
4 INCHES (4 CM) IN DIAMETER,
OR 15 PASTELIKOS
(RAISED PIES, PAGE 289)

This is a very easy dough to make. It can be easily rolled out or flattened between the palms of your hand. The quantity of flour needed is always given as "as much as it takes—when it feels like the lobe of your ear." I think that is much more sensible than giving precise measures, since the amount of water that flour absorbs varies not only with different types of flour but with flour from the same provenance from one year to another. I discovered that when I was trying bread dough and the quantities did not match recipes for pizza I had written years ago. I telephoned the British Flour Board, and they explained that this year the flour absorbed less water. For this reason, I urge you to add the amount of flour slowly towards the end, and to be ready to stop when you feel the dough has absorbed as much as it can. It should be extremely soft and malleable.

> ½ cup (125 ml) sunflower oil
> ½ cup (125 ml) warm water
> ½ teaspoon salt
> About 2½ cups (350 g) flour

In a large bowl, mix the oil, water, and salt, beating with a fork. Gradually work in enough flour to make a soft, malleable dough—stirring it in with the fork to begin, then working it in with your hands. You may roll it out right away. If you want to keep it aside for an hour or so, do so covered in wrap and at room temperature, not chilled in the refrigerator.

To make pies, see page 281.

Note

• For centuries, the Jews of Turkey used only olive oil for this, as for all their cooking. It is only in the last two or three decades that they have switched to sunflower oil.

Basic Pie Dough 2

For Use with Cheese Fillings

MAKES ABOUT 40 TURNOVERS
4 INCHES (4 CM) IN DIAMETER,
OR 15 PASTELIKOS
(RAISED PIES, PAGE 289)

This dough, which can also be used for borekas, pasteles, sambousak, and buricche, is not as malleable as "pie dough 1." But the butter gives it a lovely taste and texture.

> ½ cup (125 ml) sunflower oil
> 4 oz (125 g) unsalted butter
> ½ cup (125 ml) water
> ½ teaspoon salt
> About 3⅔ cups (550 g) flour

Heat the oil and butter in a pan over low heat until the butter melts. Add the water and salt and beat well. Add the flour gradually—just enough to make a soft, greasy dough that holds together in a ball—stirring with a fork to begin with, then working it in with your hand. The dough should be handled as little as possible, so stop mixing as soon as it holds together. Leave it to rest covered in plastic wrap at room temperature for 20 minutes before using. (Do not put it in the refrigerator; this will make it unworkable.)

This dough does not roll out as thin as "pie dough 1" and needs, instead, to be pressed between the palms of the hand (see the following recipe).

Making Borekas

The half-moon pastry or turnover is the traditional shape for borekas, sambousak, and buricche.

If using "pie dough 1": It is a very oily dough and must be rolled out without flouring the rolling pin or the surface. You want the rolling pin and surface to become oily so as not to stick to the dough. Divide the dough into 4 pieces to make rolling easier. Roll out as thin as you can, and cut into 4-inch (10-cm) rounds with a pastry cutter. Scraps can be immediately rolled into a ball and rolled again so you do not waste any part of the dough.

If using "pie dough 2": Take walnut-sized lumps and roll each into a little ball. Press and squash between your palms and pull into a 4-inch (10-cm) round.

Put a heaping teaspoon of filling in the middle of each round. Fold the dough over the filling into a half-moon shape. Then pinch the edges firmly together to seal the pies. It is traditional in all the communities to pinch, fold, and twist all around the edges.

Place the little pies on oiled trays. Brush with egg yolk mixed with a drop of water and sprinkle if you like with sesame seeds. Bake at 350°F (180°C) for about 30 minutes, until slightly golden. They are best eaten hot but are also good cold. They can easily be reheated in the oven. You can also freeze them.

Making Tapadas (Large Pies)

These are large pies made with the same pastry and the same filling as borekas. Roll out two-thirds of the dough thin and line a pie plate 10 inches (25 cm) in diameter with it, or press out the dough in the dish with the palm of your hand. Fill with the filling and cover with the rest of the rolled-out pastry. Trim the edges and pinch together to seal the pie, brush with 1 egg yolk mixed with 1 teaspoon of water, and bake in a preheated 300°F (150°C) oven for about 45 minutes, or until golden.

Borekas de Keso

Cheese Pies

MAKES ABOUT 40

These pies—common to all the Iberian Sephardim in Turkey and the Balkans—are mass-produced in a rather degraded form in Israel, where they have become a ubiquitous fast food. (Downmarket popular films are referred to as "borekas" films.) In Egypt, the Iberian Sephardim adopted the Syrian version—sambousak bi jibn (see following recipe)—leaving out the potato, which is seen as a way of making the filling cheaper.

> 1 recipe basic pie dough 2 (page 280)
> 1 egg yolk mixed with 1 teaspoon water, to glaze the pies
> 3 tablespoons sesame seeds to sprinkle on (optional)

For the cheese filling

> 14 oz (400 g) or 3 medium potatoes, boiled and mashed
> 12 oz (350 g) feta, mashed
> ½ cup (50 g) grated Parmesan
> 3 eggs
> White pepper

Mix all the filling ingredients together thoroughly. Proceed as for "Making Borekas" (page 281).

VARIATION

• To make a large cheese pie—tapada de keso—see "Making Tapadas" (page 281).

Sambousak bi Jibn

Syrian Cheese Pies

MAKES ABOUT 40

In Egypt there wasn't a party or card game without them. Together with the fila triangles with cheese, they were the teatime and Sabbath breakfast favorites of every Sephardi community. They were also a traditional specialty of Shavuot (page 37). The cheese used for the filling varied in the old days, and now it varies according to what people find most readily. But it is usually sharp, and a mixture. Among the cheeses used are feta, kashkaval, kasseri, kefalotyri, Gruyère, Parmesan, Cheddar, Cheshire, Gouda, Edam, curd, and cottage cheese.

> 1 recipe basic pie dough 2 (page 280)
> 1 egg yolk mixed with 1 teaspoon water, to glaze the pies

For the filling

> 1 lb (500 g) grated cheese (a mixture of feta and cottage, well drained, or any of the cheeses mentioned above)
> 2 eggs, lightly beaten
> White pepper

Mix all the filling ingredients together. Make the pies as indicated in "Making Borekas" (page 281).

VARIATION

• In Iraq they made them with bread dough as for pita (see page 550), containing a pinch of fennel seeds and rolled very thin.

Borekas de Espinaka

Spinach Pies

MAKES ABOUT 40

For this it is good to use frozen chopped spinach.

>*1 recipe basic pie dough 2 (page 280)*
>*1 egg yolk mixed with 1 teaspoon water,*
>   *to glaze the pies*

For the filling

>*1 lb (500 g) frozen chopped spinach, thawed*
>*2 eggs, lightly beaten*
>*½ lb (250 g) feta cheese, mashed*
>*4 tablespoons grated Parmesan*
>*A little salt if necessary*
>*Pepper*

Drain the spinach in a colander and press all the water out, then mix with the rest of the filling ingredients. Make the pies as in "Making Borekas" (page 281).

Borekitas de Berengena

Eggplant and Cheese Pies

MAKES ABOUT 16

I was thrilled to find these little pies, which are unique to the Jewish community, on the menu of a fashionable restaurant in Istanbul. When

I went to visit the caterer Rina Sarah Kam (Rinel Catering) the next day, I saw the same pies in trays ready to be sent off. Mrs. Kam explained that the restaurant trade was relatively new for her. Her main business was Jewish events and parties. She was just preparing for a *fashadoura*, a tea party given by a new mother for the women of the family to celebrate the cutting of her newborn baby's first shirt.

Her dough is a little different from the more common pie doughs 1 and 2, in that it incorporates cheese. But the other doughs can also be used.

For the dough

>*½ cup (125 ml) sunflower oil*
>*¼ cup (50 ml) warm water*
>*½ teaspoon salt*
>*2 cups (250 g) flour*
>*1 egg yolk mixed with 1 teaspoon water,*
>   *for glazing*
>*3 tablespoons grated kashkaval or Parmesan*
>   *to sprinkle on top (optional)*

For the filling

>*1 lb (500 g) eggplants*
>*4 oz (100 g) feta cheese*
>*1 cup (100 g) grated kashkaval or Gruyère*
>*Pepper*
>*Salt (optional)*

Beat the oil with the water and salt and add just enough flour (put it in very gradually at the end) to make a soft, malleable, oily dough.

Prick the eggplants with a fork and turn under the broiler until they feel soft inside. Put them in a colander and peel them. Then chop the flesh in the colander with a sharp knife to release the juices, and press them out with your hand.

Turn the eggplant into a bowl. Add the feta cheese and mix well. Then add the kashkaval or Gruyère and the pepper and mix well. You may not need to add any salt. Taste before you do.

Divide the pastry in 2 balls to make it easier to roll. Roll out thin and cut into rounds of about 4 inches (10 cm) in diameter. You don't need to flour the surface or rolling pin. The dough is so greasy it does not stick.

Take each round, roll out again, as the dough is elastic and shrinks back, and put 1 tablespoon of filling in the middle. Bring 2 opposite edges of the pastry together over the filling, press the edges very tightly, and pinch, fold, and twist all around to seal well.

Place the pies on a baking sheet. Brush the top of each with the egg yolk and sprinkle if you wish with grated kashkaval or Parmesan. Bake at 350°F (180°C) for 35 minutes, or until lightly colored.

VARIATION

• For a large version—tapada de berengena—see "Making Tapadas" (page 281). Add 2 beaten eggs to the above filling.

Borekas de Handrajo

Little Pies with an Eggplant and Tomato Filling

MAKES ABOUT 40

Handrajo, a ratatouille-type filling and a specialty of Izmir, is another famous Judeo-Spanish classic of Turkey.

2 recipes pie dough 1 or 1 recipe pie dough 2 (page 280)
1 egg yolk mixed with 1 teaspoon water, to glaze
3 tablespoons sesame seeds to sprinkle on (optional)

For the filling

1 large onion, finely chopped
5 tablespoons or more olive oil
2 eggplants weighing about 1 lb (500 g), diced
3 medium tomatoes, peeled and chopped
Salt and pepper

For the filling, fry the onion in 2 tablespoons of oil till golden. Add the eggplant and the rest of the oil and cook over low heat with the lid on, stirring often, until the eggplant is very soft. Turn the heat up high for a minute or two. Then add the tomatoes, salt, and pepper and cook till reduced and jammy (it must not be wet). Mash the eggplant lightly with a fork. Make the pies as in "Making Borekas" (page 281), filling each pie with a heaping teaspoon of handrajo.

VARIATION

• To make a large pie—tapada de handrajo—see "Making Tapadas" (page 281).

SALONIKA

THE CITY OF SALONIKA once had the largest of all Jewish communities in the Orient. It was known as the Jewish pearl of the Mediterranean and remained virtually a Jewish city for four hundred years, until the beginning of the present century. There was a synagogue, an oratory, or a Jewish school in every street, and all shops and businesses and even the post office closed on Saturdays and Jewish holidays. But the community that was the most splendid in the Eastern Mediterranean was also the most tragic.

There were Jews in Greece long before the common era. By the first century A.D., synagogues and organized communities had been founded by the apostle Paul in all the main cities. The Jews of the Byzantine Empire called themselves "Romaniot," because it was the Eastern part of the Roman Empire. After 1492, thousands of Jews fleeing the Spanish Inquisition in Spain, Portugal, Sicily, and southern Italy settled in Greece, then part of the Ottoman Empire. The greatest number settled in Salonika. By 1613, Jews constituted 68 percent of the population. The city became like a Sephardi republic in a corner of Spain, in the days when mosques, churches, and synagogues coexisted happily side by side in Spain. The Jews lived in the center of the city, by the sea, in a labyrinth of wooden houses, pressed against each other so that they ate up the air and the sky, with twisting streets below, so narrow that balconies touched across them. They were grouped in *cales* (districts) according to their provenance, around their own synagogues, which were designated as Aragonese, Andalusian, Castilian, Majorcan, Sicilian, Neapolitan, Moroccan, Provençal, Polish, and Russian.

At first, every group kept its distinctive identity, but gradually they all adopted the Spanish one. All the Jews, including the Greek-speaking Romaniots and the Ashkenazim, adopted the Castilian language, Iberian rites, Iberian dress, and Iberian customs and traditions. Even their non-Jewish Greek and Turkish neighbors spoke Spanish. The sixteenth and seventeenth centuries were a vital, glorious golden age for the Jews. They turned the port into a pivot of international trade. Through them, Salonika became "queen of the Mediterranean" and monopolized all transactions with the Levant.

But at the end of the seventeenth century, the community was affected dramatically when the sultan gave French merchants a monopoly on the traffic with Europe, as Marseilles took over the role of Venice, while at the same time imposing heavy customs duties and commercial taxes on local traders. This effectively excluded the Jews from international trade. When commerce fell out of their hands, they turned to crafts and manual work— weaving and dyeing wool, rearing silkworms, making silk kaftans for the Turkish beys and wool uniforms for the Janissaries. Those who had come from Malta were glassblowers, Majorcans made clay cooking pots in the style of their old homeland. They became shoemakers, carpenters, goldsmiths, and printers—and, famously, boatmen, dockers, and porters. There were a great number of fishermen, most Sicilian in origin and some Catalan and Andalusian. They were called "*los moros,*" because they carried on the archaic fishing traditions and jargon brought by the Moors to Spain and Sicily.

The only Jews who prospered in the situation were the "dragomen," who were employed as interpreters and intermediaries between the French and other foreigners and the Ottoman authorities. Most of them were Portuguese Marranos, newly arrived from Livorno, who continued to speak Italian and to wear Western clothes, and French-speaking Jews from Provence, who were under Italian and French protection and had the same privileges and tax exemptions as Europeans. These formed the majority of the European "colony" and were called "*francos*" (meaning "French").

For the rest of the community, cultural degradation followed economic decline. As the Jews fell into a trough of poverty, they were gripped by obscurantist cabbalistic mysticism and messianic fever. It was at this time that the young mystic from Smyrna, Shabbetai Zvi, revealed himself as the "messiah," and won over the masses and most of the rabbis. When he converted to Islam, under pressure from the sultan and to save his life, thousands of Jews converted with him. Long after Shabbetai Zvi died, many Salonikans believed that he would reappear as the savior of Israel. Waves of conversions continued, destabilizing the commu-

Young vendors in Salonika hawk L'Indépendant, *the evening Jewish newspaper in French*

nity, which never entirely recovered from the shattered messianic expectations and the resulting splits and dissensions within the synagogues. The Sabbetaians, the false messiah's followers, became a Muslim sect called *deunmeh* (meaning "apostate" in Turkish). The brand of mysticism that was born in Spain turned into Oriental sorcery. Salonikans became obsessed with miracle workers, magicians, fortune-tellers, and amulet makers. Cut off from the rest of the world, they fell into a cultural miasma of ignorance and superstition. On top of all that, they were plagued by constant attacks and pillaging by Janissaries, pirating of the seas, and kidnapping of hostages, and an accumulation of disasters, from constant epidemics of typhus, leprosy, and the plague, to great fires which destroyed the wooden houses of the Jewish quarter.

It is only in the nineteenth century, as the Turkish Empire was falling apart, that the renaissance of Jewish Salonika began. While the Balkan wars raged, and all the ancient communities of the Peloponnese were destroyed in the Greek War of Independence, which began in 1821, Salonika was transformed into a prosperous, modern, Europeanized, cosmopolitan city. Many Jews—mostly from Livorno—became representatives of European companies, obtaining European passports and protection, and some themselves became honorary consuls for countries such as France, England, Holland, Italy, Austria, Spain, and Sweden that wished to trade with the Levant. These Westernized Jews, who formed a kind of Jewish aristocracy, created new industries and instigated a cultural revolution with their modern secular ideas. Italian and French schools were opened; dozens of secular Jewish newspapers were published in the local Judeo-Spanish dialect *djidio* (the old Castilian language, which had by then absorbed Italian, Turkish, Greek, Hebrew, and French elements). Previously written in Hebrew characters, *djidio* was now in Latin characters and revitalized. A new Europeanized intelligentsia developed. The Orient Express united Salonika with London, Vienna, Belgrade, and Istanbul. The port, which was almost entirely run by Jews, was closed on Saturdays. But the renaissance was short-lived.

Salonika was occupied by the Greek army in 1912. In 1917, Greece entered the First World War, and that same year a fire destroyed virtually the whole of the Jewish quarter, including all its archives. After the Greco-Turkish treaty of 1923, which led to an exchange of populations between the two countries, one hundred thousand Greeks from Anatolia and Asia Minor were settled in Salonika in an effort to Hellenize the city and end the dominant role of the Jewish community. As an outpost of the Greek kingdom, the city lost its importance, and the community declined again, cut off as it was from its economic and cultural hinterland in Turkey. Forty thousand Jews left for Egypt, Palestine, France, America, South America, and Africa. The exodus was a continuation of the migration from other parts of Greece that had started with Greek independence a hundred years before.

Under German occupation, sixty-five thousand Jews were deported by the Nazis and the community was exterminated, as were those of Rhodes and Crete. There are very few Jews left in Greece now. The particular brand of Iberian Sephardi culture which was kept alive for four hundred years has dissolved in America, Argentina, Israel, France, and elsewhere. *Djidio* is spoken by very few people. But traces of the culture appear in the little Sephardi cookbooks produced by synagogues to raise money for charities in America and elsewhere, in recipes volunteered by women with names like Arditti, Carmona, Gattegno, and Franco.

The Jewish food of Greece varied according to the region and to the Romaniot or Sephardi background of the community. In *Cookbook of the Jews of Greece*, Nicholas Stavroulakis features dishes from Athens, Ioannina, Larissa, Volos, Komotini, Crete, and Zakinthos as well as those of the Sephardi strongholds.

The dishes that represent the mainstream Sephardi cooking of the large communities in Rhodes, Corfu, Kastoria, and especially Salonika are a special hybrid—more Turkish than Greek, often neither Turkish nor Greek—very like those of the Jews of Turkey and the Balkans and with loud echoes from Spain, Portugal, and Italy. The cooking reflects the intimacy the Jews had with Turks and Greeks and their close contacts with Jewish communities in the Ottoman world.

The cuisine was never grand, the favorite foods being avas, white haricot beans, and a large variety of pies. A typical Friday-night meal started with salt and pickled fish—garat (marinated tuna) and tarama accompanied by piaz, bean salad with olives, and arak or boza—a drink of fermented millet. It was followed by sopa de avikas, white-bean stew or soup with tomatoes and with or without meat, accompanied by huevos haminados (eggs boiled overnight). Alternatives were calf's-foot soup and beef or chicken stew with cracked wheat. The Saturday hamine was beef or chicken stew with chestnuts, chickpeas, beans, or cracked wheat. There were also stuffed vegetables, vegetable gratins, and meatballs incorporating spinach or leeks. In the seaport, fish was on every festive table, fried, grilled, baked, in a tomato sauce, with egg and lemon, or with zirwelas (a variety of acid plums), agras (verjuice), or walnut sauce. They loved bimbriyo (quince paste), naranjikas (orange preserve), and charope blanco (sugar and lemon syrup cooled and worked until it is a white fondant jam)—a specialty of Pesah.

The Salonika historian Joseph Nehama, from whose *Histoire des Israélites de Salonique* I have gleaned much of my information about the history of the community, lists dozens of dishes that the inhabitants of Salonika loved. Among these are fideos (vermicelli), calsones (cheese ravioli), sutlage (creamed rice pudding), kadaif, and baclava. Every family made wine, pekmez (concentrated raisin juice), fruit syrups, and raki from grapes, figs, and plums flavored with mastic, which was drunk at the start of every holiday accompanied by hamine eggs. Fruit preserves and jams were offered to visitors.

When the French writer Edgar Morin wrote *Vidal et les Siens*, the story of his Salonika family, he received many letters from people whose families came from the city. One of them was from Jean Carasso of Gordes, who later came to stay with me. Morin put him in touch with another Carasso, a philosophy teacher in Avignon. They sent out a newsletter,

La Lettre Sépharade, to people with names once common in Salonika, which they found through Minitel. When forty Carassos responded—including Joe Carasso, owner of the Magic Lantern, a bookshop on the Île Saint-Louis—they had a party on a bateau-mouche moored near Notre Dame. There were nostalgic speeches, a concert, and a Salonika meal with raki. Jean Carasso continued with an expanded *Lettre Sépharade* covering all Sephardi matters. One memorable day, Mireille Mazoyer, who attended the Carasso event, cooked me a Salonika lunch.

Pasteles and Pastelikos de Carne

Salonika Meat-Filled Pies

MAKES ABOUT 20

Edgar Morin wrote in *Vidal et les Siens* that he loved pastelikos and eggplant gratin (almodrote) above everything, and that for some, pastelikos is all that is left of their culture. He says that gastronomy is the kernel of a culture, and that for Salonikans pastelikos is the kernel of the kernel. The shape of pastelikos is different from the usual half-moon pasty. It is like that of the Majorcan lamb pies, empanadas de cordero, in the shape of little pots with straight sides and a lid. For centuries there was a Majorcan synagogue in Salonika, and immigrants from the island lived around it. I can imagine the women sitting outside their houses chatting and making the pies.

1 recipe basic pie dough 1 (page 280)
1 egg yolk to glaze the pies
3 tablespoons sesame seeds to sprinkle on
(optional)

For the filling

1 medium onion, chopped
3 tablespoons sunflower oil
½ lb (250 g) lean ground beef
Salt and pepper
1 hard-boiled egg, chopped
1 egg, lightly beaten
4 tablespoons finely chopped flat-leafed parsley (optional)

For the filling, fry the onion in the oil till golden. Add the ground beef, a little salt, and plenty of pepper and stir, crushing the meat with a fork, until it changes color. Add about 4 tablespoons of water and cook for 5–7 minutes more. Let it cool, then add the chopped hard-boiled egg, the raw egg, and the flat-leafed parsley.

To form the pies, take lumps of dough the size of a small egg and roll into a ball. Hollow them out with your fingers, and shape into little pots with straight sides, making the walls as thin as possible. Fill with meat mixture. Cover each pie with a lid made by flattening a tiny ball of dough between your palms. Pinch the edges together all around to seal the pies. Arrange on trays, brush the top with the egg yolk mixed with 1 teaspoon of water, and sprinkle with sesame seeds. Bake at 350°F (180°C) for 30–40 minutes, or until golden.

VARIATIONS

• Another filling, though not classic, is my favorite. I knew it from my grandmother's friends, the Salonikans who came to Egypt at the turn of the century. It is the one we used for sambousak bi lahm in the following recipe.

• Another popular filling for pasteles is handrajo (see page 284).

• It is now usual to make large-pie pasteles de carne, which are quicker to prepare. Add a mashed boiled potato to the filling and make as for "Making Tapadas" (page 281).

• Edgar Morin's beloved pastelikos, which reminded him of the blue eyes of his father, Vidal, was a large cheese pie like the tapada de keso (page 282).

Sambousak bi Lahm

Arab Meat Pies

MAKES ABOUT 20

These were our meat pies in Egypt.

1 recipe basic pie dough 1 (page 280)
1 egg yolk mixed with 1 teaspoon water,
   to glaze the pies

For the filling

1 medium onion, finely chopped
2 tablespoons sunflower oil
12 oz (350 g) lean ground lamb
Salt and pepper
¼ teaspoon allspice
½ teaspoon cinnamon
4 tablespoons pine nuts, toasted

For the filling, fry the onion in the oil till golden. Add the meat, salt, pepper, allspice, and cinnamon and stir, crushing the meat with a fork, until it changes color. Add 3 tablespoons water and cook 5–7 minutes more, then add the pine nuts.

Make little pies as explained in "Making Borekas" (page 281).

Sambousak bi Tawa

Pies Filled with Chickpeas and Chicken

MAKES ABOUT 24

My friend Sami Daniels, professor of sociology in London, remembers buying these pies from vendors at the market in the Jewish quarter in Baghdad when he came out of school. His mother sent him dozens of recipes with her letters. One evening he brought the pile of little blue square papers on which she wrote them in Arabic and translated them for me. This recipe and a few other Iraqi ones are from her. The pies were traditionally served during the Purim festival.

For the filling

½ lb (250 g) chickpeas, soaked overnight
1 large onion, chopped
3 tablespoons sunflower oil
½ lb (250 g) ground chicken or 2 boned
    and skinned breasts cut into small
    pieces
Salt
2 teaspoons cumin
¼–½ teaspoon cayenne pepper

For the dough

2⅔ cups (400 g) self-rising flour
½ teaspoon salt
About 1 cup (250 ml) of the water in
    which the chickpeas were boiled
1 egg yolk mixed with 1 teaspoon of water,
    to glaze

Drain the chickpeas and boil them in fresh water for 1 hour until they are tender. Drain and reserve their cooking water.

For the dough, mix the salt into the flour and add the lukewarm chickpea water gradually—just enough to make a soft dough that holds well together. Knead for a few minutes, until smooth and elastic, adding a little flour if it is too sticky. Cover with plastic wrap and leave for at least an hour at room temperature.

In the meantime, make the filling. Fry the onion in oil till golden. Add the chicken, salt, cumin, and cayenne pepper and cook, stirring, for a few minutes, cutting up the chicken even smaller. Blend the drained chickpeas to a paste in the food processor with about 4 tablespoons of their cooking water. Add to the chicken and onions, stir, and mix very well.

Now take little lumps of dough the size of a walnut, roll into a ball, and roll out thin on a floured surface with a floured rolling pin into rounds about 5 inches (12 cm) in diameter. Put a tablespoon of filling in the middle of each round. Fold the dough over the filling and pinch to seal well. The pies were always deep-fried in not very hot oil till browned, but baking them is in my view a better way. Arrange them on oiled trays, brush the tops with egg yolk mixed with 1 teaspoon of water, and bake at 300°F (150°C) for 35–40 minutes, or until golden.

Serve hot or cold.

VARIATIONS

- Alternative flavorings are turmeric, paprika, and curry.
- The pies are sometimes filled with chickpeas only, and no chicken, or with a mixture of chickpeas and lentils.

BURICCHE

Italian Pies

ITALIANS DESCRIBE THEM as large ravioli that you bake or fry instead of boiling. Some believe the name is derived from the Spanish word *burro* for "donkey" (in Egypt we used the word *buricco* for "donkey" instead of *asino* when we spoke Italian), but it sounds like a deformation of the Turkish "boreka." The shape of the pies is reminiscent of Spanish and Portuguese empanadas, as are some of the fillings, like one with fish, one with marzipan, and one with chopped walnuts, pine nuts, and raisins. They may have been introduced when the cities of central and northern Italy received a huge influx of Iberian immigrants after 1492. The fillings also reflect the towns where they settled and lived in ghettos for almost three hundred years. There are more than a dozen different fillings, both savory and sweet. Some, like a pumpkin filling with amaretti, are typical ravioli fillings, but others are quite fanciful. A chicken-liver filling is a legacy of the *tedeschi* communities that came from Germany. A chicken filling is a specialty of Ferrara.

The dough varies. Sometimes goose or veal fat is used. The following is a classic and excellent dough: Mix 1 cup (250 ml) olive oil with ¾ cup (175 ml) warm water and ½ teaspoon salt. Add about 4 cups (600 g) flour—enough to make a soft dough. Knead very well, divide into thirds, and roll out as thin as possible. You do not need to flour the surface. Proceed as in the method for "Making Borekas" (page 281). This makes about 36.

You may also use the basic pie doughs 1 and 2 (page 280) or store-bought puff pastry, which is used by many people. I have tried it with very good results.

Fillings for Buricche

Tuna Filling, to Make Buricche di Tonno

MAKES ENOUGH TO FILL ABOUT 18 BURICCHE

This is like something from Tunis, which had an intimate contact with the city of Livorno.

14 oz (400 g) canned tuna in brine or water
About 16 black olives, pitted and chopped
2 tablespoons capers
Juice of ½ lemon
2 tablespoons olive oil

Drain the tuna and squeeze out all the brine. Put it in a bowl, mash it, and add the rest of the ingredients.

Pumpkin Filling, to Make Buricche di Zucca

MAKES ENOUGH TO FILL
ABOUT 18 BURICCHE

This is an old specialty of Mantua and Cremona. It is very delicately flavored—savory, with a sweet almondy taste.

A 1½-lb (750-g) slice of orange
    pumpkin
1½ oz (40 g) amaretti (6 small
    amaretti)
⅓ cup (50 g) fine bread crumbs
1–2 tablespoons crystallized citrus peel
    (either orange or lemon or a combination),
    finely chopped
Grated peel of ½ lemon
Salt
A good pinch of grated nutmeg
1 egg

Peel the pumpkin, cut in small pieces, and boil in water to cover for about 15 minutes, till tender. Then drain and mash in the colander, pressing to extract as much liquid as possible. Pulverize the amaretti in a food processor, add the rest of the ingredients, and blend to a puree.

Chicken Liver Filling, to Make Buricche di Fegatini

MAKES ENOUGH TO FILL
ABOUT 12 BURICCHE

This filling originates from the German Jews who settled in Italy.

1 onion, chopped
2 tablespoons sunflower oil
½ lb (250 g) chicken livers (to kosher, salt
    all over and grill briefly on both sides
    until they change color)
3 tablespoons Marsala
Salt and pepper
¼ teaspoon allspice
1 hard-boiled egg

Fry the onion in oil till golden. Add the chicken livers, Marsala, salt and pepper to taste, and allspice, and sauté briefly, stirring. Pour into the food processor. Add the hard-boiled egg, cut in pieces, and blend briefly to a soft paste.

Empanadas de Pishkado

Little Pies Filled with Fish and Walnuts

MAKES ABOUT 18

This specialty of the Jews of Turkey is a Majorcan legacy. There was an important Jewish community in Palma in the Middle Ages. Many were forced to become Christian. A group called the *chuetas* (the word means "swine") there today are their descendants.

In Turkey, the empanadas are usually made with mackerel, which is a very oily fish. I prefer to use a white fish and moisten it with oil, since the filling would otherwise be too dry.

½ cup (150 ml) sunflower oil
⅓ cup (90 ml) warm water
Salt
About 2 cups (300 g) flour
1 lb (500 g) white-fish fillet (like cod or haddock), skinned
1 cup (100 g) walnuts, coarsely chopped
Pepper
4 tablespoons bland olive oil or sunflower oil
4 tablespoons chopped flat-leafed parsley
1 egg yolk

For the pastry, stir the oil and water together with a little salt and mix in the flour—enough to make a soft oily dough.

For the filling, poach the fish in salted water for about 8 minutes and drain. Break it up with your hands, add the walnuts, pepper, oil, and flat-leafed parsley and mix well.

Divide the dough in 2 and roll out thin on a smooth surface. (Do not flour the surface or rolling pin: the dough is so oily that it does not stick.) Cut into 4-inch (10-cm) rounds. The dough is elastic and springs back, so before you fill each round roll it out again gently. Put a tablespoon of filling in the center and fold over to make a half-moon pie. Press the edges together and twist to seal them. Arrange on a baking tray, paint the tops with egg yolk mixed with

a teaspoon of water, and bake at 350°F (180°C) for 30–45 minutes, or until golden.

Serve hot or cold.

VARIATION

• The Italian version, impannate di pesce, has a filling of cooked fish, hard-boiled egg, anchovies, and flat-leafed parsley—all finely chopped and moistened with a little olive oil.

Boyos and Boyikos

These Judeo-Spanish pies are a specialty of Turkey, especially of Izmir. Made with an oily bread dough, sometimes layered with a sprinkling of a sharp grated cheese like Parmesan, they may have various fillings. One that is unique and very good is simply fried onions. For boyos de cebollas, fry 4 large sliced onions in 4 tablespoons of olive oil over low heat, stirring occasionally, until very soft and golden (because of the quantity, it takes very long— about ¾ hour—and it is best to cover, at least at the beginning). Add salt and plenty of pepper.

For the pastry, use the dough for pita (page 550) made with 3⅓ cups (500 g) flour. Divide into 4 for easier handling and roll out as thin as possible on an oiled surface, sprinkling the top with oil and rubbing it all over with your hands. With a pastry cutter, cut into rounds of about 4 inches (10 cm) in diameter. Put a tablespoon of fried onions in the center, fold over the filling, and press the edges firmly together to seal. Brush the tops with 1 beaten egg yolk mixed with 1 teaspoon of water and sprinkle, if you like, with grated Parmesan. Bake in a preheated 375°F (190°C) oven for about 20 minutes, or until golden.

Bishak

Pumpkin Pies

This Bukharan specialty is made with an oily bread dough. Use the dough for pita (page 550). Divide into 4 for easier handling. Roll out on an oiled surface as thin as possible, sprinkling the top with oil and brushing the oil all over the sheet of dough with your hands.

For the filling, fry 2 finely chopped onions till soft and transparent in 4 tablespoons of oil. Add 1 lb (500 g) orange pumpkin cut into cubes and cook with the lid on for about 20 minutes, until the pumpkin is very soft, stirring occasionally to make sure that it does not burn. Mash the pumpkin and cook, stirring, to dry it out, adding 1 teaspoon of sugar, some salt, and plenty of pepper. Cut the dough into 4-inch (10-cm) rounds, put 1 heaping tablespoon of filling in the center, and close the pies over the filling, bringing four points up to form a pyramid and pinching the openings to seal them (as in the recipe that follows).

Arrange the pies on an oiled baking sheet, smooth side up. Brush the tops with egg yolk and bake in a preheated 375°F (190°C) oven for 20 minutes, or until golden.

Khachapuri

Georgian Cheese Pies

MAKES 12 LARGE INDIVIDUAL PIES

Lily Macal, a Georgian now living in Israel, who gave me the Georgian recipes through an interpreter, said these pies are the most popular and representative of her community's foods. They are eaten for tea, and often followed by jam. They are different from the usual Middle Eastern varieties in shape (they are square or rectangular), filling, and pastry. "Puri" means "bread," and the pastry, although layered, has a breadlike quality. The dough sounds very complicated but is easier than it seems.

> 3⅓ cups (500 g) flour
> 2 tablespoons baking powder
> ½ teaspoon salt
> 1 tablespoon vinegar
> 1 egg, lightly beaten
> A little more than ¾ cup (175 ml) warm water
> About ½ cup (125 ml) light vegetable oil
> 1 egg yolk, to glaze

For the filling

> 1 lb (500 g) Gruyère, grated
> ½ lb (250 g) fresh soft goat cheese or feta cheese
> 2 eggs, lightly beaten

Put the flour in a bowl with the baking powder, salt, vinegar, and egg, and mix well. Add the water gradually—just enough to make a soft dough that holds together in a ball, mixing first with a fork, then working it in with your hand. Knead for about 10 minutes, until smooth and no longer sticky. Pour ½ tablespoon of oil over the dough, and turn to grease it all over. Cover the bowl with plastic wrap and leave to rest for about 2 hours. It will rise a little.

For the filling, blend the grated Gruyère and goat cheese with the eggs.

Now comes the interesting part with the dough. Divide it in half for easier handling. Roll out each piece on a lightly oiled surface as thin as possible. The dough is very elastic, so you can also pull it and stretch it with your hands. It does not matter if it tears. Sprinkle with oil and gently rub the oil all over with your hands. Then fold the sheet of dough and rub oil over it again. Repeat a few times, creating layers of dough with oil in between. Leave for 15 minutes, then roll out a little and cut into 12 pieces.

Roll out each piece as thin as possible, put 2 heaping tablespoons of filling in the middle, and spread it out a little. Then bring opposite corners to meet over the filling like an envelope, pinch and twist the corner points together, and pinch the four openings to seal them. Arrange the square or rectangular pies on an oiled tray, seam side down so that they present a smooth surface. Brush the tops with the egg yolk mixed with a drop of water and let the pies stand for 15 minutes. Bake at 400°F (200°C) for 30–40 minutes, or until nicely browned. Serve hot or cold.

VARIATION

• Another common cheese filling is a combination of 1 lb (500 g) cottage cheese and ½ lb (250 g) feta cheese.

Les Fila au Fromage

Small Cheese Triangles or Cigars

MAKES ABOUT 60

These ever so light little pies, also known as "filikas," "ojaldres," and "feuilletés," were always among the most popular items on the buffet and tea tables of Oriental Jews. Today people mix all kinds of cheeses for the filling—most often feta with Gruyère or cottage cheese and Parmesan. My cousin Irene's combination sounds banal but it is delicious, and the texture is soft and slightly chewy. It is always much appreciated when I make it. It is the kind of thing you can do when you are watching television. I made 240 of them for my daughter Anna's 30th birthday party while watching 4 programs over 2 weeks. I put them in the freezer (uncooked and without brushing them with egg glaze) and baked them on the day straight from the freezer.

½ lb (250 g) Edam, grated
½ lb (250 g) Gouda, grated
½ lb (250 g) Cheddar, grated
½ lb (250 g) cottage cheese
4 eggs, lightly beaten
1 lb (500 g) filo
6 oz (175 g) butter, melted
4 tablespoons sunflower oil
2 egg yolks, to brush the tops

Mix the cheese with the eggs. Cut the filo and follow the instructions for "Making Filo Triangles" (page 298) or "Making Filo 'Cigars'" (page 300), brushing the pastry strips with a mixture of melted butter and oil and the tops with egg yolk mixed with 1–2 teaspoons water.

VARIATIONS

• Add 3 tablespoons finely chopped dill or mint to the filling and ¼ teaspoon nutmeg.
• Sprinkle with ½ cup sesame seeds before baking.
• For an alternative filling, mix 1 lb (500 g) cottage cheese with 1 lb (500 g) feta cheese (both drained of their liquid) and 4 eggs.
• In Turkey, where the pastries are called "filikas" and "ojaldres de keso," they mix feta cheese with Gruyère and fry the pies in oil.

FILA (FILO PASTRY)

THE ORIENTAL SEPHARDIM have always used the paper-thin pastry they call "fila," a legacy of the old Ottoman world, to make all kinds of pies in different traditional shapes and with a variety of traditional fillings, some of which are uniquely Jewish. It is rare now for anyone to make the pastry at home. Specialists make it by two methods. At a small workshop in London, a flour-and-water dough is kneaded until it is extremely elastic, then allowed to rest for a few hours, and pulled and stretched by two people over a large canvas on a frame with a heater placed underneath. In Istanbul, where thick and thin varieties of yufka (as it is called there) are available, the dough is rolled out by hand with thin long rolling sticks like broom handles.

Filo is now available frozen in the supermarkets, but if you can get the fresh filo from Greek or Oriental bakeries it will be better. There are different qualities of frozen filo, from very fine to rather thick. A standard size for filo sheets sold by bakeries is about 12 by 20 inches (30 by 50 cm), and 1 lb (500 g) contains about 20 sheets. Commercial frozen packs vary from a 14-ounce (400-g) box containing 12 sheets to a 12-ounce (350-g) box

containing 24. Two standard sizes that I have come across are 18 by 13½ inches (56 by 34 cm) and 12 by 7½ inches (30 by 19 cm).

Many frozen brands are unsatisfactory. Too often the sheets stick together and tear. (If they have been in packages too long, ice crystals form, and the sheets get moist and stick when you defrost.) I have found only one frozen variety out of five sold near where I live that has been invariably good. Find a good brand and stick to it.

Frozen filo must be allowed to defrost slowly for 2–3 hours. Fresh or frozen packages should be opened just before using, and the sheets used as quickly as possible, because they become dry and brittle in the air. Cut the sheets and keep them in a pile so that the air does not dry them out. Any unused sheets should be returned quickly to their plastic wrap.

There are many different shapes and fillings. The small pies are worth doing as finger foods for stand-up parties; large pies, cut up into small squares, are good for buffet meals where you can sit down with a plate and a knife and fork. For a dinner party the individual coils make a nice first course or main dish, and for a family meal a large roll is quick and easy to make.

Les Fila aux Épinards

Little Spinach Triangles

MAKES ABOUT 60

It is more common to use chopped spinach for this, but whole-leaf gives a nicer feel. Unlike the cheese filas, these do not freeze very well, because the moisture makes them go soggy.

  1 lb (500 g) filo pastry
  6 oz (175 g) unsalted butter, melted,
      or ⅔ cup (150 ml) vegetable oil
  1 egg yolk (optional)

For the filling we Egyptians use

  2 lbs (1 kg) fresh or frozen leaf spinach
  5 oz (150 g) ricotta or cottage cheese
  5 oz (150 g) feta cheese, mashed
  2 eggs
  Salt if necessary and pepper
  A good pinch of nutmeg

Wash the spinach, remove only tough stems (leave thin soft ones), and drain the leaves well. Cook them by putting them in a saucepan on low heat with the lid on for a few minutes only, until they crumple into a soft mass. (You may have to do this in batches.) Drain in a colander and, when cool enough, press as much of the water out as you can. If using frozen spinach, simply thaw and squeeze all the water out with your hands. It is usual but not necessary to chop the leaves with a sharp knife. (I leave them whole.)

Mix the spinach with the rest of the filling ingredients and make the pies following the instructions for "Making Filo Triangles" (see box), brushing the filo strips with melted butter and the tops with egg yolk mixed with 1 teaspoon of water, if you like.

MAKING FILO TRIANGLES

CUT THE SHEETS of filo into 4 rectangles about 12 by 4 inches (30 by 10 cm) and put them in a pile on top of each other. Brush the top strip lightly with oil or melted butter. Take a heaping teaspoon of filling. Place it at one short end of the strip of filo about 1¼ inches (3 cm) from the edge. Fold that end over the filling. Now pick up a corner, and, lifting it up with the filling, fold diagonally, making a triangle. Continue to fold, picking up one corner after another, until the whole strip has been folded into a triangular package. Make sure that any holes are closed so that the filling does not ooze out.

Place the little packages close to each other on a greased baking sheet and brush the tops with oil or melted butter, or better still with egg yolk mixed with a drop of water, and bake at 350°F (180°C) for 30 minutes, or until crisp and golden.

Les Fila à la Viande

Little Meat Triangles

MAKES ABOUT 30

These are popular with the Jews of Syria, Lebanon, and Egypt. The filling is called "tatbila."

> *½ lb (250 g) filo pastry*
> *Sunflower oil*
> *1 egg yolk (optional)*

For the filling

> *1 medium onion, chopped*
> *2 tablespoons sunflower oil*
> *1 lb (500 g) ground beef or lamb*
> *Salt and pepper*
> *1 teaspoon cinnamon*
> *½ teaspoon allspice*
> *2 tablespoons pine nuts, lightly toasted*

For the filling, fry the onion in the oil till golden. Add the meat and fry lightly, crushing it with a fork and turning it over until it changes color, adding salt and pepper to taste, cinnamon, and allspice. Stir in the pine nuts. To make the pies, follow the instructions for "Making Filo Triangles" (see box opposite), brushing the filo strips with oil and the tops with oil or egg yolk mixed with 1 teaspoon of water.

VARIATIONS

- Add a pinch of nutmeg and ground cloves.
- Sprinkle the pies with 2 tablespoons of sesame seeds before baking.

Other Fillings for Filo Pies

For Filikas de Balabak— Pumpkin Triangles

MAKES ABOUT 30

This is a specialty of Turkey.

For the filling

> *1½ lbs (750 g) orange pumpkin (weighed free of skin and fiber)*
> *5 oz (150 g) feta cheese, mashed*
> *2 eggs*

Cut the pumpkin into pieces and put it in a pan with a tight-fitting lid with about ½ cup (125 ml) of water. Cook with the lid on for 20–30 minutes, until soft. Drain and mash in a colander and leave it there for all the liquid to drain for about 20 minutes. Press gently, then mix with the rest of the ingredients.

Cut sheets of filo in 4 rectangles along the width. Fill and shape into triangles or cigars.

For Burag Murug—Chicken Filo Cigars

An Iraqi specialty.

> *1 lb (500 g) skinless chicken fillets*
> *1 medium onion, quartered*
> *Salt*
> *4 tablespoons chopped flat-leafed parsley*

1 teaspoon curry powder
Pinch of cayenne pepper

Boil the chicken in salted water with the onion for 20 minutes, or until soft. Drain and chop the chicken and onion coarsely. Mix in the parsley, curry powder, and cayenne. Add salt if necessary.

MAKING FILO "CIGARS"

CUT THE SHEETS of filo into 4 rectangles about 12 by 4 inches (30 by 10 cm) and put them in a pile on top of each other. Brush the top strip lightly with oil or melted butter. Take a heaping teaspoon of filling, press into a thin sausage shape, and place it at one short end of the strip of filo along the edge—about 1 inch (2½ cm) from it and from the 2 long edges. Roll up with the filling inside like a cigarette. Turn the ends in about a third of the way to trap the filling, then continue to roll, leaving the ends open (so that they look open but the filling is trapped inside). Place close to each other on a greased baking sheet and brush the tops with oil or melted butter, or better still with egg yolk mixed with a drop of water, and bake at 350°F (180°C) for 30 minutes, or until crisp and golden.

Bulemas kon Keso

Cheese Coils

MAKES 8 (1 PER PERSON)

4 sheets filo
4 tablespoons unsalted butter, melted
1 egg yolk

For the filling

½ lb (250 g) feta cheese, mashed
½ lb (250 g) Gruyère, grated
2 eggs

Mix the filling ingredients, and make the pastries following the instructions for "Making Individual Filo Coils" (see box opposite).

Bulemas kon Espinaka

Spinach Coils

MAKES 8 (1 PER PERSON)

4 sheets filo
4 tablespoons unsalted butter, melted
1 egg yolk (optional)

For the filling

1 lb (500 g) fresh or frozen leaf
   spinach
4 oz (100 g) feta cheese

MAKING INDIVIDUAL FILO COILS—FOR BULEMAS AND RODANCHAS

T HIS SHAPE is popular with Iberian Jews. They call it a "rose"; we call it a "snail." The large ones are very spectacular, and will create quite an impression when you bring them to the table.

For small individual coils, cut the sheets of filo into 2 rectangles about 12 inches (30 cm) long and 10 inches (25 cm) wide, and pile them one on top of another. Brush the top strip lightly with oil or melted butter. Put a line of filling—3 to 4 tablespoons—along one long side, about 1 inch (2½ cm) from the edge and the 2 shorter ends. Very carefully lift up the edge, fold it over the filling, and roll into a long thin roll, folding in the sides about halfway to trap the filling so that it doesn't ooze out.

To be able to coil the roll without tearing the pastry, you have to crease it first like an accordion. To do this, hold the roll with both hands and very gently push from the ends towards the center. Now curve the roll very gently in the shape of a snail and lift it onto a greased baking sheet. Repeat with the rest of the filo rectangles and filling. Place all the coils close to each other on the tray and brush the tops with oil or melted butter, or, better still, with egg yolk mixed with a drop of water, and bake at 350°F (180°C) for 30–40 minutes, or until crisp and golden.

4 oz (100 g) Gruyère, grated
2 eggs
Pepper
A good pinch of nutmeg
Salt

Wash the fresh spinach and remove any hard stems (keep the soft thin ones), then put the leaves in a pan and cook, covered, over low heat until they crumple to a soft mass. Or defrost the frozen spinach. The most important thing is to squeeze out all the water that you possibly can in a colander. Put the spinach in the food processor with the feta and Gruyère, the eggs, pepper, and nutmeg, and process very briefly. Taste and add a little salt if necessary, taking into account the saltiness of the cheese.

Make the pastries following the instructions above for "Making Individual Filo Coils."

Rodanchas de Berengena
Large Eggplant Filo Coil

SERVES 8–10

This is a specialty of Salonika. It is usually made into small individual pastries, but a large pie takes much less time and is beautiful to present as a first course. The shape and filling are uniquely Sephardi. They call it a "rose" shape. The bulemas of Turkey are similar.

> 4 large sheets filo measuring about
>   18 by 12½ inches (46 by 32 cm)
> 3 tablespoons butter, melted
> 1 egg yolk mixed with 1 teaspoon of water,
>   for glazing

For the filling

> 2 lbs (1 kg) eggplants
> 4 oz (100 g) feta cheese, mashed
> 4 oz (100 g) Gruyère, grated
> White pepper
> ¼ teaspoon nutmeg
> 2 eggs

For the filling, roast the eggplants in the hottest oven for 30 minutes, turning them once, or put them under the broiler for 15–20 minutes and turn them until the flesh feels soft and the skin is blackened. Peel and chop in a colander, letting the juices run through. Then mash with a fork and mix with the rest of the filling ingredients.

Open out the sheets of filo. Brush the top one with melted butter and put a line of filling about 1¼ inches (3 cm) thick along one long edge. Fold the edge over it and roll up, making a long thin roll, tucking the ends in to stop the filling from oozing out. To be able to coil the roll without making the pastry tear, you have to crease it first like an accordion by pushing the ends towards the center with both hands. Now carefully lift the roll and place it in the middle of a greased flat round baking dish. Curve it like a snail. Do the same with the other sheets, and place the

rolls end to end to form a long coil like a snake.

Brush the top with egg yolk mixed with water and bake at 350°F (180°C) for ¾ hour, or until browned on top. Serve hot.

VARIATIONS

- In Turkey, where they call it "bulemas," they sprinkle the top with grated Gruyère.
- Some people add a mashed potato to the filling.
- For a cheese rodancha, use the filling on page 300.

Tarte Feuilletée au Fromage
Fila Cheese Tart

SERVES 20

This is much quicker to make than the little pies and just as delightful. Use the same filling as for fila au fromage (page 296) and proceed as for "Making a Large Layered Filo Pie" (see box opposite). The very generous amount of filling makes it a good dairy entree. It is milder than the usual feta-based ones of the Greek tyropita and slightly chewy.

Tarte Feuilletée aux Épinards
Spinach Pie

SERVES 20

This is the famous Greek spanakopita, which came to us in Egypt with the Salonika Jews in the early part of the century.

Use the same filling as for fila aux épinards (page 298), and proceed as in "Making a Large Layered Filo Pie" (see box below).

VARIATION

• Add to the filling a bunch of scallions, chopped, and a bunch of dill, chopped (¼ cup chopped).

MAKING A LARGE LAYERED FILO PIE— TARTE FEUILLETÉE

THIS IS QUICK AND EASY to make. Use a large baking dish or sheet a little smaller than the filo sheets. Brush it with oil or melted butter. Place 7 sheets of filo, one on top of another, at the bottom of the dish, brushing each with oil or melted butter and letting the sheets come up along the sides. Spread the filling evenly on top. Then cover with 7 more sheets, brushing each with oil or melted butter. With a sharp-pointed knife, cut into 2-inch (5-cm) squares or diamonds with parallel lines only down to the filling, not through.

Bake at 350°F (180°C) for 45 minutes, or until crisp and golden. Cut along the cutting lines, this time going through to the bottom, and serve hot.

Boghatcha
Creamy Cheese Flan with Filo

SERVES 10

Few people know this dish. The name means "drunkard" in Judeo-Spanish—perhaps because the pastry is soaked in milk. It is a curious and wonderful pie—a version of the Turkish sutlu borek. The filo pastry with a sharp cheese filling, baked in a light creamy custard, becomes soft, like sheets of ever-so-thin pasta.

1 lb (500 g) feta, mashed
¾ lb (350 g) Gruyère cheese, grated
½ cup (75 g) grated kashkaval or Parmesan
6 eggs
½ lb (250 g) filo—7 sheets about
*   18 by 12½ inches (46 by 32 cm)*
3 tablespoons butter, melted
2½ cups (600 ml) milk

For the filling, mix the feta, Gruyère, and about ¾ of the kashkaval or Parmesan with 2 of the eggs.

Open out the sheets of filo, leaving them in a pile. Brush the top one with melted butter and put a line of filling about 1 inch (2½ cm) thick along one long side. Roll up, making a long thin roll, folding in the ends about halfway to stop the filling from oozing out. Crease the roll like an accordion by pushing the ends towards the center with both hands. Place it in the middle of a round baking dish about 12 inches (30 cm) in diameter, curving it like a snail. Do the same with the other sheets and place the rolls end to end to form a long coil like a snake. Lightly beat the remaining 4 eggs with the milk and pour over the cheese-filled coil (you do not need to add salt, because the feta cheese is very salty).

Sprinkle with the remaining kashkaval or Parmesan and bake at 350°F (180°C) for about I hour, or until the cream is absorbed and set and the top of the pastry is brown. Serve hot or cold, cut into wedges like a cake.

MAKING LARGE FILO ROLLS

THIS IS SOMETHING you can do quickly. Put 2 large sheets of filo together, brushing each with oil or melted butter. Place a row of filling about I inch (2½ cm) thick along a shorter end about 1½ inches (4 cm) from the edge and 1½ inches (4 cm) from the ends and roll up loosely. Brush the top with oil or melted butter, or with egg yolk mixed with a drop of water, and sprinkle with sesame seeds if you like. Place on a greased baking sheet and bake in a 350°F (180°C) oven for 45 minutes to I hour, until crisp and golden.

Cigares à la Viande
Moroccan Meat "Cigars"

MAKES 32

Moroccan cigars are standard fare for Jewish caterers in France and Israel. They are invariably found on menu lists for wedding and bar-mitzvah parties. In the past these pastries were always deep-fried in oil, which makes them beautifully crispy and brown, but I have found many people in Paris who bake them now. It is not quite the same, but that is what I prefer to do, and that is what we always did with similar pastries in Egypt. The meat filling, called "miga," which is blended to a soft paste, must be strongly flavored and spicy, because otherwise it goes almost unnoticed in its filo-pastry wrapping.

> 2 medium onions, chopped
> 3–4 tablespoons peanut or sunflower oil
>   (plus more to brush the filo)
> 1 lb (500 g) lean ground beef
> Salt and pepper
> 1½ teaspoons cinnamon
> ½–¾ teaspoon powdered ginger
> ¼ teaspoon nutmeg
> A good pinch of cayenne (optional)
> Juice of ½–1 lemon
> 4 tablespoons finely chopped flat-leafed
>   parsley or coriander
> ½ lb (250 g) filo—8 sheets about
>   18 by 13 inches (46 by 33 cm)

Fry the onions in oil till soft. Add the meat and stir, crushing it with a fork, until it changes color. Then add salt and pepper to taste, cinna-

PASTRY FOR NORTH AFRICAN BREIKS, CIGARES, AND BEZTELS

THE PASTRY used to make the famous Moroccan cigares, the Algerian beztels, and the Tunisian breiks, all of which have a very important place at North African weddings and bar mitzvahs today, is a paper-thin pancake called "ouarka" in Morocco and "malsouka" in Tunisia. In Israel, cigars are now on every caterer's list.

The making of the pastry is a highly skilled, painstaking operation which is now left mostly to specialists. A very soft, moist, elastic dough is made with hard durum-wheat flour and water. A special round copper tray, tinned on the outside, is placed over a fire, the tinned side on top. With a quick darting motion, a ball of the dough is dabbed over the oiled tray, leaving a thin film as it touches the metal. A whole round sheet, about 10 inches (25 cm) in diameter, is gradually built up all over the surface. As soon as it dries, it is lifted off and piled up with other sheets. In the old days these were wrapped first in a dry cloth, then in a damp one. Now they go straight into plastic wrap and stay there until they are used. You can find the hand-made pastry sold in North African markets, and you can now buy mass-produced ones in French supermarkets. I have brought back piles of these from North Africa and France and put them in my freezer, and they have kept very well. I hope they will be sold in England and America, one day.

Because the real thing is at the moment unobtainable in Anglo-Saxon countries and difficult to master, I have used filo in my North African recipes. It is a perfectly good substitute. You may also use store-bought puff pastry, which many North African Jews use in France, rolling it out very thin.

mon, ginger, nutmeg, cayenne, and lemon juice. Stir well, add about 1 cup (250 ml) water, and cook, covered, for about ½ hour, until the meat is very tender. Remove the lid towards the end to dry it out. Blend to a soft paste in the food processor and add the flat-leafed parsley.

Cut each sheet of filo into 4 rectangles about 13 by 4½ inches (33 by 11 cm) and pile the pieces on top of each other so that they do not dry out. Brush the top strip lightly with oil. Take a lump of meat smaller than a walnut and press it into a sausage shape in your hand. Place it along one short end of the strip of filo about 1 inch (2½ cm) from the edge. Roll up like a cigarette, turning the ends in about a third of the way to trap the filling, then continuing to roll with the sides seemingly open. Continue with the remaining strips of dough.

Brush the tops with oil and bake at 325°F (160°C) for about ½ hour, or until crisp and golden. Serve hot.

VARIATIONS

• For an alternative flavoring, substitute 1 teaspoon turmeric and ¾ teaspoon ginger for the spices.

• Another popular filling includes 2 crushed

garlic cloves, I teaspoon cumin, ½ teaspoon mace, a pinch of nutmeg, I teaspoon turmeric, ¼ teaspoon cayenne (omit the other spices), 2 tablespoons of vinegar instead of the lemon juice, and 4 tablespoons chopped coriander.

• In Tunisia, 2 chopped boiled eggs and I raw egg are often added to the filling of breiks à la viande. These are usually shaped in little triangles. See "Making Filo Triangles" (page 298).

• Algerian beztels à la viande have a filling similar to that of the cigars and are shaped into triangles.

• Brushing the tops with egg yolk mixed with a teaspoon of water gives the pastries a more golden color.

Cigares au Thon

Moroccan Cigars with Tuna

MAKES ABOUT 20 LARGE CIGARS

These sharp, strongly flavored pastries make an unusual and delightful appetizer.

14-oz (400-g) can of tuna in brine or
  water
A good bunch of coriander, chopped
  (⅓ cup)
Juice of 1 lemon
1–2 teaspoons cumin (optional)
¼ teaspoon cayenne or chili pepper, or to taste
  (optional)
2 tablespoons capers, squeezed to remove the
  vinegar

About 10 black olives, pitted and cut in
  small pieces
3 eggs
7 oz (200 g) filo (about half the usual
  package)
Peanut or sunflower oil

Drain the tuna and squeeze it dry. Put it in a bowl and mash it with a fork. Add the coriander, lemon juice, cumin, cayenne or chili pepper, capers, olives, and eggs and mix very thoroughly.

Cut the filo into rectangles about 12 by 5 inches (30 by 12 cm), depending on the width of the sheets. Keep them in a pile. Brush the top one with oil. Put a heaping tablespoon of the tuna mixture along a short side of the rectangle about ¾ inch (2 cm) from the edge. Roll up like a cigar. About a third of the way, fold in the ends of the cigar, so that the filling cannot fall out, then continue rolling without folding in, so the cigar looks open at its ends. Repeat with all the sheets of pastry. Arrange the cigars on an oiled baking sheet. Brush each with oil and bake at 325°F (160°C) for 35 minutes, or until crisp and lightly browned. Serve hot.

VARIATIONS

• To give the pastries a richer brown color, brush with beaten egg yolk mixed with I teaspoon of water instead of with oil.

• A few chopped pickled gherkins can be added instead of the capers.

• Cigares aux pommes de terre, filled with mashed potato (Algerians call them "beztels") are very popular in Israel, but they are not my favorites. To make the filling for them, fry 2 large onions, chopped, in 4 tablespoons olive oil on very low heat, stirring occasionally, till golden.

Peel and boil 1¼ lbs (600 g) potatoes in salted water till tender. Drain and mash, and season with salt and pepper. In a bowl, mix well with the fried onions, 2 beaten eggs, and a large bunch of parsley, chopped (½ cup), and fold in 2 chopped hard-boiled eggs.

Lahma bi Agine

Meat Pizzas

MAKES 16 7-INCH
(18-CM) PIZZAS

This type of meaty bread is part of the baker's trade in the Middle East, and one of the traditional fast-food snacks sold in the streets. The filling is usually a mix of raw meat, onions, and chopped tomatoes, and there are sometimes pine nuts. The following is popular among Aleppo Jews. You may wonder as you mix the ingredients if it could possibly turn out well, because it seems so odd (tamarind makes it all a dark brown), but it does—wonderfully. The blend of tomato paste and tamarind gives the meat a splendid taste. It is important to use the tart concentrated tamarind paste (which is made in India) or syrup (made in Italy), and not the sweet syrup (Lebanese) sold now in some stores for diluting into a drink.

For the dough

> 2½ teaspoons (1 package) active dry yeast
> ½ teaspoon sugar
> About 1 cup (250 ml) lukewarm water
> 3⅓ cups (500 g) bread flour

> 1 teaspoon salt
> 4 tablespoons sunflower oil

For the topping

> 2 onions, chopped
> 3 tablespoons sunflower oil
> 1½ lbs (750 g) lean ground lamb
> 3 tablespoons tamarind paste or tart syrup
>   (not the sweet variety of syrup)
> 2 teaspoons sugar or to taste
> ½ cup (100 ml) tomato paste
> Salt
> A good pinch of cayenne

In a large bowl, mix the yeast and the sugar with about half the lukewarm water and leave for about 10 minutes, until frothy.

Add the flour and salt and 3 tablespoons of oil and mix well, then gradually add the rest of the water—enough to make a firm dough that holds together. Knead vigorously for at least 10 minutes, until very soft and elastic. Pour the remaining tablespoon of oil into the bowl and turn the dough to oil it all over. Cover with plastic wrap and leave in a warm place for 2 hours, or until doubled in bulk.

For the topping, fry the onions in oil till soft and just beginning to color. Put in a bowl with the rest of the topping ingredients and work very well with your hands to a soft, well-blended paste. If the tamarind is too hard, soften it by diluting with 1–2 tablespoons of water in a small pan over low heat.

Punch down the risen dough and knead for a few minutes. Divide into 16 egg-sized balls (first in half, then in quarters, and so on). On a floured surface and with a floured rolling pin, roll each out as thin as possible, less than ⅛ inch (about ¼ cm) thick, into round or oval shapes. Place on oiled or floured trays and spread the filling very thickly and evenly over each, almost to the edge of the dough. Bake at 475°F (240°C) for 10 minutes. The breads should be well done but still soft and pliable enough to roll up—as some people like to eat them. Serve hot.

VARIATION

• Instead of tamarind, add sour pomegranate concentrate (molasses) and ½ teaspoon allspice (in which case do not add sugar) or lemon juice.

Torta di Erbe

Green Tart

SERVES 6–8

I made this Roman tart with green vegetables, which is also known as "pizza ebraica" (Jewish pizza), when my daughter Anna brought her new baby, Sarah, back home from the hospital—so it is associated for me with a very happy time. I realized only later that in Jewish symbolism green represents new life, a new year, a new beginning. This is one dish for which canned artichoke hearts and frozen peas will do very well.

For the dough

2 cups (300 g) flour
¼ teaspoon salt
5 oz (150 g) butter or margarine, cut in pieces

1 egg, lightly beaten
1–2 tablespoons milk or water, or more if necessary
1 egg white, to glaze the pastry

For the filling

½ lb (250 g) spinach
1 14-oz (400-g) can of baby artichoke hearts (about 7) (or frozen ones, defrosted)
1 onion, chopped
3 tablespoons extra-virgin olive oil or light vegetable oil
1 lb (500 g) frozen petits pois, defrosted
Salt and pepper
2 eggs

Make the pastry first. Put the flour in a bowl and mix in the salt. Add the butter or margarine and rub it into the flour with your hands. Add the egg and work it in. You may need a tablespoon or so of milk or water to bind the dough into a soft ball that holds together. Wrap in plastic wrap and let it rest for ½ hour at room temperature.

Wash the spinach, drain, and press as much water out as you can. Drain the artichokes and squeeze their water out gently, then cut in half. Fry the onion in oil till soft and golden. Stir in the artichokes and the peas and season lightly with salt and pepper. Put the spinach on top, press it down, and put the lid on. When the spinach crumples to a soft mass, sprinkle with a little salt and pepper and stir in all the vegetables. Continue to cook, uncovered, on low heat until the peas are very tender and most of the liquid has dried out. Then stir in the eggs and remove from heat.

Line a large greased pie plate with the dough (I used a paella pan 13 inches, or 33 cm, in diameter), pressing it in with the palm of your hand and bringing it up a little on the sides. Brush the top with egg white (you will not need the whole of the egg white), to seal the pastry and prevent it from getting soggy. Put it in a 350°F (180°C) oven for 20 minutes.

Take it out and let it cool, then fill with the vegetable mixture. Put back in the oven and bake at the same temperature for another 30 minutes. Serve hot.

Pita au Poulet

Chicken Pies with Bread Dough

MAKES 6

Make a bread dough as in the recipe for pita (page 550).

For the filling, fry 1 lb (500 g) chopped onions in 4 tablespoons peanut or light vegetable oil until soft and golden. Add ½ lb (250 g) skinless chicken fillets cut in pieces, salt and pepper, and a squeeze of lemon, and cook, stirring, for about 10 minutes. Remove from heat and mix in 4 tablespoons of chopped coriander.

Divide the dough into 12 balls. Roll out to about 4 inches (10 cm) in diameter and leave to rise for 30 minutes. Spread the filling on 6 of the rounds to within ⅓ inch (1 cm) of the edge. Cover with the remaining rounds and pinch the edges to seal the pies. Brush the tops with egg yolk mixed with a drop of water and bake in a preheated 375°F (190°C) oven for about 30 minutes, or until golden.

Mina de Carne

Passover Meat Pie with Matzos

SERVES 8

In Egypt we called it "maiena."

> 2 medium onions, coarsely chopped
> 4 tablespoons sunflower oil
> 1½ lbs (750 g) ground lamb or beef
> Salt and pepper
> 1 teaspoon cinnamon
> ½ teaspoon allspice
> Bunch of flat-leafed parsley, finely chopped
>   (about ½ cup)
> ½ cup (75 g) pine nuts
> 5 eggs, lightly beaten
> 2½ cups (600 ml) chicken stock
>   (you may use 2 bouillon cubes)
> 8 matzo squares

Prepare the filling. Fry the onions in 3 tablespoons of oil till soft and golden. Add the meat, salt and pepper to taste, cinnamon, and allspice and cook, stirring and breaking up the meat, for about 8 minutes, until it changes color. Add the flat-leafed parsley. Fry the pine nuts in the remaining oil until slightly browned and add them too. Remove from heat and let it cool slightly, then add 3 beaten eggs and stir very well.

For the crust, put the warmed chicken stock in a bowl and soak 4–5 matzo squares in it until they are soft. Be careful not to make them too soggy. Lift them out quickly and fit 4 matzo squares in 2 layers in the bottom and sides of a 12-inch (30-cm) baking dish, overlapping and trimming the edges. Fill with the meat mixture and cover with the rest of the matzos, softened in the stock. Pour ½ cup (100 ml) of stock all over the pie (it will seep through the crust), then pour the rest of the beaten eggs over the top. Bake at 350°F (180°C) for 45 minutes.

Mina de Espinaka

Matzo and Spinach Pie

SERVES 8

A pie made with spinach, or spinach and cheese, was eaten during the Passover week in the Judeo-Spanish Ottoman world.

> *2 lbs (1 kg) spinach*
> *5 eggs*
> *½ lb (250 g) feta or cottage cheese*
> *Salt and pepper*
> *¼ teaspoon nutmeg*
> *8 matzo squares*
> *2 cups (500 ml) milk, warmed*

Make the filling first. Wash the spinach and remove any hard stems. Drain and squeeze the excess water out, then put the spinach in a pan with a tight-fitting lid. Steam for a minute or two, until the leaves collapse into a soft mass. (You might need to do this in batches.) Mix the spinach, including the green juice, with 3 eggs (beaten) and the cottage cheese. Season with salt, pepper, and nutmeg.

For the crust, dip 4–5 squares of matzo in the milk until only just softened and fit 2 layers on the bottom and sides of a 12-inch (30-cm) shallow oiled baking dish. Cover with the spinach filling. Soak the remaining matzo sheets in milk and arrange in 2 layers on top. Beat the remaining eggs with what is left of the milk and pour all over the pie. Bake in a preheated 350°F (180°C) oven for about 45 minutes.

Soups

MANY OF THE SOUPS in this chapter are substantial. Some were eaten in the morning for breakfast, some at wedding parties. Today they would represent a meal. Fish soups are to be found in the chapter on fish.

Sopa de Huevo y Limón

Egg-and-Lemon Soup

SERVES 6

In his *Cookbook of the Jews of Greece*, Nicholas Stavroulakis says that in Salonika this soup was served to break the Yom Kippur fast. In Egypt it was part of the meal before the fast. We called it *"beid ab lamouna."* One of the most popular soups in the Sephardi world, it is variously made with whole eggs, as in this recipe, or with egg yolks alone.

> *1 chicken carcass and some giblets or*
> *chicken wings to make the stock*
> *1 large onion, quartered*
> *2 carrots, cut in large pieces*
> *2 celery stalks and leaves, cut in large pieces*
> *A few parsley stalks*
> *Salt and pepper*
> *½ cup (100 g) rice*
> *3 large eggs*
> *Juice of 1–2 lemons*

Put the chicken carcass and giblets or wings in a pot with the onion, carrots, celery, and parsley stalks. Add 2¾ quarts (2½ liters) of water and bring to the boil. Remove the scum, add salt and pepper, and simmer, covered, for I hour to obtain a rich stock. Strain through a fine sieve and return to the pot. Simmer to reduce the stock to about 2 quarts (1¾ liters) stock. Adjust the seasoning.

Add the rice and simmer 20 minutes or until tender. Just before serving, beat the eggs in a bowl, add the lemon juice (the soup should be tart), and beat in a ladleful of stock. Pour this mixture into the soup, which should be barely simmering, and beat constantly until the soup thickens—but do not let it boil or the eggs will curdle. It should be creamy.

CHICKEN SOUPS

IN THE SEPHARDI WORLD, chicken soup does not have the place it has in Ashkenazi culture, but there are many versions. The most common are with rice or vermicelli. North Africans may add couscous or semolina dumplings. Sometimes a pinch of saffron or turmeric gives a golden color and slight aroma, and eggs beaten in at the end give a lovely thick texture. Some are more elaborate, such as the Tunisian "soupe de poulet aux joujoux," which has vermicelli and hard-boiled eggs cut in pieces and a raw egg beaten in at the end.

VARIATIONS

• Instead of rice, you may add vermicelli or tiny little pastine.

• Some like to thicken the soup further by stirring in I tablespoon of cornstarch mixed with a little cold water after the rice is added.

• A Moroccan *bouillon de poule aux oeufs* is chicken broth, yellowed by ¼ teaspoon saffron or turmeric, and with 2 eggs beaten in at the end.

• A Passover specialty in Georgia is khengali, walnut balls, in chicken soup. Lightly beat 2 eggs, then beat in 2 cups (250 g) ground walnuts and ¼ teaspoon salt. Roll into walnut-sized balls, drop into boiling chicken broth, and simmer for about 10 minutes.

Minestra Dayenu

Chicken Soup with Matzos

SERVES 6

This recipe came in a letter from Nedelia Tedeschi in Turin. It is the traditional Passover soup. *Dayenu,* meaning "that would have been enough" in Hebrew, is the chorus of a song that is part of the Haggadah—the story of the Exodus.

> *7½ cups (1¾ liters) well-flavored chicken stock*
> *3 matzos, cut in small pieces*
> *3 egg yolks*
> *1 teaspoon cinnamon*

Bring the chicken stock to the boil, throw in the matzo pieces, and simmer ½ hour, until the matzo is very soft and bloated. In a soup tureen, beat the egg yolks with the cinnamon and 4–5 tablespoons of cold water, then gradually pour in the soup, stirring constantly.

Shorba bi Djaj

Chicken Soup with Rice

SERVES 6

This thick, creamy, aromatic soup was eaten on cold winter mornings for breakfast in Baghdad. It was made with a whole chicken, but it is easy enough to use chicken wings.

16 chicken wings
3 celery ribs and a bunch of celery leaves, chopped
⅔ cup (125 g) short-grain rice
Salt
4 cardamom pods
Juice of ½–1 lemon
½ teaspoon turmeric
1 teaspoon cinnamon

Put the chicken wings in a pot with 2¾ quarts (2½ liters) of water. Bring to the boil and remove the scum. Then put in the rest of the ingredients and simmer for 1½ hours, or until the rice has softened so much that it gives a creamy texture to the soup. Lift out the chicken wings. When they are cool enough to handle, remove the skin and bones and put the meat back into the soup. Serve hot.

VARIATION

• The Calcutta Baghdadi version of chicken-and-rice soup, simply called "shorba" —which means "soup"—has I small chopped onion and ½ teaspoon ground ginger. (For the Jews who moved from the Arab world to India, see page 368.)

Bulgarian Yogurt and Cucumber Soup

SERVES 6

During the Second World War, Bulgarian Jews were saved by the king and the Church, but at the time of the communist takeover tens of thousands made their way to Israel. Their simple, fresh-tasting, healthy dishes had a great impact on the Israeli diet and food production. Bulgaria is famous for its reputedly life-prolonging yogurt culture, *Bacillus bulgaricus*, and this refreshing summer soup is part of the heritage.

1½ large cucumbers, peeled and coarsely grated or diced
Salt
3 cups (750 ml) natural yogurt
⅔ cup (150 ml) sour cream
4 garlic cloves, crushed
2 tablespoons olive oil
A bunch of dill, finely chopped (about ½ cup)
6 ice cubes

Sprinkle the cucumber with plenty of salt and leave to drain for I hour in a colander. Then rinse and drain again. In a serving bowl, beat the yogurt and sour cream with the garlic, olive oil, and dill. Stir in the cucumber, taste, and add salt if necessary. Chill and add ice cubes before serving.

Jewish yogurt vendors in Salonika

Dueh

Persian Yogurt Soup

SERVES 6

This recipe comes from *A Persian Jewish Cook Book* by the Sisterhood of the Persian Hebrew Congregation in Skokie, Illinois. They call for "sour cream," but it can also be made with yogurt or a mixture of the two. The pickled cucumbers give an unusual, sharpish flavor.

2 cups (500 ml) yogurt or sour cream or
  a mixture of the two
1 cup (250 ml) cold water
Salt
1 bunch scallions, finely chopped
1 lb (500 g) pickled cucumbers, peeled and
  finely chopped
⅓ cup (50 g) raisins or sultanas
  (optional)
A bunch of dill, finely chopped (¼ cup)
6 ice cubes

Beat the yogurt and/or sour cream in a bowl and add the rest of the ingredients.

Shorbet Sabanekh bel Zabady

Spinach and Yogurt Soup

SERVES 6

We called it "labaneya." It is one of my favorites.

1 lb (500 g) fresh or frozen leaf spinach
1 onion, chopped
2 tablespoons oil
1 or 2 cloves garlic, crushed
5 cups (1¼ liters) chicken stock or
*   water*
4 scallions, finely chopped
½ cup (100 g) rice
Salt and pepper
2 cups (500 ml) yogurt, lightly beaten
2 teaspoons dried mint

Wash the fresh spinach, remove the stems, and drain; or defrost frozen spinach. Squeeze the water out and cut into ½-inch (1½-cm) ribbons.

Fry the onion in the oil till soft. Add 1 crushed garlic clove and cook gently, stirring, for 2–3 minutes. Add the spinach.

Cover with stock or water, add the scallions and the rice, season with salt and pepper, and simmer 20 minutes, until the rice is tender. Beat the yogurt with another crushed garlic clove, if you like, and mint and beat it into the soup. Heat through, but do not let the soup boil or it will curdle.

VARIATIONS

• For a Turkish touch, garnish with a dribble of 1 tablespoon paprika mixed into 2 tablespoons of sizzling-hot butter.

• Persian Jews make a similar yogurt and spinach soup with rice, which is flavored with dill. They call it pshal dueh.

Melokheya

SERVES 6

This famous Egyptian soup derives its name from the leaf that gives it its distinctive taste, dark-green color, and glutinous texture. I have never found out why it is called "Jew's mallow," but Egyptian Jews are madly fond of it, like everybody else in Egypt. I have heard of many exiles trying to grow it unsuccessfully in various countries (only in Colombia have they managed to produce plentiful crops). In Milan, relatives planted seeds in the garden of their apartment complex only to find, when they settled down for the grand banquet after weeks of watering and tending, that they had mouthfuls of weeds.

Melokheya is now available dried and frozen (the latter gives better results) in Middle Eastern stores, and occasionally you can find the fresh green leaves. Accompanied by rice, which is added to the soup in the plate, it is a substantial meal in itself.

2 lbs (1 kg) fresh or frozen melokheya or
*   1 lb (500 g) dried*
1 chicken
2 bay leaves
3 or 4 cardamom pods, slightly cracked
1 onion, cut in half
Salt and pepper
10 cloves garlic, minced or finely chopped
2–3 tablespoons oil
1 tablespoon dried ground coriander
Plain rice to accompany

Fresh leaves must be picked off the stems, washed, squeezed dry, and shredded very thin. Frozen melokheya comes finely chopped and only needs defrosting. Dried melokheya, sold in whole-leaf form, needs to be crumbled with the hands or reduced to a powder briefly in a blender or processor, then sprinkled with hot water and allowed to absorb the moisture for 5 minutes before being used.

Put the chicken in a large pot, cover with 2¾ quarts (2½ liters) water, and add the bay leaves, cardamom, onion, salt, and pepper. Bring to the boil, remove the scum, and simmer for 1 hour. Strain the broth and return it to the pot. Cut the chicken into serving pieces and set aside.

Just before you are ready to serve, bring the broth to the boil. Add the melokheya and simmer for 3–5 minutes. Do not overcook. The melokheya remains suspended in the broth.

For the finishing touch, fry the garlic (yes, it is a very garlicky soup) in oil till it is golden and the aroma rises, then stir in the coriander. Quickly pour this mixture (it is called "taqliya") into the soup and cook a minute longer.

Serving note

• Our family ritual was to eat the melokheya in two servings—first on its own, then with plain white rice. The chicken, reheated, was served separately. Others like to serve the chicken in the soup and have toasted or fried pita bread for dipping.

VARIATIONS

• Instead of chicken, you can use 2 lbs (1 kg) of meat—beef or lamb—cubed. Shin of veal is also popular.

• As flavoring, you may add the juice of ½ lemon and a pinch of chili or cayenne pepper.

Shorbet Ads
Lentil Soup

SERVES 6

Jacob gave Esau bread and a pottage of lentils. Lentils are often mentioned in the Talmud and the Bible. They have always had an important place in the Sephardi diet. For centuries they sustained the poor communities—often mixed with rice or with cracked wheat or noodles, or eaten as a salad with an oil-and-lemon dressing. In several communities they were an obligatory part of the Thursday-evening meal, which was traditionally meatless. Large green and brown lentils are used for most dishes, but for soups the little split red ones are used.

The following was the very basic Thursday soup we had in Cairo. When I was last there, in winter, it was offered to me in a one-table café on a medieval market street. They asked if I wanted scallions. When I said yes, a little boy ran out and got two from a nearby stall. They were peeled ceremoniously at the table and handed over. Lentil soup is the soup that has the most variations, and they are all worth trying.

1 large onion, finely chopped
2½ cups (500 g) split red lentils
7½ cups (1¾ liters) meat or chicken stock
  or water
Salt and pepper
1 teaspoon cumin
Juice of ½–1 lemon
Extra-virgin olive oil to sprinkle on,
  to taste

In a saucepan put the onion, lentils, stock or water, a little salt, and pepper, and simmer ½ hour, or until the lentils have disintegrated. Add water if the soup needs thinning. Then stir in the cumin and lemon juice and adjust the seasoning. Let people help themselves to a trickle of olive oil.

VARIATIONS

• Stir in at the end 1 large, coarsely chopped onion fried in 2–3 tablespoons of oil until very brown—almost caramelized.

• Omit the cumin and stir in before serving 4 crushed cloves of garlic fried in 3 tablespoons of olive oil with 2 teaspoons dried crushed mint.

• Serve with tiny bread croutons, toasted or fried in oil with crushed garlic.

• The Baghdadi Jews of India add 1 teaspoon turmeric, and 2 dried chopped chilies or a good pinch of cayenne pepper.

• Add ½ cup (100 g) rice, or vermicelli broken in your hands, or bulgur 15 minutes before the end of the cooking.

• Add 2 peeled and chopped tomatoes during the cooking and let them soften before serving.

• Add 1 lb (500 g) shredded fresh leaf spinach or ½ lb (250 g) frozen 10 minutes before the end of cooking.

• At my aunt Latifa's, it was "ads bi rishta"—a lemony lentil soup with noodles—every Thursday. Ten minutes before serving, throw in 5 oz (150 g) noodles, or tagliatelle broken into small pieces. Fry 2 chopped onions in 2 tablespoons olive oil till brown, add 4 crushed cloves of garlic and 1 tablespoon of crushed dried mint, then stir them in at the end with a trickle of olive oil.

Bessara
Dried Fava Bean Soup

SERVES 6

According to the Bible, fava beans are one of the foods the Jews hankered for during their Exodus from Egypt. They have been the basic food of Egypt since the time of the Pharaohs (specimens have been found in ancient tombs). In Egypt the soup we made was flavored only with salt, pepper, lemon juice, and flat-leafed parsley and was considered to be especially good for when you were sick. The following Moroccan version—eaten at Passover, because "that is what the Hebrews ate in Egypt"—is deliciously aromatic. You must use the large skinless variety or—as they are called on packages—split fava beans.

1 lb (500 g) skinless split dried fava
   beans
Salt
5 garlic cloves, chopped
2–8 tablespoons extra-virgin olive oil
1½ teaspoons paprika
1½–2 teaspoons cumin
¼ teaspoon turmeric
A pinch of cayenne or chili pepper
   (optional)
Juice of 2 lemons
A large bunch of coriander, chopped
   (½ cup)

Soak the beans in water for 2 hours. Drain and put into a pot with 2¾ quarts (2½ liters) of water. Bring to the boil, remove the scum, and simmer, covered, for 2 hours, until the beans are so soft they fall apart. Add salt, and mash the beans with a potato masher (this is quite satisfactory), or put the soup in a blender or through a vegetable mill to reduce it to a cream, then pour back into the pot.

Fry the garlic in 2 tablespoons of oil till golden, then add the paprika, cumin, turmeric, and, if you like, cayenne. Add to the soup and simmer ¼–½ hour longer, adding water if the soup is too thick. Before serving, stir in the lemon juice and coriander. Trickle a little olive oil over each bowl.

VARIATIONS

• Accompany with croutons and add a touch of extra paprika and cayenne in the olive oil you sprinkle on at the end.

• Adding merguez—little hot, spicy North African sausages—makes this a complete meal. Blanch the sausages in boiling water before adding them, cut in pieces, to the soup.

• For a Tunisian version, make a sauce by mixing 1½ teaspoons harissa with about ¾ cup (175 ml) of the cooking water, the juice of 1½ lemons, ⅔ cup (150 ml) olive oil, 2 crushed garlic cloves, and 1 teaspoon cumin. And pass it around for people to help themselves.

Soupe de Pois Chiches
Moroccan Meat and Chickpea Soup

SERVES 6

This was eaten on the Sabbath. The fore-knuckle or shin of veal gives a rich gelatinous quality.

1 lb (500 g) foreknuckle of veal sawn into large pieces
1 lb (500 g) chickpeas, soaked for at least an hour
8 cloves garlic, peeled
Salt and pepper
Juice of 1 lemon
A bunch of coriander, chopped (about ½ cup)

Put the meat in a pot with 2¾ quarts (2½ liters) of water. Bring to the boil and remove the scum. Add the chickpeas and whole garlic cloves and simmer for about 2 hours, until the meat and chickpeas are very tender, adding salt and pepper after an hour.

Take out the meat and blend the chickpeas to a cream in a food processor with a little of the stock, then pour back into the pot. Cut or pull the meat into small pieces and return them to the pot along with the scooped-out marrow of the bones. Bring to the boil and add water if necessary to make a light creamy texture. Stir in lemon and coriander and cook a few minutes more before serving.

VARIATION

• In Egypt we did not puree the chickpeas but left them whole. Sometimes we colored and flavored the soup with ½ teaspoon of turmeric.

Potakhe

Bean or Chickpea Soup with Spinach

"Potakhe" is the Moroccan Jewish spelling of the Spanish word for the thick soups that combine vegetables and legumes in Spain. This soup is sometimes also made with meat.

> 1 cup (200 g) dry white haricot beans or
>   chickpeas, soaked for 2 hours or overnight
> Salt and pepper
> 4–5 garlic cloves, crushed in a press or
>   finely chopped
> 4 tablespoons extra-virgin olive oil
> 2 lbs (1 kg) fresh or frozen spinach
> Juice of 1 lemon

Boil the beans or chickpeas in a large pot with 2¾ quarts (2½ liters) of water for 1½ hours, or until very tender, adding salt and pepper to taste after 45 minutes. Add garlic, fried in the olive oil, and more water if necessary. Wash and drain the spinach and remove any tough stems. Add it to the soup with the lemon juice. Put the lid on and cook a few minutes, until the spinach crumples. Stir well and serve hot.

Potakhe de Potiron

*Yellow Split Pea and
Pumpkin Soup*

In Morocco, this golden soup was served on the first night of Rosh Hashanah—the Jewish New Year. It is sometimes cooked with meat and marrow bones. The important thing is that the pumpkin have a good taste—they don't always.

> 1¼ cups (250 g) yellow split peas
> 1 large onion, chopped
> 2¾ quarts (2½ liters) chicken stock
> Salt and pepper
> 4 tablespoons sunflower oil
> 1 teaspoon cinnamon
> ¼ teaspoon ginger
> ¼ teaspoon saffron
> 1 lb (500 g) orange pumpkin, cubed
> 3 tablespoons finely chopped flat-leafed
>   parsley

Put the yellow split peas and the onion in a pot with the stock. Bring to the boil and simmer for ½ hour, or until the split peas are tender. Add salt and pepper to taste, the oil, cinnamon, ginger, and saffron, and put in the pumpkin. Simmer until the pumpkin falls apart. Sprinkle with flat-leafed parsley before serving.

VARIATION

• Chickpeas may be used instead of yellow split peas. They will need soaking for at least an hour.

Harira

Moroccan Bean and Vegetable Soup

SERVES 12 OR MORE

For Muslims, those rich soups full of fresh and dried vegetables and pasta are the specialty of Ramadan—when they are eaten every night to break the fast. Jews too have adopted the soups for their festive occasions. This one is hot, with plenty of black pepper, velvety with the addition of a flour-and-water paste, deliciously rich with the marrow bones, and fragrant with herbs and spices.

> 1 lb (500 g) fatty meat—lamb or beef—
>   cut into small cubes
> 3 or 4 marrow bones
> 18 cups (4¼ liters) water
> 1¼ cups (250 g) brown or green lentils
> 1¼ cups (250 g) chickpeas, soaked for
>   an hour at least
> 3 onions, chopped
> 2 tablespoons sunflower oil
> Salt
> 1½ teaspoons black pepper
> 2 lbs (1 kg) tomatoes, peeled
> ½ teaspoon powdered ginger
> ½ teaspoon saffron (powdered or crushed
>   pistils)
> ⅔ cup (100 g) flour
> 4 oz (100 g) vermicelli, broken into
>   small pieces with your hand
> A large bunch flat-leafed parsley,
>   finely chopped (1 cup)
> A large bunch coriander, finely chopped
>   (1 cup)
> Juice of 1 lemon, or more to taste

Put the meat and bones in a very large pot with the water and bring to the boil. Remove the scum, then add the lentils and chickpeas.

In a frying pan, fry the onions in the oil till golden and add them to the soup. Simmer 1½ hours, adding salt to taste and the black pepper after about an hour. Blend the tomatoes to a cream in a food processor and pour into the soup. Add the ginger and saffron and more water as required.

Mix the flour to a paste with cold water and add to the soup, stirring vigorously to avoid the forming of lumps, until the liquid thickens and the soup acquires what North Africans call a "velvety" texture. Add the vermicelli and simmer 15 minutes. Then add the parsley, coriander, and lemon juice and cook a few minutes more, until the vermicelli is tender. Serve in deep bowls.

VARIATIONS

• Instead of meat, you can have chicken; instead of chickpeas, fava beans, dried or fresh; instead of vermicelli, you can have rice.

YEMEN

THE JEWS OF YEMEN are one of the most ancient of Jewish communities, possibly dating back to the ninth century B.C., when, according to the Bible, a romantic encounter took place between King Solomon and the queen of Sheba. Professor Yehuda Nini of Tel Aviv University told me their story as we sat in a London coffeehouse. Jews were prominent in ancient Yemen. They fought many wars and even formed a Jewish kingdom in the middle of the fifth century A.D., which lasted 150 years. Many local tribes converted to Judaism. It was the Ethiopian Christian king who, at the bequest of the Byzantine emperor, fought and finally destroyed the Jewish kingdom of Yemen. According to legend, the last Jewish king, Yussef Dunwass, rode on his white horse into the sea rather than be captured.

When Islam became the state religion, after the Muslim conquest in the seventh century, the Jews chose to keep to their own special way of life and were allowed to maintain their separateness. The laws of Islam gave them protected status, but they had to pay a special tax and live within certain restrictions. One of these was that they were not allowed to

Yemeni silversmiths

wear bright colors outside their quarters. When they visited Muslim quarters, they changed into indigo-blue clothes. But most Jews lived side by side with Muslims, in small villages where there were no Jewish quarters, and were dispensed from that obligation. Although they were in some ways separate, they were integrated in the local society. They followed every occupation, from farmer and artisan to musician, shopkeeper, teacher, and doctor—and, famously, silversmith. They lived the same lives as the rest of the population and ate the same food. The only difference was that they kept the Jewish dietary laws. They were a pious community. It was messianic ideas that made them leave for Palestine as early as 1881. In 1949, thirty thousand were airlifted to Israel in an operation called "Magic Carpet." Six thousand more went to the United States. There are still Jews left in Yemen—in Sada, Haidan, Sagen, and Wadi Amlah.

Years ago, when the Sunday *Times Magazine* of London did a series on diet and health, Yemeni food came out healthiest based on an Israeli study of heart disease and cancer within their different immigrant communities. Now that a generation of Yemenites born in Israel who adopted the general diet is still showing a low rate of these diseases, it looks as though the reason may be genetic.

When I have asked Yemenites about their food, they have usually replied that there is not much to say. They do not eat dairy products such as milk, cheese, yogurt, or cream, except for samneh (clarified butter). In Yemen they did not eat very much at all. Theirs is a frugal diet based on bread—different kinds of bread—and very little meat. Cracked wheat (bulgur), called "haris," is a staple, eaten hot with clarified butter and honey for breakfast or cooked with meat bones, tomatoes, onion, and spices for a main meal. The main party food of celebration is a meat-and-tomato soup. The highly prized delicacies that appear at weddings are the offal dishes—all very hot and peppery and cooked with garlic and spices.

My cousin Mali Baer took me to a small Yemeni restaurant in Rehovoth, where there is a large Yemeni community, and where she is deputy mayor. We had a taste of everything, from bone soup to lung stew and tripe. A young Israeli journalist who accompanied us would touch only the hummus. Most of the dishes had the same spicy, peppery taste, as though the same mix had been used. And it had, because it is a Yemeni custom to use the same spice mixture for most things.

Although Yemeni cooking is considered primitive in Israel, based as it is on simple soups and cracked wheat and on offal dishes like udder, tripe, intestines, lungs, oxtail, lambs' testicles, and ox penis, some of the foods, like their Sabbath "breads," have become very popular Israeli national foods and are sold frozen in supermarkets. There is jihnun—a kind of rolled-up puff pastry which is cooked overnight in a pot with fat; a yeast pastry called "kubaneh"; lahuh, a spongy pancake made with fermented wheat or sorghum batter; and melawah, layers of paper-thin dough brushed with clarified butter and cooked in a frying pan. Other Yemeni foods that have had a great impact are the now famous hot, peppery relishes, like hilbeh and zhoug, which are eaten with bread as an accompaniment to most things.

The cooking of the Jews of Aden, in the south of Yemen, is similar to that of the Yemenites but with a difference. Since medieval times, the port city had an important position as a crossroads, and as the community prospered for a time under Ottoman rule, it acquired cultural sophistication with the British.

When the British occupied Aden in 1839 they reported only 500 residents, of whom the majority were Jewish. The city became a prosperous free port, and by 1916 the Jewish population had increased to 3,700. Some of the new settlers came from India and the Middle East, but for the most part they were from the Yemeni port of Mokka. The Jewish area in the old city, known as "the Crater," was located in the interior of an extinct volcano overlooking the bay. The British dug a tunnel through the mountainside connecting it to the commercial center around the port, where many of the Jews worked. In the late nineteenth century, most had been craftsmen—silversmiths, mat weavers, carpenters, bookbinders, and fez makers—but by the 1940s most were shopkeepers and merchants.

The community was closely knit and religious. The synagogue (there were ten) was the focal point of life, and the Beth Din, the Jewish court of law, had enormous power. Festivals were celebrated elaborately, with preparations going on for weeks. Births and circumcisions involved almost the entire community, with members gathering around the house and singing in the street. At funerals almost all of the Jewish poplulation would follow the body, which was carried on foot to the cemetery. Wedding celebrations lasted a week, with parties on rooftops, and music accompanying every event.

Most of the Adenis are now settled in Israel. A small community established itself in London's Stamford Hill, near the Hassidic community, where I visited Shoshana Yefet, whose husband is a musician. I watched Mrs. Yefet prepare Sabbath dishes and was offered a tasting. The Adenis have breads and relishes similar to those of the Yemenites. Hariss is meat stew with meat bones, onions, and cracked wheat. Mehawag, a fried mix of vegetables including potatoes, onions, eggplants, zucchini, okra, and tomatoes, with garlic, chilies, spices, and tamarind, is particular to them, as is Eedam, a spicy fish soup left overnight in the oven to be eaten on Saturday. It is made with fish heads and tuna fish (canned tuna is often used these days), onion, garlic, and a spice mixture that includes turmeric, cumin, coriander, cardamom, and black pepper. A large amount of flour makes it velvety thick and creamy. It is eaten with jihnun (a type of puff pastry) and eggs, which are also put in the oven overnight.

Ftut

Yemeni Wedding Soup

SERVES 4

The usual Yemeni meal consists of soup. This one, with meat or chicken and marrow bones, is the grand one served at weddings in Israel. I asked a fashionable Israeli chef whose family came from Yemen for his version. He said that if he adds any embellishment, like a bay leaf or parsley, there are immediate objections. It is flavored with *hawayij*—a spice mixture that contains black pepper, caraway seed, turmeric, and cardamom—which every Yemeni family keeps in a jar for constant use.

> 1 lb (500 g) slightly fatty beef, cut in
>   2-inch (5-cm) pieces
> 2 marrow bones
> Salt and plenty of black pepper
> ¼ teaspoon ground caraway seed
> ¼ teaspoon ground turmeric
> ¼ teaspoon ground cardamom
> 1 large potato, cubed
> 2 medium zucchini, cut in cubes
> 1 tomato, peeled
> 2 scallions, sliced

Put the meat and marrow bones in a pot with 7½ cups (1¾ liters) water. Bring to the boil and remove the scum. Add salt, pepper, and spices and simmer for 1 hour, or until the meat is tender. Add the vegetables and cook ½ hour more. Extract the bones and discard, but first scrape the marrow out and add it to the soup.

Gondy

Iranian Chicken Soup with Chickpea Dumplings

SERVES 6

This soup is eaten by Persian Jews on Friday nights. Dried limes give it a musty lemony flavor. You can find them and the chickpea flour in Oriental and Indian shops (where it is sold as gram flour). The dumplings here are a mixture of chickpea flour and beef, but ground raw chicken can be used instead of the meat.

> 1 small roasting chicken
> 2 medium onions
> Salt and pepper
> ¼ teaspoon turmeric
> 3 dried limes or juice of 1 lemon, or to taste
> 8 oz (250 g) lean ground beef
> 1 cup (100 g) chickpea (gram) flour
> ½ teaspoon ground cardamom

Put the chicken in a large pot with 3 quarts (3 liters) of water. Bring to the boil and remove the scum. Add 1 coarsely chopped onion, salt and pepper, the turmeric, and the limes, pricked in several places with the point of a knife or cracked with a hammer to release the maximum flavor and so that the water can penetrate and soak them entirely. They are dark brown inside and emanate a wonderfully evocative aroma. If you do not have limes, add fresh lemon juice before serving. Simmer for 45–55 minutes, until the chicken is tender.

Make the meatballs: Mix the ground meat

with the remaining onion, finely chopped or grated, and the chickpea flour and season with salt, pepper, and ground cardamom. Knead well with your hands until it binds together (you can put it all in a food processor, starting with the onion). Rub oil on your hands and roll the paste into little balls the size of a small walnut.

Lift the chicken out of the soup and drop the balls in. Simmer 20–30 minutes longer. Remove the skin and bones from the chicken, cut the chicken meat into pieces, and return to the soup to heat through.

Serve in bowls with plain basmati rice.

VARIATIONS

• To the chicken stock you may add from the start 2 ribs of celery and their leaves, chopped, and ¾ cup (150 g) yellow split peas, previously soaked for 1 hour.

• To the chicken stock add 2 large diced potatoes, 2 large diced carrots, 1 tablespoon tomato puree, and a pinch of cayenne.

Oshee Kifte

Chickpea and Tomato Soup with Chicken Quenelles

SERVES 8

In Bukhara and Samarkand this soup was served at the end of a party meal. It is delicate in taste—a little tart—and the chicken balls or kifte have a lovely light texture.

2¾ quarts (2½ liters) clear chicken stock
1¼ cups (250 g) chickpeas, soaked in water overnight
1 large onion, chopped
1 lb (500 g) tomatoes, peeled and cut in pieces
Salt and pepper
1 or 2 tart fresh or dried apricots, chopped
A bunch of coriander, chopped (about ½ cup)

For the chicken kifte

1 small onion
3 chicken fillets weighing in total ¾ lb (350 g), preferably breast, without skin
2 small eggs
1 large slice of good white bread, crusts removed, soaked in water and squeezed dry
A little salt and pepper

In a large pot put the stock, chickpeas, onion, and tomatoes and simmer for 1 hour, or until the chickpeas are tender, adding salt and pepper when they have begun to soften.

In the meantime, make the kifte (chicken balls). Finely chop the onion and chicken in the food processor. Add the eggs, bread, salt, and pepper and blend to a soft paste. Take lumps, smaller than a walnut, and roll into little balls.

Drop the balls into the simmering soup, add the apricots, and simmer for 10–15 minutes. Add the coriander before serving.

Fish

FISH IS A SYMBOL of abundance and procreation in Jewish lore, because, according to the Bible, God blessed the fish in the sea so that they would grow and multiply. In Morocco, a fish dinner was offered by newlyweds to their families and friends a few days after the wedding. In Salonika, *el día del peshe* (the day of the fish; "peshe" in Salonika dialect derives from the Italian word for fish) was the day when a bride stepped over a dish of fish which was then offered around by guests.

Fish was believed to be out of the reach of the evil eye, because it was in the water, which provided protection. One of my uncles was a cabbalist. People went to him for amulets and good-luck charms. He would draw a fish on a piece of paper and write a message in it and give it to them. I was struck by the idea that fish were full of *fel*—beneficial virtues.

For the New Year, a fish was served with the head left on so that "Jews would be at the head rather than the tail," or, according to some, so that "they may be ahead with good deeds and serve as a model of goodness." Joelle Bahloul writes in *Le Culte de la Table Dressée* that in Algeria, on the last meal of Passover, some homes served a fish dressed with flowers and wild herbs.

In all Sephardi communities, fish was appreciated and prestigious. It was eaten on Friday night and at the end of the Sabbath and was often part of the meatless Thursday-evening meal too. It was grilled, poached, fried, or simmered in a sauce and eaten cold. Fish roe and fish fritters, fish balls and little pies were eaten as appetizers with drinks. Fish was present at holiday feasts and on picnics. In North Africa, outdoor meals were enveloped with the smells of grilled fish with cumin.

As for the choice of fish, there was plenty around the Mediterranean. In the sea towns, where many of the Jewish communities were concentrated, fish represented the great and grand dish. Tunisia and the city of Salonika were especially famous for their fish dishes.

TO COOK A LARGE FISH IN FOIL

IN THIS MANNER OF COOKING, the fish is steamed in its own juice. It can be a whole large fish, weighing about 9 lbs (4 kg), or the fillets put together and the head—if you want it for the presentation—wrapped separately. Brush a large sheet of foil with 2 tablespoons of extra-virgin olive oil. Place the fish or fillets in the middle and sprinkle lightly with salt. Wrap in a loose aluminum-foil parcel, twisting the foil edges together to seal it. Bake at 400°F (200°C). Remove the parcel with the head after 25 minutes. Open the foil of the main parcel to test the fish for doneness after about 45–60 minutes, by cutting it with the point of a knife and seeing if it begins to flake. Let it cool in the foil.

Pesce Sott'Olio per il Sabato

Cold Fish in Olive Oil

This wonderful Italian way of preparing fish for Saturday—which keeps it moist and juicy—is made with a firm white fish such as bream, bass, John Dory, cod, or haddock. Salmon is not a traditional Italian fish, but I have used it too in this way, with great success. The fish can be poached or baked. I usually bake it in foil.

To bake the fish in foil, see box at left. When it is cold enough to handle, remove the skin and bones and put the fillets, in large pieces, in a serving dish. Beat the juice of 1 lemon with ½ cup (125 ml) of very light extra-virgin olive oil and the cooking juice from the fish in the foil. Add very little salt and white pepper and pour over the fillets. Leave to marinate for several hours or overnight, covered in the refrigerator.

Serve as it is or with a salsa verde (recipe follows).

Salsa Verde per Pesce

Green Sauce for Cold Fish

SERVES 8 OR MORE

In Italy, everyone has a version of salsa verde. It can be mild or sharp and piquant, or even sweet and sour. The oil-based sauce is usually made up to taste with green things like flat-

Salsa Verde (cont.)

leafed parsley, mint, capers, pickled gherkins, and green olives, thickened with bread, potato, hard-boiled egg yolk, or pine nuts, and flavored with anchovies and garlic. The following mixture is exciting and refreshing.

A very large bunch of flat-leafed parsley
    (2 cups), stems removed
½ cup (75 g) pine nuts
5 small pickled gherkins
8 pitted green olives
3 crushed garlic cloves
3 tablespoons wine vinegar or juice of
    ½ lemon
Salt and pepper
1 cup (250 ml) very light extra-virgin
    olive oil

Put all the ingredients except the oil in a food processor and blend. Add the oil gradually—enough to make a light paste.

Anjuli

Fish Salad with Coconut Milk

SERVES 6

This delectable fish salad is eaten on the Sabbath in India. It is often topped by fried eggplants, but I prefer it without them. It is so simple and so good. The fish and potatoes are cooked in coconut milk (I used the canned variety), which gives them a voluptuous flavor.

2½ cups (600 ml) rich coconut milk
    (see page 235) or use a half-and-half
    mixture (or thereabouts) of canned
    coconut milk and coconut cream
Juice of 1 lemon
Salt
3 thick fish steaks weighing about 2 lbs
    (1 kg)—a firm white fish such as
    cod, haddock, or flounder
1½ lbs (750 g) new potatoes, cut in
    ½-inch (1½-cm) slices
1 hot chili pepper, cut in half, seeded
A dozen scallions, thinly sliced

Put the coconut milk in a wide, shallow pan with the lemon juice and a little salt. Bring to the boil and put in the fish steaks. Simmer for about 10 minutes, or until the fish becomes translucent and begins to flake when you cut into it with a pointed knife, turning the slices over if necessary (if they are not covered by the coconut milk). Lift out the fish carefully. When it is cool enough, remove the skin and bones.

Put the potatoes in the pan, add the chili, and cook for 40–60 minutes in the coconut milk, until the potatoes are tender, adding a little water if the liquid boils away. Taste after 30 minutes and remove the chili pepper if you feel the sauce is getting too hot. Let cool. With your fingers, break the fish into pieces, then on a serving plate mix with the potatoes and the reduced coconut sauce. Sprinkle with plenty of scallions and chill, covered, in the refrigerator. Serve cold.

Sardina

Fish and Mango Salad

This fish salad is a popular Saturday dish in the Bombay Baghdadi community. The recipe is adapted from Mavis Hyman's book *Indian Jewish Cooking*. It is one of her favorites and one of mine too. It is usually made with green mangoes but it is also very good with slightly unripe ordinary ones.

> 2 lbs (1 kg) firm white fish fillet such as
>   haddock or cod
> 6 tablespoons light extra-virgin olive oil
> 2–3 mangoes chopped fine or diced
> 2–3 tablespoons finely sliced scallion
> Salt and pepper
> ¼–1 fresh green chili, seeded and finely
>   chopped

Fry the fish in 4 tablespoons of oil over moderately high heat for about 7–10 minutes, or until the flesh becomes translucent and begins to flake, turning it over once. Remove to a serving dish, let it cool, then break it up into flakes. Add the mangoes, scallion, salt, pepper, and green chili and sprinkle on the remaining oil. Mix thoroughly and serve cold.

Seviche

Marinated Raw Fish

In 1654, Portuguese descendants of *conversos* (Marranos) fleeing persecution in Brazil were invited to settle on the Dutch West Indies island of Curaçao. By the eighteenth century the Jewish community there had become immensely prosperous. A little book called *Recipes from the Jewish Kitchens of Curaçao* (1982), compiled by the sisterhood of Mikve Israel–Emanuel and sent to me by Dalia Carmel of New York, is full of exotic recipes from the once glittering community. In this recipe, which I've adapted, the fish—"cooked" by the lemon juice—has a sharp, refreshing taste. It makes a wonderful hors d'oeuvre. The recipe is for red snapper or sea bass, but any white fish will do. The fish must be very fresh. Ask the fishmonger to skin and bone it.

> 1 lb (500 g) raw fish fillet (see recipe
>   introduction)
> 1 garlic clove, crushed in a press
> Salt
> A good pinch of cayenne or chili pepper
> ½–¾ cup lime juice
> 1 mild onion, finely chopped
> 2 tablespoons finely chopped flat-leafed
>   parsley
> 2 tablespoons finely chopped coriander
> 2 small (Bibb) lettuces to serve on

Cut the fish into bite-sized pieces and put them in a small bowl. Mix the garlic, a little salt, and cayenne or chili pepper with the lime juice and pour over the fish so that it covers the fish entirely. Marinate for at least 2 hours, covered, in the refrigerator.

Just before serving, drain the fish and mix with the onion, flat-leafed parsley, and coriander. Serve on baby lettuce leaves.

Samak Tarator

Cold Fish with Pine Nut Sauce

SERVES 12

This was a party favorite with the Aleppo community in Egypt. The sauce, called "nougada," is the Jewish version of the Arab tarator. It differs in that it is made with oil rather than fish stock. It is meant to be quite lemony and garlicky. You can use any large fish, such as bream, bass, John Dory, haddock, or salmon. Ask the fishmonger to fillet and skin the fish, but keep the head, if you like, for the presentation. Because pine nuts are very expensive today, you can use less of them and more bread.

> *1 large fish weighing about 9 lbs (4 kg),*
> *   skinned and filleted*
> *2 slices white bread, crusts removed*
> *2½ cups (350 g) pine nuts*
> *Juice of 4 lemons or to taste*
> *3–5 garlic cloves or to taste, crushed*
> *½ cup (125 ml) sunflower oil*
> *¼ cup (60 ml) extra-virgin olive oil*
> *Salt and white pepper*

Snippets of flat-leafed parsley to
*   garnish*

Cook the fish in foil (see box on page 327). Let it cool in the foil before transferring onto a serving dish. Keep the juices for the sauce. Place the head at the end so as to make the shape of a whole fish.

For the sauce, soak the bread in water and squeeze dry. Put it in the food processor with the pine nuts, reserving 2 tablespoons for the garnish, the lemon juice, garlic, oil, a little salt and pepper, and enough of the fish juices— about ¾ cup (175 ml)—to make a cream the consistency of mayonnaise. Cover the fish entirely with the sauce.

Garnish with snippets of flat-leafed parsley and with a few toasted pine nuts.

Poisson en Escabèche

Pickled Fried Fish

SERVES 4–6

A fish pickle called "escobeche" is featured in *The Jewish Manual*, a cookbook that was published in England in 1846. "Take some cold fried fish, place it in a deep pan, then boil half a pint of vinegar with two tablespoonfuls of water, and one of oil, a little grated ginger, allspice, cayenne pepper, two bay leaves, a little salt, and a tablespoon of lemon juice, with sliced onions; when boiling pour it over the fish, cover the pan, and let it stand twenty-four hours before serving."

The dish must have come from Portugal or

Majorca, where similar ones exist today, when the Marranos settled in England in the seventeenth century. Although it is no longer cooked by Jews in England, I have come across many modern Sephardi recipes for escabèche, particularly in North Africa. The word comes from the medieval Arabic *sikbaj*, derived from the Persian, meaning "sour." It was used in medieval Spain to denote dishes containing vinegar, verjuice, lemon, or sour pomegranate juice. Whole small fish, fish fillets, or steaks are fried (sometimes they are first coated in flour), then marinated in a vinegar mixture.

The following recipe is adapted from Violetta Autumn's *A Russian Jew Cooks in Peru*. It does not have as much vinegar as the escabèches made to keep several days, but it should be prepared several hours in advance, or the day before, so that the fish has time to absorb the marinade.

> 2 lbs (1 kg) fish fillet, cut in pieces
>   (use any firm white fish)
> Salt
> A bland-tasting olive oil for shallow-frying
> 3 small onions, cut in half, then sliced
> 1 chili pepper, seeded and finely chopped
> ⅓ cup (90 ml) white-wine vinegar

Lightly salt the fish, then shallow-fry quickly in not too hot oil, turning over once, until it is slightly golden and the flesh begins to flake when you cut into it. Drain on paper towels and arrange on a serving dish.

Fry the onions with the chili pepper in 4 tablespoons of oil until the onions are very soft. Add the vinegar, simmer for 5 minutes, then pour over the fish. Refrigerate, covered, and serve cold. Violetta Autumn garnishes with olives and sliced hard-boiled eggs.

VARIATIONS

• Fry 6 sliced garlic cloves with the fried onions, add 1 teaspoon of paprika, and pour in ½ cup (125 ml) white-wine vinegar and ½ cup (125 ml) dry white wine. Pour over the fish arranged on a serving dish with a thinly sliced lemon. Serve sprinkled with chopped flat-leafed parsley.

• For Algerian sardines en escabèche, fry 2 lbs (1 kg) sardines with plenty of sliced garlic and marinate in a mixture of extra-virgin olive oil with 2 tablespoons wine vinegar, 2 teaspoons paprika, 1 tablespoon cumin, ½ teaspoon cayenne or chili powder, and salt. I found the flavors a bit too powerful for my taste.

Sogliole Marinate
Marinated Soles

SERVES 6

This is a very famous and very old Venetian specialty, also known as "pesce in saor." I tasted it first at a banquet for Italian regional chefs at the celebrated Gritti Palace Hotel. The table was set on the terrace overlooking the Grand Canal. The dish was our first course, representing the cooking of Venice. I have since found out, through the Venetian writer Maffioli, that it originated in the Jewish ghetto, where it was prepared on Friday to be eaten cold on Saturday. It is a version of the Portuguese escabèche. The fish—you can use Dover or lemon sole (the poor used sardines)—are fried, then marinated in a sweet-and-sour sauce made with vinegar, white wine, raisins, and pine nuts.

2 onions weighing about 1 lb (500 g)
2 tablespoons extra-virgin olive oil
3–4 tablespoons white-wine vinegar
1 cup (250 ml) dry white wine
Salt and pepper
2 tablespoons raisins
2 tablespoons pine nuts, lightly toasted
6 little soles weighing about 3 lbs (1½ kg)
Flour
A bland-tasting olive oil or vegetable oil for frying

For the sauce, fry the onions in the 2 table-spoons of extra-virgin oil till very soft and just beginning to color. Then add vinegar, white wine, a little salt and pepper, raisins, and pine nuts and simmer for about 10 minutes.

Dredge the fish in flour seasoned with salt, so that it is well covered all over, and deep-fry very quickly in hot oil, turning them over once. Drain well on paper towels and place in layers on a serving platter, pouring some of the sauce over each layer. Leave in the refrigerator for a few hours or overnight before serving.

VARIATION

- Red mullet or sardines can be substituted.

Mai Birion Ovi Sir

Bukharan Fried Fish with Garlic and Coriander Sauce

SERVES 4

In Samarkand, fish was always the first course for the Sabbath and parties, and it was only ever done in this way. I ate the dish as part of a memorable Friday-night family dinner at the home of Penina Mirzoeff, who gave me the recipe. "Ovi sir" is the name of the sauce, meaning "garlic water." It gives the fish a very strong taste, which you will like very much if you like raw garlic and coriander. In Samarkand, freshwater fish such as carp was used, because the city is surrounded by rivers. But you can use hake, cod, haddock, halibut, or other firm white fish.

4–6 garlic cloves or to taste
Salt
A large bunch of coriander, finely chopped
*   (1 cup)*
4 fish steaks (see recipe introduction)
Flour
Corn or sunflower oil for frying
4 slices white bread

For the sauce, pound the garlic in a mortar with a little salt and add the chopped coriander (or blend the two in a food processor), and beat in about 1 cup (250 ml) of water. Sprinkle the fish steaks with salt, dust with flour, and deep-fry in oil for about 5–10 minutes, turning over once, till done and browned on both sides. Drain on paper towels. In the same oil, fry the slices of bread till brown, turning them over, and drain on paper towels. Bring the fish and the sauce to the table so that people can decide whether they want their fish smothered in the sauce. The bread too has sauce poured over.

VARIATION

- Families who love garlic leave the fish soaking in the sauce a day ahead and eat it cold. (In this case it is called "siroo.")

Saluna

Iraqi Sweet-and-Sour Fish

SERVES 4

Iraqi Jews were especially fond of sweet-and-sour flavors. This dish sounds too sweet, but it is surprisingly delicious.

> *1 large onion, sliced*
> *1 small pointed (semihot or mild) green*
>   *pepper, sliced (available in Indian and*
>   *Oriental stores)*
> *Light vegetable oil*
> *2 large beefsteak tomatoes, peeled, cut in half,*
>   *then in slices*
> *Salt and pepper*
> *Juice of 2 lemons—about ½ cup (125 ml)*
> *3 tablespoons sugar*
> *1½ tablespoons tomato paste*
> *4 cod fillets weighing about 2 lb (1 kg)*

Fry the onion in 2 tablespoons of oil with the green pepper till soft and transparent, stirring often. Add the tomatoes and sprinkle with salt and pepper.

Make a sweet-and-sour syrup by simmering the lemon juice with the sugar, a little salt, and the tomato paste until the sugar dissolves.

In another frying pan, briefly shallow-fry the fish in hot oil, turning the fillets over so that they are lightly colored but still undercooked. Then transfer them to the frying pan with the onions and tomatoes. Pour the syrup over the fish and vegetables and cook 10 minutes, or until the fish is done.

VARIATIONS

• One teaspoon curry powder, 1 teaspoon cumin, and a pinch of turmeric are optional flavorings that can be mixed into the lemon syrup.

• Use 4 tablespoons wine vinegar or 3 tablespoons pulverized dried lime (see page 236) instead of the lemon juice, and 4 tablespoons of date syrup (dibis) instead of sugar.

Triglie con Uvette e Pinoli

Red Mullet with Raisins and Pine Nuts

SERVES 4

Romans have had a passion for red mullet since ancient times because of its fine flavor, firm flesh, and beautiful color. This old Roman Jewish classic is eaten at Yom Kippur. The raisins and pine nuts give away its Sicilian origin. The majority of Jews in Rome are descended from immigrants from the south who were fleeing the Inquisition in the early sixteenth century, when the island and southern Italy were ruled by Spain.

Have the fish scaled and cleaned, but leave the heads on, and ask the fishmonger to reserve the liver—it is a delicacy. If you cannot find red mullet, use other small or medium whole fish, such as bream or red snapper.

4 red mullet weighing about 2 lbs
   (1 kg)
Salt
6 tablespoons extra-virgin olive oil
4 tablespoons wine vinegar
Pepper
1 teaspoon sugar
4 tablespoons raisins, soaked in water for
   ½ hour
5 tablespoons pine nuts

Season the cavities of the fish and put back the livers. Arrange them in one layer in a shallow baking dish so that a head is near a tail. In a cup, beat the oil and vinegar with the salt, pepper, and sugar and pour over the fish. Sprinkle with raisins and pine nuts. Bake at 375°F (190°C) for 20–30 minutes, or until cooked.

Triglie alla Mosaica

Red Mullet in Tomato Sauce

SERVES 4

Livorno is a Tuscan seaport famous for its fish dishes—many of them of Jewish origin. The port city was once predominantly Jewish. The community was formed in the seventeenth century by Marranos from Spain and Portugal who were invited to settle by the Grand Duke Ferdinando I de Medici and allowed to revert to their old religion. These Marranos were among the first to introduce tomatoes in Italy—which was the second country after Spain to adopt the New World vegetable. They did so through their contacts with the Marranos of South America, who had emigrated as New Christians to escape the pressures of the Inquisition. The New Christians had been among the first who sailed with Christopher Columbus, and they became involved in the early trade of New World vegetables. That may be why some old classics with tomatoes—like this one—were called "alla mosaica" (referring to the prophet Moses and meaning Jewish).

If you cannot find red mullet, use other small or medium whole fish such as bream or red snapper.

4 red mullet weighing about 2 lbs
   (1 kg)
4 garlic cloves, chopped
4 tablespoons extra-virgin olive oil
1 lb (500 g) ripe tomatoes, peeled and
   chopped
Salt and pepper
1–2 teaspoons sugar
3 tablespoons chopped flat-leafed
   parsley

Have the fish scaled and cleaned, but leave the heads on and keep the liver. In a large frying pan that can hold the fish in one layer, fry the garlic in oil till it begins to color. Add the tomatoes, salt, pepper, and sugar (the amount depends on the flavor of the tomatoes) and simmer for 10 minutes. Then put the fish in and simmer 7 minutes, or until done. It looks beautiful, red on red. Add the flat-leafed parsley before serving.

Pishkado kon Salsa de Tomat

Fish with Tomato Sauce

SERVES 4

Fish cooked with tomatoes is characteristic of every Judeo-Spanish community. It is also a Passover dish. It is done with whole fish such as red mullet (a favorite), sardines, mackerel, and bonito, and with fish steaks or fillets.

> 2 garlic cloves, crushed
> 4 tablespoons olive or sunflower oil
> 4 large tomatoes, peeled and chopped
> 1 small mild or semihot pointed green pepper, seeds removed and sliced thin (optional)
> 1 teaspoon or more sugar
> Salt and pepper
> Juice of 1 or more lemons
> 4 individual fish or 2 lbs (1 kg) fish pieces (see recipe introduction)
> 4 tablespoons finely chopped dill or flat-leafed parsley

In a large frying pan, fry the garlic in oil till it begins to change color. Add the tomatoes and green pepper, season with sugar and a little salt and pepper and cook 10 minutes, until the sauce is thick. Then add the lemon juice and the fish. Cook 10 minutes, or until the flesh is opaque and flaky. Add the dill or flat-leafed parsley a few minutes before the end.

VARIATIONS

• In Salonika, Nicholas Stavroulakis (*Cookbook of the Jews of Greece*) adds a little white wine and a pinch of cinnamon but no lemon to the sauce.

• Another way is to put the fish in a hot oven, cover it with the peeled and chopped tomatoes, sprinkle with salt, pepper, 2 tablespoons of oil, the lemon juice, and the herbs and bake 20 minutes, or until done.

Poisson à la Grecque

Fish Baked in the Oven

SERVES 8

This dish came to Egypt with the Salonikan Jews. Delicately flavored sea bass is wonderful cooked this way, but you can use other large fish. Roasting at a high temperature gives a crisp skin before it is overcooked.

> 4 lbs (2 kg) fish such as sea bass
> 2 large onions, cut in thick slices
> Extra-virgin olive oil
> Salt and pepper
> Juice of ½ lemon
> 2 large tomatoes, sliced thick
> A bunch of flat-leafed parsley, chopped
> 1 lemon, sliced thin
> ½ cup (100 ml) dry white wine

Have the fish scaled, gutted, and cleaned but leave the head on. Rinse and dry.

In a large frying pan, fry the onions gently in 3 tablespoons extra-virgin olive oil till soft and lightly colored. Arrange in a baking dish and place the fish on top. Brush the fish with oil, season with salt and pepper, and sprinkle with lemon juice. Arrange the tomatoes around the fish, on top of the onions. Sprinkle the tomatoes with salt, pepper, and flat-leafed parsley, cover with the lemon slices, and dribble 2 tablespoons extra-virgin olive oil on top. Pour in the wine and bake at 425°F (220°C) for about 30 minutes. Test for doneness by cutting with a pointed knife at the thickest part to see if the flesh has turned white.

VARIATION

• Thick fish steaks can be used. In this case put a little onion and tomato and a lemon slice on top of each, to prevent their drying out.

Poisson en Sauce Épicée

Fish in a Peppery Tomato Sauce

SERVES 3

I have tasted and cooked many versions of this dish—Algerian, Moroccan, Tunisian, and Libyan. All kinds of fish can be used—large or small. Grouper, hake, cod, and tuna are often used. It is as good cold as it is hot. Harissa is very hot, so start with the lesser quantity and add more later if you want to.

> 1 medium onion, coarsely chopped
> 2 tablespoons peanut or sunflower oil
> 3 or 4 garlic cloves, crushed
> ½–2 teaspoons harissa (see page 242) or

> 2 teaspoons paprika and ¼ or more
>   teaspoon cayenne
> 1 lb (500 g) tomatoes, peeled and chopped
> Salt
> 1–2 teaspoons sugar (depending on the
>   flavor of the tomatoes)
> 2 tablespoons capers
> 3 fish steaks (use any firm white fish)
> 4 tablespoons chopped coriander

In a large frying pan, fry the onion in oil till soft and slightly golden. Add the garlic and, when it begins to color, add the harissa and stir well. Then add the tomatoes, salt, sugar, and capers (squeezed to remove the vinegar) and stir well. Put the the fish steaks in, sprinkle with salt, and pour some sauce on top.

Cover and simmer for 10 minutes, then turn over the steaks, sprinkle with coriander, and cook, covered, for another 5 minutes, or until the fish begins to flake.

VARIATIONS

• Instead of harissa or cayenne you can have a whole hot chili pepper—slit and seeded.

• A Tunisian version adds 2 tablespoons of tomato paste, 1 teaspoon of ground coriander, and 1 tablespoon of vinegar.

• In Marrakesh I watched a woman cook a whole lot of small fish in a clay tagine for the Friday-night dinner. She poured in a glass of extra-virgin olive oil and arranged a layer of sliced tomatoes at the bottom, then laid the fish on top with 6 whole garlic cloves. She seasoned with salt and cayenne pepper, sprinkled with chopped coriander, and covered with the rest of the tomatoes. She then left the dish to simmer on an open fire more than ½ hour.

The port of Salonika, once almost entirely run by Jews

Poisson Hraymi

Peppery Garlicky Fish

SERVES 4

North African Jews and, famously, those from Libya are fond of this very peppery-hot garlicky fish. In 1941, under the Italian occupation which began in 1911, 25 percent of the population of Tripoli was Jewish, and now the greater part of the Jewish community has settled in Italy. Libyan Jewish cooking is a mix of Italian and North African, with both pasta and couscous, and there is also a Spanish touch from the original fifteenth-century settlement. A few Jewish restaurants in Rome offer "Cucina Tripolina." Start with very little harissa or cayenne and add more to taste.

6–8 garlic cloves, crushed
5 tablespoons extra-virgin olive oil
1–2 teaspoons paprika
½–2 teaspoons harissa (see page 242)
    or ¼–½ teaspoon cayenne pepper or
    to taste
½ teaspoon ground cumin (optional)
½ teaspoon ground coriander (optional)
2 tablespoons tomato paste
Juice of 1 lemon
Salt
4 white-fish steaks or skinned fillets
    weighing about 2 lbs (1 kg)
4 tablespoons chopped coriander

In a frying pan, fry the garlic in the oil until it only just begins to color. Stir in the paprika, harissa or cayenne, optional cumin and/or ground coriander (if you like), and tomato paste. Add the lemon juice, a little water—about ¾ cup (175 ml)—and a little salt. Stir well and simmer for 5 minutes. Then put in the fish and cook 7–10 minutes, turning over once, until the flesh just begins to flake. Serve hot, sprinkled with chopped coriander.

Poisson Sauce Rouge

Fish with Red Pepper Sauce

SERVES 4

Among the Moroccan fish dishes is this sumptuous one with a coulis of roast peppers. It is a Passover and Sabbath special.

> *3 fleshy red bell peppers*
> *3 or 4 cloves of garlic, peeled*
> *Salt and pepper*
> *2 lbs (1 kg) white-fish steaks or fillets*
> *4 tablespoons peanut or sunflower oil*
> *Juice of ½–1 lemon*
> *3 tablespoons chopped flat-leafed parsley*

For the sauce, grill or roast the peppers and peel them (see box, page 253). Blend them to a cream with the garlic, salt, and pepper in the food processor. Pour into a saucepan and heat through until the sauce begins to bubble. (Be careful not to leave it too long on the fire, for it burns easily.)

Sauté the fish in the oil for about 10 minutes, turning it over once and adding salt and pepper and the lemon juice. Serve with the sauce poured over and sprinkled with parsley.

VARIATION

• You may add a little cayenne to the sauce.

Pishkado kon Agristada

Fish with Egg-and-Lemon Sauce

SERVES 4

Also called "pishkado kon uevo e limón," this is one of the most charasteristic Sephardi ways of cooking fish. The sauce is known to us all as Greek and Turkish, but it also appears in early Iberian communities in countries such as England, Holland, and Denmark—where the Ottoman and Greek influence was hardly felt. The earliest Jewish cookbook published in England, in 1846, which had mostly Portuguese dishes, is full of egg-and-lemon sauces. The one for fish was adopted by the Eastern European immigrants, and "halibut with egg-and-lemon sauce" is one of the common Friday-night dishes in Britain today.

If I have to name one city that was famous for this specialty, it is Salonika. There, it was a Saturday dish to be eaten cold. Any kind of white fish can be used—sole, haddock, cod, halibut, swordfish.

> *2 lbs (1 kg) fish—cut in steaks or fillets*
> *Salt and white pepper*
> *2 tablespoons extra-virgin olive oil*
> *Juice of 1 lemon*
> *2 eggs*
> *3 tablespoons finely chopped flat-leafed*
>   *parsley*

Put the fish in a pan that can accommodate it in one layer. Pour in just enough water to cover. Add salt, pepper, oil, and half the lemon juice. Bring slowly to the boil and poach very gently, so the surface of the water barely trembles, for 5–10 minutes, until the flesh just begins to flake. Lift the fish out carefully and arrange on a serving dish, leaving the water in the pan. There should be about 1 cup (250 ml).

To make the sauce, beat the eggs with the rest of the lemon juice, then beat in a few tablespoons of the cooking water. Now pour this mixture into the pan with the hot cooking water and stir constantly over a very low flame until it thickens. Do not let it boil. Add the parsley. Pour over the fish and refrigerate, covered with plastic wrap.

VARIATIONS

• For a thicker sauce, mix 1 tablespoon flour or cornstarch with a little water to a paste, then stir into the cooking water and simmer 10 minutes before adding the beaten-egg mixture.

• A large whole fish about 4 lbs (2 kg) may be baked wrapped in foil (see page 327), then skinned and served cold with an agristada sauce made separately (see page 247).

• Nicholas Stavroulakis gives a glamorous version of the sauce with white wine in his *Cookbook of the Jews of Greece:* Beat 2 eggs, 4 or 5 garlic cloves crushed in a press, salt, and pepper with the juice of 2 lemons, then beat in ½ cup (125 ml) dry white wine. Pour into a pan and heat over low heat, stirring all the time, until the sauce thickens.

• In Morocco they pour the sauce (they call it "sauce blanche") over fried fish balls.

Ragout de Morue
Stewed Salt Cod

SERVES 6

The Iberian Sephardim acquired a taste for salt cod in Spain and Portugal and maintained their fondness within the Muslim world, although it was not liked there. In Algeria they were encouraged in their affection by the French colonists.

There are several varieties of salt cod, ranging from a mild, slightly salted, but not dried type to heavily salted, hard, dried ones. They all need desalting by soaking in changes of water, but the time varies from a few hours to more than 24, depending on the degree of saltiness and dryness. In the south of France, where many North African Jews have settled, the fish is sold already desalted.

> 2 lbs (1 kg) salt cod, desalted for 24 hours
>   (unless advised otherwise; see recipe
>   introduction)
> 1 large onion, chopped
> 3 tablespoons extra-virgin olive oil
> 2 garlic cloves, chopped
> 4 tomatoes, peeled and chopped
> 2 lbs (1 kg) small new potatoes
> Black pepper or cayenne or chili powder (optional)
> 2 bay leaves
> A few sprigs of flat-leafed parsley
> ¼ teaspoon saffron powder
> Salt if necessary

The salt cod should be thoroughly desalted. Remove the skin and cut the flesh into cubes.

In a pan, fry the onion in the oil till soft and

golden. Add the garlic and stir till the aroma rises. Add the tomatoes, potatoes, pepper or chili, bay leaves, and parsley stems (reserve leaves), and cover with water. Simmer for 20 minutes, or until the potatoes are tender and the sauce is reduced. Add the saffron and the drained salt cod and simmer for 10 minutes, or until done. Add the reserved parsley leaves, chopped, and taste before adding salt if necessary, taking into consideration the saltiness of the fish.

Serve with ajada, the garlicky mayonnaise (see page 247).

VARIATION

• Sometimes the salt-cod pieces are rolled in flour and deep-fried in hot oil before adding them to the stew (see page 351).

Poisson aux Citrons Confits

Fish with Pickled Lemon

SERVES 4

This is a popular North African way of cooking fish, with lemons preserved in salt. Their skins are soft and their flavor is mellow.

> 4 tablespoons peanut or sunflower oil
> ¾ cup (175 ml) water
> 1 teaspoon paprika
> ¼ teaspoon turmeric (optional)
> Salt and pepper

> 4 tablespoons chopped coriander
> 1 large fish such as bream weighing about 3 lbs (1½ kg) or 4 fish steaks
> 2 or 3 pickled lemons (see page 239)

Beat the oil and water with the paprika, turmeric, salt, pepper, and chopped coriander and marinate the fish in this for about ½ hour.

Rinse the pickled lemons under the cold tap and cut into small pieces. Spread half over the bottom of a baking dish. Lay the fish on top and pour the marinade over it. Cover with the rest of the lemons and bake in a 425°F (220°C) oven for 20 minutes, or until the fish is done.

Peshe kon Nuez

Salonikan Fish with Walnut Sauce

SERVES 4

The walnut sauce is in the style of the one used in the famous Turkish Circassian chicken. (The word "peshe"—instead of "pishkado"—for fish is an example of the Italian input in the Judeo-Spanish dialect of Salonika.)

> 2 lbs (1 kg) white-fish fillets
> Juice of ½–1 lemon or 4 tablespoons vinegar
> Salt and pepper
> 1 slice white bread, crusts removed
> 1 cup (100 g) walnuts
> 3 or 4 garlic cloves, crushed

2 tablespoons extra-virgin olive oil
2 tablespoons finely chopped flat-leafed
    parsley

Put the fish in a pan with just enough water barely to cover and the lemon juice or vinegar, salt, and pepper. Bring to the boil and let it barely tremble for 7–10 minutes, until the flesh just begins to flake when you pierce it with the point of a knife. Lift out the fish and place it on a serving dish, leaving the cooking water in the pan.

For the sauce: Soak the bread in the cooking water, then blend it in a food processor with the walnuts, garlic, oil, flat-leafed parsley, and enough of the cooking water to make a thick cream. Pour over the fish and serve cold.

Sateni

Georgian Fish with Walnut Sauce

SERVES 6

This dish has been adopted by the Jews in Georgia for Sabbath and holiday meals. The walnut sauce with tamarind is delicately flavored and delicious, but it has an unappealing brown color. It is traditionally sprinkled with pomegranate seeds, but you can garnish with plenty of chopped flat-leafed parsley or coriander to make it look good. I served it with bright-red quartered plum tomatoes. Freshwater fish, such as carp or perch, are generally used in Georgia, but other firm fish, like haddock, halibut, or cod, will do very well. Marinating the fish in ginger, garlic, and tamarind is an embellishment. Usually it is simply salted and fried.

1 tablespoon tamarind paste
½ cup (125 ml) boiling water
4 garlic cloves, crushed in a press
Juice from a 2-inch (5-cm) piece of
    ginger crushed in a garlic press
Salt
6 fish steaks about 1¼ inches (3 cm)
    thick

For the walnut sauce

2 large onions, finely chopped
4 tablespoons light vegetable oil
4 garlic cloves, crushed in a garlic
    press
1 tablespoon tamarind paste
1¾ cups (200 g) walnuts, ground or
    finely chopped
Salt
½ teaspoon cayenne or chili powder
1 tablespoon cider or wine vinegar
1–1½ cups (250–350 ml) water

Oil for frying
Seeds scooped out from half a pomegranate,
    to garnish (optional)
3 tablespoons chopped flat-leafed parsley or
    coriander, to garnish

Dissolve the tamarind in the boiling water in a saucepan, then remove from the heat. Add the garlic and ginger juice and a little salt and let it cool. Turn the fish steaks in this marinade and leave for about 1 hour to absorb the flavors.

For the walnut sauce, fry the onions in the oil till very soft. Add the garlic, and stir until the aroma rises. Add the tamarind paste and stir until it dissolves. Add the walnuts, salt, and cayenne or chili powder and stir very well. Finally, add the

Fish with Walnut Sauce (cont.)

vinegar and enough water to make a thick, creamy sauce, and cook, stirring, 5–10 minutes more.

Now shallow-fry the fish in oil, turning it over once, for 10 minutes, or until the flesh begins to flake. Arrange the pieces on a serving dish and pour the sauce on top. Serve cold, garnished with pomegranate seeds (if you like) and chopped parsley or coriander.

Boulettes de Poisson à la Sauce Tomate

Fish Balls in Tomato Sauce

SERVES 4

All the Oriental communities make fish balls or fingers in various kinds of sauces, tomato being the most common. In Egypt we called them "blehat." Because they are round and contain fish, their symbolism made them a New Year's dish. I prefer this Moroccan version to ours. It can be served with couscous or rice, or cold with bread.

For the sauce

> *3 cloves garlic, finely chopped*
> *2 tablespoons peanut or vegetable oil*
> *2 large tomatoes, peeled and chopped*
> *3 tablespoons tomato paste*
> *1 teaspoon sugar or to taste*
> *Salt*
> *1 hot fresh chili pepper or ¼ teaspoon*
> *   cayenne*

For the fish balls

> *1 lb (500 g) ground white fish*
> *4 tablespoons dry white bread crumbs or*
> *   matzo meal*
> *1 egg, lightly beaten*
> *¼ teaspoon ground ginger*
> *A good pinch of nutmeg*
> *Salt and pepper*
> *3 tablespoons finely chopped coriander or*
> *   flat-leafed parsley*

> *1 lemon, cut in wedges, to serve with*

Make the sauce first. In a wide pan, fry the garlic in oil till the aroma rises. Add the tomatoes, tomato paste, sugar, salt, and chili pepper or cayenne. Add about 2 cups (500 ml) of water and bring to the boil. If you leave the chili pepper in throughout the cooking, the sauce might end up too hot for you, so taste the sauce and remove the pepper when you feel the sauce is hot enough.

For the fish balls, mix all the ingredients together and work to a firm paste with your hands. (If you use the food processor to grind the fish, do so very briefly or it can turn into a creamy puree.) Take lumps of paste the size of a small walnut and roll into little balls. Drop them one by one into the sauce and simmer for 20–25 minutes, turning them over once.

Serve accompanied by lemon wedges.

VARIATIONS

• These are alternative flavorings that often go into North African fish balls, to choose from: ½ teaspoon mace, ¼ teaspoon turmeric, a pinch of saffron powder, 1 teaspoon grated fresh ginger, ½ teaspoon cinnamon, ½ teaspoon allspice, 1 or 2 minced garlic cloves.

• For an Egyptian version, add ½ teaspoon of ground coriander, 1 teaspoon of cumin, and 2 minced garlic cloves instead of the ginger and nutmeg.

Kefta de Poisson au Coriandre et Citron Confit

Stewed Fish Cakes with Coriander and Preserved Lemon

SERVES 6

You can use fresh peeled and diced lemon instead of preserved lemon in this very flavorsome Moroccan dish. The combination of lemon with coriander and turmeric goes very well with fish. You may use one type of white fish such as cod, haddock, or whiting or a mixture.

For the sauce

> 1 large onion, chopped
> 5 tablespoons peanut or sunflower oil
> ¼ teaspoon turmeric
> Coarsely chopped skin of 1 preserved lemon, or a fresh lemon, peeled and diced
> Salt and white pepper
> 4 tablespoons chopped coriander

For the kefta

> 2 lbs (1 kg) white-fish fillet or ground fish
> 1 slice white bread, crusts removed, soaked in water
> ½ onion, grated or finely chopped
> Salt and white pepper
> ½ teaspoon mace
> ¼ teaspoon turmeric
> ½ teaspoon powdered ginger
> 4 tablespoons chopped coriander
> 1 egg

Begin with the sauce. In a large frying pan, fry the onion in the oil until soft. Then add the turmeric, the preserved or fresh lemon, salt, white pepper, and coriander.

Buy ground fish or chop it fine yourself. You can use the food processor, but start by processing the rest of the kefta ingredients first—the bread (squeezed dry), the onion, a little salt and white pepper, mace, turmeric, ginger, coriander, and the egg—before adding the fish. Process very briefly to a soft paste. Wet your hands before taking lumps of fish mixture the size of a small clementine, roll into a ball, and flatten slightly. Put the fish cakes in the sauce in the frying pan and sauté gently on low heat for about 15–20 minutes, turning over once.

GAYA KON AVRAMILA

Rockfish with Plum Sauce

THIS IS the ceremonial Friday-night dish of the Jews of Turkey. A type of rockfish called "gaya" that looks like an eel is used. Although it does not have scales, gaya is considered kosher, and indeed only the Jews eat it. It is referred to as "pishkado de djudios" (the Jewish fish), and gaya kon avramila is described as the Jewish national dish of Turkey. The fish is cooked in the juice of small sour yellow-green plums called "avramila," and these relate to the tradition that Abraham sat under a plum tree following his circumcision. I never tasted gaya or the rare plums avramila. A Jewish caterer in Istanbul said that ordinary tart, unripe greengages could be substituted, and that red mullet or red gurnard or a large whole fish like hake could be used instead of gaya. I did try it with hake and a sauce of boiled and pureed greengages (I gave it a sweet-and-sour flavor with a bit of lemon and sugar, as the original one has), but it was not very good, so I leave you with the information and no recipe, in the hope that one day you might get to taste the real thing.

Pastilla au Poisson
Fish Pie with Filo Pastry

SERVES 6

Pastilla—a large pie made with paper-thin pancakes called "briouats" and a pigeon or chicken filling—is the great Moroccan party dish. The less common fish filling is especially favored by Jews. The paper-thin pancakes are made by dabbing a tray placed over a source of heat with a very soft ball of dough. The process requires very special skill, and very few people can do it, even in Morocco. It is a specialist's job and very labor-intensive. Mass-produced briouats (also called "warka") are now widely available in France. The best alternative is to use filo pastry, although that does not quite reproduce the very special crisp effect of briouats.

1 large onion, coarsely chopped
Peanut or light vegetable oil
2 or 3 garlic cloves, crushed in a press
1½ lbs (750 g) tomatoes, peeled
2 teaspoons sugar
Salt and pepper
¼–½ teaspoon ground cloves
1½ lbs (750 g) firm white-fish fillet, skinned
¼ lb (100 g) small button mushrooms, quartered
A large bunch of fresh coriander, chopped
4 eggs, lightly beaten
12 sheets filo pastry
1 egg yolk

Prepare the filling. In a large frying pan, fry the onion in 2 tablespoons of oil till soft. Add the garlic and fry till slightly colored. Put the tomatoes in the blender and reduce them to a liquid, then pour them in. Add sugar, salt, pepper, and cloves and simmer 5 minutes. Put in the fish and simmer 5 minutes, turning it over once (it should be slightly underdone), then lift it out and set it aside.

Now add the mushrooms to the tomato sauce and simmer 8 minutes. Stir in the coriander (this is the major flavoring) and the eggs and cook gently, stirring occasionally, until the sauce sets to a thick cream. Break up the fish into small pieces, remove any bones, and mix it into the sauce.

Open the packet of filo only when you are ready to use it, for it dries out. Brush a large round pie plate or baking dish with oil. Fit a sheet of filo in so that the edges hang over the edges of the dish. Brush with oil and repeat with 3 more sheets, brushing each with oil. Spread half the filling on top and cover with 5 sheets of filo, brushing each with oil. Spread the remaining filling over these. Bring the edges of the filo up over the filling. Cover with the remaining sheets, brushing each with oil. Cut the corners off and tuck the edges in around the side of the pie plate or baking dish. Paint the top with egg yolk mixed with a drop of water and bake at 375°F (190°C) for about 40 minutes, or until crisp and brown.

Fish Curry

SERVES 4

This recipe, contributed by Mrs. M. Reuben to the "Bene Israel Cook Book" (distributed in manuscript by the Jewish Religious Union Sisterhood in Bombay), calls for fresh coconut and up to 5 green chilies. I have used dried coconut and canned coconut milk, and I chili was enough for my taste. Although the Bene Israel are famous for very hot spicing, many families, including Sophie Jhirad's (page 367), do not like their food too hot. It is an exciting, beautifully green dish, to be served with rice.

½ fresh coconut, brown skin removed and cut
    into pieces, or 1 cup dried coconut and
    ½ cup coconut milk (page 235)
2 cups fresh coriander
1 or 2 green chilies, cut open and seeded
1 teaspoon cumin
6 or 7 garlic cloves, crushed in a press
3 tablespoons sesame, peanut, or vegetable oil
    (preferably sesame)
½ teaspoon turmeric
Juice of ½ lime or lemon
Salt
1½ lbs (750 g) white-fish fillet

Put the coconut, or dried coconut and coconut milk, in the food processor with the coriander, chilies, and cumin, and blend to a paste. Fry the garlic in the oil very quickly until it is only barely colored. Add the turmeric and the coconut paste and stir for a minute or two. Add about 2 cups (500 ml) of water, the lime or lemon juice, and some salt. Stir and bring to the boil, then put in the fish and simmer for about 10–15 minutes, or until the fish is cooked.

Serve hot with rice.

Cacciucco alla Livornese

Fish Soup

SERVES 8

Livorno had a very old and important Jewish community. In the seventeenth century it was one of the most preeminent in Western Europe. When the city was developed into a free port in 1593 by the grand dukes of Tuscany, they invited Jews to settle, including lapsed Marranos, who were promised immunity despite the Inquisition, which operated also in Italy. They were never made to live in ghettos, as was the case in the rest of Italy, and that attracted a huge number of settlers to the city, which became an important rabbinic and intellectual Jewish center.

This fish soup can be a stunning meal in itself, with a variety of fish. You may use a mixture of anything from sole, flounder, turbot, and brill to red or gray mullet, bass, bream, cod, John Dory, hake, and salmon. It is simple and beautiful and delicate of flavor.

5 lbs (2½ kg) assorted fish—you can have fillets, steaks, and whole fish
4 garlic cloves, finely chopped
2 fresh red or green chilies, cut open and seeded
4 tablespoons extra-virgin olive oil
3 lbs (1½ kg) tomatoes, peeled and chopped
A bottle of dry white wine
3–4 teaspoons sugar
Salt and pepper
½ teaspoon saffron pistils or saffron powder (optional)
6 tablespoons chopped flat-leafed parsley
8 slices toasted bread to accompany

Clean and wash the fish. Cut larger fish into pieces and leave smaller ones whole. Using fish steaks, cut by the fishmonger, makes it easier to cook and to serve.

In a large pan, fry the garlic and chilies in the oil until the garlic begins to color. Add the tomatoes, cook 10 minutes, then add the wine, sugar, a little salt, and pepper, and simmer for 30 minutes. Add saffron if you like. Put in the fish and poach 6–20 minutes (the timing will depend on the type and thickness of the fish). You may need to use 2 pans. Alternatively, you can transfer the tomato-and-wine stock to a large casserole (I use a large Spanish clay dish), put the fish in, and cook it in the oven, covered with foil.

Serve in bowls (removing the chilies), sprinkled with chopped parsley, accompanied by toasted bread.

Caldero

Fish Soup with Rice

SERVES 12 OR MORE

This fabulous dish is a specialty of Oran in Algeria. It is very like a Spanish (Valencian) dish of the same name which is derived from the clay pot it is cooked in. "Caldeirada" is also the Portuguese name for fish soup. Jews in Oran served it at Rosh Hashanah. The heads of the fish were left on for symbolic reasons. It is a wonderful dish, and although it sounds elaborate it is easy—a matter of organization and planning—and it represents a grand meal in itself.

The most important—and usually also the most difficult—part is getting the fish bones and heads to make a good fish stock. Get at least 6 fish frames (heads and bones) from white, not oily, fish. Remove the gills, because they give an unpleasant taste.

The stock is flavored with fried garlic, tomatoes, and the sweet dried Spanish peppers called "ñoras," and is used to cook the accompanying rice and to poach a selection of fish—any firm fish. I used haddock fillet, a red snapper, and a small hake. (In the Mediterranean they would use bream, John Dory, red mullet, or red gurnard.) The dish is served with a garlic mayonnaise called "al-i-oli" in Spain and "ajada" (see page 247) by Sephardim. A North African note enters with a peppery sauce made by mixing a little harissa (see page 242) into some of the stock and passing it around.

8–12 garlic cloves (very much according to taste)

1¼ cups (300 ml) light extra-virgin olive oil or a mixture with sunflower oil

3 tomatoes, peeled and chopped

2 dried ñoras (Spanish dried round sweet dark wine-colored peppers) or other dried sweet peppers

3 lbs (1½ kg) white-fish bones, rinsed, to make the stock

Salt

Peel of 1 orange

2 bay leaves

A large bunch of flat-leafed parsley or coriander (the stalks are used to make the fish stock)

2 egg yolks

Juice of 1 lemon

½–¾ teaspoon good saffron powder

2½ cups (500 g) rice, preferably round Spanish or Italian Arborio

1 tablespoon pastis or raki (optional)

6–9 lbs (3–4 kg) fish (see recipe introduction)

1 teaspoon or more harissa (see page 242), or 1 teaspoon paprika and ½ teaspoon cayenne

Chop 4–6 cloves of garlic and fry them in 2 tablespoons of oil in a large saucepan until golden. Add the tomatoes and the ñoras or dried sweet peppers and cook for 5 minutes. Put in the rinsed fish bones and about 13 cups (3 liters) of water, then add salt, the orange peel, bay leaves, and parsley or coriander stalks (reserve leaves). Bring to the boil, remove the scum, and simmer about 30 minutes, then strain in a colander.

Prepare the ajada (garlicky mayonnaise). All the ingredients must be at room temperature. Crush 4–6 cloves of garlic and put them in a warmed bowl. Add the yolks and a little salt and beat for 5 minutes, until the paste is thick and sticky. Then beat in the remaining oil very gradually, pouring it drop by drop and beating with a wooden spoon or electric whisk. When the sauce thickens and about half the oil has been used, add a little of the lemon juice and start pouring in the oil in a thin trickle, beating all the time and making sure that it is properly absorbed, until the sauce is very thick. Then beat in the rest of the lemon juice to taste. (If the sauce separates, you can start again, with a fresh egg yolk.) Keep covered in the refrigerator until ready to serve.

Cook the rice: Put 5 cups (1¼ liters) of the strained stock back into the pan and stir in ¼ teaspoon saffron powder and bring to the boil. Add the rice and simmer, covered, for about 20 minutes, till tender.

Now cook the fish: Put the rest of the stock in a large earthenware casserole (I use a large flameproof Spanish *cazuela*). Stir in the rest of the saffron and the pastis or raki, bring to the boil, put in the fish, and simmer 15–20 minutes, or until the fish just begins to flake, adding the chopped parsley or coriander leaves at the end. You can set the dish, covered with foil, to cook in the oven. It will take longer to cook, but it will be easy to reheat, if you need to, at the same time as the rice—which should also be covered in an ovenproof dish.

In deep bowls, serve the rice first, and the fish on top, with plenty of stock poured over. Let people help themselves to the ajada (mayonnaise), and to a peppery sauce made with the harissa, or a mixture of paprika and cayenne, mixed into 2 ladlefuls of stock.

Grilled Fish

Grilling over charcoal is one of the very pleasing Sephardi ways of cooking fish. Cooking under an overhead broiler, or over a bed of pumice-stone rock heated by gas, or on a plancha or griddle are good alternatives.

One specialty is fish kebabs. Turkish Jews use swordfish, because it has very firm flesh that does not break up on the skewer. There is continuing discussion by rabbinical authorities as to whether swordfish is forbidden, since it does not have scales, but Turkish Jews consider it kosher because it has scales during its first months of life. Other firm fish are also used.

For fish kebab, cut the fish into 1-inch (2½-cm) cubes and thread them onto flat-bladed skewers with alternate pieces of green pepper and firm tomato wedges of about the same size.

Oil the grill or broiler rack and let it become very hot before you put the fish on, so that the surface is seared and the juices are sealed in. Turn the pieces over once and do not overcook. The fish is ready when the flesh just begins to flake if you cut into it with a pointed knife.

For small whole fish, the traditional Mediterranean favorites for grilling are red mullet and sardines. Clean and scale them but leave the heads on. Sardines are so oily they do not need oil or a marinade—only salting, when they have been cooked, and lemon wedges to serve with.

Sauces and Marinades for Grilled Fish

Marinate the fish in one of the following sauces for about an hour before cooking, or simply pour the sauce over the fish after it is done. The recipes produce enough for 2 lbs (1 kg) fish.

1. For a fresh-tasting herby sauce, beat 5 tablespoons of extra-virgin olive oil with the juice of 1 lemon, salt, and pepper. You may add a small onion liquefied in a blender, or 2 crushed garlic cloves and 2 tablespoons of chopped herbs, such as flat-leafed parsley, dill, coriander, or fennel.

2. A very popular hot and spicy sauce is the Moroccan chermoula, which is also used with fried fish and in stews. Beat 5 tablespoons extra-virgin olive oil with the juice of 1 lemon or 3 tablespoons wine vinegar, 3 crushed garlic cloves, salt, 1 teaspoon cumin, 1 teaspoon paprika, a good pinch of cayenne or powdered chili, and plenty of chopped coriander (about ½ cup).

MASGOUF IN IRAQ

WHEN JEWISH FAMILIES in Baghdad had big parties like weddings, which usually took place in the gardens of houses, they hired specialists to come and prepare masgouf. The specialists were the boatmen (*ballamchi*) on the river Tigris who brought in the fish every evening and cooked it on the riverbank in Baghdad. When the boats came in at around nine-thirty in the evening, the boatmen went up to people sitting in the riverside cafés to take orders and proceeded to clean and cook the fish on the bank. By the time they were ready, the men in the cafés were drunk on arak and beer. In the summer, the riverside was dotted with the flames of brushwood fires against which were silhouetted the fish roasted upright.

Among the happiest memories of Baghdad Jews are the picnic parties on the river Tigris. On hot summer nights, parties set out in the high-prowed *ballam* (boats) with a supply of bread, fruit, and cold drinks, singing and playing the *oud* and tambourine. The boatmen towed their catch behind by strings through the gills. They stopped upriver and started brushwood fires while they prepared the fish. They would cut the fish down the

The river Tigris as it flows through Baghdad, in a turn-of-the-century photograph

back, clean it, and rub it with salt. They hung each fish upright on 4 pointed stakes planted in the ground, cut side towards the fire, 14 inches (36 cm) from the fire, so that they cooked slowly while the topping of chopped onions and tomatoes was prepared with condiments and spices. When the fire burned down, the fish were put directly on the embers and covered by the juicy topping. For wedding parties in private gardens, the boatmen were hired to cook the fish in exactly the same way as they did on the riverbank.

Iraqi Jews were so fond of doing fish in this way that many try to reproduce the effect on a barbecue or in the oven. But it can never taste the same without the aroma of the burning brushwood. The choice of fish in the Tigris was limited to 4—biz, shabbut, bunni, and dhakar—all closely related to the barbel, roach, and tench, in the carp family, of European waters. In Iraq, they liked shabbut, which has very firm, fatty flesh and is very large—larger ones can feed up to 8 people. Carp might be the equivalent in Europe, but other fish are preferred. Favorites for grand parties in London are sea bass, bream, and salmon, the last being most commonly used. Because shabbut tasted a little muddy, they used strong condiments and spices, such as curry powder and Worcestershire sauce, to flavor it. With salmon or sea bass, that is not done.

TO PREPARE MASGOUF WITH SALMON UNDER THE BROILER: Have the fishmonger clean and scale the fish and slit and open it out from the back, so that you can open it out flat. Alternatively, and more easily, ask him to fillet the fish and keep the skin on.

Brush the fish with mild extra-virgin olive oil and season with salt. Lay the whole fish or the fillets, skin side up, on a large shallow dish (laying it on foil makes turning over easier). Put it under the preheated broiler and cook for 6–8 minutes, until the skin is crispy. Turn over and cook the flesh side for about 2 minutes or until done.

Now sprinkle the fish with the juice of 1 lemon and cover with a layer of diced ripe firm tomatoes—about 4 or 5. Sprinkle with salt and pepper and continue to cook under the broiler until the tomatoes are hot and the fish is done. Serve with pickled cucumbers or mango chutney (page 241).

Beignets de Poissons

Deep-Fried Fish

Deep-frying fish in olive oil was a method learned in Andalusia. The Iberian Sephardim have spread the art among their corelgionists throughout the Mediterranean. In Turkey—which is an olive-oil-producing country—though the general population never uses olive oil to fry fish, the Jews have always used it.

Fry small and medium fish whole, with the head on or off, and large fish cut into steaks or fillets. Season the fish with salt, then cover entirely but lightly with flour. Alternatively, dip in flour, then in beaten egg. Or make a batter by mixing ¾ cup (125 g) flour with 1 egg and beating in approximately ¾ cup (175 ml) water—enough to achieve the texture of light cream.

Very small fish must be fried quickly at a high temperature until they are crisp and golden. Larger fish and thick steaks take longer and need a lower temperature, so that they have time to cook inside. Turn over once and drain on paper towels before serving. The oil can be reused up to 4 times, but of course the first time will be the best. It must be filtered to get rid of impurities each time. Serve sprinkled, if you like, with chopped parsley or coriander and accompanied by lemon wedges.

You can marinate the fish in a sauce for an hour before deep-frying. More commonly, the fish is dipped in the sauce after frying, sometimes to be heated through in the oven so that the sauce is absorbed. This is a custom of North African and Bukharan Jews. For a North African chermoula, see page 348, and for the Bukharan garlic sauce ovi sir, see page 332.

Croquettes de Poisson

Spicy Fish Fritters

SERVES 4–6

We made these these spicy fish cakes in Egypt. North Africans have similar ones. They make an excellent hot or cold appetizer for parties. Any white fish can be used, or a mixture. If you want to grind the fish yourself in the food processor, do so very briefly; otherwise it will turn into a creamy puree which you will have to pick up with a tablespoon.

> 1 lb (500 g) ground white fish
> 4 tablespoons fine dry bread crumbs or
>   matzo meal
> 1 egg, lightly beaten
> About ½ teaspoon salt
> White pepper
> 3 tablespoons chopped flat-leafed parsley
>   or coriander
> 2 garlic cloves, minced or crushed in a
>   press
> 1 teaspoon ground cumin
> ½ teaspoon ground coriander
> Flour to dip the cakes in
> Olive or light vegetable oil for frying
> Lemon wedges to serve with

Mix all the ingredients except flour, oil, and lemon together and work with your hand to a soft paste. Take lumps the size of a walnut or a small egg, roll into a ball, and flatten slightly. Dip in flour, coating them all over, then deep-fry in batches in medium-hot oil, turning over once, until crisp and golden brown. Drain on paper towels. Serve hot or cold with lemon wedges.

VARIATION

• For Italian polpettine di pesce, mix in 10 small finely chopped anchovy fillets and flavor with a good pinch of nutmeg instead of cumin and coriander. Dip the fish cakes in fine bread crumbs or matzo meal instead of flour before frying.

Arook Tahin bel Samak

Calcutta Fish Cakes

SERVES 4

These tasty hot and spicy "Baghdadi" fish cakes are a Friday-night special in Calcutta. The beautiful parsley-green fritters also make perfect finger food for a party. You may use flounder, turbot, cod, or haddock, or the raw ground-fish mixtures sold by Jewish fishmongers for gefilte fish.

> *½ green chili pepper, seeded*
> *A bunch of scallions (about 9 thin ones)*
> *A large bunch of flat-leafed parsley (1 cup)*
> *1 teaspoon curry powder or to taste*
> *A good pinch of cayenne pepper or to taste*
> *3 tablespoons flour*
> *1 lb (500 g) raw ground fish or skinned*
> *   fish fillet*

About ½ teaspoon salt
Oil for frying

Finely chop the chili pepper, scallions, and flat-leafed parsley in a food processor. Add the curry powder, cayenne, and flour, and blend. Add the fish fillet and a little salt, and process very briefly (a few seconds only) with the rest of the ingredients. If using store-bought ground fish, turn into a bowl with the rest of the ingredients, mix with a fork, and work to a paste that holds together with your hand.

Heat a little oil in a frying pan and drop the mixture in by the tablespoon, pushing it off with another spoon. Flatten the fritters a little in the pan and fry on both sides till lightly browned but still soft inside. Drain on paper towels and serve hot with chutney.

VARIATIONS

• Instead of curry powder, use ¼ teaspoon turmeric and the juice of a ¾-inch (2-cm) piece of ginger crushed in a garlic press.

• The original Iraqi version of arook bel samak ("arook" means "fritter")—a Friday-night dish in Iraq too—is quite different. It is fried fish fillet served with a spicy flour-and-water batter that is fried separately in the same oil as the fish. For the batter fritter: Chop in the food processor half a small hot fresh chili pepper, 1 medium onion, 5 scallions, 1 tomato, and a bunch of flat-leafed parsley (½ cup). Add 2 cups (250 g) flour, a little salt, and a scant cup (225 ml) of water—enough to make the consistency of thick cream. Drop the batter into the oil and fry at not too high heat, turning over once. Some people like to add ½ teaspoon curry powder and a pinch of cayenne.

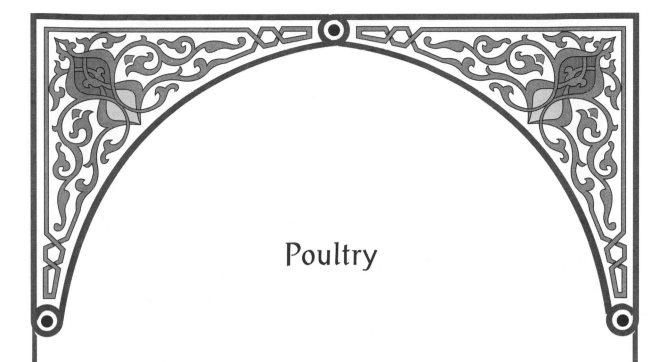

Poultry

Chickens were part of a number of rituals in Oriental Jewry. In the Maghreb, they were slaughtered to inaugurate a new home and to celebrate a betrothal, and they were brought as sacrifices on pilgrimages to shrines and tombs, where people went to ask for help in curing an illness and women went to find or to keep a husband or to become pregnant.

Chicken is the food of Yom Kippur in all Jewish communities, because of the custom of *kapparoth*—the ritual whereby a chicken is killed as a substitute sacrifice for every member of the family. The chicken is whirled over their heads—a cock for males, a hen for females—while a prayer is said that the slaughtered bird may serve as a substitute for the named person. In countries where this custom continued to be practiced, every family was left with a large number of chickens that had to be eaten quickly.

Jacques Hassoun describes the slaughter of chickens in Egypt in his book *Juifs du Nil* (*Jews of the Nile*). Two or three days before Kippur, Jews, even those who lived in the upper-class areas, had live chickens in their bathrooms and terraces, a cock for each male, a hen for each female of the family, to be sacrificed before the night of the festival. Some families brought them to the markets, which were transformed for the occasion into slaughterhouses. The sacrificer stood on a table, in the light of dozens of lamps, amid the squalling of birds, the screams of the crowd, and the shouts of poultry vendors. Every family went forth with their cocks and hens. With a murmur of "This is in the place of that," the head was cut off and presented to the crowd of paupers pressed around the sacrificer. Every family kept only two or three of their chickens for the soup and dish that constituted the meal

לשנה טובה תכתבו

זאל זיין דאָס אַ כפרה
פאַר דיר, פאַר וויַיב און קינד,
פאַר פריַינד, פאַר כּל-ישׂראל —
אויף אַלע אינזערע זינד!

The kapparoth *ritual on the eve of Yom Kippur*

on which every Jew had to survive for the following twenty-six hours. The rest was given to the poor.

Madame Zette Guineadau (*Les Secrets des Cuisines en Terre Marocaine*) describes the chickens waiting in the darkness of the butchers' streets in Morocco in the days before Yom Kippur, in cages, tied up, suspended live by the feet, clucking, before falling by the hundreds in the dusty alleys of the mellah (Jewish quarter). The slaughterer went around the houses, whirling the birds over the heads of all the people in turn, calling

their names, invoking the prayer of Kapparah, cutting the birds' throats. The chickens had to be plucked and cooked before the fast. For the sake of ease, they were simply boiled or sautéed and later combined with other ingredients. For this reason, many chicken dishes are associated with the fast of Yom Kippur. The lunch on the day before the fast was a chicken couscous garnished with raisins and onions or pumpkin. In the early evening, two more chicken dishes were eaten. After the meal, when the sun went down, the men hastened to the synagogue dressed in white and wearing sneakers. The door opened on a paradise of lights and chants and supplications towards God. The day after Kippur more chicken dishes were eaten.

At one time chicken was more expensive then meat. It was a grand dish reserved for the Sabbath and holidays, and the major dish at wedding feasts. In North Africa it was used in many stews as an alternative to meat and was considered the better, more refined choice. Most of the chicken dishes that follow are in the category of Sabbath and festive dishes. Stuffing gave birds a festive air. Nowadays it is common to cook the stuffing separately and to serve it with the bird. In North Africa celebratory dishes had a touch of sweetness, with fruit or honey.

I have not included recipes for some of the more elaborate dishes, like the one that, according to an old Jewish tradition in Tunisia, is prepared before a wedding. A large chicken, boned and stuffed with ground veal, pistachios, and hard-boiled eggs, was colorfully "clothed" and elaborately decorated and sent by the families of the fiancée to the future in-laws on the Saturday before the wedding as a symbol of the couple's happiness and a promise of a large progeniture.

El Hamam del Aroussa

The Bride's Pigeons

SERVES 6

In Morocco, 2 stuffed pigeons in an onion sauce with lemon and honey were served to young Jewish couples on the wedding night to wish them a sweet life full of love. If you cannot get the tender Mediterranean-type baby pigeons or pigeonneaux, use poussins or Cornish hens instead. When I made this dish, there were six of us and we could just about manage 3 poussins between us. The recipe is elaborate, with a long list of ingredients, but it is truly wonderful and worth making, not only for a wedding night.

> 3 young tender pigeons, poussins, or Cornish hens
> Juice of 1 lemon
> 3 tablespoons peanut or sunflower oil
> Salt and pepper
> ½ cup (75 g) almonds, toasted or fried and coarsely chopped, to garnish

For the stuffing

> 1 onion, coarsely chopped
> 4 tablespoons sunflower oil
> 1 lb (500 g) ground beef or veal
> 1¾ cups (350 g) long-grain rice
> Salt
> ⅔ cup (100 g) pitted prunes
> ⅔ cup (100 g) dried apricots
> ⅓ cup (50 g) dried raisins
> ¾ cup (100 g) walnuts, coarsely chopped

> ½ cup (100 g) almonds, coarsely chopped
> Plenty of black pepper
> 1½ teaspoons cinnamon
> 1 teaspoon mace
> ¼ teaspoon nutmeg
> ¼ teaspoon ground ginger

For the sauce

> 3 large onions, about 2 lbs (1 kg), coarsely chopped
> 4 tablespoons peanut or sunflower oil
> Salt and plenty of black pepper
> A good pinch of saffron powder or crushed pistils
> ½ teaspoon mace
> 1–1½ tablespoons honey
> Juice of ½ lemon

Rub the pigeons, poussins, or Cornish hens with a mixture of lemon, oil, salt, and pepper.

To make the filling: Fry the onion in the oil till soft. Add the ground meat and stir and crush it until it changes color. Boil the rice in plenty of salted water for 20 minutes, then drain and add it to the meat. In the meantime, chop the prunes and apricots together in the food processor, then put them to soak in cold water for 10 minutes with the raisins. Drain and add them to the ground meat and rice with the walnuts and almonds. Add salt and pepper to taste, cinnamon, mace, nutmeg, and ginger. Fill the birds with as much stuffing as they will take and put them in a baking dish. Put the remaining stuffing in another baking dish.

Make the sauce: In a large frying pan with a lid, fry the onions in the oil, covered and on a very low flame, for about ¾ hour, until very soft, stirring occasionally. Add salt, pepper, saffron, mace, honey, and lemon juice and ½ cup (125 ml) water and stir very well.

Put the stuffed birds in a baking dish, breast side down, with the sauce poured over. Roast in the oven at 350°F (180°C), turning them over once, for 45–60 minutes, or until they are browned and the juices that run when you cut into the thigh are no longer pink. Heat through the extra stuffing, covered, in the oven at the same time. Serve the birds in their sauce, sprinkled with toasted chopped almonds, accompanied by the extra stuffing.

To serve, cut the birds in half down through the breastbone on one or the other side of its keel with a large, very sharp carving knife, using a strong, steady pressure.

Djaj Mahshi

Stuffed Chicken

SERVES 8

This was a regular Sabbath and festive dish in many Middle Eastern countries. A very large chicken was stuffed with the traditional rice-and-ground-meat stuffing called "hashwa," then was boiled or roasted while more stuffing was cooked separately. Turkey (deek hend) was stuffed in the same way. Now it is common to roast the bird and to cook the stuffing separately and serve it as an accompaniment. The proportions of rice and meat vary. The mixture here, which is particularly meaty, was considered grandest.

> 2 chickens
> 4 tablespoons vegetable oil
> Juice of 1 lemon
> 4 garlic cloves, crushed or minced
> Salt and pepper

For the stuffing (hashwa)

> 1½ lbs (750 g) ground beef
> 5 tablespoons sunflower oil
> 1¼ cups (250 g) long-grain or Patna rice
> Salt and pepper
> 2 teaspoons cinnamon
> ½ teaspoon allspice
> 2 cups (500 ml) meat or chicken stock, or water with 2 dissolved bouillon cubes
> ¼ cup (50 g) split almonds
> ⅓ cup (50 g) pistachios
> ⅓ cup (50 g) pine nuts

Rub the chickens with a mixture of the oil, lemon juice, garlic, salt, and pepper. Put them in a baking dish breast side down (this keeps the breast meat, which tends to be dry, moist and juicy), and roast at 350°F (180°C) for the first 45 minutes, then turn the birds breast side up and cook for 20 minutes more, or until the breasts are browned and the juices that run from a thigh when you cut it with a pointed knife are no longer pink.

For the stuffing, in a large pan fry the ground beef in 3 tablespoons of oil, turning it constantly and breaking up lumps, until it has changed color and the moisture has disappeared. Add the rice and stir well for a few minutes. Then add a little salt (taking into account the saltiness of the stock), pepper, cinnamon, and allspice. Bring the stock to the boil, then pour over the meat and rice. Mix well and simmer, covered, for about 25 minutes, until the rice is tender, adding a little stock or water if it becomes too dry, and adjusting the seasoning to taste.

Fry the mixed nuts in the remaining oil until they just begin to color and mix them into the rice before serving.

VARIATIONS

• A festive way of presenting the stuffing is to press it into an oiled mold, heat it through in the oven before you are ready to serve, and turn it out on a serving platter. Sprinkle with the fried nuts.

• For a Baghdad flavor, add to the stuffing ¼ teaspoon cardamom, a good pinch of ground cloves, and nutmeg.

• Use the same stuffing for turkey, pigeons, and quails.

Hamam Mahshy bi Lahm

Pigeon Stuffed with Meat

SERVES 4

All Egyptians have a tenderness for pigeons. A ground-meat stuffing was popular in the Jewish community. It makes a rich meal, served with rice. Use Mediterranean-type baby pigeons (pigeonneaux), squabs, or small poussins.

1 onion
Juice of ½ lemon
4 tablespoons corn or light vegetable oil
Salt and pepper
1 teaspoon ground cardamom
1 teaspoon cinnamon
½ teaspoon allspice
4 baby pigeons, squabs, or poussins

For the stuffing

1 large onion, chopped
2 tablespoons light vegetable oil
¾ lb (350 g) lean ground beef
2 tablespoons raisins or sultanas
4 tablespoons pine nuts, lightly toasted till golden
Salt and pepper
1 teaspoon cinnamon
¼ teaspoon allspice

Put the onion (cut in pieces), the lemon juice, oil, salt and pepper, cardamom, cinnamon, and allspice in a blender or food processor and liquefy. Rub the birds with this mixture inside and out.

For the stuffing, fry the onion in oil till golden. Add the meat and stir, crushing it with a spoon and turning it over, until the color changes. Add the raisins, pine nuts, salt, pepper, cinnamon, and allspice and cook 5 minutes more.

Spoon the stuffing into the birds and secure the openings with toothpicks. Arrange in a baking dish, breast side down. Roast in a preheated 350°F (180°C) oven for 20 minutes. Turn them over and roast for another 10 minutes, or until they are golden brown and the juices no longer run pink when you cut into the thick part of a thigh.

VARIATIONS

• Another very popular stuffing is cracked wheat or bulgur. Boil 2 cups of water in a pan. Add I cup (175 g) of cracked wheat, salt and pepper, and I teaspoon of cinnamon and cook with the lid on, on very low heat, for 10–15 minutes, until the water is absorbed. Stir in 4 tablespoons of chopped walnuts or pine nuts.

• Quails are also stuffed with the same stuffing. They are best braised in a pan in the onion, oil, and spice mixture for about 15 minutes, turned over a few times. The stuffing will do for 8 quails.

Couscous pour Farcir la Volaille

Moroccan Couscous Stuffing for Chicken, Turkey, or Pigeon

SERVES 6–8

This deliciously rich and nutty stuffing is best served as a side dish with a roast or pot-roasted bird. The couscous available here is precooked and only needs moistening with stock or water and heating through, which makes it very easy.

2½ cups (500 g) packaged couscous
About 3½ cups (800 ml) turkey or chicken stock (you may use water and 1½ bouillon cubes)
Salt
½ teaspoon saffron powder
1 teaspoon cinnamon
½ teaspoon mace
¼ teaspoon nutmeg
4 tablespoons peanut or light vegetable oil
1 cup (200 g) blanched almonds, toasted and coarsely chopped
⅔ cup (100 g) pine nuts, toasted
⅓ cup (50 g) pistachios, coarsely chopped
¾ cup (100 g) raisins or chopped dried apricots (tart, not sweet ones), soaked in water for ½ hour
1 tablespoon or more sugar (optional)

Put the couscous in a bowl. Warm the stock, adding a little salt (taking into account the saltiness of the stock), saffron powder, cinnamon, mace, and nutmeg. Pour only about 2¼ cups (500 ml) of the stock over the couscous. Mix very well and leave for 20 minutes, until the couscous has absorbed the stock. If it is not quite tender, add a little more stock. Stir, breaking up any lumps with a fork, and rub the grain between your hands, to air it and make it light and fluffy. Stir in the oil, chopped almonds, pine nuts, pistachios, raisins or apricots, and, if you like, sugar, and mix well. You can leave the couscous at this stage until you are almost ready to serve. All you need is to heat it through. Do this in the oven in an ovenproof serving dish covered with foil. Just before serving, moisten with a little of the remaining heated-through stock.

• A usual companion to poultry stuffed with couscous is an onion sauce made by frying 2 lbs (1 kg) sliced onions in 4–5 tablespoons of peanut or sunflower oil for 1 hour, adding salt and pepper, 1 teaspoon of cinnamon, and 1 tablespoon of honey at the end.

Poulet aux Dattes

Chicken with Dates

SERVES 6

This Moroccan combination has roots that go back to medieval Baghdad.

> 6 chicken quarters
> 4 tablespoons peanut or sunflower oil
> 2 large onions, 1 lb (500 g), coarsely
>   chopped
> 2 teaspoons cinnamon
> ¾ teaspoon mace
> ¼ teaspoon nutmeg
> 1 tablespoon honey
> Salt and plenty of black pepper
> ½ lb (250 g) dates, pitted
> Juice of ½–1 lemon
> A pinch of saffron
> ½ cup (100 g) blanched almonds, toasted or fried

In a large pan, sauté the chicken pieces in the oil for a few minutes, until lightly colored, turning them over once. Remove them and put the onions in. Cook them on low heat until soft, then stir in the cinnamon, mace, nutmeg, and honey, and pour in about 1¾ cups (400 ml) of water. Stir well and put in the chicken pieces. Bring to the boil, add salt and pepper, and simmer for 25 minutes. Now add the dates, lemon juice, and saffron and cook for another 5–10 minutes, or until the chicken is tender. It is important to taste and adjust the seasoning, for the right balance of flavors is a delicate matter in this dish. It usually needs plenty of black pepper to counteract the sweetness. Serve with the almonds sprinkled on.

Treya

Chicken with Spaghettini or Noodles

SERVES 6

This is a chicken dish that my father's family made in Egypt. I found a mention of a similar one with the same name in a thirteenth-century Syrian cooking manual. Recently I heard from a friend who is from Beirut that it was the Saturday dish of the Wadi—the Jewish quarter, where the synagogue, Alliance school, and kosher butcher were situated. There, it was left overnight at the baker's oven. I have also found a similar dish that is made for wedding parties in Morocco. The following recipe combines methods and flavors from the 3 countries. It is homely but deliciously satisfying, the appeal being that the pasta is partly cooked in the richly flavored chicken sauce. (Ideally, it should be cooked in the stock made from the chicken carcass, as in the variation.) The noodles were once made at home. If you want to make the pasta yourself, use the recipe for pasta on page 152.

> 6 boneless, skinned chicken fillets weighing
>   about 1 lb 10 oz (800 g), cut into
>   strips
> 3 tablespoons corn or sunflower oil
> Seeds from 4 cardamom pods
> Juice of ½–1 lemon
> ¾ teaspoon powdered ginger
> Salt and pepper
> ½ teaspoon saffron pistils or powder (optional)
> 1 lb (500 g) spaghettini, vermicelli, or
>   thin fresh noodles
> 2 teaspoons cinnamon

Put the chicken pieces in a large pan with the oil, cardamom seeds, lemon juice, ginger, salt, pepper, and saffron (if using). Cover with about 2 cups (500 ml) of water and simmer, covered, for 20 minutes.

In the meantime, cook the pasta in boiling salted water until only half cooked and still a little hard. Drain, and turn into the pan with the chicken. Stir well in the sauce and cook for a few minutes longer, covered, on low heat, until tender. Serve hot, sprinkled with cinnamon

VARIATIONS

• Instead of partly boiling the pasta in water, boil it until done *al dente* in a seasoned stock made with the chicken carcass.

• In Becky Hakim-Douek's Beirut version, allspice is the flavoring, instead of cinnamon. Layers of vermicelli and boned chicken pieces are arranged in a baking dish and stock is poured on top. The discarded chicken skin is spread over

that, and the dish is baked in the lowest oven overnight.

• A similar dish, called "intria" or "ministra," was served at Jewish weddings in Morocco. For 6, in a large pan fry 1 large chopped onion in 3 tablespoons of oil till very soft. Add 6 chicken pieces and sauté until lightly browned. Add salt, pepper, 1 teaspoon cinnamon, ¾ teaspoon ground ginger, and about 4 cups (1 liter) water and simmer ¾ hour. Then add ½ teaspoon saffron powder or crushed saffron pistils or turmeric and 1 lb (500 g) thin soft fresh noodles or vermicelli and cook, stirring, until the pasta is tender. Add a bunch of flat-leafed parsley or coriander, finely chopped (½ cup), and serve hot.

• In Egypt some people served treya with an apricot sauce called "mishmisheya." Simmer ½ lb (250 g) dried apricots of a tart, not sweet, variety with the juice of ½ lemon and about 2½ cups (600 ml) water until they are very soft, then blend in a food processor to obtain a soft cream.

Chicken Sofrito

SERVES 4

The word "sofrito" is a tender word that arouses a great deal of feeling in Sephardi communities. It is a method of cooking slowly in a mixture of oil and very little water—adding water gradually as the sauce becomes reduced—which results in a taste and a feel quite different from those of a stew.

Chicken sofrito was one of our Friday-night dishes at my parents' home. My mother was a little touchy about always doing the same thing while I was producing ever more new dishes as part of my research, but it was one of our family traditions. It was also traditional to deep-fry potatoes cut into small cubes and to throw them into the sauce at the end, but my mother substituted tiny boiled new potatoes when she came to England. She always made 2 or 3 chickens, and cold chicken sofrito was eaten on Saturday.

> 2½ tablespoons sunflower oil
> Juice of ½ lemon
> ½ teaspoon turmeric
> Salt and white pepper
> 2 or 3 cardamom pods, cracked
> 1 chicken, quartered

In a large pan or casserole put the oil, lemon juice, a cup of water, the turmeric, salt, pepper, and cardamom, and bring to the boil. Then put in the chicken pieces. Cover and cook over very low heat, turning the chicken over frequently, and adding water if necessary, until the chicken is very tender. There should be a good amount of sauce.

Serve with plain rice or roz bil shaghria (page 460) sprinkled with toasted pine nuts.

VARIATION

• Add 2 garlic cloves crushed in a press, and instead of turmeric and cardamom add ½ teaspoon ground ginger and ¼ teaspoon saffron powder.

Poulet aux Coings

Chicken with Quinces

SERVES 6

This is a sumptuous dish of which the Jews from many different countries are very fond. It is the seductive flavor and perfume of the quinces that makes it special. Joelle Bahloul (*Le Culte de la Table Dressée*) says that it was eaten the evening before the fast of Yom Kippur among the wealthier families who lived around Algiers. The following is a Moroccan version which was prepared for holidays and grand occasions when quinces were in season. I urge you to try it.

> 2 large onions weighing about 1½ lbs
>   (750 g), coarsely chopped
> Peanut or light vegetable oil
> 1 teaspoon cinnamon
> 1 teaspoon ground ginger
> 6 chicken portions
> Salt and pepper
> 2 quinces weighing about 2¾ lbs (1¼ kg)
> Juice of 2 lemons
> 2 tablespoons honey

Heat the onions in 3 tablespoons of oil in a large heavy-bottomed frying pan and stir in the cinnamon and ginger. Lay the chicken pieces on top and sprinkle with salt and pepper. Put the lid on and cook on very low heat for about 30 minutes, turning the chicken over once. The chicken fat and the onion juice should produce a rich sauce, but you may like to add a little water if you feel it is a bit dry. Remove the chicken pieces and place them in a large baking dish that you can bring to the table.

Wash and scrub the quinces and cut them into quarters. (This fruit is extremely hard, so you will need a strong, sharp knife.) You do not need to peel and core them. Simply cut away the ends. Put the quarters quickly—before they begin to darken—into boiling water acidulated with the juice of 1 lemon and simmer until just tender, for about 20–30 minutes. Be careful not to overcook. Drain and, when cool enough, cut away the hard cores and slice each quarter in half.

Fry the quince slices in batches in shallow oil until brown (this gives them a caramelized taste), then lift them out and put them in the onion sauce in which the chicken was cooked. Stir in the honey and the juice of the remaining lemon and cook over very gentle heat, with the lid on, for about ½ hour, until very tender. Put the quince and sauce with the chicken in the baking dish and heat through.

VARIATIONS

• Lightly fried slivered almonds, or sesame seeds toasted dry, can be sprinkled on before serving. I prefer the dish without them.

• A quarter-teaspoon saffron powder may be added at the same time as the honey.

• Two tablespoons of sugar can be used instead of honey.

• Another common version is to add ½ cup raisins, I cup prunes, I cup apricots, soaked in water and drained, after the quinces have been fried.

• A Judeo-Spanish version from Bulgaria called "pojo con bimbriyo" has the chicken and quince fried separately, then put together and cooked with salt and pepper and liquid caramel (made by heating 2 tablespoons sugar until it browns and adding a teacup of water). The dish is cooked slowly with the lid on until the quince is tender.

Fesenjan

Duck with Pomegranate and Walnut Sauce

SERVES 4

When the traveler Rabbi David D'Beth Hillel traveled in Asia in the early nineteenth century (see page 366), he wrote about two kinds of pomegranate syrup he tasted with Israelites in Mosul; both came from Bahadina, in Kurdistan. One was as sweet as honey, and the other sour. "They are made," he wrote, "by drying the grains of the pomegranates, and after that they boil them with water until it has a good taste."

The Jews of Iraq, Iran, and Syria are fond of using the sour pomegranate concentrate or molasses—a dark-brown treacly syrup that is now available in Middle Eastern stores. Mixed with sugar, the result is a divine sweet-and-sour flavor. The following is a simplified version of a famous Iranian dish which survives in Jewish homes in London and Los Angeles.

2 tablespoons sunflower or light vegetable oil
4 duck breasts
1 large onion, chopped
Salt and pepper
3 tablespoons sour pomegranate concentrate
½ cup (75 g) walnuts, finely chopped
2–3 teaspoons sugar or to taste

In a large frying pan, heat the oil and put the duck breasts, skin side down. Sauté gently for 5 minutes, until they release some of their fat. Then add the onion and fry very gently until soft, stirring occasionally, and sprinkling with salt and pepper. Turn the duck breasts over when they are brown on the skin side and turn them again when the flesh is lightly colored. Remove when they are still underdone and set aside.

Strain off the duck fat and return the onions to the frying pan. Add the pomegranate concentrate and walnuts and about ½ cup (100 ml) water and stir very well. Add sugar to taste and return the duck breasts to the pan. Simmer gently in the sauce until they are done.

VARIATION

• Chicken can be used instead of duck.

Poulet aux Olives

Chicken and Olives

SERVES 4

A North African favorite. It is better to pit the olives, but it is more important that you use olives with a good flavor.

> 1 large onion, finely chopped
> 3 tablespoons sunflower oil
> 3 crushed garlic cloves
> ½ teaspoon ground ginger
> 1 chicken, quartered
> 2 tomatoes, peeled and chopped
> ¼ teaspoon powdered saffron
> Salt and pepper
> 7 oz (200 g) green or reddish-brown olives
> Juice of ½–1 lemon
> 4 tablespoons chopped coriander leaves

Fry the onion in the oil till soft. Add the garlic and ginger and stir well. Add the chicken pieces and cook, turning the pieces over, until they acquire a bit of color. Then add the tomatoes, saffron, a little salt (taking into account the saltiness of the olives), pepper, and water to half-cover.

Cook on very low heat for ½ hour, or until the chicken is tender, turning over the pieces and adding water if it becomes too dry. Blanch the olives in plenty of boiling water. Drain and add to the chicken and cook another 10 minutes. Stir in the lemon juice and coriander and serve hot.

VARIATION

• Serve with 2 preserved lemons (see page 239), rinsed and cut in pieces.

Poulet aux Pois Chiches

Chicken with Chickpeas

SERVES 4

This is one of the dishes my mother made when the grandchildren visited. Now they have adopted it. It is very soupy, with a lot of lemony sauce, and is served with plain rice.

> 1 large onion, chopped
> 3 tablespoons oil
> 1 teaspoon turmeric
> 1 chicken, quartered
> 1¼ cups (250 g) chickpeas, soaked for
>   2 hours or overnight
> Juice of 1 lemon
> 2 cardamom pods
> Salt and white pepper

Fry the onion in the oil till soft. Add the turmeric and stir well. Then put in the chicken pieces and sauté, turning them over once, until they have taken a little color. (Do not use chicken fillets: they would become too dry and you need the bones to produce some stock.)

Put in the drained chickpeas and cover them and the chicken pieces with water. Add the lemon juice and the cardamom pods, slightly cracked. Bring to the boil, remove the scum, and simmer, covered, for about 1 hour, or until the chickpeas are tender. Add salt and pepper when they have begun to soften. Serve hot with plain rice.

VARIATION

• Instead of turmeric, use ¾ teaspoon ground ginger.

Maqlub bi Djaj

Chicken with Rice

SERVES 4

Also called "pilau bi djaj," this is a traditional and attractive way of presenting homely food on Friday night in Oriental Jewish homes.

> *1 chicken*
> *1 onion, left whole*
> *Salt and white pepper*
> *3 cardamom pods*
> *1¾ cups (350 g) long-grain rice*
> *4 tablespoons pine nuts*

Cover the chicken and onion with water in a large pot. Bring to the boil, remove the scum, add a little salt and pepper and the cardamom

and simmer for 45 minutes, or until the chicken is tender. Lift it out and remove skin and bones, keeping the meat in relatively large pieces. Put them in a bowl covered with a little of the stock.

Strain the rest of the stock and reduce to 2¾ cups (650 ml). And while it is simmering, throw in the rice. Cook, covered, on very low heat for about 20 minutes, until the liquid is absorbed and the rice is tender.

To assemble the maqlub, sprinkle the bottom of an oiled, shallow round mold (like a pie plate) with pine nuts. Arrange the chicken pieces on top and fill the pie plate with the rice. Pour a few tablespoons of the stock left with the chicken pieces over the rice. Press down with your hands to pack all the ingredients firmly together. Cover with foil and bake long enough to heat through. Turn out onto a serving dish so that the chicken and pine nuts come out on top.

VARIATIONS

• Add ½ teaspoon of turmeric to the water at the start and 2 tablespoons of soaked raisins in the mold with the pine nuts. Blanched almonds may be used instead of pine nuts.

Capsicum Chicken

SERVES 4

This recipe was sent by Queenie Hallegua, who lives in Cochin, the famous spice city of India. It is often served on Friday night. Mrs. Hallegua's quantities—5–8 fresh green chilies and 1 tablespoon cayenne or chili powder—make the dish much too hot for me. I have adapted it to my taste, but you might prefer the larger measures.

3 large onions, sliced

4 tablespoons sesame or sunflower oil

3 small fresh hot green chilies, slit and
　seeded

4 curry leaves

½ teaspoon turmeric

2 large tomatoes, peeled and chopped

3 garlic cloves, crushed in a garlic press

1½-inch (4-cm) piece of ginger, grated, or
　juice of the piece crushed in a garlic
　press

A pinch of cayenne or chili powder

1 chicken, quartered, or 4 chicken pieces
　(boned and skinned if you like)

2 large red bell peppers, seeded and diced

2 teaspoons tamarind paste diluted in
　½ cup (125 ml) boiling water

Salt

1–2 teaspoons sugar (optional)

Fry the onions in the oil till soft. Add the green chilies and curry leaves and fry, stirring, until the onions are golden. Now stir in the turmeric, add the tomatoes, garlic, ginger, and cayenne, and simmer for 10 minutes. Add the chicken pieces and the bell peppers and pour in the diluted tamarind. Add enough water just to cover, season with a little salt, and simmer for about 30 minutes, or until the chicken is tender and the sauce reduced, tasting and adding a little sugar if it is too sour.

Serve with rice or Indian bread. I remove the chilies before serving.

THE THREE JEWISH COMMUNITIES OF INDIA

THE JEWS OF INDIA are an object of fascination to other Jews because of their Indianness and darkness of color and their separation into three distinct groups: the Cochinis, the Bene Israel, and the Baghdadis. Mystery and romance surround their origins, and there is the extraordinary centuries-old total isolation of the largest group, the Bene Israel, who were "discovered" and emerged into the mainstream of Jewish life less than three hundred years ago.

The Cochinis, long settled on the Malabar coast in southwestern India, with only a handful now left, were themselves divided into subgroups: the White Jews, the Black Jews, and the Meshuarim or freed slaves and their descendants, attached to both groups. The White Cochinis' ancestors arrived at various times from as early as the thirteenth century from Spain, in the sixteenth century from Portugal, Holland, and later from the Middle East. They came to trade, attracted by the spices. The White Cochinis maintained that the Black Jews, who were the large majority (about 90 percent), were the descendants of converted slaves, and relegated them to an inferior position, banning them from their synagogues, not allowing intermarriage, and refusing to recognize the validity of their ritual slaughter. The Black Jews claim they were in the region many centuries before the White

Jews. According to their legends, their ancestors were part of the Lost Ten Tribes, who came at the time of King Solomon for spices. Whatever the truth, the famous Jewish traveler Benjamin of Tudela mentions that he saw them on a visit to India in 1167, and Marco Polo talks of his encounter with them in 1293. Copper plates said to be from the tenth century, kept in the Pardesi Synagogue, record princely privileges granted to a Jew, a certain Joseph Raban, and his descendants by the then ruler of Malabar.

Black and White Cochinis maintained separate religious institutions. Until the mid-nineteenth century, when slavery was abolished, their slaves or Meshuarim—the descendants of offspring of unions between Jews and slave concubines—were allowed to worship in their respective synagogues but were treated like outcasts. All the Cochinis spoke the local Malayalam language and for centuries dressed like their Malayali neighbors and shared their customs, but the White Jews became Anglicized and Westernized during the British Raj.

Originally settled in Cranganore, the entire community moved from there to Cochin in the fifteenth century to escape attacks from South Arabian and Portuguese invaders. The maharajah invited them to build their temple next to his. The synagogue, a light airy building with blue-and-white Chinese floor tiles and a Dutch crystal chandelier, stands next to a Hindu temple. The Jews settled into a quarter now known as Jew Town. They were always involved in the pepper-and-spice trade. The precious aromatics—pepper, tamarind, cinnamon, cloves and nutmeg, cardamom, ginger, and turmeric—grow profusely in the hinterland, and their smell permeates the city. The Black Jews were small traders and artisans—handling, drying out, and grinding the spices. The White Jews were the traders. They were at their most glorious during the Dutch occupation, from 1665 to 1795, when they flourished as middlemen, shipowners, and financiers. When Cochin became a backwater, the community deteriorated.

The nineteenth-century traveler Rabbi David D'Beth Hillel described the city in his *Travels*, written between 1824 and 1832 (now published in *Unknown Jews in Unknown Lands*, edited by Walter Fischel [Ktav]): "Cochin is built upon an arm of the sea on the Malabar coast—the view of the fort which is now in decay is occupied by numerous streets of handsome houses resembling a town in Europe. The English officers and respectable Dutch, Portuguese and country-born families reside there." Among the foods they ate that he had not come across before, he listed coconut, mangoes, guava, tamarind, coffee, pepper, and saffron. He described the coconut at length and the way oil was made from it—an activity Jews were engaged in: "The fruit is broken into six or eight pieces which are placed in the sun to dry; the fruit is changed from a delicate white to a brown colour and becomes as hard as a stone; the oil is pressed by an oil mill. It is used for all purposes by the poor classes—for food, for the head and skin and for burning light." Vinegar and a type of sugar were also made from the coconut, as well as a fermented drink, neera, from the water of the unripe fruit.

By far the largest of the communities and the most wholly Indian in the way they dressed, spoke, lived, and ate are the Bene Israel, or Children of Israel. They lived for centuries, entirely unknown to the rest of world Jewry, in villages in the Kolaba district of the Konkan region of Maharashtra—on the west coast, south of Bombay—until Cochini Jews "discovered" them in the mid-eighteenth century. The Cochinis recognized them as Jews because they kept the Sabbath, practiced circumcision on the eighth day, made a distinction between "clean" and "unclean" food (they would not eat fish without scales or fins), and recited the Shema prayer—although that was the only Hebrew prayer they knew, and they had no religious books. The Cochinis sent teachers to instruct them in the observances of Judaism. Since then the Bene Israel have gradually moved into Bombay, where most of those who remain in India now live. Their mother tongue is Marathi, one of the main languages of western India, and their surnames are those of their old villages in the Konkan. Sophie Jhirad, who is a Bene Israel living in London, told me about her community and provided most of the information and recipes I've used here. Some are from her mother and friends, some are out of a typewritten manuscript entitled the

Sophie Jhirad (standing, right), who contributed recipes from her mother and other relatives, with her family in Karachi, 1944

"Bene Israel Cookbook," which is produced by the Jewish Religious Union Sisterhood in Bombay. I first met her at a Jewish symposium in Oxford, where, dressed in a beautiful sari, she gave a riveting talk about food habits in her community.

According to Bene Israel tradition, their ancestors were part of the Lost Ten Tribes of Israel, who were shipwrecked off the coast of India in King Solomon's time, in the second century B.C. The Bene Israel were traditionally farmers and oil pressers and were known to their neighbors as Shanwar Telis (Sabbath-observing oilmen). They pressed sesame, which was the main oil used for cooking, peanut oil, and, especially, coconut oil, which was not used for cooking. They were also professional soldiers. They fought for Hindu maharajahs and Muslim nabobs and served in the armies and navies of the British East India Company and the Bombay and Indian armies. When they moved to Bombay, they took on a variety of occupations, including scholarly ones. The first synagogue built outside Bombay was built by the Bene Israel. In the Konkan they had many little synagogues, some no more than a large hut. The people did their own ritual slaughtering. Their rabbis and hazzans (cantors) were usually from Cochin. In the nineteenth century, their emancipation, through knowledge of English and Hebrew, brought about a religious revival and adherence to traditional orthodoxy.

The newest and most affluent Jewish community, based in Bombay and Calcutta, is made up of people of Middle Eastern origin who are known as the Baghdadis, because a majority are descended from Jews from Iraq. The first settlers, in the early nineteenth century, were merchants who traded between Basra, Baghdad, the Persian Gulf, and Zanzibar in the West, and the Malay coast, Siam, and China in the East. They dealt in Venetian ware, mirrors, gold leaf, copper, and coral, foodstuffs such as coffee, raisins, almonds, coconuts, myrrh, saltpeter, and spices. They also traded in indigo, sandalwood, and elephant tusks. They began to settle and established trading houses. There followed a stream of Jewish immigrants, mainly from Syria and Iraq and also from Yemen and Iran, and the community became large and important. Now it has virtually disappeared.

The first Jew to settle in Calcutta, in 1798, was Shalom Cohen of Aleppo. A merchant and jeweler, he became the leader of the community, setting on it the stamp of Aleppo. Calcutta is known now mostly for its squalor and violence, but it was once the glorious imperial City of Palaces, the political heart of the country. The most British of Indian cities, it started as a trading post of the East India Company and became the capital of British India, remaining so until 1912.

David Sassoon, the legendary figure who founded the larger and more prosperous Bombay community, came from Baghdad in 1832, and since its beginnings the community took its mores and styles from Baghdad. A few fortunes were made early on in the opium trade with China, in general merchandising, land, shipping, and later industry. The Sassoons, who had been courtiers and merchant princes in Baghdad, became fabulously wealthy in Bombay. Bombay was British—it was leased to the East India Company—and their mercantile tolerance offered enormous opportunities for enterprising traders. One of the Sassoons' activities was as middlemen in the exchange between Britain, China, and the Gulf ports of cotton goods from Manchester for silks, pearls, and spices. Another was the silk trade in the overland caravan route. Their greatest source of wealth was opium, which was grown and refined in India and shipped to China. They built the giant docks and the first cotton mills of Bombay and contributed to developing the city into the second largest in Asia.

In his book *Turning Back the Pages: A Chronicle of Calcutta Jewry*, Esmond David Ezra describes the more provincial, less entrepreneurial city of Calcutta, where everyone kept open house. "Much of the informal entertaining of relatives and close friends took place in the bedrooms. . . . They would all relax on the beds or on chairs brought in for the purpose and chatter for hours. Occasionally tea or light refreshments would be taken in to them by the servants." It was mostly a very modest community. They all lived and worked in a relatively small area of the city and saw a great deal of each other. Gambling—card games and horse racing—had a strong hold on the community.

The Bombay and Calcutta Baghdadis were never Indianized. They kept themselves to themselves, as did all the communities in India. Nor did they mix with the Bene Israel or the Black Cochinis. Tudor Parfitt, author of *The Thirteenth Gate: Travels Among the Lost Tribes of*

Israel, found the different Jewish communities "living at peace with their Muslim and Hindu neighbours but not with each other." The Baghdadis enjoyed a special status under the Raj as white non-Indians—although some are coffee-colored. They felt British and emulated the British. But they kept their Oriental (Arab) rites and customs even as they identified with Europe and the British Raj. They had dressed in Turkish and Arab style and continued to speak Arabic among themselves for more than a hundred years, until English began to take its place at the turn of the century. The older generation—which idealized Baghdad as their "Garden of Eden"—still have Arab names. The young, for whom England was the mother country, are called Daphne and Mavis, but their language is suffused with sometimes deformed Arab words.

The Jews of India were secure and respected and never suffered any kind of persecution in the multireligious society of Hindus, Muslims, Buddhists, Christians, Parsees, Zoroastrians, and Armenians. Nonetheless, after Indian Independence and the establishment of the State of Israel, they began to leave for Israel, Britain, Australia, Canada, and America.

The dishes of the Bene Israel and Cochinis are quite wonderful, even stunning. They are among the best in this book. Every time I cook them, my guests ask for the recipes. Throughout the centuries, these two communities had a free and intimate relationship with their Hindu and Muslim neighbors and fully participated in the life of the general community, so that their cooking is closely related to that of the two regions in which they lived, the Kerala and the Konkan, both of which have a particularly delicious aromatic cuisine.

Cochini cooking is southern Indian, with coconut milk and grated coconut, a very wide variety of spices, and plenty of hot peppers. The food is chili-hot. Arab influence can be felt in the cooking of the White Cochinis, because the latest immigration was from Baghdad.

Bene Israel cooking is western Indian, and more specifically Maharashtrian, although the Jews have their own special touch and have several dishes that are different from those of their Muslim and Hindu neighbors in the Konkan. The community also adopted some dishes in Bombay and in other parts of the country where they settled. They add more onion than the Hindus, make greater use of tomato and coconut, and employ lemon where curds or yogurt might be used by Muslims. They love fresh herbs as well as dried spices and have their own preferences in flavoring, blending tamarind, lemon, coconut, cinnamon, cardamom, cumin, and little dried red chilies with a touch of raw sugar in a delicate marriage of sweet, savory, hot, and sour. In the Konkan, as in Cochin, the coconut is ubiquitous. It is grated and used fresh or dry. The juice known as coconut milk, made from ground coconut and water, goes into stews, curries, and rice dishes. Rice, which is grown in the Konkan, is used extensively even to make pancakes, pastries, and puddings. Fish is a great favorite here too. But, being so plentiful and cheap, it is not considered special enough for the Sabbath, festivals, or for great occasions such as weddings (except for Rosh Hashanah). For special occasions they serve chicken and mutton dishes. They have many sweet preparations attached to the various festivals. The fabulous Alphonso mangoes grow in the Konkan. The

Bene Israel who lived in villages or small towns kept their own hens, ducks, and occasionally also turkeys in their back yards. To make matzo, they would buy their own special wheat, clean it, and either grind it themselves or take it to the mill to be ground in front of them. They extended the laws of kashrut by deciding that fish and milk could be neither cooked nor eaten together. Respect for Hindu sensibilities ensured that beef did not enter their kitchen. This taboo became so ingrained that some became convinced that beef was not kosher.

The cooking of the Baghdadis is a hybrid. To Iraqi and Syrian dishes they added Indian flavors. They adopted some Indian foods, especially chutneys and bhajis and breads, such as puris and chapatis, and English foods like bread pudding, which they adapted. During World War II, the Calcutta community was doubled with a flood of Jews fleeing from Rangoon, and these too brought new cooking styles. In the nineteenth century, the freed Cochini slaves escaping from their outcast condition in Cochin had come to work and cook in the homes of the Bombay and Calcutta Baghdadis. In later years, they were replaced by Hindus and Muslims. Flower Elias and Judith Elias Cooper write about the "Jewish" cooks, who were much in demand. They were not Jews but Muslims who had worked in Jewish households for many years and knew how to cook the traditional dishes. These cooks trained each other. It is they who were responsible—with the Black Meshuarim from Cochin, who preceded them—for creating the unique hybrid Baghdadi cuisine, which marries Middle Eastern, Bengali (Calcutta), Maharashtrian (Bombay), and Cochin styles—the sweet and sour with the hot and spicy.

In Bombay there were many meat and especially lamb dishes, but in Calcutta there were no facilities for the ritual slaughter of cows, sheep, and goats, and they never had a *shohet* (professional slaughterer). One came from Bombay for the festivals, so they had meat sometimes only once a year, at Rosh Hashanah. Because of that, they were particularly strong and imaginative in preparing chicken, fish, and vegetables. In the old days, a *shohet* came to the houses to slaughter chickens, but later Indian cooks took the live chickens to the *shohet*, who had a stand at the market. The Jews adopted the Bengalis' passion for freshwater fish and dislike of saltwater fish (they say it is not sweet enough), and they ate the fish from the Ganges estuary and from lakes and pools. Servants made Indian breads like chapatis and parathas every day, mostly in brick or clay ovens. They did not make many desserts, but they ate many sweetmeats—mostly flavored withrose water and cardamom— sending them to each other on trays covered with silk handkerchiefs on Jewish holidays. And they bought ready-made Indian sweets. The oldest established Jewish confectioner, and baker, Nahoum and Sons, is still in business, going strong in the new covered market. Once upon a time, he was thronged before the holidays. In the old days, a *mir cuchini* (man who made sweets) went from house to house making little sweets based on coconut. Some poor Jewish families produced halek (thickened date juice), which was eaten sprinkled with crushed walnuts and almonds as an accompaniment to matzo at Passover and used as a sweetener the rest of the year.

Minty Carrot Chicken

SERVES 4

This recipe, which was also sent from Cochin by Mrs. Queenie Hallegua (Hallegua is the Portuguese name of one of the old established families), is not peppery hot. I made it with the optional ginger and garlic and left out the optional chilies. The fresh minty flavor is the distinctive feature. It may seem ordinary, but it is quite delightful.

3 large onions, sliced
3 tablespoons sesame or sunflower oil
2 garlic cloves, crushed (optional)
Juice of 1½-inch (4-cm) piece of ginger
    crushed in a garlic press, or the grated
    piece (optional)
2 green chilies, slit and seeded (optional)
1 teaspoon turmeric
1 chicken, quartered, or 4 chicken pieces
    (skinned and boneless if you like)
Salt
1¼ lbs (600 g) carrots, sliced lengthwise and
    cut into 1-inch (2½-cm) lengths
3 tablespoons finely chopped fresh mint leaves

Fry the onions in the oil till soft and golden, stirring occasionally. The next 3 ingredients—garlic, ginger, and chilies—are optional. If you are using them, put them in now. Stir in the turmeric. Put in the chicken pieces and sauté for about 10 minutes, adding salt to taste, and turning the pieces over once. Then add the carrots and just enough water to cover.

Add a little more salt and cook uncovered for 15 minutes, or until the chicken and carrots are done and the liquid is reduced. Add the mint and cook a few moments more. Serve hot with Indian bread or rice.

Macalcal or Masala Chicken
Chicken in a Coconut Sauce

SERVES 6

This Bene Israel (Indian) dish is not in the least hot. There are sweet and delicate flavors in the voluptuous sauce. Serve it with rice.

4 medium onions, about 1 lb (500 g),
    coarsely chopped
4 tablespoons sesame or sunflower oil
6 garlic cloves, crushed in a press
Juice of 2½-inch (6½-cm) piece of ginger
    crushed in a garlic press, or the grated
    piece
1 teaspoon turmeric
6 chicken pieces—thighs and breasts (boneless
    and skinless)
Salt
Plenty of white pepper
1 lb (500 g) new potatoes, cut in thick slices
1 can of unsweetened coconut milk, or 3 oz
    (75 g) creamed coconut (see page 235)
    cut into pieces and diluted in
    1¼ cups (300 ml) boiling water
1 teaspoon sugar
¾ cup (100 g) cashew nuts or split almonds
2 tablespoons raisins

In a large pan, fry the onions in oil till soft and golden, stirring occasionally. Because there is so much onion, that takes a long time, and it is best to start with the lid on (which steams them). Add the garlic and cook, stirring, for a few minutes. Then add the ginger and turmeric and stir well.

Put in the chicken pieces and season with salt and white pepper. Cook 5 minutes and turn over the chicken pieces. Add the potatoes and coconut milk and enough water to cover—about I cup (250 ml). Add sugar and adjust the seasoning. Then simmer for 30–45 minutes, or until the chicken and potatoes are very tender. Add the cashew nuts or almonds and the raisins and cook a few minutes more. Serve hot.

Chittarnee
Sweet-and-Sour Chicken in Onion Sauce

SERVES 6

This dish is uniquely of the Baghdadi Indian community. In Bombay meat was often used instead of chicken, but in Calcutta chittarnee was always made with chicken, because the community never had a *shohet* and they only ate meat when one came to the city from Bombay to slaughter for the festivals.

Bene Israel woman grating a coconut in Cheul, the Konkan

2 lbs (1 kg) onions, grated or finely
    chopped
4 tablespoons peanut or vegetable oil
2 or 3 garlic cloves, crushed in a press
Juice of a 1-inch (2½-cm) piece of fresh
    ginger crushed in a garlic press, or
    1½ teaspoons grated ginger
1 teaspoon turmeric
1 teaspoon ground cinnamon
1½ teaspoons coriander
¾ teaspoon ground cardamom
A good pinch of cayenne or red chili powder
    or to taste
2 bay leaves
6 boneless and skinless chicken fillets (breasts
    and thighs) weighing about 1¾ lb
    (800 g), cut into smaller pieces
Salt
1 lb (500 g) tomatoes, peeled and chopped,
    or a 14-oz (400-g) can of chopped
    tomatoes
2–3 tablespoon wine vinegar
2 teaspoons sugar or to taste

Put the onions in a large pan with the oil and cook very gently with the lid on, stirring occasionally, until they are very soft and golden. Because there is so much onion, this can take up to ½ hour. Add the garlic, ginger, spices, and bay leaves and stir for 5 minutes. Put in the chicken pieces, season with salt, and sauté for 10 minutes, turning them over once. Now add the tomatoes and simmer, uncovered, for 30 minutes, or until, as they say, "all the excess liquid has dried out and the gravy glistens with the oil." Finally, stir in the vinegar and sugar and cook 10 minutes more. Serve hot with rice.

La Minima

Chicken and Calves' Brains Cake

SERVES 10

This famous Jewish Tunisian dish, also pronounced "minina," is eaten on Rosh Hashanah. Jewish Tunisian restaurants in Paris have it on their regular menu as a cold appetizer, and it can usually be seen displayed on the counter. You find it served at weddings and bar mitzvahs in France. Nowadays it is often made without the brains, which are a symbolic New Year's ingredient (see page 28), but they do give the dish a marvelous creamy texture.

1 calf's brain or 2 lambs' brains
2 tablespoons vinegar
3 chicken breasts or thigh fillets (without
    skin and bones) weighing about
    1 lb (500 g)
Salt
9 eggs, lightly beaten
Pepper
¼ teaspoon nutmeg
3 hard-boiled eggs, cut in small pieces
3 lemons, cut in wedges

Soak the brain or brains in water with 1 tablespoon of vinegar. Carefully remove the thin outer membranes and wash under cold water. Poach in fresh boiling water with the remaining vinegar for 3 minutes, or until it firms. Cut into small pieces. Simmer the chicken in salted water for 15–20 minutes, then drain and chop it.

In a bowl, mix the chicken and the beaten

eggs, add salt, pepper, and nutmeg, and fold in the hard-boiled eggs and the brains.

Grease a large nonstick cake pan or mold with oil and pour in the mixture. Cover with foil and bake in a preheated 400°F (200°C) oven for 45–60 minutes, until firm—remove the foil after ½ hour. Let the minima cool before turning out. Serve cold, cut into squares or like a cake, accompanied by lemon wedges.

VARIATION

• An Algerian version called "meguena" has a macédoine (mixture) of cooked vegetables such as sliced green peas, diced carrots, and sliced mushrooms—instead of the chicken.

La Pastilla
Individual Chicken Pies

MAKES ABOUT 25

There is a belief among the Jews of Morocco that their ancestors were responsible for bringing the country's great festive pie from Andalusia. Now, in Paris, for weddings, they make it in small individual parcels. It is a very good idea for a dinner party too. The filling is always a great and delightful surprise to guests. The following recipe has the sharp lemony flavor of Tétouan. The variation, with sugar and

The oil-pressing house in Cheul, the Konkan. Only one family of oil pressers remains here.

cinnamon sprinkled over the top, is from Fez.

One pie should be enough per person. I have given large quantities because it is an ideal dish for a large party: the pastry parcels can be made in advance and reheated, and there is no need to cut or carve anything. Filo pastry is a very good substitute for the Moroccan ouarka (see page 305).

2 chickens
Salt
3 lbs (1½ kg) onions
4–5 tablespoons light vegetable oil
12 eggs
Pepper
¾ teaspoon ginger
2 teaspoons cinnamon
Juice of 2 lemons
A large bunch of coriander, finely chopped
  (1 cup)
A bunch of flat-leafed parsley, finely
  chopped (½ cup)
1¾ cups (300 g) blanched almonds
25 sheets filo
3 egg yolks

Put the chickens in a very large pot with water to cover. Bring to the boil, remove the scum, add salt, and simmer 45 minutes, until tender.

Fry the onions in the oil till very soft and golden. You will need to cook them in 2 pans because of the large quantity, and they will take very long to cook. Put the lid on and stir occasionally.

Lift out the chickens when they are done, remove skin and bones, and cut the meat into smallish pieces. Reduce the stock by boiling to concentrate it.

In another pan, beat the eggs lightly and beat in 1 cup (250 ml) of the reduced stock. Add a little salt and pepper, the ginger, cinnamon, lemon juice, coriander, and parsley. Stir with a wooden spoon over medium-low heat for about 10 minutes, or until the eggs set to a creamy soft scramble. Add the almonds, toasted or lightly fried and coarsely chopped, and the chicken pieces and mix well. That is the filling. Let it cool.

Take the filo sheets out of their packages when you are ready to use them. I used 2 packages of 14 oz (400 g) each; the sheets were 18½ by 12½ inches (47 by 32 cm). Keep them opened out, in a pile. Brush the top one lightly with oil. Put a good portion of filling—about 3 heaping tablespoons—about 4 inches (10 cm) from a short edge, and equidistant from the 2 long edges. Fold the short edge over the filling, then the bottom long edge. Carefully pick up the filling with the wrapping and fold it over to the side. Then fold the top edge over it. Now continue to fold over until you have a package about 4½ inches (11 cm) square. It sounds complex but it is very easy and obvious when you do it. Do the same with the rest of the filling and sheets of filo. Of course, you may improvise and wrap it your own way.

Arrange all the parcels side by side on oiled trays or on greaseproof or wax paper. Brush the tops with the egg yolks mixed with a tablespoon of water and bake at 350°F (180°C) for about 30 minutes, or until crisp and brown. Serve hot.

VARIATION

• For a Fez-style version, omit the lemon juice and dust the pastries, as they come out of the oven, with 3–4 tablespoons confectioners' sugar, or to taste, and 1–2 tablespoons cinnamon.

Gayna kon Berengena Assada

Chicken with Eggplant Sauce

SERVES 6–8

Chicken and chicken balls smothered in an eggplant sauce and served with rice is a famous Sabbath dish in Turkey. The sauce is a Jewish version of a classic Turkish one, using stock instead of milk.

>   *1 whole chicken*
>   *Salt and pepper*
>   *1 onion, peeled*
>   *2 bay leaves*
>   *2 chicken breasts weighing about ¼ lb*
>   *(350 g), skin and bones removed*
>   *½ cup (75 g) ground almonds*
>   *1 slice bread, crusts removed*
>   *1 egg*
>   *3 lbs (1½ kg) eggplants*
>   *6 tablespoons sunflower oil*
>   *4 tablespoons flour*

Put the whole chicken in a large pot. Cover with water and bring to the boil. Remove the scum, then add salt, pepper, the whole onion, and the bay leaves. Simmer for 40 minutes.

At the same time, make the chicken balls. Put the chicken breasts in the food processor with the almonds, the bread (soaked in water and squeezed dry), the egg, and a little salt and pepper, and blend to a soft paste. Roll into balls the size of small walnuts and drop into the pan with the chicken. Simmer for 10–15 minutes, or until the chicken and chicken balls are very tender. Remove from the heat.

For the sauce, broil or roast the eggplants and peel them into a colander (see page 256), then chop them with 2 pointed knives and mash them with a fork, letting their juices run out. Heat the oil in a saucepan and stir in the flour. Add 2 cups (500 ml) of the strained hot chicken stock—very little to begin with, then gradually, a little at a time—stirring vigorously (as in making a béchamel) so that no lumps form. Cook for 5 minutes, then stir in the mashed eggplants and cook for another 5–10 minutes. Taste, and adjust the seasoning.

Serve the chicken cut in pieces and the chicken balls on a bed of eggplant sauce, accompanied by plain rice. If you have enough stock, cook the rice in one and a half times its volume of stock or a mixture with water.

VARIATIONS

• Add 2 peeled and chopped tomatoes to the sauce when you put in the eggplants.

• Another popular dish is berengena assada kon baba—duck with the eggplant sauce.

Pollo Fritto

Chicken Pieces Fried in Batter

SERVES 2–4

This Tuscan way of cooking small pieces of chicken has become a Hanukah specialty in Italy. The frying oil commemorates the oil that burned for 7 days when there was only enough for 1 day. It is sometimes part of a fritto misto, which may include sweetbreads, small pieces of brains, and tiny lamb chops. The chicken is cut in small pieces—usually including skin and bones, but you can use skinless fillets if you like.

> 8 small pieces of chicken cut from the breast
>   or leg
> Juice of 1 lemon
> Salt and pepper
> Flour
> 1 egg, lightly beaten
> Light vegetable oil for frying, about 1 inch
>   (2½ cm) deep

Marinate the chicken pieces for 1 hour in the lemon juice, a little salt, and pepper. Just before you are ready to eat, roll them all in flour, then in beaten egg (prepare a soup plate of each, and the chicken pieces can all be in at the same time). Heat the oil in a heavy pot and deep-fry the chicken till golden. If the oil is too hot, the batter will burn before the chicken is done.

If you want to make a large quantity, you may reheat in the oven.

VARIATION

• The Tunisian "Livornese" version—poulet en beignets—is a chicken cut in small pieces marinated in a mixture of 3 tablespoons of extra-virgin olive oil, the juice of 1 lemon, 2 crushed garlic cloves, 3 tablespoons finely chopped flat-leafed parsley, salt, and pepper, then dipped in a batter made with ⅓ cup (75 g) flour beaten with 1 egg and a little water—just enough to obtain a light cream—plus salt and pepper. Deep-fry in medium-hot oil and serve with lemon quarters.

Arook bel Murug
Indian Baghdadi Chicken and Rice Croquettes

SERVES 4

This exquisite delicacy with a splendid ginger flavor was a real discovery for me. It is from the Baghdadi Jewish community of India, adapted from the book *Awafi*. It is also easy to make. Round risotto-type rice is best used, because it is sticky and binds well. It makes good finger food and can be served as a main dish with relishes to accompany.

> ½ cup (125 g) Italian round rice
> Salt
> ½ lb (250 g) chicken-breast fillets (without
>   skin and bones)
> 1 garlic clove, crushed
> 1-inch (2½-cm) piece of ginger, grated,
>   or the juice obtained by crushing it in
>   a garlic press
> ½ teaspoon garam masala
> ½ teaspoon turmeric
> 4 tablespoons chopped flat-leafed parsley
> Light vegetable oil for frying, about 1 inch
>   (2½ cm) deep

Boil the rice in salted water for 15 minutes only, then drain. Grind the chicken to a paste in the food processor. Add the rest of the ingredients (except the oil) and blend briefly. Then add the cooked rice and blend briefly again.

Oil your hands, because the mixture is sticky. Take walnut-sized lumps and roll into fingers 2½ inches (6 cm) long. Deep-fry in oil until golden, turning them over once.

VARIATION

• You may, alternatively, arrange the croquettes in an oiled baking dish and bake them in a 350°F (180°C) oven for 40 minutes.

Arook Thayin

Chicken Croquettes Burmese Style

SERVES 6

Jews from Calcutta, Cochin, Persia, and Iraq began to settle in Burma, in Southeast Asia, in the mid-nineteenth century. It was Jews of Baghdadi origin who organized the congregation, and it is their style of cooking that influenced the Jewish style that developed locally. During the Japanese occupation, almost all the community fled, many of them to India. This recipe is one of many given to me by Mrs. Philomène Jacobs of the Baghdadi community of India. These delectable fritters—soft and creamy, gingery and peppery—make splendid finger food.

4 scallions, very finely chopped
½–2 fresh green chilies, seeded and very finely chopped
¼ cup chopped coriander leaves
3 chicken-breast fillets weighing about 12 oz (350 g)
3 tablespoons flour

4 eggs
Juice of 1½-inch (4-cm) piece of fresh ginger crushed in a garlic press, or the grated piece
Salt
Light vegetable oil for deep-frying, about 1 inch (2½ cm) deep

Chop the scallions, chilies (half a chili is enough for me), and coriander in the food processor. Then add the chicken, flour, eggs, ginger, and salt, and process until the chicken is finely chopped and all the ingredients are well blended (I have overprocessed the chicken to a paste by mistake, and the result was also delightful). Chill, covered, for 1–2 hours.

Deep-fry by the heaping tablespoon (dip the spoon in oil so that the mixture does not stick) in medium-hot oil, turning over once, until browned all over. Drain on paper towels. The recipe makes about 14 2½-inch (6-cm) fritters and up to 36 tiny ones. Serve hot or cold.

VARIATION

• An Indian Baghdadi arook thaheen is made with a pinch of turmeric.

Djaj Meshwy–
Poulet Grillé

Grilled Chicken

SERVES 4

This is a very simple way of cooking chicken, but the garlic, lemon, and olive oil make it special.

4 chicken portions, boned if you like
4 tablespoons extra-virgin olive oil
Juice of 1 lemon
4 garlic cloves, minced or crushed in a
    press
Salt and pepper
2 tablespoons chopped flat-leafed
    parsley

Marinate the chicken in a mixture of olive oil, lemon juice, garlic, salt, and pepper. Cook over embers or under the broiler—about 4 inches (10 cm) from the fire—turning over a few times so that they do not burn. The important thing is not to overcook. Legs take 35–40 minutes, boned breasts about 10–15 minutes. Serve sprinkled with parsley.

VARIATIONS

- I have tasted other versions, one with cinnamon, another with fennel seeds.

Simman Meshwy–Cailles Grillées

Grilled Quails

SERVES 4 OR 8

Quails are popular in Egypt. They used to migrate there; now they are farmed. They are important to the Jews because they feature in the Bible: Moses made them fall from the sky when the Hebrews were hungry in the wilderness. The usual way of cooking them is to cut them open and grill them flattened out.

8 quails
2 medium onions, quartered
4 tablespoons extra-virgin olive oil
1 teaspoon coriander
1 teaspoon cinnamon
1 teaspoon ground cardamom
Salt and pepper
1–2 lemons, cut in wedges

Lay each quail breast down and split it open along the whole backbone by sawing through with a serrated knife or by cutting with kitchen shears. Crack the breastbone and flatten the quail out. Cut the wings and legs at the joints, just enough to spread the quails out, then pound them as flat as you can on a board (you might find it easier to do that between sheets of greaseproof or wax paper).

Prepare a marinade. Put the onions, oil, coriander, cinnamon, cardamom, salt, and pepper in a blender or food processor and liquefy. Marinate the quails in this for about 1 hour, then grill on a barbecue or under the broiler. Grill for 5–6 minutes on each side, or until golden and the juices no longer run pink when you cut into a thigh. Serve with lemon wedges.

VARIATIONS

- For an alternate marinade, use the one given in preceding recipe for grilled chicken.
- I am not so keen on the usual Egyptian flavoring of 1 teaspoon coriander and 2 teaspoons cumin, but you might like it.
- Do the same with Mediterranean-type baby pigeons (pigeonneaux), squabs, or very small poussins. They will take about 15 minutes to cook.

Polpettone di Tacchino

Turkey Galantine

SERVES 14

This recipe was sent by Nedelia Tedeschi of Turin as the Piedmontese quaietta 'd pito. It is a very old dish—an *antica ricetta*—of the Italian Jews of Italy. I made it for Passover, as they do, and wondered if it was worth all the effort, but the family and guests all thought it was. Because it is cooked in stock, it is one of the few ways of cooking turkey in which the meat does not come out dry. The same dish is also made with chicken. Some versions include cow's udder (a delicacy in Rome and Ancona), hard-boiled eggs, and truffles. The following is with pistachios.

> 1 turkey weighing about 8½ lbs (4 kg)
> Salt and white pepper
> 14 oz (400 g) veal (you can buy ground veal)
> ¾ teaspoon nutmeg
> 2 eggs, lightly beaten
> 2 garlic cloves, finely chopped or crushed in a garlic press
> ½ cup (75 g) pistachios

Remove the skin of the turkey, taking care not to tear it: First singe the turkey over a flame to loosen it. With a very sharp knife, cut the skin top to bottom down the back, then cut around the wings and leg ends. Carefully pull the skin right off as though removing a shirt, cutting away from the flesh with a pointed knife where it clings. Reserve the skin.

Now bone the turkey. In a very large saucepan put the carcass with bits of meat on it and the neck. Cover with water, add salt and pepper, and bring to the boil. Remove all the scum and simmer for about 1 hour.

In the meantime, discard nerves and tendons from the leg meat and grind it to a soft paste with the veal in the food processor. Do it in batches and turn into a bowl. Add ½ teaspoon salt, pepper, nutmeg, eggs, and garlic. If you don't mind the effort, it is best to blanch the pistachios for a few minutes in boiling water and to remove the skin before adding them—otherwise chop them coarsely so that the green shows. Mix thoroughly with your hands.

Wash the skin and lay it out flat, outside part down. It looks small, but it stretches enough to wrap the turkey loaf. Place the filling down the middle, lengthwise, like a fat roll, and pat it firmly. Pull the skin over it and wrap it well. Any bare parts can be patched with pieces cut from the skin that covered the legs. Some people darn any holes with thread, but I don't think it is necessary as long as the galantine is properly tied. Tie the roll firmly at intervals with strong thread, especially where the patches are.

Remove the carcass and bones from the pan and lower the turkey roll in carefully, curving it gently to fit into the pan. It should be entirely covered by stock. Simmer for about 1½ hours. Serve hot or cold. Either way it should stay in the stock until you are ready to eat, so that it remains moist. Lift out, cut off the threads, and serve cut in slices.

GARNISHES

• On Saturday the polpettone is served cold, garnished with sliced hard-boiled eggs, olives, and radishes.

ABOUT MY AUNT RÉGINE

M Y AUNT RÉGINE, whose family came from Syria, gave me the identical recipe to the above polpettone many years ago. She called it a "galantine." She lives in Paris now, in the Avenue Carnot, near the Étoile. I thought I should say something about her somewhere in the book because so many of her recipes are included and because she complained that I only talked about the Doueks (she is the widow of my uncle Jacques, and I had been asking her about him). She insisted that her family, the Picciottos, were worth a mention. To prove it, she gave me a photocopy of a chapter in the *Revue d'Histoire Diplomatique*, written by Bernard Le Calloc'h (whom she met in her building), all about the Picciottos, who were a dynasty of consuls in the service of France in the Levant between 1784 and 1894. The Picciottos were among the Marrano families who settled in Livorno and moved to Aleppo in the eighteenth century. They were successful merchants who became consuls general for Tuscany, France, and Austria—a role that was passed on from one generation to the next, and which bestowed on the family a title and the particle "de" in front of the name. This explains some of the mysteries of the Italian influence in Aleppo, and also the refinement and sophistication of Régine's recipes.

Aliyah

*Stewed Chicken with Tomatoes
and Coriander*

SERVES 6

The word "aliyah" refers to the immigration of Jews to Israel. That was the name given to me by Lily Macal, who said this dish was eaten on the Sabbath in the Georgian town of Koulashi. It was served with gomi, a cornmeal porridge similar to polenta and mamaliga. The cornmeal in Georgia is mostly white, but you can use yellow.

1 lb (500 g) onions, finely chopped
3 tablespoons vegetable oil
3 garlic cloves, crushed in a garlic press
1 chicken, cut in pieces (or 4 fillets, skinned and boned)
1 lb (500 g) tomatoes, peeled and chopped
Salt and pepper
1 tablespoon tamarind paste
1 bay leaf
A large bunch of fresh coriander, chopped (¾ cup)
3 tablespoons chopped basil

For the cornmeal gomi

2 cups (275 g) cornmeal
8 cups (2 liters) water
½ teaspoon salt

Fry the onions in the oil till soft. Add the garlic and fry a few minutes more. Then add the chicken and tomatoes, salt, pepper, tamarind, and bay leaf and cook for about ½ hour, until the chicken is tender and the sauce reduced, turning the chicken pieces over once. Remove the bay leaf and stir in the coriander and basil.

To make gomi, follow the method for making mamaliga (page 159), using the above measures. The result will be creamy. You may also use precooked instant polenta, which is not bad.

Serve the gomi in little bowls and the chicken in a separate dish for people to help themselves. It is the custom in Georgia for guests to help themselves from serving dishes placed on the table.

Satsivi

Chicken in Walnut Sauce

SERVES 8 OR MORE

"Satsivi" is the name of the sauce that appears in every Georgian feast, sometimes over roast or grilled birds—turkey, duck, chicken, or quail— or as an accompaniment to cooked vegetables or fried eggplants. It has a rich brown color and a complex, spicy flavor in which sour pomegranate—the fresh juice or the molasses—often plays a part. There is something very Persian about it. To the Jews, satsivi with chicken is a cold Saturday dish which does not need reheating.

1 large chicken
Salt and pepper
A few parsley stalks
2 bay leaves

For the walnut sauce

2 large onions, finely chopped
4 tablespoons sunflower oil
6 garlic cloves or to taste, minced or crushed in a press
1¾ cups (200 g) walnuts, ground or finely chopped
Salt
1½ teaspoons ground cinnamon
¼ teaspoon allspice
¼ teaspoon ground cloves
1½ teaspoons ground coriander
1 teaspoon paprika
¼–½ teaspoon cayenne or red chili powder
2–3 tablespoons cider or wine vinegar
1 tablespoon pomegranate concentrate or molasses or tamarind paste

Put the chicken in a large pot, cover with water, and bring to the boil. Remove the scum, add some salt and pepper, the parsley stalks, and the bay leaves, and simmer, covered, for about 1 hour. Lift out the chicken (reserve the stock), and when cool enough remove the skin and bones and cut into medium pieces. Set aside, covered with a little stock. Reduce the stock in the pan to about 2 cups (500 ml) by boiling it down.

For the sauce, fry the onions in oil till very soft. Add the garlic and stir until the aroma rises. Add the walnuts, salt, and spices and stir for a few minutes. Now stir in enough of the strained chicken stock to make a light creamy sauce. Add the vinegar and pomegranate concentrate, or the tamarind paste, and cook, stirring, for a few minutes more. Arrange the chicken pieces on a serving dish and pour the sauce on top. Serve cold. This makes a marvelous buffet dish.

PROSCIUTTO E SALAME D'OCA

Cured Goose "Ham" and Salami

Goose and goose fat came into the Jewish cooking of Italy through the German Jews who sought refuge there in the sixteenth century. (There are many families called "Tedeschi" and "Tedesco," which mean "German.") It was used to make prosciutto and salame, which have become famous Jewish specialties of the Veneto, Ferrara, and Ancona in particular. For prosciutto d'oca, goose legs and thighs are salted for about five days and the liquid is drained off; then they are hung up to dry for four weeks. Salame d'oca is a sausage made with seasoned ground goose meat mixed with plenty of goose fat or the thick fat you find around veal kidneys, all stuffed into the neck skin or rolled into a large piece of skin and hung up to dry for six to eight weeks. They both keep well and are served sliced thin as an appetizer.

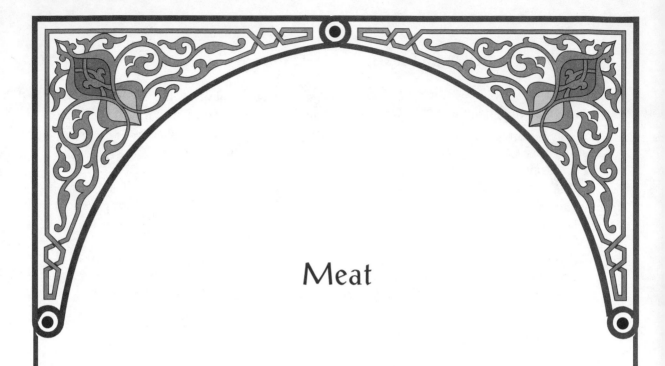

Meat

MANY SEPHARDI COMMUNITIES were poor and could afford meat only on festive occasions. Because the only real meals they had were on the Sabbath and holidays, most of the dishes in this chapter are celebratory dishes. According to North African tradition, this often meant sweetness and making use of fruit, honey, or sugar. Fruit cooked with meat is one of the characteristics of Sephardi cooking, the origin of which can be traced to ancient Baghdad during the Sassanian Persian period.

Mutton and lamb were the traditionally favored meats of the Oriental Sephardim. But in the early part of this century, mutton lost its prestige with modern Westernized urban families. Associated with the Arab way of life, and seen as the meat of the past and of backwardness, it inspired disgust as being too fatty and indigestible and having too strong a smell. Though it was often replaced by beef or veal, lamb (as op-

posed to mutton) was still well esteemed and eaten on special and grand occasions such as the New Year, Passover, and at weddings. Only those who lived in the countryside and had their sheep slaughtered in the village thought that lamb had no taste compared with mutton and that it was good for no one but sick people and very little children.

In France today, beef is used by North African families on festive occasions and it is served with the Sabbath couscous. The only Jews who eat mutton in France are the descendants of the Judaized Berbers from the countryside and the mountains, who had lived like Muslims and were seen as backward and primitive. They still love fat and offal, eat the mutton's head on the New Year, overcook their meat until it falls apart, and spice their food so that it is hot and peppery. Bear these changes in mind and suit your taste as to which meat you use.

Kebabs and Shashlik

Grilled Meats on Skewers

Lamb, usually shoulder, is the traditional meat for this. Turkish and Balkan Jews like their kebab cubes to be about 1–1¼ inches (2½–3 cm). North Africans prefer tiny cubes for their brochettes. Many like their grilled meats *nature*—that is, simply turned in oil with salt and pepper before cooking. But you may like to try marinating in one of the marinades that follow. You can cook the meat under an oven broiler, but it tastes better, of course, over dying embers.

Have 2 lbs (1 kg) meat for 6 people. Cut it into cubes and thread it on skewers. Use those with flat blades, which hold the meat well when you turn them. Pieces of onion and bay leaves are sometimes threaded in between the morsels for flavor, and pieces of fat are squeezed in as lubricant. Oil the grill, so that the meat does not stick. Let the fire die down to embers. Cook, turning the meat over once and being careful not to overcook. It should be brown outside and still tender and juicy inside. Depending on the size and type of meat, this takes from 7 to 15 minutes.

Serve very hot, sprinkled with salt and pepper and accompanied by lemon wedges. A Moroccan way is to pass around finely chopped mild onion, flat-leafed parsley, and ground cumin in little bowls. Serve with rice or with warmed pita bread and a cucumber-and-tomato salad.

Marinades and Sauces for Grilled Meats

Marinate for an hour or longer in one of the following marinades, or use it as a sauce to pass around in little bowls when serving.

- Mix the juice of 1 lemon with 4 tablespoons of olive oil, salt, and pepper. A little wild thyme or marjoram gives a Greek touch. A little dried mint gives a Moroccan touch.
- Mix about ⅔ cup (150 ml) of light vegetable oil with the juice of 1 lemon, 4 crushed cloves of garlic or 1 grated onion, salt, and pepper.
- For a Turkish flavor, turn 1 large onion into juice in the food processor and add salt, pepper, and 1 teaspoon cinnamon.
- An old Hugarian marinade is oil mixed with a good amount of paprika and a little lemon zest.
- For a Tunisian marinade, dilute 1 tablespoon harissa (see page 242) in a glass of water with the juice of 1 lemon. Add ½ teaspoon caraway, ½ teaspoon coriander, salt, and 3 tablespoons olive oil.
- For another Tunisian marinade, dilute 1 teaspoon of harissa in ⅓ cup (80 ml) of water and stir in 1 teaspoon of cumin, salt, the juice of 1 lemon, and 4 tablespoons olive oil.

PRESERVED MEAT

ONCE UPON A TIME, the use of preserved meat was common. The usual way of preserving it was cooking it in fat—like the French preserved goose in *confit d'oie*. That preparation was part of my father's childhood memories. Large quantities of chopped lamb or beef fat were put, with chopped onions, in a large heavy pot over a low flame until the fat melted down and the onions were golden. Then chunks of meat were put in and cooked on very low heat for about an hour. The meat was kept in glass or earthenware jars with the fat poured over to cover it entirely.

There were also those who simmered the meat in oil and kept it covered in oil. In North Africa and the Balkans they cured spiced meat by drying and smoking.

A recipe for "mutton ham" given in *The Jewish Manual*, published in London in 1846, is similar to curing ham: "Choose a fine leg of mutton, rub it in daily with a mixture of three ounces of brown sugar, two ounces of common salt, and half an ounce of saltpetre, continue this process for a fortnight then hang it to dry in wood smoke for ten days longer."

When I was in Granada, Spain, at a center for research on the history of Spanish food called El Molino, I was told Jewish cooking was one of the major influences there. I asked for an example and was given "the way of roasting pig." In response to my disbelief, the mustachioed gastronome explained that the Marranos cooked suckling pig in the way they had cooked baby lamb. Converted Jews made a point of cooking pork to protect themselves from charges by the Inquisition of continuing to practice their old religion. Rabbi Abraham Levy, head of the Sephardi congregation in Britain, told me that he gets a number of inquiries from people in Spain and Portugal curious about their ancestry who claim that it was the practice for generations in their families to hang hams outside the door. That was one of the ways Jews tried to prove their abandonment of their faith. The "mutton ham" may be one of the legacies that Marrano families who returned to Judaism kept from their time as New Christians. The anonymous author of *The Jewish Manual*—believed to be Lady Judith Montefiore—was the wife of Sir Moses, whose family was from Livorno of Marrano descent.

GRILLED MEATS

THE SEPHARDIM ENJOYED good weather in the old countries and indulged as often as possible in outdoor cooking and eating. Old Arab houses had inner courtyards and outdoor ovens and grills where all the cooking took place. It was also common to barbecue on balconies.

One of the impacts of Oriental Jewry on Israel has been the custom of picnicking and barbecuing. On summer evenings and weekends, you see hundreds of little fires in parks and along the seafront, and the seductive smell of roasting meat envelops the streets.

Different meats, from beef and veal to lamb, mutton, and chicken, are used. Most often the meat is cubed and skewered, but cutlets and steaks are also done on the grill. Offal—such as liver, heart, kidneys, spleen, sweetbreads, and testicles—cut in cubes or slices, is very popular, as are merguez sausages. The "Jerusalem grill" of mostly chicken giblets has become an institution to which every community adds its own traditional spicing. There is a custom among North African Jews of barbecuing meats during Passover, because that is how the Hebrews must have cooked in the wilderness during the Exodus from Egypt.

Kofta Meshweya

Grilled Ground Meat Patties

SERVES 6

Grilled ground lamb kofta was our favorite grill in Egypt. You can cook the meat wrapped around skewers or as patties. It needs to be a little fatty so that it remains moist and juicy. Most of the fat melts away in the fierce heat.

> *2 lbs (1 kg) ground lamb or beef with a good*
> *amount of fat*
> *2 medium onions, grated or very finely chopped*
> *1 bunch flat-leafed parsley, finely chopped*
> *(½ cup)*
> *Salt and pepper*

Mix all the ingredients and work with your hands to a paste that holds together. Divide into 8 lumps and pat each around a wide flat-bladed skewer by squashing the skewer into the minced meat in the palm of your hand and pressing the meat over and around it. Alternatively, shape the meat into hamburgers.

Cook over a charcoal fire on an oiled grill about 4 inches (10 cm) from the fire, or under an oven broiler, for 7–10 minutes, until lightly browned, turning over once. Serve hot with a salad and pita bread or rice.

VARIATIONS

• A Turkish way is to flavor with I teaspoon cinnamon and a pinch of cayenne.

• A Syrian-Lebanese way is to sprinkle with the sharp maroon-colored spice called "sumac" or lemon juice when you serve.

• A very herby and spicy Moroccan mixture has I bunch of coriander and a sprig of mint with 2 crushed cloves of garlic, I teaspoon of cumin, I of paprika, and a good pinch of cayenne.

• Burmese Jews (they call grilled meat patties "shoftas") flavor with 2 teaspoons grated ginger and 2 tablespoons finely chopped coriander or mint.

Zeroa
Cold Shoulder of Lamb

Although traditionally, in most countries, the roasted shank bone alone appears on the Seder plate, in Egypt we had a whole cold boiled shoulder of lamb for our Passover ritual. It was one of the gastronomic highlights of the holiday, and each year we remarked how moist and juicy and delicious it was and we wondered why we never made it at other times of the year. We ate the cold meat with our date-and-raisin paste haroset (page 619). When I was one of the judges of a Krug/Telegraph cooking competition and each of the judges had to bring a picnic dish to Raymond Blanc's Manoir des Quat' Saisons, I brought zeroa with haroset, and it was very well received.

To cook the zeroa: Trim some of the excess fat off the meat and cook the shoulder whole as it is, on the bone. Simply boil in salted water to cover (that is all we did) for about 2 hours, until it is very tender. Let it cool in its own broth and

refrigerate, covered. When the fat congeals on the surface, remove it carefully, and leave the meat in the broth until you are ready to serve.

VARIATIONS

• In Morocco, rolled shoulder of lamb—sometimes stuffed with crushed garlic cloves and chopped mint and flat-leafed parsley—was steamed for 2 hours in the top of a *couscoussier* with the lid on and boiling water underneath. To finish, it was turned in a pan in hot oil with a pinch of powdered saffron to give it a golden color. It was served hot or cold with little bowls of salt and cumin for everyone to dip into.

• Apricot and sour cherry sauces (pages 392 and 393) also make good accompaniments.

Vitello Sott'Olio
Cold Veal in Olive Oil

SERVES 8

Cold veal is Sabbath food in Italy. An old way was to cook it "in gelatina" with a calf's foot to produce a jelly. This way, simply boiled and dressed with oil and lemon, and accompanied with a salsa verde, results in moist, tender meat with delicious sharp flavors.

2 lbs (1 kg) veal brisket or rolled shoulder
  or breast
2 stalks celery

1 onion
1 carrot
Salt and pepper
Plenty of light-tasting olive oil
Juice of 1 or more lemons

Put the meat in a large pot with the vegetables and cover with water. Bring to the boil, remove the scum, add some salt and pepper, and simmer for about 2½ hours, or until very tender. Remove from the stock, put it in a bowl just large enough to contain it, and cover with olive oil. Leave overnight and serve cold, thinly sliced. Dress with the olive oil, which should preferably be a little bland, and the lemon juice.

Accompany, if you like, with the following salsa verde.

Salsa Verde

This herby green sauce is usually made up to taste, but here is something to go by: Blend in the food processor a large bunch of flat-leafed parsley (2 cups), stems removed, 1 hard-boiled egg yolk, 1 2-oz (50-g) can anchovy fillets, 4 tablespoons matzo meal moistened with a little of the meat stock, 3 tablespoons capers, 2 crushed garlic cloves, the juice of 1 lemon, and ½ cup (125 ml) or more light olive oil—enough to make a thick cream.

Agneau aux Pruneaux

Lamb with Prunes

SERVES 6

Moroccan Jews adopted the local Muslim tradition of serving meat stews sweetened with honey or sugar on festive occasions. During Passover, mutton or lamb tagines—as stews are called, after the clay pots they used to be cooked in—were eaten, to commemorate the lamb sacrificed by the slaves on the eve of the Exodus. This one with prunes is the most popular. I would rather have it without the honey. The prunes are sweet enough, and the spicing is very subtle.

1 large onion, finely chopped
2 garlic cloves, finely chopped
4 tablespoons peanut or light vegetable oil
2 lbs (1 kg) boned lamb shoulder or fillet of
    neck, cubed and trimmed of excess but not
    all fat
Salt and pepper
½ teaspoon saffron powder
½–1 teaspoon ginger
¼ teaspoon nutmeg
1 lb (500 g) pitted prunes
2 teaspoons cinnamon
1–3 tablespoons honey or sugar (optional)
1 tablespoon sesame seeds
½ cup (100 g) blanched almonds or ½ cup
    (75 g) coarsely chopped walnuts

Fry the onion and garlic in the oil till soft. Add the meat and turn to brown it lightly all over. Add salt, pepper, saffron, ginger, and nutmeg. Cover with water, stir well, and simmer for 1½ hours, or until the meat is very tender, adding a little water if it becomes too dry. Add the prunes, cinnamon, honey or sugar (if using), and plenty of black pepper to mitigate the sweetness. Simmer about 15–20 minutes longer. The sauce should be reduced.

Toast the sesame seeds and almonds or walnuts separately in a dry pan. They should be only very slightly toasted. Serve the lamb hot, sprinkled with sesame seeds and almonds or walnuts.

VARIATIONS

• You may stuff the pitted prunes with walnut halves or blanched almonds.

MERGUEZ

North African Sausages

THESE HOT AND SPICY North African sausages can be found in kosher butcher shops and charcuteries all over France. They are made of lamb or beef ground with fat and mixed with allspice, ground fennel, and coriander and plenty of garlic and harissa (see page 242). They are usually grilled or fried, and feature in egg and couscous dishes and in soups. Cut into small pieces, they make hearty appetizers.

• In *Saveurs de Mon Enfance*, Fortunée Hazan-Arama gives a recipe for mouton aux pruneaux et aux pommes, which was served at Pesah. For this use only half the quantity of prunes and add 1 lb (500 g) peeled and quartered apples.

• A festive dish of the Jews of Fez is agneau aux dattes—lamb with dates—using ½ lb (250 g) of pitted dates instead of prunes, and less or no honey, since the dates are sweet.

Agneau aux Raisins Secs et aux Amandes

Lamb with Raisins and Almonds

SERVES 6

This is a Passover specialty of Fez and Meknes in Morocco. As usual for festive occasions, it is sweetened. Start with only a tiny bit of honey—it may not be to your taste—and add more if you like. It is a lovely dish, the kind the Arabs left all over the Southern Mediterranean.

> *1 lb (500 g) small pickling onions, peeled*
> *5 tablespoons peanut or light vegetable oil*
> *2 lbs (1 kg) lamb shoulder or fillet of neck,*
>   *cubed and trimmed of excess but not*
>   *all fat*
> *Salt and pepper*
> *¼ teaspoon saffron*
> *¾ teaspoon ginger*
> *1⅔ cups (250 g) seedless raisins*
> *1 teaspoon cinnamon*
> *1–3 tablespoons honey (optional)*
> *½ cup (100 g) blanched almonds*

Put the onions in a large pan with 3 tablespoons of oil and the meat, and sauté, stirring, until the meat changes color. Add salt, pepper, saffron, and ginger. Cover with water and simmer for 1½ hours, or until the meat is tender. Add the raisins and cinnamon and cook another 15 minutes. Add the honey, if using, and cook 15 minutes more.

Lightly fry the almonds in the remaining oil until slightly colored. Chop them coarsely or leave them whole. Serve the lamb hot with the almonds sprinkled on top.

Khoresht Beh

Quince Stew

SERVES 6

This is a Persian stew to be eaten with rice. Its success depends on getting the sweet-and-sour flavor and delicate spicing right by tasting. At a gastronomic congress in Jerusalem I was asked to demonstrate it. I found myself having to make enough to give a tasting to 100 people. It was pretty hard going in the kitchens of the ultra-religious hotel, with the rabbinical supervisor looking over my shoulder, and young cooks refusing to be helpful because it was not part of their union-agreed duties, and pretending not to speak English. It took me half an hour to find a sharp knife and a teaspoon, and it was agony getting the cooks to fetch the meat and find quinces at a sufficiently kosher supplier, and having to ask for salt and each spice. I would give the Egyptian name and an Iraqi or Palestinian in the kitchen would shout the Hebrew one. I would mumble searchingly "malh ... malh ..." (bringing words out that I had locked away for 40 years) and "meleh!" came screaming from the other side of the kitchen. In the end it was all great fun. I cooked a gigantic cauldron-full. It took me late into the evening, and one of the cooks put it away in the cool room. The next day, horror of horrors, the cauldron had disappeared. Everyone was mobilized to look for it, but it was never found. The happening was reported by the press, and during the weeks I stayed in Israel I was often asked—by a librarian at the Museum of the Diaspora in Tel Aviv, a bank clerk, etc.—"What happened to the quince stew?" It had acquired a certain mystique, and everyone asked how it was made. There are various versions, but this is the one I used in Jerusalem—minus the yellow split peas (the cooks did not find any).

2 large onions, coarsely chopped
3 tablespoons sunflower oil
2 lbs (1 kg) shoulder of lamb, beef, or veal, trimmed of fat and cut in 1-inch cubes
1½ teaspoons cinnamon
¼ teaspoon nutmeg
Salt and pepper
½ cup (100 g) yellow split peas, soaked in water for 1 hour (optional)
2 large ripe quinces, washed, cored, and cut in thick slices (peeled or not)
4 tablespoons lemon juice
1½–2 tablespoons sugar or to taste

In a large pan, fry the onions in the oil till soft, add the meat, and cook the pieces, turning them, till they are brown all over. Add water to cover, the spices, salt and pepper, and simmer 1 hour.

Stir in the yellow split peas, and add the

quinces and water if necessary. Simmer about ½ hour, or until tender (the cooking time varies, depending on the variety of quince and their ripeness), adding lemon and sugar for the last 15 minutes.

VARIATIONS

• Another delectable meat-and-quince recipe said to be "Georgian style" among the Jews of Turkey, called "komshuyani," is given in the Turkish book *Sefarad Yemekleri:* For 4, fry 1 large chopped onion in 4 tablespoons sunflower oil till soft. Add 1½ lbs (750 g) lamb cut in cubes and turn to brown it all over. Add salt, pepper, 1 teaspoon ginger, and ½ teaspoon allspice. Add 1 lb (500 g) tomatoes, peeled and chopped, and water to cover, then simmer 1 hour with the lid on, till the meat is tender. Add 1 lb (500 g) quince, peeled and sliced, the juice of 1 lemon, and 2 tablespoons or more sugar. Add water if necessary and simmer for 25 minutes, or until the quince is tender and the sauce reduced. Serve the meat surrounded by the slices of quince. I served it to a friend from Iraq and he said the dish was eaten in his community too.

• There is a similar Bulgarian recipe for veal with quince and prunes, called "hamin dulce," in which 2 tablepoons of sugar, melted and browned, give a delicious caramel flavor.

Lahma Mahshi bil Karaz
Shoulder of Lamb with Rice Stuffing and Sour Cherry Sauce

SERVES 10–12

The combination of lamb with apricots has been popular in the West for some time, but lamb with sour cherries has not yet become fashionable. In the old days, Syrian Jews used sour cherries as an alternative to apricots. They used fresh ones and pitted them. Now that I can find them pitted and dried from California at the supermarket, I have started using these. Stuffed breast of lamb was our special Passover dish in Egypt. We cut a pouch to stuff it, but it is easier to cook the stuffing separately, and the shoulder is meatier than the breast and, because it is very fatty, ideally suited to being roasted.

> *2 shoulders of lamb*
> *Salt and black pepper*
> *1–2 tablespoons sunflower oil*
> *½ lb (250 g) dried pitted sour cherries*
> *Juice of ½ lemon*

For the stuffing

> *1 medium onion, chopped*
> *3 tablespoons sunflower oil*
> *5 oz (150 g) ground beef*
> *1¼ cups (250 g) long-grain rice*
> *Salt and pepper*
> *4 tablespoons pine nuts*
> *3 tablespoons currants or raisins (optional)*

Rub the shoulders with salt, pepper, and oil and place them in a baking dish. Roast at 400°F (200°C) for about 1½–2 hours, or until the meat is browned and done to your taste. Pour the fat out of the dish after about 1 hour, and pour more out again before serving.

In the meantime, soak the dried cherries in water to cover for ½ hour, then simmer in the same water for about ½ hour, until they are soft and the liquid is reduced, adding the juice of ½ lemon.

Prepare the stuffing so that it is ready at the same time as the meat, or heat it up again, covered, in the oven. In a large saucepan, fry the onion in oil till golden. Add the ground meat and stir, crushing it with a wooden spoon, until it changes color. Add the rice and stir until well coated, then pour in 2 cups (500 ml) of water. Add salt and pepper and simmer undisturbed with the lid on for about 25 minutes, or until the water has been absorbed and the rice is tender. Stir in the pine nuts and, if using, the currants or raisins.

Serve the meat with the stuffing, and pass the cherry sauce around for people to help themselves.

VARIATION

• For an apricot sauce, which is more commonly used than dried sour cherries: Simmer ½ lb (250 g) dried apricots—a tart, natural, not sweetened or honeyed variety—in water to cover with the juice of ½ lemon until very soft. Blend to a cream in the food processor.

Kofta bil Karaz
Meatballs with a Sour Cherry Sauce

SERVES 6

This is something Syrian Jews make for parties, served on toasted bread. It is very elegant and exquisite.

> 1½ lbs (750 g) lean lamb
> Salt and pepper
> 1 teaspoon cinnamon
> ½ teaspoon allspice
> 3 tablespoons finely chopped flat-leafed parsley
> ½ cup (75 g) pine nuts, lightly toasted
>   (optional)
> Light vegetable oil
> 1 large onion, coarsely chopped
> 1¼ lbs (600 g) morello cherries, pitted, or
>   10 oz (300 g) dried pitted sour cherries
>   soaked for ½ hour in just enough water
>   to cover
> Juice of 1 lemon or 2 tablespoons tamarind
>   paste
> 1–2 tablespoons of sugar or to taste (optional)
> 12 slices bread, crusts removed

Blend the meat to a paste in a food processor. Add about ¾ teaspoon salt, pepper, cinnamon, allspice, and parsley and blend a little longer, until well mixed. Then work the pine nuts, if using, into the paste with your hands. Take lumps of paste the size of small walnuts and roll into little balls, pushing the pine nuts to the center as much as possible. Fry quickly in shallow oil, turning them over

Meatballs with Cherry Sauce (cont.)

until lightly browned and still pink and juicy inside.

Make the cherry sauce. In another pan, fry the onion in 2 tablespoons of oil till soft. Add the cherries and half-cover with water (the dried ones with their soaking water). Add the lemon or tamarind and sugar if you like (it depends on the sweetness of the fruit and your taste). Simmer, stirring, until the cherries are soft. Put the meatballs in the sauce and simmer 5–10 minutes.

Toast the bread in the oven till lightly colored. I have used different kinds of bread and have found a brioche type particularly good.

Serve the meatballs, hot or cold, with their sauce, on the slices of toast. The bread soaks up the delicious flavorsome sauce and becomes soft and bloated.

VARIATION

• I have tried to use a cherry compote and also canned cherries in syrup, both with good results. In these cases, drain the cherries well and do not add any sugar.

THE BABYLONIAN JEWS IN THE LAND
—— OF THE TWO RIVERS ——

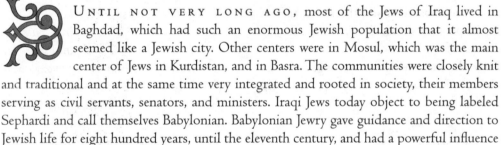 UNTIL NOT VERY LONG AGO, most of the Jews of Iraq lived in Baghdad, which had such an enormous Jewish population that it almost seemed like a Jewish city. Other centers were in Mosul, which was the main center of Jews in Kurdistan, and in Basra. The communities were closely knit and traditional and at the same time very integrated and rooted in society, their members serving as civil servants, senators, and ministers. Iraqi Jews today object to being labeled Sephardi and call themselves Babylonian. Babylonian Jewry gave guidance and direction to Jewish life for eight hundred years, until the eleventh century, and had a powerful influence on the Sephardi world, especially in North Africa and Spain, but the Jews of Iraq gained little from Iberian Sephardi culture except the liturgy, which they adopted in the seventeenth century.

Theirs was the oldest community of the Diaspora, and its ties with the Holy Land have always been strong. It was established in 586 B.C., after the destruction of the First Temple, when the Babylonian monarch Nebuchadnezzar conquered Judea and deported the population to Babylon. When the Persian King Cyrus allowed the exiles to return to the land of Israel fifty years later, the majority decided to stay. Almost all the Jews of Iraq are descended from those brought as captives twenty-five hundred years ago and settled on the banks of the rivers Tigris and Euphrates, in Mesopotamia, near the city of Babylon. Their ancestors built what was until the ninth century A.D. the leading community of the Jewish dispersion. It was a self-governing community, with its own courts and administration, centers of learning, and established nobility. Until the tenth century, it was lead by exilarchs—Jewish "princes" in exile who traced their ancestry to the House of David. Their spiritual leaders—called *geonim* (plural of *gaon*)—were scholars at the head of the great academies where two hundred years earlier the Babylonian Talmud, one of the monuments of Jewish learning, was composed.

In 227 A.D., Babylon came under the rule of the Persian Sassanians, who maintained their hold for four centuries. In the eighth century, Baghdad became the capital of the Muslim Empire. It also became the center of Babylonian Jewish life and learning. Under both Persian and Muslim Arab rule, a new class of wealthy Jewish merchants arose who were involved in international trade, and in particular the silk trade between China and the Mediterranean world.

When Baghdad declined in the tenth century, the Jews became very poor. Their unique position in the Jewish Diaspora and intellectual and religious standing were lost, while their lot fluctuated through centuries of Mongol, Persian, and Ottoman rule. At the end of the

Jewish family home with courtyard in Baghdad, Iraq, 1891

The Sassoon family of Baghdad (who founded the Bombay community) and the family of Rabbi Yossef Hayim, 1870

nineteenth century, although many of the city's Jews had emigrated to Kurdistan, Persia, Syria, Egypt, India, and the Far East, they were still the largest minority in the population. After Salonika, the Baghdad community was the most numerous, important, and prosperous in the Ottoman Empire. And when the British occupied Baghdad in 1917, Jews represented well over a third of the inhabitants, which also included Sunnis, Shias, Christians, Kurds, Turks, and Persians.

The community was made up of a small number of rich bankers and merchants; a middle class of doctors, lawyers, engineers, small traders, retailers, and government employees; a large poor class which included artisans; and a group of professional beggars. Many Jews were educated through the Alliance Israélite Universelle schools, which taught French and English. Jews literally monopolized the foreign trade, dealing with the network of Baghdadi Jews who had settled in India, England, and the Far East. They traded in sugar, coffee, pharmaceuticals, metals, haberdashery, precious stones, jewelry, wool, skins, guns, and carpets.

A chief item was cloth from Manchester, which they re-exported to Persia. The main city markets were dominated by Jews, and everything closed on Saturday.

The Jews of Baghdad spoke Arabic with a distinctive accent, and among themselves a Judeo-Arabic dialect with Persian words. Half of them did not have surnames and were known by their fathers' first names, the most popular being Hezkel, Salman, Daniel, and Sasson. Even when most of the well-to-do had moved away from the Jewish quarter in the old city, they went back to shop for food at the Souk Hannoun, where you could buy live poultry and have it slaughtered by a *shohet*. The *shohet* was usually also a Hebrew teacher who taught in people's homes. He would sometimes be asked to slaughter a chicken when he came, or the occasional sheep, or even a cow in sacrifice if somebody had had a bad dream or was sick. The meat would be given to the poor. There were several synagogues and several Jewish schools, including the Alliance (see page 229), the midrash, and one for blind students. Schoolchildren always wore boots, because the sewers overflowed when it rained and it was always muddy. They bought lablabi (boiled chickpeas) from Jewish vendors, and a mixture of sumac and zahtar in paper cones, to eat on their way home.

Iraqi Jews had a fixed weekly menu. Thursday was for kichree (lentils and rice), vegetables, and dairy foods. On Friday the fishermen brought the fish in early from the river, in time for the Jews to prepare fried fish and arook. They also had chicken soup with chicken pieces and rice. On Saturdays in winter they went to synagogue early, and when they returned for breakfast ate tabyit—chicken stuffed with and also buried in rice—which had cooked overnight. Then they sat in the sun on the balcony or the roof terrace with their hamine eggs, fried eggplant, mango pickle, and bread, or they took these to a picnic on an island in the river. In the summer they set out porous water jugs, which sweated and kept the water cool on the terraces. They also left pots of kubba—meat dumplings in a bamia (okra) stew, which had been prepared on Friday—on the roof terrace, for the Saturday lunch. At night they slept on the terrace to catch the breeze.

Because of their strict adherence to Jewish dietary traditions, everything was made at home. Jewish women from the old quarter hired themselves out and went from house to house to do seasonal jobs like preparing large trays of tomato paste, which was left out to dry on rooftops; sheets of dried apricot called "qamardine"; manna (see page 23), which they also called "abba kadrassi" ("from the sky"), and a date syrup called "halek" (see page 627). They also made sausages with sheep-intestine casings. People had their own wood-burning ovens (tandoors) in the house. Cooks came around every day to make bread for them and sometimes also breakfast. The tandoor was also used for grilling and roasting meat and for stewing. On the Sabbath, Jewish women called out to Muslims passing in the street to turn on their lights.

Though Muslims came to eat in Jews' homes, Jews could only have tea in Muslim homes. So their dishes took shape in their own particular way. Even if they ate like the rest of the population, they had many dishes of their own, and also characteristic flavors. They were particularly fond of the sweet-and-sour in their stews, which they called "hamud," meaning "sour" (when a stew was not sweet and sour it was called "helou," which means "sweet," although it was not necessarily sweet), and obtained with a mixture of vinegar, tamarind, or pomegranate concentrate, and sugar. Various characteristics that seem to be a legacy of the old cuisine of the Baghdad Caliphate—which was based on Sassanian Persian styles, such as sweet-and-sour flavors, little meat dumplings, and stews with meat and fruit—could be found in Jewish dishes more than in Muslim.

For reasons of geography, the dishes of the Jews of Basra were very Persian and also Indian. Those of Mosul were more Turkish and Kurdish. There were Kurdish Jews in Persia and Turkey, but the majority were in Iraq, and their center was Mosul. They lived in villages and small towns in the mountainous regions of Kurdistan. They were craftsmen, peddlers, and merchants, and many lived off the land. They spoke ancient Aramaic, not Arabic. Their cooking, based on cracked wheat and legumes, is rough and rustic. The distinctive characteristic is the great variety of kubba (dumplings) that go into soups and stews.

In the eighteenth and nineteenth centuries, under Turkish rule, repressive measures resulted in large numbers of Iraqi Jews immigrating to India, China, Indonesia, and the Sudan. The communities they formed in these new countries kept up the old cooking traditions, but their dishes acquired new flavors and local touches, and they developed special dishes of their own.

After the creation of the State of Israel, the Jews in Iraq were subjected to harassment, discrimination, and extortion. In 1951, there was a mass exodus. In an airlift known as "Operation Ezra and Nehemiah," all but a few left the country, mainly for Israel.

Kofta Mishmisheya

Meatballs in Apricot Sauce

SERVES 4

Iraqi Jews are fond of this dish, which is served with plain rice. It is interesting to note that a similar meat stew with apricots, called "mishmishiya," appeared in a thirteenth-century Baghdad cookbook. You must use natural, tart dried apricots for this, not the sweetened or honeyed dried ones more commonly available. Getting the right balance between the natural sweetness of the fruit and the sharpness of dried lime and fresh lemon juice is important.

1 large onion, chopped
3–4 tablespoons sunflower oil
1½ lbs (750 g) ground lamb
1 teaspoon ground dried lime (from Indian and Oriental stores)
¼ teaspoon ground cloves
¼ teaspoon allspice
Salt and pepper

3–4 tablespoons tomato paste
7 oz (200 g) dried apricots, soaked in water
   for ½ hour
3–4 tablespoons currants or raisins
Juice of 1 lemon or to taste
1 teaspoon sugar

In a large frying, pan fry the onion in oil till golden. With your hands, work the meat into a paste with the dried lime, cloves, allspice, ¾ teaspoon salt, and pepper, and roll into walnut-sized balls. Add them to the pan and cook, turning them to brown them all over. Stir in the tomato paste, add the drained apricots and the currants or raisins, and cover with water. Simmer for about 25 minutes. Crush the apricots a bit with a fork, add lemon juice and sugar and a little salt and pepper, and simmer for another 20 minutes.

Hamim de Kastanya

Lamb with Chestnuts

SERVES 6–8

This Judeo-Spanish stew from Turkey is a delight, and peeling chestnuts after roasting them is easier than you think.

   2 lbs (1 kg) lamb from the shoulder or
      neck
   1 large onion, chopped
   4 tablespoons sunflower oil
   Salt and pepper
   1½ teaspoons cinnamon
   ½–1 teaspoon allspice
   1½ lbs (750 g) chestnuts

Juice of ½ lemon (optional)
3 tablespoons chopped flat-leafed parsley
   (optional)

Trim the meat of much but not all of its fat and cut it into about 1¼-inch (3-cm) cubes.

Fry the onion in the oil on very low heat, stirring occasionally, until golden. Add the meat and turn to brown it all over. Add salt and pepper, cinnamon, and allspice, cover with water, and bring to the boil. Remove the scum and simmer 1½–2 hours, until the meat is very tender.

To peel the chestnuts, make a slit on one side with a sharp-pointed knife and grill under the broiler, turning them over once, until they are only slightly colored and the skins can come off easily. Peel them while still hot. Fifteen minutes before the end of cooking the lamb, add the chestnuts. If you like, add the lemon juice and serve sprinkled with parsley.

Veau Sofrito

Braised Veal with Turmeric and Lemon

SERVES 6

Many very different dishes are called simply "sofrito." Every community knows exactly what they mean by it, but the dish is always different. I was very surprised to find that what Turks called "sofrito" was meatballs cooked in the juice of acid plums. Our "sofrito" in Egypt was foreknuckle (shin) of veal—called "mosate"—cooked with lemon, garlic, and turmeric, and with potatoes thrown in at the end. The connective tissue of the shin produced a rich, gelatinous sauce. There is controversy about the potatoes. Fundamentalists say they should be cubed and deep-fried in oil first. When I told my cousin that I preferred not to fry the potatoes beforehand, she replied, "Then don't do it at all. That is not a sofrito." However, after phoning around and getting a consensus, I found that many people had switched to a lighter version. When she had grown old and tired, my mother bought peeled new potatoes from the supermarket to throw in. Sofrito was a traditional Friday-night dish.

> 2 lbs (1 kg) shin or foreknuckle of veal, cut
>   in large pieces
> 3 tablespoons sunflower oil
> Salt and pepper
> ½ teaspoon turmeric (optional)
> 1 onion, cut in half
> 1 lb (500 g) potatoes, cut in small cubes,
>   or tiny new potatoes
> Oil for deep-frying (optional)
> Juice of ½ lemon

In a pan, brown the meat on all sides in the oil. Add salt and pepper and turmeric and half-cover with water. Put in the onion and simmer very slowly, covered, for 1½ hours, turning the meat every so often, and adding water by the glassful as it becomes reduced.

If you like, deep-fry the potatoes in oil until golden and drain on paper towels. Then throw them in with the meat and cook for 15 minutes, stirring, so that they absorb the sauce. Alternatively, add the new potatoes and more water to cover and simmer 25 minutes more. Add the lemon juice before serving.

VARIATION

- Tunisians use a cubed shoulder of lamb in their sofrito, include plenty of garlic, and add a lemon, peeled and cut in slices.

Ingriyi

Sweet-and-Sour Meat and Eggplant

SERVES 8 OR MORE

There are different versions of this Iraqi Jewish dish. The following, using cubed rather than ground meat, and tamarind and sugar for flavoring, is the most delicious. Lamb was the traditional meat, but now beef is also used.

There is a curiously similar recipe (without tomatoes, of course) called "tabahiya" in a thirteenth-century Arab cooking manual attributed to one Ibrahim al Mahdi.

> 2½ lbs (1¼ kg) lamb or beef, cubed
> Salt
> 2 large eggplants, weighing about 2 lbs
>   (1 kg), cut in ½-inch (1¼-cm) slices
> 2 lbs (1 kg) onions, sliced
> Sunflower oil for frying
> 2½ lbs (1¼ kg) large tomatoes, peeled and
>   sliced
> Pepper
> 2 tablespoons tamarind paste
> 1–2 tablespoons sugar or to taste

Simmer the meat in water to cover with a little salt for 1½–2 hours, until tender.

Sprinkle the eggplant slices with salt and leave for 1 hour to draw out their juices.

Fry the onions in 3 tablespoons of oil over low heat till very soft and really brown, which gives them a caramelized taste.

Rinse and dry the eggplant in a tea towel, then fry briefly in very hot oil, turning over once, until lightly browned. Drain on paper towels. Alternatively, you can brush the slices with oil and cook them under the broiler.

In a baking dish, assemble layers of eggplant slices, drained meat (keep the stock), onions, and tomatoes, sprinkling each with a little salt and pepper.

Heat about 1 cup (250 ml) of the meat stock in a small pan and stir in the tamarind and sugar. When the paste has dissolved, pour evenly over the layers. Bake at 350°F (180°C) for 30–40 minutes. Serve hot with rice.

VARIATIONS

• Instead of cubed meat, use ground meat and fry it in 2–3 tablespoons of oil for 10 minutes, stirring often.

• Instead of tamarind, use the juice of 1 lemon.

• Ingriyi became the traditional festive and Sabbath dish of the Bombay community, which was formed in a great part by Jews from Iraq. But they make it with chicken instead of meat. It is served hot with rice on Friday night, and again, cold, on Saturday.

Moussaka

SERVES 8

This is the way it was made by Jews in Egypt. It is less heavy and more fresh-tasting than the usual versions.

2 lbs (1 kg) eggplants, cut in thin slices
Salt
Oil for frying
2 medium onions, coarsely chopped
4 cloves garlic, crushed
2 lbs (1 kg) ground lamb or beef
1½ teaspoons cinnamon
½ teaspoon allspice
Pepper
2 tablespoons tomato puree (a pure, unflavored type)
A bunch of flat-leafed parsley, finely chopped (½ cup)
1½ lbs (750 g) tomatoes, thinly sliced
1 teaspoon sugar or more (optional)

Sprinkle the eggplant slices with salt and leave them for about an hour, then rinse and dry them on a tea towel or paper towels. Fry in very hot oil very briefly, turning them over once, so that they are only lightly browned all over and do not have much time to absorb too much oil (they are cooked further later). Drain on layers of paper towel and cover with more paper towels to get rid of the excess oil. Instead of frying, you may brush the eggplants with oil and grill them under the broiler.

Fry the onions in 2 tablespoons of oil until soft and golden, add the garlic, and fry till the aroma rises. Add the ground meat, cinnamon, allspice, salt, and plenty of pepper. Crush the meat with a fork and mix well until it changes color. Add the tomato puree and cook for about 10 minutes, then stir in the flat-leafed parsley.

Assemble the moussaka in a baking dish. Arrange a layer of fried or broiled eggplant slices at the bottom. Cover with a layer of tomato slices. (If the tomatoes are not tasty enough, sprinkle them with a teaspoon or more of sugar.) Sprinkle lightly with salt and spread the ground-meat filling on top. Cover with a second layer of eggplant and tomato slices. Bake uncovered for 30–45 minutes at 350°F (180°C).

VARIATIONS

• Zucchini may be used instead of eggplant.

• Another favorite is a potato moussaka. Use layers of thinly sliced new potatoes—about 2 lbs (1 kg)—instead of the eggplant. It will need longer cooking—1½ hours or longer.

Loubia

Black-Eyed Pea Stew

SERVES 8

This was a Rosh Hashanah (New Year's) dish in Egypt. The black-eyed peas symbolized fertility and the hope for many births in the family. They were in season, and we used them fresh. In London my mother always used dried beans. Last year I was offered fresh ones from France for the occasion, and I jumped at it. My daughter, just arrived from New York, offered to pod them. It was such an effort for so few tiny beans that we kept saying they must have been mad to do this in Egypt. Of course, it was the cook who did it.

1 onion, chopped
3 tablespoons sunflower oil
2 garlic cloves, minced or crushed in a press
1½ lbs (750 g) lamb or veal, cubed

1 lb (500 g) tomatoes, peeled and chopped
3 tablespoons tomato paste
1 lb (500 g) dried black-eyed peas, soaked for 1 hour
1 teaspoon cinnamon
½ teaspoon allspice
Salt and pepper
1–2 teaspoons sugar

Fry the onion in the oil till golden. Add the garlic, and when the aroma rises add the meat. Stir to brown it all over. Add the tomatoes and tomato paste.

Drain the black-eyed peas, and simmer in fresh water for 15 minutes, then drain and add them to the meat. Add cinnamon and allspice and cook for 2 hours, adding salt and pepper to taste and the sugar after about 1 hour.

Avas

Haricot Bean Stew

SERVES 6

This is the beloved stew of Salonikans, also called by the endearment "avicas" (alluding to the smallness of the beans). It was served on Friday night with rice, and enough was made so that it could be eaten again on Saturday. Sephardi families in Palestine adopted it as the washday dish avicas con arroz.

2 onions, chopped
3 tablespoons extra-virgin olive oil or vegetable oil
3 garlic cloves, chopped
1½ lbs (750 g) beef or lamb, cubed

1 lb (500 g) small dry white haricot beans,
    soaked for 2 hours or overnight
1 lb (500 g) tomatoes, peeled and chopped
1–2 teaspoons sugar or to taste
Salt and pepper
Juice of 1 lemon
1 lemon cut in wedges (optional)

Fry the onions in the oil till golden. Add the garlic and, when it begins to color, add the meat and stir to brown it all over. Then put in the beans and tomatoes, add sugar, and cover with water. Simmer for 2–3 hours, until the meat and beans are very tender, adding salt and pepper when they begin to soften, and the lemon juice just before serving. Serve with plain rice, accompanied, if you like, with lemon wedges.

VARIATIONS

- In the Arab world, the dish is called "yakhni fassoulia." Three tablespoons of tomato paste is used instead of tomatoes, and I teaspoon of allspice is added.

- In Tunisia, boeuf aux haricots blancs is flavored with ½ teaspoon of harissa and 2 teaspoons of cinnamon or cumin, with a bunch of coriander, chopped, added at the end. Spicy sausages called "merguez" are sometimes fried and served in the stew.

- In Algeria, meatballs are dropped into a pot of beans cooked with tomatoes. For the meatballs, blend in a food processor I lb (500 g) ground beef, I slice bread soaked and squeezed, I egg, salt, pepper, a pinch of nutmeg, ½ teaspoon ground cumin, ½ teaspoon ground caraway, and 2 teaspoons dried mint. Roll into little balls and cook with the beans for the last ½ hour.

- In another Judeo-Spanish dish, avas kon espinaka, 1½ lbs (750 g) spinach is added at the end and cooked covered until softened.

Ragout aux Épinards
Tunisian Meat Stew with Yellow Split Peas and Spinach

SERVES 6–8

1 large onion, chopped
4 tablespoons extra-virgin olive or light
    vegetable oil
5 garlic cloves, chopped
1½ lbs (750 g) beef, cubed
1 cup (350 g) yellow split peas
Salt and pepper
1½ teaspoons cinnamon
1½ lbs (750 g) spinach
A few sprigs of mint, chopped, or 3 teaspoons
    dried mint

You will need a very large pan, because the spinach is bulky before it cooks down. In the pan, fry the onion in the oil till soft and golden. Add the garlic and stir till the aroma rises. Add the meat and cook, stirring, to brown all over.

Add the yellow split peas, cover with water, and bring to the boil. Remove any scum, then simmer for 1 hour. Add salt, pepper, and cinnamon, and water if necessary, and cook for ½ hour longer, or until the meat and split peas are very tender. Now put in the spinach and the mint. The spinach is usually cut into ribbons, but I prefer to leave it whole, and I do not remove the stems if they are thin. Cook, covered, until the spinach crumples to a soft mass, and serve hot.

VARIATION

- Replace the yellow split peas with chickpeas soaked for 2 hours or overnight.

Lahma bi Bamia

Meat with Okra

SERVES 4

One of the usual, everyday meals of Jews in Egypt was a meat stew with a vegetable such as okra, green beans, or peas. This was also true for many Oriental communities.

1 lb (500 g) okra
2 cloves garlic, finely chopped
2 tablespoons sunflower oil
1 lb (500 g) lamb or beef, cubed
1 lb (500 g) tomatoes, peeled and chopped
Salt and pepper
1 teaspoon sugar
A bunch of coriander, coarsely chopped
(½ cup)

Wash the okra and trim the stem ends. Fry the garlic in the oil, add the meat, and cook, stirring, until browned all over. Add the tomatoes and water to cover. Season with salt, pepper, and sugar and simmer 1 hour, or until the meat is tender. Add the okra, and simmer about 25 minutes, until tender. Add the coriander. Serve with plain rice or roz bil shaghria (see page 460).

VARIATIONS

• Jews from Iraq give it a sweet-and-sour flavor by adding the juice of 1 lemon or 2 tablespoons of tamarind, ½–2 tablespoons of sugar, and 1 tablespoon of dried mint. They call it "bamia hamud."

• In Iraq and Turkey they used tiny dry okra (bamia) when the vegetables were out of season.

They bought them threaded on a string. These must be simmered for 15 minutes in boiling salted water before being rinsed in cold water and added to the stew.

• For lahma bi fassoulia hadra, green beans are used instead of okra.

Lamb with Red Chilies and Tamarind

SERVES 12–14

My guests raved about this dish, and it really is magnificent. The recipe was contributed by a Mrs. L. Samuel for the "Bene Israel Cook-Book," distributed in manuscript by the Jewish Religious Union Sisterhood in Bombay. In India, mutton is used, but lamb will do very well. Because it is very easy to make in large quantities, I strongly recommend it for a party. The recipe has been adapted to make it easier, with already ground spices and store-bought tamarind paste and creamed coconut. You can also buy boned shoulder and clean tiny new potatoes, which do not need peeling. The beauty of this dish is the sweet-and-sour, hot-and-spicy symphony of flavors. The secret is to taste and, starting with these quantities of aromatics, increase them if you wish, to your liking. Bene Israel dishes are usually very hot, but some families like their food not hot at all. Though there are many chilies in this recipe, they are the very tiny ones, which can be bought in packages at Indian and Oriental stores. You may of course use fewer—as few as 3 or 4. My way is to take them out during the cooking, when I have tasted the stew and found it peppery enough. This is easy to do, for they float on the surface.

2 lbs (1 kg) onions, sliced or coarsely chopped

6–8 tablespoons vegetable oil

4½ lbs (2 kg) lamb shoulder or fillet of neck or a mixture of the two

6–10 large garlic cloves, crushed

1 teaspoon cumin

2 teaspoons ground coriander

3 teaspoons ground cinnamon

2 teaspoons ground cloves

8–10 tiny dried red chilies

3 lbs (1½ kg) tiny new potatoes

3½ oz (90 g) creamed coconut in a hard block or 8 oz (250 g) canned coconut cream (for both, see page 235)

3 tablespoons tamarind paste (can be found in Indian and Oriental stores)

3 tablespoons sugar

Fry the onions in 3–4 tablespoons of oil on very low heat until soft and golden, keeping the lid on and stirring occasionally to keep the onions from burning. It may take 30–45 minutes because of the large quantity.

Trim off skin and excess, but not all, fat from the meat and cut it into 1½-inch (4-cm) pieces. Fry in 3–4 tablespoons of oil in batches in a large, heavy-bottomed pan, turning the pieces to brown them all over.

Add the garlic, cumin, and coriander to the onions and stir well for a minute or so, then add the spiced onions to the meat. Cover with about 4 cups (1 liter) of water and bring to the boil. Remove the scum and add cinnamon, cloves, and chilies, then simmer, covered, on low heat for 1½–2 hours, or until the meat is very tender. I prefer to remove the chilies at this stage.

Now put in the potatoes, peeled or simply well washed (I do not peel them), and add about 2½ cups (600 ml) of water—just enough to cover. Add the creamed coconut cut into pieces or the canned coconut cream, the tamarind, and the sugar and simmer for another 30–40 minutes, until the potatoes are tender. There should be a lot of sauce.

Serve with plain rice, chapatis, or bread.

Veau aux Topinambours et Petits Pois

Veal with Peas and Jerusalem Artichokes

SERVES 6

This North African dish can also be made with lamb.

2 lbs (1 kg) breast or shoulder of veal, cubed

3 garlic cloves, finely chopped

4 tablespoons peanut or light vegetable oil

Salt and pepper

1 lb (500 g) Jerusalem artichokes, peeled

Juice of ½ lemon

1 lb (500 g) tiny green peas (petits pois), fresh or frozen

Sauté the meat with the garlic in the oil till lightly browned. Add salt and pepper and water to cover and cook for 1½ hours. Add the Jerusalem artichokes, more salt and pepper and water to cover, if necessary, and the lemon juice. Cook another 15 minutes; then add the peas and cook 4–5 minutes or until they are tender.

Agneau aux Fèves Vertes et aux Amandes

Lamb with Fresh Fava Beans and Almonds

SERVES 8

This ancient Berber dish was served between Purim and Pesah in Morocco. Fava beans are the food of Passover because that is what the Hebrews ate when they were slaves in Egypt. In the Berber villages, new green almonds—it was their season, too—were used.

> 4 tablespoons peanut or light vegetable oil
> 2 lbs (1 kg) mutton or lamb, cut in large pieces
> 2 cups (500 ml) water
> Salt and pepper
> ½ teaspoon mace
> 2 onions, chopped
> 1 cup (200 g) green or blanched almonds
> 1 lb (500 g) fresh fava beans (weighed after shelling)
> 1 tablespoon honey

Heat 2 tablespoons of oil in a large pot, put in the meat, and turn it to brown slightly all over. Add the water and bring to the boil. Season with salt and pepper and add the mace. Simmer for 2 hours, adding a little water if necessary. In a separate pan fry the onions in the remaining oil until golden, then stir in the almonds. Add the onions and almonds and the fava beans to the meat and stir in the honey. Cook on low heat for 15 minutes, or until the almonds and beans are tender.

Kofta à la Sauce Tomate

Meatballs in Tomato Sauce

SERVES 6

Served with rice, this is one of the homely everyday dishes of virtually every Sephardi community. We called them "blehat." In Turkey they call them "yullikas." In the old days people fried the meatballs first, but now you often find them simply poached in the sauce. Sometimes they are briefly roasted in the oven at high heat to brown them slightly and firm them before stewing.

> 1¼ lbs (600 g) ground lamb, beef, or veal
> 1 large onion, finely chopped or grated
> About ½–¾ teaspoon salt
> Pepper
> 1 teaspoon cinnamon
> ½ teaspoon allspice
> Sunflower oil for frying (optional)

For the tomato sauce

> 4 garlic cloves, minced or crushed in a press
> 2 tablespoons sunflower oil
> 2 lbs (1 kg) tomatoes, peeled and chopped, or a 28-oz (800-g) can of tomatoes
> Salt and pepper
> 2 tablespoons tomato puree
> 1–2 teaspoons sugar

Mix the meat with the onion, salt, pepper, cinnamon, and allspice and knead to a soft paste. Make little balls or ovals the size of a small walnut. You may fry very briefly in oil, shaking the

KOFTA—BOULETTES— ALBONDIGAS— YULLIKAS—MEATBALLS

THE JEWISH FONDNESS for meatballs is legendary. One explanation given is that they were a way of making meat go far, another that they were a way of tenderizing otherwise tough kosher meat. But it also has to do with the delicacy of spicing that can be achieved.

John Cooper (*Eat and Be Satisfied*) found a recipe for albondigas in the *Libro Novo*, published in Venice in 1549. They were meatballs made with ground veal, herbs, raisins, and hard-boiled egg yolks, and they were cooked in a saffron soup. It sounds as though the dish came to Venice with the Iberian refugees. *The Jewish Manual*, published in England in 1846, has an Iberian-inspired almondegos soup with veal meatballs and a ground-almond and egg-and-lemon finish.

Meatballs are part of an ancient Arab heritage (the word "albondigas" comes from the Arabic). Early Arab cooking manuals are full of recipes for them. They have remained the versatile mainstay of Oriental Jews, served also on the Sabbath and grand occasions. Formed into little round balls or tapered or made into cigars or small oval shapes or hamburger-type patties, they are usually cooked in a sauce, or in a stew with vegetables and sometimes also fruit. Meatballs in which vegetables are worked in with the meat are uniquely Jewish. They are part of the Judeo-Spanish tradition of Turkey and the Balkans and also of Tunisia. Rice and cracked wheat are worked into the meat in Iraq and Iran. Jews of Turkey and the Balkans add 1 or 2 slices of soaked bread, squeezed dry, and an egg to the ground meat, which gives it a softer, creamy texture.

Meatballs are particularly tasty because aromatics are incorporated into the meat paste. You can guess from the flavor where the cook has come from. Those from Egypt season with cumin and ground coriander. Those from Turkey favor cinnamon and allspice. Moroccans use many spices and often keep a spice mixture specially for meatballs in a jar. A spice mixture for meatballs given by Rivka Levy Mellul in *La Cuisine Marocaine* comprises 2 teaspoons mace, 1 teaspoon black pepper, 1 teaspoon ground ginger, 1 teaspoon white pepper, 1 teaspoon cinnamon, 1 teaspoon turmeric, and 1 teaspoon nutmeg.

pan, to brown them slightly all over, then drain on paper towels. Alternatively, put them on a baking sheet and roast them for about 7 minutes in the hottest oven, until slightly colored.

For the tomato sauce: In a large saucepan, fry the garlic in the oil till colored. Add the tomatoes, salt, pepper, tomato puree, and sugar and simmer 15 minutes. Then put in the meatballs and simmer another 20 minutes.

Serve with rice.

VARIATIONS

• Tunisian meatballs may have 3 table-spoons chopped flat-leafed parsley or coriander, I tablespoon chopped mint, a small onion chopped fine, a crushed garlic clove, I teaspoon cinnamon, I teaspoon rosebud powder, and ½ teaspoon harissa.

• Spices in an Indian Baghdadi kofta include ¼ teaspoon ground ginger and ¼ teaspoon turmeric. Another version has I tablespoon garam masala and a pinch of chili powder.

• Some people like to incorporate an egg and I or 2 slices of bread soaked in water and squeezed dry, which bind the meat and result in a softer texture.

• Some drop the meatballs in the sauce without preliminary frying or roasting and cook them for 25 minutes. This gives them a slightly different texture.

• For a Syrian version called "Daoud Pasha," stuff each meatball with a few pine nuts.

• In Salonika they sometimes added I tablespoon of honey instead of sugar to the tomato sauce.

• Italian Jews make polpette alla giudea on the same principle but with a very special flavor. Soak 4 oz (100 g) bread, crusts removed, in water, and squeeze dry, then blend with I lb (500 g) ground meat, 2 crushed cloves of garlic, a bunch of flat-leafed parsley finely chopped, salt, pepper, a pinch of nutmeg, and 2 eggs. Take small lumps and shape into flat patties. Fry them in oil, turning them over once. Cook I lb (500 g) peeled and chopped tomatoes with the grated peel of ½ lemon, 2 tablespoons vinegar, 2 teaspoons sugar, salt, and pepper for 10 minutes. Add a tablespoon each of chopped

flat-leafed parsley and basil. Drop in the meat patties, and cook 5 minutes longer.

Albondigas di Prasa
Leek Meatballs

SERVES 4

Years ago, after my Middle Eastern cookbook first came out, I received several letters telling me that I had forgotten to include the leek meatballs of Izmir. One correspondent sent a recipe, and this is it. It is a uniquely Jewish dish, and you are unlikely ever to find it in a public place. When I was in Turkey last year, a Jewish caterer gave me the address of a restaurant that offers Jewish food. It turned out to be a small workers' café near the grand bazaar called Kaşer Levi Lokantasi. To reach it, you have to pass through a courtyard, into a warehouse, and up a flight of stairs. I got lost and telephoned, and a young waiter came out to fetch me. The owner, a young Muslim, explained through a Jewish client that his father had been the cook for a Mr. Levi who had died 22 years ago, and he had carried on after his father in exactly the same way as in the time of Mr. Levi. He explained that the food was "half kosher." His albondigas di prasa were on large trays, as were several other things featured in this book. They were quite surprising—soft and creamy inside and more like fritters than meatballs.

1 lb (500 g) leeks
2 small potatoes, weighing about ½ lb (250 g)
½ lb (250 g) lean ground beef
2 eggs

Salt and pepper
Flour
Sunflower oil for frying

Trim and wash the leeks and cut them into pieces, then boil them with the potatoes until they are very soft. Drain and, when the vegetables are cool enough to handle, press them between your palms as hard as you can to get all the water out that you possibly can. This is very important in order to make the meatballs firm.

Now put the leeks, potatoes, meat, and 1 egg into the food processor with about ¾ teaspoon salt and pepper and blend to a soft paste. Shape into little round flat cakes about 2¼ inches (6 cm) wide and dip in flour on a plate. As you are ready to deep-fry, dip each into the remaining beaten egg, then lower gently into sizzling oil. Lower the heat, so as not to brown them too quickly, and turn over once. Drain on paper towels and serve hot.

VARIATION

● The fritters are often served with a fresh tomato sauce (see page 548) made a little sharp with a squeeze of lemon juice.

Albondigas de Espinaka

Meatballs with Spinach

SERVES 4

These meatballs, a specialty of Salonika, have a meaty texture but are so green that the meat seems secondary.

14 oz (400 g) spinach
7 oz (200 g) ground lamb, beef, or veal
2 slices bread, crusts removed, soaked in
    water and squeezed dry
2 eggs
About ¾ teaspoon salt
Pepper
¼ teaspoon nutmeg
Flour to roll the balls in
Sunflower oil for frying

Wash the spinach and remove tough stems, then drain and squeeze the water out. Put the leaves in a pot on low heat, with the lid on, for a minute or so, until they soften (they will steam in the water that clings to them), then drain again. When the spinach is cool enough, press all the water out with your hands (it must be as dry as possible). Put it in a food processor with the rest of the ingredients except the flour and oil and blend to a paste. Shape into little flat cakes (they are soft and not very easy to handle) and dip them in flour on a plate. Sprinkle with more flour and fry in shallow oil, turning them to brown on both sides. Drain on paper towels and serve hot or cold.

VARIATION

● They can be accompanied by a fresh tomato sauce (see page 548).

Albondigas de Berengena

Eggplant and Ground Meat Fritters

SERVES 6

These fritters are wonderfully soft and creamy and quite delicious, with the intriguing flavor of roasted eggplant.

> 2 lbs (1 kg) eggplants
> 12 oz (350 g) ground lamb
> Salt and pepper
> 2 eggs, lightly beaten
> Flour to dip in
> Sunflower oil for frying

Grill or roast, then peel the eggplants (see box, page 256). Put them in a colander and chop them with 2 sharp knives, pressing out the juice. Transfer them to a bowl, add the meat, about 1 teaspoon salt, pepper, and eggs, and mix well. Work with your hands till well blended. The mixture will be very soft. Using 2 tablespoons, take a heaping tablespoonful of the mixture, push it onto a plate covered with flour, and sprinkle the top with flour. Continue to make little cakes covered with flour. Shallow-fry in hot oil, turning over once, until browned all over. Drain on paper towels and serve hot or cold.

Kofta Shawandar Hamudh

Meatballs with Sweet-and-Sour Beets

SERVES 4

This Iraqi dish is usually made with kubba—meat dumplings in a ground-rice shell (see page 418)—but most people now make it simply with meatballs. It reminds me of borscht, with its sweet-and-sour taste and riveting beet color, which looks extraordinary on rice. It is an old Iraqi Jewish classic and has many fans, but it is not one of my favorites.

> 1½ lbs (750 g) raw beets
> 1 onion, coarsely chopped
> 3 tablespoons light vegetable oil
> 1½ lbs (750 g) ground beef or lamb
> 5 tablespoons chopped flat-leafed parsley
> 1 teaspoon cinnamon
> Salt and pepper
> Juice of 2 lemons or more to taste
> 1½ tablespoons sugar or to taste

Peel the beets, cut them in half, and simmer in water to cover for 1 hour. Fry the onion in the oil until golden. Work the ground meat, flat-leafed parsley, cinnamon, about ¾ teaspoon salt, and pepper to a paste and roll into walnut-sized balls. Put them in the frying pan with the onions and turn them, to brown them slightly all over. Then drop them and the onions into the pan with the beets. Add lemon and sugar to taste (the sweet-and-sour taste is very individual) and simmer 20 minutes. Serve hot with rice.

Nanaeya

Meatballs with Garlic and Minty Sweet-and-Sour Sauce

SERVES 4

This was a Passover dish in Baghdad. It was made as a stew with meat cubes, or with meatballs, as in this recipe. It was considered an everyday dish to serve with rice, not a party dish, because it was simple. But today nostalgia has glamorized it, and it is served at parties. Those who put in a lot of garlic (new young garlic which is not too powerful is used) call it "thoumia" ("thoum" means "garlic"). It has a strong and delicious flavor—garlicky, minty, and slightly sweet and sour. I like it both hot and cold.

1½ lbs (750 g) ground lamb
Salt and pepper
A bunch of flat-leafed parsley, finely chopped
  (½ cup)
1½ large onions, chopped
3 tablespoons light vegetable oil
6 or more garlic cloves or to taste (use new,
  young garlic if possible), finely chopped
Juice of 1½ lemons
1½ tablespoons sugar
A large bunch of fresh mint, finely chopped
  (1 cup)

Make the meatballs first. Mix the meat with about ¾ teaspoon salt, pepper, and parsley and work to a soft paste with your hands, then roll into balls the size of small walnuts.

For the sauce, fry the onions in the oil till soft. Add the garlic and the meatballs and cook, turning the meatballs to brown them all over. Now pour in water not quite to cover the meat and bring to the boil. Add a little salt and pepper and simmer for about 25 minutes, until the meatballs are very tender and the sauce is reduced, turning them over once. Mix the lemon juice, sugar, and mint and pour over the meat. Cook for 15 minutes more. (I was told to put in the lemon-and-mint sauce a few minutes before the end, but I forgot and put it in at the same time as the water, and it was very good.)

VARIATION

• Two chopped tomatoes may be added after the meat is browned.

Kibbeh Mahshiyeh

Syrian Stuffed Fried Kibbeh

SERVES 6

This is the national dish of Syria and Lebanon. Women staked their reputations as perfect wives and hostesses on these. There is a mystique attached to them. It was said that you could not get married if you did not know how to make them. Having a long finger helps, and women with longer fingers considered themselves lucky. When we heard, in Egypt, that Rita Hayworth had insured her legs for a huge sum, one woman asked her husband to insure her finger. For the older generation it is still the foremost food served to guests. A few widowed women of my mother's generation have made a living since they left Egypt by sending fried kibbeh all over the world by plane for bar mitzvahs, weddings, and even card games. When I started giving Middle Eastern cooking classes, my aunt Yvette in California asked my mother how good my kibbeh were. That was the real test of my worth. My father could not believe that any student could possibly learn to make them. You had to have years of practice.

Leg of lamb was the preferred meat for the shell. It was "porged" of sinews, nerves, and veins by kosher butchers, and therefore allowed. In countries where porging is not practiced, other, permitted cuts are used and all the fat and ligaments removed. Fatty shoulder was once the preferred meat for the filling, but now lean beef and veal are also used. The cracked wheat must be the finest grind, which is not as widely available here as the medium one. The usual ratio of meat to wheat is twice as much meat as cracked wheat, but that varies.

For the kibbeh shell

>*1¼ cups (250 g) fine cracked wheat (bulgur)*
>*1 small onion, quartered*
>*1 lb (500 g) lean tender lamb*
>*1 teaspoon salt*
>*Pepper*

KIBBEH—KUBBA—KOBEBA

WHEN MEMBERS of my family travel and see relatives abroad, they come back with stories of freezers filled with all manner of kibbeh made long ago in preparation for their visit. You could call them dumplings, but they are a many-splendored thing that defies characterization. Kibbeh are the hallmark of Syrian cooking—the standard by which once upon a time women were judged—even if it was the cook who made them. They represented refinement and elegance. There are dozens of versions involving pounded mixtures of meat and cracked wheat or rice stuffed with a meat filling. Iraqi and Kurdish Jews call them "kubba." In Egypt we called them "kobeba."

Kibbeh are a matter of skill: of making a paste of perfect consistency so that the shell will not fall apart; of using your finger to hollow out the shell to make its walls as thin as possible without breaking; of flavoring the ground-meat filling in an exquisite manner. "Kibbeh" means "ball-shaped" in Arabic, but traditional shapes vary from balls and stocky little ovals to long thin ones and flat round ones.

The meat and wheat or rice used to be pounded with a metal pestle and mortar (the ringing of the metal is in the background of so many of our memories); now they are turned into a paste in the food processor, but it still takes time to hollow the shell and stuff the dumplings. For this reason, and despite their cultural importance, I doubt that all the numerous versions of kibbeh that were particular to the Jews will be kept up.

For the meat filling or hashwa

1 medium onion, finely chopped
2 tablespoons oil
½ lb (250 g) lean ground beef
Salt and pepper
½ teaspoon allspice
½ teaspoon cinnamon
⅓ cup (60 g) pine nuts, lightly toasted

Light vegetable oil for frying

For the shell: Soak the cracked wheat in cold salted water for 10 minutes, then wash in a sieve under cold running water and drain. Squeeze excess water out. Puree the onion to a paste in the food processor. Add the meat (cut in pieces), salt, and pepper and process to a soft paste. Remove the meat and mix with the cracked wheat. Process the mixture in 2 batches until it is blended to a soft, smooth doughlike paste. You may need to add a tablespoon or two of cold water. Leave it to cool, covered, in the refrigerator; this will make it less sticky and easier to work.

For the filling: Fry the onion in the oil till soft. Add the meat and cook, stirring and crushing it with a fork, until it changes color. Season with salt, pepper, allspice, and cinnamon and stir in the pine nuts.

To shape and stuff the kibbeh: Keep wetting your hands with cold water. Take a lump of kibbeh paste the size of a small egg. Hold it in your left hand and make a hole in the middle with the forefinger of your right. Enlarge the hole and shape the kibbeh into a hollow, tapered oval with thin walls—less than ¼ inch (¾ cm) thick—by rotating your finger in quick clockwise movements, pressing the sides on the palm of your hand while at the same time opening and closing your cupped hand. Patch any holes with a wet finger.

Fill each shell with about 1 tablespoon of filling. Wet the open rim and pinch it closed, tapering the ends. Leave the kibbeh covered in the refrigerator until you are ready to cook them. Deep-fry in medium-hot sizzling oil to a rich brown color, turning them over once. Drain on paper towels and serve, preferably hot.

VARIATIONS

• To the shell mixture add ½ teaspoon of allspice and 1 teaspoon of cinnamon, or ½ teaspoon of ground coriander and 1 teaspoon of cumin.

• Instead of frying the kibbeh, you can bake them at 375°F (190°C) for 20–30 minutes.

Kibbeh bil Sanieh
Layered Meat and Cracked Wheat Pie

SERVES 8–10

Kibbeh on a tray ("sanieh" means "tray") is the homely everyday version, which takes less time. There are top and bottom layers of shell or crust made of a cracked-wheat-and-meat paste sandwiching a fried-meat-and-pine-nut filling. It is traditionally cooked on a round pie plate.

For the shell

2½ cups (500 g) fine-ground cracked wheat
    (bulgur)
About 2 teaspoons salt
1 large onion, quartered
1 lb (500 g) lean lamb
Pepper
2 teaspoons cinnamon
½ teaspoon allspice

For the hashwa (filling)

1 large onion, chopped
3 tablespoons sunflower oil
1½ lbs (750 g) ground lamb, preferably
    fatty
Salt and pepper
1 teaspoon cinnamon
½ teaspoon allspice
¾ cup (100 g) pine nuts

2–3 tablespoons sunflower oil

For the shell, soak the cracked wheat in plenty of cold salted water for about 15 minutes (the salt prevents it from going mushy). Then rinse in cold water in a sieve in the sink. Press the excess water out with your hands.

Process the onion first in a food processor. Add the meat and blend to a paste. Take out the paste and mix with the cracked wheat and flavorings, then process, in batches, to a soft, well-blended doughlike paste.

For the filling, fry the onion in the oil till soft. Add the ground meat, salt, pepper, cinnamon, and allspice and fry, turning and crushing the meat with a fork, until it has changed color. Add the pine nuts and mix well.

To assemble the pie, grease a large pie plate or shallow baking dish with oil. The traditional round shape looks good, but a square is more practical when it comes to cutting into portions. Press half the shell paste evenly on the bottom, about ½ inch (1½ cm) thick. Spread the filling on top and cover with the rest of the paste. This last layer of shell needs to be built up gradually. Wet your hands, take large lumps of the paste, flatten them between your palms, and lay them on top of the filling until it is entirely covered. Patch up any holes and press down firmly with your hands.

With a pointed knife, cut crisscrossing straight or diagonal parallel lines right through to the bottom, making square or diamond shapes, and run the knife around the edge. Brush or sprinkle the top with 2–3 tablespoons sunflower oil and bake in a preheated 375°F (190°C) oven for about 25 minutes.

Serve hot or cold, with a salad.

VARIATIONS

• Some people prefer to use beef or veal instead of the traditional lamb, or to have lamb for the shell and beef or veal for the filling.

• Flavor the shell with 2 teaspoons cumin and ¼ teaspoon hot cayenne pepper instead of cinnamon and allspice.

• Add 4 tablespoons of tomato paste to the shell mixture. It is used both for the taste and for the red "meaty" color it lends.

• Add to the filling 4 tablespoons each of soaked raisins and chopped walnuts instead of the pine nuts.

• There is a popular version in which the shell or crust is thick and the filling is meager.

KOBEBA WITH GROUND RICE

Rice Dumplings with Meat Filling

THESE LITTLE round dumplings, which are an entirely Jewish specialty of Syria and Iraq, are extremely versatile. They are cooked in soups and stews and with vegetables and even fruit. My own favorite is my mother's kobeba hamda, which she made every Passover (because they contain rice rather than bulgur). It is in the rice chapter (page 466), because the dumplings are in a sauce for rice. I chose to demonstrate it at a Jerusalem gastronomic congress, because it is festive and uniquely Jewish. I was very proud of my choice and thought it would be original. But when I came down to the preparation kitchen of the hotel, where Jewish cooks of different origins were preparing their specialties, every one of them, it seemed, was doing a type of kobeba, kubba, or kibbeh as they are variously called. Later I was told that Jerusalem has become the capital of kubba. We had to prepare hundreds to give as tastings after the demonstration. One

of the demonstrators, who worked next to me, was an Iraqi Kurd. We eyed each other's progress. She was unbelievably fast and much more skilled than I was, which depressed me. We could not communicate at all, with no language between us (not even my poor Arabic) and only a Palestinian cook to interpret. After the congress, I was taken to eat at a modest restaurant called Ima ("mother"), which specializes in kubba. The Kurdish woman rushed out of the kitchen to kiss me. The restaurant was hers. I tried every one of her kubba dishes (there were several). They were delightful, but I have to say our dishes are more refined and sophisticated—theirs more rustic.

When the last generation who makes kobeba or kubba has disappeared (I expect these dishes will not be carried on, because they take too long), I hope Jerusalem keeps up her reputation as the capital, and that some food producer will decide to make them commercially, so that a whole little world of our culinary culture does not disappear.

A Basic Kobeba Dumpling with Ground Rice

SERVES 8

I have tried many recipes for these dumplings. The main difference is the proportion of meat to rice in the shell. The old way was to soak rice in water for an hour, then to drain it and pound it to a paste. Now this can be done in a food processor. A simpler way is to use ground rice. Since the whole procedure takes time, it is usual for people to make larger quantities than they need and to freeze for later use. In Egypt they were Passover foods.

For the shell

> ½ lb (250 g) lean ground beef
> 1½ cups (300 g) ground rice
> Salt
> About 6 tablespoons water

For the filling

> ¾ lb (350 g) ground beef
> 1 medium onion, grated
> Salt and pepper
> ½ teaspoon allspice
> 1 teaspoon cinnamon

For the shell, put the meat, ground rice, and about ½ teaspoon salt through the food processor and process thoroughly. (It is important that the meat be very lean, or the dumplings can fall apart.) Then add just enough water to produce a soft, dryish paste that holds well together.

Work the filling ingredients to a paste by hand.

To make the dumplings, take lumps of the ground-rice-and-meat paste, a little smaller than a walnut, and roll into a ball. (Some people wet their hands so that the paste does not stick, some flour them, some oil them.) Make a dent in the middle of each dumpling with your finger, then pinch the sides and lift them up as though you were shaping a pot, making the shell as thin as possible. Stuff with 1 teaspoon of filling and bring the shell up over the filling, pinching the edges together to close the dumplings, then roll into a ball. Although many people deep-fried their kobeba in oil before stewing them, to give them a golden color and to firm them, some people now roast them briefly first in a hot oven. In my family we simply poached the kobeba in stock or a stew for about 25 minutes. They should not be overcooked.

VARIATIONS IN THE FLAVORING OF THE FILLING

• Finely chopped flat-leafed parsley or celery leaves can be added to the filling.

• In Iraq the filling had parsley or celery leaves, ½ teaspoon of ground cardamom, or 1 teaspoon of pulverized dried limes (see page 236).

• In Calcutta the filling was flavored with ginger, garlic, turmeric, and chopped fresh coriander.

TRADITIONAL SYRIAN-EGYPTIAN KOBEBA STEWS

• Drop the kobeba in boiling stock to cover with sliced desert truffles (you can find them canned or in jars) and simmer for 25 minutes.

• In a pan put 8 artichoke hearts cut in half, 1 lb (500 g) fresh fava beans, 4 sliced celery stalks and leaves, and about 2½ cups (600 ml) stock. Bring to the boil, add 2 tablespoons oil, the juice of 1 lemon, 1 teaspoon sugar, salt, and pepper, and drop in the kobeba. Simmer for 25 minutes. Add 2 teaspoons dried mint towards the end.

• Fry 1 large chopped onion in 1 tablespoon sunflower oil until golden. Add ½ lb (250 g) chickpeas, previously soaked and boiled, and 1 lb (500 g) tart, natural dried apricots. Cover with about 2½ cups (600 ml) stock or water and simmer for 50 minutes. Add the kobeba, salt, pepper, the juice of 1 lemon, and water to cover, and simmer for 25 minutes longer.

• Put 2 quinces, washed and sliced but not peeled or cored, in 2½ cups (600 ml) of stock. Add salt, pepper, ½ teaspoon allspice, ½ teaspoon nutmeg, the juice of ½ lemon, and 1 teaspoon of sugar or to taste, and simmer for ¾ hour. Lift out the quince pieces and cut away the cores, then return them to the pan. Add the dumplings and more water to cover and simmer for about 25 minutes.

• Cook the dumplings in stock with 2 or 3 eggplants previously cubed, fried, and drained on paper towels, 3 chopped garlic cloves, salt, and pepper.

• Cook 2 lbs (1 kg) sliced leeks in stock with 2 tablespoons of oil, 2 whole garlic cloves, the juice of 2 or 3 lemons, and ¼ teaspoon turmeric for ½ hour. Throw in the kobeba and cook 25 minutes longer.

Kubba Bamia

Okra Stew with Meat Dumplings

SERVES 6–8

This Iraqi Friday-night dish, using semolina for the shell instead of the usual ground rice and meat blended to a paste, was given to me many years ago by Mrs. Daisy Saatchi. She invited me to lunch, and watching her cook and tasting the new dishes she offered was an occasion I remember with particular delight.

For the kubba (dumplings)

> *1 lb (500 g) fine semolina*
> *Salt*
> *1 lb (500 g) lean ground beef*
> *1 large onion, grated (sprinkled with salt and*
> *   left to draw out its bitter juices)*
> *2 dried limes (see page 236)*
> *Pepper*
> *Flour*

For the stew

> *1 large onion, chopped*
> *2 tablespoons oil*
> *2 garlic cloves, minced or crushed in a press*
> *3 oz (75 g) tomato paste*
> *A small bunch of celery leaves, chopped (¼ cup)*
> *A small bunch of flat-leafed parsley or*
> *   coriander, chopped (¼ cup)*
> *Juice of ½ lemon or 1 dried lime*
> *1 teaspoon sugar*
> *Salt and pepper*
> *2 lbs (1 kg) small, young, tender okra*

For the dumpling shell, put the semolina in a bowl with ½ teaspoon of salt. Moisten with just enough water, by the tablespoon, to make a firm paste and work it with your hands until it is doughy and elastic. For the dumpling filling, mix the meat, onion, dried limes ground fine in a food processor, and a little pepper.

Dusting your hands with flour so that they do not stick, take a walnut-sized lump of semolina dough, roll it into a ball, and flatten it thin in the palm of your hand. Place a teaspoon of filling in the center, bring the semolina dough up over the filling, and close the gap. Shape into a ball, then roll in flour so that it does not stick. Continue with the rest of the dough and filling, arranging all the dumplings on a plate.

In a large saucepan, fry the onion in oil till golden. Add the garlic and fry until it begins to color. Add the rest of the ingredients and enough water so that it will cover the dumplings when they are added. Bring to the boil and simmer a few minutes, then drop in the dumplings very gently. They will remain submerged until they are cooked. They should be done in about 25 minutes, when the semolina becomes soft and they begin to float. Release them gently from the bottom and sides of the pan if they are stuck.

VARIATIONS

• Add I lb (500 g) peeled and chopped tomatoes (or a medium—14-oz; 400-g—can of peeled tomatoes) and omit the tomato paste.
• Instead of okra, zucchini or eggplants and tomatoes may be used. The dish can also be made with a yellow pumpkin.

• For the more common and traditional ground-rice version of the dumpling, use the basic recipe on page 416.
• Jews of Baghdad put in mint instead of coriander leaves and make it sweet and sour with the juice of I lemon and I–2 teaspoons of sugar.

Kubba Halab
Meat-Filled Rice Croquettes

SERVES 4

This is an Iraqi dish. Its name indicates that it is of Aleppan origin, but there is nothing like it in Aleppo. It is a little out of favor, because it is fiddly and people don't like frying any more, but it is very nice, especially when the croquettes have just been fried. Any rice can be used. I have tried different ones, and I prefer it with basmati.

> 1½ cups (300 g) basmati rice
> Salt
> 1 onion, finely chopped
> 2 tablespoons sunflower oil
> 4½ oz (125 g) lean ground beef
> Pepper
> 2 tablespoons slivered almonds

Throw the rice in plenty of boiling salted water and cook for about 18–20 minutes, until soft. Then drain.

For the filling, fry the onion in the oil till soft. Then add the ground meat, salt, and pepper and cook, stirring and crushing the meat

Chalghi Baghdad Jewish musicians who played at Jewish and Muslim weddings and events. Here they are in Cairo in 1932 to take part in a competition of Arab musicians, where they won first prize, awarded by King Fouad. The famed Daoud al Kuwaiti is holding the oud *(lute).*

QOUZI

Whole Roast Baby Lamb with Rice Stuffing

THIS FAMOUS BEDOUIN DISH was adopted by many Jewish communities as the great celebratory dish for weddings and grand parties. At the wedding of one of my cousins, where half a dozen baby lambs were served, I was photographed beside one—it is in a sitting position on a large tray with a bunch of flat-leafed parsley stuffed in its mouth. In cities the lamb was usually sent to be cooked in the public bakehouse oven.

Qouzi was especially popular with the Jews of Iraq. It was the custom for families to go out on picnics in the countryside, where Jews had land. Sami Daniels remembers large parties at Diala, a village south of Baghdad. A baby lamb was roasted on an open fire while a rice stuffing was cooked in huge metal bowls *(tosht)*. The animals were ritually slaughtered by Jewish butchers, who porged the hindquarters so the whole lamb could be eaten. The cooking was done by local people with a Jewish supervisor overseeing, so that it was in accordance with the laws. The meat was cooked to such tenderness that it could be pulled off with the hand. People ate with their hands, and at the end of the meal they cleaned their hands with soil.

For weddings, families got together days in advance and brought their cooks to share in the preparations. They produced hundreds of little pies, kibbeh, stuffed vegetables, and pilafs. Specialists were brought in on the day to cook the qouzi in the garden. While bands, singers, and belly dancers entertained the guests, the aroma of the lambs roasting on the spit wafted around them. At one time 90 percent of Iraqi musicians and composers of traditional music were Jewish. They played the *oud* (lute), the *kanoun*, and the *kamanja*. Two brothers, Saleh and Daoud al Kuwaiti, were famous composers. Selima Mourad was a famous Jewish singer who performed at weddings.

The lamb was rubbed inside and out with a mixture of onion juice, oil, and lemon and cooked for 3–4 hours. The stuffing was like the one called hashwa on page 356.

Meat-Filled Rice Croquettes (cont.)

with a fork, until it changes color and the water has evaporated. Stir in the almonds.

To make the shell, turn the cooked rice to a soft yet firm paste in the food processor. Because it is sticky, you will need to oil your hands to handle it. Have a little oil in a cup, and also some brushed over a plate. Take a walnut-sized lump of rice paste and roll it into an oblong. Then flatten between your palms so that the shell is as thin as possible without breaking. Put a teaspoonful of the filling in the middle and lift the sides up, closing them over the filling. Gently pat the croquette into an oblong and patch any holes. Place on the oiled plate. Repeat with the rest of the rice and filling. Deep-fry the croquettes in medium-hot oil until lightly golden and drain on paper towels.

In Iraq kubba were the kind of thing that was taken cold on picnics. But I prefer them hot, with a salad and pickles.

VARIATIONS

• Some people add ¼ teaspoon of turmeric to the cooking water, so that the rice becomes yellow. Some roll the croquettes in a beaten egg or in egg white before frying.

Ajja bi Lahma
Meat Omelettes

SERVES 4–6

Meat omelettes are popular with the Oriental Sephardim. They were often the main part of a light evening meal, served with a salad or fried eggplant. Because they could be eaten cold, they were common Saturday fare. They were taken on picnics and were often to be seen on buffet tables. They are made by mixing eggs with either raw or cooked ground meat—

lamb, beef, or veal. I prefer to fry the meat very briefly first. The omelettes can be thick and large and cut like a cake, or cooked by the half-ladleful like small fritters as in this recipe, which makes ideal finger food for a party; but the large cakelike version given in the variation may be the one you will adopt.

1 large onion, chopped
2 tablespoons sunflower oil
½ lb (250 g) ground lamb, beef, or veal
Salt and pepper
½ teaspoon allspice
6 eggs, lightly beaten
4 tablespoons finely chopped flat-leafed parsley
Light vegetable oil for frying

Fry the onion in the oil till golden. Add the meat and stir for a few moments, until it changes color, adding salt, pepper, and allspice. Let it cool, then mix with the eggs and flat-leafed parsley. Using a ladle, pour dollops of about 2–3 tablespoons of the mixture—do a few at a time—in hot, shallow oil in a frying pan. Or,

better still, use a nonstick pan lightly brushed with oil. Turn over when the eggs have set on the bottom to cook the other side.

Serve hot or cold.

VARIATIONS

• For the large version, heat 2 tablespoons of oil in a 9- or 10-inch (23- or 26-cm) frying pan, pour in the meat-and-egg mixture, and cook, covered, until the eggs at the bottom have set. Then put under the broiler to cook the top and brown it a little.

• A Judeo-Spanish version called uevos kon karne has 2 peeled and chopped tomatoes added to the meat.

• For a Tunisian maakoude à la viande, add 3 crushed garlic cloves, 2 slices of bread soaked in water, squeezed, and crumbled, and 2 chopped hard-boiled eggs. Serve with lemon wedges.

• Tunisian meguena aux boulettes de viande has tiny meatballs poached in stock or water or sautéed in a little oil, then mixed with beaten egg seasoned with salt, pepper, and allspice.

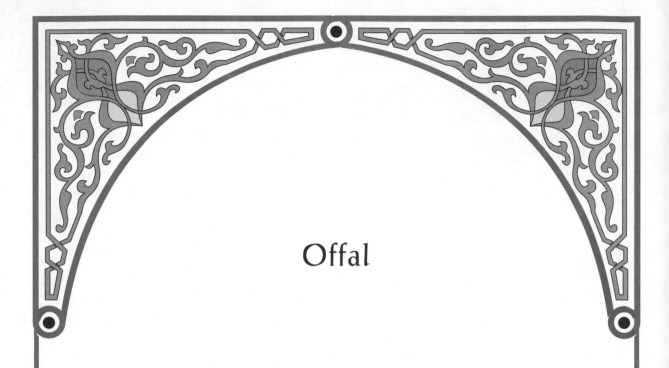

Offal

In Egypt in the early part of this century, kosher butchers came to the house to take orders and deliver meats.

My grandfather once caught his kosher butcher buying offal from an Arab at the market in Cairo. The butcher excused himself, saying: "You all want offal. How many animals do you think I would have to kill to have enough for all of you?" The offal everybody was after included liver, brains, sheep's head, tongue, spleen, stomach, heart, tripe, testicles, cow's udder, feet, and intestines.

Even though offal was poor food, these morsels were considered a delicacy. Every community had its favorites. The Judeo-Spanish Sephardim were especially fond of brains and also of feet. North African Jews adored tongue, spleen, and tripe. Only the Yemenites and North Africans have kept up their dishes. Though the

Anglo-Saxon environment has not been propitious for this kind of cuisine, French kosher butchers display a marvelous array of beautifully cut, cleaned, and sometimes ready-cooked pieces. Some of the dishes combine a variety of offal. Tunisian aakode is a stew of stomach, tripe, stuffed intestine, testicles, and penis with harissa, cumin, paprika, and tomato paste. Algerian faad d'agneau is the lungs, heart, liver, esophagus, and entrails of a lamb, cooked with garlic, tomato, onion, and parsley. Moroccan tagine del guezar is stewed liver, spleen, heart, lungs, head, feet, and beef-intestine sausage filled with liver, cooked with a yellow sauce (garlic and turmeric) or a red sauce (cumin and paprika).

Most popular is the North African mixed grill, méchoui d'abats, which includes kidney, liver, heart, sweetbreads, and testicles, usually from lamb or veal, as well as merguez (spicy sausages). Everything is cut into ¾-inch (I-cm) cubes or in slices and marinated in a mixture of lemon juice, olive oil, salt, and pepper, or in a sauce made with olive oil, lemon juice, harissa (page 242), ground caraway, cumin, and coriander, threaded on skewers (brochettes) and turned over a brazier.

Some of the offal dishes are famous. The higado kon vinagre of Turkey is liver cooked with wine vinegar. You find foie au cumin, liver with cumin, throughout North Africa—grilled, fried, or stewed, but always with the same flavorings of garlic, vinegar, cumin, and paprika, or harissa.

Langue farcie aux câpres, tongue stuffed with capers, is a Tunisian specialty. An incision is made in a partly cooked veal tongue with a long pointed knife, through its length, from the root end, without piercing the skin. The resulting pocket is stuffed with a mixture of chopped hard-boiled eggs, garlic, capers, and parsley. It is cooked in plenty of water with a little lemon juice and tomato paste, a sprig of thyme, and a bay leaf and served cut in slices. Langue farcie aux olives has chopped green olives instead of capers. In Turkey, tongue is cooked with black olives or with several heads of garlic. In the Arab world, small lambs' tongues are cooked in a sauce with vegetables such as green beans or okra.

Lamb's head was a New Year's dish in every community. The head was split in half, the tongues and brains left in (the eyes and ears were removed). It was sprinkled with oil, garlic, and spices and roasted in the oven for an hour, turned over once.

Stuffed spleen is one of the great delicacies.

A pocket is cut through the side and stuffed with a variety of fillings—a prestigious North African one is chopped liver or sweetbreads mixed with soaked and squeezed bread, lots of garlic, cumin, paprika, chili, and egg to bind it—and baked.

"Patcha" (the word is Turkish) is the name of many calf's-foot or lamb's-trotter dishes. But patcha in Baghdad was a stuffed lamb's tripe cooked with a calf's foot and lambs' tongues. Naim Dangoor, from whom I have learned a great deal about Baghdad cooking, nostalgically described this much-loved Saturday dish, which was cooked overnight in the dying embers of the fire, with eggs sitting on the lid, covered with a blanket to hold in the warmth. Stuffed lamb's tripe, called "im flus" ("with coins") because the tripe has circular lines, was also very popular as a wedding-party dish, when it was cooked as individual packages. So many were needed for a wedding that a cook came from Israel bringing dozens of kosher stomachs. The tripe was cut in four and washed with vinegar and coarse salt. Each piece was stuffed with rice, meat, and tomatoes and flavored with turmeric, cardamom, cloves, cinnamon, and rose petals, sewn up, and put in a large pot with the calves' feet and lambs' tongues.

It is interesting to note that a stew of meatballs, sheep's feet, head, tripe, and intestines stuffed with spicy ground meat, flavored with cinnamon and coriander and cooked in a vinegar, mustard, and raisin sauce was sold at the market in thirteenth-century Andalusia for the Sabbath (according to Lucie Bolens, *La Cuisine Andalouse et l'Art de Vivre, XIe–XIIIe Siècle*).

Meyoyo con Agristada

Brains with Egg-and-Lemon Sauce

I love brains, but we can't get them now in Britain, because of "mad cow disease." Years ago I would buy them just for myself and eat them simply poached and dressed with oil and lemon as my children looked on in horror. Brains cooked with agristada is a Judeo-Spanish favorite.

To serve 4, soak 2 calves' or 4 lambs' brains in cold water with 1 tablespoon of vinegar for 1 hour. Remove the membranes in which they are encased and rinse under the cold tap. Lower gently into boiling salted water acidulated with a teaspoon of vinegar and simmer gently for 10–15 minutes, until firm. Lift the brains out and cut in slices.

Serve hot or cold with agristada (egg-and-lemon sauce, page 247) poured over.

Fritas di Meyoyo

Brain Fritters

SERVES 6

These delicate fritters, crisp outside and deliciously soft and creamy inside, are popular throughout the Sephardi world.

> 2 calves' or 4 lambs' brains
> 1½ tablespoons vinegar
> Salt
> Flour

White pepper
> 2 eggs, lightly beaten
> Light vegetable oil for frying, about 1 inch (2½ cm) deep
> 2 lemons, cut in wedges

Soak the brains in cold water with 1 tablespoon of vinegar for 1 hour. Remove the membranes carefully and rinse in cold running water. Lower into boiling salted water, acidulated with ½ tablespoon of vinegar, and simmer for 4 minutes, until they begin to firm.

Lift them out, cut in thick slices, and let them dry. Dip in flour seasoned with salt and pepper, then in the egg, so that they are well coated all over. Deep-fry in hot oil, turning over once, till golden brown all over. Drain on paper towels and serve hot with lemon wedges.

Tagine de Cervelle à la Tomate

Brains in Tomato Sauce

SERVES 4

A North African favorite and, like all brain dishes, a specialty of the New Year (see page 28).

> 2 calves' or 4 lambs' brains
> 1½ tablespoons vinegar
> 4 cloves garlic, finely chopped
> 3 tablespoons peanut or vegetable oil
> 1 lb (500 g) tomatoes, peeled and chopped, or a 14-oz (400-g) can of peeled tomatoes
> Salt
> 1–2 teaspoons sugar

Juice of ½–1 lemon
1 hot chili pepper, cut in half and seeded
3 tablespoons finely chopped parsley or coriander

Soak the brains in cold water with the vinegar for 1 hour. Fry the garlic in the oil till golden. Add the tomatoes, salt, sugar, lemon juice, and chili pepper and cook for about 15 minutes.

Remove the membranes in which the brains are encased and rinse in cold running water. Gently lower into the tomato sauce and simmer for another 10 minutes, until the brains are firmed. Cut them into 8 pieces (for calves' brains) or 4 pieces (for lambs') before serving hot or cold.

VARIATION

• Add 1 teaspoon of cumin to the tomato sauce and ½ preserved lemon, rinsed and chopped up.

Sopa de Patcha

Calf's Foot or Lamb's Trotter Soup

SERVES 6

In Turkey this was once an early-morning or late-evening meal.

2 calves' feet or 4 lambs' trotters (ask the butcher to cut them in 4)
Salt
1 egg (optional)
⅔ cup (150 ml) white-wine vinegar or lemon juice
7 garlic cloves, finely chopped

Scrub and wash the feet well. Cover with cold water in a large pan; boil vigorously for 5–10 minutes, until the scum appears; then pour the water out with the scum and cover with fresh water. Add a good pinch of salt and simmer for about 3–4 hours, until the meat comes away from the bone, adding water as necessary.

Strain the soup. Take the meat off the bone and return it to the broth. Add water if necessary to make about 6 cups (1½ liters), and bring to the boil again. Just before serving very hot, you may beat the egg in a little bowl with some of the hot broth, and pour it into the soup, beating vigorously—off the heat, so that it does not curdle.

In a serving bowl, make a little sauce to pass around. Mix the vinegar or lemon juice with the garlic. Let people pour a little of this in their soup.

VARIATIONS

• Avas kon patcha has white haricot beans cooked with the feet.

• In Syria and Egypt, patcha, also called kawareh, was cooked with chickpeas and flavored with 1 teaspoon of turmeric. Half an hour before the end, potatoes were added.

• In Salonika, where it was a Sabbath dish, chickpeas and eggs in their shells were added.

• There is another Turkish soup, with 4 chopped tomatoes and 4 potatoes, and served with lemon wedges.

• In Tunisia, areugma is the soup flavored with plenty of garlic, 1 teaspoon of harissa (see page 242), 1 teaspoon of paprika, and 1 teaspoon of cumin.

OSBAN—GHEH—MUMBAR

Stuffed Intestine—a Sausage

I HAVE BEEN GIVEN numerous recipes for stuffed intestine casings (sheep's intestines are mainly used) from different parts of the Sephardi world, but I have not tried them. I shall describe them, for they are a very old and important part of Sephardi culture. The cleaning of intestines was a whole ritual—they were washed, turned inside out, scrubbed with hot water and vinegar, then rinsed several times in cold water. Today in Israel they sell them clean and ready in frozen packages. The intestine is filled, and the extremities are tied in a knot. It is pricked with a pin in a few places so that it does not burst during the long, slow cooking.

The Tunisian osban, which is cooked with the Passover dish called "msoki" (page 498), is stuffed with ground meat or liver and spinach, mixed with chopped mint, parsley, coriander, and celery leves, minced garlic, chopped onion, and rice, seasoned with salt, pepper, and harissa. On festive occasions the large intestine and a part of the stomach are also stuffed.

Syrian Jews stuffed intestine casings with a ground-shoulder-of-lamb-and-rice filling flavored with allspice and cinnamon. They called it "gheh." The sausage was knotted every 6 inches (15 cm) to make small sausages and was often cooked together with lambs' trotters and chickpeas.

In Iraq, mumbar was filled with ground meat, chopped liver, and rice flavored with powdered cloves, cardamom, cinnamon, and pepper.

Derbali

Spicy North African Tripe Stew

SERVES 6

Tripe was much loved in North Africa. This is a flavorsome, gutsy way to prepare it. The tripe had to be scrubbed hard, rinsed, and soaked in water with vinegar, then blanched and cooked for 3–5 hours. Now it is sold cleaned and partially or ready-cooked. You need to find out when you buy it how long it needs to be cooked.

2 lbs (1 kg) tripe, sold partially cooked
2 onions, chopped
3 tablespoons olive or vegetable oil
8 garlic cloves, finely chopped
1 lb (500 g) little new potatoes
1 teaspoon harissa (page 242), or
    1 teaspoon paprika and ¼ teaspoon
    cayenne or red-chili powder
Juice of 1 lemon
1 teaspoon ground caraway
1 teaspoon ground coriander
1 teaspoon ground cinnamon
Salt
3 tablespoons chopped flat-leafed parsley

Cut the tripe into 1½-inch (4-cm) squares. Fry the onions in the oil till soft and golden. Add the garlic, and fry until it begins to color. Add the potatoes and cover with water. Stir in the harissa, or the paprika and cayenne, and the lemon juice, caraway, coriander, cinnamon, and some salt. Simmer until the potatoes are tender. Now put in the tripe and cook for between 20 minutes and 1½ hours (depending on how much precooking it has had), adding water as necessary, until it is tender and the sauce is reduced. Serve hot, sprinkled with parsley.

VARIATIONS

• You may add 1 preserved lemon, rinsed and chopped up.

• Algerian shkemba—tripe in a red sauce—is a village dish with plenty of garlic, paprika, chili peppers, cumin, and a little vinegar, prepared during Passover.

• For shmeunka, a Tunisian tripe soup, cook 4 cubed turnips and 3 carrots with 5 garlic cloves, 1 teaspoon paprika, ½ teaspoon coriander, 4 bay leaves, and a pinch of cayenne for 30 minutes before adding the tripe.

• Tahfifa is tripe cooked with cabbage and pumpkin.

Dafina and Hamin—
the Sabbath Pot

A FEW YEARS AGO, at the bakehouse in Marrakesh, I saw a number of Jewish pots. These are recognizable by the way the lids are stuck down. Once upon a time, the public oven was crowded with Jewish pots on the Sabbath. Families would send their bread and pastries to be baked on the Friday morning and retrieve these when they brought their pots in the afternoon, to be left all night in the dying embers. The pots were carried to the oven in procession by a maid or an errand boy accompanied by the children of the family. They were sealed with a flour-and-water paste, or lids were held tightly down with wire and tape and other contraptions, so that the stew did not dry out, and also to make sure that no nonkosher ingredient could find its way in. The baker scribbled a number in chalk and gave a piece of paper

with the number. The pots were placed in the requested positions in the stone oven, which was sealed for the night with clay before a Jewish "guardian." On Saturday, as the men came out of the synagogue, the bakery was crowded with women and children making sure that the little maids and errand boys picked up the right pots.

In Egypt the inhabitants of the Jewish quarter could put their pots in the embers that heated the water at the public baths. Several Middle Eastern communities continued to have access to a neighborhood bakehouse until they left. The socializing this entailed was one of the highlights of the Sabbath preparations. Another traditional way of cooking the Saturday meal at home before the advent of ovens was in the ashes of a brazier or *kanoun*. The pot was covered by a thick blanket or cushions or old coats to keep it hot when the fire died down.

The Sephardi equivalent of the Ashkenazi cholent is infinitely varied. Every community had more than one. The Saturday dishes of Morocco are the most varied. Every town—Essaouira, Fez, Meknes, Marrakesh, Casablanca, Rabat, Salé, Tangier, Ouezzane, and Debdou—had its own special version. And there were dafinas for when the Sabbath fell on feast days like Yom Kippur or Passover or the 9th of Ab.

The Sephardi Saturday meal-in-the-pot is known by various names. The general name "dafina," which means "buried" in Arabic, indicates that the cooking pots were once cooked in a hole in the ground with burning embers. There are many mentions of dafina in old accounts, including the court proceedings of the Inquisition in Spain. Another name is "hamin," meaning "hot." In Morocco it is called "skhena," which also means "hot." In Iran they call it "khalebibi," and in Kurdistan "mabote." In Egypt, where it was made with young green wheat, it was simply called "ferik," meaning "wheat," whereas in North Africa and Yemen it is called "harissa" when it is made with cracked wheat.

Because of the labor involved and the type of ingredients—such as stuffed intestines, tongue, and calf's foot—dafinas have not always been kept up when people emigrated. But they are on the menus of North African Jewish restaurants in Paris and Marseilles. They are complex dishes which make use of many ingredients and comprise a variety of components, which on special occasions can represent five dishes, including the dessert. In less hurried times, their preparation was one of the joys of the Sabbath, remembered with affection. Female relatives would get together to share the work,

sometimes with the help of the children. There was chopping and mincing and stuffing and shaping meat loaves or meatballs. Assembling the components was an art. They used thin muslin and nylon fabric to wrap up rice ("serra" is the Moroccan word for the bag tied at both ends); foil to wrap meat loaves and sweets; little metal containers like old round cigarette boxes, small biscuit tins, and little plates to hold side dishes, so that all the parts were kept separate.

A basic dafina may be composed of knuckle of veal, shin of beef, breast or shoulder of lamb. Sliced calf's foot gives the stew a delicious rich quality. There are usually chickpeas or beans, rice or wheat, potatoes or sweet potatoes, sometimes green vegetables like fava beans and spinach, and always hard-boiled eggs, which acquire a brown color and creamy yolk consistency and are called "uevos haminados" and "uevos adafinados" (see page 246). On special festive days there may be a meat loaf called "kora," sometimes referred to as "pudding," or a stuffed chicken, or sausages of beef and rice called "relleno de arroz," and also a sweet. Sometimes sweet things like raisins, dates, prunes, and quinces are included, with added sugar or honey, on special occasions, as are also desert truffles. In North Africa dafinas—pronounced there "t'fina"—are usually accompanied by couscous left over from the day before.

Many of the people I have talked to were slightly mocking about their Sabbath pot and said that it was not the best example of Jewish gastronomy but had an important place in their culture. It is usually stodgy and heavy on the stomach and not a beautiful sight, but the aroma is magnificent, and the stew has a deliciously rich texture with lots of sauce and a delicate flavoring.

As the preparation of the Sabbath dish is

surrounded by ritual, so is the serving. Potatoes and eggs are served first, with plenty of sauce or broth (the eggs are usually peeled and put back in the pot before serving, to make things easier), and salt, cumin, and cayenne are passed around for people to help themselves. Then the rice or wheat is served, followed by the meat and chickpeas, and the extras—the sausages and meat loaves.

Although all the dishes in this section are meant to be left overnight in the lowest possible oven because of the laws of the Sabbath, they can of course be cooked on the stove for a few hours only. You will need a large, heavy-bottomed pot or casserole.

Moroccan Dafina

SERVES 6

The following is a basic recipe for a traditional Moroccan dafina (also known as "skhena" in Morocco), which is similar to dafinas (sometimes pronounced "adafine") around the Sephardi world. Extra components, such as meat loaf, rice, or cracked wheat in a bag, can be placed in the pot, on top of the other ingredients. Recipes for these follow.

1 cow's or calf's foot, cut in 4 slices, or 2 marrow bones (optional)
2 lbs (1 kg) breast, foreknuckle, or shin of beef, cut in large pieces
½ lb (250 g) chickpeas, soaked for 1 hour or overnight
1 whole onion

1 lb (500 g) peeled new potatoes
6 hard-boiled eggs
Plenty of pepper
⅓ teaspoon nutmeg
⅓ teaspoon mace
1 teaspoon cinnamon
Salt

Wash, then blanch the cow's or calf's foot (if using) in boiling water until the scum appears, then throw out the water. Put the calf's foot or marrow bones in a large pan with the meat. Cover with plenty of water, bring to the boil, and remove the scum. Add the rest of the ingredients except the salt, and more water to cover. Simmer for 3 hours, adding salt to taste after about 1 hour, or leave overnight in the lowest possible oven.

VARIATIONS

• Add 1 tablespoon of honey or quince jam, 4 chopped dates, or 2 tablespoons of sugar heated in a little pan until it caramelizes, then diluted in a little water.

• Add ½ teaspoon saffron, turmeric, or powdered ginger.

• Instead of chickpeas use white haricot beans, soaked overnight.

Kora–Boulette–Relleno–"Pudding"

Meat Loaf to Put In with the Dafina

SERVES 6

Kora is a many-splendored thing. There are endless versions, all of them well flavored, rich, and exciting. The loaf, or sausage, is stuffed in an intestine casing or wrapped in cloth and cooked with the dafina.

> 1 lb (500 g) ground beef
> 1 egg, lightly beaten
> 4 tablespoons chopped flat-leafed parsley
> 5 tablespoons fine bread crumbs or matzo meal
> ½ teaspoon salt
> Pepper
> ¼ teaspoon nutmeg
> 1 teaspoon cinnamon
> ¼ teaspoon ground ginger
> 3 tablespoons oil
> 2 cups (250 g) walnuts or hazelnuts, chopped (optional)

Mix all the ingredients together in a bowl and work to a soft paste with your hand. Shape into a long fat roll, and wrap in a thin muslin cloth, tying up the ends. Or wrap in foil that has been brushed with oil. Place on the top of the other ingredients in the pot. Serve cut in slices.

VARIATION

• For the luscious kora of Essaouira, also called "pudding" souiri, mix 1 lb (500 g) fatty ground beef, 1 egg, 3 tablespoons bread crumbs, ½ cup (100 g) raisins or dates cut into small pieces, ½ cup (100 g) chopped almonds or walnuts, salt, pepper, ¼ teaspoon nutmeg, and 3 tablespoons oil.

Serra

Rice Stuffing in a Bag for Dafina

SERVES 6

The rice stuffing is cooked in a bag, an intestine casing, or a separate closed metal container placed in the pot.

> 1¼ cups (250 g) long-grain rice
> 7 oz (200 g) ground beef (optional)
> 1 onion, chopped
> 3 tablespoons raisins
> Salt and pepper
> 1 teaspoon cinnamon
> ¼ teaspoon saffron
> A pinch of ginger
> 3 tablespoons vegetable oil
> 1 egg, lightly beaten

Mix all the ingredients together, put them in a muslin or cloth bag, and tie up the ends, leaving enough room for the rice to expand. Or put it in a closed container, like a metal box, with 2¾ cups (650 ml) water, and place in the pot with the adafina. In the bag, it will cook in the dafina liquid. In the closed container, it will cook in its own water.

SKHENA IN MARRAKESH

I WAS INVITED to watch the Friday preparations of a Jewish family in the medina (old residential quarter) in Marrakesh. They were twelve—father, mother, grandmother, and nine children. The tiny door, which seemed to lead into a hovel, opened into a paradise of cobalt and turquoise mosaics, a fig tree, an orange tree, climbing vines, and perfumed jasmine. The family lived in a few rooms on the upper floor, all of which gave onto a gallery of balconies overlooking the courtyard. The father was a white-magic man. I was introduced to the family by a doctor in Marrakesh who sent him patients. The magic man ostensibly had a shop selling mineral water and soft drinks but carried on his real business in the back. He explained that he practiced "white" magic. The lizards, bats, and animals that could be seen in the spice shops at the souk were for black magic—for setting spells and the evil eye on other people. His job was to undo these spells and help people. They came with all kinds of problems—women with problems of jealousy and fear of rival women or co-wives, men because of fear of waning sexual performance. The magic man wrote messages on small pieces of paper, rolled them up, stuffed them in an amulet, and tied them around their necks. His business was thriving, and that is why they had stayed on when most of their extended family had left.

They had a brand-new oven, but it was covered with a lace tablecloth and stuck on the front was a portrait of the Moroccan rabbi Abouhassira, who died in Egypt, and

Interior of a North African Jewish home

whose tomb, near Alexandria, is an important place of pilgrimage (planeloads and coaches arrive from Paris and Israel every year with musicians, singers, and packed foods for two days of reveling). All the cooking was done on braziers on the balcony. They had many fires going and produced more than fifteen dishes. The Saturday pot had a ground-meat roll, chickpeas, rice, hard-boiled eggs, and a chicken stuffed with dates and a sweet almond paste—when I looked horrified at the amount of sugar that went in, the father said, "Don't worry, you can have that as the dessert!" I trooped along with the grand-mother and the children behind the little maid who carried the pot on her head to the public oven. Before coming home, we all went on to the public baths. The family had a modern bathtub at home, but only the father used it. At the Sabbath table he asked me if I had any marriageable daughters. I asked if it was for his sons. He replied, "No. It's for me," and they roared with laughter.

When I was in Israel, at Beth Hatefut-soth, the Museum of the Diaspora, looking for photographs for my book at the picture library, there I found a photograph of them on their balcony cooking skhena, the Satur-day pot. A few photos away in the library was Dr. Guido Riso Levy, who was my GP in Cairo, smiling in his galabia (robe), fatter and much older than when I was a little girl but still the ladies' man. It made me a little sad to think that their lives were museum pieces.

Festive Skhena of Marrakesh and Essaouira

Stew with Stuffed Chicken and Chickpeas

SERVES 10

This Moroccan meal was prepared for the breaking of the fast of Yom Kippur.

1¼ cups (250 g) blanched almonds
½ lb (250 g) pitted dates
1 very large chicken or 2 small ones
1¼ lbs (600 g) ground beef
2 eggs
3 tablespoons fine dry bread crumbs or matzo
    meal
¼ teaspoon nutmeg
1 teaspoon cinnamon
Salt and pepper
1½ cups (300 g) chickpeas, soaked for 2 hours
10 waxy potatoes, peeled

8 hard-boiled eggs in their shells
½ teaspoon saffron
4 tablespoons peanut or light vegetable oil

For the chicken stuffing, blend the almonds and dates to a paste in a food processor, adding 3 tablespoons of water. Stuff the chicken with this and sew up the openings or secure with toothpicks.

For the meat loaf, put the ground meat in a bowl with the eggs, bread crumbs or matzo meal, nutmeg, cinnamon, salt, and pepper, and work to a paste with your hand. Shape into a loaf, and wrap in a muslin cloth and tie it up, or wrap in foil brushed with oil so that the meat does not stick.

In a very large pot put the drained chickpeas and the potatoes. Put the chicken and the eggs on top and lay the meat loaf over them. Cover entirely with water and add salt, pepper, saffron, and oil. Simmer for 2 hours, or leave in the lowest oven overnight.

TUNISIA—BERBERS AND "LIVORNESE"

THE JEWS OF TUNISIA lived (and some still do) for the most part in cities near the sea, mostly in Sousse, Sfax, Bizerte, Monastir, and Tunis, which accounts for their reputation for fish dishes. There were also a few rural communities, and there were Jews who lived a nomadic life. They all led a very traditional Jewish life, and their cooking was different from that of the general population and as varied as the community was mixed.

It is not known if the native Jews originally came from Jerusalem after the destruction of the Temple, as they claim, or if they came with the Phoenicians, with whom they had a famous affinity (there is a Jewish hill cemetery in the ruins of Carthage), or whether they are descended from Berber tribes. Their origin is probably mixed.

The ancestors of the Jews in the extreme south—some of whom lived in tents or in dwellings made with olive and palm branches and a few in troglodyte caves—had fought with the Berbers against Arab rule since the seventh century and took refuge with the Berbers on the island of Djerba and the Sahara. Family names of many Tunisian Jews indicate Persian, Iraqi, and Palestinian origins. There has been a close connection since the ninth century between Tunisian and Babylonian Jewry, with Talmudic scholars moving backwards and forwards to Spain, which led to the founding of an important and famous Talmudic school in Kairouan. In the tenth century, during the Fatimid Caliphate, Jews attained positions of power, and a Jewish court culture of poets, scholars, and *bons vivants* blossomed, to leave its mark on later times. Part of the legacy of that period is a number of dishes with a curious similarity to old Baghdad dishes.

In the fifteenth century, Andalusian Jews migrated, escaping with the Moors from Spain. They built Andalusian houses with tiled courtyards and inner gallery balconies. The ancient town of Testour is an old Jewish Andalusian settlement that still draws families back on nostalgic holidays and on pilgrimages to the tomb of Rabbi Es Saad Fradj Chaoua. Andalusian influence is especially marked in the cooking of the Jewish communities—more so than in the Muslim population.

In the sixteenth century, Jews came from the Italian port of Livorno in Tuscany to finance ransoms and arrange the release of Jewish hostages captured by pirates. Tunisia was a notorious base for pirates. It thrived on captured shipping, contraband, and speculation in ransoms throughout the seventeenth century. The Livornese were subjects of the Tuscan grand duke, and many of them were of Portuguese Marrano origin. They were invited to stay on by the local beys as treasury officials, diplomats, and consuls. A flow of immigrants

187. TUNIS — Souk-El-Grassa

The souk el Grana, *the Livornese Jewish quarter, Tunis*

from the Tuscan port city, which had an enormous Jewish population, continued until the nineteenth century. In 1741, two separate Jewish communities, a Tunisian and a "Livornese" (also called "Grana" and "Gorni"), were formed. The Livornese asked for autonomy, on the pretext of having a different liturgy. Today all the European Jews of Tunisia—whether they have come from Italy, France, Gibraltar, Malta, or other parts of the Mediterranean—call themselves "Livornese" and consider themselves superior to the "Twansa" or "Tuns," as the indigenous Tunisian Jews are called—even the very rich ones. The Livornese never intermarried with native Jews, refused to speak Judeo-Spanish, and continued to speak Italian. They gave their children Italian names, sent them to Italian schools and to the university in Pisa. They have family names like Cesana, Castelnuovo, Errera, Giaccomo, Trionfo, Lumbroso, and Angelo. They had their own rabbis, synagogues, cemeteries, and charities, and they clung jealously to their way of life and also to their cooking, which is a Tunisian, Italian, and Portuguese mix. They established themselves in cities on the coast and went into maritime trade, especially with Italy. At Sousse they went into the olive-oil business. Some became very rich bankers and merchants, but many were weavers, tailors, shoemakers, dyers, and silversmiths. Some lived in abject poverty as domestics or on charity.

Apart from the "Tuns" and the "Livornese," there was a population of Oriental Jews from the Ottoman territories who came with the occupying Turks in the nineteenth century and brought their foods, including baklava, Turkish delight, and Turkish coffee.

The Jews of Djerba are the most distinct and insular group. There was once a very large community and Jewish villages on the island, known for its date palms and its fig and olive trees. The synagogue of Al Ghariba is believed to be built on the site of one of the earliest synagogues in the world, founded in the sixth century B.C., after the exile from Jerusalem. Jews were among the Berbers who took refuge from the Arabs on the island in the eighth century A.D. In the 1950s, there was a massive emigration to Israel, and only about a thousand remain on the island, living a pious, puritanical, archaic life. You can see them weaving, as they have always done, and sewing the local costume—a beige-and-brown burnoose. The women go about in long skirts, their heads covered with a large cloth and a big straw hat. The dazzling multicolored tiled synagogue is a place of pilgrimage and a tourist attraction. The old Jewish quarter is a huddle of brilliant whitewashed houses with palm-branch roofs and clusters of mauve bouganvillea. Tiny rooms, faced with blue-and-green mosaics, bare of furniture, with stone elevations to sleep on, open onto small inner courtyards. Once upon a time, all life, including cooking, went on in these patios.

The courtyard—which often also served as the kitchen—of a Jewish home in the hara *in Tunis, c. 1900*

Large clay pots like Roman amphorae were used for storage, clay pots also kept water cool, and clay dishes were for cooking over charcoal. Clay vessels were also the communal dishes. At night families got together to hear the elders read verses from the Bible.

In the cities, ever since the Middle Ages, indigenous "Tuns" have lived in the margin of the Muslim population in haras—quarters inhabited only by Jews. They wore local clothes, though they were not allowed bright colors, especially white or green (which is the color of Islam), and their skull caps had to be black. The *hara* in Tunis is squeezed between the Arab medina and the souks. From the middle of the nineteenth century, it became the most overcrowded and insalubrious part of the city, with no running water or electricity; whole families occupied tiny rooms like hovels. Those who could moved out in the 1930s to buildings in the new town built by the French, but they stayed together in enclaves such as the Avenue de Londres and the Rue d'Angleterre, where you could once hear their Judeo-Arabic dialect and where, during Sukkot, you could see palm huts on balconies and roof terraces and hear Hebrew songs. Those who remained in the old *hara* were mostly artisans—tailors, potters, leatherworkers, and silversmiths. The men wore large, baggy pale-gray or blue pants, brown or black waistcoats, and red hats with large blue tassles. The women wore bouffant pants, silk jackets, and scarves covered with gold medals. The "Livornese" lived in a separate quarter of the old city, called the *souk el Grana.* The wealthier ones built Tuscan-type villas in the consular area of the Avenue de Paris.

In the nineteenth century, when Tunisia was part of the Ottoman Empire, British, French, and Italian powers offered nationality and protection to a number of Jews as a way of establishing influence in the outposts of empire. Under French colonization, the Jews won their "emancipation," and many of them became French. Since the country's independence in 1956, with the flood of *pieds noirs* (French North Africans) arriving, France has inherited their cooking. Their liberal use of the fiery red-pepper paste called "harissa" makes it one of the hottest and spiciest of any Jewish cuisine (though not as hot as the Yemeni and Ethiopian). Some dishes are incredibly elaborate and time-consuming. The Jewish couscous made for Friday night is a world in itself, containing a homemade beef sausage, little meatballs, a number of vegetables, and a variety of stuffed vegetables. I have counted at least thirty ingredients in one version.

T'Fina Pkaila

Meat Stew with Beans and Spinach

SERVES 8

This traditional Sabbath dish of Tunisia and Algeria is also prepared for everyday meals. Restaurants in France have it on the menu. Calf's foot, marrow bones, or knuckle give it a lovely gelatinous texture, but other cuts of meat are also used.

> 2 lbs (1 kg) spinach
> ⅓ cup (90 ml) extra-virgin olive oil or light
>   vegetable oil
> 2 lbs (1 kg) knuckle of veal or shin of beef,
>   or slightly fatty shoulder
> 2 marrow bones (optional)
> 8 oz (250 g) white haricot beans, soaked
>   overnight
> 6 or more garlic cloves, peeled
> Black pepper
> Salt

Wash the spinach, remove any tough stems, and drain well. It is usually shredded, but does not have to be. Put the leaves in a large pan with the oil and cook with the lid on, stirring occasionally, until they crumple into a soft, dark mass.

Turn them out of the pan and put the meat and marrow bones in. Cover with about 6 cups (1½ liters) of water, bring to the boil, and remove the scum. Add the drained beans, garlic, pepper, and spinach and bring to the boil again. Simmer on very low heat for about 3½ hours, adding about 1½ teaspoons salt or to taste for the last ½ hour, and water, if required. Alternatively, leave overnight in the lowest possible oven.

VARIATIONS

• Instead of the marrow bones, add I calf's foot sawn into slices by the butcher.

• You may use sliced cardoons or Swiss chard instead of spinach.

• Add a small can of tomato paste and I teaspoon sugar.

• Serve if you like with a little sauce made by diluting I teaspoon of harissa or cayenne in ½ cup (125 ml) water.

• Osban (page 426), a large hot spicy sausage, is often put in the pot.

• Algerians add small new potatoes and hard-boiled eggs in the shell, and sometimes use chickpeas instead of beans.

• A "boulette" (meat loaf) can be added to the pot. For this, mix and work to a soft paste with your hand 10 oz (300 g) ground beef with 4 oz (100 g) soaked bread squeezed dry, ¼ teaspoon nutmeg, ¼ teaspoon mace, I teaspoon cinnamon, salt and pepper, a pinch of harissa or cayenne, 3 tablespoons chopped flat-leafed parsley, and I lightly beaten egg. Then shape into an oval loaf.

Hamin Toscano con Pomodori e Polpettone

Meat Loaf with Beans and Tomatoes

SERVES 6

This Italian Sabbath dish incorporates the old Tuscan bean pot with tomato.

> *1 onion, chopped*
> *⅓ cup (90 ml) extra-virgin olive oil*
> *1 lb (500 g) tomatoes, peeled and chopped, or a 14-oz (400-g) can of peeled tomatoes*
> *10 oz (300 g) dried cannellini or white haricot beans, soaked overnight*
> *Salt and pepper*
> *1 lb (500 g) ground beef or veal*
> *2 eggs, lightly beaten*
> *4 tablespoons fine dry bread crumbs*
> *¼ teaspoon nutmeg*
> *4 tablespoons chopped flat-leafed parsley*
> *Flour*

In a large saucepan, fry the onion in 2 tablespoons of the oil till soft. Add the tomatoes and simmer for 10 minutes. Then add the drained beans, cover with about 6 cups (1½ liters) of water, and simmer, covered, on very low heat for about 1½ hours, adding salt and pepper when the beans have begun to soften.

In the meantime, put the ground meat in a bowl with the eggs, bread crumbs, nutmeg, salt, pepper, and parsley, and work to a soft paste with your hand. Shape into 2 oval rolls. Roll in flour and brown them all over in the remaining oil in a frying pan. Lift them out carefully and put them in the pot with the beans. Add water, if necessary, to cover, and cook, covered, for 40 minutes longer. Serve with the meat cut in slices.

Ferik

Whole Wheat Casserole

SERVES 6

This was one of our Egyptian Saturday dishes, which we also called "hamin." You need young green wheat for it—the type now obtainable in Middle Eastern stores as "ferik" (the usual wheat you find in health-food stores is too old and tough). It is a stodgy but heartwarming dish.

> *1 lb (500 g) young green wheat*
> *1¼ lbs (600 g) onions, coarsely chopped*
> *4 tablespoons light vegetable oil*
> *1 shoulder of lamb, cut in large pieces, or 6 small shins*
> *Salt and pepper*
> *2 teaspoons cinnamon*
> *1 teaspoon allspice*
> *6 hard-boiled eggs in their shells*

Wash the wheat in a bowl of water and drain. In a large pot, fry the onions in oil on a very low flame till soft. Then add the meat and turn to brown it all over. Cover with about 9 cups (2 liters) of water, bring to the boil, and remove the scum. Add the wheat, salt, pepper, cinnamon, and allspice. Put the eggs on top. Leave to cook all night, tightly covered, in the

HARISSA IN MEDIEVAL SPAIN AND THE ORIENTAL WORLD

Lucie Bolens writes in *La Cuisine Andalouse et l'Art de Vivre, XIe–XIIIe Siècle* that harissa—a porridge of pounded wheat and chopped meat—was eaten by Jews on Saturday in medieval Spain, where it was widely popular and sold by vendors in the street. It was meant to be two-thirds wheat and one-third meat. Vendors cheated by adding red clay to make it appear as though there were more meat while souk inspectors went around checking. It was cooked so long that the meat fell apart, then served with melted fat poured over and with sprinklings of cinnamon. This soft, creamy porridge, which represented the best of Andalusian cooking in the thirteenth century, was of Persian Sassanian origin. Another dish also called "harissa" was rice with chicken or mutton left to cook overnight, then pounded and mashed to a cream and served with mutton fat and cinnamon.

Harissa (nothing to do with the North African pepper paste of the same name) was the Saturday breakfast dish in several Oriental communities. It was left to cook overnight and eaten for breakfast with a sprinkling of cinnamon. A friend from Iraq, Sami Daniels, remembers that a Muslim cook was hired just to come and pound it to a creamy paste. The dish has been kept up by Jews of Yemeni and Adeni origin.

A book entitled *Recipes from Baghdad*, published by the Indian Red Cross in Baghdad in 1946 with an introduction by the queen mother of Iraq and a long list of contributors, many of them Jewish, gives a recipe for "Persian Harisa": Half a kilo each of mutton and whole wheat are left to cook overnight with bones and enough water so that it does not dry out. When all the water has been absorbed, the bones are removed and the mixture is passed first through a coarse, then a fine sieve, until it has the consistency of thick cream. It is eaten hot, seasoned with salt and a sprinkling of cinnamon, with melted fat poured over. The dish may also be eaten with a little sugar. The recipe lists chickpeas in the ingredients but does not mention how they are used. Nowadays people use cracked wheat (burghul, or bulgur) rather than whole wheat, and the food processor makes it easy to turn into a cream. A Syrian version of harissa, in which the ingredients are not mashed, but left whole, is called burghul bi dfeen.

lowest possible oven; or simmer 3 hours, or until the meat and wheat are very tender, adding water as required. There should be quite a lot of liquid at the end, when serving.

VARIATIONS

• For a Tunisian t'fina de blé arricha, add a cow's or calf's foot (cut in 4 pieces) and ½ teaspoon turmeric.

• For an Algerian oriza au blé, add 2–3 whole heads of garlic in their skin, 6 small new potatoes, or I lb (500 g) cubed sweet potato and 3 dried ñoras (dried sweet dark wine-colored peppers). You may add I teaspoon harissa (the North African pepper paste, that is) diluted in a little water, or I teaspoon paprika and ¼ teaspoon or more cayenne, and, if you want it sweet, 3 tablespoons sugar and I teaspoon cinnamon.

Burghul bi Dfeen

Meat Stew with Wheat

SERVES 6

This is the Syrian version of harissa, which is not all mashed to a cream.

> *2 medium onions, sliced*
> *5 tablespoons sunflower oil*
> *1 lb (500 g) lamb or beef shoulder or breast, cubed*
> *½ cup (100 g) chickpeas, soaked for at least 1 hour*
> *Salt and pepper*

2 cups (350 g) cracked wheat (medium or preferably coarse grind)
Cinnamon

Fry the onions in 2 tablespoons of oil till golden. Add the meat and stir, turning the pieces to brown them all over. Add the drained chickpeas, cover with water, and simmer for about 2 hours, until the meat and chickpeas are very tender, adding salt and pepper after about I hour. Add the cracked wheat and enough water to make up the liquid in the pan to at least 4 cups (I liter). Add a little more salt and pepper and cook for about 20 minutes, or until the liquid has been absorbed and the cracked wheat is tender. It should be very moist; add water if it seems dry. Stir in the remaining oil and serve sprinkled with cinnamon.

VARIATIONS

• For an Algerian t'fina de blé concassé, add a beef marrow bone, 6 chopped garlic cloves, I teaspoon paprika, and a little hot chili powder. In another t'fina the cracked wheat is replaced by barley.

Tabyit

Chicken and Rice

SERVES 8

This chicken stuffed with rice and cooked in rice was the traditional Sabbath dish of Baghdad. In still quite recent times, when hardly any family had an oven in Baghdad, it was cooked in a large copper cauldron with a very wide bottom and a narrower mouth, sitting on a *kanoun* or brazier that was built into the floor and wall of every home. It stayed on the slowly dying fire overnight from Friday, the heat kept in with quilts and special kitchen cushions made out of rags and burlap placed over it. A large number of eggs were placed on the lid, which had a high rim, to cook in the steam, and become the famous creamy-textured hamin eggs. At the same time, beets were also sometimes set to cook slowly in the ashes.

The eggs were eaten for breakfast, when the men came back from the synagogue, together with slices of fried eggplant, beets, tomato sal-

ads, and a favorite mango pickle which was sour and watery—not sweet or hot. At lunchtime on Saturday, the steaming pot was placed in cold water to help unstick the rice from the sides and turned out like a large cake with the chicken inside. Young brides were given as a wedding present a silver palette to help them remove the favored crusty bits that clung to the bottom and sides and to lay these on the top.

When I asked Naim Dangoor—who publishes *The Scribe*, a newsletter for the Iraqi community—about cooking in Baghdad, he invited me to meet him with his wife and his sisters Eileen Kalastchy and Doreen Dangoor. We spent the afternoon talking about cooking and life in Baghdad. After that, for almost two years, I called Eileen and Doreen regularly to ask them for recipes and for tips as I was trying the dishes. This is Eileen's way of making tabyit, translated to our facilities. (If you use a nonstick pot, it can be turned out and presented like a crusty cake.) The rice, cooked in the chicken stock with a mixture of gentle spices and tomato, comes out salmon pink, creamy soft, and aromatic. The stuffing is mixed with the chopped giblets. A large chicken—preferably a stewing hen—should be used, and long-grain rice rather than basmati. Every family had a mixture of ground spices for making tabyit, which included cardamom, cinnamon, ginger, nutmeg, allspice, cloves, and black pepper.

Haham Ezra Dangoor with his wife, Habiba, and their sons, 1895

> 4 cups (800 g) long-grain rice
> Salt
> 1 large stewing hen
> 1 large onion, chopped
> 2 large tomatoes, chopped (no need to peel them)
> Pepper
> 2 tablespoons tomato paste
> 1 teaspoon ground cardamom

1 teaspoon cinnamon
½ teaspoon ginger powder
¼ teaspoon nutmeg
½ teaspoon allspice
¼ teaspoon ground cloves

For the stuffing

½ cup (100 g) rice (from the original 4 cups;
    see procedure)
The giblets (gizzard, heart, and liver), cut in
    very small pieces
3 tomatoes, chopped unpeeled
¼ teaspoon salt
Pepper
½ teaspoon cinnamon
¼ teaspoon nutmeg
¼ teaspoon ground cardamom
A pinch of ginger
A pinch of ground cloves

First soak the rice. Pour boiling water over it, add 2 tablespoons of salt, and leave for 1 hour, then drain and rinse.

Take about ½ cup (100 g) of the drained rice for the stuffing and mix with the rest of the stuffing ingredients. Fill the chicken cavity about three-quarters full, to leave room for the rice to expand. Sew the opening or secure with a toothpick.

In a large, preferably nonstick pot, put the onion and tomatoes and stir well. Prick the chicken skin to release the fat and place the chicken on top. Leave on low heat for about 15 minutes, turning the chicken around. Plenty of fat will run out. Lift out the chicken and cook the onion and tomato in the chicken fat until the tomato sauce has dried out and begins to sizzle in the fat. Now put the chicken back into the pan and add water almost to cover. Bring to a boil and remove the scum, add ½ teaspoon salt and pepper, and simmer, covered, for almost 2 hours.

Lift the chicken out and measure the stock. It should measure about 7 cups (1⅔ liters). Reduce it by boiling if there is more, or remove some. Add more salt (about 1–1½ teaspoons—it needs quite a bit, because of the large quantity of rice to be added) and pepper and stir in the tomato paste and spices—cardamom, cinnamon, ginger, nutmeg, allspice, and cloves. Add the drained rice and cook, covered, on very low heat for about 10 minutes, until the water has almost disappeared. Then push the chicken deep into the rice. Cook in a preheated 400°F (200°C) oven for 30 minutes, then reduce to 250°F (120°C) and cook for 2–3 hours or overnight. Alternatively, cook on top of the stove on the lowest heat, and with a mat to disperse the heat, for 1 hour, then put into the lowest possible oven.

To serve, plunge the pot in cold water to help loosen the bottom crust. Serve inverted, or with the golden crust scraped off and placed on top. Accompany with pickles, a tomato salad, a plate of radishes, and a bunch of flat-leafed parsley.

VARIATIONS

• Naim Dangoor says that sometimes, in winter, more water was added and it became like a porridge, which they called "shorba" (soup).

• Iraqi Jews have carried tabyit to India and Burma and all the countries where they emigrated, and kept it up for centuries. A Burmese version adds garlic; an Indian one colors the rice with turmeric.

Grain—Rice, Bulgur, Pasta, and Couscous

Basic Ways of Cooking Rice

Rice is usually soaked in warm salted water for 10 minutes, then rinsed in a colander to remove the starchy powder that makes it sticky. The highly processed American long-grain does not need to be soaked or washed. The amount of water absorbed by the grain differs among the different varieties, and even among the same variety, depending on the harvest and the age of the grain. Rice is measured by volume, and the water required to cook it, as a general rule (although this varies), is about 1½ times the volume. One pound (500 g) rice (enough for 6) fills 2½ cups (600 ml), so the amount of water needed is 3¾ cups (900 ml). When a smaller quantity of rice is cooked, a

little more water is needed, as the amount of evaporation in proportion to the rice is greater.

1. Fried Rice

This rice is hardly fried, but that is how it is known. Heat 3 tablespoons of oil in a pan. Add 2 cups (400 g) of rice and stir until each grain is well coated and translucent. Add 3 cups (750 ml) of water or stock and some salt (about 1 teaspoon, unless the stock is already salted), bring to the boil, then lower the heat to a minimum and cook, covered and undisturbed, for about 18 minutes. Turn off the heat and steam for 5 minutes, until the water is absorbed and the rice is tender. My mother used a nonstick pan and turned the rice out like a cake.

RICE

E XCEPT FOR NORTH AFRICA, where the basic food is couscous, the Sephardi staple is rice. It comes with almost every meal. Rice first came into the Jewish world during the Babylonian exile in Mesopotamia, through Persia. It is mentioned in the Babylonian Talmud. The grain was adopted by one Sephardi community after another as it spread with Islam through the Middle East and the Mediterranean. Each community adopted the ways of preparing it that developed locally. In each community rice came to form part of the Friday-night meal. Certain embellishments were developed to give it a festive air, like coloring it yellow with saffron or turmeric, or sprinkling with almonds and pistachios, pressing it into a ring mold to give it a beautiful shape, or baking it in a pie crust. Each community used several different varieties of grain, some of which grew locally. In Iraq the most prestigious was the thin, slightly yellow, and aromatic ambar; in Iran it was the thin delicately flavored dom siah. The Jews of India used Patna and basmati. In Egypt we had an unremarkable long-grain and a roundish rice.

Soon after *A Book of Middle Eastern Food* came out nearly thirty years ago, I received a letter from a Muslim in Egypt saying that what I had described as "an Egyptian way of making rice" was a Jewish way. Egyptians used butter or clarified butter—not oil, as we did. When I started researching Middle Eastern recipes in the early sixties, there was a great deal of mystique surrounding the cooking of rice. There were many different ways, and everyone believed fiercely in his or her own. There were rituals, such as stretching a cloth under the lid and plunging the pan in cold water, and inexplicable touches that bordered on the magical. Syrian and Egyptian Jews fried their rice first, before pouring water over it. Egyptians cooked it uncovered, Syrians with the lid on. Turkish Jews used stock. Bukharan Jews cooked their rice in a cloth bag (see page 456) that was tied up more or less tightly according to how much liquid you wanted the grain to absorb. If there was little space for the rice to expand, it would come out in separate grains and fluffy. If it had a lot of space, it ended up bloated and soggy. For the Sabbath, the bag was put in a pot on top of the various ingredients that constituted the Saturday meal. Iranians were the great artist-perfectionists. They poured boiling salted water over their rice and soaked it overnight. They drained it and threw it in fresh boiling salted water, let it boil for 5 minutes, then drained it and put it back in the pan to steam with a cloth stretched under the lid. The pan was often lined with thinly sliced potatoes so that the dish could be turned out like a cake.

Nowadays people try to make life easier for themselves. The ways of making rice have been simplified. The types of rice used are those available in the supermarket—American long-grain, Patna, and basmati. Basmati is the most favored, for its aromatic qualities and fluffy separateness. Short-grain round rice is used for milk puddings and stuffing vegetables, because it sticks together, and in Italy, of course, for risottos.

People used different kinds of oil to cook rice, depending on the country—it could be sesame or peanut oil; in Egypt it was sesame or corn oil; in Turkey, for five centuries and until a few decades ago, it was olive oil—but now sunflower oil has generally been adopted in Europe.

2. Boiled Rice

Boil 3 cups (750 ml) of water with 1 teaspoon of salt. Add 2 cups (400 g) of rice and simmer, covered, on very low heat for 18 minutes, or until tender. Stir in 3 tablespoons of oil.

3. Steamed Rice

This is my favorite way for basmati, and it is based on the Iranian style.

Soak 2 cups (400 g) of rice in plenty of cold water with 1 tablespoon of salt for at least 1 hour. (Do not be afraid of the large amount of salt—it drains away with the water.) In a large pan with a tight-fitting lid, bring about 9 cups (2 liters) of water to a rolling boil with 3 tablespoons of salt. Pour in the drained rice, stir well, and boil hard for 10 minutes. Strain quickly, while the rice is still a little underdone. Put 1 tablespoon light vegetable oil in the pan, pour the rice back in, and stir in 2 more tablespoons of oil. Cover tightly with the lid and steam on the lowest heat (with no extra water) for 20 minutes, or until tender.

To Reheat Rice

It is best to reheat large quantities of rice in the oven or microwave, for the bottom burns easily.

Riz au Saffran

Saffron Rice

SERVES 6

This golden rice—in Arabic, "roz bi zaafran" —was a festive and Friday-night favorite in Oriental communities. Depending on the country, different types of rice were used and different methods of cooking. Using stock instead of water makes it extra delicious.

3¾ cups (900 ml) water or stock
3 tablespoons sunflower or light vegetable oil
About 1 teaspoon salt
½ teaspoon powdered saffron
2½ cups (500 g) basmati or long-grain rice

Bring the water or stock to the boil with the oil and salt. Add the saffron and pour in the rice. Let it come to the boil again and stir well, then lower the heat to a minimum and cook gently, with the lid on, for about 20 minutes, until little holes appear on the surface and the rice is tender. Leave to rest, covered, for a few minutes before serving. Pack if you like in an oiled ring mold and turn out before serving.

VARIATIONS

- Another way is to stir the rice in hot oil over very low heat until it is well coated and translucent, then add hot water or stock, salt, and saffron.
- Garnish if you like with 1 chopped onion fried in vegetable oil till golden, or ⅔ cup (100 g) raisins soaked in boiling water for a few minutes and ½ cup (100 g) flaked or chopped almonds toasted under the broiler or fried in 2 tablespoons of oil.
- Sprinkle with a mixture of toasted pine nuts and chopped almonds and pistachios.

Risotto Giallo del Shabbat

Saffron Risotto

SERVES 4

According to the Italian writer Giuseppe Maffioli, in *La Cucina Veneziana* (1982), the Jews of the Venice Ghetto had a much greater variety of risotti than the local population, combining the rice with vegetables such as peas, artichokes, zucchini, spinach, eggplant, celery, and tomatoes, and sometimes with chicken livers and bits of chicken or kosher sausage. And they had their own way of making the risotti, which they called "pilaf." They would add the liquid all in one go instead of a little at a time as it becomes absorbed (the way Italians make risotti). It was a method adopted from the *levantini* who lived in the ghetto. Risi colle uvette—rice with raisins—an old Venetian Jewish classic, is like a pilaf served cold as a first course in Turkey today.

Risotto giallo is an old Jewish specialty of Ferrara and Venice, served on the Sabbath as a first course or as a side dish. It is said to be the origin of the famous risotto alla milanese. The Jews dealt in saffron and other spices and used them more than the general population. The old traditional way was to fry the rice in goose or veal fat or in bone marrow, but most people now use sunflower oil. The combination of stock, saffron, and wine gives this creamy rice a most seductive quality.

> 1½ cups (300 g) Italian risotto rice
>   (preferably Arborio)
> 3 tablespoons sunflower oil
> 4 cups (1 liter) boiling chicken stock
>   (you may use bouillon cubes)
> ½ cup (125 ml) dry white wine
> About ¾ teaspoon salt
> ½ teaspoon saffron powder or threads

In a large pan, stir the rice in the hot oil till it becomes translucent, then add the boiling stock and white wine (there is more liquid than usual, and the result is very moist) and stir well. Simmer, covered, for about 20–25 minutes, until the rice is done *al dente*, adding salt, if necessary, and the saffron towards the end.

VARIATIONS

• For a risotto giallo ai funghi, stir in at the end 10 oz (300 g) sliced mushrooms fried in 3–4 tablespoons oil with 2 finely chopped garlic cloves and seasoned with a little salt.

• If there is no meat in the meal, you may stir in 2 tablespoons butter and ½ cup (50 g) grated Parmesan at the end.

Coconut Yellow Rice

SERVES 6

This is a Sabbath dish of the Bene Israel community. The recipe, from Mrs. Norah Solomon, calls for the milk obtained from a fresh coconut, but it is also very successful made with creamed coconut or canned unsweetened coconut milk.

2 cups (400 g) rice
2½ oz (65 g) creamed coconut
    (see page 235), cut in pieces
4 cups (1 liter) water
3 cardamom pods, cracked
½ teaspoon turmeric
About 1 teaspoon salt

Wash the rice. Put the rest of the ingredients in a saucepan and bring to the boil. Stir, and when the creamed coconut is completely dissolved, add the drained rice. Bring to the boil, then simmer, covered, on very low heat for 25 minutes, or until done. Add more boiling water if the rice becomes too dry (it can easily burn at the bottom).

VARIATIONS

• Instead of creamed coconut, use a 14-oz (400-ml) can of coconut milk mixed with 2¼ cups (500 ml) water.

• Mrs. Elisheva Moses cooks the rice in a mixture of coconut milk and stock, adds a cinnamon stick and 5 cloves, and serves it for a party garnished with fried onion, fried nuts and raisins, and silverleaf paper.

PERSIA

THE PERSIAN COMMUNITY is one of the oldest in the Diaspora. It dates back to the Babylonian exile in the fourth century B.C. For two centuries, the Jews in exile in Mesopotamia and in the homeland in Palestine were under Persian rule; and the Persian community was attached to the Babylonian, and depended on the early Babylonian yeshivot (Jewish academies). Its culture today is similar in its everyday Jewish practice to that of the Jews of Iraq. Their cooking too is similar.

The Jews of Persia were known for their wealth in ancient and medieval times. As merchants, they were part of the network that connected the West with China in the silk trade and with India in the spice trade. They were prosperous and relatively well integrated through the Sassanian period, in the third century A.D. and the Muslim Arab period. Their position deteriorated with the Shiite Safavid regime, whose rigid way of interpreting the Koran excluded and marginalized them. There was a revival of Jewish life during the Sunni Mogul Empire, which was liberal towards minorities. But when the Moguls moved to India and the Shias returned to power at the beginning of the sixteenth century, the Jews were again oppressed and marginalized. The shahs did not allow them at court or in any position of power and influence. Shah Abbas was an exception and allowed them to settle in his capital, Isfahan, but they were expelled in 1656 and forced to convert to Islam. Many immigrated to Iraq, Syria, Bukhara, Samarkand, Baku, and Georgia. A very small community was left in Persia in the eighteenth century—and they lived miserable, humble lives, quietly and afraid.

In a chapter entitled "Parsi, Jewish & Armenian Women" from a 1930s book (with my apologies, I can't trace it any more), the writer says:

> In most large cities there is a Jewish quarter which, bad as a moslem city can sometimes be, is even worse. Jewish women are not veiled but they adopt the black outdoor chador worn by all Persian townswomen and keep their faces well covered. In their own houses they wear long full skirts with a jumper-like upper garment and a jacket, a muslin scarf is pinned under the chin. They speak Persian and English and French which are looked upon as languages of advancement. Many are educated in French and English schools.
>
> The girls are betrothed when they are eight or nine but not married until they are about sixteen. They have Biblical, Hebrew and also Persian names. (Kafi means "enough" and is given when a boy would have been a much more welcome arrival than a girl. The name is often given and one is sorry for the bearer of the name).

He writes that many Jewish women do embroidery and visit many shrines that are places of pilgrimage, like Queen Esther's burial place, near Isfahan. He adds that, though Persians have never persecuted the Jews, they treat them with the utmost contempt.

In the nineteenth century, the entire Jewish community of Meshed was forced to convert to Islam but continued to practice Judaism in secret. Some managed to escape to Afghanistan, where they returned to Judaism at the end of the century. A large number went together on a hajj (pilgrimage) to Mecca as Muslims, then on to Medina and to holy Muslim sites in Jerusalem. There they stayed, returning to Judaism, and they built a special quarter for themselves with a beautiful synagogue.

With the accession of the Pahlavi dynasty (the late shah's father) in 1925, the position of the Jews in Iran improved enormously. The transformation was so great that most left the hinterland for Teheran. Some, who were close to Riza Shah and his son Muhammad Riza, lived very grandly. But many of the poor and middle classes went to Israel in 1948 in an operation called "Magic Carpet." The wealthy are now mostly in Los Angeles.

The foreword to a little book entitled *Persian (Jewish) Cook Book: Presented by The Sisterhood*

Postcard depicting a Jewish doctor and his family, Iran

of the Persian Congregation, Skokie, Illinois, begins: "The recipes listed in this book have been lovingly prepared for many years in much the same way as they were generations ago in the Urmia and Eravon areas of Persia. In the second decade of the twentieth century began their migration to the city of Chicago." It continues, "Our people possessed the talent of making a little food go a long way, therefore this book has numerous recipes for soups." Their food is poor food compared with the jeweled rice and other grand dishes adopted by the wealthy community in the time of the shah.

Shirin Polo

Sweet Jeweled Rice

SERVES 6

This is now a favorite at Iranian Jewish weddings, where it is served with roast chicken, cut into small pieces and sprinkled on top of the rice. My brother went to one such wedding in London where a band played Iranian music. He raved about the rice. There are various versions—usually with candied orange peel and almonds and all kinds of dried fruit. The following, with dried pitted sour cherries and cranberries (which can be found in some supermarkets), is a delight. It sounds difficult but it is not. You may use store-bought candied peel, but a homemade one tastes better.

2½ cups (500 g) basmati rice
About 1¼ teaspoons salt
Finely pared peel of 2 oranges, finely shredded
½ cup (100 g) sugar
⅓–½ cup (50–75 g) dried pitted sour
    cherries
⅓–½ cup (50–75 g) dried cranberries
5–6 tablespoons sunflower oil
¼ teaspoon saffron powder
1 cup (100 g) split blanched almonds

Wash the rice, then soak it in cold water with 1 tablespoon of salt for at least 1 hour.

To make candied peel, pare off the orange peel, leaving behind the white pith, and shred it finely. In a small pan, boil the peel in plenty of water for ½ hour to remove the bitterness, then drain. In the same pan put the sugar with ⅓ cup (80 ml) of water and bring to the boil. Add the drained peel and simmer for about 20 minutes. Soak the sour cherries and cranberries in water for 15 minutes.

Bring about 9 cups (2 liters) of water with about 2 tablespoons of salt to the boil (do not worry—the salt will be drained away) in a large saucepan. Pour the drained rice into the fast-boiling water, let it come to the boil again, and boil hard for about 8 minutes, or until the rice is partly cooked and still a little firm, then drain in a colander. Pour the oil in the bottom of the pan. Stir the saffron in and pour the rice back in. Mix in the candied peel (drained of syrup), the drained cherries and cranberries, and the almonds, and stir very well, so that all the rice is evenly colored yellow with the saffron and imbued with oil.

Put the lid on and steam on the lowest heat for 20 minutes until tender. Or put the rice in a baking dish, cover with foil, and bake at 350°F (150°C) for 30 minutes.

Note:

• It is always best to reheat the rice, if necessary, in the oven, for it tends to burn at the bottom of the pan when it is dry.

VARIATIONS

• Instead of the sour cherries and cranberries, use chopped dried apricots and chopped dates.
• Add coarsely chopped pistachios as well as almonds.
• Use ⅓ cup (50 g) commercial chopped candied peel instead of making your own.
• Omit the candied orange peel if you don't like its sweetness.

Purdah Pilau

Rice and Chicken in a Pie

SERVES 10

This is a party dish of Iraqi Jews. "Purdah" means "veiled" and implies that the rice is "hidden" by the pastry. It is a complex dish, with pieces of chicken, vermicelli, and almonds mixed in with the rice. The spicing is delicate and it looks good. People used to make their own very thin pie crust, but these days filo pastry is used.

1 chicken

2 onions, quartered

1 teaspoon cinnamon

½ teaspoon allspice

¼ teaspoon cardamom powder

Salt and pepper

Juice of ½ lemon

½ cup (50 g) vermicelli broken up in your
    hand

1¾ cups (350 g) American long-grain or
    Patna rice

¼ cup (50 g) blanched almonds

Sunflower or light vegetable oil

¼ cup (50 g) pine nuts

7 large sheets filo pastry

1 egg yolk

Put the chicken in a pot with about 9 cups (2 liters) of water to cover. Bring to the boil, remove the scum, then add the onion, cinnamon, allspice, cardamom, salt, and pepper. Simmer, covered, for 45 minutes. Lift out the chicken and, when it is cool enough to handle, skin and bone it and cut it into small pieces. Strain the stock and boil down to reduce to about 3½ cups (800 ml), then add the lemon juice.

Break the vermicelli into small pieces with your hands and toast them under the broiler for a few minutes, until browned, stirring so that they brown evenly. (Watch them, for they brown very quickly.) Pour the rice and vermicelli into the boiling stock, add a little salt, and cook, covered, for about 15 minutes, or until little holes appear on the surface of the rice. Remove from the heat before all the stock has been absorbed.

Fry the almonds in 2 tablespoons of oil, stirring, until golden. Add the pine nuts and stir till they are slightly browned. Mix the nuts and the chicken pieces with the rice and let the mixture cool.

Line a round baking dish or a large springform cake pan about 11 inches (28 cm) with greaseproof or wax paper, and brush with oil. Fit 4 sheets of filo in the dish or cake pan to cover the bottom and sides, brushing each with oil, and letting them overlap and hang out over the rim. Fill with the rice-and-chicken mixture. Bring the hanging pastry edges up and fold them over the rice. Cover with 3 more sheets of overlapping pastry, brushing the first 2 with oil. Trim the corners with scissors and tuck the edges down into the sides of the pan to close the pie. Brush the top with the egg yolk mixed with 1 teaspoon of water and bake in a 350°F (180°C) oven for about 30 minutes, or until the top is golden. Lift the pie out carefully and serve hot.

VARIATION

● Instead of using filo, you can make a piecrust. Beat ¾ cup (175 ml) sunflower oil with 6 tablespoons warm water and ½ teaspoon salt, then mix in about 3 cups (425 g) flour. Break the dough into 2 lumps, one two-thirds of the dough, the other one-third. Roll each out thin and use the large one for the bottom and the small one for the top. Trim the edges, and seal the pie by pinching them together. It is a very soft dough, which does not stick and does not need dusting with flour to roll out because it is so greasy, but it needs careful handling. The best way to lift it up is to roll it gently around the rolling pin. If there are any tears, patch them with a small piece of leftover dough.

BUKHARAN JEWS

UNTIL THE SIXTEENTH CENTURY, the Iranian-speaking Jews, whose origins date back to the ancient Persian Empire, formed a single community. It was split in two by the establishment of the Shiite Safavid monarchy, which separated Iran from Sunni Central Asia. The latter split in the eighteenth century into the states of Bukhara and Afghanistan. Ever since, the three communities have had little contact with each other or with the outside world, but some similarities in the cooking—in particular the rice dishes and the use of fruit with meat and rice—bear witness to the old unity.

The Bukharan Jews remained cut off from the rest of Jewry until 1793, when a messenger from Tétouan in Morocco, Joseph Maman al-Maghribi, allegedly shocked by their ignorance and seeing groups forced into conversion to Islam, decided to stay. He became their leader and initiated the Hibbat Zion (Love of Zion) movement, which was eventually to bring thousands of Bukharan Jews to Jerusalem, first on yearly pilgrimages, then as settlers.

Traditional types of Bukharan Jews

They began settling in the city in the late nineteenth century, and emigration grew between 1917 and 1924, when the Russian Revolution brought them under Bolshevik rule. For a long time they had their own quarter with their own synagogues in Jerusalem, and the community kept its distinctive ethnic identity. Recently, newcomers from the Soviet Union, arriving in Israel and the U.S. with their multicolored silk clothes and old cooking traditions, have revived the old identity.

The Bukharan Jews, who lived in cities like Samarkand, Bukhara, Tashkent, Dushanbe, Kokand, and various small towns of Uzbekistan, have a reputation for good eating and hospitality, traditions they shared with the local Muslims. Unlike the Afghani Jews, who were mainly poor mountain people, and the Persian Jews, who had been very poor until they became freer and prosperous under the shah, Bukharan Jews always lived well. As they tell you, there was always a cow or a sheep to kill. Their big celebratory meals are legendary.

Penina Mirzoeff, who lived in Samarkand until 1925, gave me the Bukharan recipes I have included and told me about the community, which was thriving and prosperous until the Russian Revolution. Jews were mostly merchants. They were involved in the early silk trade, when Samarkand was on the camel-caravan silk route from China. More recently, they brought goods from Moscow and sold them at regional markets. They produced the multicolored flower-printed silks which Bukharans are famous for. Everything they used and wore was in pure silk—dresses, headscarves, curtains, bedcovers, cushions. Silk coats and hats were embroidered with real gold thread. The Jews were also involved in precious stones—in lapis lazuli and sapphires. Mr. Mirzoeff's family traded in furs from Afghanistan.

A large minority were rich. There were no beggars in the community. Even the poor were employed, peddling bits of cloth, and had their own little houses. In Samarkand they lived mostly in the old town, which was near the market and the business bazaar. Some lived outside it, in larger houses. All the houses had inner courtyards with big gates for carriages and small doors for privacy. There were summer buildings and winter buildings, because the climate was very extreme and severe, and also stables. They all kept a cow and chickens and had their own supplies of milk and eggs, and they had horses. Servants, who were Muslim fellahin, had special quarters. Usually the cook was Jewish. The women of the house also took part in the cooking.

Every house had a big cellar for preserves. Fresh onions and carrots were kept covered with earth. Grapes and apples were hung up to dry. Melted-down sheep's-tail fat was kept in jars. In September they prepared tomato juice and wine and distilled their own arak. They boiled down grape juice to a thick brown syrup called "shini," which was eaten like honey on bread, or diluted in water to make a cold drink for guests or into boiling water to make tea. It was given especially to nursing mothers. Melon peel, carrots, and grapes were cooked in the syrup to make sweet preserves. Little eggplants were pickled in vinegar. Fresh foods were kept in enormous domed baskets which were hung in a cold place in the open air. There were also iceboxes. Some families had wells in the courtyard and drew their own fresh water. In the old town, peddlers came around selling water for washing in sheepskin bags. Cooking was done on open fires in the middle of the courtyard and in communal clay ovens.

Festive meals were usually in the courtyards. At ordinary gatherings the women sat on one side of the table, the men on the other; at weddings they were in different rooms. Wedding parties went on for seven days and seven nights, and people were invited for dinner every night. The cooking was done over a bonfire in huge cauldrons while musicians played drums, accordions, and other musical instruments.

When the Bolsheviks captured Samarkand, they threw the people out of their grand houses, and whole families were forced to squeeze into one or two rooms. Some were sent to Siberia, because they were rich.

The Jews had lived close to the Muslims and in the Muslim style. They ate sitting on the floor on thick blankets covered with silk and cushions. When they moved to the new town, where the Russians lived, they adopted Russian styles, including eating at table. And they appended "-off" to the end of their names. They spoke the same language, wore the same clothes, and ate the same food as the Muslims. You can detect various influences in their cooking, apart from Persian and Turkish echoes. They have Mongolian mantu (steamed meat dumplings) and Indian samosas. Russian dishes like pechonki, kotleti, piroshki, borscht, and shashlik were adopted, and a few dishes, like stuffed vegetables, came through the Jerusalem Sephardim. Theirs was a meat-rich diet. At gatherings it was usual to put a whole chicken, four lamb chops, and three ribs of beef in front of three people. Cooked vegetables never came to the table except in a stew. Vegetables were served raw, chopped up as a salad, dressed only with salt and lemon. Pasta was common but rice was the grand prestigious food. The national dish, plof, a rice dish cooked with grated carrots, chopped onions, raisins, chicken, and meat, was considered the "shah of foods" and served on special occasions to honor guests. Bukharan food is very natural in flavor and mostly seasoned only with salt and pepper. The only aromatics are garlic, turmeric, saffron, and fresh coriander, with sometimes a tiny bit of cinnamon.

Bukharan Jews always had a Jewish education. Rabbis came from Jerusalem. To have a good family name, you had to be religious. It was considered an honor to be a cantor and to give your services free. Families baked their own bread, including a fine crispbread called "tnouk," at home. A woman went around to the houses to make it for them. Even under communism, old people continued to keep the Sabbath and to have their animals ritually slaughtered by a *shohet* who visited the houses secretly at strange hours, such as four in the morning. In the old days, preparations for the Sabbath began on Wednesday. Quilted silk covers made from old clothes were used to wrap foods and cover large pots and tea urns to keep them hot.

The traditional Friday-night Bukharan meal begins with boyjon (eggplant puree mixed only with salt and garlic) and a salad of chopped tomato, cucumber, lettuce, onion, and coriander dressed with salt and lemon, followed by fried fish in a garlic-and-coriander sauce. The main dish, yakhni, is two kinds of boiled meat and chicken. The meats are brought whole to the table and sliced just before serving, with a little stock poured over, and boiled vegetables—carrots, potatoes, leeks, turnips—to garnish. The Friday-night special is khalti barsh—rice with chopped meat and liver and plenty of chopped coriander cooked together in a linen bag. The technique of cooking rice in a bag immersed in stock or water is Jewish. I have never come across it elsewhere. The method was devised as a way of cooking rice overnight without its burning or turning into a creamy mush. The closed bag does not give too much space for the grain to grow and stops it from absorbing too much liquid and becoming bloated and soggy. The result is rice with a very distinctive flavor and texture. For Saturday there is khalti savo, a different rice, also cooked in a bag, sometimes containing chopped fruit.

The only dessert at the end of a Bukharan meal is fruit or a compote of fresh or dried fruit, and, to finish, nuts and halvah with green tea. There are not many Bukharan pastries. A favorite, prepared for visitors who drop in on the Sabbath and festivals, is deep-fried ribbons of thin dough sprinkled with confectioners' sugar. They are served with chai kaymokee—green tea aerated and darkened by continuous ladling, then mixed with clotted cream, butter, and milk, and sometimes sprinkled with chopped almonds or walnuts.

KHALTI BARSH

Bukharan Rice with Meat in a Bag

Penina Mirzoeff described the method of cooking rice in a bag ("khalti" means "sack" or "bag") for Friday night. It is typically Jewish and was devised as a way of cooking the grain overnight without letting it get bloated and soggy. A hand-sewn linen bag is filled with a rice mixture: 2½ cups (500 g) basmati or American long-grain rice, ½ lb (250 g) finely chopped tender meat, ½ lb (250 g) calf's or chicken liver (salted and grilled briefly on either side to make it kosher) cut into small pieces, a huge bunch of coriander (2 cups chopped), salt, and pepper. The rice is pressed down and the bag is filled and tied up tightly. It is filled only three-quarters full, to leave just enough room for the rice to expand but not enough for it to get bloated and soggy after hours immersed in a pan of boiling water. When the rice is served, turned out of the bag, it is very soft and very green.

The rice is also left to be eaten cold on the Saturday, in which case it turns into a firm loaf that is served cut into thick slices. Nowadays, in the West, most Bukharans no longer use the bag, since it is a bother to keep it clean and it needs to be boiled to be sterilized. It is simple enough to cook it in the usual way in a pan with 3 cups (750 ml) of water, but the idea of the bag is a nostalgic one and represents a unique way of life.

Plof

Bukharan Rice with Chicken and Carrots

SERVES 6

Plof is the Bukharan national dish, the king of dishes, the celebratory dish for large family gatherings, served at weddings, engagements, and bar mitzvahs to honor guests. It is always served at the end of the meal, after all the other foods—nearly always consisting of fried fish in garlic-and-coriander sauce, eggplant puree, pickles, chopped mixed salad of tomato, cucumber, lettuce, and coriander, and great quantities of chicken and meat, which are brought out whole and cut up at the table.

The art of making plof is not to mix the ingredients but to cook them in layers. The result, when you turn it out, inverted, is a topping of meltingly soft—and in parts caramelized—vegetables and browned chicken over a fluffy, lightly colored rice infused with the flavors of the vegetables. The rice is often mixed with sharp, tiny brownish-red barberries or little black raisins. You can now find the dried barberries in Iranian and Oriental stores.

2½ cups (500 g) basmati or American
long-grain rice
Salt
3¾ cups (900 ml) boiling water
2 large onions, sliced
1 lb (500 g) carrots, cut into thin juliennes
4 tablespoons corn or light vegetable oil
1 lb (500 g) chicken fillets (I prefer
thigh), cubed
Pepper
2–3 tablespoons raisins or barberries
(optional)

Wash and drain the rice. Put it in a bowl with 1 teaspoon salt and pour the boiling water over it. Mix well and leave to soak for about 1 hour.

Fry the onions and half the carrots in the oil until the onion is very soft. Add the chicken, season with salt and pepper, and cook, turning the pieces over, for about 10 minutes. Cover with the remaining carrots and sprinkle with plenty of pepper. Leave on a very low fire for a few minutes longer.

Mix the barberries or raisins, if using, into the rice, and pour the rice with its soaking water over the carrots, distributing it all over the top, without mixing it in or disturbing the layers. Simmer, with the lid on, for about 30 minutes, or until the water has been absorbed and the rice is very tender. You may or may not need to add a little water if it becomes too dry before it is cooked. You can reheat the pan before serving, in the oven or over very low heat.

Invert the pan onto a serving dish. In Bukhara there is an art to dishing out the plof from the cauldron—first the rice, then the carrots, meat, and onions on top—onto trays for groups of five or six, from which guests help themselves, eating from the side nearest to them.

VARIATION

- Meat can be used instead of chicken.

Savo

Bukharan Rice with Fruit

SERVES 6

This soft, fruity rice with a delicate flavor and brown hue is a modern adaptation of a traditional Bukharan Sabbath rice that is cooked overnight in a linen bag immersed in a bone soup, also full of fruit (see box on page 456 for the method of cooking rice in a bag). When it is cooked in a bag it is called "khalta savo." This way—cooking the rice for a long time, with the stock from the soup, in a baking dish or casserole in the oven—reproduces the texture and flavor of the traditional dish. In the old days, fresh or dried fruit was used, depending on the season. Although a little diced meat was also usually included, I prefer this meatless version. Prepare the soup first, then use it to cook the rice.

For the soup

5 cups (1¼ liters) meat or chicken stock (you may use bouillon cubes)
3 tart or sweet apples, quartered and cored
1 quince (if available), quartered
2 tablespoons raisins
4 dried apricots
4 dried pitted dates
3 pitted prunes
1 teaspoon cinnamon
Salt

For the rice

2½ cups (500 g) basmati or American long-grain rice
½ teaspoon cinnamon
¼ teaspoon saffron powder or threads (optional)
Salt
1 apple with skin, cored and chopped
1½ tablespoons raisins
3 dates, chopped
½ quince (if available), chopped

Put all the soup ingredients in a pan and simmer for about 1 hour.

Wash and drain the rice, and mix thoroughly with the rest of the ingredients and a little salt in an oven dish or casserole. Pour in about 3½ cups (900 ml) of the strained broth from the soup (this quantity takes into account the liquid that the fruit will give out; if you use more the rice will be sticky and pasty), and stir well. Reserve the rest of the soup, including the fruit. Bake, covered with foil or a lid, in a 350°F (180°C) oven for about 3 hours. Serve hot, accompanied by the remaining soup with the fruit, heated through.

VARIATION

• For another Sabbath meal, mix with the rice 1 lb (500 g) grated carrots fried in 4 tablespoons of vegetable oil on a high flame until brown and caramelized, 4 chopped tomatoes, 3 tablespoons raisins, ½ chopped apple, and ½ chopped quince. The caramelized carrots give the rice a light brown color. You might also add ½ lb (250 g) cubed lamb or chicken.

Kichree

Rice and Red Lentils

SERVES 4

This Iraqi version of a dish that originated in India (it is related to kedgeree) was cooked every Thursday evening by Jewish families in Baghdad as part of the light dairy meal that is supposed to rest the stomach in preparation for the rich Sabbath food.

It is one of those dishes that everyone has a special way of making. The proportion of rice and lentils varies; some color it with turmeric, some with tomato paste; and there are various ways of serving. The most popular are with a cheese topping and with yogurt. You can use any type of rice except short round rice, which becomes a mush after long cooking. The following is the way my friend Sami Zubaida, a sociologist and gourmet and now culinary historian, makes it.

> 4 garlic cloves, minced or crushed in a press
> 3 tablespoons light vegetable oil
> 2 teaspoons cumin
> 2 tablespoons tomato paste
> 1 cup (200 g) rice—basmati, Patna, or American long-grain
> 1 cup (200 g) red lentils
> About 1 teaspoon salt
> Pepper
> 3 oz (75 g) butter, cut into pieces

For the optional cheese side dish or topping

> 1 large onion, sliced
> 3 tablespoons oil
> 12 oz (350 g) halumi cheese or mozzarella, sliced

Fry the garlic in the oil till it just begins to color. Stir in the cumin and tomato paste. Add the rice and lentils (in this case they do not need to be washed) and stir over very low heat until all the grains are coated. Cover with 4 cups (1 liter) boiling water. Add salt and pepper, bring to the boil, and simmer, covered, on very low heat for about 45 minutes, until the rice is very soft. Be careful that it does not dry out or burn; add water if necessary. Stir in the butter and let it melt in. Keep the lid on. Serve topped with yogurt or with the cheese topping that follows.

For the topping: In a large frying pan, fry the onion in the oil until golden. Lay the cheese on top and leave the pan on low heat. Serve when the cheese begins to bubble.

VARIATIONS

- For the topping, 2 large slices of tomatoes can be added to the onions and allowed to soften before the cheese goes in.
- Eggs fried in butter can be served on top.
- Indian Jews flavor the dish with garam masala, cardamom, cinnamon, and cumin—all fried with plenty of garlic.

Megadarra

Brown Lentils and Rice

SERVES 4–6

In Syria it was called "mudardara," but for us in Egypt it was "megadarra." Accompanied by yogurt, it was a regular part of traditional Jewish dairy meals on Thursday nights, and on Saturdays it was eaten cold. It may seem that the recipe calls for a large amount of onions—but when they are crisp and brown and caramelized it will seem that there are not enough.

> *3 large onions weighing about 1½ lbs*
> *(750 g), cut in half and sliced*
> *½ cup (125 ml) olive oil*
> *1½ cups (250 g) large brown lentils*
> *1¼ cups (250 g) long-grain rice*
> *About 1 teaspoon salt*
> *Pepper*

Fry the onions in the oil, stirring often, until they turn a rich golden brown.

Rinse the lentils and cook them in 4½ cups (1 liter) of water for 20 minutes. Now add half the fried onions and the rice. Season with salt and pepper and stir well. Put the lid on and cook on very low heat for another 20 minutes, or until the rice and lentils are tender, adding water if it becomes too dry.

At the same time, put the remaining onions back on the fire and continue to fry them, stirring often, until they are a dark brown and almost caramelized.

Serve the rice hot or at room temperature with these onions sprinkled on top.

Roz bil Shaghria

Rice with Vermicelli

SERVES 4

This everyday Arab rice is served with all kinds of meat dishes, and also forms part of Jewish dairy meals, accompanied by yogurt and salad.

> *½ cup (50 g) vermicelli, broken into pieces*
> *about 1 inch (2½ cm) long in your*
> *hand*
> *2 tablespoons sunflower oil*
> *1¼ cups (250 g) long-grain rice*
> *3 cups (750 ml) water*
> *About 1 teaspoon salt*

Toast the vermicelli in a dry frying pan on the range, or on a baking sheet under the broiler, until they are brown, stirring so that they brown evenly. Watch them, for they brown very quickly.

Heat the oil in a saucepan over medium heat, add the rice, and stir until the grains are well coated. Pour in the water, add the browned vermicelli and some salt, and stir well. Then simmer, covered, for about 18 minutes, or until the rice is tender and the water absorbed. Turn off the heat and steam with the lid on for another 5 minutes.

VARIATIONS

• Fry 1 chopped onion in the oil until golden before adding the rice, and stir in a handful of boiled or canned chickpeas.

• Jews from Iran do not fry their rice but boil it with the toasted noodles until not quite done, then drain and steam it. They also add black raisins.

- This rice can also be colored yellow. Add ¼ teaspoon of saffron powder or turmeric to the cooking water.

Roz bil Ful Ahdar

Rice with Fresh Fava Beans

SERVES 6–8

All kinds of dishes with fava beans, from soups to stews, are associated with Passover, partly because it is early spring when their season begins and they are at their tender best, partly because they are supposed to be what the Hebrews ate during their bondage in Egypt. There are versions of this rice dish throughout the Sephardi world. This one, with sugar and lemon, garlic and dill, has a lovely flavor. It is best made with fresh fava beans, but frozen ones will also do. When it is part of a dairy meal, it is served with yogurt.

> *1 lb (500 g) shelled fava beans*
> *Salt*
> *4 cloves garlic, crushed*
> *2 tablespoons sunflower or light vegetable oil*
> *Juice of ½ lemon*
> *1 teaspoon sugar*
> *2½ cups (500 g) basmati or American*
>   *long-grain rice*
> *A very large bunch of dill, finely chopped*
>   *(1 cup)*
> *3 oz (75 g) butter, cut into pieces,*
>   *or 4 tablespoons light vegetable oil*

I like to cook the fava beans separately, because you can never be sure how long they will take. In the spring, when they are very young, they cook in hardly any time. As they get older, they can take up to ½ hour. You can now sometimes buy them already shelled in supermarkets, but they are easy enough to shell. Most people do not bother to remove the white outer skin, although it is considered more refined without. Boil the beans in a small pan in salted water until tender and drain.

Fry the garlic in the same (dried) pan in the oil until the aroma rises. Add the lemon juice, sugar, and beans and cook, stirring, a minute or two, so that they absorb the flavors.

In the meantime, in a large, heavy-bottomed pan boil plenty of salted water. Throw in the rice, stir, and let it boil hard for about 10 minutes. While the rice is still underdone and a little hard, throw in the dill, stir, then quickly drain in a colander. (A little of the dill will run out with the water but most will stick to the rice, and you will have a beautiful speckled effect.) Pour the rice back in the pan, and stir in the beans and the butter. Put the lid on and steam on a very low flame for about 20 minutes, until the rice is tender. Be careful that it does not burn at the bottom.

VARIATIONS

- Add 14 oz (400 g) quartered frozen artichoke hearts, defrosted (or the weight of a package).

- For a Persian version, put ½ teaspoon saffron powder in the rice water before you throw in the dill.

Arroz kon Espinaka

Rice with Spinach

SERVES 6

A dish in the Judeo-Spanish tradition of Istanbul.

> 1½ lbs (750 g) fresh spinach
> 1 large onion, coarsely chopped
> 4 tablespoons sunflower or light vegetable oil
> 2½ cups (500 g) rice
> 3¾ cups (900 ml) stock or water
> About 1¼ teaspoons of salt (less if the stock is salted)
> 1 teaspoon sugar
> Juice of ½ lemon or more to taste
> Pepper

Wash and drain the spinach, and cut it coarsely or leave it whole. You do not need to remove the stems. Fry the onion in the oil in a large pan till soft. Add the rice and stir well. Then add the stock or water, salt, sugar, and spinach. Stir well and cook the rice for about 20 minutes, until tender. Stir in the lemon juice and pepper, to taste, before serving.

Green Pea Pulau

SERVES 6

An Indian Bene Israel recipe from Sophie Jhirad's mother.

> 2 tablespoons sesame, peanut, or light vegetable oil
> 1 2-inch (5-cm) cinnamon stick
> 5 or 6 cloves
> 2 medium onions, finely sliced
> 2½ cups (500 g) rice—basmati, Patna, or American long-grain
> 1 lb (500 g) fresh or frozen green peas
> 3½ oz (90 g) creamed coconut (sold in packages in Indian groceries; see page 235)
> About 1½ teaspoons salt
> Seeds of 8 cardamom pods or 1 teaspoon ground cardamom (optional)
> A good pinch of nutmeg (optional)

Heat the oil in a large saucepan. Add the cinnamon and cloves and when they begin to sizzle add the onions and fry over low heat, stirring occasionally, till golden. Remove about half the onions and keep aside to use as garnish, then add the rice and stir until it is well coated. Add the peas and mix well.

Bring to the boil 4 cups (1 liter) with the creamed coconut cut in pieces, and stir over low heat until dissolved. Pour over the rice. Add salt and cardamom and nutmeg if you are using them. Stir well and cook, covered, over very low heat for 20 minutes, till the rice is done, adding a little water if it becomes too dry and the rice is sticking at the bottom.

Serve garnished with the remaining fried onion.

VARIATIONS

• For an alternative garnish: add to the onion ½ cup (100 g) cashew nuts or blanched split almonds, toasted or fried in oil till lightly browned, and 2 tablespoons raisins, boiled in water for a few minutes and drained.

• A special accompaniment for a dairy meal is green coriander chutney (see page 240) mixed with enough yogurt to make a thick sauce.

Ginger Garlic Rice

SERVES 6

This Bene Israel recipe is also called "spiced pulao," but the large amount of ginger and garlic, which are turned into a paste with onion and turmeric, makes it quite different from any Indian spiced-rice dishes I have eaten. Mrs. Joseph, whose recipe it is, uses as much as 8 or 9 garlic cloves. The size of cloves varies, of course. I used 5 very large ones, and it was certainly not too much. This is a dry rice with very little fat and goes well with all the Indian stews.

2½ cups (500 g) basmati rice
1 medium onion
5–8 garlic cloves
1½-inch (4-cm) piece of ginger, peeled
½ teaspoon turmeric
3 tablespoons peanut or light vegetable oil
8 peppercorns
5 cloves
6 cardamom pods

3 cinnamon sticks
About 1¼ teaspoons salt

Wash and drain the rice. Blend the onion, garlic, ginger, and turmeric with I tablespoon of oil to a paste in the food processor.

Heat the remaining oil in a pan. Add the peppercorns, cloves, cardamom pods, and cinnamon sticks and fry for a minute or so, until they pop. Add the garlic-and-ginger paste and stir for a few minutes on low heat, until a wonderful aroma rises from the pan. Put in the drained rice and stir vigorously. Add salt and 3¾ cups (850 ml) of water and stir well. Bring to the boil, then simmer, covered, over very low heat for about 18 minutes. Turn off the heat and leave, covered, to steam for another 5 minutes.

VARIATION

• On festive days and private celebrations such as weddings, it was served with a generous sprinkling of blanched almonds and raisins on top. The raisins should be soaked or simmered for a few minutes in water, until they are soft.

Riso coi Carciofi

Rice with Artichokes

SERVES 4

The Jews in the Venice Ghetto had a greater variety of vegetable risotti than the Venetians, using peas, zucchini, eggplant, cabbage, potatoes, spinach, and artichokes. My own favorite is this rice with artichokes—"risi coi articiochi," in the Venetian dialect. The particular combination comes from the inhabitants of the ghetto who migrated from Sicily in the sixteenth century. Both rice and artichokes were grown on the island, where they had been introduced by the Arabs as early as the tenth century, centuries before they became a staple of northern Italy. I make the dish with frozen artichoke bottoms, which are expensive but very good, but of course it is better still, though arduous, to use fresh young artichoke hearts. In Venice, where artichokes are cheap, you can buy the hearts from vendors, who are seen cutting away the leaves and stalks at flashing speed and dropping them into bowls of acidulated water.

> 2¼ cups (500 ml) water
> 2¼ cups (500 ml) dry white wine
> 8 tablespoons sunflower or light vegetable oil
> 1¾ cups (350 g) Italian risotto rice
>   (preferably Arborio)
> Salt and pepper
> 14 oz (400 g) frozen artichoke hearts,
>   defrosted, or young fresh hearts
>   (to prepare, see page 509) boiled in salted
>   water for about 10 minutes

Bring the water and wine to the boil. In another pan, heat 4 tablespoons of oil, add the rice, and stir until it is well coated and translucent. Then pour in the water and wine, add salt (about ¾ teaspoon) and pepper, and cook, covered, on very low heat for about 20 minutes, or until the rice is tender but firm and there is still a little liquid left.

At the same time, cut the artichoke hearts into slices and fry quickly in 4 tablespoons of oil, adding a little salt and stirring all the time, until very slightly browned. Drain off the oil and mix the artichokes with the rice before serving.

VARIATIONS

• For riso e melanzane (rice with eggplants), a specialty of Rome, fry 1 lb (500 g) cubed eggplants in oil with 1 chopped garlic clove, then stir into the rice, adding chopped flat-leafed parsley.

• For risi colle uette (dialect for "uvette," or raisins), stir ¾ cup (100 g) raisins into the rice before adding the wine and water or broth.

Bomba di Riso al Formaggio

Rice Cake with Cheese

SERVES 10 AS A FIRST COURSE

·

Italian rice cakes are a southern Italian legacy—a world apart from the risotti of the north. They are among the dishes kept up by the Jews since the time, in the sixteenth century, when they were banished from the south and the islands. This creamy dairy version is particularly scrumptious.

> 2½ cups (500 g) Italian risotto rice
>   (preferably Arborio)
> Salt
> Pepper
> ½ teaspoon nutmeg
> 4 eggs, lightly beaten
> 1¼ cups (250 g) ricotta, mashed
> ¼ cup (25 g) grated Parmesan

11 oz (300 g) mozzarella, chopped
Oil and bread crumbs or matzo meal for the mold

Boil the rice in plenty of salted water for about 18 minutes, or until tender. Drain and let it cool and dry out for a few minutes, then mix with the rest of the ingredients. Turn into an oiled and bread-crumbed mold or baking dish and bake at 350°F (180°C) for about 25 minutes, until the eggs set and the cheese melts. Turn out and serve hot.

VARIATION

• A little powdered saffron can go into the pan when the rice is boiling.

Roz ou Hamud

Rice with a Green Vegetable Sauce

SERVES 6

Rice served with a sauce of green vegetables in a chicken broth flavored with mint and lemon was a Sabbath-and-holiday favorite in our community in Egypt. The usual everyday version has only one or two green vegetables with a little potato that is allowed to disintegrate as a thickener. This festive version has a greater variety of vegetables, and ground pine nuts or almonds are used as the thickener. It is quite magnificent. I sometimes have it as a soup, with rice added when serving.

Carcass of a chicken or 16 chicken wings for a good broth

2–3 leeks, cut into ¾-inch (2-cm) slices
1 head celery with leaves, cut into ¾-inch (2-cm) slices
Salt and white pepper
3 large garlic cloves, chopped
Juice of 1½–3 lemons, to taste
1 teaspoon sugar or to taste
3 zucchini, cut in ½-inch (1½-cm) slices
6 artichoke hearts, fresh or frozen, cut in half (optional)
½ cup (4 oz) pine nuts or blanched almonds, ground in a food processor
2 tablespoons dried mint
2½ cups (500 g) plain rice, freshly cooked (see page 444)

In a large pot put 9 cups (2 liters) water and the chicken wings or carcass. Bring to the boil, remove the scum, and simmer for 1 hour. Lift out the carcass and wings, remove skin and bones, and return the bits of meat to the pot. Put in the leeks, celery, salt, pepper, garlic, lemon juice, and sugar and simmer for about ½ hour. Now add the zucchini and artichoke hearts, and simmer 15 minutes longer. Add the ground pine nuts or almonds (the pine nuts give a particularly fine flavor) and mint and cook 5–10 minutes more. It is important to taste and adjust the flavorings. Serve in soup bowls over the hot rice.

VARIATIONS

• One or two diced potatoes are sometimes used as a thickener instead of pine nuts. They are boiled in the sauce from the start, until they fall apart.

• My cousin Irene makes her hamud very tart, with 3 lemons, 2 lbs (1 kg) of leeks as the only vegetable, and a pinch of turmeric.

Kobeba Hamda

Ground Rice Dumplings in Hamud Sauce with Rice

SERVES 6

A Passover specialty in our family was ground-rice dumplings filled with minced meat, cooked in the hamud sauce of the preceding recipe, and poured over rice. It was so popular among the Syrian Jews of Egypt that it was eaten all year round. I chose to demonstrate it at a Jerusalem gastronomic congress, because it is festive and uniquely Jewish. In preparation for the congress, I had tried it on my father. He criticized my dumplings, saying that his mother's shells were thinner. They do require skill. So make them when you have time to sit down and apply yourself.

> 11 oz (325 g) lean ground lamb or beef
> 2 tablespoons finely chopped flat-leafed parsley
> About ¼ teaspoon salt
> Pepper
> A good pinch of allspice
> 1¼ cups (250 g) rice flour

For the filling, mix 4 oz (100 g), or about a third, of the meat with the parsley, salt, pepper, and allspice and work them to a paste with your hands.

For the shell, put the remaining 7 oz (200 g) of meat and the ground rice in a food processor with salt (about ¾ teaspoon) and pepper. Adding a few tablespoons of water, turn the mixture to a soft but firm dough.

To make the dumplings, put a little oil on your hands so that the dough does not stick, and roll it into balls the size of small walnuts. Hollow each ball with your finger and shape it into a little pot, pinching the sides up all around and making the shell as thin as possible without breaking it. Fill each with about a teaspoon of filling, then close the shell up over the filling and roll into a ball. Drop the balls into the boiling broth (see preceding recipe for roz ou hamud) at the same time as the zucchini and artichokes. Serve in soup bowls over rice.

VARIATION

• For an easier but rather heavy, less appealing version, put through the food processor 8 oz (250 g) ground lamb or beef with ⅓ cup (65 g) ground rice, ¼ teaspoon allspice, salt and pepper, and just enough water, by the tablespoon, to make a smooth paste. Roll into marble-sized balls, drop into the boiling broth, and cook for 30 minutes.

Khoreshte Ghormeh Sabzi

Meat and Green Herb Sauce for Rice

SERVES 6

Iranian Jews ate like the rest of the population, with few distinctive dishes and few differences, apart from those resulting from the dietary laws. This sauce for rice—an herby stew—is one of the most popular dishes in Iran, and it remained a favorite with the Jews when they left. The special qualities are the symphony of flavors from a variety of herbs—the most commonly used are parsley, chives, and fenugreek, but some versions also include dill and coriander—and the unique bitter-sour flavor derived from the herb fenugreek and from dried limes (see page 236). Fresh fenugreek (a rare herb) can be found in Iranian and Oriental stores in the summer, and packages of dried fenugreek are available all year round. Only a little is used, because it has a very powerful flavor. The dried limes can also be found in Oriental and Indian stores in various forms, whole, broken in pieces, and powdered. If you can't find the powdered form, add an extra whole one or grind it yourself.

1 large onion, finely chopped
6 tablespoons light vegetable oil
1½ lbs (750 g) beef or lamb, cut into
*   1-inch cubes*
4 dried limes
1–2 teaspoons ground dried lime
Salt and pepper
2 leeks, green part included, chopped
A bunch of scallions (about 8), green part
*   included, chopped*
A large bunch of flat-leafed parsley, chopped
*   (about 1 cup)*
A bunch of coriander, chopped (about ½ cup)
*   (optional)*
A small bunch of dill, chopped (about ¼ cup)
*   (optional)*
A small bunch of fresh fenugreek leaves,
*   chopped (about ¼ cup), or 2 tablespoons*
*   dried leaves*
2½ cups (500 g) basmati rice, cooked as on
*   page 446*

Fry the onion in 2 tablespoons of oil till soft. Add the meat and turn the pieces until browned all over. Add 3¾ cups (900 ml) of water, bring to the boil, and remove the scum, then turn down the heat. With the point of a knife, make little holes in the dried limes and put them in as well as the ground dried lime. Add salt and pepper.

As soon as you have put the meat in, prepare the green vegetables and herbs. Chop the leeks and scallions finely in the food processor. Then chop the herbs. My impulse is usually to put the herbs in at the last minute, but in this recipe it is quite different: they are sautéed first, then cooked with the meat for a long time. Heat the remaining 4 tablespoons oil in a large pan and put all the fresh vegetables and herbs in together. Sauté, stirring often, over medium heat for about 15 minutes, until they begin to darken. Then add to the meat (if you are using dried fenugreek leaves, put them in at this stage) and simmer for about 1½–2 hours, until the meat is very tender. As the limes soften, squeeze them with a spoon against the side of the pan, so that they absorb the liquid and cease to float on the surface.

Serve very hot over plain white rice.

VARIATION

• Usually, red kidney beans or black-eyed peas (soaked for a few hours) are added for the last 30 minutes of cooking, but in my view the stew is better without them.

Khoreshte Gheimeh
Meat and Yellow Split Pea Sauce for Rice

SERVES 6

This is another of the fondly remembered Iranian stews served as a sauce for rice. It is exquisite, delicately spiced, with dried lime as the dominant flavor.

1 large onion, chopped
2–3 tablespoons oil
1½ lbs (750 g) lamb or beef, cut into
    1¼-inch (3-cm) cubes
4 cups (1 liter) water
½ teaspoon turmeric
1 teaspoon cinnamon
¼ teaspoon nutmeg
A few grinds of black pepper
4 dried limes (see page 236)
¾ cup (200 g) yellow split peas, soaked
    in water for 1 hour
Salt
2½ cups (500 g) basmati rice, cooked as on
    page 446

Fry the onion in the oil till soft. Add the meat and sauté, turning to brown it all over. Add water and bring to the boil. Remove the scum and add turmeric, cinnamon, nutmeg, and pepper. Pierce a few little holes in the dried limes with the point of a knife and put them in. Simmer for 1 hour, then add the drained split peas and cook ½–1 hour more, or until the meat and split peas are very tender, adding salt towards the end.

Serve over the plain white rice.

VARIATION

• The dish is usually served topped with fried diced potatoes, which are sometimes added in the pan, to sit on the surface of the stew and soak up some of the sauce.

Burghul bi Banadura

Cracked Wheat with Tomatoes

SERVES 4

Kurdish Jews use cracked wheat more than any other community does. This is my interpretation—the quantity of tomatoes is extravagant—of one of their everyday foods. It is best to use fresh tomatoes, but canned ones will also do.

2 lbs (1 kg) tomatoes, peeled, or a 28-oz
    (800-g) can of tomatoes
6 tablespoons sunflower or light vegetable
    oil
1 teaspoon sugar
Salt and pepper
2 cups (325 g) coarse- or medium-ground
    bulgur (cracked wheat)

Turn the tomatoes to a cream in a blender or food processor. They should measure about 4 cups (1 liter). If they do not, add water to make up that volume. Put the tomato in a large pan. Add 3 tablespoons of the oil, sugar, salt (about 1 teaspoon), and pepper. Bring to the boil, stir in the cracked wheat, and simmer, covered, for 10 minutes. Then take off the heat and leave, covered, for about 10 minutes, until the wheat has absorbed the tomato juice and is plump and tender. Stir in the rest of the oil and serve.

Burghul bi Jibn

Cracked Wheat with Cheese

SERVES 6

This was one of the Jewish dishes of Aleppo—and a Thursday-night special. Halumi cheese, which has a firm, chewy texture and is quite salty, was used. Mozzarella has a similar texture but is not salty enough, so if you must substitute it you need to season well.

> *2 large onions, sliced*
> *3 tablespoons sunflower or other light*
> *   vegetable oil*
> *3 cups (500 g) coarse or medium bulgur*
> *   (cracked wheat)*
> *Salt and pepper*
> *½–¾ lb (250–350 g) Greek halumi cheese,*
> *   cut into small cubes*
> *3 oz (75 g) butter, cut into small pieces,*
> *   or 4 tablespoons additional sunflower*
> *   or light vegetable oil*

Fry the onions in 3 tablespoons of oil till golden. Add the cracked wheat and 4½ cups (1 liter) of boiling water. Season with salt (about 1 teaspoon) and pepper and stir well, then cook on very low heat with the lid on for about 10–15 minutes, or until the water has been absorbed and the cracked wheat is tender. Mix in the cheese and the butter or extra oil and heat through until the cheese is soft.

CRACKED WHEAT— BURGHUL—BULGUR

CRACKED WHEAT ("burghul" in Arabic), now more commonly known by the Turkish name "bulgur," is wheat that has been boiled, then dried and ground. Throughout the Middle East, it is the food of the countryside and the mountains. Jews were on the whole city people and their staple was rice, but cracked wheat was also part of the diet. Bulgur was the main staple of the Yemeni and Kurdish Jews and of the Jews of Aden. When it is cooked as a pilaf, like rice, the coarse- or medium-ground grain should be used. Quantities of bulgur are measured by volume; generally, about one and a half times the amount of water or stock is used to cook it. Three cups of bulgur weighs 1 lb (500 g) and needs about 4½ cups (1 liter) of water or stock.

VARIATION

• I particularly like a version with eggplants: Fry 1 lb (500 g) cubed eggplant in oil till lightly browned. Drain on paper towels and mix into the cracked wheat with the cheese.

Burghul Pilav

Cracked Wheat with Almonds, Raisins, and Pine Nuts

SERVES 6

In many communities in the Arab and Ottoman worlds, cracked wheat is served as an alternative to rice and as a filling or accompaniment to poultry such as pigeons, chickens, and turkey. The raisins and nuts turn the grain into a festive dish. This way of preparing it is quick and easy.

> 4½ cups (1 liter) stock or water
> 3 cups (500 g) coarse burghul
>   (cracked wheat)
> About 1¼ teaspoons salt
> Pepper
> ½ cup (100 g) blanched almonds
> 5 tablespoons sunflower or light vegetable oil
> ½ cup (75 g) pine nuts
> ⅓ cup (50 g) raisins, soaked in water
>   for ½ hour

Bring the water or stock to the boil in a pan. Add the cracked wheat, salt, and pepper and stir, then cook, covered, on very low heat for about 10 minutes, or until the liquid is absorbed. Turn off the heat and leave, covered, for 10 minutes, or until the grain is tender.

Fry the almonds in 1 tablespoon of oil, stirring and turning them until beginning to color. Add the pine nuts and stir until golden. Stir the nuts, the drained raisins, and the remaining oil into the cracked wheat in the pan and heat through.

PASTA

PASTA APPEARS in the Oriental Jewish diet in many forms. The main ones are the Arab rishta and treya (noodles), shaghria (vermicelli), and tiny grainlike ovals called "lissan al ass-four" (birds' tongues). Pasta is dropped in soups and stews and combined with rice, lentils, meat, or chicken. North African Jews have several types of tiny semolina and water or egg pasta, which they used to make at home, rolling the dough between their fingers or their palms. Jews of Spanish origin make great use of fideos (vermicelli). A curious dish in Jewish Turkey has dry vermicelli fried in sunflower oil till golden brown, then cooked with just the right amount of salted water in the pan and turned out like a cake. And, of course, the Jews of Italy have a wide variety of pasta dishes. A Jewish scholar, Kalonymus ben Kalonymus, who lived in Italy in the fourteenth century, included macaroni and tortelli in a list of Purim dishes. Pasta still forms part of traditional Italian Sabbath and festive meals and is eaten cold on Saturday.

Caveos di Aman

Vermicelli Salad with Olives and
Hard-Boiled Eggs

SERVES 6

In her book on Sephardi cooking, Suzy David gives a pasta salad that was eaten in Bulgaria at Purim to commemorate the Persian Haman's cruelty towards the Jews. It is made with black olives and hard-boiled eggs, both of which are symbols of mourning.

> *1 lb (500 g) vermicelli or spaghettini*
> *Salt*
> *6 tablespoons extra-virgin olive oil*
> *Juice of 2 lemons*
> *Pepper*
> *30 black olives, pitted if you like and cut*
>   *in pieces or left whole*
> *3 hard-boiled eggs, cut in wedges*

Cook the pasta in boiling salted water until done *al dente*. Drain, and dress with the olive oil and lemon juice beaten with salt and pepper. Mix in the olives—and garnish with hard-boiled eggs cut in wedges. Serve at room temperature.

Rishta bi Ats

Brown Lentils with Noodles

SERVES 10

For a traditional Thursday meatless meal, this Syrian specialty is dressed with melted butter rather than oil, and served accompanied by yogurt.

> *1 lb (500 g) large brown or green lentils*
> *Salt*
> *1 large onion, coarsely chopped*
> *3 tablespoons light extra-virgin olive oil*
> *4 garlic cloves, minced or crushed in a press*
> *1 lb (500 g) tagliatelle*
> *3 oz (75 g) butter or ⅓ cup (90 ml)*
>   *light extra-virgin olive oil*
> *A bunch of flat-leafed parsley or coriander,*
>   *finely chopped (⅓ cup)*
> *Black pepper*
> *2 lemons, cut in wedges (optional)*

Rinse and drain the lentils, then boil them in water for about 25 minutes, or until tender, adding salt to taste towards the end.

Fry the onion in 3 tablespoons of oil till brown, then add the garlic and stir until the aroma rises.

Cook the pasta in boiling salted water until done *al dente*, then drain. Combine with the drained lentils in one pan or the other. Add the butter or olive oil, parsley or coriander, and black pepper. Stir well and heat through. Serve with lemon wedges if you like.

VARIATIONS

• Blend the lentils in a food processor with a little of their cooking water to a creamy texture, or use red lentils, which disintegrate by themselves.

Rishta wa Calsones

Tagliatelle and Large Ravioli Stuffed with Cheese

SERVES 4

In Aleppo this was a famous Jewish dish. In Egypt, it was one of our regular Thursday-evening dairy meals. The name "calsones" made us giggle, because it was our word for under-pants. We never wondered as to its origin. It must have come with the Italian Jews who joined the Aleppo community. They did so at different times, beginning in the sixteenth cen-tury, when there was a mass migration towards the East, following the expulsion of Jews from the South. In the eighteenth and nineteenth centuries many came from Livorno. Their descendants, referred to as "signorim," repre-sented, with those of Iberian descent, a kind of Jewish aristocracy. This is one of their dishes that was generally adopted. Some fami-lies made calsones into half-moon shapes, some into squares or rectangles. They were al-ways served mixed with rishta (tagliatelle) and dressed with plenty of melting butter and sometimes also yogurt. Of several fillings, a mild one with a mixture of mozzarella and ricotta that is close to the white cheese—gebna beida (page 271)—we made at home is my favorite.

Pasta dough, made with with 4 eggs and 2⅔ cups (400 g) flour (page 152), divided into two (one part to make tagliatelle, one for ravioli)

For the filling
4½ oz (125 g) mozzarella
7 oz (200 g) ricotta
1 egg, lightly beaten
Salt and pepper

1 egg yolk, to make the dough stick
4 oz (100 g) butter or to taste
Yogurt at room temperature to pass around

Make the pasta dough following the in-structions on page 152. Make tagliatelle (see noodles, page 153) with one-third of the dough.

Use the rest to make the ravioli. Divide into 4 pieces for easier handling, and roll out as thin as possible. Cut into rounds about 3¼ inches (8 cm) in diameter.

Blend the filling ingredients in a food pro-cessor. Place a heaping teaspoon of cheese mix-ture in the middle of each round. With your little finger, smear around the edges with a thin line of egg yolk to make the dough stick better. Fold the round in half over the filling and press firmly to seal the edges.

Boil the tagliatelle and ravioli in different saucepans, in salted water, for about 5 minutes, or until done *al dente*. Drain, and serve mixed to-gether, dressed with plenty of melting butter. Pass yogurt around for people to spoon some over the pasta if they wish.

Tortelli di Zucca Gialla

Pumpkin Ravioli

SERVES 8

This specialty of Mantua—a city that once had a very rich Jewish culture—is said to be a Jewish legacy. The community had a golden age during the Renaissance, under the Gonzaga duchy. It was famous for its theater groups, which performed at court, for its musicians, its scholars, and its printing presses.

The pumpkin has been associated with the Jews since the early days of its arrival in Italy, because they had a special familiarity with it through their Marrano and Sephardi connections, who dealt with New World and Spanish and Portuguese products. And they always had a special fondness for it.

It is the sweet orange-fleshed variety that you need for this recipe. These days, tortelli or ravioli filled with pumpkin are among the most well-liked stuffed pasta around the world. They are even mass-produced and sold in supermarkets. There are many versions of the filling. The following is the old Jewish one. In Mantua today the almonds are often replaced by amaretti biscuits, which have a slightly bitter almond flavor, and a popular addition is the powerful mostarda di Cremona (fruit in syrup with mustard essence).

For the filling

> 1¼ lbs (600 g) orange pumpkin (weighed after cleaning)

4 tablespoons grated Parmesan
Salt and white pepper
¼ teaspoon nutmeg
⅓ cup (75 g) finely chopped or ground almonds
3 or 4 drops of almond extract
½ cup (75 g) raisins, soaked for ½ hour and squeezed
1 tablespoon sugar or to taste (optional)
2 eggs, lightly beaten

Pasta dough (page 152), made with 4 large eggs and 2⅔ cups (400 g) flour
1 egg yolk, to make the dough stick, if necessary
4 oz (100 g) butter, or to taste, for the dressing

Make the filling. Peel the pumpkin, remove the seeds and stringy bits, and cut it in pieces. Put it in a pot with a tight-fitting lid. Pour in about ½ cup (125 ml) of water and steam, with the lid on, for 15–20 minutes, until very soft. Then drain and mash the pumpkin to a puree with a fork in a colander, allowing the juices to escape. Dry the puree further by stirring over low heat in the pot to evaporate the excess moisture. Let it cool, then add the rest of the filling ingredients and mix well.

Divide the pasta dough into 4 for easier handling and roll out as thin as possible. Cut into rounds about 3¼ inches (8 cm) in diameter.

Place 1 tablespoon pumpkin mixture in the middle and fold in half over the filling. Then press firmly to seal the edges. If necessary, to make the dough stick better, with your little finger smear a thin line of egg yolk around the edges.

Boil in salted water for 4 minutes, or

Pumpkin Ravioli (cont.)

until done *al dente*. Drain and serve with melted butter.

VARIATION

• Matzo meal may be substituted for the finely chopped or ground almonds to absorb excess moisture.

Tagliolini Freddi alla Salsa di Pomodoro

Cold Pasta with Tomato Sauce

SERVES 6

Whereas Spaniards introduced tomatoes to southern Italy, it was Marranos of Spain and Portugal who brought them to the north. That explains why the Italian writer Maffioli, in *La Cucina Veneziana*, describes this salsa as a Jewish sauce of the Venice Ghetto. It is eaten cold on Saturday and tastes different from southern-Italian sauces, partly because of its slight sweet-and-sour flavor.

> 3 garlic cloves, finely chopped
> 2 tablespoons extra-virgin olive oil
> 2 lbs (1 kg) ripe tomatoes, peeled and chopped, or a 28-oz (800-g) can of peeled tomatoes, chopped
> Peel of 1 lemon (optional)
> 2 tablespoons wine vinegar
> 3 teaspoons sugar
> Salt
> A good pinch of cayenne or red chili powder

> A bunch of flat-leafed parsley or basil, chopped
> 1 lb (500 g) tagliolini (thin tagliatelle) or spaghettini

Fry the garlic in the oil till just colored. Add the tomatoes, lemon peel, vinegar, sugar, salt, and cayenne or chili powder and simmer for about 25 minutes, or until the sauce is thick. Remove the lemon peel and add flat-leafed parsley or basil.

ITALIAN COLD PASTA JEWISH STYLE

IN APRIL 1995 on the occasion of a conference on the history, archaeology and culture of the Jewish communities in Italy entitled "The Jews of Italy: Memory and Identity" at the Institute of Jewish Studies, University College London, the Italian Cultural Institute in Belgrave Square staged a roundtable and concert and offered a buffet dinner for 150 people. I was asked to organize a traditional Italian Jewish menu with a kosher caterer. It was not difficult to find suitable cold dishes, because of the large repertoire of cold Saturday dishes, especially pasta. When nobody in Italy ate cold pasta, Jews were eating what is now known as pasta salad. The dishes are old and traditional and quite distinctive.

Cook the tagliolini or spaghettini in boiling salted water till done *al dente*, drain, and mix with the tomato sauce. Serve at room temperature.

Bigoli in Salsa all'Ebraica con Acciuga

Pasta with Anchovy Sauce

SERVES 6

Giuseppe Maffioli describes this, in *La Cucina Veneziana*, as an old Jewish dish. Bigoli are a Venetian whole-wheat pasta (you can substitute other, preferably short, pasta), and the sauce is the archaic version of a popular Sicilian one. The Venice Ghetto was divided in 3, with Jews of different origins in their own separate quarters, where they kept up their separate traditions. It is a strongly flavored sauce with plenty of anchovy and garlic. I love it with lots of anchovy—I put in 3 cans.

> 1 lb (500 g) bigoli or other pasta, preferably short and whole-wheat
> Salt
> ½ cup (125 ml) light extra-virgin olive oil
> 2 or 3 cans anchovy fillets, each can weighing about 4 oz (100 g), chopped
> 5 or 6 garlic cloves, finely chopped or crushed in a press
> A large bunch of flat-leafed parsley, finely chopped (¾ cup)
> Plenty of pepper

Cook the bigoli or other pasta in boiling salted water till done *al dente* and drain.

At the same time, make the sauce. Heat the garlic in 3 tablespoons of the oil. When the aroma rises, add the anchovies and stir until they almost melt. Dress the pasta with this and the remaining oil. Add the flat-leafed parsley and plenty of pepper and mix well. Serve hot or cold.

VARIATIONS

• A can of tuna, drained and chopped, and/or a handful of chopped capers may be added.

Tagliolini con la Bagna Brusca o Salsa Agresta

Tagliolini with Egg-and-Lemon Sauce

SERVES 6

This is a Saturday dish, meant to be eaten cold. The egg-and-lemon sauce—also called "salsetta garba"—is a specialty of the Marches, said to be of Greek origin.

> 2 cups (500 ml) flavorsome chicken stock
> 2 eggs
> 2 egg yolks
> Juice of 1–2 lemons
> 1 lb (500 g) tagliolini (thin tagliatelle)
> Salt
> 3 tablespoons olive oil
> Pepper

Make the sauce first. Bring the chicken stock to the boil. In a bowl, beat the eggs and yolks and lemon juice, then beat in a little of the hot broth. Pour this mixture into the rest of the simmering broth, stirring vigorously over low heat until the sauce thickens, but do not let it boil or the eggs will curdle. Let it cool.

Cook the tagliolini in boiling salted water until done *al dente* and drain. Dress with olive oil, salt, and pepper and stir so that they do not stick together. Let them get cold before mixing with the sauce.

VARIATIONS

• For a thicker sauce, before you add the egg and lemon to the broth mix I tablespoon of cornstarch or arrowroot to a paste with a little water and pour into the simmering broth, stirring until it thickens, and simmer for about 15 minutes.

• Instead of lemon, agresto (verjuice), the very sharp juice of immature grapes, was once used.

Tagliatelle Frisinsal

Tagliolini with Roast Chicken, Raisins, and Pine Nuts

SERVES 6

In the Venice Ghetto, this pasta ("frisinsal de tagiadele," in the local dialect) was served on Friday night. In other parts of Italy it was also a Sabbath dish—variously called "bescia-lac," "ruota di Faraone," and "hamin"—which sometimes included beef or goose sausage. This version with roast chicken pieces and a sauce based on the gravy from the roast, flavored with herbs, is particularly delicious.

1 chicken
2 tablespoons extra-virgin olive oil
Salt and pepper
2 or 3 sprigs of rosemary, finely chopped
2 sprigs of sage, finely chopped (optional)
⅓–¾ cup (50–100 g) raisins, soaked
*   in water for ½ hour*
⅔ cup (100 g) or more pine nuts, lightly
*   toasted*
1 lb (500 g) thin tagliatelle

Rub the chicken with oil and sprinkle with salt and pepper, then place it breast down in a baking dish. Roast in a preheated 350°F (180°C) oven for 1–1½ hours, until well browned, turning it over towards the end to brown the breast. It is done when the juices do not run pink when you cut into the thigh. Bone the chicken and cut into small pieces.

For the sauce, pour the gravy, including the fat, into a saucepan. Add the finely chopped rosemary and the sage, if you like (I leave it out), the drained raisins (you might find the larger amount too much), and pine nuts. Begin to simmer the sauce when you are ready to cook the pasta.

Boil the pasta in plenty of salted water until done *al dente*, then drain and mix with the sauce and the chicken pieces.

VARIATION

• A dish called "pastizzo di polenta," using cornmeal polenta (see page 487) instead of pasta, is baked with layers of polenta and the frisinsal ingredients.

JEWISH ITALY

PEOPLE ARE OFTEN surprised to hear that there are Jews in Italy. This is because theirs is a small community—it was much reduced by emigration following the Fascist racial laws of 1938 and by the Nazi deportations—and it is also very integrated and assimilated into Italian society. In fact, the Jewish presence in the Italian peninsula is the oldest in Western Europe and was uninterrupted for two thousand years.

Until recently, when a few cookbooks were published, almost nothing at all—apart from the famous carciofi alla giudia, little Roman artichokes opened out like sunflowers and deep-fried—was known about the food of Italian Jews, not even by the Italian Jews themselves. This is partly because Italy is regionally diverse (until unification in 1870, it was divided into separate states), and the cooking of the Jews furthermore reflects the individual histories of their once numerous communities.

At one time or another they were in almost every region. Their traces can be found in street names like "Via della Sinagoga" and "Piazza Giudea" and quarters called "Giudecca." There are remains of old synagogues; reliefs and frescoes representing symbols of Jewish

Piazza Giudea, Rome. Etching by A. Franzetti

identity like a menorah (candelabra) and an oil flask; tombstones and catacombs with Hebrew lettering. A *Guide to Jewish Italy* by Annie Sacerdoti in collaboration with Luca Fiorentino gives the Jewish sites in various cities as well as the historical background of the old communities. It is uncanny how there is a dish in the Jewish repertoire to match each of the sites.

A cookbook contributed by members of the Italian Jewish women's association ADEI (Associazione Donne Ebree d'Italia) called *La Cucina nella Tradizione Ebraica*, edited by Giuliana Ascoli Vitali-Norsa, identifies the recipes as "al uso marchigiano," "alla romana," "di Ferrara," "alla padovana," "vecchia ricetta veneta," "vecchia ricetta anconetana," "all'uso fiorentino," "alla livornese," "alla piemontese," "di Trieste," and so on, revealing the main centers where Jews once had an important and intense presence.

Now they are mostly concentrated in Rome, Milan, and Turin, and the old historic communities, which were once dispersed throughout the peninsula, have disappeared or lost their identity. As Jews gained equal rights and full emancipation after the kingdom of Italy was created in 1870, they abandoned orthodoxy and assimilated. The old family dishes are among the few things that remained as a testimony to their past.

Jews have lived in Rome and in southern Italy and the islands of Sicily and Sardinia since the second century B.C. Many came from the Mediterranean outposts of the Roman Empire, attracted to the center of power. The community grew enormously as thousands of prisoners were brought back as slaves after the conquest of Jerusalem by the Roman general Pompey in 61 B.C., and as a result of revolts against Roman occupation and the destruction of the Holy Temple by the Emperor Titus in the year A.D. 70. (The Arch of Titus portrays the Jewish slaves carrying a menorah.) In the first century of the Empire there were up to 50,000 Jews in Rome. They lived in the Trastevere area, the Suburra, and in Porta Capena.

The earliest and largest colonies of Jews existed in the Italian south—in the little ports around the Bay of Naples, in Puglia, Basilicata, Calabria, Sardinia, and most particularly in Sicily, where the Jewish population was 100,000—until the Inquisition banished them from that part of the Italian peninsula, which was under Spanish rule in the beginning of the sixteenth century.

In Sicily, the Jews enjoyed eighteen centuries of tranquil existence. They grew oranges, produced silk, and mined minerals, were cheese-makers and artisans, cloth merchants and doctors. They were among the colonies of the Diaspora that had the richest culture and traditions, being at the heart of Mediterranean traffic and benefiting from the cultural and economic impact of foreign occupiers, including Arabs, Normans, Angevins, and Aragonese. Under Muslim rule, from 831 to 1061, the Jewish population increased greatly with new immigrants from Muslim lands. They traded with the East and dealt in silks and perfumes; became Arabized in their tastes and looked to North Africa and the East, especially to Egypt, for their culinary standards. The Arab influence on Jewish cooking in Italy remains until today.

In 1492, on the orders of Ferdinand the Catholic of Spain, the Jews were banished from Sicily and Sardinia, and a few years later from southern Italy. It was said that over thirty-five thousand left Sicily alone. There has been little or no Jewish population in those parts since then, but the foods the Jews took with them when they fled to central and northern cities—vegetables like eggplants and artichokes, garnishes of raisins and pine nuts, sweet-and-sour flavors, marzipan pastries, and the custom of deep-frying batter-coated morsels in oil—all of which came to Sicily with the Arabs, are still associated with the Jews. Many of the dishes labeled "alla giudia" or "alla ebraica" throughout Italy are like those of the Italian south. Some, like cassola, the creamy ricotta cake sold by a Jewish bakery on the Via del Portico di Ottavia in the old Jewish Ghetto of Rome, are archaic Sicilian.

The massive emigration of Jews from the south and their arrival in cities of central and northern Italy coincided with the arrival there of a flow of escapees from German lands at the same time as thousands of refugees from Spain and Portugal. The crisis that this huge influx created resulted in their segregation in special quarters and the imposition of restrictions. Venice was the first city, in 1516, to force Jews to live in a special quarter with walls behind which they were locked in at night. The quarter was called *ghetto* after the hard-*g* Jewish pronunciation of the Venetian word for "foundry," because it was situated near an old foundry that made cannons. The *ghetto* became the model for all the ghettos of Europe, which also adopted the name. Forty years later, Pope Paul IV issued a decree obliging Jews in the Papal States to live in ghettos. In most cities where they lived in the Italian peninsula, the Jews were confined in ghettos for up to three hundred years. But restrictions varied and were enforced with a certain elasticity, and in many cases were in theory rather than in practice. The ghettos continued to exist until Napoleon's armies occupied Italy in 1796 and tore down their gates, in accordance with the principles of the French Revolution.

From the sixteenth century on, the history of the Jews swung between periods of security and tolerance and periods of segregation and restrictions. There were never persecutions on the scale suffered by Jews in the rest of Europe, and although they were marginalized, a kind of symbiosis and friendly relations generally prevailed with the rest of the population. They were often expelled, but because Italy was a patchwork of independent states—republics, dukedoms, principalities, papal and city states—they could escape from one to another, sometimes to return when the situation changed. At a time when every state was entirely ignorant of the cooking of its neighbors and no other group moved as they did, the ways of cooking they brought from one state to another remained forever linked with them.

The cooking was different in every ghetto. Local regional styles were absorbed, and dishes from other lands adapted. Some communities were destitute, some were close to royal courts and an aristocracy. The Roman Ghetto was the most desperately cramped, and its inhabitants were the poorest in Italy, forbidden to own property, forced to wear yellow badges and red hats, and excluded from most professions except moneylending, dealing in old clothes and bric-a-brac, and street peddling. Many of them were *friggitori*—vendors famous for their deep-fried morsels, mainly of fish and vegetables. Their type of fritto misto, once considered vulgar, is very fashionable now and the specialty of many Roman restaurants.

Very little remained of the grand dishes enjoyed by Roman Jews in better times, like those described by the Jewish scholar Kalonymus ben Kalonymus (1286–after 1328), known as Maestro Callo. Among the meats he listed as foods eaten at Purim were lamb, gazelle, venison, chicken, pigeon, turtledove, goose, capon, swan, duck, pheasant, partridge, moorhen, and quail. He also mentioned macaroni, tortelli, and tortelletti, various pies and tarts, pancakes and fritters, foccaccia, mostaccioli, gingerbread, macaroons, chestnuts, and salad.

A fashionable restaurant called Piperno near the Rome synagogue in the old ghetto, which is now the intellectual hub of the city, was described in the *Guida Italia* as "not quite the temple of Jewish food—the oldest, poorest, and tastiest food of Rome." Many of the dishes, like ceci coi pennerelli (chickpeas with bits of meat from the knuckle) and aliciotti con l'indivia (anchovies with chicory), reflect the pauperization of the old community—anchovies being the poorest fish. Other Roman dishes, like the caponata alla giudea with eggplant, concia di zucchine (fried and marinated zucchini), and cassola, are testimony to the swamping of the Roman community by refugees from Sicily and the south.

In the Venice Ghetto, Jewish cooking was exotic and cosmopolitan. Since the twelfth century, when Venice was the only Italian city to trade with the Levant, it allowed foreign merchants, among them Levantine and German Jews, to reside near but not in the city and to open warehouses and offices. The first Jews allowed in the city were Germans invited in as moneylenders in 1382. They were permitted to reside only on the island of Spinalunga, now known as the Giudecca, and later in Mestre. When Jews from southern and central Italy and from around the Veneto flooded in, followed by exiles from Provence and Marranos from Spain and Portugal, the city dealt with the invasion by separating the communities into three ghettos. The *tedeschi* (German Jews), who were poor secondhand dealers and pawnbrokers and ran the Monte di Pietà—the poor people's banks—were settled in the *ghetto nuovo* with Italians (from Sicily and the local inland province); the Oriental *levantini*, who came as merchants from Turkey, Syria, and Egypt, were put in the adjoining *ghetto vecchio*; and the Spanish and Portuguese *ponentini*, in the *ghetto nuovissimo*. The ghettos became more and more cramped, so new floors were added on to houses that grew into *grattacielli* (skyscrapers) nine stories high; corridors and balconies were turned into rooms; and the streets were so narrow that people could hold hands across windows.

But despite the squalid conditions and the vulnerable position of the inhabitants, commerce was allowed to flourish. There were many large-scale international merchants—a few were even shipowners. They were mainly of Portuguese Marrano and Levantine origin. They dealt in precious cloth and *objets d'art* from the Levant and controlled the trade in wool, sugar, silk, spices, grain, and dried fruit and nuts. An intense artistic and intellectual life also blossomed in the ghetto. Printing houses brought out hundreds of books. Venice became a Jewish intellectual capital. It was the major point where Iberian, German, and Levantine Jews coexisted, and an international meeting place for traveling Jews.

The inhabitants were locked in at night, but during the day were free to move around the city. Christians came into the ghetto as soon as the gates were opened in the morning to do business and attend fairs and to enjoy the celebrations, such as the Purim carnival and other street festivals. The Jews had a symbiotic relationship both with the poor Venetians and with the Signoria, who at the same time detested and wooed them. By the end of the seventeenth century, when the political and economic power of the city declined because of Ottoman competition and the discovery of America, crippling taxes were being imposed on the community, and restrictions reduced them to dealing in secondhand goods. So many moved away. In 1797, when the French occupied Venice, the ghetto gates were broken and restrictions lifted.

When I visited the old Ghetto of Venice and asked a rabbi about Venetian Jewish cooking, he directed me to the Casa di Riposo Israelitico (Jewish old people's home), where they also serve meals to tourists during Jewish holidays. One of the ladies in charge of the cooking answered my question by pointing to the three synagogues (scole) that stood together in the piazza—the *spagniola*, the *levantina* and the *tedesca*. They represented, she said, the different styles (a fourth one was Italian) that make up the Venetian Jewish style.

The coexistence in the ghetto bore fruit in the kitchen. The *levantini* brought riso pilaf and risi colle uette (rice with raisins, eaten cold, as in Istanbul today). The Iberian *ponentini* introduced salt-cod dishes, frittate (vegetable omelettes), almondy sweets, orange cakes, flans, and chocolate cakes (more about these later). The *levantini* and *ponentini* introduced the range of spices and aromatics that they dealt in. The Arab combination of pine nuts and raisins came both with the Sicilians and the *levantini*.

The *tedeschi* introduced goose and duck, beef sausages and goose salame, pesce in gelatina (jellied fish) and polpettine di pesce (gefilte fish), penini de vedelo in gelatina (calf's-foot jelly) and knaidlach, which became "cugoli." An example of the interweaving of cultures is pastizzo di polenta, with raisins and pine nuts. Another is the buricche—little pies halfway between Portuguese empanadas and Turkish borekas but with fillings unique to Italy, such as fish with hard-boiled egg; or anchovies and capers with fried eggplant and zucchini; or pumpkin with crushed amaretti and chopped crystallized citrus peel. A bakery in the old ghetto sells the old Jewish pastries, and at Passover you can find pane azzimo (matzos) hand-made in the old ways, with holes or with a lattice design.

In *La Cucina Veneziana* (1982), Giuseppe Maffioli writes that the Jews were not liked in the past because of their activities as usurers but that, within a generation after they left the ghettos, they were regarded as extraordinary and prestigious citizens. Daniele Manin (1804–1857), the last doge of Venice, was descended from the Jewish family of Medina. Wealthy Jewish families such as the Franchettis, Luzzattis, Treves, Morenas, and Vidals acquired palaces on the Grand Canal, while the poor stayed in the ghetto. Jewish cooking had an important impact on the local cuisine. Among the Jewish dishes adopted by Venice that

Maffioli cites are various vegetables "alla giudia," salt-cod dishes, almond pastries, and puff pastry. The Jews introduced the eggplant, which the Venetians at first feared would drive them mad. Maffioli says that the Jews had so much *"fantasia"* (imagination) that despite their forbidden foods they had a more varied diet and made greater use of vegetables than the Christians. He attributes the Venetian tradition of making risotti with every possible type of vegetable—artichokes, zucchini, fennel, celery, carrots, peas, tomatoes, cabbage, potatoes, and spinach—to them, and he believes that the famous Milanese riso giallo (rice with saffron) is the Sabbath riso col zafrán. Pesce in saor, fried and marinated fish with raisins and pine nuts, was also adopted from the Jews.

The cooking of the communities in the different Italian cities reflected the origins of the inhabitants. Continual persecutions in Germany and the Rhineland sent waves of refugees, from as early as the thirteenth century, which intensified in the fourteenth, at the time of the Black Death, across the Alps, spreading throughout Lombardy and the Veneto. Jews from Germany represent the origin of the majority of communities of upper Italy. The communities of Trentino and Alto Adige had so many German Jews that they adopted the German rites in their synagogues, and their cooking was very German, with stuffed goose, potato cakes, cabbage, dumplings, and apple fritters.

In the Piedmont (the old duchy of Savoy), a large part of the communities of Turin, Casale-Monferrato, Alessandria, and Vercelli were made up of an influx of Jews from Provence which started in the fifteenth century and continued until the nineteenth. A first wave was expelled from Provence by Charles VI in 1394, and almost all the Jews of Cuneo came from Avignon in 1570. The cooking had a strong French accent. One of the French-style dishes that recently came to me in a letter from Turin is a polpettone—a galantine of turkey or chicken with minced veal and pistachios. Other Provençal dishes that have come into the Jewish tradition are patate e pomodori of Ferrara, which is like a tian with baked layers of potatoes and tomatoes, and the curious Tuscan sweet spinach tart, torta di mandorle e spinaci, which is a specialty of Nice.

Trieste was a very cosmopolitan port city. Since the eleventh century, German, Spanish, French, and Levantine Jews had settled there, and when Iberian Jews came in large numbers, their Sephardi synagogue rite was adopted. In the nineteenth century, Jews came from Corfu fleeing the Greeks, and when Austria annexed Trieste, many flooded into the city from all over the Hapsburg Empire. The Jews of Trieste were professionals and intellectuals. They became affluent, founded banks and insurance companies; they were judges and were elected to the Vienna Parliament. Some became part of the Hapsburg nobility and were given titles. Their cooking was a varied mix that included Hungarian dishes like gulyás (goulash) and palacinche (stuffed pancakes), and the yeast cake putizza of Austrian descent.

In many cities the Renaissance provided a tolerant background for Jews and for the Marranos who arrived from Spain and Portugal. It idealized talent and learning and created an atmosphere of opportunity. Jewish wealth helped its cultural flowering. Since the fourteenth and fifteenth centuries, moneylending banks had mushroomed all over Italy.

Such work was forbidden to Christians, and the Jews were called upon to assume it. Christian guilds and merchants, resisting their competition, pushed them out of other trades. Moneylending became a Jewish preserve. In certain areas moneylenders were subjected to crippling taxation, which led to higher interest rates, and resentment from borrowers. But their services were in demand, and they were invited into many cities, where they financed economic expansion as well as the local nobility, who became their protectors. Thousands of Jews settled in such cities as Ferrara and Modena, where they prospered under the protection of the dukes of Este; Verona and Padua, where the Viscontis and the Sforzas treated them well; and Mantua, where the community, which included many Jews from Provence, became important under the Gonzagas. In Florence, Pisa, Luca, Siena, and many little Tuscan centers, Jewish fortunes were tied to the Medici, who protected them. Lorenzo invited Jew-

Ghetto in Siena, once known as the "Little Jerusalem." There were five great Hebrew academies at the end of the nineteenth century.

ish scholars to his court in Florence. Many sophisticated old Jewish recipes—like the buricche ferraresi (little pies filled with chicken), the arancini canditi padovani (balls of orange paste), and the tortelli di zucca mantovani (pumpkin tortelli)—are linked to the cities where Jewish life flourished and cooking reached a high level of sophistication.

The sixteenth and seventeenth centuries were the age of great Jewish merchants. Many were Sephardim and Marranos from Spain and Portugal, and they spread all over the country, participating in the beginnings of capitalism. Their maritime trade was the dominant force in cities like Ancona, Ferrara, Livorno, and Venice. Some had their own ships. They traded with their relatives and coreligionists around the Mediterranean, including their New Christian connections in Spain and Portugal. Through these contacts they introduced New World food products such as tomatoes, pumpkin, potatoes, corn, and haricot beans, the seeds and plants brought back to Spain and Portugal from South America by the Conquistadors. That is why red mullet cooked with tomatoes is called "triglie alla mosaica" in

Livorno, and a tomato sauce in Venice is called "alla giudia." Pumpkin too, despised for a long time by the general population, was considered Jewish. Many pumpkin dishes are still Jewish favorites. This period was also an age of intellectual brilliance for the Jews. Italy became the world center of Jewish printing and bookmaking, and there were prominent Jewish physicians, musicians, actors, poets, and playwrights. A refined cuisine developed in this kind of environment.

The most glorious community was that of Livorno. There, Jews enjoyed a degree of freedom and prestige unknown in any other city. In 1593, the Grand Duke Ferdinando I dei Medici turned the city into a free port and invited in merchants of all nations, and Jews in particular. In a public manifesto known as "La Livornina," he promised them tax exemptions, freedom of commerce, and freedom of religious practice—including reverting to Judaism and building synagogues, as well as personal protection. The great majority of Jews who flooded in were Portuguese Marranos, and it is they who shaped the character of the community and the style of cooking. Their Sephardi synagogal rites were adopted as well as their language, which was Portuguese (it later turned into the Judeo-Livornese dialect *bagito*), and their written language, which was Castilian. The Marranos controlled the port administration; they manufactured arms, produced soap, paper, tobacco, and coral; and they had printing houses. They were rich and cultured and had had a century of life as Christians, mingling and marrying into the Iberian upper classes (the less advantaged Jews of Spain and Portugal left a hundred years earlier, in 1492). Portuguese delicacies like uova filate or filli d'oro (threads of egg yolk cooked in syrup) and Monte Sinai and bocca di dama (made with eggs and almonds) are among their legacies. A number of Livornese chocolate cakes owe their existence to contacts with Marranos in Amsterdam. That community started the first chocolate factory with cocoa sent by New Christians in South America.

The dishes of Livorno had an impact beyond the borders of Italy, because Livornese Jews sent relatives to various North African and Levantine cities, like Tunis, Tripoli (in Libya), Izmir, Aleppo, and Alexandria, to develop interfamily commerce. A Livornese community in Tunisia, which was born in 1685, became enormous and still has a powerful identity today among the *pieds noirs* in Paris. The many North African dishes, including cuscussu, pastries filled with dates, and dates filled with marzipan, are testimony to the continuing connection with Tunisia, and also with the Jews who came from Tripoli in 1511 and those who arrived in 1770 from Oran (Morocco), banished by the Spanish governor of the city, the marquis of Los Velez. When Livorno lost its importance in the second half of the nineteenth century, many Jews followed their relatives, especially to Tunis and Libya. By an irony of fate, the small community that is left in Livorno today has a majority of Jews from Tripoli, who were expelled by Colonel Qaddafi after the Six-Day War. So *cucina tripolina* is making an impact in Livorno as it is in Rome.

There is a curious gastronomic link between Livorno and nineteenth-century London. A cookbook entitled *The Jewish Manual* (pages 183–84), published in 1846 and assumed to be by Lady Judith Montefiore, includes many recipes very similar to those cooked in Livorno today. The family of Lady Judith's husband, Sir Moses Montefiore, came from Livorno. London Jewish high society at the time was dominated by families of Marrano and Sephardi origin, and Italian, Spanish, and Portuguese dishes were much in evidence on the grander tables.

Though every trace of such food has disappeared from Anglo-Jewish tables, testimony to the old Italian Jewish culture survives on the tables of families from Istanbul, Salonika, Damascus, Cairo, and Tunis—cities where there were once Jews with names like Ancona, Viterbo, Ventura, di Pisa, Romano, and Senigallia. In Salonika there were once synagogues called Napoli, Puglia, Palermo, Siracusa, and Sardegna. If our community in Egypt had an Italian flavor (in Alexandria most Jews spoke Italian at home), it was partly thanks to the Livornese. Because the town hall in Livorno was burned down during the Second World War and all the records were lost, when the Jews began to leave in the 1950s, many stateless families managed to get Italian passports through the embassy, claiming that they had lost their birth certificates.

My uncle Joe Sassoon (he had a British passport) settled in Milan with his family in the fifties. When he joined the Jewish club, it turned out to be Halabi (Syrian from Aleppo). He described it to us as a "cattle market" where Jewish girls were sent from all over the world to find a rich husband. Middle-aged bachelors sat in a circle around them and asked if they knew how to cook and play the piano. When I was in my late teens, my parents kept threatening to send me there. The Milan community grew after 1870, with the economic and industrial development of the city. Now it is dominated by Syrian and Persian Jews, Lebanese Jews have settled mainly in Rome, and Libyan Jews are in Livorno.

Quadrucci coi Spinaci

Pasta Squares with Spinach

SERVES 6

This recipe is adapted from Donatella Limentani Pavoncello's book *Dal 1880 ad Oggi: La Cucina Ebraica della Mia Famiglia*. It is simple and good. It is best, of course, to make your own pasta (page 152) but you can use store-bought fresh lasagne and cut them into small squares.

1½ lbs (750 g) spinach (frozen whole-leaf spinach will do)
2 medium onions, chopped
2 tablespoons sunflower oil
1 lb (500 g) fresh, preferably green, lasagne
Salt
3 oz (75 g) butter, cut in pieces
Pepper
1 cup (100 g) grated Parmesan

Wash the spinach and remove thick stems (thin ones can be left). Drain well, and squeeze out the excess water. (If using frozen spinach, defrost it.)

In a very large pan, fry the onions in oil till golden, then put in the fresh spinach. Put the lid on and let it cook by steaming in the water that clings to it, stirring occasionally. As soon as it crumples into a soft mass—it does so very quickly—take it off the heat and sprinkle lightly with salt. (Frozen spinach needs only a few minutes' cooking with the onion.)

Cut lasagne into 1¼-inch (3-cm) squares. Drop the pasta into plenty of vigorously boiling salted water and cook until done *al dente*. Drain and mix in the pan with the spinach and butter.

Serve hot, sprinkled with pepper and grated Parmesan.

Pasticcio di Maccheroni con Fegattini e Polpettine

Pasta Pie with Meatballs and Chicken Livers

SERVES 10

A special feature of this very complex and grand Italian Friday-night dish is the combination of sweet crust and savory filling. Because the bottom crust gets soggy, I prefer to have it simply as a topping.

For the pie dough topping

1⅔ cups (250 g) flour
A pinch of salt
3 tablespoons sugar
4 oz (125 g) chicken fat or vegetable
  shortening, cut in pieces
1 egg, lightly beaten
1 egg yolk to paint the crust

For the filling

1½ lbs (750 g) ground veal, beef, or lamb
Salt and pepper
A good pinch of nutmeg
Sunflower oil for frying
2 large onions, coarsely chopped
1 lb (500 g) chicken livers (to kosher,
  sprinkle with salt and grill briefly on
  both sides)
2 cups (500 ml) white wine
1 lb (500 g) short macaroni (maccheroncini,
  penne, ziti)

To make the pie crust, mix the flour with salt and sugar in a bowl. Add the chicken fat or vegetable shortening and rub into the flour with your hands. Add the egg and mix well into the dough. You may need to add a tablespoon or so of water to bind the dough together or to add a little flour if it is too sticky. Do not work it any further. Wrap in plastic wrap and leave to rest while you prepare the filling.

In a bowl put the ground meat, about ¾ teaspoon salt, pepper, and nutmeg. Work well with your hands to a soft paste and roll into balls the size of large cherries. Shallow-fry quickly in ⅓ inch (¾ cm) hot oil, shaking the pan and turning the meatballs to brown them all over. They should be undercooked and still pink inside. In another large pan, fry the onions in 5 tablespoons of oil till soft and beginning to color. Add the chicken livers. Sauté very briefly, stirring and turning them over quickly.

Add salt and pepper and the white wine and cook a few minutes more, then take off the heat.

Boil the macaroni in salted water until still a little underdone, then drain. Mix well with the chicken livers and their sauce and the meatballs and pour into a large baking dish, about 13 inches (33 cm) in diameter.

Roll out the pie dough on a floured surface with a floured rolling pin, lift it up by wrapping it around the rolling pin, and lay it over the baking dish, pressing it so that it sticks to the sides of the dish. Brush with the egg yolk mixed with 1 tablespoon of water and bake for 30 minutes at 350°F (180°C), or until lightly browned. Serve hot.

Making Cornmeal Porridge–Polenta

SERVES 4–6

Cornmeal porridge, which originates in the New World, was not embraced by every country in the Old. Jews adopted it in Italy as polenta, in Romania as mamaliga, and in Georgia as gomi.

I have got an easy way of making this that I picked up in Italy: instead of stirring for ¾ hour, I bake it. There are different types of cornmeal—white or yellow (the most common), ground fine or coarse. Areas have their preferences, but they can all be used.

> 2 cups (300 g) cornmeal
> 6¼ cups (1½ liters) cold water
> 1½–2 teaspoons salt

Mix the cornmeal with about half the amount of cold water. Bring the rest of the water to boil with the salt in a large pan or pot that can go in the oven. Pour the cornmeal mixture into the pan, stirring vigorously. Bring to the boil slowly, on very low heat, stirring all the time so that lumps do not form. Cook for a few minutes, stirring, until the paste thickens. Put the pan in the oven with the lid on. Bake at 400°F (200°C) for 1 hour.

If you want to cut it in slices, let it cool and turn it out on a board or platter before you do.

VARIATIONS

• For a creamy polenta, use as much as 13 cups (3 liters) water or a half-and-half mixture of water and milk.

• A precooked, "instant" polenta is quite acceptable.

Making Couscous with the Processed (Pre-cooked) Packaged Couscous

I shamelessly make it in the easiest way, as prescribed in some of the package instructions, with very good results. It is so easy you can make it for very large parties.

For 6 people, put 1 lb (500 g) medium-ground couscous in a bowl. Add 2½ cups (600 ml) warm water with ½–1 teaspoon of salt gradually, stirring so that the water becomes absorbed evenly. After about 10 minutes, when the couscous has become a little plump and tender, add 3–4 tablespoons of peanut or light vegetable oil and rub the grain between your hands to air it and break up any lumps. Heat it through by steaming in the top part of a *couscoussier* or double boiler (it is ready as soon as the steam passes through the grain) or, more simply, in the oven, covered with foil. I usually make it for a large number of people by heating it right in the huge ovenproof clay dish I serve it in. There is nothing easier. A small quantity for 2 or 3 can be heated in a saucepan, stirring so as not to burn it. Before serving, break up any lumps very thoroughly.

There are various traditional ways of glamorizing the grain for festive occasions and the Sabbath.

Saffron Couscous

Add ¼–½ teaspoon of powdered saffron to the water before moistening the couscous.

"Couscous de Cérémonie"

Festive Presentations and Garnishes for Couscous

For grand occasions like weddings and bar mitzvahs, the grain is piled high, given a pyramid shape, decorated, and also accompanied by sweet garnishes or side dishes, because sweetness symbolizes happiness.

DECORATIONS

• Sprinkle the grain with cinnamon and confectioners' sugar and whole or chopped toasted blanched almonds, making a design with lines fanning down like rays from the top.
• Cover with walnut halves and raisins (soaked in water and drained).
• Make a ring of dates—skinned, pitted, and stuffed with blanched almonds—around the bottom of the pyramid.
• Serve the grain mixed with boiled chickpeas and raisins and make a design with these on the top.

La Soupe de Légumes pour le Couscous

Basic "Soup" with Meat and Vegetables to Serve with Couscous

SERVES 6–8

This is a basic "soupe à la Juive" that is served with couscous, whether it be the simple everyday dish or a ceremonial party affair. To serve, moisten the grain with a little of the broth and shape the grain into a mound. Put the meat on top and the vegetables down the sides, and bring the remaining broth to the table in a separate bowl.

On the Sabbath and festive days, the grain is served separately. It is prepared in large quantities, decorated as indicated above (see "DECORATIONS"), and sometimes also accompanied by extra side dishes and garnishes, such

COUSCOUS

THE THEME of a Jerusalem congress on Jewish food in 1993 was "Gefilte fish or couscous?" Couscous, the most famous of North African foods, has had an enormous impact in Israel. Ruth Sirkis, my Israeli publisher, had phoned once, years ago, to ask if there was an easy way to prepare fish couscous for a few hundred people. I wondered if it was for a wedding party. No, she said, it was for the army: soldiers wanted couscous instead of gefilte fish on Friday.

There is probably more couscous than gefilte fish served on Friday night in Jewish families in France too. Twenty years ago, I was invited to a ball in Orléans by a woman who was hoping to translate my first book into French. It turned out to be a Hanukah party. The community had always kept a low profile. But everything had changed since the arrival of North African Jews, who were always getting together for celebrations. And for the first time the old established community of Vieille France and Eastern European Jewry had joined them. The reason was extraordinary. Rumors had spread in the city that girls who went into Jewish shops had been drugged and spirited away to Saudi Arabia, where they were sold as sex slaves. Jewish shops had been attacked, and an anti-Semitic cabbal had continued for months. The community became frightened and decided to get together to show solidarity. Certainly the atmosphere at the ball took them far away from their troubles in Orléans. There was chanting and belly dancing. People snatched the microphone to sing passionately songs like "Un Soir à Casa" and "Fez Tu Es Mon Amour." The meal consisted of spicy salads, roast lamb, and mountains of splendidly decorated couscous. It is difficult now to go to a Jewish event in France without its turning into an opportunity for North African music and song. North African–style weddings have become fashionable. I have heard many accounts of *henna* nights in tents, where the bride is transported on a large tray, dressed in velvet and gold, and bedecked with jewels; a band plays and singers perform, while great platters of Moroccan goodies and mountains of ornate couscous are served.

The name "couscous" refers to the hard semolina grain on which it is based, as well as to the stew or soup and the side dishes that go with it. For North African Jews, though not for those of Morocco, couscous is the Friday-night dish. Couscous with meatballs—a dish cooked by Muslims for their great feast of the year, Eid el Kibir—is the Friday-night dish of Algerian and Tunisian Jews. They make large quantities, so that it can be eaten again on Saturday to accompany the dafina (see page 428). There are also festive couscous dishes, including sweet ones, for different holidays, and grand ceremonial ones for weddings and bar mitzvahs. Typically Jewish are the "boulettes"—meatballs, chicken balls, or fish balls—which are part of the Friday-night meal. The night before Yom Kippur (page 30), the couscous is with chicken; during Sukkot (page 31), there are sweet potatoes and raisins in the soup; at Rosh Hashanah (page 28), there are more sweet ingredients—quinces, sweet potatoes, and yellow raisins—and nothing black—no olives and no eggplants.

In the past, families would buy whole hard wheat in big sacks and have it ground at the mill while they watched, to make sure that they got their own grain back. They could have it ground to different degrees of fineness. At home they sifted and separated it, then moistened it, and rubbed fine flour into it with their hands.

The cooking of the grain by steaming in a *couscoussier*—a pot made usually of aluminum but also of clay, with a steamer or strainer that fits on the top—was equally painstaking and time-consuming. You started by moistening the grain with a little water, stirring in salt and oil, and airing it by picking it up and rubbing it between your hands over the bowl or putting it in a large sieve and throwing it up in the air. Then the grain was steamed in the top part of the *couscoussier* for one hour over a bubbling broth. After that it was turned into a large bowl and water was added. When the steaming grain was cold enough, it was rubbed between the hands so as to break up and separate any lumps. It was left for half an hour to absorb the water, then aired again by combing and turning it over lightly with the fingers, put back in the steamer and steamed for another

half-hour, and finally turned out to have any lumps broken up before serving.

You can understand why couscous is surrounded by mystique, and why its preparation arouses great passions among the people whose traditional cooking it is and also among those who have adopted it as a fashionable and exotic new food. When I was in America recently, I was pursued by a journalist who telephoned me in Boston and New York to find out if I thought processed, packaged couscous was acceptable and how I dealt with it. There was great controversy, it seemed, between California chefs and some famous food writers. I said I did not believe in being "*plus royaliste que le roi*" (more royalist than the king), or in making life difficult for myself or others. Anyway, nowadays, it is virtually impossible to find the unprocessed grain outside North Africa.

Today in North Africa, there are two types of commercially processed grain sold in packages—the precooked one, which is sold abroad, and one that is commercially "rolled" but not precooked. In 1993, I visited a couscous factory in Sfax. It was during an Oldways International Symposium which took us on a fabulous gastronomic tour of Tunisia. We were received with flags and welcome banners, and treated to a tasting of dozens of sumptuous couscous dishes—both savory and sweet—and to a demonstration by Berber women in exotic dress of the old traditional ways of rolling couscous by hand. Then the owner of the factory took us in small groups to see the processing of the grain—the grinding, steaming at great pressure, and drying. Earlier, American symposiasts had insisted that even the commercial grain needed to be steamed twice. When I asked the manufacturer what he advised, he said, "Once it has absorbed an equal volume of water, all you need really is to heat up the grain, either in a saucepan, in the oven, or a microwave, and to break up any lumps. If people steam it, it is because they are used to doing that. It is a ritual—part of the culture."

Basic "Soup" to Serve with Couscous (cont.)

as those described in the recipes that follow on page 492.

> *1 large chicken or 2 lbs (1 kg) beef or lamb*
> *1 or 2 marrow bones*
> *12 cups (3 liters) water*
> *¾ cup (150 g) chickpeas, soaked for 2 hours or overnight*
> *Salt and pepper*
> *4 medium onions, cut in half*
> *4 tomatoes, peeled*
> *1 lb (500 g) carrots, cut into four pieces*
> *1 lb (500 g) turnips, quartered*
> *1 cabbage heart, quartered*
> *1 lb (500 g) zucchini, cut into 4 pieces*
> *1 lb (500 g) orange pumpkin, cut into slices*
> *½ teaspoon powdered saffron*
> *A large bunch of parsley, chopped (⅓ cup)*
> *A large bunch of coriander, chopped (⅓ cup)*
> *1 tablespoon harissa, for the sauce to accompany*

Put the chicken or meat and bones in a large pan with the water. Bring to the boil and remove the scum, then add the chickpeas. Simmer for 1 hour (or 1½ hours for meat). Add salt and pepper, the onions, tomatoes, carrots, and turnips, and cook 20 minutes. Add the cabbage, zucchini, pumpkin, and saffron and cook 20 minutes more. Just before serving, stir in the parsley and coriander.

Make a hot sauce to accompany: mix the harissa with a ladle of soup, and pass the sauce around for people to help themselves.

VARIATIONS

• Add other vegetables, such as a sliced celery stalk, fava beans, peas, and quartered artichoke hearts.

• Add 1 teaspoon cinnamon and ½ teaspoon mace.

Festive Side Dishes to Serve with Couscous

For *oignons confits et raisins secs* (caramelized onions and raisins): Fry 2 lbs (1 kg) sliced onions in about 4 tablespoons of oil till very brown, stirring often—it takes at least ½ hour. The onions brown more evenly if you let them soften with the lid on to begin with, so that they steam. When they are really brown, add 3 tablespoons of sugar, 1 teaspoon of cinnamon, and 4 oz (100 g) raisins (soaked and drained), and cook a few minutes more.

For *pruneaux aux noix* (prunes stuffed with walnuts): Stuff 1 lb (500 g) pitted prunes each with a walnut half and simmer in water to cover for ½ hour.

For *pois chiches et raisins secs* (chickpeas and raisins): Cook these separately and serve them in separate bowls. Soak 1 lb (500 g) chickpeas for 1 hour, then drain and simmer in fresh water for 1 hour, or until tender, adding salt when they begin to soften. Serve hot with some of their cooking water. Simmer 1⅔ cups (250 g) raisins in water for about 10 minutes. Some people add 2–3 tablespoons of sugar.

Hlou aux Abricots et Potiron

Apricot and Pumpkin Accompaniment for Couscous

SERVES 6–8

In Tunisia, a sweet side dish made with pumpkin combined with apricots, greengages, quinces, or chestnuts is served hot or cold to accompany couscous on festive occasions. It is a specialty of Rosh Hashanah, when the gold of the pumpkin symbolizes the hope that the New Year will be prosperous.

> ¼ cup (50 ml) peanut or light vegetable oil
> ¾ cup (150 g) sugar
> 1 large onion, coarsely chopped
> ½ lb (250 g) orange pumpkin, cubed
> ½ lb (250 g) fresh apricots, pitted, or
>   dried ones, soaked for ½ hour and
>   drained
> *Juice of ½ lemon*

Heat the oil with the sugar until the sugar begins to caramelize and turn brown. Add 1 chopped onion and cook for 5 minutes. Add the pumpkin and apricots, the lemon juice, and enough water to cover—about 1 cup (250 ml)—and cook for about ¾ hour, to a jam-like consistency, adding water if it becomes too dry. Serve hot or cold in a bowl to accompany the couscous grain.

- For hlou aux reines claudes, use greengages instead of apricots.
- For hlou aux coings, use 2 quinces cut in small dice instead of the apricots.
- For hlou aux marrons (particularly delicious), use chestnuts instead of the apricots. To peel them, make a slit on one side and cook them under the broiler, turning them over once, until they are lightly browned and the skin is loosened. Then put them in with the pumpkin.

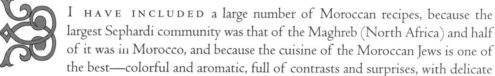

MOROCCO–LEGACIES FROM BAGHDAD AND ANDALUSIA IN THE BERBER WORLD

I HAVE INCLUDED a large number of Moroccan recipes, because the largest Sephardi community was that of the Maghreb (North Africa) and half of it was in Morocco, and because the cuisine of the Moroccan Jews is one of the best—colorful and aromatic, full of contrasts and surprises, with delicate flavoring derived from a very long list of spices and aromatics, sometimes peppery hot and sometimes sweet. Morocco was the seat of the great Berber empires, the Almohads and the Almoravids, which dominated all of North Africa and part of Spain for centuries. The culinary refinements and sophistication are a legacy of their courts and a result of the fusion of local Berber practices with the styles of the Baghdad Caliphate and those of Andalusia.

In Morocco, Jewish cooking is still rated as one of the four best styles in the country, on the level of those of Fez, Tétouan, and Marrakesh. I heard this from many non-Jewish sources as I traveled across the country. People remembered with nostalgia the foods they ate at their Jewish friends' homes. There had been a strong Jewish presence in all the Maghrebi countries (Libya, Tunisia, Algeria, and Morocco) since Roman times, centuries before the advent of Islam. The origin of this presence is uncertain, but it is believed that Jews arrived from Cyrenaica (now Libya) and Egypt in the first century, when revolts against the Romans were crushed and the Alexandrian community was destroyed. They took refuge in the mountains and spread Judaism among the indigenous Berber population. By the time the Arabs conquered the area in the seventh century, the Berbers counted a large number of Jewish tribes. Indeed, the last resistance to the Arabs in Tunisia was led by Jewish tribes and a Jewish queen called Kahena. The Jewish tribes of Algeria and Tunisia, faced, like all the Berbers, with forced conversion to Islam, fled to Morocco, where the conquerors had a weaker hold. That is why there were many more Jews in Morocco than in the rest of the North Africa. Then a flow of Jews from Palestine and Babylonia arrived in the wake of the Muslim armies.

The Jews of Morocco were part of the new and vibrant civilization that was created in the Muslim Maghreb and Andalusia in the early Middle Ages, and their own culture flourished with the constant traffic of scholars and immigrants between Baghdad, Granada, Córdoba, and Fez. Fez was the spiritual center and the seat of Talmudic learning. It is here that the famous Andalusian Hebrew poetry with Arab metrics was born, and it is here too that one of the most refined styles of Jewish cooking developed.

When the Almohads, a fanatical, puritanical Berber tribe from the High Atlas Mountains, swept through the Maghreb and Muslim Spain in 1145, a period of Jewish martyrdom, massacres, and forced conversions began. Many communities were destroyed. As Jews fled from Morocco to Christian Spain, thousands of refugees from Spain headed for Fez, where they were met only with hardship and famine. For centuries the Jews never truly recovered from the material degradation and intellectual impoverishment caused by the Almohad persecution and repression. They remained vulnerable and unpopular, serving the rulers as a marginal group, having to wear special clothes and special shoes to indicate their identity. They were placed in special quarters called "mellahs" at their own request, for their protection against a hostile populace. The mellah of Fez, situated near the royal palace, was founded in 1438—on the model of the *juderias* of Spain. Eventually every city had a mellah and there were also mellahs in the mountain villages in Berber country in the south.

The position of the Jewish community improved when the Sephardim and Marranos of Spain and Portugal arrived, fleeing in little boats, starting in 1492 and thereafter. They settled in coastal cities and centers like Fez, Meknes, and Tétouan. The newcomers very quickly came to play a central role in the development of the country and in external trade. With their superior culture, skills in printing and weaving, and expertise in armaments manufacturing, and also their ability to speak different languages and to trade with their exiled connections, they had much to offer. They became commercial intermediaries between foreign traders and their Muslim neighbors. Some served as consuls and diplomatic representatives to European governments on behalf of the sultans. Rewarded with special rights and privileges from which the old community was barred, many acquired wealth and rose to influential positions.

As soon as they settled, they formed separate communities, maintaining the communal organizations and the manners and customs of Spain. They dominated Jewish life, especially in the north, establishing a cultural, economic, and communal hegemony over the native Jews, whom they regarded as inferiors. Their privileged position—they remained the intellectual elite and bourgeoisie of lawyers, doctors, financiers, and royal advisers—and the resentment it created in the old community survived until modern times. They called the native Jews *berberiscos,* and were known by them as *megorashim* (the banished—because they were banished from Spain) and *forasteros* (strangers). Tensions and splits between the two communities lasted hundreds of years.

From the late Middle Ages on, all North African Jewry shared in the general economic and cultural decline of the region. They suffered a double isolation in their mellahs—in

Morocco, and from the world outside. European travelers noticed their degradation. A Frenchwoman, Madame Pascal Saisset, wrote in *Heures Juives au Maroc:* "*Un cercle manque à l'enfer de Dante, il n'avait pas vu le Mellah de Marrakech*" ("A circle is missing in Dante's inferno, he had not seen the mellah of Marrakesh"). In the imperial city full of gardens and luxurious palaces, brilliant with color and smelling of the mountain air, the Jewish quarter was packed with people dressed in black, crowded on top of each other, busily carrying on their activities in gold- and silversmithing, brocade embroidery, dyeing, weaving, sewing, processing beeswax, ostrich feathers, and leather, selling cloth, beads, and bric-a-brac, pastries and confectionery. The mellah smelled of the refuse of their trades, of meats and fish grilling on charcoal, and pastries frying in oil. The mingled odors of cumin and paprika, saffron and turmeric hung in the air over the houses. Some of the houses were large, around courtyards, but most were no more than hovels.

Though there was hardly any air to breathe, and despite the apparent misery, a rich spiritual and intense social life flourished within the walls of the mellahs. The inhabitants were fervently pious. Everywhere you could hear their prayers and chants. And they lived in a gripping world of superstition and magic—visiting cabbalists and "sorcerers," driving away "devils," countering the "evil eye," making vows and sacrifices. They went on pilgrimages and worshipped at shrines of saints. Professional singers and storytellers entertained at parties; professional mourners wailed at funerals. Circumcisions, bar mitzvahs, engagements, and weddings, which lasted for days, were celebrated in great pomp, with mountains of food and old women screaming "youyous" of joy.

With the arrival of French colonialism in the nineteenth century, the more privileged families adopted French as their language and Western ways, and assimilated with the Europeans. The populations of the mellahs burst out of their walls and spread into neighboring areas of the medinas, or old residential quarters, and into new, modern European districts. But the great majority remained traditional and religious. With the independence of the North African states and the creation of the State of Israel came the mass migration of North African Jews.

Many of the upper-class Jews of Tangiers, which had once been Spanish Morocco, went to Spain. At that time, Madrid had sponsored research on Spain's "golden past," and a Jewish scholar had found thousands of files with family names of Jews who were related to the old Spanish nobility. Many of the educated and affluent Jews of Casablanca and French Morocco went to France and French Canada. The inhabitants of the old mellahs and Berber villages went to Israel.

The lifting of the entire population of mellahs secretly in one night and their transplanting to the "Promised Land" make dramatic stories, but for some the tale ended sourly, with resettlement in isolated places, out in the desert. They became the proletariat of Israel, the "black" Jews, seen as backward. The Moroccan community in Israel is now the largest single group and forms half of all the Sephardi population. Although their cuisine has had the greatest impact, it is seen as inferior, poor food. Israeli friends make a face when

Jewish vegetable merchant in Morocco

I mention certain foods. It may be that the more sophisticated dishes have not reached Israel, or that they became degraded as the "poor" southern-Italian food was in America. One only hopes that the young Israeli chefs start making the most of their legacies the way American chefs have discovered the regional cuisines of Italy. They should look at France, where Moroccan dishes are so appreciated that they have been adopted by other Sephardi communities for grand events like weddings and bar mitzvahs.

Morocco is a country with a highly variegated culture, and its diversity was reflected in the Jewish population. Differences in language, clothing, music, architecture, and food ran along geographical lines dividing northern, central, and southern Morocco, with some overlap and also local substyles.

In Tangiers and Tétouan, in Mediterranean northern Morocco—where a large number of people had names like Toledano, Bejar, Leon, and Cordoba, and where Jews kept up *haketia*, a Judeo-Spanish dialect mixed with Berber and Arabic, longer than anywhere elsewhere—Spanish influences were strong. Jewish craftsmen made coffers in the Iberian tradition and mirror frames like the windows of an Andalusian palace, and Jewish women cooked dishes with a marked Spanish influence.

In central Morocco, the cities of Fez, Meknes, Rabat, and Salé were bastions of Muslim Arab heritage. Jews had quickly dropped Spanish for Arabic, and in the nineteenth century dropped Arabic for French. The Jews of Fez, who were famous for their work in jewelry and filigree, for spinning the gold and silver threads used in brocades, and for their

On the patio of a Jewish home in Tangiers, c. 1900. Many of the Jews in this city were of Spanish descent and spoke a Judeo-Spanish dialect.

silky-soft leather goods, were also noted for their highly refined cooking, which combined Andalusian styles with elements from old Baghdad—like meat cooked with fruit.

The south was Berber country, where Jews lived in villages in the Atlas Mountains and in the desert (they were "*les hommes bleus*," dressed entirely in blue). Even in the towns, like Agadir and Sousse, the Jews were Berbers. They wore little black *kipas* and black *jelabas*. Metalwork was a specialty of the south, and this was the only region where women too were artisans, making clothes, blankets, and carpets.

One city in the south that was famous for its prestigious Jewish cooking was Mogador, now Essaouira, on the seacoast, not far from Marrakesh. It was founded in 1760 as a trading port by the Sultan Mulai Abdullah. He called on the Jews to come and live there and gave them all kinds of privileges to tempt them. They started trade with Europe, including Britain and Germany, bringing products from Africa by camel caravan through the desert, including spices and almonds from the East. They became known as "*tujjar al-Sultan*" and "*les marchands du roi*" (the king's merchants) and came to represent half the population. The community was prosperous, with a mixed population of "Andalusian" traders and a "*petit peuple*" of Berber artisans. The women sewed at home, making clothes—*haiks, jelabas, farajias,* and kaftans—which were sold in the weekly markets in neighboring towns and in the local souk. There, a hundred tiny shops—some no bigger than a cupboard, and almost all of them Jewish—were squeezed into the main street. They all closed on Saturday, obliged by the municipality.

All the Jews of Mogador lived in a mellah until around 1860, when some began to move out. The houses, white with blue doors, some of them built around a courtyard, were repainted constantly. There were thirty-five synagogues in the mellah. Fabulously grand houses were built around the main synagogue, with their windows looking into it. Everyone went to the synagogue every day. The community was very religious and cabbalist. Because they did not have two kitchens or two sets of dishes and they had only one sink, some people did not touch milk. For the same reason, there was little tradition of dairy food, and cheese was nonexistent. Every Moroccan town had its Jewish saint. In Mogador it was Rabbi Nessim ben Nessim. His tomb—near a spring, surrounded by olive and pomegranate trees—is a holy place of pilgrimage which still attracts many Jews, who come to spend three days praying and cooking méchoui (grills) in the open.

Mogador was cool, because it was on the Atlantic, so it became a holiday place for families from Marrakesh when it was too hot in the city. That is how the cooking of the city became widely known. The Jewish women of Mogador were famous especially for their sweets and had a very large repertoire of *petits-fours,* preserved fruits, and jams. Their famous wedding cake, called "le paille" (from the English word "pie"), is an extraordinary *pièce montée* on a meringue base. Because the south is Berber country it is also couscous country. But in Mogador, as in the rest of Morocco (and contrary to the rest of North Africa), couscous was never a Friday-night dish, although it was a festive dish of celebration. Favorite fish dishes were boulettes de poisson (fish balls). In general there were no first or second courses; everything was on the table at the same time, including a large number of cold dishes. People rave about the oil from the argan tree, which grows only in these parts and was used to make a whole range of wonderful salads and cold vegetable dishes. The meal finished with fresh fruit and dried fruit and nuts. They did not usually drink at mealtime. Mahia was for before or after the meal. They drank red kosher wine or sweet homemade wine on Friday night. Rabbi Jacob was a famous label that is still found on restaurant lists in Morocco today.

Couscous aux Boulettes du Vendredi Soir–Msoki

Tunisian Couscous with Stuffed Meatballs

SERVES 12 OR MORE

The special Friday-night couscous is one of the highlights of Tunisian Jewish cuisine. On festive Friday nights (when it falls on a holiday), the dish becomes a grandiose affair. When it was first described to me by Celine Perez, who lives in Paris, it didn't seem posssible that so much time and effort could be put into one meal. It consists of a vegetable stew, "boulettes" (meatballs), osban (a herby sausage in a beef intestine casing), and the grain.

The stew is made with meat and marrow bones and a selection of seasonal vegetables. The meatballs are extraordinary. Variously referred to as "boulettes royales" and "de cérémonie" and as "les farcis" (stuffed vegetables), in a way they are mock stuffed vegetables with pieces of vegetable stuck in them. These meatballs are dipped in flour and egg, then deep-fried and stewed in tomato sauce. I have made them like that, encrusted with all kinds of vegetables and fried, for a party, and they were splendid. But I have since been given easier and new, lighter ways of making them, which I have adopted.

The osban sausage is stuffed with a mixture of ground veal, diced tripe, rice, and spinach flavored with onion, garlic, harissa, cinnamon, allspice, powdered rosebuds, and nutmeg. Most people in France now have dropped the osban, or they buy it ready-prepared from kosher butchers.

Apart from all these, there is the grain. I hope that I have not frightened you, because now that I have made this grand affair a few times for parties I find it not too difficult, only complex. I make it in a special way that is not the most traditional but is the most pleasing to me, and which guests find stunning. The vegetable stew is without meat or bones but has more vegetables than usual (make your own selection), and the peppers are roasted separately rather than stewed (they taste better and look beautiful). The meatballs (I prefer lamb) are encrusted with pieces of potato and artichoke bottoms. (I use frozen ones—they are sometimes labeled "hearts").

For the vegetable stew

- 5 red and yellow peppers
- 10 tiny onions, peeled
- 6 carrots, cut in 1¼-inch (3-cm) slices
- 3 leeks, cut into four pieces
- 1 lb (500 g) new potatoes
- 6 small turnips, cut in half or quartered
- A small head white cabbage, cut in wedges
- 3 tomatoes, peeled and quartered
- 12 cups (3 liters) water or chicken stock (you may use 6 bouillon cubes)
- 5 garlic cloves, crushed in a garlic press
- Salt and pepper
- 2 teaspoons cinnamon
- ½ teaspoon allspice
- 1 teaspoon ginger
- ½ teaspoon mace
- 4 zucchini, cut in thick slices
- 1 lb (500 g) orange pumpkin, weighed peeled and cut into slices
- A large bunch of flat-leafed parsley, finely chopped (1 cup)
- A large bunch of coriander, finely chopped (1 cup)

For the "boulettes" and their tomato sauce

- 3 garlic cloves, crushed in a garlic press
- 2 tablespoons peanut or sunflower oil
- 2 lbs (1 kg) tomatoes, peeled and chopped, or a 28-oz (800-g) can of peeled, chopped, or pureed tomatoes
- 2 tablespoons tomato paste
- 2 teaspoons sugar
- Salt and pepper
- Juice of ½ lemon
- 3 lbs (1½ kg) ground lamb or beef
- 2 slices bread, soaked in water and squeezed dry
- 1½ teaspoons cinnamon
- ½ teaspoon allspice
- 14 oz (400 g) frozen artichoke bottoms, quartered
- 1 lb (500 g) new potatoes, peeled and quartered

Tunisian Couscous with Stuffed Meatballs (cont.)

For the grain

2 lbs (1 kg) couscous
Salt
½ cup (125 ml) peanut or sunflower oil

For the hot sauce

1½ teaspoons harissa, or 1 teaspoon paprika
and ½–1 teaspoon cayenne, or to taste

For the vegetable stew: Roast and peel the peppers (see page 253) and cut them in half. Keep them aside to add to the stew when you are ready to serve. It is easier to peel the little onions if you blanch them in boiling water first and peel them while they are still a little hot.

In a large saucepan put the onions, carrots, leeks, potatoes, turnips, cabbage, and tomatoes. Add the stock or water, garlic, salt and pepper, cinnamon, allspice, ginger, and mace. Bring to the boil and simmer for about ¾ hour, or until the vegetables are tender, tasting to see if the seasoning and spices are right, then take off the heat. About 15 minutes before you are ready to serve, bring to the boil again, and add the zucchini and pumpkin. Five minutes before the end, add the flat-leafed parsley and coriander. Put in the peppers and heat through. There should be plenty of liquid. Add water if necessary.

For the boulettes and their sauce: Start with the tomato sauce. Fry the garlic in the oil till lightly colored. Add the tomatoes, tomato paste, sugar, salt, pepper, and lemon juice and bring to the boil, then simmer gently.

Put the ground meat and bread in a bowl with salt, pepper, cinnamon, and allspice and work to a soft paste with your hands. Take a walnut-sized lump, roll it into a ball, and press

2 pieces of artichoke or 2 pieces of potato into it so that they stick out a little. Repeat with the rest of the meat. Drop the balls into the tomato sauce and add enough water to cover, then simmer gently, covered, for about 45 minutes, until very tender.

To cook the grain: Follow the instructions on page 487 and heat through in the oven, covered with foil, for about 20 minutes before serving.

To serve: Pour the vegetable stew in a very wide, shallow dish so that all the vegetables can be seen, and put the peppers on top. They are quite spectacular. In another dish, break up the grain with a spoon and shape it into a mountain. Serve the meatballs in a separate bowl. Make a hot sauce for everyone to pass around by mixing the harissa or paprika and cayenne in about 3 ladlefuls of the vegetable broth.

VARIATIONS

• For simpler, more common "boulettes," see page 407.

• Msoki de la pâque juive, a famous Tunisian Passover Seder dish, is similar and consists of the stew, meatballs, and osban but without the couscous and with 1 lb (500 g) matzos, broken into pieces, thrown into the stew at the end. The Passover stew has mainly green vegetables, including fava beans, peas, spinach, artichoke hearts, zucchini, leeks, fennel, green cabbage, cardoons, and beets.

• It is exciting to find that in Livorno, in Tuscany, the Jews make a similar couscous with meatballs, which they call "cuscussu moksci con polpette." The vegetables included are all green—there is cabbage, lettuce, spinach, and cauliflower in the stew—and the polpette (meatballs) are made with zucchini, celery, and artichokes.

Couscous de Poulet

Chicken Coucous

SERVES 8–10

This too is a North African Friday-night special. Tunisians accompany it with boulettes de poulet—chicken balls cooked in tomato sauce (see following recipe). I have listed quite a few vegetables as suggestions; you do not need to have them all.

For the soup

1 chicken
½ cup (100 g) chickpeas, soaked for at least an hour
3 onions, chopped, or 1 lb (500 g) tiny onions (to peel them more easily, blanch them first in boiling water)
4 tomatoes, peeled and chopped
4 carrots, peeled and cut into large pieces
4 turnips, peeled and quartered
1 small cauliflower cut into florets, or 1 small white cabbage cut into wedges
4 new potatoes, peeled and cut into thick slices
2 cloves garlic, crushed
Pepper
1 teaspoon powdered ginger
1 teaspoon cinnamon
5 cloves
½ teaspoon mace
Salt
1 lb (500 g) fava beans, fresh or frozen (optional)
1 lb (500 g) orange pumpkin, peeled and cut into thick slices
4 zucchini, thickly sliced

For the grain

1½ lbs (750 g) couscous
1 teaspoon salt
6 tablespoons peanut or light vegetable oil

For the hot chili sauce

2 teaspoons harissa, or 1½ teaspoons paprika and ½ teaspoon cayenne or chili pepper, or to taste

For the soup, put the chicken in a large pot with about 11 cups (2½ liters) water. Bring to the boil and remove the scum. Add the drained chickpeas and all the other ingredients except the salt, fava beans, pumpkin, and zucchini. Simmer for 1 hour, or until the chickpeas and chicken are done. Add the salt, the fava beans, pumpkin, and zucchini 10–15 minutes before serving.

For the grain, follow the instructions on page 487, and heat through in the oven, covered with foil, for about 15 minutes, or until very hot, before serving.

Serve the soup and grain in separate dishes. Make a hot sauce to pass around in a little bowl by mixing the harissa or paprika and cayenne with about 3 ladles of the soup.

VARIATION

• For a different presentation, boil 1¼ cups (250 g) chickpeas and ¾ cup (100 g) raisins separately and serve the grain mixed with the drained raisins and chickpeas. Omit the chickpeas from the soup.

Boulettes de Poulet pour le Couscous

Couscous with Chicken Balls

SERVES 8–10

In Tunisia these are served as a side dish with chicken couscous on Friday night or special occasions like weddings. They are also called "les boulettes de la mariée" (the bride's chicken balls). The tomato sauce is usually a little tomato paste in a mixture of oil and water, but I prefer using fresh or canned tomatoes. Buy boned and skinned chicken pieces (breast or thigh) for this.

> 2 lbs (1 kg) tomatoes or a 28-oz (800-g)
>   can of peeled or chopped tomatoes
> Salt and pepper
> 1–2 teaspoons sugar
> 1 onion
> 2 slices white bread, crusts removed
> A bunch of flat-leafed parsley, finely chopped
>   (about ½ cup)
> 3 garlic cloves, crushed in a garlic press
> 2 eggs
> 1 lb (500 g) chicken fillets
> ½ teaspoon allspice
> ½ teaspoon cinnamon

For the tomato sauce, put the tomatoes, quartered and with their skins, or the canned ones, in the food processor and blend to a cream. Pour into a pan, add salt, pepper, and sugar, and bring to the boil.

For the boulettes, blend the onion, bread, parsley, garlic, and eggs to a cream. Then add the chicken, salt, pepper, allspice, and cinnamon and process briefly to a paste. Take tablespoons of the mixture, and rubbing your hands with oil, roll into balls the size of a walnut, and drop into the tomato sauce. Simmer for 30–45 minutes.

Couscous aux Légumes Verts

Couscous with Green Vegetables

SERVES 8

This springtime couscous makes a delightful meal.

For the soup

> 4 green bell peppers
> 1 large onion, chopped
> 3 tablespoons peanut or sunflower oil
> 6 crushed garlic cloves
> 2 lbs (1 kg) stewing lamb or beef, cut in large
>   chunks
> 11 cups (2½ liters) water
> Salt and pepper
> ¼ teaspoon nutmeg
> 1 lb (500 g) new potatoes
> 3 celery stalks, cut in large slices
> 1 teaspoon fennel seeds
> 1 lb (500 g) fresh fava beans (you may use
>   frozen ones)
> 1 lb (500 g) artichoke hearts or bottoms, cut
>   in half (you may use frozen ones)
> 2 zucchini, cut into thick slices
> 2 fennel bulbs, cut into thick slices
> Juice of 1 lemon
> A bunch of mint leaves, finely chopped (⅓ cup)

For the grain

> 1½ lbs (750 g) couscous
> Salt
> 6 tablespoons peanut or sunflower oil

For the hot sauce

> 1 teaspoon harissa, or 1 teaspoon paprika
>   and ½ teaspoon cayenne

Roast, peel, and seed the peppers as described on page 253, and cut in half. Keep them aside until you are ready to serve.

Fry the onion in the oil till golden. Add the garlic and stir for a moment or two. Then add the meat and turn the pieces to brown them slightly all over. Cover with water and bring to the boil. Remove the scum, add salt, pepper, and nutmeg and simmer for 2 hours.

Add the potatoes, celery stalks, and fennel seeds and simmer for 20 minutes longer. Then add the fava beans, artichoke hearts, zucchini, fennel bulbs, and lemon juice and simmer another 15 minutes, or until the vegetables are tender. Five minutes before serving, add the mint and the roasted peppers.

While the stew is cooking, prepare the couscous. Follow the instructions on page 487, and heat through in the oven, covered with foil, for 15–20 minutes before serving. Serve the soup in a wide, shallow dish so that the meat and all the vegetables can be seen. An alternative way of serving is to shape the couscous in a cone, then arrange the meat in a hollow on the top and the vegetables around the sides.

Make a hot sauce to pass around by mixing the harissa or paprika and cayenne with 3 ladlefuls of the broth.

Couscous à la Courge Rouge et aux Raisins Secs

Couscous with Orange Pumpkin and Raisins

SERVES 6

This delicate-tasting golden couscous is eaten at Rosh Hashanah (page 28). The homemade liquor mahia (page 626) is served with it.

> 1½ lbs (750 g) beef, lamb, or veal, cubed
> 1 marrow bone, if possible
> 6 cups (1½ liters) water or more
> 1 cup (200 g) chickpeas, soaked for at least
>   1 hour
> 3 medium onions, quartered
> Salt and white pepper
> 4 carrots, cut in half lengthwise
> 1 large sweet potato, cubed
> 1 or 2 hot fresh chilies, slit open and seeded
> ½ teaspoon saffron
> 1½ lbs (750 g) orange pumpkin, peeled, seeds
>   and fibers scraped off, and cut in large
>   slices
> ¾ cup (100 g) golden raisins
> 1 lb (500 g) couscous
> 4 tablespoons vegetable oil for the grain
>   (see page 487)
> 1 teaspoon cinnamon
> 1–2 tablespoons confectioners' sugar (optional)
> ½ cup (100 g) coarsely chopped toasted
>   almonds (optional)

For the "soup," cover the meat and marrow bone with water and bring to the boil. Remove the scum and add the chickpeas and onions.

Couscous with Orange Pumpkin and Raisins (cont.)

Simmer 1½ hours, then add salt and pepper, the carrots, sweet potatoes, and chilies, and more water if necessary. (During the cooking, taste the soup and remove the chilies when it seems peppery enough.) Cook 15 minutes and add saffron, pumpkin, and raisins. Cook another 20 minutes, until the pumpkin is tender.

While the stew is cooking, prepare the couscous. Follow the instructions on page 487, and heat through in the oven for about 15–20 minutes before serving. Sprinkle a design with cinnamon and the confectioners' sugar or almonds if you like.

Pour a few ladles of stock on top of the grain and serve the meat and vegetables in a separate bowl. Or, if you dispense with the garnishes on the grain, arrange the pieces of meat in the middle and vegetables all around the sides.

Couscous au Poisson

Tunisian Fish Couscous

SERVES 8

When I was a schoolgirl in Paris, I often went to eat fish couscous at the Pavillon Tunisien in the Cité Universitaire, where I had friends. Tunisians are the only ones who make it in North Africa. They passed it on to Sicily when the Arabs were there, more than 600 years ago. The Tuscan city of Livorno adopted it through the Jewish connection with Tunis (page 484). A distinctive Jewish touch is the boulettes de poisson (fish balls) that come with it. They are either fried, then cooked in a sauce, or simply poached in the sauce. In Tunisia the fish may be gray mullet, grouper, or bream, but you can use cod, haddock, hake, and other white fish.

For the fish soup

> *1 large onion, sliced*
> *2 tablespoons oil*
> *4 carrots, cut in 1-inch (2½-cm) slices*
> *3 turnips, quartered*
> *2 celery stalks, cut in 1-inch (2½-cm) slices*
> *4 medium potatoes, quartered*
> *5 tomatoes, peeled and quartered*
> *1 tablespoon tomato paste*
> *Salt and pepper*
> *Juice of ½–1 lemon*
> *½ teaspoon saffron*
> *4 large fish steaks (see headnote)*
> *3 tablespoons chopped coriander or flat-leafed parsley (optional)*

For the fish balls

> *1 recipe boulettes de poisson (page 342) or kefta de poisson au coriandre et citron confit (page 343)*

For the grain

> *1½ lbs (750 g) couscous*
> *6 tablespoons oil*
> *Salt*

Fry the onion in the oil till soft and lightly colored. Add the carrots, turnips, celery, potatoes, and tomatoes and cover with about 6 cups

(1½ liters) water. Stir in the tomato paste, add salt and pepper, bring to the boil, and simmer for about 20 minutes. Add lemon juice and saffron, put in the fish, and cook 10 minutes more. Serve sprinkled, if you like, with coriander or parsley.

Prepare the recipe for boulettes de poisson à la sauce tomate or the one for kefta de poisson au coriandre et citron confit.

To cook the grain, follow the instructions on page 487, and heat through in the oven for about 20 minutes before serving.

Serve the grain, the soup (cut the fish steaks in half), and the fish balls in separate bowls.

VARIATIONS

• You may add 1 teaspoon of paprika to the soup, and you may put in 1 small chili pepper, slit and seeded, which you take out when you feel the soup is hot enough.

• Other vegetables that sometimes go in the fish soup are zucchini and pumpkin slices.

• The Jews of Livorno flavor their cuscussu di pesce with cinnamon and ground cloves.

ual vegetables, the most popular being fava beans and peas.

To serve 6: Prepare 1 lb (500 g) couscous following the instructions on page 487, mix in 4 oz (100 g) butter, and shape into a cone with a flat top. Serve the grain crowned with about 2 lb (1 kg) fava beans or peas (fresh or frozen), boiled separately in salted water and mixed with 2 oz (60 g) more butter. You may sprinkle with 3–4 tablespoons of raisins or sultanas, soaked in water for 20 minutes, then drained, or, if you like, with lines of cinnamon and confectioners' sugar down the sides of the cone.

It is the custom to serve milk or buttermilk to drink in little glasses at the same time. Some people today also pour yogurt over the dish.

VARIATIONS

• Zucchini or orange-pumpkin slices may be used instead of beans or peas, and the grain may be covered with plenty of sliced onions fried in oil until golden.

Couscous au Beurre et aux Fèves Fraîches ou aux Petits Pois

Couscous with Butter and Fava Beans or Green Peas

During Shavuot, couscous was prepared with butter instead of oil and served with individ-

Couscous Sucré "Seffa"

Sweet Couscous

SERVES 6

Sweet couscous is a festive Jewish dish in North Africa. In Morocco it was served at Hanukah in bowls with wooden spoons. When it is made with butter, it is the custom to serve cold milk or buttermilk with it, in little tea glasses.

1 lb (500 g) couscous
½–1 teaspoon salt
4 oz (100 g) unsalted butter, cut into pieces,
    or 6 tablespoons peanut or light vegetable
    oil (it is great with the rare argan oil;
    see page 234)
1 tablespoon cinnamon
3 tablespoons confectioners' sugar or to taste
¾ cup (100 g) raisins or sultanas, boiled in
    water for 10 minutes (optional)
Buttermilk or milk to accompany

Prepare the couscous following the instructions on page 487. You can use butter instead of oil. Serve shaped in a cone, sprinkled with lines of cinnamon and confectioners' sugar down the sides and, if you like, with the drained raisins or sultanas.

VARIATIONS

• You may add 1 tablespoon or more orange-blossom water or ½ teaspoon saffron powder to the water moistening the couscous.

• For couscous sucré aux fruits secs, sprinkle with 1¼ cups (250 g) mixed toasted pine nuts, chopped almonds, and pistachios.

• For couscous aux grains de grenade, a specialty of Rosh Hashanah (page 28)—the pomegranate seeds representing the wish that there should be many children born—empty the shiny pink seeds of a pomegranate on top of the grain (omit the raisins or sultanas).

• For couscous aux dattes, arrange dates and chopped almonds on top (omit the raisins).

• For couscous sucré au lait, pour hot milk over the couscous just before serving.

• In Morocco, a fat-grained type of couscous called "berkoksh" (it can be bought there in packages), which is like a tiny pasta, was served at Purim (page 33) with hard-boiled eggs representing the eyes of Haman. The grain was soaked in water and steamed, seasoned with either salt or sugar, and smothered in butter and hot milk. It was accompanied by buttermilk and yogurt and served in the morning, when people came back from the synagogue, and in the evening, when they played cards.

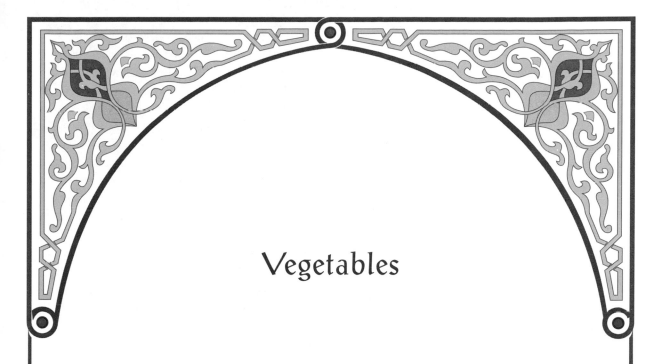

Vegetables

THE SEPHARDIM have a reputation as vegetable lovers even by Mediterranean standards. Certain vegetables have been especially popular with them, and some have been associated with them, such as eggplants and artichokes, especially in Spain and Italy. Although these vegetables were brought to the south of these countries by the Arabs, the Jews took the credit, because it was they who introduced them to the north when they fled the Inquisition. Jews remained forever fond of them.

Jews have also been associated with the vegetables from the New World. In the Islamic world, they made a greater use of tomatoes, peppers, potatoes and pumpkin than did the general population. A great number of Marranos (converted Jews, also known as New Christians) were on the Spanish and Portuguese boats that sailed to the Americas in 1492 and later. They became

involved in the trade of gold and silver as well as of tomatoes, peppers, hot chilies, potatoes, green beans, and corn to the mother country and elsewhere. Marranos in Spain and Portugal were also involved in the trade that brought seeds and foodstuffs to every port in the Mediterranean, where they dealt most often with their Marrano and Sephardi contacts. Jews adopted the new vegetables enthusiastically. In the sixteenth and seventeenth centuries, waves of Marranos fleeing the Inquisition brought the ways of making use of them that had been developed in Spain. One of these, the famous Spanish sofrito—a sauce of fried onions and tomatoes, which is the start of so many dishes—became a kind of signature tune of Sephardi cooking.

Jews were always known as onion and garlic eaters. In Istanbul, when Jews avoided the plague during a terrible epidemic, it was said that the virus did not penetrate the Jewish areas because of the smell of garlic. In the Exodus in the Bible, the Hebrews remembered nostalgically the leeks, onions, and garlic they had eaten in Egypt. The first sonnet ever written in Hebrew was in praise of these vegetables. It was part of a work, the *Mahberot* (*Compositions*), written by the greatest Hebrew poet of medieval Italy, Immanuel ben Solomon of Rome, called Manoello (1260–c. 1328). My friend the Israeli poet and songwriter Danny Almagor sent me this translation by Allen Mandelbaum, which appeared in the American Jewish periodical *Commentary* in 1951:

From the Hungry, Praise

I gaze on manna and on quail,
but voices warn, "Approach not here";
the banquet now is but a dream
bereft the grandeur of my soul.

For heart's redeemer is the onion,
onion, garlic, leek, my peace,
upon my head fit coronal,
and for my soul-ills, unction.

Garlic is earth's stag and blossom,
Grace did bear him, Glory robed him,
over him—the Great Bear and her sons.

And wheel in wheel, like heaven's spheres,
the onion's skin; the leek, Elisha's
wand, in wondrous miracles.

The Biblical allusions in the poem are to the Jews in the wilderness who fed on quails that fell from the sky and on manna that appeared on trees.

Certain vegetables have symbolic significance and are used in ritual celebration. During Passover, fava-bean soups and fava-bean dishes of all kinds are eaten, because the Hebrews ate fava beans during their captivity in Egypt. For Rosh Hashanah, green vegetables such as spinach, chard, peas, fresh fava beans, and artichokes represent renewal and happiness, beans such as black-eyed peas and chickpeas represent plenty—that there should be more children and more prosperity. In *La Cuisine Juive Marocaine*, Viviane and Nina Moryoussef give a recipe for the symbolic "seven vegetables for Rosh Hashanah" that has a pound (five hundred grams) each of carrots, turnips, and leeks cut in half lengthwise, quinces and orange pumpkin cut in pieces, and a bunch of beets cooked with a glass of oil, two glasses of water, and half a package of saffron. Most but not all families add half a glass of sugar and one teaspoon of cinnamon towards the end so that the year "should be sweet." Madame Guineaudeau in *Les Secrets des Cuisines en Terre Marocaine* has a Jewish feast-day bean-and-vegetable pot of chickpeas, beans, and various vegetables such as zucchini, leeks, spinach, and pumpkin flavored with cinnamon and ground cloves. Algerians too make a soup with "seven vegetables." Seven is a lucky number, because, according to Jewish lore, the world was created in seven days and there are seven days in a week and the Sabbath is the seventh day.

In the Sephardi repertoire you find vegetables in all kinds of guises—in stews, with meatballs, combined with ground meat, mashed with cheese and eggs, partnered with legumes, and also stuffed. Another distinctly Sephardi way of preparing vegetables is to combine them with eggs or cheese or with both. These meatless dishes—they are referred to these days as "gratins," "soufflés," and omelettes—are part of the dairy table, eaten as light evening meals, as snacks, and as appetizers. Thick vegetable omelettes are "fritadas"

CARCIOFI ALLA GIUDIA

Deep-Fried Artichokes

THIS FAMOUS Roman specialty is the only dish widely recognized as Jewish in Italy. I will always remember my pleasure when I first tasted it at Piperno's in the old Roman Ghetto. The restaurant has an artichoke design on its menu, and, I believe, had much to do with popularizing the dish. They serve the crisply fried artichokes, which look like delicate bronze chrysanthemums with curly petals, all the year round; they store them partially cooked in the freezer to serve when artichokes are not in season, because that is what tourists invariably ask for.

This way of cooking artichokes can only work with the special little Roman artichokes that you can eat whole, leaves and all, when they are young and tender (a variety also found in Spain). If you are able to find such artichokes, here is how to prepare them. It is not easy. Roman Jews have a knack.

Squeeze the juice of 1 to 2 lemons into a bowl of cold water. To prepare the artichokes, pull off the small outer leaves, and peel and trim the stem. Then with a sharp knife cut away the tougher end parts of the leaves, leaving more and more of the leaf as you near the center. With the help of a knife with a rounded end, bend the leaves back like the petals of a flower, then cut away and discard the tiny inner spiky leaves and the fuzzy choke, scraping it off and being careful not to break the artichoke bottom.

Drop each artichoke, as soon as it is pared, into the bowl of acidulated water to prevent the cut parts from discoloring. Leave to soak for a few minutes, then dry them. Now press the artichokes down on a plate, bottoms up and leaves opened out, flattening them as much as you can without breaking them. Sprinkle with salt and pepper. Cook the artichokes in olive or sunflower oil, over low heat, for about 15 minutes, bottoms up to begin with, then turning them over once. Finally turn them again, leaves down, and raise the heat to very high. When the oil is bubbling, sprinkle cold water over it with your fingers 3 or 4 times. This makes the leaves curl up and become crisp and brown. Lift out quickly and drain on paper towels. Serve at once.

to Jews of Iberian descent, "ajjas" for Jews in the Arab world. Cheese dishes are referred to as "kon keso" by the "Espagnoli," and "bi jibn" or "bi gebna" by Arabized communities. The main cheeses used are the Sephardi staples—kasseri, referred to as "kasher" in Turkey; the hard sharp kashkaval, used for grating; and the ubiquitous white salty feta, which is sometimes soaked in water to remove some of the saltiness. Also typical are the vegetables cooked in olive oil or dressed with oil and lemon and served cold, which have an important place at the cold Saturday table. You will find these in the appetizer-and-salad section.

Fritto Misto di Verdure

Deep-Fried Vegetables Roman Style

The old Roman Ghetto has a very old tradition of deep-frying. It has been famous since early times for its *friggitori*, vendors who deep-fried all kinds of foods, "robba fritta," from salt cod and offal meats to vegetables, fruit, and sweets. People came from all over the city for these delicacies. Although eating fried things was considered a little vulgar, it is now very fashionable, and restaurants specialize in fried vegetables, which are featured as "Jewish style."

All kinds of vegetables can be deep-fried. Some are simply floured, others are dipped in batter. Small mushrooms can be left whole. Potatoes are cut in thin slices, zucchini and onions into thick ones. Orange pumpkin should be cut into small thinnish slices. Tiny, tender artichokes are trimmed. Cauliflower and broccoli florets must be boiled in salted water for 5 minutes, drained, and allowed to dry before being dipped in batter. Zucchini or pumpkin flowers are done too.

For the batter (la pastela)

> 1 cup (150 g) flour
> ½ teaspoon baking soda
> ¼ teaspoon salt
> 1 tablespoon olive oil plus more for frying
> 1 cup (250 ml) cold water
> Lemon wedges to accompany

In a bowl, mix the flour with the baking soda, salt, and oil. Then beat the water in gradually with a fork. Beat thoroughly to a smooth cream and let rest for about ½ hour before using.

Dip the vegetables in the batter and fry in batches in 1½ inches (4 cm) of medium-hot olive oil till crisp and golden, then lift out with a slotted spoon and drain on paper towels. Reheat, if you need to, in the oven. Serve very hot, accompanied by lemon wedges.

Finocchi Gratinati

Baked Fennel

SERVES 6

Here is a favorite Italian Jewish way of preparing fennel that emphasizes the delicate anise flavor.

> 3 largish fennel heads, cut in 4 lengthwise
> Salt
> 4 tablespoons extra-virgin olive oil
> 3 garlic cloves, minced or crushed
>   in a press
> 4 tablespoons chopped flat-leafed parsley
> 4 tablespoons bread crumbs

Boil the fennel in salted water for about 15 minutes, or until tender but not floppy, then drain and arrange in an oven dish. Mix the oil with the garlic, parsley, and a little salt and pour over the fennel. Turn the vegetables so that they are covered with the dressing all over. Sprinkle with bread crumbs and bake in a 400°F (200°C) oven for 15–20 minutes, or until lightly golden.

• For a dairy version, mix the garlic and parsley with 2 oz (50 g) melted butter and pour over the vegetables, then turn the pieces in the butter to coat them. Sprinkle with salt, pepper, and 5 tablespoons grated Parmesan and bake.

Torzelli

Cooked Belgian Endive

Chicory was much favored by Jews in Italy, where it is called "indivia," and where there are many varieties, white, red, and green, small and compact and curly-leafed. They are eaten as salad but they are also cooked, which produces a pleasant, slightly bitter flavor. The small, smooth-leaved one known here as Belgian endive is most commonly used. Cut a slice off the root end and boil whole in salted water for a few minutes, until just tender. Drain well and dry in a tea cloth, then shallow-fry very briefly in ¼ inch (½ cm) of sizzling-hot oil, turning them until lightly golden. Drain on paper towels.

Alternatively, boil briefly, then bake in a hot oven with a sprinkling of salt and pepper and a little vegetable oil until slightly colored.

Zucca Disfatta

Pumpkin Puree

SERVES 4–6

Pumpkin is not to everyone's taste in Italy, where it was once reviled as poor food. It is true that the taste of pumpkin varies considerably and that it is not always good. But the Jews have always liked it and used it, especially in Ferrara, where it is known for its fine flavor. It was probably Jews who introduced the New World vegetable to that city, through the Marrano connection. This dish was prepared to end the fast of Yom Kippur.

1½ lbs (750 g) orange pumpkin
1 onion, chopped
2 tablespoons sunflower or light vegetable oil
Salt
1½ teaspoons sugar or to taste
½ teaspoon cinnamon (optional)
3 tablespoons chopped flat-leafed parsley (optional)

Cut the pumpkin peel away and remove the seeds and fibrous bits, then cut the pumpkin into cubes.

Fry the onion in the oil till golden. Add the pumpkin and cook with the lid on. It will release a lot of water. Simmer until the pumpkin falls apart. Then mash it with a fork and continue to cook, allowing the liquid to evaporate. Add salt and sugar to taste, and sprinkle if you like with cinnamon and parsley.

Pumpkin Puree (cont.)

VARIATIONS

• Add 2 teaspoons finely chopped candied citrus peel.

• In a Jewish recipe of Venice called "zucca in tecia," the Italian writer Maffioli adds white wine and rosemary at the same time as the pumpkin.

Budino di Zucca Gialla

Pumpkin Flan

SERVES 4

This creamy specialty of the Veneto is my favorite Italian pumpkin dish. Everyone marvels at how good it is.

> 1 lb (500 g) orange pumpkin (weighed when skin, seeds, and stringy bits have been removed)
> 2 oz (50 g) butter
> 3 tablespoons flour
> 1 cup (250 ml) milk, warmed
> ½ teaspoon salt or to taste
> White pepper
> 2–3 teaspoons sugar
> 3 eggs, lightly beaten
> Butter and flour for the pan

Peel the pumpkin, remove seeds and stringy bits, and cut it in pieces. Put these in a pan with a tight-fitting lid with about ½ cup (125 ml) of water, and steam for 20–30 minutes, until soft. Then, if any water remains, cook with the lid off until the liquid disappears.

Make a stiff béchamel sauce: melt the butter in a pan, add the flour, and stir vigorously for a few minutes, then add the milk gradually, stirring all the time to avoid lumps, and simmer for about 8 minutes.

Mash the pumpkin to a puree with a fork. Add the rest of the ingredients (except the butter and flour for the pan) and beat. (You may blend everything together to a cream in a blender or food processor.) Taste to adjust the flavoring. This is all-important with pumpkins. They grow particularly sweet in the Veneto, and that is why you will probably need to add sugar to approximate the taste. Pour into a greased and floured, preferably nonstick, baking dish or mold (a ring mold or a round *bomba* will do very well) and bake at 350°F (180°C) for about 45 minutes. Turn out and serve hot.

Green Beans in Tomato Sauce

SERVES 4

Many vegetables are cooked in this way, which begins "Fry onions in oil, add garlic, then tomatoes," as does the Spanish sofrito. Olive oil is used if the dish is to be eaten cold.

> 1 onion, coarsely chopped
> 3 tablespoons light extra-virgin olive oil or sunflower oil
> 4 garlic cloves, finely chopped
> 1 lb (500 g) tomatoes, peeled and chopped
> 1 lb (500 g) French beans, topped and tailed
> Salt and pepper
> 1 teaspoon sugar

Fry the onion in the oil till soft and golden. Add the garlic, and when the aroma rises, add the tomatoes and French beans. Season with salt, pepper, and sugar, add water if necessary to cover the beans, and simmer 15–25 minutes, or until the beans are tender and the sauce is reduced a little.

VARIATIONS

• Add the juice of ½ lemon if you will be eating the dish cold.

• Cook zucchini cut in slices 1 inch (2½ cm) thick in the same way. They need only 10 minutes' cooking.

Mattar Paneer

Peas and Cheese Curry

SERVES 4

This classic Indian dish made a delicious dairy meal for Indian Jews, accompanied by plain rice. It is prepared with white cheese such as the one on page 271, but mozzarella may be used instead.

> 1 large onion, chopped
> 2 tablespoons butter
> 1 garlic clove, chopped
> 1 teaspoon turmeric
> ½ teaspoon ground coriander
> ¼ teaspoon chili powder
> 1 inch (2½ cm) fresh ginger, grated, or the juice from it, extracted by squeezing in a garlic press
> 2 tomatoes, peeled and chopped
> 1 lb (500 g) fresh or frozen peas (preferably petits pois)

½ teaspoon cinnamon
½ teaspoon cardamom
Salt and pepper
½ lb (250 g) mozzarella, cut into 1-inch (2½-cm) cubes

Fry the onion in the butter on low heat until golden. Add the garlic and stir until it begins to color. Stir in the turmeric, coriander, chili, and ginger, and cook for a minute or two.

Add the tomatoes and peas, and cover with about 1 cup (250 ml) of water. Add cinnamon, cardamom, salt, and pepper, and simmer, covered, for 5–10 minutes, until the peas are tender. Add the cheese and cook for about 8 minutes longer, or until the cheese is soft.

Bamia

Okra in Tomato Sauce

SERVES 6

Okra is one of the most popular vegetables among Middle Eastern Jews.

> 1 lb (500 g) okra, preferably young and small
> 1 medium onion, cut in half and sliced
> 3 tablespoons sunflower or light olive oil
> 2 garlic cloves, chopped
> 1 lb (500 g) tomatoes, peeled and chopped
> Salt and pepper
> Juice of 1 lemon
> 1–2 teaspoons sugar or to taste
> A small bunch of flat-leafed parsley or coriander, chopped

Trim or cut off the conical caps of the okra and wash them, then drain. Fry the onion in the oil till soft and golden. Add the garlic and fry till the aroma rises. Now add the okra and sauté gently for about 5 minutes, turning the pods over.

Add the tomatoes, salt, pepper, lemon juice, and sugar and simmer 15–20 minutes, or until the okra are tender and the sauce is reduced. (In the old days, they cooked okra for a very long time, until it almost fell apart.) Stir in the parsley or coriander and cook a minute more.

Serve hot with rice or cold as a side dish or starter.

VARIATION

• In Iraq, 1–2 dried limes, cracked open with a hammer, were often used instead of lemon juice. They give a distinctive, delicate musty flavor. Two teaspoons of dried ground limes may also be used.

Bamia bel Tamarhendi
Okra with Tamarind Syrian Style

SERVES 6

It is not pretty to look at—the tamarind, a dark-brown, almost black paste, gives the dish a muddy brown color—but it is delicious, especially cold.

1 lb (500 g) okra, preferably small ones
1 medium onion, chopped
3 tablespoons sunflower or light olive oil
2 cloves garlic, crushed
1 tablespoon tamarind paste
Salt and pepper
1 tablespoon sugar
½ teaspoon allspice

Trim or cut off the conical caps of the okra and wash them well.

Fry the onion in the oil till soft and beginning to color, then add the garlic and fry till the aroma rises. Add the tamarind, crushing it with a fork until it melts. Now put in the okra and barely cover with water. Add salt, pepper, sugar, and allspice and simmer, uncovered, for about 20 minutes, or until the okra is tender and the sauce much reduced (people used to like okra soft and limp, but they are also very nice a little crisp). Serve cold.

FRIED EGGPLANT SLICES

EGGPLANT—OR AUBERGINE, as it is known in Europe—is *the* Sephardi vegetable, and fried slices are a ubiquitous side dish at their tables.

Cut the eggplants into ⅓-inch (¾-cm) thick slices. Sprinkle generously with salt and leave in a colander to drain for 1 hour. Then rinse off the salt, drain, and dry with a tea towel or paper towels.

Jews of Arab lands fry the slices as they are. Fry quickly in hot olive or vegetable oil, about ¼ inch (½ cm) deep, turning over once, until lightly browned and tender, then drain on paper towels.

Jews of Iberian descent dip them in lightly beaten egg seasoned with salt, or first in flour, then in egg, before frying in not-too-hot oil. Italian Jews sometimes also dip the slices a third time in fine bread crumbs. The point of these coatings is to stop the eggplant from absorbing too much oil.

Nowadays many people prefer to broil or roast the eggplants rather than fry them. To do so, brush the slices generously with oil and cook under the broiler, turning over once, or roast in a very hot oven until browned.

Eggplant slices are served in many different ways. A common method is to sprinkle them with fried chopped garlic and parsley. Another is to top them with yogurt or fresh tomato sauce (page 548). A delicious Syrian way is dressed with a pomegranate syrup diluted in water in the proportion of 1 tablespoon of concentrate to 2 of water.

Fried Zucchini Slices with Yogurt

SERVES 4

This is a Turkish way of eating zucchini that spread throughout the Ottoman world.

1 lb (500 g) zucchini
Light olive or vegetable oil for frying
Salt and pepper
2 tablespoons chopped fresh dill or mint
1 cup (250 ml) yogurt to pour over

Trim and cut the zucchini lengthwise into 4 long slices, about ⅓ inch (¾ cm) thick. Film a frying pan with oil and fry the slices quickly over high heat until brown, turning them over once. Drain on paper towels. Sprinkle with salt and pepper and the dill or mint and serve hot with yogurt poured over.

Artichoke Hearts and Fava Beans

SERVES 6

This was the Friday-night standby at my parents' home in London. In Egypt, vendors used to come to the kitchen door and sell artichokes by the crate. My mother was so fond of the dish that, although she would not take the trouble to cut artichoke hearts free of leaves and chokes, she compromised and cooked the frozen vegetables.

> 1 lb (500 g) fresh shelled or frozen fava beans
> 1 lb (500 g) frozen artichoke hearts (or bottoms), quartered or cut in half
> Salt and pepper
> 4 tablespoons light olive oil
> 2 garlic cloves, crushed in a press or finely chopped
> Juice of 1 lemon
> 1 teaspoon sugar or more to taste
> 2 sprigs of mint or dill, finely chopped

Put all the ingredients in a pan together with water barely to cover and simmer gently for 15–20 minutes, or until the vegetables are tender and the liquid is reduced.

Serve hot or cold.

Piselli al Ebraica

Peas Jewish Style

SERVES 4

I wonder why this recipe is defined as Jewish style in Italy. Some supermarkets sell tiny fresh peas, but frozen ones will do.

> 1 medium onion, finely chopped
> 3 tablespoons sunflower or light vegetable oil
> 2 lettuce leaves, cut in thin ribbons
> 1 lb (500 g) shelled peas
> ½ cup (125 ml) dry white wine
> Salt and pepper
> 1 teaspoon sugar

Gently fry the onion in the oil till soft. Add the lettuce and peas and stir well. Then add the wine, salt, pepper, and sugar and simmer until the peas are tender—very young petits pois take 5 minutes, older peas may take up to 20.

Spinaci con Pinoli e Passerini

Spinach with Pine Nuts and Sultanas

SERVES 6

This is a famous Venetian Jewish specialty. I found the same dish in Spain. The raisins and pine nuts are an Arab combination, which could have come through the *levantini*, the *spa-*

nioli, or even the Sicilian Jewish inhabitants of the ghetto.

> *1½ lbs (750 g) spinach*
> *1 onion, chopped*
> *3 tablespoons sunflower oil*
> *3 tablespoons pine nuts*
> *2 tablespoons raisins or sultanas, soaked*
> *   in water for 15 minutes*
> *Salt and pepper*

Wash the spinach in plenty of water. You do not need to remove the stems unless they are big and hard. Drain, and squeeze out the excess water.

In a very large pan (spinach is bulky), fry the onion in the oil till soft. Add the pine nuts and stir till lightly browned. Add the drained raisins or sultanas and stir. Then press the spinach down into the pan with no added water. Put the lid on and leave over low heat until the spinach crumples into a soft mass. Season with salt and pepper and stir well. Serve hot or cold.

Épinards aux Pois Chiches

Spinach and Chickpeas

SERVES 6

This combination is common to all the Sephardi communities, among whom it was often a New Year's dish, the chickpeas representing plenty and their roundness symbolizing the hope that the year would be well rounded, and the spinach representing newness. Joelle Bahloul writes in *Le Culte de la Table dressée* that it was eaten on the Sabbath by Algerian families from Constantine.

> *1 large onion, coarsely chopped*
> *2 tablespoons sunflower oil*
> *½ lb (250 g) chickpeas, soaked in water for*
> *   2 hours or overnight*
> *2 tomatoes, peeled and chopped*
> *Salt and pepper*
> *1½ lbs (750 g) spinach*

Fry the onion in the oil till soft, then add the drained chickpeas and the tomatoes. Cover with water. Simmer 1 hour, until the chickpeas are tender, adding salt and pepper when they begin to soften and water if necessary, letting it reduce when the chickpeas are done. Wash and drain the spinach and squeeze the water out (unless the stems are thick and hard you do not need to remove them). Place on top of the chickpeas. Put the lid on, so that the spinach is steam-cooked. As soon as the spinach flops (within minutes), add a little salt and stir. Serve hot.

VARIATIONS

• A Judeo-Spanish version called "espinakas kon avas" is with white haricot beans instead of chickpeas.

• A tablespoon of tomato paste may be used instead of tomatoes.

Pumpkin Kofta Curry

SERVES 4

This vegetarian stew from India is most appealing, with an exquisite combination of flavors and different shades of orange and gold. The recipe is slightly adapted from one by Mrs. S. Joel in the *Bene Israel Cook Book* of India. (I made it with orange pumpkin rather than white and used only 2 fresh hot chilies instead of 5 or 6.) Serve it with plain rice.

For the pumpkin kofta

> 1 lb (500 g) orange pumpkin (weighed after
>   peeling and scraping)
> 3 tablespoons finely chopped coriander leaves
> 1 green chili, finely chopped
> 2 garlic cloves, crushed in a garlic press
> 1¼-inch (3-cm) piece of fresh ginger, grated,
>   or the juice extracted by crushing in
>   a garlic press
> ½ cup (75 g) chickpea (gram) flour
> Salt

For the curry sauce

> 1 teaspoon ground coriander
> 1 teaspoon ground cumin
> 1–5 red chilies (1 might be enough for you)
> ¼–½ teaspoon ground turmeric
> 1 teaspoon poppy seeds (optional)
> ½ cup dried unsweetened coconut
> 2 large onions, chopped
> 4 tablespoons sesame or peanut oil
> 3 or 4 tomatoes, peeled and chopped
> 1 tablespoon sugar or to taste

> Salt
> About 2 oz (60 g) solid creamed coconut,
>   cut in pieces (see page 235)

For the kofta (dumplings), peel the pumpkin and scrape off the fibrous part with the seeds. Cut it in pieces and put it in a pot with a tight-fitting lid. Add about ½ cup (100 ml) of water and steam, with the lid on, for about 20 minutes, or until very soft. Then drain and mash in a colander and press all the water out. Mix with the rest of the kofta ingredients. Rub your hands with oil and shape the mixture into walnut-sized balls.

For the sauce, blend the first 6 ingredients to a paste in the food processor. Fry the onions in the oil till soft and golden, then add the paste and stir over low heat until it begins to brown. Add the tomatoes, about 2 cups (500 ml) water, the sugar, salt, and creamed coconut. Then simmer for about 10 minutes. Drop the kofta in the simmering curry sauce and cook for about 15 minutes. (Mrs. Joel fries them in oil first.) Serve hot with rice.

Shalgham Helu

Turnips with Date Syrup

This is an Iraqi specialty. Turnips are very popular in Iraq. They are sold in the streets stewed in date syrup (see dibis, page 627). People also prepare them at home. You can now find commercially produced date syrup in Oriental stores. Peel 1 lb (500 g) of small white turnips and cut them in half. Cover with water in a pot and add salt and 2 tablespoons of date syrup. Simmer for about 30 minutes, until they are tender and the water is reduced.

VARIATION

• Brown sugar is sometimes used instead of date syrup.

Patatas Kocas

Potatoes and Tomatoes

SERVES 6

This is a simple and very tasty Judeo-Spanish way of cooking potatoes. I use waxy new potatoes, which do not fall apart, but others like it with floury potatoes, which do fall apart.

> *2 lbs (1 kg) potatoes, cut in half or quartered*
> *1 lb (500 g) tomatoes, peeled and chopped*
> *2 cups chicken stock or enough to cover the*
> *   potatoes (you may use a bouillon cube)*
> *4 tablespoons extra-virgin olive oil*
> *Salt and pepper*

Put all the ingredients together in a pot and simmer 30–40 minutes, until the potatoes are done. Cover the pot to begin with, and take the lid off towards the end to reduce the sauce to very little.

Pommes de Terre aux Olives

Potatoes with Black Olives

SERVES 6

Turmeric gives the potatoes a pale-yellow tinge, and olives, customary in a salad, make an exquisite combination in this hot Moroccan dish.

> *2 lbs (1 kg) small new potatoes*
> *Salted water*
> *½ teaspoon turmeric*
> *4 garlic cloves, minced or crushed in a press*
> *4 tablespoons extra-virgin olive oil*
> *Pepper*
> *4 oz (100 g) black olives (omitted*
> *   if you like)*
> *A small bunch of coriander leaves,*
> *   coarsely chopped (¼ cup)*

Simmer the potatoes—peeled or simply well washed—in salted water with the turmeric until tender. Drain, and put into a shallow baking dish with the garlic, olive oil, salt, pepper, and olives. Mix very well and bake at 350°F (180°C) for 30 minutes. Serve sprinkled with coriander.

ALOO MAKALLA

Whole Deep-Fried Potatoes

THERE IS ALWAYS one dish that just about everyone from a certain country mentions when I say I am looking for Jewish recipes. Potatoes fried whole, called "aloo makalla," is the one for the Baghdadi Jews of Calcutta. The first time I ate them was at the London home of Bernard and Philomène Jacobs. Bernard had been tracing the origin of Jewish dishes as well as of Jewish family names in Baghdad, and they had invited me out of the blue—to my great delight. Aloo makalla is unique to the Calcutta Baghdadi community. The potatoes are traditionally eaten every Friday night, on festivals, and for every kind of celebration. "Aloo" is the Hindi word for potato, and "makalla" is derived from the Arabic for "fried." Another name is "jumping potatoes": the golden potatoes are meltingly soft inside but so crisp and hard outside that they are difficult to cut, and "jump" on the plate. Despite all that time in the oil, they don't come out like soggy fries but are dry inside. I can see why this is one of the dishes that the new generations want to keep up.

To cook aloo makalla, choose medium-sized, preferably old potatoes. Peel them, and boil them in salted water for 5 minutes. Then drain and cool and let them dry. Now pack them into a large pan and pour enough corn or sunflower oil to cover them completely. Bring to the boil and simmer on the lowest heat for 45–60 minutes, or until a golden-brown crust is formed, turning them over so that they brown evenly. The time depends on their size and variety. Turn up the heat to high for a few minutes if they have not browned. You can turn off the heat and leave them in the oil until you are ready to serve, then turn the heat on again and cook for 5 minutes more. Lift them out with a slotted spoon and drain on paper towels.

Pommes de Terre Douces

Sweet Potatoes

SERVES 6

Sweet potatoes are much used in stews and appear quite often in the Saturday pot. They are also eaten boiled, with dollops of butter. This Moroccan way is one of the nicest.

2 lbs (1 kg) sweet potatoes
Salt
3 oz (75 g) butter
½ cup (125 ml) milk
1 teaspoon cinnamon
Pepper
2 large onions, sliced
3 tablespoons sunflower oil

Peel the sweet potatoes and boil them in salted water. Mash with the butter and milk till smooth. Add cinnamon, salt, and pepper and mix very well. Fry the onions in the oil till golden and serve on top of the mashed sweet potatoes.

Brinjal Albaras

Layered Eggplant Dish

SERVES 6

The beauty of this wonderful dish of the Bene Israel of India is the extraordinary symphony of flavors. The method of layering vegetables in a saucepan, and cooking them over a flame with hardly any liquid, was quite different from anything I knew but worked perfectly well. You need a large, shallow, heavy-bottomed casserole or pot with a tight-fitting lid.

> 1¼ oz (45 g) creamed coconut (see page 235) or a small can of unsweetened coconut milk
> 5 garlic cloves
> ½ hot fresh green chili pepper, seeded, or more to taste
> 1-inch (2½-cm) piece of fresh ginger
> ¼ teaspoon ground cloves
> ½ teaspoon ground cinnamon
> ½ teaspoon ground turmeric
> A good bunch of coriander leaves (½ cup)
> Salt and pepper
> 3 tablespoons peanut or light vegetable oil
> 1 lb (500 g) onions, cut in ⅓-inch (1-cm) slices
> 1½ lbs (750 g) potatoes, cut in ⅓-inch (1-cm) slices
> 1 lb (500 g) eggplant, cut in ⅓-inch (1-cm) slices
> 1 lb (500 g) tomatoes, cut in ⅓-inch (1-cm) slices

Dissolve the creamed coconut (if using) in ½ cup (100 ml) boiling water. Put the garlic, fresh chili, ginger, cloves, cinnamon, turmeric, coriander, a little salt, pepper, and the dissolved coconut cream or the canned coconut milk in a food processor and blend to a paste.

Dip each vegetable in this paste. Cover the bottom of the casserole or pot with the oil and put in the vegetable slices in layers, beginning with a layer of onions, then potatoes, followed by eggplants, and finishing with tomatoes. Put the lid on, and cook on a very low flame for about an hour, until the vegetables are very soft. They cook in their own juices, turn an earth color, and become richly imbued with the aromatic flavors. Turn out carefully on a serving platter so that the vegetables remain in layers.

Serve hot with bread or chapatis.

Almodrote de Berengena

Eggplant Flan

SERVES 8

This is one of the best-loved and most distinctive Jewish dishes of Turkey, the one everyone mentions as the favorite. A similar dish of mashed eggplant, eggs, and cheese is mentioned in the records of the Court of the Inquisition in Spain as one that gave away Christian converts attached to their Jewish faith. The only similar dish I found is the papeton d'aubergines of Provence. Is there a link and a story?

A mixture of feta and kashkaval cheese is traditionally used, but other cheeses, like Cheddar and Gruyère, are also used (by Turkish Jews in England) with very pleasing effect.

> *4 lbs (1¾ kg) eggplants*
> *8 oz (250 g) feta cheese*
> *2 eggs, lightly beaten*
> *2 large slices white bread, crusts removed*
> *1 cup (100 g) grated kashkaval or*
>   *Gruyère*
> *5 tablespoons sunflower oil*

Roast and peel the eggplants as instructed in the box on page 256. Put them in a colander and press with your hand to squeeze out as much of the juices as you can. Then chop the flesh with 2 knives or, as is also the custom in Turkey, mash it with a wooden spoon. Do not use a food processor—that would change the texture.

In a bowl, mash the feta cheese with a fork. Add the eggs, the bread (soaked in water and squeezed dry), the kashkaval or Gruyère (reserving 2–3 tablespoons), and 4 tablespoons of oil. Beat well. Add the eggplants and mix well. Pour the mixture into an oiled baking dish, sprinkle the top with 1 tablespoon of oil and the remaining grated cheese, and bake at 350°F (180°C) for about 1 hour, until lightly colored.

VARIATION

• For almodrote de kalavasa, use boiled and chopped zucchini instead of eggplants.

Marcoude aux Aubergines
Eggplant Omelette

SERVES 6

Egg dishes, called "marcoudes," eaten hot or cold, are very popular hors d'oeuvres in Tunisia.

> *4 medium eggplants, weighing about 2½ lbs*
>   *(1¼ kg)*
> *2 large onions, weighing about 1 lb (500 g)*
> *5 tablespoons olive oil*
> *4 garlic cloves, crushed*
> *6 large eggs*
> *¾ cup coarsely chopped flat-leafed parsley*
> *1 teaspoon ground caraway seed*
> *½ teaspoon ground coriander*
> *Salt and pepper to taste*
> *1 lemon, cut in wedges*

Grill or roast the eggplants and peel and chop them as instructed in the box on page 256.

Fry the onions in 3 tablespoons of oil on very low heat till very soft and golden, stirring occasionally. Add the garlic and stir until it is lightly colored and the aroma rises.

In a bowl, beat the eggs lightly. Add the mashed eggplants, the fried onion and garlic, parsley, caraway, coriander, salt, and pepper and mix well.

Heat the remaining oil in a large, preferably nonstick skillet. Pour in the eggplant mixture and cook, covered, over very low heat for about 10 minutes, until the bottom sets. Then put the frying pan under the broiler until the top sets firm and is lightly browned.

Serve hot or cold with lemon wedges.

A JUDEO-SPANISH STRONGHOLD
IN TURKEY

DRIVING ALONG the Bosporus on the way to a fish restaurant, I saw the word "Ortaköy" and shouted to the taxi driver to stop. My grandmother Eugénie lived in Ortaköy, a suburb of Istanbul, when she was a girl, and we grew up on her stories of earthquakes, raging fires, epidemics, and Armenians running into her house for protection. The waterfront is a charming trendy development now, packed with cafés, restaurants, and art galleries. At the back, among dilapidated wooden houses with jutting balconies and bay windows, I saw a row of eighteen houses where my grandmother might have lived. She told us that eighteen was a lucky number, and that the wood was to protect the houses from earthquakes but it made them vulnerable to fires. I found a long list of Alphandarys (her name) in the records of the little synagogue nestling between a mosque and a Greek Orthodox church, and I spotted what might have been my ancestors in the old community photographs on the wall.

In my grandmother's days, there were forty synagogues and sixty thousand Jews in Istanbul. The community is tiny now. On the Golden Horn, among the mosques and churches and covered bazaars, and through the winding lanes on the hills looking down on the Bosporus, you can find decaying synagogues, old Jewish schools, medieval graveyards, Stars of David, mezuzahs, and Hebrew lettering—testimonies to the once enormous Jewish community which flourished in Istanbul.

The community represented one of the largest group in the mixed population of the cosmopolitan city (other important minorities were Armenian and Greek Orthodox) and played an important part in Istanbul's economic and cultural life. Jews practiced in all kinds of professions, from street vendor, seaman, and porter to jeweler, carpet dealer, printer, doctor, and banker.

A few families lived in affluent parts of the city along the Bosporus in beautiful wooden villas called *yali*, but most in-

*My grandmother Eugénie Alphandary Sassoon,
who came from Istanbul, in Paris in 1903*

habited overcrowded, insalubrious, dilapidated quarters. In a little publication entitled *Balat—Faubourg Juif* (*Balat—Jewish Quarter*), Marie Christine Varol has pieced together life in one of the biggest and poorest Jewish quarters, which a French traveler once described as "a serpent sprawled on the Golden Horn." The streets lived to the rhythm of the Sabbath and Jewish holidays. Sweets and toys and "Haman's ears" pastries were sold at Purim, dice was played, and children performed theatricals depicting the hated Haman and the heroic Esther. At Pesah, the *shammash* (synagogue beadle) went through the streets shouting, "*Ya empeso la buyuk hames*"—that it was time to remove the last crumb of bread. Trellises covered with leaves were erected in balconies during Sukkot. Children walked in processions with long candles at night during Simha Torah. At Shavuot, crowds of friends took picnics on boats. On Friday at five o'clock, the *gabbay* (synagogue official) went around asking shops to close, and the *shammash* went around the houses asking everyone to "*Ashender k'es tarde*" ("Light up, because it's late"). On

"The Eighteen," a row of eighteen houses built by a Jew and rented out to Jews—including my grandmother's family—in Ortaköy

Saturday morning Muslims made the rounds offering to light fires; the *shammash* called Jews to prayer with shouts of "*Altos sinyores, ya van a dizir Baruh shemah.*" After the synagogue, the men got together in each other's houses to chat over raki and cold *mezze*. In the afternoon, after the family lunch, it was visiting time, and families went to the *gazino* to listen to music and poetry. In the "casinos," fortune-tellers read cards and matchmakers introduced young men and women.

The *hammam* or *banyo* (public bath) had special pools—different ones for men and women—for ritual purification, where the water was blessed by the rabbi. They were used especially on Fridays, when people went in large groups of family and friends, bringing *mezze* as snacks to eat. On the night of a *henna*, the day before a wedding, the women of the family accompanied the bride to the *banyo* for the *mikvah* (ritual bath) with great pomp and fanfare, carrying luxurious bath accessories, "*el bogo de la novya*," which were sent by the groom with an escort of musicians. The bride was submerged seven times into the water, and the ladies ate pastries and sweetmeats while the band played. Another type of ladies' party for which special pastries were prepared was for the birth of a child—called *kortar el fachadura* (cutting the blouse), when the baby's first shirt was cut.

At an Oxford Symposium on Food and Cookery, a famous food columnist from Turkey, Tuğrul Şavkay, said that he had recently eaten Jewish dishes he had never seen before. He asked if I could explain how it was that Jewish cooking remained unknown even though Jews had been in Turkey for five hundred years. I reminded him that several years earlier, when we had traveled together through Turkey on a gastronomic tour, he had often commented that he had never encountered many of the dishes offered to us. Turkey has a rich heritage of regional and ethnic cuisines which remain unknown outside the region and the community. It is true that it is not easy to find Jewish foods outside Jewish homes. A great part of their cuisine is quite different from what the Muslims eat.

The only restaurant serving Turkish Jewish food I could find in Istanbul was Kaşer Levi Lokantasi, a small workers' café near the bazaar run by a young Muslim who carried on with the same dishes on the menu after his father died. His father had been the cook when a Mr. Levi ran the restaurant until his death more than twenty years ago. But I was thrilled to find borekitas stuffed with eggplant puree on the menu of a trendy new restaurant with a view of the Golden Horn, and later to meet the caterer who produced them for the restaurant. Rina Sarah Kam caters for bar mitzvahs, weddings, Jewish holidays, and special events like the *kortar el fachadura*.

There are a few small Jewish caterers who cook traditional Jewish foods for private homes and now also provide restaurants. Some of the specialties have become fashionable. A woman who sold jewelry in the hotel I was staying in made borekitas for a newly opened restaurant while she watched television at night. A few Muslim caterers also specialize in Jewish food. A woman called Suna Suzer—wife of the owner of the Pera Palace Hotel—caters for the Jewish club on Prince's Island. Under the supervision of a rabbi, she cooks Jewish specialties learned from elderly Jewish ladies. For the quincentenary celebrations of the expulsion of Jews from Spain, she made a giant cake that was a model of the first Turkish ship that went to pick up the Jews from Spain when they were banished. Lately there has been a revival of interest in Sephardi culture and food within the community. I had been to a dinner at the home of one of the leading members of the community a few years ago when the food was all *nouvelle* and classic French cuisine. Suna catered for the same man's latest party with traditional Jewish dishes.

Many of the dishes popular in the community are the same as those of the non-Jewish population, but in the minds of its members the Spanish heritage is all-important, and indeed it is obvious. Cookbooks recently published in France on the cooking of the Jews of Turkey are entitled *Cuisine Judeo-Espagnolle*. In a book called *Sefarad Yemekleri*, a collection of recipes contributed by a number of women to raise funds for an old people's home, the foreword begins: "Our ancestors who moved from Spain to this land five centuries ago brought their traditions, their customs and their eating habits. Some of these eating habits are still being used."

Until about twenty years ago, the Jews of Turkey cooked everything—even hot meat dishes—with olive oil, as they had done in Spain, which shocked both the Muslims and the Ashkenazim. Nowadays they consider olive oil old-fashioned, heavy, and strong-tasting and use sunflower oil instead. One of their strong points is a range of vegetarian egg-and-cheese dishes, because it was usual to have a meat meal at lunch and a dairy one in the evening. Among these is almodrote de berengena—roasted and mashed eggplant mixed with cheese and egg. A similar dish is mentioned in the records kept by the Court of the Inquisition in Toledo in which a woman was accused of keeping Jewish traditions because she cooked this dish to be eaten cold on Saturday (from testimonies against 111 women studied by Cynthia Levine).

Another strong point is the pies, many of which are distinctive, with a pastry, shape, and filling that are different from the norm. There are pies stuffed with eggplant puree and cheese, and pies with a chopped ratatouille-type filling called "handrajo," and Majorcan-type empanadas with a fish-and-walnut filling. Caterers are especially proud of a modern borekita filled with lokum (Turkish delight), but this is my least favorite. Jews make the usual Turkish vegetables stuffed with meat or rice, but they also have some filled with cheese, and they have special ones like stuffed leeks. Other particularities are the mixtures of meat with mashed vegetables, such as spinach, leeks, and eggplant, in meatballs (albondigas). Many of their almond pastries are the kind that Spanish nuns produce today, and their quince paste is like the membrillo of Spain.

Sfongo

Spinach and Potato Pie

SERVES 6

This dish is served as a dairy meal accompanied by hard-boiled eggs during the Passover week in Turkey. When Lizi Behmoaras, a journalist on the Jewish paper of Istanbul, came to interview me, I asked her for recipes. A few days later, her beautiful mother, Jaklin Katalan, turned up at my hotel with a stack of handwritten recipes. This is one of them.

2½ lbs (1¼ kg) potatoes
1–2 oz (30–60 g) butter
½ cup (125 ml) milk
Salt and pepper
2 eggs, lightly beaten
¾–1 cup (75–100 g) freshly grated
    kashkaval or Parmesan
1½ lbs (750 g) spinach
A good pinch of nutmeg
2 tablespoons olive oil

Boil the potatoes in their skins till soft. Then peel them and mash them with a potato masher or fork. Add the butter, milk, salt, pepper, eggs, and grated cheese, reserving 2 tablespoons, and mash and beat well until smooth and well blended.

Wash the spinach, drain, and press to get rid of excess water. Cook over low heat in a pan with the lid on for a minute, until the leaves soften. They will steam in the moisture that clings to them. Season with salt, pepper, and nutmeg and mix well.

In an oiled baking dish, spread half the quantity of mashed potatoes. Cover with the spinach, then spread the remaining mashed potatoes on top. Sprinkle with the remaining grated cheese and the oil and bake at 400°F (200°C) for 40 minutes, until lightly colored.

Prasifouchi

Leek Pâté

SERVES 6

This creamy pâté makes another traditional dairy evening meal in Turkey during the Passover week.

> *2 lbs (1 kg) leeks*
> *Salt*
> *1 potato weighing about ½ lb (250 g)*
> *3 eggs, lightly beaten*
> *⅔ cup (60 g) grated kashkaval or Parmesan cheese*
> *¼ teaspoon nutmeg*
> *Pepper*
> *3 tablespoons sunflower oil*

Trim and wash the leeks, then boil in salted water till very soft. Drain, and press all the water out with your hands. Boil and drain the potato.

Puree the leeks in a food processor. Add the rest of the ingredients, including the potato cut into pieces—reserving 1–2 tablespoons of grated cheese and a tablespoon of oil for the top. Blend briefly. Pour the mixture into a greased baking dish. Sprinkle with the remaining cheese and oil and bake at 400°F (200°C) for 35–40 minutes, or until it is firm and the top is lightly browned.

Note:

• You can bake the mixture in a well-oiled mold for an attractive presentation. It is easy to invert.

Fritada de Espinaka

Spinach and Cheese Cake

SERVES 6

The Judeo-Spanish word for an omelette-type cake is more Italian than Spanish, as indeed is the style of adding mashed potato for a firmer texture. This is a legacy of the Jews who left Italy at various times for Ottoman lands.

> *14 oz (400 g) spinach*
> *5 eggs*
> *1 medium potato, boiled, peeled, and chopped*
> *7 oz (200 g) feta cheese, mashed*
> *¼ teaspoon nutmeg*
> *Pepper*
> *2 tablespoons olive or light vegetable oil*

Wash the spinach. Remove the stems only if they are tough. Drain, and put the spinach in a large pan on low heat with the lid on. It will steam and collapse very quickly into a soft mass. Drain, and when it is cool enough, press the excess water out. Cut the spinach coarsely or leave it whole.

In a bowl, lightly beat the eggs. Add the potato, spinach, cheese, nutmeg, and pepper and stir well.

In a frying pan, heat the oil. Pour in the spinach-and-egg mixture and cook over a low flame for about 10–15 minutes, until the bottom of the omelette has set. Then cook under the broiler until firm and lightly browned.

Turn out and serve hot or cold, cut in wedges. A usual accompaniment is yogurt.

VARIATION

• Instead of feta cheese, use a mixture with cottage cheese.

Tav Sponaw

Spinach Omelette

SERVES 4–6

Spinach omelette is a common everyday dish in almost every Sephardi community. You find it served for light evening meals, late Saturday lunches, and buffet parties and picnics. Its greenness, which symbolizes renewal, makes this a natural for Rosh Hashanah. Although it is often referred to as an omelette, it is hardly that. There are a great many versions. The most usual is simply spinach and egg flavored with salt and pepper. This Persian one is herby and aromatic.

1 lb (500 g) spinach
4 tablespoons sunflower or light vegetable oil
4 eggs
A bunch of scallions (about 12), trimmed and sliced
4 tablespoons chopped fresh coriander
A few sprigs of mint, chopped
A few sprigs of dill, chopped
Salt and pepper
½ teaspoon nutmeg or allspice

Wash the spinach and remove any thick stems. Drain, and squeeze out the excess water. Put the leaves in a large pan with 2 tablespoons of oil. Cover and steam them until they flop into a soft mass. It takes minutes only. When the spinach is cool enough, press the excess water out in a colander and slice the leaves coarsely with a sharp knife.

In a bowl lightly beat the eggs. Add the cooled spinach, scallions, coriander, mint, dill, salt, pepper, and nutmeg or allspice and mix well.

Heat the remaining oil in a large, preferably nonstick, frying pan. Pour in the spinach mixture and cook on very low heat with the lid on for about 15 minutes, until the bottom of the flan has set. Then put the pan under the broiler to cook the top. When it has set, turn out on a serving platter.

Eat hot or cold. This is usually served with yogurt in a meatless meal.

VARIATIONS

• Alternatively, pour the spinach mixture into a greased baking dish and bake at 350°F (180°C) for 45 minutes.
• Add 1 cup (100 g) very coarsely chopped walnuts.

- Add ½ lb (250 g) cottage cheese and ½ cup (60 g) grated kasseri or Parmesan.
- Frozen spinach will do.

Salq bi Gebna

Spinach with Cheese

SERVES 4

A very simple Oriental way of using spinach.

1 lb (500 g) spinach
2 tablespoons corn or sunflower oil
6 oz (175 g) feta cheese
Pepper
A good pinch of nutmeg

Wash the spinach, drain, and press out the excess water. Do not remove the stems. Put it in a pan with the oil and cook, covered, on very low heat for minutes only, until the leaves soften. Add the cheese and crush it with a fork. Sprinkle with pepper and nutmeg. Cook, stirring, for a few minutes longer, until the cheese melts.

VARIATION

- You can crack open 4 eggs over the spinach and let them poach slowly. Sprinkle with salt and pepper.

Mufarka

Spiced Spinach with Scrambled Eggs

SERVES 6

This Indian Baghdadi dish was eaten for breakfast in Calcutta. It has an intriguing and delicious flavor. The recipe is based on one from the book *Awafi* ("To your health"), published in Sydney, Australia, to celebrate the Silver Jubilee year of the Sephardi Synagogue.

1¼ lbs (600 g) spinach
1 large onion, chopped
3 tablespoons peanut or light vegetable oil
2 garlic cloves, finely chopped
1-inch (2½-cm) piece of fresh ginger, grated, or the juice extracted by crushing in a garlic press
¼ teaspoon turmeric
A pinch or up to ½ teaspoon cayenne or red chili pepper
Salt
4 eggs, lightly beaten

Wash the spinach and remove any thick stems. Drain, and cut into strips about ¾ inch (2 cm) wide. In a large pan, fry the onion in the oil till soft and just beginning to color. Add the garlic and, when the aroma rises, add the ginger, turmeric, and cayenne or chili pepper and stir well. Now put in the spinach, sprinkle with salt, and press down the leaves. Put the lid on and cook until the spinach crumples into a soft mass. Stir well. Add the eggs and cook, stirring, until they are softly scrambled.

Tortino di Spinaci

Spinach Cake

SERVES 6–8

This is an old Italian Jewish dish which reflects a mixed heritage—the anchovies-and-capers partnership is very Italian, the raisins and pine nuts are a Sicilian and Arab touch. The recipe is from *La Cucina nella Tradizione Ebraica*, a collection put together by the Adei Wizo Jewish women's organization, which I have used constantly as source and guide. The book is a monument to Italian Jewish culture, and deserves to be widely celebrated.

> 1½ lbs (750 g) spinach
> 4 small anchovy fillets
> 2 cloves garlic, crushed
> 2 tablespoons capers, squeezed to remove
>   excess vinegar
> 5 tablespoons sunflower oil
> 2 eggs, lightly beaten
> A little salt and pepper
> ½ cup (60 g) pine nuts
> 1–1½ tablespoons currants or raisins
> 2 tablespoons fine dry bread crumbs
>   to dust the baking dish

Wash the spinach. You do not need to remove the stems unless they are tough. Squeeze out the water between your hands. Put the leaves in a large pan and steam them with the lid on (and no extra water) over low heat until they crumple into a soft mass—it takes minutes only. Drain, and when cool enough to handle, press all the water out. Chop the anchovy, garlic, and capers finely (or turn them into a paste in the food processor) and fry in 2 tablespoons of the oil for a minute or so, then mix with the spinach in a bowl. Add the eggs, salt and pepper, raisins, and pine nuts (briefly fried in 1 tablespoon of oil until lightly colored). Mix well and pour in a nonstick mold or baking dish greased with the remaining oil and dusted with bread crumbs. Bake at 350°F (180°C) for 30–40 minutes, and turn out like a cake.

Frittata di Carciofi

Artichoke Omelette

SERVES 6

For this exquisite Italian omelette I use frozen artichoke hearts or bottoms.

> 14 oz (400 g) frozen artichoke hearts or
>   bottoms, defrosted
> Olive or light vegetable oil for frying
> 5 eggs
> Salt and pepper
> A good pinch of nutmeg
> 4 tablespoons grated Parmesan (optional)
> 2 tablespoons chopped flat-leafed parsley

Cut the artichokes in half, then in slices, and fry very quickly in a little medium-hot oil (about ⅛ inch (2 mm)) till slightly browned. Drain on paper towels. Beat the eggs lightly. Add salt, pepper, nutmeg, Parmesan (if you like), and parsley. Beat well and mix in the artichokes. Heat an oiled nonstick frying pan, pour in the egg mixture, and cook over low heat with the lid on until the bottom has set. Then put under the broiler and cook the top. Slip it out of the pan and serve hot or cold.

Fritada de Tomat

Tomato Cake

SERVES 6

1 potato, boiled and mashed
4 eggs, lightly beaten
½ cup (60 g) grated kashkaval or Parmesan
1 lb (500 g) tomatoes, peeled and chopped
4 tablespoons chopped flat-leafed parsley
Salt (very little) and pepper

Put the mashed potato in a bowl, and beat in the eggs. Add the grated cheese, the tomatoes, parsley, salt (taking into account the saltiness of the cheese), and pepper. Pour into an oiled baking dish and bake at 375°F (190°C) for about 40 minutes, or until firm.

Marcoude de Pommes de Terre

Potato Omelette

SERVES 8

Sephardi Jews in several countries have made potato omelette a specialty. It is served as a first course or a snack meal, and every country has its own version. In North Africa it is referred to as "omelette juive." My favorite is the classic marcoude of Algeria and Tunisia.

2 lbs (1 kg) potatoes
2 onions, coarsely chopped
4 tablespoons olive or sunflower oil
4 garlic cloves, minced or crushed in
  a press
6 eggs, lightly beaten
Salt and pepper
1 teaspoon turmeric
Juice of ½ lemon
A large bunch of flat-leafed parsley,
  chopped (½ cup)

Boil the potatoes till soft, then peel and mash them. Fry the onions in 3 tablespoons of oil till soft and slightly golden, then add the garlic and fry till the aroma rises. Mix the mashed potatoes with the fried onions and garlic and beat in the eggs. Add salt and pepper, turmeric, lemon juice, and parsley and mix well. Grease a baking dish with the remaining oil and pour in the omelette mixture. Bake at 425°F (220°C) for 45 minutes, or until set. Serve hot or cold, cut in pieces.

VARIATIONS

• For a very simple "frittata di patate," served by Jews in Italy as a first-course, alternative to minestrone, on Friday night, boil and mash 1 lb (500 g) potatoes and beat in 4 eggs, salt, pepper, and 3 tablespoons finely chopped mint or parsley or a mixture of these. Heat the 2 tablespoons of oil in a nonstick pan and pour in the mixture. Cook until the bottom of the omelette is set and lightly browned. Turn over and do the other side by slipping the omelette onto a plate with a spatula and slipping it back, upside down, in the pan. Or brown the top under the broiler.

• A very pleasing Judeo-Spanish version—bimuelos de patatas, or potato fritters—favored in the Balkans, is made with a sharp cheese and can be prepared as the Italian frittata above or fried in oil like fritters. Boil, peel, and mash

3 potatoes weighing about 1½ lbs (750 g). Beat in 4 eggs and about ⅓ cup (40 g) grated Parmesan. For the fritters, drop by the heaping tablespoon into a frying pan filmed with sizzling oil and fry on medium heat, turning over once, till brown all over. There is a curious custom of eating the fritters with a dusting of sugar or with a dribble of honey.

Beid bi Banadoura

Egg and Tomato

SERVES 2

This is a popular breakfast and evening snack all over the Oriental Jewish world.

> 3 garlic cloves, finely chopped
> 1 tablespoon light olive or sunflower oil
> 2 tomatoes, peeled and sliced
> Salt and pepper
> 2 eggs

Fry the garlic in the oil until golden and add the tomatoes, salt, and pepper. When the tomatoes have softened, break the eggs on top and cook until they set.

VARIATIONS

• In Persia they serve the eggs with yogurt or sour cream poured on top.

• Tunisians chop the tomatoes and turn them into a sauce before dropping in the eggs and make it peppery with ¼ teaspoon of harissa (page 242).

Shakshouka

Fried Peppers and Tomatoes with Eggs

SERVES 4

This name is used for all kinds of dishes involving fried vegetables with eggs broken on top. A variety of vegetables, from potatoes and fava beans to artichoke hearts and zucchini, are used in Tunisia, where the dish originated, but it is the version with onions, peppers, and tomatoes that has been adopted in Israel as a popular evening meal.

> 2 onions, chopped
> 3 tablespoons light vegetable oil
> 2 green or red bell peppers, seeded and cut
>   in small pieces
> 1 hot fresh chili pepper, seeded and thinly
>   sliced (optional)
> 4 tomatoes, peeled and chopped
> Salt and pepper
> 4 eggs

Fry the onions in the oil till golden. Add the peppers and fry until they are soft. Add the tomatoes and simmer 10 minutes. Then crack the eggs open on top and cook 3–4 minutes more, until they set. Serve hot with bread.

VARIATIONS

• You may stir and scramble the eggs instead of leaving them whole.

• Add ½ lb (250 g) merguez (spicy sausages; see page 390), cut in small pieces, and 3 boiled and sliced potatoes.

• For a Bulgarian version with cheese, fry

3 red peppers sliced in rings in 3 tablespoons of vegetable oil until soft, then add 4 peeled and sliced tomatoes, sprinkle with salt and pepper, and cook a few minutes. Stir in 4 lightly beaten eggs and about 4½ oz (125 g) mashed feta cheese and cook till the eggs set.

Kalavassika kon Keso

Zucchini and Cheese Gratin

SERVES 6

There are dozens of zucchini-and-cheese recipes in the Sephardi repertoire. Some use a mixture of cheeses with fried onion added in, some have béchamel sauce poured over. In this Judeo-Spanish version, the usual blandness of zucchini is lifted with the strong-tasting feta cheese and the mint, which gives its little perfume.

> *1 lb (500 g) zucchini*
> *12 oz (350 g) feta cheese*
> *2 eggs, lightly beaten*
> *Pepper*
> *A good pinch of nutmeg*
> *2 teaspoons dried mint or 3–4 sprigs of*
>   *fresh mint*

Wash and trim the zucchini. If they are small, cut them in half lengthwise; if they are large, into thick slices. Boil them in salted water for a few minutes, until only slightly tender. They must be still crisp. Drain and arrange tightly in a shallow baking dish.

Crush the feta with a fork and add the eggs, pepper, nutmeg, and mint. Mix well and pour over the zucchini. Bake in a preheated 350°F (180°C) oven for about 30 minutes, until the top is colored. Serve hot or cold with yogurt.

VARIATIONS

• Instead of the feta cheese, use an equal mixture of cream or cottage cheese and grated kashkaval or Parmesan and add 2–3 tablespoons chopped dill instead of mint.

• For another very pleasing version we made in Egypt as "cousa bi gebna," fry 1 large sliced onion in 2 tablespoons of oil till golden. Boil 1 lb (500 g) thinly sliced zucchini in salted water for minutes only, until softened but a little underdone. Drain and mix with the fried onion, 2 beaten eggs, 6 oz (175 g) grated Cheddar, pepper, and ¼ teaspoon of nutmeg. Pour into a baking dish and bake for 30 minutes.

Ful Medammes

Dried Fava Beans with Hard-Boiled Eggs

SERVES 6

Dried brown fava beans are much used by Middle Eastern Jews. They come in different shapes and sizes, from the small Egyptian ones to the large, flat Iraqi ones, which are served as a *mezze* sprinkled with olive oil, lemon juice, and dried mint, or, as in Iraq, with pennyroyal and sometimes a sprinkling of crushed garlic. In Egypt, a dish of fava beans with hamine eggs was the cheap Sabbath lunchtime meal in families that were large, modest, and hospitable. My father called it a "tfadalou," meaning "welcome." It was accompanied by salads—babaghanoush, potato with garlic, and tomato, pepper, and onion. On Friday, in the Jewish quarter of Cairo, families would bring pots of beans and eggs to the public baths and leave them in the ashes of the fire. They would retrieve them on Saturday morning and eat the beans for breakfast. It was the famous Egyptian national breakfast, with the difference that the eggs were also cooked all night and acquired a brown color, the yolk a creamy texture. When my father became a widower in his mid-nineties, he bought stacks of cans of Egyptian beans and tried to convince his new housekeeper that it was real gourmet food.

> 1 lb (500 g) Egyptian fava beans, soaked
>   overnight or 2 28-oz (800-g) cans
>   of ful medammes
> 6 or more garlic cloves, finely chopped
> Salt
> Extra-virgin olive oil
> 6 hard-boiled eggs or hamine eggs
>   (page 246), peeled
> 2 or 3 lemons, quartered
> Pepper

Drain the dried beans and simmer with the garlic in water to cover for 1½ hours, or until tender, adding salt towards the end. If using canned beans, heat through with the garlic fried in 2 tablespoons of the oil.

Serve hot in bowls or soup plates with a hard-boiled or hamine egg, quartered lengthwise, for each person. Pass around the bottle of olive oil, a plate of lemon quarters, and salt and pepper for people to dress their own beans.

Accompany if you like with mixed Israeli salad (page 248) and tehina (page 274).

Aubergines Medias
Eggplant Halves with Cheese

SERVES 4–8

A woman from Aleppo gave me this recipe more than thirty years ago. The Jews from Spain who settled in the Syrian city were referred to as *medias*, which means "half," because, unlike the local Jews, they continued to cut their stuffed vegetables in half, long after they had become totally Arabized.

> 4 small eggplants, about 4¾ inches (12 cm)
>   long, or 2 large ones (total weight about
>   1¼ lbs) (500 g)
> Salt
> Oil for frying
> 8 oz (250 g) feta cheese or a mixture
>   with cottage cheese, drained
> 1 egg, lightly beaten
> Pepper
> 2 teaspoons dried mint
> ¼ teaspoon nutmeg

Cut the small eggplants in half and the large ones crosswise in thick slices—about 1 inch (2½ cm). Sprinkle generously with salt and let them sit for 1 hour to draw out the juices. Then rinse and dry them with a tea towel or paper towels and fry very briefly in about ½ inch

(1¼ cm) hot oil, turning them over once, until lightly colored and tender when you prick them with a fork. They should be slightly undercooked. Drain on paper towels and arrange in a baking dish cut side up. (Alternatively, you can brush them with oil and grill them under the broiler, turning them over once, until browned.)

In a bowl, mash the feta cheese with a fork, then mix with the cottage cheese (if using). Add the egg, pepper, mint, and nutmeg and mix well. Cover the eggplants with the cheese mixture and bake at 350°F (180°C) for 20–30 minutes, or until the filling has set firmly. Serve hot.

It is usually accompanied by a cucumber-and-yogurt salad (page 270).

VARIATIONS

• For a wonderful Syrian version with tomato sauce: Fry 2 or 3 crushed cloves of garlic in 1 tablespoon of oil, add 1 lb (500 g) peeled and chopped tomatoes, salt and pepper, and a teaspoon of dried mint and simmer 15 minutes. Then pour over the stuffed eggplants and bake.

• For a sharper flavor, add 4 tablespoons of grated kashkaval or Parmesan to the cheese mixture.

• A custom in Turkey and the Balkans is to add 1 mashed potato to the cheese mixture for a firmer topping (in this case, add another egg). They call it "berengena kon keso al horno."

Rulos de Berengena
Eggplant Roll Stuffed with Meat

SERVES 6

Also called "revoltinos," this is referred to as a "mock" stuffed vegetable. It is a very popular food for Jewish parties in Turkey today. Caterers have it on their lists. It is served in the only restaurant in Istanbul that serves Jewish-style (they call it "half-kosher") dishes, which is run by a Muslim (see page 525)—a little hole-in-the-wall where merchants from the bazaar come for a lunchtime snack.

4 eggplants, long in shape and medium-sized, each weighing about ½ lb (250 g)
Salt
2 lbs (1 kg) tomatoes, peeled and chopped
1–2 teaspoons sugar
Pepper
3 tablespoons chopped flat-leafed parsley
1 medium onion, finely chopped
2 slices bread, soaked in water
12 oz (350 g) lean ground beef
½ teaspoon allspice
Vegetable oil for frying

Peel the eggplants and slice them lengthwise about ⅓ inch (¾ cm) thick. (If you can only find very large, round ones, cut them in half before slicing.) Sprinkle with salt and leave for 1 hour to drain.

Make a tomato sauce: put the tomatoes in a pan, add sugar, salt, and pepper, and simmer 15–20 minutes, till soft.

Prepare the meat stuffing: In the food processor, finely chop the parsley and onion and add the soaked bread squeezed dry. Then add the meat, ½ teaspoon salt, pepper, and allspice and blend to a soft paste.

Rinse the eggplant slices and dry them with paper towels. Fry briefly in very hot oil, about ⅓ inch (¾ cm) deep, until only just browned, turning over once. Drain on paper towels. (Alternatively, you may broil the eggplant slices instead of frying them. Brush generously with oil and cook under the broiler, turning over once, until lightly browned.)

Take walnut-sized lumps of meat paste, roll into balls, and wrap a slice of eggplant around each. Hold together with a toothpick pierced right through the roll.

Divide the tomato sauce between 2 pans so you can fit the rolls in a single layer. Put in the rolls carefully, and simmer for about 25 minutes.

Stuffed Brinjal

Indian Stuffed Eggplants

SERVES 4–8

They do not look very appetizing, but they are absolutely scrumptious, with an extraordinary combination of flavors. The recipe is adapted from one by Mrs. S. Joel of the Bene Israel.

STUFFED VEGETABLES— MAHSHI—DOLMA

STUFFED VEGETABLES are an important part of Sephardi culture. They are festive and celebratory dishes, considered grand and refined. They reveal the skill of the cook and the wish to honor a guest. They also represent an ideally complete food, combining as they do vegetables with various ingredients such as meat or cheese, rice, dried fruit, and nuts.

It is usual in the Arab world for a variety of vegetables to be hollowed and stuffed with a mixture of ground meat and rice with spices, and put to cook together in the same pot—firm ones at the bottom, fragile ones at the top. This is not my favorite way, because they end up tasting the same, and I have not included it. Every community has its special and favorite fillings and distinctive ways of hollowing and cooking. The Judeo-Spanish communities of the old Ottoman world are particularly strong on meatless versions, because dairy meals were very much part of the old way of life. Vegetables to be eaten cold were stuffed with rice, and vegetables to be served hot were stuffed with cheese. The old way of cooking stuffed vegetables in most countries was to fry them first—sometimes in an egg-and-flour batter—then to stew them, but it has become common practice now to bake them.

The original had fresh little chilies in the paste, but it is easier to control how hot the result is by using cayenne or chili powder.

1 large onion, chopped
3 tablespoons sunflower oil
5 cloves garlic, crushed
½ cup (50 g) dried grated coconut
1 tablespoon tamarind paste
1 tablespoon dark-brown muscovado
 (unrefined) or other brown sugar,
 or more to taste
1 teaspoon ground coriander
½ teaspoon ground cumin
Salt
½ teaspoon or more cayenne or ground chili
 pepper
1½-inch (4-cm) piece of ginger, grated, or the
 juice extracted by pressing in a garlic press
A small bunch of coriander leaves, chopped
 (¼ cup)
4 small eggplants, weighing about 1 lb
 (500 g)
1½ oz (40 g) creamed coconut (in block
 form) or 1¼ cups (300 ml) canned
 coconut milk (see page 235)

For the filling, fry the onion in the oil till golden. Add the garlic and grated coconut, and when lightly colored, add tamarind paste and brown sugar. Add a few tablespoons of water to dilute the tamarind, so as to make a soft paste. Then add the ground coriander, cumin, salt, cayenne or chili powder, ginger, and fresh coriander.

Trim the ends of the eggplants and cut 4 slices lengthwise but not right through, so that they do not separate at the stem end. With a little spoon, spread the paste in the slits and pack the stuffed eggplants in a pan.

In another pan, boil about 2½ cups (600 ml) of salted water with the creamed coconut until that has dissolved and pour over the eggplant. Alternatively, mix the canned coconut milk with the same amount of water. Put the lid on and simmer the eggplant for about an hour. Serve hot or cold.

Sheikh el Mahshi Betingan

Eggplants Stuffed with Ground Meat and Pine Nuts

SERVES 4

This famous Arab dish is called "sheikh" because the filling is all meat, and therefore grand.

4 small eggplants or 2 large ones, total
 weight about 1¼ lbs (500 g)
Salt
1 onion, chopped
Sunflower or other light vegetable oil
1 lb (500 g) ground lamb
Pepper
½ teaspoon allspice
¼ cup (50 g) pine nuts
2 garlic cloves
1 lb (500 g) tomatoes, peeled and chopped
1 teaspoon sugar

Peel the eggplants. Cut the small ones in half lengthwise, the large ones crosswise in slices of ¾ inch (about 2 cm). Sprinkle generously with salt and let them degorge their juices for 1 hour.

Prepare the filling. Fry the onion in 2 tablespoons of oil till golden. Add the ground meat, salt, pepper, and allspice and cook, turning and crushing the meat with a fork, for a few minutes, until it changes color. Add the pine nuts, toasted slightly if you like.

Make the tomato sauce. Fry the garlic in I tablespoon of oil until it begins to color. Add the tomatoes, salt, pepper, and sugar and simmer for 15 minutes.

Now rinse and dry the eggplants with paper towels and fry very briefly in about ½ inch (1¼ cm) very hot oil, turning them over once, until lightly browned. They should be undercooked, as they will cook further in a sauce. Drain on paper towels and arrange in an oven dish cut side up. Spread a little filling on each and pour the tomato sauce between them. Bake at 350°F (180°C) for 30 minutes. Serve hot.

Mahasha

Stuffed Peppers Indian Style

SERVES 6

The word "mahasha" is the deformation by the Baghdadi Jews of India of the Arab word "mahshi," which means "stuffed." The dish is a curious Arab-Indian hybrid. The vegetables are stuffed as in the Arab world, but the filling—an aromatic mixture of rice and chicken—is entirely different. In Calcutta and Bombay, all kinds of vegetables, including eggplants, onions, small cucumbers, lettuce, and vine leaves,

were stuffed with the same filling and served at buffet parties.

I have used peppers, which make a colorful first course with an unexpected flavor. Choose medium-sized peppers for a first course; big ones can be a main meal.

1¼ cups (250 g) Patna or American
     long-grain rice
Salt
½ lb (250 g) chicken fillets (breast or thigh meat)
1-inch (2½-cm) piece of ginger, grated, or
     the juice extracted by crushing it in a
     garlic press
2 garlic cloves, minced, or crushed in a press
3 tablespoons peanut or vegetable oil
Juice of 1 lemon
1–2 teaspoons sugar
½ teaspoon turmeric
2–3 tablespoons finely chopped fresh mint
Pepper
6 medium bell peppers, weighing about
     2¾ lbs (1⅓ kg)

Cook the rice in plenty of boiling salted water for about 15 minutes, until only just tender, then drain. Chop the chicken, using the food processor if you like. Put the rice and chicken in a bowl and mix with the rest of the ingredients except the peppers.

To stuff the peppers, with a sharp-pointed knife cut a circle around the stem ends and reserve as caps. Remove the cores and seeds with a spoon, and fill with the rice mixture. Trim the underside of the caps and replace them. Arrange side by side in a shallow baking dish, pour about a finger of water at the bottom, and bake at 375°F (190°C) for 45–55 minutes, or until the peppers are tender.

Serve hot or cold.

• To make stuffed tomatoes, use large "beefsteak" tomatoes. Cut a little circle around the stem end and slice a lid. Scoop out the seeds with a pointed spoon, being careful not to break the outer flesh and skin. Stuff with the above filling and bake till soft—for a large beefsteak tomato, this can take from 45 minutes to almost 1 hour.

Pipiruchkas Reyenadas de Arroz

Peppers Stuffed with Rice

SERVES 6

Like most cold vegetables with no meat, this is commonly served at buffets. It makes a good starter or light meal. Choose peppers that can stand on their base. Round short-grain or Italian risotto rice is best used, because it is sticky and binds together.

> 1 large onion, finely chopped
> 6 tablespoons extra-virgin olive oil
> 1¼ cups (250 g) short-grain or Italian risotto rice
> Salt and pepper
> 1–2 teaspoons sugar
> 3 tablespoons pine nuts
> 3 tablespoons raisins
> 1 large tomato, peeled and chopped
> 2 teaspoons dried mint
> 3 tablespoons chopped dill or flat-leafed parsley
> Juice of 1 lemon
> 6 medium green or red bell peppers

For the stuffing, fry the onion in 3 tablespoons of the oil until soft. Add the rice and stir until thoroughly coated and translucent. Pour in 2 cups (450 ml) of water and add ⅔ teaspoon salt, pepper, and sugar. Stir well and cook, covered, for 15 minutes, or until the water has been absorbed but the rice is still a little underdone. Mix in the pine nuts, raisins, tomato, mint, dill or parsley, lemon juice, and the rest of the oil.

To stuff the peppers, cut a circle around the stem end of each and reserve as a cap (with the stem). Remove the cores and seeds with a spoon and fill all the peppers with the rice stuffing. Replace the caps. Arrange side by side in a shallow baking dish, pour about a finger of water at the bottom, and bake at 375°F (190°C) for 45–55 minutes, or until the peppers are tender. Watch them after 45 minutes and turn off if it looks as if they may be falling apart. Serve cold.

VARIATION

• Add ¼ teaspoon allspice, ¼ teaspoon cinnamon, and ¼ teaspoon ground cloves to the rice. And instead of the chopped tomato use 1 tablespoon tomato paste.

Pipiruchkas Reyenadas de Keso

Peppers Stuffed with Cheese

SERVES 6

This most wonderful dish from the Judeo-Spanish communities of the Balkans is my favorite stuffed vegetable. It makes a brilliant first course or main dish. (Mozzarella can be used instead of halumi cheese, but it will need salting.)

> 6 red or yellow bell peppers
> 2 garlic cloves
> 2 tablespoons sunflower oil
> 1 lb (500 g) tomatoes, peeled and chopped
> Salt and pepper
> 1–2 teaspoons sugar
> 6 slices halumi or mozzarella cheese weighing about ¾ lb (350 g)

Roast the peppers, peel them, and remove the stems and seeds (see page 253), trying not to tear them (if you do, it doesn't much matter).

Make a tomato sauce: Fry the garlic in the oil till it begins to color. Add the tomatoes, a little salt, pepper, and sugar and simmer for about 15 minutes.

Slip 1 large slice of cheese inside each pepper and arrange side by side in a baking dish. Pour the tomato sauce over them and bake at 350°F (180°C) for about 20 minutes, until the cheese is soft. Serve very hot.

Tomatoes Stuffed with Rice

SERVES 8

This comes from Syria. Tamarind, which gives the rice a brown color and sweet-and-sour flavor, is a Jewish touch. The large beefsteak tomatoes make it a main dish. For a buffet, use small tomatoes.

> 1 medium onion, chopped
> 3 tablespoons olive oil
> 1¼ cups (250 g) round short-grain or Italian risotto rice
> 2 cups (450 ml) water
> Salt and pepper
> 1 tablespoon tamarind paste
> 1–2 teaspoons sugar
> 2 teaspoons mint
> 3 tablespoons raisins (optional)
> 3 tablespoons pine nuts
> 8 firm large (beefsteak) tomatoes

For the stuffing, fry the onion in the oil till golden. Add the rice and stir until well coated and translucent. Add the water, ½–⅔ teaspoon salt, pepper, tamarind, and sugar and stir well to dissolve the tamarind. Simmer, covered, for 15 minutes, until the water is absorbed, then mix in the mint, raisins, and pine nuts.

Cut a circle around the stem end and slice a cap from each tomato. Remove the center and seeds with a pointed spoon. Fill with the stuffing and replace the caps. Arrange in a shallow baking dish and bake at 350°F (180°C) for 40 minutes, or until the tomatoes are soft, keeping watch so that they do not fall apart too quickly.

VARIATIONS

• Smaller tomatoes—you can use 16— need only 20–30 minutes' baking.
• Omit the tamarind and add the juice of 1 lemon, ¼ teaspoon of allspice, 1 teaspoon of cinnamon, and ¼ teaspoon of ground cloves just before stuffing. In addition to mint, you may use chopped flat-leafed parsley and dill.

Tomates Yenas de Keso

Tomatoes Stuffed with Cheese

This Balkan dish makes a good first course.

> *8 medium tomatoes, weighing about 2 lbs (1 kg)*
> *Salt*
> *½–1 teaspoon sugar*
> *4 oz (100 g) feta cheese*
> *4 oz (100 g) cottage cheese*
> *2 eggs, lightly beaten*
> *¼ teaspoon nutmeg*
> *1 teaspoon dried mint*
> *Pepper*

With a sharp-pointed knife, cut a little circle around the stem end of each tomato, slice a lid, and reserve. With a pointed spoon, scoop out the seeds, being careful not to break the outer flesh and skin. Place the tomatoes in an oiled baking dish cut side up and sprinkle lightly with a little salt and sugar.

Mash the feta cheese with a fork. Add the cottage cheese, eggs, nutmeg, mint, and pepper and mix well. Fill the tomatoes with this. Put the lids on and bake at 400°F (200°C) for about 30 minutes, or until the tomato is soft (be careful that it does not overcook and fall apart). Serve hot.

VARIATIONS

• You can cut large tomatoes in half, fill them, and bake, then brown the tops under the broiler. For a sharper filling, add 4 tablespoons grated kashkaval or Parmesan and reduce the amount of cottage cheese.

Sheikh el Mahshi Tamatem

Tomatoes Stuffed with Meat, Nuts, and Raisins

This Syrian and Egyptian stuffed tomato is considered the grandest, because the filling is meat. It can be served as a starter or a main course.

> *4 extra-large tomatoes*
> *1 onion, chopped*
> *3 tablespoons sunflower oil*
> *8 oz (250 g) lean ground beef*
> *Salt and pepper*
> *1 tablespoon raisins*
> *2 tablespoons pine nuts or coarsely chopped walnuts*
> *½ teaspoon cinnamon*
> *½ teaspoon allspice*
> *3 tablespoons finely chopped flat-leafed parsley*

Cut a circle around the stem end of each tomato and cut out a cap. Remove the center and seeds with a pointed spoon.

For the filling, fry the onion in the oil till golden. Add the meat, a little salt, and pepper. Turn the meat over and squash it with a fork until it changes color. Stir in the raisins and pine nuts or walnuts and add cinnamon, allspice, and parsley.

Stuff the tomatoes with the filling and cover with the caps. Put them close to each other in a baking dish with a finger of water at the bottom. Bake at 350°F (180°C) for about 30–40 minutes, or until the tomatoes are soft, being careful that they don't fall apart. Serve hot.

VARIATIONS

• A Balkan way is to stuff the tomatoes with raw ground meat worked to a soft paste with 2 slices soaked bread squeezed dry and I egg, seasoned with salt and pepper, allspice, cinnamon, and flat-leafed parsley.

• For tomatoes stuffed with a meat-and-rice filling, use the stuffing called "hashwa" on page 356.

• For 8 frenkes—stuffed green tomatoes, a Jewish specialty of Istanbul—stuff 8 medium-sized green tomatoes with a mixture of 10 oz (300 g) minced lamb or beef, I slice of white bread, soaked in water and squeezed dry, salt, pepper, and 3 tablespoons chopped parsley.

Mahshi Cousa

Stuffed Zucchini

SERVES 6

Stuffed zucchini was the great dish in Egypt—I saw hundreds of them being hollowed and filled, and I did many myself. Scooping out the insides with a long thin corer was quite an art. When women had only the kitchen to busy themselves with, it was a pleasure to sit down with company in front of a mountain of zucchini. There are dozens of ways of making them—different in every community. A Syrian and Lebanese way, which was also ours in Egypt, is to stuff them with a mixture of rice and meat and cook them in tomato sauce.

12 medium zucchini

For the filling

½ lb (250 g) lean ground lamb or beef
¾ cup (150 g) short- or long-grain rice
Salt and pepper
½ teaspoon cinnamon
¼ teaspoon allspice

For the sauce

4 garlic cloves, crushed
1 tablespoon corn or sunflower oil
2 lbs (1 kg) tomatoes, peeled and chopped, or a 28-oz (800-g) can of peeled or chopped tomatoes
Salt and pepper
1–2 teaspoons sugar or to taste

Slice off the stem ends. Using an apple corer or the special long thin gadget for hollowing zucchini (you'll find them in Arab markets), scoop out the center pulp, being careful not to break the skin or to pierce the other end. You can develop a knack for making a small, quick twisting motion when you get near the end, which detaches the pulp and allows you to pull it out. The pulp is not needed for this dish. You can boil or steam it and serve it as a salad, dressed with oil and lemon. (If the zucchini are too long for your corer to reach the end, you can cut them in half.)

Mix all the filling ingredients together in a bowl and knead well with your hand. Push into the zucchini with your fingers and fill not more than three-quarters full, to allow for the expansion of the rice; otherwise the zucchini will tear.

Make the sauce in a large pan. Fry the garlic in the oil till it begins to color. Add the tomatoes, salt, pepper, and sugar and simmer 10 minutes. It should have a good sweet-and-sour flavor. Now put in the stuffed zucchini. If the tomato sauce does not cover the zucchini, add water so that it does. Simmer, covered, for about 1 hour, until the zucchini are very tender. Uncover the pan towards the end, to let the sauce reduce.

VARIATIONS

• Substitute the ground-meat-and-pine-nut stuffing called "sheikh el mahshi" (page 541). In that case, you can fill the zucchini completely, for there is no rice to expand.

• Add 2 teaspoons of tamarind and 1 teaspoon of sugar to the filling ingredients.

Rouleaux de Poireaux Farcis

Stuffed Leek Rolls

MAKES ABOUT 22, SERVING 6

When I was in Istanbul once, a member of the old Ottoman aristocracy who had been married to an Egyptian prince was lamenting the old Ottoman recipes that nobody made any more. I asked her for examples and she mentioned stuffed leeks. Well, the Jews anyway have kept them up. This was one of our recipes. It is a very elegant but time-consuming delicacy to serve on special occasions.

> 4 very fat leeks
> Salt
> 1 lb (500 g) ground beef
> Pepper
> 1 teaspoon cinnamon
> ¼ teaspoon allspice
> 1½ tablespoons tamarind paste
> 1½ tablespoons sugar

Cut the tough green ends off the leeks so that you have white rolls about 6 inches (15 cm) long. With a sharp knife, make a slit very carefully along one side of each leek, only through to the center (do not cut right through). Boil the leeks in salted water till softened. Drain and cut a slice off the root end of each leek, freeing the layers from each other. You will have wide rectangular strips.

Season the ground meat with salt, pepper, cinnamon, and allspice and work to a soft paste with your hands. Put about 1 heaping tablespoon of filling in a line along the larger side of each rectangle of leek, leaving about 1 inch (2½ cm) at each end, and roll up like a long thin cigar. Continue with all the leaves. When they get too narrow, put 2 together to make a roll. Pack all the leek rolls side by side, seam side down—close to each other, so that they don't open—in a large, shallow, heavy-bottomed pan. Dissolve the tamarind and sugar in 2½ cups (600 ml) of boiling water and pour over the leeks. Cook, covered, over very low heat for about ¾ hour. Remove the lid towards the end to reduce the sauce. Serve hot or cold.

VARIATION

- Turkish Jews dip their rolls in egg and flour and fry, then cook them in stock with a little tomato paste. They call them "chufleticos."

Oignons Farcis

Onion Rolls Stuffed with Meat in Tamarind Sauce

SERVES 6–8

This was a favorite buffet party dish in the Syrian community in Egypt. I have demonstrated it at various fund-raising charity events, because the preparation is fascinating and the taste is wonderful.

3 large mild onions
1½ lbs (750 g) finely ground beef
Salt and pepper
1½ teaspoons cinnamon
½ teaspoon allspice
4 tablespoons finely chopped flat-leafed parsley
1–2 tablespoons tamarind paste
2 tablespoons sugar
3 tablespoons light vegetable oil

Peel the onions and cut off the ends. With a sharp knife, make a slit on one side of each, from top to bottom, through to the center—and no farther. Throw into a big pan of boiling water and boil for 10–15 minutes, until they soften and begin to open so that each layer can be detached. Drain, and when cool enough to handle, separate each layer carefully.

For the filling, work the ground meat with about ¾ teaspoon salt, pepper, cinnamon, allspice, and parsley. Put a lump the size of a small walnut into each curved onion layer and roll up tightly. Line the bottom of a wide, shallow pan with discarded bits of onion (this is to protect the rolls). Pack the stuffed onion rolls tightly on top.

Dissolve the tamarind paste and 1 tablespoon of sugar in about ⅔ cup (150 ml) of boiling water, add the oil, and pour over the onions; add more water to cover if necessary. Place a plate on top to hold the onions down and prevent them from unrolling, and simmer, covered, on very low heat, adding more water as required, for about 45–60 minutes, until they are very well done and the water is absorbed.

Now arrange them in 1 layer on a flat, heatproof serving dish, sprinkle the top with the remaining sugar, and caramelize under the broiler. This gives them a nice warm wrinkly look. They are best served hot but are also very good cold.

Kharshouf Mahshi

Artichoke Bottoms Stuffed with Meat

SERVES 6–8

This is famous as one of the grand old Jerusalem dishes. It was also a favorite of the Jews of Egypt—a specialty of Passover, when vendors came to the kitchen door to sell them by the crateful. Awad, our cook, spent hours cutting away the leaves. It is not one of the kitchen jobs any of us is prepared to do now except on rare occasions. But frozen artichoke bottoms—a flat, cup variety, produce of Egypt (which you can find in Oriental stores)—are perfect for this. (Canned artichokes will not do at all, either in shape, size, or flavor.) Veal was the meat we used as filling, but you can use beef or lamb. In the old days, the stuffed bottoms were dipped in beaten egg and bread crumbs and deep-fried. Now we simply bake them. They are served as a first course, and, like many stuffed vegetables, the feature in buffet meals. The dish is also one of the highlights of the Jerusalem kitchen.

14 oz (400 g) frozen artichoke bottoms
    (about 10)
1 onion, chopped
2 tablespoons sunflower oil
2 tablespoons pine nuts
10 oz (300 g) ground veal, lamb, or beef
2 tablespoons finely chopped flat-leafed parsley
About ½ teaspoon salt
Pepper
A pinch of nutmeg
½ teaspoon allspice or cinnamon
1 small egg, lightly beaten
Juice of ½ lemon

Defrost the artichokes. Fry the onion in the oil till golden. Add the pine nuts and stir till lightly colored. Mix the meat, parsley, salt, pepper, nutmeg, allspice or cinnamon, and egg, and work to a soft paste with your hands. Then work in the onions and pine nuts. Take lumps of the meat mixture and fill the artichoke bottoms, making little mounds. Place them in a shallow baking dish.

Mix the lemon juice with about ⅔ cup (150 ml) of water and pour into the dish. Cover with foil and bake at 350°F (180°C) for ½ hour, or until the meat is done. Serve hot or cold.

Carciofi Ripieni

Stuffed Artichoke Bottoms

SERVES 4

Artichokes have been associated with Jews in Italy since Jews introduced them to Rome, Venice, and other cities when they fled from Sicily in the sixteenth century. I use the frozen artichoke bottoms, which are a produce of Egypt. You can find them in Oriental stores. They are very expensive, but they taste natural compared with any of the canned varieties. They come in packages of 14 oz (400 g), and you get about 9 flat cups or "bottoms." The combination of anchovy, garlic, and lemon is intriguing. The dish makes a good appetizer.

2 oz (50 g) or about 5 small anchovy fillets,
    finely chopped (optional)
2 garlic cloves, crushed
A good bunch of flat-leafed parsley, finely
    chopped (about ½ cup)
2 oz (60 g) bread crumbs
6 tablespoons olive oil
2–3 tablespoons lemon juice
14 oz (400 g) artichoke bottoms

Mix all the ingredients except the artichokes into a paste. Fill the artichoke bottoms with this stuffing. Put in a baking dish side by side. Pour enough water—about I cup (250 ml)—to half-cover the artichokes (it should not reach the filling) and bake at 350°F (180°C) for about 25 minutes, or until they are tender. Serve cold.

Urug Patata–Potato Chaps

Stuffed Potato Cutlets

SERVES 4

This Iraqi specialty—mashed-potato fritters filled with a spicy meat filling—is not difficult to make, but it is time-consuming. It is the kind of food that was prepared when women spent the whole day in the kitchen, or when they had servants to make it for them. It is exquisite—a good main dish to serve with salad. Mrs. Daisy Saatchi cooked it for me, and the recipe is hers.

> 2 lbs (1 kg) mealy baking potatoes
> Salt
> 1 egg, lightly beaten
> Pepper
> 1 large onion, chopped
> 3 tablespoons sunflower oil
> ¾ lb (350 g) lean ground beef
> Seeds of 1 or 2 cardamom pods or 1 teaspoon
>   ground cardamom
> 1 teaspoon cinnamon
> ½ teaspoon allspice
> A good pinch of nutmeg
> ½ teaspoon cumin

> ½ teaspoon coriander
> 3 tablespoons finely chopped flat-leafed parsley
> A small bowl of fine bread crumbs or matzo
>   meal
> Light vegetable oil for frying

For the potato casing: Wash the potatoes well in their skins and boil them in salted water until tender when you pierce them with a knife; do not overcook or they will be too watery. Drain, peel, and mash well while still hot with a potato masher. The mashed potatoes must be dry. If they are not, dry them by stirring them over a low flame to evaporate the moisture. (Another way to cook, so that the potatoes are not at all wet, is to bake them in their skins till they are very soft.) Let the mashed potatoes cool a little, then add the egg, salt, and pepper and work very well with your hands to a soft dough.

For the filling: Fry the onion in the oil till golden. Add the meat and fry, breaking it up with a fork and stirring, until it changes color. Add salt, pepper, spices, and a little water, barely to cover. Simmer until the water is entirely absorbed and evaporated, then stir in the parsley.

Oil your hands, take lumps of mashed potatoes the size of a small tangerine, and flatten each into a round in the palm of your hand. Put a tablespoon of filling in the middle and bring up the mashed potato from the sides over the filling to form a closed ball. Turn all the balls in bread crumbs or matzo meal so that they are covered all over, and flatten them into cakes. Fry a few at a time in sizzling medium-hot oil, about ½ inch (1¼ cm) deep, carefully turning them to brown them all over. Drain on paper towels before serving very hot.

VARIATIONS

• A little curry powder may go into the filling.

• A particularly flavorsome filling is the one made by the Baghdadi community of India, using veal or chicken instead of beef. They season with ½ teaspoon of ground ginger, I teaspoon garam masala, ¼ teaspoon turmeric, and I large chopped tomato.

• Some people dip the cakes in flour, then egg, then bread crumbs, to make a thicker crust.

• A Moroccan version has the fritters dipped in finely chopped almonds instead of bread crumbs. The meat filling is sometimes replaced by chopped hard-boiled eggs.

• For an easy meat-and-potato pie, just have a layer of meat filling covered by a layer of mashed potato in an oven dish and bake at 425°F (220°C) for about 20–30 minutes, or until the top is browned.

Oshi Tos Kadu

Stuffed Pumpkin

SERVES MORE THAN 20

This is a festive Bukharan specialty. It is quite spectacular. When I went out to buy a pumpkin, the smallest I could find was a 14-pound (6-kg) one. Since I had 15 people coming for dinner, I decided to take it. What with all the many courses, we ate only half. I will still give you the measures for a large one, for it takes no more time to make than a small one, and it is cheap and looks so beautiful. But of course you can cook a smaller one and reduce the amount of stuffing accordingly. The stuffing is usually meat and rice, but I particularly like this meatless one.

*1 orange pumpkin weighing about 14 lbs
  (6 kg)*
Salt
1 tablespoon sugar
2 onions, coarsely chopped
½ cup (125 ml) light vegetable oil
4 cups (800 g) long-grain rice
*¼ teaspoon saffron powder or ½ teaspoon
  threads*
3 tart apples
Juice of ½ lemon
⅓ cup (60 g) raisins or sultanas
*A large bunch of coriander, chopped
  (¾ cup)*

With a strong, sharp knife, cut out a round lid about 8 inches (20 cm) in diameter around the stem end and lift it out. Scrape inside and scoop out and discard the seeds and loose fibers. Remove some of the flesh from the lid and also from the sides by hacking it with the knife (reserve it to make little pies—bishak, page 295—or a sweet). Sprinkle inside with a little salt and the sugar, and stand it on a double piece of foil in a baking pan large enough to hold it.

Make the filling: Fry the onions in 2 tablespoons of the oil till golden. Bring a large pot of salted water to the boil and throw the rice in. Let it come to the boil again, and simmer for about 12 minutes, until the rice is still a little underdone; then drain and pour into a mixing bowl. Mix the saffron powder with 1–2 tablespoons of boiling water—or crush saffron threads in a little coffee cup before soaking in the boiling water, then mix well with the rice.

Peel and core the apples, and coarsely chop them in a food processor, adding the lemon juice to prevent them from browning. Add them to the rice with the fried onions and the raisins, the remaining oil, and the coriander. Stir well and season with salt and pepper.

Fill the pumpkin with the rice mixture and put the lid on. Pour about ¾ inch (2 cm) of water in the baking pan and bake at 375°F (190°C) for about 2½ hours, or until the pumpkin is soft and the rice very tender. Serve hot, cut in slices.

VARIATION

• For a meat filling for a 3-lb (1½-kg) pumpkin, to serve 6–8: Fry 1 chopped onion in 2 tablespoons of vegetable oil until golden. Add ½ lb (250 g) ground beef and fry, stirring and crushing it with a fork, until it changes color. Season with salt and pepper and mix with 1 cup (200 g) of rice that has been boiled in plenty of salted water until still a little underdone, then drained. Add a large bunch of coriander, chopped (1 cup), 4 tablespoons of raisins, and 3 chopped tomatoes, and mix well. Stuff the pumpkin and bake for almost 2 hours.

FRESH TOMATO SAUCE

Serves 6

TOMATOES were gradually introduced in every Mediterranean country following the discovery of the New World. They had an extraordinary impact on the cooking of the area, and this sauce became one of its recurring themes (you will find it incorporated in recipes throughout this book). It originated in Catalunya and was adopted early on by the Jewish communities with their New Christian contacts in Spain and South America. I prefer it with garlic.

1 medium onion, chopped, or 2 garlic cloves,
    finely chopped or crushed
2 tablespoons olive oil
6 ripe plum tomatoes, peeled and chopped
Salt and pepper to taste
1–2 teaspoons sugar

Sweat the onion or garlic in the oil until the aroma rises. Add the tomatoes, salt, pepper, and sugar and simmer for about 10 minutes to reduce a little.

Breads

THE SEPHARDIM do not have a common Sabbath bread like the Ashkenazi hallah; nor do they have everyday breads in common. The most widespread bread among them is the Arab flat-bread with a pocket, known here as "pita." Jewish festive breads are often sweet and aromatic, with orange or lemon zest or with aniseed. It was common in some countries, as in Iraq, for professional bakers to come around the houses and make the breads. In North Africa, families sent their breads to the public bakery, and a young employee of the bakery would bring them back.

I have not attempted to cover the many different breads, which are made with semolina, corn, millet, and rice flour, and am featuring only a few of the most common and most accessible. Yemenites are famous for their Sabbath and festive breads, and these have become popular foods in Israel, where they can be bought frozen in supermarkets. There is jihnun, a yeast-less flour-and-water dough rolled out to paper-thinness, brushed with oil or fat, and folded several times, rolled out again, brushed with oil or fat, then rolled up into little bundles and placed in a pot full of melted fat to cook overnight in a very low oven. The effect is that of a greasy puff pastry. "Tawa" or "mellawah" is the same dough but not rolled up. It is a round, many-layered disc, cooked in a frying pan and served spread with honey. "Kubaneh" are flat cakes of risen yeast dough, left to cook overnight, like jihnun, in melted fat in a covered pot. "Lahun" is a spongy flour-and-water pancake. The batter, made with wheat flour or cornstarch, is left to ferment for days and then poured onto hot oil in a large frying pan.

A similar spongy type of pancake with an unusual sour flavor is the famous Ethiopian bread "injeera," which is made with teff flour (teff is a type of millet). The process is long and complex, with many steps, and the batter is left to ferment for 2–3 days. It is used as a plate to serve the food on, and also to pick up food with the hand. Large ones can cover a small table.

In India, Bene Israel housewives make fresh bread for every meal. On weekdays it is bhakri, made from millet, and chapatis—thin pancakes made with either wheat or rice flour. For the Sabbath, chapatis are sweet and made with coconut milk. "Hamotsi" is a sweet chapati cooked on a dry griddle rather than in oil. Two of them are baked, and they are broken when reciting the Sabbath blessings. "Sandhans," which are served to accompany the meal before Kippour, are steamed rice cakes made with coarse-ground rice, coconut milk, and sugar, and may be colored with saffron. "Satpadar" are large sweet pancakes also made with rice flour and coconut.

Matzah

Unleavened Passover Bread

Most communities had a Jewish bakery that produced "matzah" (this is the Hebrew and Sephardi pronunciation of "matzo") locally. The flour used was a special flour blessed by a rabbi, for which the growing of the wheat, harvesting, milling with special millstones, and storage were supervised to make sure that nothing could contaminate it and that no dampness could cause any fermentation. Our unleavened bread was produced in a village called Mit Ghamr. Villagers who came to do the baking were asked to have a bath, were given special clothes, and stayed inside the

bakery compound for the entire baking period. They produced large round thin crisp sheets, which were the most common type of matzah.

There were other types of unleavened bread. Food historians and anthropologists Valery and Gerald Mars brought back two types, one latticed and one with little holes, from a Jewish bakery in Venice.

Housewives also made unleavened bread at home, with the special hard wheat bread flour and warm pure fresh water such as spring water—two cups of flour to one cup of water. According to Jewish Law, no more than eighteen minutes should elapse from the time the ingredients are mixed to the moment they are baked, so that there is no risk of fermentation. The dough must be kneaded for at least five minutes, so that it is no longer sticky and can be rolled out. A common way is to take lumps the size of a walnut and roll them out as thin as possible, then prick them all over with a fork. The sheets of dough are transferred, to heated baking sheets and baked at 475°F (245°C) for about six to eight minutes, or until vaguely golden. As it cools the bread becomes crisp and hard.

Pita–Khubz–Lavash

MAKES 7

Not many people bother to make these flat pocket breads now, since they are so readily available in all the supermarkets in Western countries. They are best eaten straight out of the oven, and because they harden very quickly, you must right away freeze those that you are not going to eat.

2 teaspoons dry yeast
A pinch of sugar
About 1 cup (250 ml) warm water
3⅓ cups (500 g) white bread flour or
  a mixture with whole-wheat flour
1 teaspoon salt
1 tablespoon olive or sunflower oil plus
  a little more to grease the dough

Dissolve the yeast with the sugar in about half the quantity of water and leave for about 10 minutes, until it froths. In a large bowl, mix the flour with the salt and oil, and add the yeast mixture and enough of the remaining water so that the dough holds together in a ball. Begin by mixing with a fork, then work it in with your hand. Knead for about 10 minutes, until smooth and elastic. Pour ½ tablespoon of oil in the bowl and roll the dough around in it to grease it all over. Cover the bowl with plastic wrap and leave in a warm place for about 1½ hours, until doubled in bulk.

Punch down and divide into 7 equal pieces. Roll out each piece on a lightly floured surface with a lightly floured rolling pin to about 7 inches (18 cm) in diameter and a thickness of ¼ inch (¾ cm). Let stand on floured trays, covered with a lightly floured cloth, for about 30 minutes, or until they have risen. Then transfer onto lightly floured hot baking sheets and bake in a preheated 425°F (220°C) oven for 8–10 minutes, or until the breads have puffed up fully and are a very pale gold. Wrap them in cloth or in plastic wrap as they come out, to keep them soft and pliable. Freeze those that you are not going to use right away.

Pain Juif à l'Anis

Algerian Anise Bread

MAKES 6

This aromatic North African bread is a festive bread eaten to break the fast of Yom Kippur.

2 teaspoons dry yeast
1½ tablespoons sugar
About ¾ cup (175 ml) or more warm water
3⅓ cups (500 g) flour
1½ teaspoons salt
1 egg
2 tablespoons peanut or sunflower oil plus
  a little more to grease the dough
2 tablespoons aniseed
1 egg yolk, to glaze the breads

Dissolve the yeast and ½ teaspoon of the sugar in ½ cup of the warm water. Add about a cup of the flour and stir vigorously till smooth. Leave this sponge (batter) for 30 minutes, until doubled in bulk.

Put the remaining flour in a large bowl, add the rest of the ingredients except the egg yolk, and mix well. Add the risen sponge. Work it in with your hands and add enough warm water to make a soft dough that holds together in a ball. Knead for 10 minutes, until very soft and elastic. Pour ½ tablespoon of oil in the bowl and roll the dough around to grease it all over. Cover the bowl with plastic wrap and leave in a warm place for 1½ hours, or until doubled in bulk.

Punch down the dough, divide into 6 balls, and place at a distance from each other on a baking sheet, on parchment paper. Leave covered with a cloth for 30 minutes, to allow the dough to rise again. Brush the tops with the egg yolk mixed with 1 teaspoon of water and bake in a preheated 400°F (200°C) oven for 30–40 minutes, until browned on top. Tap at the bottom of a roll. If it sounds hollow, it is done. Cool on a rack.

VARIATIONS

- Two plaited breads, each with 2 strands, can be made instead of the rolls.
- Milk may be used instead of water.

Mounettes aux Raisins et aux Noix

North African Sweet Breads with Nuts and Raisins

MAKES 12

Many festive Sephardi breads are similar to these sweet cakey buns with nuts and raisins. The dough takes a long time to rise because of the sugar content, and it is good to leave it overnight.

1 tablespoon dry yeast
½ cup (100 g) sugar
About ⅔ cup (150 ml) warm water
3⅓ cups (500 g) flour
1 egg
¼ cup (50 ml) peanut or light vegetable oil, plus a little more to grease the dough
Grated zest of 1 orange
½ cup (50 g) walnuts or ¼ cup (50 g) almonds, coarsely chopped

⅓ cup (50 g) raisins
1 egg yolk, to glaze

Dissolve the yeast with ½ teaspoon of the sugar in the warm water and leave for 10–15 minutes, until it froths.

Put the flour in a bowl with the rest of the sugar, the egg, oil, and orange zest and mix very well. Add the dissolved yeast, stirring it in with a fork to begin with, then working it in with your hand. Add a little flour if necessary or a drop more water, to make a soft dough that holds together. Knead vigorously for about 10 minutes. Put about ½ tablespoon of oil in the bowl and roll the dough around to grease it all over. Cover with plastic wrap and leave in a warm place for 3 hours or overnight, or until doubled in bulk.

Punch down the risen dough and incorporate the nuts and raisins, working them in with your hand. Now divide the dough into tangerine-sized balls. Place them a little apart from each other on parchment or wax paper on baking sheets. Brush the tops with the egg yolk mixed with 1 teaspoon of water. Let rise again for 20 minutes, then bake in a preheated 400°F (200°C) oven for 20 minutes, or until they are a nice brown and sound hollow when you tap them.

VARIATION

- A Yom Kippur version has ½ teaspoon saffron, crushed and soaked in a tablespoon of water, added to the flour.

Note:

- It is interesting to know that a variety of breads, large and small, usually with egg, called "mona di pascua," are made by pastry shops during Easter in Spain.

Mouna au Lait

Sweet Bread with Milk

MAKES 1 LOAF

This is another North African sweet bread.

2 teaspoons dry yeast
A little more than ½ cup (150 g) sugar
½ cup (125 ml) warm milk
4⅔ cup (600 g) flour
2 eggs
Grated zest of 1 orange
3 tablespoons peanut or sunflower oil plus
  a little more to grease the dough
2 tablespoons melted butter
1 egg yolk, to glaze

In a little bowl, dissolve the yeast and ½ teaspoon of the sugar in the milk. Add about ¾ cup (100 g) of the flour and beat vigorously. Let this sponge froth and rise to double its bulk.

Beat the eggs with the remaining sugar and the orange zest in a large bowl. Add the oil and melted butter and beat well. Add the remaining flour and mix thoroughly with a fork. Then add the sponge and work it in with your hand. Add a little more flour or milk if necessary to make a dough that holds together in a ball. Knead for about 10 minutes, until very smooth and elastic. Drop ½ tablespoon of oil in the bowl and turn the dough around to grease it all over. Cover with plastic wrap and leave to rise in a warm place for 3½ hours or overnight, until doubled in bulk.

Punch the dough down, shape into a round, and place on a large floured tray. Cover with a lightly floured tea towel and leave to rise again for 1½ hours. Make little cuts around the top with a pointed knife, brush with egg yolk mixed with 1 teaspoon of water, and sprinkle with sugar. Bake at 375°F (190°C) for about 45 minutes, or until the bread is golden brown and sounds hollow when you tap the bottom.

VARIATION

• To make little "mounettes au lait," divide the dough into 8 little balls and bake for 30–35 minutes.

To Make Mofleta

Use the same dough as for pita (see page 550) but with 2 tablespoons of sunflower oil instead of 1. The quantities will make about 20 pancakes. Put a large, lightly oiled frying pan over medium-low heat. Take lumps of the dough the size of an egg, and roll out on a lightly oiled surface as thin as you possibly can, then pull and stretch the dough to make it even thinner. Lift a thin round sheet of dough carefully and lower it gently into the frying pan. Cook for about 2 minutes on one side, then turn over and cook the other side for another minute or so, until both sides are lightly colored. Then continue with the rest of the dough.

By tradition, as a pancake is done, a new one is slipped under it, and the cooked one remains on top. In this way a little pile is formed. It is a way of keeping the mofletas warm and pliable— they quickly harden when they get cold. Another way of keeping them soft is to wrap them in a cloth or, better still, put them in a plastic bag. Reheat in the oven wrapped in foil.

Eat the pancakes warm, spread with butter and honey.

LA MOFLETA DE LA MIMOUNA

MOROCCAN JEWS hold a unique celebration called the Mimouna at the end of Passover. The festival is nowhere mentioned in classical Jewish texts, but it has the earmarks of an ancient rite of spring. It was the custom, in Morocco, for Jews to visit each other at night and to dance in the street. The whole community, in every city, held open house. It was also an occasion for the public demonstration of friendly relations between Jews and Muslims. Muslims would bring flowers, ears of grain, greens, honey, milk, bread, and fresh butter to their Jewish friends. Those with whom Jews had deposited foods for the duration of the Passover week (for this custom, see page 34) would bring them back then, and Jews would invite Muslims to partake of the Mimouna delicacies—something they also did throughout Passover. It was an old custom for young Jews to dress up in Muslim clothes lent to them by Muslim friends. The tradition dated back to a time when the Islamic law forbidding Jews to dress like Muslims was enforced. The day after the Mimouna, Jews went in great crowds on picnics in the country. Muslim landowners would allow them to picnic on their private land on the outskirts of town, and Jews would send them a thank-you gift.

Israel has adopted the Mimouna, which has turned into a mass carnival in Jerusalem's Sacher Park, drawing hundreds of thousands of celebrants from all over the country—singing and belly-dancing and gorging themselves with food. At home, Israelis from North Africa follow their old open-door traditions and invite all their neighbors in to eat.

The festive table of the night of the Mimouna is garlanded with leaves and grasses and green ears of wheat, symbolizing the renewal of nature after winter. A platter of flour in which lie five fava beans, five dates, five ears of wheat, and five coins symbolizes the hope for plenty. Some have a fish on the table, representing fertility. The table is laden with dairy foods and great platters of fruit, confectionery, and pastries. All the food is sweet—there is nothing sour or salty.

The first leavened bread after Passover, a type of thin pancake called "mofleta," has pride of place. It is eaten with butter and honey and accompanied by milk, which symbolize abundance, sweetness, and happiness, and also Israel, the land of milk and honey. Eating mofleta is believed to bring good luck.

Kahk

Savory Bracelets

MAKES ABOUT 46

I have found the same dry, hard, savory little bracelets covered with sesame seeds in many communities. The name comes up in the Talmud and in medieval Arab manuscripts (although we don't know what they were like). My mother kept a boxful almost all the time, to serve with *mezze*, and filled plastic bags for us to take home after her Friday-night dinners. It is the kind of thing you can't stop eating.

> 1 tablespoon dry yeast
> About ½ cup (125 ml) warm water
> A pinch of sugar
> 3⅓ cups (500 g) bread flour
> 1 teaspoon salt
> 1½ teaspoons ground cumin
> 1 teaspoon ground coriander
> 6 oz (175 g) margarine
> 1 tablespoon sunflower oil
> 1 whole egg, lightly beaten
> About 5 tablespoons sesame seeds

Put the yeast in a little bowl with about half of the water, a pinch of sugar, and 2 tablespoons of the flour and beat vigorously. Leave until it froths.

Put the remaining flour in a large bowl and mix in the salt, cumin, and coriander. Add the margarine and the oil and work into the flour with your hand. Add the yeast mixture and the remaining water—just enough to make a dough that sticks together in a ball. Knead for 10 minutes. Pour ½ tablespoon of oil in the bowl and roll the dough around to grease it all over. Cover the bowl with plastic wrap and leave for 1½ hours, or until almost doubled in bulk (it does not rise very much). Punch down. Take lumps smaller than a walnut and roll them between your palms into long, thin rolls 4 inches (10 cm) long and ⅓ inch (1 cm) thick. Make little bracelets by bringing the ends together and pinching them. Brush the tops with beaten egg and dip them top side down into a bowl of sesame seeds. Arrange the bracelets—a little apart from each other, for they grow—on greased baking sheets or on baking sheets lined with parchment paper. Let rise for 20 minutes. Bake in a 375°F (190°C) oven for about 30 minutes, then lower the heat to 225°F (100°C) and bake for another 15–20 minutes. Leave to cool. They last a very long time in a biscuit tin.

VARIATIONS

• For the above recipe I have used my cousin Liliane Gershon's measures and my mother's flavoring with ground spices. For Liliane's alternative flavoring, substitute 2 tablespoons whole roasted cumin seeds and a pinch of the little black nigella or onion seed.

• Instead of cumin and coriander, mix the flour with ground fennel and a little ground fenugreek. Some people add a grain or two of pulverized mastic.

• It is usual in this recipe to use margarine, but you can substitute butter or ½ cup (125 ml) sunflower oil.

Desserts

IN ALL THE OLD Sephardi communities, everyday family meals ended with fruit or a compote or with an assortment of dried fruit and nuts. Desserts were for special occasions such as the Sabbath, Jewish holidays, and celebratory events.

A Quick and Easy Way of Making Granitas— Basic Method

Blend the fruit to a light, creamy pulp and pour it into ice-cube trays. Cover with plastic wrap and let the pulp freeze hard for 6 hours or overnight in the freezer. Just before serving, put the frozen cubes, in batches, in the food processor and turn them into a very fine, soft frothy slush. Or do this in advance and pour the granita into a serving bowl and back into the freezer covered with plastic wrap. Take it out 15 minutes before serving.

Granita au Melon

Melon Granita

SERVES 6

Buy very ripe melons with a sweet fragrance that you can smell from a distance.

6¼ cups (1½ liters) melon pulp, obtained from
    2 melons, weighing about 5 lb (2½ kg)
Juice of 1 lemon
¾ cup (150 g) sugar or to taste
½–1 tablespoon orange-blossom water

Cut open the melons, peel and remove the seeds, and cut the flesh in pieces. Put in the food processor with the lemon juice, sugar, and orange-blossom water, and blend to a liquid pulp. The amount of sugar depends on how sweet the melons are, and the amount of orange-blossom water depends on whether it is concentrated or diluted, which varies—so you must taste. Continue as in the "basic method" on page 556.

a paste in a blender or food processor. Add the syrup and blend to a cream. Continue by following the "basic method" on page 556.

Mango Granita

Mangoes are my favorite fruit. For entertaining, I serve them cut up in slices. Occasionally I turn the flesh into a granita. The main thing is to find ones that taste good and are not stringy. Peel, remove the pit, and blend to a cream in the food processor. Continue as in the "basic method" on page 556.

Bouza bi Mish Mish

Apricot Granita

SERVES 8–10

Apricots are much-loved fruits among Oriental Sephardim. The quality we get these days never has the intense flavors of my childhood, but adding sugar and lemon helps.

2 lbs (1 kg) apricots
1 cup (200 g) sugar or to taste
¾ cup (200 ml) water
Juice of ½ lemon

Wash the apricots and remove the pits and stems. Put the sugar in a pan with the water and lemon juice and bring to the boil (this amount of sugar gives a tart, not too sweet taste). Simmer 5 minutes and let cool. Turn the apricots to

GRANITAS

G RANITAS OR water ices were popular because they were refreshing in the hot-weather climates, and because they were without cream and could be served after meat. People made them at home in a bucket with a churn, surrounded by a freezing mixture of crushed ice and salt. They made them with various fruits and most commonly with oranges, melons, and apricots. They are a lovely sweet to offer, because of their wonderful fresh fruit flavor.

Orange Granita

Now that we can buy freshly squeezed orange juice, this could not be easier. Add sugar to taste and proceed as in the "basic method" on page 556.

Flan à l'Orange
Orange Flan

SERVES 8

This is simply marvelous—one of the great high points of Sephardi gastronomy. I found a similar dessert called "budino di arancia" in Italy. Orange flans, like orange cakes, are part of the Iberian legacy. This one has the texture of a crème caramel with a little crunchiness produced by finely chopped almonds, and a refreshing orange flavor.

> *¾ cup (150 g) sugar, or to taste*
> *1 cup (200 g) blanched almonds*
> *Grated zest of 1 orange*
> *7 eggs*
> *1¼ cups (300 ml) freshly squeezed orange juice*
> *3 tablespoons orange brandy (optional)*

In a metal flan mold, make a treacly caramel: Put in 4 tablespoons of sugar and heat over the fire until it melts and turns a darkish brown, stirring so that it does so evenly. Then pour in about 1½ tablespoons of boiling water, let it bubble, and stir to dilute the caramel evenly. Then, holding the mold with a cloth (it will be very hot), turn it around until the liquid caramel has reached every part of the mold. Let it cool.

Grind the almonds in the food processor. (Don't use commercially ground almonds: they won't give the texture.) Add the rest of the sugar, the orange zest, and the eggs and blend well. Then add the orange juice and brandy and blend further.

Pour into the mold and place in a pan of water. Bake, at 350°F (180°C) for about 1¼ hours or longer, until set, covering the mold with a lid or with foil for the first ¾ hour.

Chill. Cut around the edge of the flan before unmolding upside down.

Salade d'Oranges

The most common and popular North African dessert is orange slices sprinkled with a little orange-blossom water and cinnamon. Remove all the pith when you peel them, and slice them thickly.

Tatli Tharid
Stewed Cherries on Bread

SERVES 8

This Turkish sweet was adopted by several Sephardi communities, including the Syrians of Egypt. It is one of my favorites and can be easily made for a large number of people, so bear it in mind when cherries are in season. In Egypt we made it with a brioche-type bread, but hallah or a good country bread will do very well.

8 large slices brioche or bread about ½ inch
  (1¼ cm) thick
2 lbs (1 kg) black cherries
12 oz (340 g) morello or black-cherry
  jam
Juice of ½–1 lemon
1¼ cups (300 ml) kaimak (see page 562),
  clotted or heavy cream, mascarpone, or
  thick strained yogurt to accompany

Trim the crusts off the bread and lightly toast the slices (you can do that in the oven if you like). Wash and drain the cherries and remove the stems. Some people remove the pits but I do not (it is all right to let people spit them out).

Put the jam in a large pan with ⅔ cup (150 ml) water and bring to the boil (I used a "reduced-sugar" jam, but you might prefer a sweeter one). Add the cherries and lemon juice and simmer gently for 20 minutes, or until the cherries are soft. Let them cool, and strain their juice into a bowl.

Arrange the toasted bread on a serving plate and ladle some of the juice over each piece, soaking the bread so that it is soft but not so that it falls apart. Top with the stewed cherries and serve with the kaimak, cream, mascarpone, or yogurt.

VARIATION

• A similar sweet is made with apricots. Pit 2 lbs (1 kg) apricots. Put them with 12 oz (340 g) of apricot jam, the juice of ½ lemon, and ⅔ cup (150 ml) water in a large saucepan. Cook, stirring, for a few minutes, until the apricots begin to soften, and continue as above.

Composta di Fichi
Fresh Fig Compote

SERVES 6

This Italian fig compote is ideal for when figs are not at their best (as is often the case with imported ones)—the treatment gives them a splendid flavor.

6 figs
¾ cup (150 g) sugar
6 tablespoons water
Grated zest of 1 lemon
A squeeze of lemon juice
5 tablespoons rum

Peel the fig skins carefully, trying not to tear into the pink flesh. Simmer the sugar and water with the grated zest and the squeeze of lemon juice for 5 minutes. Then put in the figs and cook a few minutes more, until soft, turning them over once. Add rum and let them cool.

Khoshaf
Dried Fruit and Nut Compote

SERVES 8

Compotes of dried fruit macerated (not cooked) in perfumed water were ubiquitous in every community in the Ottoman and Arab worlds. Each community had its special combination of fruit and nuts. This was ours. A special touch was to blanch the pistachios and peel them, a task worth the effort.

> 1 lb (500 g) dried apricots
> 1 lb (500 g) pitted prunes
> 2 cups (300 g) raisins or sultanas
> ½ cup (100 g) pine nuts
> ½ cup (100 g) blanched almonds
> ½ cup (100 g) blanched pistachios
> 2 tablespoons orange-blossom or rose water
> 6 cups (1½ liters) cold water

Put all the ingredients together in a glass bowl with the water and leave to soak, covered, for 24 hours. Serve in bowls.

Crème d'Amardine

Apricot Cream

SERVES 6

This cream used to be made with the sheets of pressed dried apricot sold as "qamardine" or "apricot leather." You can easily find them, but the flavor is not as good as it once was, and you had better use dried apricots—a natural, unsweetened, tart variety. It is just a matter of soaking and blending—something that you must do to taste, since the flavor of the apricots and the strength of the orange-blossom water varies. With wonderful-tasting dried apricots, you might leave out the lemon and sugar.

> 1 lb (500 g) dried apricots
> 3 cups (750 ml) water

> 1 tablespoon orange-blossom water or more to taste
> Juice of ½ lemon or to taste (optional)
> 2 tablespoons sugar or to taste (optional)
> 4 tablespoons chopped pistachios or almonds
> 1 cup (250 ml) kaimak (see page 562), clotted cream, heavy cream, mascarpone, or strained yogurt to accompany (optional)

Rinse the apricots and soak them overnight in the water, to cover. Put them through a blender or food processor with enough of their soaking water to make a thick cream, adding orange-blossom water, lemon juice, and sugar. Serve sprinkled with chopped pistachios or almonds, accompanied by cream or yogurt.

VARIATION

• It is also very good to blend the creams or yogurt with the pureed apricots.

Coings en Gelée

Quinces in Their Jelly

SERVES 4–6

Quinces are very important to the Sephardim, who have many ways of cooking them, including jams, jellies, and pastes. They are one of my favorite foods, and I never pass up a chance to eat them. This way of preparing them, from the Jewish community of Istanbul, is one of the most appealing. The recipe was given to me by Jaklin Katalan when I was there.

I have never found quinces at a supermarket or at an ordinary greengrocer, but for many years now they have been appearing in Greek and

Middle Eastern groceries from around October until February. Do get them when you have a chance.

2 lbs (1 kg) quinces (2 large fruit)
Juice of ½ lemon
½ cup (100 g) sugar
6 cloves
A few drops of vanilla extract
⅔ cup (150 ml) kaimak (see page 562),
   clotted cream, heavy cream, or mascarpone

Wash the quinces well and use a brush to remove the light down that covers their skin in patches. Peel them and cut them into slices ¾ inch (2 cm) thick. (It is easier to core the slices when they are cooked than to core the whole fruit, because it is extremely hard.) The seeds are important, for they produce the distinctive red jelly. Cook the quinces as soon as they are sliced: the flesh discolors quickly.

Put them in a pan with the lemon juice, sugar, and cloves. Cover with about 2½ cups (600 ml) water and simmer until the fruit is tender and the syrup turns into a reddish jelly, adding the vanilla about half the way through the cooking time and water if necessary. It takes more than an hour for the jelly to form. If the fruit becomes tender too quickly (the time varies depending on its ripeness), lift out the slices, reduce the syrup, return the fruit to the pan, and cook until the syrup becomes reddish and thick. The sugar has a hardening effect and prevents the fruit from falling apart. Lift out the quince slices, cut away the cores with a sharp knife, and arrange them in a serving dish. Pour the syrup on top. It will turn into a jelly as it cools.

Serve chilled or at room temperature, with dollops of clotted cream, whipped heavy cream,

or mascarpone. In Turkey the cream used is the very thick kaimak made from buffalo's milk (page 562).

Cotognata

Quinces in Wine

SERVES 4

This Italian sweet is different from other quince compotes in that it is cooked in wine, which gives a delicious rich taste.

1¼ cups (250 g) sugar
1½ cups (350 ml) red or white wine
10 cloves
2 teaspoons cinnamon
2 large quinces, each weighing about 1 lb
   (500 g)

Put the sugar and wine in a wide pan with the cloves and cinnamon and bring to the boil.

Wash and scrub the quinces well to remove the light down that covers them, and cut them in half. They are extremely hard, so you will need a strong knife. Do not peel them. Trim the ends but leave the cores and seeds, which produce the jelly. Put the quinces in the syrup and add enough water to cover them. Simmer gently for about 1 hour, or until tender, turning them over once so that they cook through evenly, and adding a little water if necessary. In the end the syrup should be greatly reduced. Serve them hot or cold in their syrup.

VARIATION

• You can finish them off, cut side up, in the oven.

Pumpkin Halwa

SERVES 4

This Bene Israel sweet depends very much on the good taste of the pumpkin.

- 1 lb (500 g) orange pumpkin, peeled and coarsely grated
- 1¼ cups (250 g) sugar
- Seeds of 3 cardamom pods or ½ teaspoon ground cardamom
- ⅔ cup (150 ml) clotted or heavy cream
- ½ cup (75 g) coarsely chopped almonds and pistachios

Steam the pumpkin in a pot with a tight-fitting lid and about ½ cup (125 ml) of water. It will release a lot of juice. Cook with the lid off for a few minutes to evaporate some of the water. Add the sugar and cardamom seeds and cook until thick and slightly jammy. Let it cool before folding in the cream and nuts. Serve chilled or at room temperature.

Dondurma Kaimak

Mastic and Rose Water Ice Cream

SERVES 6

So many people from Egypt and elsewhere in the Middle East are forever searching for this mythical ice cream made with buffalo's milk thickened with sahlab (the ground root of a

KAIMAK
Thick Cream

KAIMAK IS the thick cream that comes to the top when buffalo milk is simmered, then left to rest for several hours. It is so thick you can cut it with a knife. People bought it rolled up, from vendors, and cut it into strips or squares. The nearest thing to it is clotted cream, but heavy cream or mascarpone can also be used.

type of orchid—orchis mascula) and flavored with rose water and mastic. I have been looking for it in several countries for nearly forty years, but nothing has matched up to the very rich, chewy-textured ice cream (it would pull into long threads) of my childhood. My efforts to re-create it myself with sahlab have not been successful. Sahlab, also called salep, is very expensive, and I am sure that the various samples I bought were adulterated. In Israel I was invited to dinner by Rosita Sevilla, who comes from Turkey and writes about food. For the dessert, she had made a wonderful approximation of this ice cream using a rich custard. Here is a version. Although it does not have the chewy texture of the original, the taste is right. The mastic, which gives the distinctive flavor, is sold in small hard lumps, like crystals, which must be pounded to a fine powder with a pestle and mortar or wrapped up in strong paper and crushed with a hammer.

4 egg yolks
½ cup (100 g) sugar
1¼ cups (300 ml) light cream
2 tablespoons rose water or to taste
1¼ cups (300 ml) heavy cream
½ teaspoon powdered mastic (obtained by
   pounding 2 or 3 grains mastic with a
   mortar and pestle, or wrapping them in
   paper and crushing with a hammer)

Beat the egg yolks and sugar to a thick, pale cream in a bowl. Bring the light cream to the boil and gradually pour over the yolk mixture, beating all the time. Put the bowl in a pan of boiling water or in the top part of a double boiler and stir, or lightly beat, until the mixture thickens into a custard. Add the rose water and sprinkle the mastic over the whole surface (if it falls in one place, it sticks together in a lump) and stir well. Let cool. Beat the heavy cream until firm and fold it into the cooled custard. Cover with plastic wrap and freeze overnight.

VARIATIONS

• For another version, beat 6 egg yolks with ⅔ cup (125 g) sugar to a thick, pale cream. Bring to the boil 2½ cups (600 ml) light cream and gradually pour onto the yolk mixture, beating all the time. Add ½ teaspoon powdered mastic and 2 tablespoons rose water and cook, stirring over boiling water, until the mixture thickens.

• Some people cheat and use store-bought vanilla ice cream. For this, blend with the flavorings—mastic and rose water—and put back into the freezer.

• Another instant alternative is to blend ½ lb (250 g) mascarpone with 2 egg yolks, 1½ tablespoons rose water, 5 tablespoons sugar, and ½ teaspoon powdered mastic.

Torta di Mandorle e Spinaci

Almond and Spinach Dessert

SERVES 6–8

This old Florentine recipe is a curiosity. For a long time I could not bring myself to make it. Although I ate and liked the sweet tourte de blettes (a tart with Swiss chard or spinach) in Nice, the thought of a spinach dessert was off-putting. Yet the the dish was important, because my friends David Plant and Nikos Stangos, who have a home in the ancient walled city of Lucca, told me that Catholic locals mysteriously hinted at their Jewish origins and pointed to this family dish as part of their Jewish heritage. Anyway, I made it and found it tasty and kept eating a little more throughout the day. Since I have only encountered anything like it in Nice, I wonder if there is any connection with the Jews who were banished from Provence and found refuge in Italy in the sixteenth century (page 482).

1 lb (500 g) spinach
1¼ cups (200 g) blanched almonds
1 cup (200 g) sugar
4 egg yolks
2 egg whites
Confectioners' sugar to sprinkle on

Wash the spinach and remove any tough stems. Drain and squeeze the excess water out. Put the leaves in a pan with the lid on and steam in the water that clings to them, for a

Almond and Spinach Dessert (cont.)

minute or two only, until they collapse into a soft mass. Drain and press out as much water as you can.

Finely chop the almonds in the food processor. Add the sugar, egg yolks, and spinach and blend to a cream. Beat the egg whites stiff and fold them in. Pour into an oiled baking dish, and bake in a 375°F (190°C) oven for 35 minutes. Serve hot or cold, sprinkled with confectioners' sugar.

ALEPPO (SYRIA) WAS THE PEARL
—— OF THE JEWISH KITCHEN ——

A LARGE PROPORTION of the recipes in this book are Syrian, and most particularly from Halab (Aleppo). They are part of my background, and they are among the most prestigious dishes of the Middle East. Many come from my cousin Irene Douek Harari's notebooks. They were handed down by her grandmother, my father's sister Latifa, who was famous for her cooking. Irene, who lived in Latifa's extended family home when she was small, now lives near me in Hampstead, and we exchange recipes and memories.

Latifa had eighteen children—though not all of them survived. She kept an open house, and visitors called at all times of the day. On Saturdays the garden of the family villa in the leafy suburb of Kubbeh was filled with people. A constant flow of refreshments was passed around, from coffee, pastries, and confectioneries in the morning and whiskey or beer with *mezze* at midday to sherbets, sweetmeats, and jams in the afternoon. There was no oven in the house—they had fatayels (Primus stoves) and braziers—and the Jewish cook Nessim would send trays of delicacies—chorek, ghorayebah, baklawa, kibbeh, and bread—to the public oven.

When my father was ninety-four, we were sent a tape recording that Latifa's husband, Moussa, made in Canada before he died at the age of 104. He told how he had left Aleppo for America at eighteen and stopped in Alexandria to take a transatlantic ship. Because of an epi-

My great-uncle Moussa Douek came from Aleppo. He had this photograph with his wife's picture in his lapel taken when he was abroad on business, to show her he was thinking of her.

demic in Aleppo, the authorities confiscated his suitcases to fumigate them. They took so long to return them that he missed his ship. The next one left two weeks later, so he went to look for his brother in Cairo. Walking through the streets, he saw a tiny boy on a balcony and asked his name. It was my father, his nephew. My grandfather would not let his younger brother stay in the house because he had daughters at home. One day while he was walking in the souk, a Muslim asked Moussa why he looked miserable. He told him he wanted to get to America. The man replied, "Stay here—this *is* America!" and gave him a job. Days later, somebody sold him a twenty-pound lottery bond which he could pay for in monthly installments. The next month, he won two thousand pounds. His employer let him buy a corner of the warehouse in which rubbish had been kept. And that was how his fortune started. He then married his niece, who was fourteen. In later years, he became the provider for the large extended Douek family, supporting widowed sisters-in-law, providing dowries for nieces, and giving jobs to impoverished relatives. He was also a bit of a tyrant with those who worked for him and squeezed relatives who were competitors out of business. Their home represented a corner of Aleppo where there was always an open house, and Latifa spent her days preparing food.

When I went back to Cairo after thirty years' absence, I found Moussa's name still on the warehouse. As I stood a good distance away in the khan (market), looking at it with beating heart, somebody came out and asked if I was a relative of Moussa Douek. A large crowd—old men in kaftans, young ones in jeans, women in chadors—gathered around from neighboring stores to see me. They offered me coffee. An old man brought out photographs of my family. I went to visit Latifa's tomb in the Jewish cemetery in the desert outside Cairo. Bedouins with sheep and goats who have made their homes in nearby mausoleums rushed to take down washing and tidy up. I was invited as a "relative" to drink tea in one of these mausoleums. Another had been turned into a bakery with a stone oven. I was offered some of the bread. There were chickens running around. The Doueks are now dispersed all over the world, Latifa and Moussa's children mostly in Montreal. But when we visit relatives we are offered the old delicacies.

Syrian cooking has survived in an extraordinary way in communities abroad, even though the great migration from Syria was in the very early days of the century—much earlier than from the rest of the Middle East (when the Suez Canal was built, and the caravan trade through Syria collapsed, Jews lost their means of survival). One reason is that the large communities, to be found now mostly in Manchester, North and South America, and the Caribbean islands, are closely knit and their feeling of identity is particularly strong. To give you an example, years ago, when the *Jewish Chronicle* featured my Passover recipes accompanied by a photograph of me and my two daughters with a few words about my Syrian ancestry, I received phone calls from Milan, New York, Mexico, and Rio de Janeiro from people of Syrian origin asking for my daughters in marriage on behalf of their sons.

In his social history of the New York Syrian community, *Aleppo in Flatbush*, Joseph Sutton describes the Halabis who live in Brooklyn and on Long Island. They make good wives and husbands, he says; the men are good businessmen and the women are submissive, devoted, and prudish. They entertain each other lavishly and are addicted to playing cards. When they entertain, they may even hire a moving van to stack their furniture in, to make room for card tables. Businessmen travel together to Manhattan from Long Island in buses converted to hold card tables. I met the octogenarian Mr. Sutton in New York. He gave me his second book,

The synagogue of Aleppo, where my great-grandfather was chief rabbi

Aleppo Chronicles: The Story of the Unique Sepharadeem of the Near East in Their Own Words, a collection of taped memories. It gave my father enormous joy to find his grandfather described as "walking majestically holding a staff," and a relative confiding, "Each time my fiancé approached I ran to the far side of the room." The way my father talked about his childhood in Cairo, it seems it was a continuation of Mr. Sutton's Aleppo.

Another book, *The Natural History of Aleppo* by Dr. Alex Russell, an eighteenth-century English doctor, shows that life for Jewish families in the ancient city did not change very much for hundreds of years. He describes the Jews as "living under the eye of their rabbis." Their rabbis were my ancestors the Douek ha Cohens and the Sassoons, who were also merchants. What follows is family lore illumined by Dr. Russell and Mr. Sutton.

A synagogue is said to have been established in Aleppo in the time of King David, nearly three thousand years ago. According to legend, the city got its name, Halab, which means "milk" in Aramaic Hebrew and Arabic, when the patriarch Abraham stopped there to milk his flocks. It was the base and terminus of the ancient caravan trade between East and West. From the Middle Ages until the nineteenth century, it was one of the most important commercial centers in the world, and its Jewish community was famous for international trading. "Aleppo" was the way merchants from Venice, who came to trade, pronounced "Halab." Jews carried on their business in souks and khans, which were like underground cities with vaulted roofs and arches. They financed the camel caravans that came and went from the khans bringing silks, spices, perfumes, and jewels from the East. These goods, as well as Syrian wheat, olive oil, sesame, and pistachios, were shipped to Europe from Lebanon. At the same time, bales of cloth and other goods from Europe were loaded onto the caravans that set off again for the Arab world and the Asian interior.

Until 1905, all the Jews lived within the old city walls in the Jewish quarters of Bahsita, the Saha, and Haret el Yahoud. After that, all except the very poor gradually moved to Djamiliyeh, which had wide, leafy streets. According to my relatives and Mr. Sutton's interviewees, they were treated with respect and affection by the Muslim population. They wore Arab clothes, and European clothes for special occasions. They all spoke Arabic—even those who came from Spain and Portugal and from Venice and Livorno, such as the Lisbonas, Silveras, Pintos, Laniados, Anconas, and Picciottos. These families were considered gentry and were the leaders of the community. Some became pashas; some were consuls of European countries and were given titles such as "baron" by the Austro-Hungarian emperor and acquired a French "de" in front of their names. They were called "*franj*" (meaning "French" or "European") and "*signorim*" by the rest of the community. Another name for them was "*medias*," which had to do with the way they cut their vegetables to be stuffed: they cut them in half, unlike the native Jews, who left them whole and hollowed them. My aunt Régine, who is a de Picciotto, a family that produced a dynasty of consuls, is the source of a great number of recipes. There is more about her in introductions to her recipes.

Extended families—parents, married children, and grandchildren—lived together in the same house, a large *hosh* built around an inner courtyard. It looked like nothing from the outside, with no windows and a small door. But these little doors opened with huge keys to reveal tiled courtyards with scented fruit trees, climbing vines, and fountains. All the rooms gave onto the courtyard or onto a gallery balcony overlooking the courtyard. (When I remarked to somebody who had lived in a *hosh* that it must have been wonderful, she said, "Imagine having to run out in the cold at night when you need to go to the toilet!") Divans along the walls served as beds at night. During the day they were covered by Persian rugs. Thin mattresses on the floor were used by most of the family and put away during the day. Large trays on folding legs served as tables. The rooms were heated by charcoal braziers and lit by candles and oil lamps. Cooking was done on the brazier or a Primus. The cellar was filled with jars of pickles, jams, and preserves and with supplies of rice, oil, and wine. If there was not a well in the courtyard, you had to fetch water from one in the street. A friend, André Sharon, recently returned from a visit to Syria with photographs of their old family house, which is now the town hall (his mother's family name is still engraved on the building). The tiled courtyard, fountain, and mosaic seating fitted my grandparents' descriptions.

Life was tranquil, simple, and happy. Women married by arrangement, sometimes as young as thirteen, usually with much older men and often someone from the same family—an uncle or cousin. A broker arranged a dowry. They had many children—thirteen was usual. My great-grandfather married again when his wife died—he was seventy-five—and his new wife gave him three more children. But it was unlikely for a widow to remarry. The ideal woman was respectful and submissive and a good cook. The family's reputation depended on her honor and virtue, its happiness on her cooking. For a family to be consid-

The Straight Street in Damascus. The city had a large Jewish population.

ered a "good" family, there had to be a long line of women of impeccable virtue. The women of Damascus were reputedly flirtatious, flighty, and spoiled. Men of Aleppo were afraid to marry them. The Damascenes dressed well, and those who could afford it were covered with jewels. Joseph Sutton tells how Baron Edmond de Rothschild was entertained by the community in Damascus. Asked to contribute funds, he looked at their gold and diamonds and replied, "I think you should subsidize me!"

Aleppo was more provincial than Damascus. Relatives, friends, and neighbors spent most of their time in each other's courtyards. Someone would play the *oud* (lute); stories and jokes would be told and poems recited. And they played cards. In the summer they picnicked in orchards where figs, apricots, and mulberries, pistachios and almonds grew. There were visits to fortune-tellers and magic men and to saints' tombs. Magicians, puppet theaters, and Arab bands toured the streets, and musicians played in cafés. During Muslim saints' days, the streets were all lit up, and acrobats, jugglers, and musicians came to entertain.

There were constant Jewish festivities. Wedding celebrations went on for many days with several festive dinners and musicians playing. Wealthy relatives lent their homes for the wedding ceremony. There was also the *hammam* or *mikvah* (the bride's ritual bath), attended by female relatives and friends. The bathhouse was rented and decorated for the occasion, which could last all day. A Bedouin woman was mistress of ceremonies, and female musicians and singers entertained. Large ceremonial trays covered with perfumes, silk robes, inlaid wooden clogs, flowers, and a purse with money to pay for the *hammam* were sent by the bridegroom. The bride's mother and relatives brought platters of sweetmeats and delicacies. Guests could bathe and also have a massage. It was on such occasions—when they could see the shape of young girls' hips—that women chose brides for their sons.

The bathhouse was the most congenial meeting place for women. They would go there on Friday afternoons, after their Sabbath preparations. They had baths and massages and gossiped. The men went at a different time. On Saturdays men and women went to the synagogue and visited relatives. Bedouin women would go through Jewish streets with pans of lighted charcoal shouting "Fire! Fire!" and were called in to do some cooking. For the Feast of Tabernacles (Sukkot), myrtle from Antioch, and citrons and palm branches from Tripoli would be distributed by the rabbis. Every family constructed a tabernacle (a hut) with branches in the courtyard, on the roof terrace, or on balconies. The family members ate there and sometimes slept there. During feasts they entertained constantly and sent platters of sweetmeats to each other. Muslims came to visit and were offered coffee, sweetmeats, and sherbets.

As the importance of Aleppo diminished with the opening of the Suez Canal, many Jewish families became destitute. In 1908, when the Young Turk Revolution overthrew Abdul Hamid II, the minorities in the Ottoman Empire became equal with Muslims and eligible to join the army. Jews who had previously been released on payment of a small tax found themselves subject to conscription. This was a further incentive for young men and their families to leave and seek their fortune in Egypt and across the Atlantic. After the foundation of the State of Israel in 1948, the position of the Jews in Syria became precarious, and many crossed into the new Jewish state.

They brought with them exquisite dishes with delicate flavorings and elaborate procedures. In the seventh century, when Damascus became the first center of Islam, ruled by the Umayyad Caliphate, a court cuisine had developed in Syria to which Jews had access as court advisers, physicians, and financiers. Years ago I came across an analysis by the French Orientalist Maxime Rodinson of a thirteenth-century culinary manuscript of Syrian origin. It was written in the Ayyubid period by someone close to the court, with references to the sultan and the royal kitchens. Mr. Rodinson listed the names of seventy-four dishes and described them. Many are very like the recipes given to me by my aunts. The Jews also inherited the poor foods of the area—the lentils and legumes, grains and vegetables—because most of them were poor.

The dishes of my aunt Latifa and her cook Nessim were the traditional ones of Jewish Syria. On Thursday night there was always lentil soup, rishta bi ats (homemade tagliatelle with brown lentils), or rishta wa calsones (tagliatelle and ravioli stuffed with cheese) and fried fish. On Friday night there was chicken or veal sofrito with little fried potatoes cooked in the sauce under the chicken, kobeba and rice with pine nuts and pistachios. These and dozens more Syrian dishes are what we get when we visit our families in Los Angeles, Mexico, and Colombia, Paris and Geneva.

Sutlage–Muhallabeya
Fragrant Milk Pudding (Basic Recipe with Variations)

SERVES 6

Milk puddings with ground rice are ubiquitous in the Middle East. For the Jews they are the all-purpose dessert of the dairy table and the traditional sweet of Shavuot and Purim. In Turkey and the Balkans such a dish was called "sutlage"; in Syria and Egypt, as in the rest of the Arab world, it was "muhallabeya." Every community has its own traditional flavorings and presentation. Use the basic recipe, and add the flavorings from one of the variations that follow. Each one transforms the pudding into something special.

> *½ cup (100 g) rice flour*
> *5½ cups (1¼ liters) cold milk*
> *½ cup (100 g) sugar*
> *For the flavorings and garnishes, see the variations*

In a little bowl, mix the rice flour with a cup of the cold milk, adding it gradually and mixing thoroughly to avoid lumps. Bring the rest of the milk to the boil in a pan. Pour the rice flour-and-milk mixture in, stirring vigorously, then cook on very low heat, stirring continuously until the mixture thickens. If you don't stir every so often, the milk will thicken unevenly and form lumps. Let the cream cook gently for a few minutes more (in all, 15–20 minutes). Stir in the sugar and cook until dissolved. Stir with a wooden spoon, being careful not to scrape the bottom of the pan, because the cream always sticks and burns at the bottom, and you want to leave that part behind, untouched. The cream might seem too light, but it does thicken when it cools. Pour into a large bowl or into small individual ones and serve cold.

FLAVORING VARIATIONS

- The most common way is to add 1–2 tablespoons orange-blossom or rose water towards the end of the cooking and to garnish with a sprinkling of chopped almonds and pistachios.
- For a Judeo-Spanish version from Turkey, boil the milk with a stick of vanilla or add a few drops of vanilla extract or the zest of ½ lemon. Serve sprinkled with 1 teaspoon cinnamon.
- My favorite pudding is with cardamom—a popular flavoring with Indian, Iraqi, and Iranian Jews. Add 1 teaspoon ground cardamom and 1 tablespoon rose water a few minutes before the end of cooking.
- Instead of rice flour, you can use cornstarch or a mixture of rice flour and cornstarch.

Régine's Festive Muhallabeya

My aunt Régine gave me the following recipe for a grand and delectable version of muhallabeya. It is from Aleppo and was called "keshk el fo'era," which meant (ironically) that it was for the poor. Régine's family were grandees from Livorno who settled in Aleppo and became a dynasty of consuls for Tuscany, France, and Austria. Régine was one of the most beautiful women in Egypt, and the most elegant. She brought all the latest designs from the French couture houses to be copied by dressmakers in Cairo—and we all copied them. She brought the same elegance and refinement to her cooking.

For her festive muhallabeya, follow the preceding basic recipe and add 1–2 tablespoons orange-blossom water towards the end of the cooking. Pour into a crystal (or glass) serving bowl and let it cool.

Make a honey syrup: Bring to the boil 3 tablespoons honey with ½ cup (125 ml) water. Stir well and add 1 tablespoon orange-blossom or rose water. Let it cool, and pour over the cold, firmed cream. It will seep in gradually. Chill, covered, in the refrigerator. Before serving, sprinkle with ¾ cup (150 g) finely chopped pistachios or a mixture of pistachios and almonds. Régine made a design with the different-colored nuts.

Arroz kon Leche

Rice Pudding

SERVES 6

If there was an everyday Sephardi dessert, this was it. It was eaten hot or cold, for breakfast, or in the evening after a light meatless meal, or when visitors came in the middle of the day. Flavorings differed in each community. I have given them as variations to the basic recipe that follows. I make the pudding regularly (it is nothing like the rice puddings you may remember from school days) and use it as a bed for poached fruit.

1 cup (200 g) Italian risotto or short-grain round rice
1½ cups (350 ml) water
4 cups (1 liter) milk
¾ cup (175 g) sugar or to taste

Put the rice in a large pot with the water. Bring to the boil and simmer, covered, for about 6 minutes, or until the water is absorbed, watching and stirring so that the rice does not dry up and stick to the bottom of the pan. Add the milk, bring to the boil, and simmer on very low heat for 30–45 minutes, or until the rice is very soft and the milk almost absorbed (there should be some liquid left), stirring occasionally so that the rice does not stick. Stir in the sugar and one of the following flavorings and cook for a few minutes longer.

Serve hot or cold, accompanied if you like with a fruit compote.

FLAVORING VARIATIONS

• For a Judeo-Spanish version, flavor with a vanilla bean at the start of the cooking, or with a few drops of vanilla extract towards the end, and serve sprinkled with cinnamon. (Some people also add the zest of ½ lemon.)

• An Arab version known as "roz bi halib" (rice with milk) is flavored with 1 tablespoon rose water and ½ teaspoon ground mastic stirred in at the very end. Mastic is a resin from a tree which you can buy in small grains or crystals in Greek and Oriental stores. You have to pound it yourself to a powder with a pestle and mortar, or wrap it up in a piece of paper and crush it with a hammer. It gives a marvelous flavor which we Oriental Sephardim are very fond of, but you must use very little, for otherwise the taste becomes unpleasant.

- For a splendid Iranian version called "shirberenj," add I teaspoon ground cardamom and ½ teaspoon saffron powder or crushed saffron pistils.

- Use ½ cup (90 ml) honey instead of sugar.

- For a baked version, pour into an oven dish and let it cool, then pour over the top I beaten egg mixed with ½ cup (125 ml) milk. Bake in a 425°F (220°C) oven for 20 minutes, or until a brown crust forms.

- For a caramel version, heat 4 tablespoons sugar until brown, add I tablespoon water, and let it bubble, then pour over the pudding, making circular lines. Bake for 30 minutes and serve hot or cold. (In this case, use 4 tablespoons less sugar at the start, or you might find it too sweet.)

- In Jewish Aleppo, a very thick, sticky rice pudding, made thicker by using less milk, was cooked with honey instead of sugar and eaten in bowls with milk poured over. It was called "brekhito."

BAKED RICE PUDDING IN CAIRO

WHEN I FIRST went back to Cairo after thirty years, I went to see the place where both my parents were born. It had then been a new suburb which had been reclaimed from marshlands and developed by a civil engineer called Sakakini Pasha, after whom the quarter was named. Another name for the area was "Daher." It was once entirely inhabited by Jewish immigrants, mostly from Syria. My father told me there had been a bakery to which people brought their milk puddings to be baked, and these came out with a golden-brown crust quite unlike the usual white creams of Egypt.

I found the old rococo palace that had belonged to Sakakini Pasha, with the streets converging towards it like the rays of the sun. The old inhabitants of the area believed the palace moved and turned on a kind of pivot and fantasized about the romances that went on inside. Now the palace, with all its little angels, was covered with black soot; the streets were hung with washing, and inches of water covered the ground. Facing the palace was a tiny dairy. The milk pudding I ordered came with a brown crust. When I explained that my parents were born here, the shopkeeper said, "In that case it's on the house." For the recipe, see the last two variations of the preceding recipe, arroz kon leche.

Kheer

Coconut Creamed Rice Pudding

SERVES 8–10

This Indian pudding is eaten by the Bene Israel community in India after the fast of Gedalish, at the time of the year when the new rice paddy is just getting ready. It is a rice pudding made without milk and therefore can be eaten after a meat meal. The following, prepared with canned coconut milk, is an adaptation of Mrs. R. Daniels' recipe made from the juice obtained from ground coconut. It is very rich, and I can only eat a few spoonfuls. I suspect the original may have been more diluted and lighter. It is for those who are fond of coconut.

> 2 cans or 3¾ cups (800 ml) coconut milk
>   (see page 235)
> ¾ cup (150 g) rice flour
> 1 cup (250 ml) water
> 5 cardamom pods
> ⅔ cup (125 g) sugar or to taste
> 2 tablespoons blanched almonds, slivered or
>   coarsely chopped
> 2 tablespoons pistachios, coarsely chopped

Bring the coconut milk to the boil in a pan. Mix the rice flour with the water into a paste and pour into the simmering coconut milk, stirring all the time. Bring to the boil, stirring, and continue to stir until the mixture thickens. Then add the cardamom and simmer over low heat for about 20 minutes, stirring occasionally. Add the sugar towards the end. Pour into a serving dish and sprinkle with almonds and pistachios. Serve cold.

VARIATIONS

- Chopped almonds and pistachios may be stirred into the cream.
- Mavis Hyman, in her book *Indian-Jewish Cooking*, gives a similar dish called "dodail" prepared by the Baghdadis of Calcutta. She uses ground cardamom and 1–2 tablespoons of rose water as flavorings and, instead of regular sugar, jaggery or muscovado (unrefined brown) sugar, both of which have a distinctive taste and give the pudding a light-brown color.
- Another sweet, called simply "halwa" (meaning sweet), made by the Bene Israel for Rosh Hashanah, weddings, and other happy occasions, has the same ingredients but is much thicker, with a larger quantity of rice flour and also a little cornstarch. It is cooked for about 2 hours, poured in a shallow dish, and when it cools it is cut into lozenges.

Balouza

Rose-Flavored Jelly

SERVES 12–16

I ate this rose-scented cornstarch jelly at a small restaurant in Jerusalem called the Eucalyptus Inn. They told me they added rose-petal jam to a recipe in my first book. The advantage, for the restaurant that serves meat, is that there is no milk in it.

Rose-Flavored Jelly (cont.)

1 cup (150 g) cornstarch
9 cups (2 liters) water
1 cup (200 g) sugar
1–2 tablespoons rose water
½ cup (125 ml) rose-petal jam or to taste
½ cup (100 g) blanched almonds, chopped
½ cup (75 g) pistachios, chopped
½ cup (75 g) raisins or sultanas, soaked in
    water for 15 minutes

Mix the cornstarch with 1 cup of the water until dissolved. In a large pan, heat the rest of the water. Before it is too hot, pour the cornstarch mixture in, stirring vigorously with a wooden spoon, and bring to the boil slowly, stirring constantly to prevent lumps from forming. (You can salvage a lumpy mixture by beating with an electric beater or blending in a food processor.) Simmer gently over the lowest possible heat, stirring often, until the mixture thickens enough to coat a spoon or to form a little ball when you drop a bit onto a cold plate, adding sugar towards the end. Pour into a wide, shallow bowl and chill. When the mixture has set into a stiff jelly, chop it up with a knife and stir in the rest of the ingredients.

VARIATIONS

• The balouza is sometimes flavored with 2 grains of mastic resin pounded to a powder.
• Naim Dangoor from Baghdad recalls that at Hanukah they used to make a pudding they called "halawa" (it means "sweet") with cornstarch, sugar, oil, and water cooked to a creamy paste, which was eaten with bread. Families who had a bereavement sent around big flatbreads like the Indian nan, spread with halawa and

folded, and inscribed with the name of the bereaved.

Belila

Whole Wheat or Barley in Syrup with Nuts

SERVES 12

At one time in Syria, cooked young green wheat and also barley were sold in the streets bathed in syrup, and people would buy these and embellish them with nuts and tiny silver balls and a drop of orange-blossom water. This was the traditional offering to friends and neighbors who looked in when there was a happy event, like a baby's first tooth. It is made with whole young wheat or with pearl barley.

2½ cups (500 g) young wheat or pearl barley
2¼ cups (500 g) sugar or to taste
2–3 tablespoons orange-blossom or rose water
2 teaspoons cinnamon
¾ cup (100 g) pistachios, coarsely chopped
½ cup (100 g) almonds, slivered or chopped
¾ cup (100 g) coarsely chopped walnuts
    (optional)
¾ cup (100 g) seedless raisins or sultanas,
    soaked in water and drained (optional)

The wheat needs to be soaked in cold water overnight. Drain off any bits of husk that float to the top, then rinse and drain in a colander. The barley needs only to be rinsed and drained. Put the grain in a pot with plenty of water. Bring to the boil and simmer for ½–1½ hours, until very tender (the time varies considerably, depending mainly on the age of the wheat), adding water if it becomes too dry. Drain again, and pour into a large serving bowl. (In the old days it was served in a silver bowl.)

Now boil the sugar with 3 cups (750 ml) of water and the juice of ½ lemon until the sugar has dissolved. Add the orange-blossom water and simmer for a moment or two, then pour over the grain.

Serve hot or cold in little bowls or teacups, sprinkled with cinnamon, nuts, and raisins. There should be quite a lot of syrup in each serving. Alternatively, pass the nuts and raisins around in a bowl for people to help themselves.

VARIATION

• For a milky version of belila, boil the wheat or barley in water as above. Boil 3 cups (750 ml) milk with 1 lb (500 g) clear honey and add 2–3 tablespoons of orange-blossom water. Serve the grain hot or cold, with the milk poured over, sprinkled with nuts and raisins and a little cinnamon.

Apam
Bread Pudding with Coconut Milk

SERVES 6

This glorious pudding from the Calcutta community is a reflection of the Anglicized character of that city, which was the capital of the British Raj until 1911. It is also an example of the way coconut milk was used instead of milk by the Jews so that puddings could be eaten after meat. I made it with creamed coconut milk, sold in block form, but you can use unsweetened canned coconut milk.

4 cups (900 ml) water
7 oz (200 g) creamed coconut
   (see page 235), cut in pieces
½ cup (100 g) sugar
A few drops of vanilla extract
6 eggs, lightly beaten
3 tablespoons split or slivered almonds
3 tablespoons little black seedless raisins
6 slices bread, crusts removed

Boil the water. Add the creamed coconut, and simmer until it dissolves. Add the sugar, stir, and when it is dissolved add the vanilla. Let it cool a little, then beat in the eggs. Stir in the almonds and raisins. Put the bread in a wide baking dish and pour the milk mixture on top, making sure that the almonds and raisins are spread evenly over the bread. Bake at 350°F (180°C) for about 45 minutes, or until golden. Serve hot or cold.

VARIATION

• Instead of creamed coconut dissolved in water, use 5 cups (1¼ liters) of unsweetened canned coconut milk.

Cassola
A Sweet Ricotta Pancake

SERVES 8

This is an old Roman recipe and one of my favorites. There are more sophisticated, modern versions, but this one is simple and won-

A Sweet Ricotta Pancake (cont.)

derful. It enchanted a dinner party of food writers gathered together after the Oxford Symposium on Food and Cookery. I served it with figs lightly poached in a syrup with rum (page 559). It is good with any fruit in syrup.

1 lb (500 g) ricotta
1 cup (200 g) sugar
5 eggs
2 tablespoons oil

Blend the ricotta and sugar with the eggs in a food processor. Heat the oil in a large nonstick frying pan. Pour in the mixture and cook on very low heat until the bottom has set firmly. Then put under the broiler and cook the top until it is firm and browned. (It should still be soft and creamy inside.) Slip it onto a serving plate. It is lovely hot or cold.

VARIATIONS

• Modern versions include flavoring with the grated rind of 1 lemon or with 5–6 tablespoons of cognac and sprinkling with cinnamon.

Farka

Tunisian Couscous Cake with Dates and Nuts

SERVES 10

1 lb (500 g) couscous
¾ cup (175 g) superfine sugar
Juice of ½ lemon

2 tablespoons orange-blossom water
12 oz (350 g) pitted dried dates
5 tablespoons peanut or light vegetable oil
2 teaspoons cinnamon
½ cup (100 g) almonds
¼ cup (50 g) hazelnuts
⅓ cup (50 g) pistachios
¾ cup (100 g) walnuts
2 tablespoons confectioners' sugar

Put the couscous in a bowl. Boil 2½ cups (600 ml) water with the sugar and lemon juice until the sugar dissolves. Stir in the orange-blossom water and pour over the couscous. Mix very well, so that the syrup is absorbed evenly. Leave for about ½ hour, until the grain is tender, turning it over occasionally and breaking up any lumps. Try the grain, and if it is not quite tender add a little water.

Put the dates in a pan with 1 cup (250 ml) water and simmer until they are very soft and the water is absorbed, then crush them with a fork. Add the oil, 1 teaspoon cinnamon, and mashed dates to the couscous and work them in with your hands.

Toast the almonds and nuts very lightly under the broiler. Save a handful of almonds and pistachios to decorate, chop the rest very coarsely, then work them into the couscous mixture, breaking up any lumps. Press the mixture into a large round cake pan or baking dish and heat through in the oven, covered with foil. Turn out onto a serving dish and pat back into shape if necessary. When you are ready to serve, dust all over with confectioners' sugar and the remaining cinnamon, and garnish with the whole almonds and pistachios.

Scodelline

Egg and Almond Cream

SERVES 6

This golden cream made with egg yolks and almonds is part of the Portuguese legacy which came to Livorno with Marrano settlers and is still to be found there and among the "Livornese" community of Tunis (they call it "scoudilini"). It is so rich that you can only eat a few teaspoonfuls. It is served in very tiny pots. In Tunis you also find it as a filling for sponge cake and in little tartlets (barquettes). I like to offer a dollop alongside a slice of cake, as a sauce or custard.

> ⅓ cup (75 ml) water
> ⅓ cup (75 g) sugar
> A little squeeze of lemon juice
> ½ cup (75 g) ground almonds
> 1 or 2 drops (not more) almond extract
>   (optional)
> 6 egg yolks, lightly beaten
> 1 teaspoon grated lemon or orange zest
>   (optional)
> ½–1 teaspoon cinnamon

In a small pan, boil the water with the sugar and lemon juice for 5 minutes. Stir in the almonds and almond extract. (This is to give the flavor of a few bitter almonds, which are traditionally added, but do not add more than 2 drops or the taste will be unpleasant.) Remove from the heat and beat in the egg yolks. Add grated lemon or orange zest if you like, then put the pan in a larger pan of boiling water (a *bain marie*) and stir constantly until the mixture thickens to a thick cream.

Pour into 6 tiny pots and serve cold, sprinkled with cinnamon.

VARIATIONS

• Judith Jackson has a Portuguese recipe for "scudalini," also called "jemma." It is without almonds. Make a thick, sticky, vanilla-flavored syrup by boiling ½ cup (100 g) sugar and ⅓ cup (75 ml) water with a vanilla bean split in half. Beat in 6 egg yolks and cook in a double boiler, stirring, until the mixture thickens. I saw her make it when we were lecturing and demonstrating together at the Sephardi synagogue on Lauderdale Road, on the occasion of an exhibition on "The Jews and the Golden Age of Spain," sponsored by the Spanish embassy. The recipe is from Judith's mother, Tess Levy Blackburn, who was born in Lisbon in 1903. The family, of Iberian origin, had moved to Gibraltar and Portugal from Marseilles in the nineteenth century. Tess used to fill minuscule marzipan pies called "queijinhos" with jemma. Now she puts the egg cream in jars to spread on bread.

Monte Sinai con Uova Filate

Almond Pastry with Egg Threads

SERVES 10

This is a very curious Italian Jewish sweet—an almond pastry base topped with egg yolk threads cooked in syrup. It is very Portuguese and almost identical to a sweet called "Bola d'Amor" in *The Jewish Manual*, published in London in 1846 (see pages 183–84), presumably by Lady Judith Montefiore, whose husband's family was from Livorno.

They still make it in Livorno to celebrate Purim. The pastry came to the city in the sixteenth century with the Marranos, who settled in large numbers. It is sometimes molded in the shape of a Star of David. It is very rich, so serve only tiny portions.

For the macaroon pastry base

> ½ cup (100 g) sugar
> Grated zest of 1 orange
> 1⅓ cups (200 g) ground almonds
> 1 egg
> 3 tablespoons finely chopped preserved citrus
>   peels

For the egg threads

> 2¼ cups (500 g) sugar
> 1 cup (250 ml) water
> 1 tablespoon lemon juice
> 1–2 tablespoons orange-blossom water
> 8 egg yolks

For the pastry base, put the sugar in a pan with 4 tablespoons of water and bring to the boil. Simmer a few minutes, until thick and sticky, but do not let it brown. Add the orange zest and ground almonds, stir vigorously, and remove from the heat. Let it cool a little, then beat in the egg.

Line the bottom of a round cake pan or baking dish about 9½ inches (24 cm) in diameter with foil or greaseproof paper. Pour in the almond mixture. It will make a very thin layer. Bake in a preheated 300°F (150°C) oven for 30 minutes. Let it cool, then invert onto a serving plate and peel off the foil or paper.

To make the egg threads, prepare a syrup in a wide pan by boiling the sugar with the water and lemon juice until it is thick enough to coat a spoon. Pour about half the egg yolks into a colander and let them run through the holes into the boiling syrup, moving the colander in a circling motion, so that the yolks make threads. Help the yolks through with a spoon. When the surface of the syrup is full of egg threads, push them in with the back of a fork and let them cook a few seconds, till set but still soft. Lift them out with a slotted spoon and drain on paper towels. Continue with the remaining yolks. Add water to the syrup if it becomes too thick. Put the cooked yolk threads in the (washed) colander and rinse off some of the syrup with cold water, then let them dry. Spread the preserved citrus peel on the pastry base and the egg threads on top.

Bruscadelle
Toasted Bread in Red Wine

This is not so much a sweet as an old custom. In Piedmont they break the fast of Yom Kippur with slices of toasted brioche-type bread (use hallah) sprinkled lightly with sugar and cinnamon and left to soak in the local strong red wine until they are very soft and soggy.

Pastries, Sweetmeats, and Fruit Preserves

IN A WORLD where the ideal was to be constantly surrounded by family and friends, where visiting was the main recreation and entertaining the most desirable activity, pastries had a very important place. Visitors calling unexpectedly at any time in the morning or afternoon would be graciously received with little cups of strong black coffee or tea or a cold syrup like almond milk or tamarind and sweet delicacies. In Egypt women spent much of their time together. In my grandmother's day they entertained each other by playing the lute. In my mother's time they played cards—games like *poula, canasta, j'achète, quatorze cartes,* and *coum-cam*—or they chatted and did their *petits points.* In the evenings card games were arranged around the men. On the Sabbath and on Sundays entire families visited each other. Every family kept stocks of pastries, sweetmeats, and jars of fruit preserves which they set out artfully on silver or crystal platters.

Among my father's bachelor-day stories were those of his invitations by families that had daughters. The parents always said their daughters had made the sweets they offered him, even when he recognized them as those sold by the vendor in the street. Pastry-making was one of the commercial activities of the inhabitants of the Haret el Yahoud (the Jewish quarter) and their pastries were readily identifiable.

A wide variety of pastries were ever-present at weddings, engagements, and ritual-bath ceremonies, and at every Jewish holiday, when it was the custom to spend the time visiting. Sweet things were a symbol of joy and happiness. Platters full of mixed petits-fours and little pastries were exchanged by families and sent around to non-Jewish friends and neighbors. Those whose children were to be married were constantly sending tray-fulls to future in-laws.

SUGAR

Jews were involved historically in the sugar trade. In 1532, Portuguese Marranos transplanted the cultivation of sugar cane from Madeira to Brazil, and when they fled from Portuguese Brazil to the West Indian islands owned by the Dutch, French, and English, they established plantations and introduced techniques for drying and crystallizing sugar (John Cooper, *Eat and Be Satisfied*). They helped the Dutch to establish sugar industries in Barbados, Jamaica, and Surinam and to produce sugar in Martinique. Jews also owned sugar refineries in Amsterdam and Egypt, as well as in Poland and Russia.

Konafa à la Crème

SERVES 12

This crisp vermicellilike pastry with a cream filling, which is eaten hot with a fragrant syrup poured over, was an important party dish in our community in Egypt, as it was in Syria. Muslims made it with a bland white cheese, Jews favored a cream filling with ground rice. It is very easy to make, but the pastry sold here under the Greek name "kadaif" is not easy to find. Only a few Oriental stores and the occasional bakery that sells fresh filo have it.

For the syrup

2½ cups (500 g) sugar
1¼ cups (300 ml) water
2 tablespoons lemon juice
2 tablespoons orange-blossom water

For the filling

½ cup (125 g) plus 1 tablespoon rice flour
5½ cups (1¼ liters) cold milk
4 tablespoons sugar
⅔ cup (150 ml) heavy cream (optional)

For the pastry

1 lb (500 g) konafa (kadaif)
8 oz (250 g) unsalted butter, melted
⅔ cup (100 g) pistachios, coarsely chopped,
    to garnish

Make the syrup first. Boil the sugar, water, and lemon juice for 10–15 minutes, then add the orange-blossom water. Let it cool, then chill in the refrigerator.

For the filling, mix the rice flour with enough of the cold milk to make a smooth paste. Boil the rest of the milk. Add the rice flour paste, stirring vigorously with a wooden spoon. Leave on very low heat and continue to stir constantly until the mixture thickens, being careful not to let it burn on the bottom. Add the sugar and stir well. Let it cool before adding the heavy cream and mixing well.

Put the konafa pastry in a large bowl and pull the strands apart to loosen them. Pour on the slightly cooled melted butter, then work it in with your hands, so that the strands are thoroughly coated. Spread half the pastry at the bottom of a 12-inch (30-cm) round pie plate.

Spread the cream over it evenly and cover with the rest of the pastry. Press down and flatten with the palm of your hand. Bake in a preheated 350°F (180°C) oven for about 1 hour. Then raise the temperature to 425°F (220°C) for about 10 minutes, until the pastry colors slightly.

Just before serving, run a sharp knife around the pie to loosen the sides and turn out, inverting it onto a large serving dish. Pour the cold syrup all over and sprinkle the top with the chopped pistachios.

Alternatively, you can pour only half the syrup before serving and pass the rest around in a jug for people to help themselves to more.

Notes

• If you want to brown the top of the pie (though that is not usual, some like to do it), run the bottom of the pan over a burner before turning it out upside down.

• You can make 2 small pies, and one can go in the freezer, before baking, for another time.

VARIATIONS

• For a cheese filling—one of my special favorites—use homemade gebna beida (white cheese, page 271) or mix 1½ lbs (750 g) ricotta with ¾ lb (350 g) grated or chopped mozzarella. (There is no added sugar.) This too is served hot with syrup poured over. We called it "konafa bi gebna." In Jerusalem "knafe bi jibn" is made with semolina, but in Nablus it is made as we do with konafa. In Lebanon, where they call it "osmanlia," they make it with crushed or chopped konafa (mafrouka).

• For a nut filling, spread 4 cups (500 g) chopped walnuts or pistachios and 3½ cups finely ground almonds. (If you are using walnuts, mix them with 1 teaspoon of cinnamon.) This pastry is served cold.

Baclawa
Multi-Layered Nut-Filled Pastry

MAKES ABOUT 50 PIECES

Baclawa was associated with celebration in all the Jewish communities throughout the Middle East. Muslims prepared it during Ramadan, and Jews made it for most of their festivals. Family members always offered to make it for special occasions like weddings and bar mitzvahs as a gesture of affection. The pistachio filling was considered the grandest. Everyone was a purist and a traditionalist, but there were different fillings and different philosophies about how finely the nuts should be chopped and whether the syrup should be hot or cold when it touched the hot pastry. Families inherited their special tricks, which were passed down, and they were contemptuous of other ways. To depart from my mother's way (her recipe is in my book of Middle Eastern food), I am giving my cousin Irene's recipe, which she inherited from her grandmother, my aunt Latifa.

Baklawa was always made on a round tray. The sheets were placed so that the corners came up all around the tray, and these were trimmed with scissors. But it makes more sense to use a rectangular tray. As it is very rich and sweet (though not as sweet as commercial varieties), portions should be very small.

3½ cups (500 g) pistachios, walnuts, or almonds
3 tablespoons superfine sugar
6 oz (175 g) unsalted butter
½ cup (100 ml) sunflower oil
1 lb (500 g) filo (use the finest sheets you can get) (see page 297)

For the syrup

2¼ cups (500 g) sugar
1 cup (250 ml) water
Juice of ½ lemon
2 tablespoons orange-blossom water

For the filling: Grind or chop the nuts or almonds medium fine and blend with the 3 tablespoons of sugar. Melt the butter with the oil. Pour about 4 tablespoons of the butter mixture over the nuts and mix well.

Grease a 12-inch (30-cm) baking pan or dish. Fit half the pastry sheets in the tray, one at a time, brushing each generously with the melted-butter-and-oil mixture, easing the filo into the corners, folding and overlapping as required, and trimming the edges as it spills over the rim. Spread the nut or almond mixture evenly over the sheets. Cover with the remaining sheets of filo, one at a time, brushing each, including the top, with the melted-butter-and-oil mixture.

With a sharp-pointed knife, cut parallel lines right through all the layers to the bottom, making small diamond shapes about 2–3 inches (5–7 cm) long and 1½–2 inches (4–5 cm) wide

(you can make them tiny if you like). Bake in a preheated 325°F (180°C) oven for about 1 hour. If it is not browned, raise the heat to 400°F (200°C) for a few minutes until golden.

While the pastry is in the oven, make the syrup: Simmer the sugar and water with the lemon juice for 10 minutes, then add the orange-blossom water. Let it cool.

Take the baclawa out of the oven, cool for 5 minutes, and pour the syrup all over, particularly along the cut lines. Then put it in the oven for 5 minutes more at the same high heat (this last procedure is unorthodox and frowned upon, but it was Latifa's secret trick, and the pastry made this way is among the best I have eaten). If you do not want the pastry too sweet, reduce the amount of syrup by up to half. Serve cold.

VARIATIONS

• In Turkey and Iraq they perfume the syrup with rose water.

• If walnuts are used, 1 teaspoon of cinnamon is added to them.

• A popular filling in Baghdad is finely ground blanched almonds flavored with 1 teaspoon ground cardamom.

Note

• According to Mavis Hyman (*Indian Jewish Cooking*) in Calcutta, gifts of jewelry from a bridegroom to a bride would be sent with a dish of baklawa "to sweeten the mouth." The filling she gives for 1 lb (500 g) of pastry is: 6½ cups (1 kg) ground blanched almonds mixed with ¾ cup (175 g) sugar, 6 tablespoons rose water, and the crushed seeds from 8–10 cardamom pods. It is divided in 3 equal parts, to make 3 layers of filling between the sheets.

Rose aux Amandes

Marzipan Coil in Filo Pastry

SERVES 12

This is a splendid pastry and easy to make. In Morocco they call it a "snake" ("m'hencha"), but the Jews there call it a "rose." It is made for special occasions like weddings. Since it is quite rich, the portions should be small. Serve it for tea, or after dinner with coffee. When I made it, I noted on my sheet "really wonderful"—and it is. You must try it.

> 1½ cups (250 g) blanched almonds
> ¾ cup (150 g) sugar
> 2 eggs, lightly beaten
> Grated zest of 1 lemon
> 1 or 2 drops (no more) almond extract
>   (optional)
> 4 tablespoons butter, melted
> 3 sheets of filo
> 1 egg yolk for glazing
> Confectioners' sugar to sprinkle on
> 1 teaspoon cinnamon to sprinkle on

For the filling, grind the almonds with the sugar in the food processor. Add the eggs, lemon zest, almond extract, and 2 tablespoons of the melted butter and blend to a creamy paste.

Open out the sheets of filo when you are ready to use them and keep them in a pile. Brush the top one lightly with melted butter. Put a line of filling about ¾ inch (2 cm) thick along one long edge and roll up into a thin roll, tucking the ends in to stop the filling from oozing out. To curve the roll without tearing the filo, you have to crease it first like an accordion by pushing the ends towards the center with both hands. Lift the roll up with both hands and place it in the middle of grease-proof or wax paper or a greased sheet of foil on a flat baking sheet or the detachable bottom of a tart pan. Curve it very gently, like a snail shell. Do the same with the other sheets, rolling them up with the filling inside, curving the rolls, and placing them end to end to make a long coil.

Brush the top with the egg yolk mixed with a drop of water and bake at 350°F (180°C) for ¾ hour, or until crisp and browned on top.

Serve cold, sprinkled with confectioners' sugar and cinnamon.

Sansaticos

Nut-Filled Filo Triangles
in Syrup

MAKES ABOUT 40

> 1 lb (500 g) filo (see page 297)
> 5 oz (150 g) butter, melted, or about
>   ¾ cup (175 ml) light vegetable
>   oil

For the syrup

> 1¼ cups (250 g) sugar
> ⅔ cup (150 ml) water
> 1 tablespoon lemon juice
> 3 tablespoons liquid honey
> 1–2 tablespoons rose water

For filling 1

3 cups (350 g) walnuts, coarsely ground
1 cup (175 g) sugar
1–1½ tablespoons cinnamon
Grated zest of 1 orange

For filling 2

3 cups (350 g) hazelnuts, coarsely ground
1 cup (175 g) sugar
Grated zest of 2 oranges

For filling 3

3 cups (350 g) blanched almonds or
*   pistachios, coarsely ground*
1 cup (175 g) sugar
1 tablespoon orange-blossom water
1 tablespoon rose water

To make the syrup, boil the sugar and water with the lemon juice for about 10 minutes, until thick enough to coat a spoon, then add honey and rose water and cook a minute longer.

Prepare one of the fillings by mixing the ingredients listed.

Take the sheets of filo out of the package when you are ready to use them. Leave them in a pile and, using scissors, cut them in half along the width, so as to have rectangles approximately 14 by 9 inches (36 by 23 cm), and put them together in 1 pile. Brush the top sheet lightly with melted butter or oil and fold it in half, bringing the long sides of the strip together, making a strip about 4 inches (10 cm) wide. Brush the strip with butter or oil and put a heaping tablespoon of filling at one short end, about

1¼ inches (3 cm) from the edge. Fold the edge over the filling, then fold diagonally again and again, wrapping the filling in a triangular package. Repeat with the rest of the cut sheets of filo and put each triangular package on a greased baking sheet.

Brush the tops with melted butter or oil, and bake in a preheated 350°F (180°C) oven for 30 minutes, or until crisp and golden. Do not let them get too brown. Dip the pastries as they come hot out of the oven, a few at a time, into the cold syrup, leaving them in for a minute or two. Lift them out and serve hot or cold.

VARIATIONS

• These pastries may also be deep-fried in not-too-hot oil, then drained and dipped in syrup.

• For the Tunisian filling called "breik aux amandes," mix 4 cups (400 g) ground almonds with 1 cup (200 g) sugar, the grated zest of 1–2 oranges, 2 drops of almond extract, and 3 eggs. This makes enough for about 40 pastries, using 1 tablespoon of filling for each cigar or triangle. Bake or deep-fry, and dip (or not) in syrup.

• In Algeria they make the same pastries and call them "beztels aux amandes." They perfume the syrup with the grated zest of 1 lemon.

Assabih bi Loz–Cigares aux Noix

Nut Fingers

MAKES ABOUT 56

"Assabih" means "fingers" in Arabic. That is what we called them. In Turkey and North

Africa they are called "cigars." They are slim rolls of filo pastry stuffed with chopped almonds, pistachios, or walnuts, baked or deep-fried, and sprinkled with confectioners' sugar or soaked in syrup. A Jewish favorite in every Middle Eastern community, they were present at parties and celebrations and were brought to the *mikvah* (ritual bath) by the bride's mother to offer to the women relatives from both sides who accompanied the bride to the bath. The bridegroom sent a basket with a bathrobe, towels, wooden bath clogs encrusted with mother-of-pearl, soaps, and perfumes.

Our own favorite in Egypt was "assabih bi loz"—almond fingers.

3½ cups (500 g) ground almonds
1¼ cups (250 g) superfine sugar or to taste
6 tablespoons orange-blossom water (see
    below)
1 lb (500 g) filo
6 oz (175 g) unsalted butter, melted
Confectioners' sugar to dust with

For the filling, mix the ground almonds, superfine sugar (the quantity here is less than the usual for this pastry), and orange-blossom water. (The quality we get here is a diluted variety. If you have the concentrated orange-blossom water, 3 tablespoons are enough. Mix it with 3 tablespoons of water.) Work the mixture with your hand until the moisture, combined with the oil in the almonds, binds it slightly together.

Cut the sheets of filo into rectangles, about 4 inches (10 cm) on one side, the width of the sheets in the other. Put them in a pile so that the strips do not dry out. Brush each strip lightly with melted butter. Put 1 heaping teaspoon of filling along 1 short end of each rectangle. Roll up like a cigarette. A third of the way, tuck in the

ends to trap the filling and continue to roll so that the roll looks like an open cigar. Arrange on a greased baking sheet. Brush the tops with butter and bake in a preheated 350°F (180°C) oven for 30–40 minutes, or until crisp and golden. Let them cool before dusting with confectioners' sugar.

VARIATIONS

• For a delicious Baghdad flavor, add ½ teaspoon of ground cardamom to the filling.

• For a splendid filling—considered the grandest—use ground or finely chopped pistachios.

• For another delicious filling, use coarsely chopped walnuts instead of ground almonds, and rose water instead of orange-blossom water, and mix with 1–2 teaspoons of cinnamon or the grated rind of 1 orange.

• For "assabih in syrup," use only 4 tablespoons of sugar in the filling. Deep-fry the pastries in oil, drain on paper towels, or bake them as above till crisp and brown, then dip for a few seconds in cold sugar syrup. The syrup is made by boiling 2¼ cups (500 g) sugar, 1 cup (250 ml) water with the juice of ½ lemon, then adding 1 tablespoon rose or orange-blossom water.

Breik aux Dattes
Date Pastries

These Tunisian pastries are made with the pastry called "malsouka," but you can use filo and prepare the pastries following the methods for making filo cigars (page 300) or triangles (page 298). You may bake or fry them, and dip them or not in a syrup.

Date Pastries (cont.)

For the filling, to make enough for about 36 pastries, using 14 oz (400 g) filo: Blend to a soft paste 12 oz (350 g) of a soft variety of dried pitted dates, ¼ cup (50 g) chopped almonds, ½ teaspoon cinnamon, the grated zest of ½ orange, and 2 egg yolks. Use a tablespoon of filling for each pastry.

For the syrup, put 1 lb (500 g) sugar and 1 cup (250 ml) water in a pan. Bring to the boil and add 2 teaspoons lemon juice and the grated zest of ½ orange. Simmer for 10 minutes, stir in 3 tablespoons of honey and 2 or 3 drops of vanilla extract, and cook for a moment more.

Arrange the pastries on a greased baking tray, brush the tops with oil or melted butter, and bake in a preheated 350°F (180°C) oven for 30–40 minutes, until crisp and brown. As they come out of the oven, plunge in batches into the cold syrup. Leave for a minute, then transfer to a serving dish. Alternatively, sprinkle with confectioners' sugar. Serve hot or cold.

Bulemas Dulses de Balabak

Filo Coils with Sweet Pumpkin Filling

MAKES ENOUGH FILLING FOR 8 PIES

These pies are a specialty of the Georgian Jews who settled in Istanbul. They are shaped in a coil (they call it a "rose") like the rodanchas

on page 301. Make filo coils as described on page 301. Use the filling below with 4 sheets of filo, 4 tablespoons oil to brush the sheets, and 1 egg yolk mixed with 1 teaspoon of water to brush the tops of the pies.

> 2 lb (1 kg) pumpkin
> ½ cup (100 g) sugar or to taste
> 4 eggs, lightly beaten
> 1 teaspoon cinnamon

Peel the pumpkin and remove seeds and fibrous bits. Steam in a saucepan with about ½ cup (125 ml) water, with the lid on, for 20 minutes, or until soft. (It will release its own water.)

Drain, chop, and mash in a colander. Leave for 10 minutes to allow the juices to drain, and press as much out as you can with your hand. Dry the pulp further by turning it back into the pan and stirring over low heat. Let it cool a little, then mix with the rest of the ingredients.

Les Cornes de Gazelle

Pastry Crescents Filled with Almond Paste

MAKES 24–26

I was unable to go to the wedding of my friend Raymonde Bendaoud's son Giles in Paris. One of the highlights, as she later described to me, was the hundreds of cornes de gazelle she had brought along from Fez. These legendary Moroccan pastries (the name means "gazelle's horns") are a specialty of that city, but they are now part of every Jewish North African celebration.

The oil-based pastry in this particular recipe has a delicate orange perfume, and the filling you crack into is lovely and creamy and not too sweet.

For the pastry

> 3¼ cups (500 g) flour
> 2 eggs, lightly beaten
> ½ cup (125 ml) vegetable oil
> 6–8 tablespoons fresh orange juice, or as required

For the filling

> 3¼ cups (350 g) ground almonds
> 1 cup (200 g) sugar
> 1 egg, lightly beaten
> 1 egg yolk
> Grated zest of 1 lemon or 1 orange
> 1 or 2 drops of vanilla extract (optional)

For the pastry, mix the flour with the eggs and the oil very thoroughly. Then bind with just enough orange juice to hold it together in a soft, malleable dough. Wrap in plastic and leave to rest for ½ hour.

Mix the filling ingredients to a soft paste. Divide the pastry dough into 4 for easier handling, then roll out as thin as possible on a floured surface into sheets. Cut into 4-inch (10-cm) squares. Take a lump of almond paste and shape into a thin little sausage a finger long. Place in the middle of a square, diagonally, on the bias, about ⅓ inch (1 cm) from the corners. Fold the dough over the filling (a wide-bladed knife helps to lift the dough) and roll up, then very gently curve into a crescent, turning the ends away so that the corner point is on the outside of the crescent. Arrange on oiled baking sheets and bake in a preheated 375°F (190°C) oven for 30 minutes. The crescents should not turn brown, but only just begin to color. They

Jewish feast, Algiers, 1835

will be soft. Do not try to move them until they are cool and firm. Dip in confectioners' sugar to cover completely.

VARIATIONS

• Some people cut the pastry into rounds, place a line of filling in the middle, and fold the pastry over the filling to make a half-moon shape. They pinch the edges together, trim some of the excess rounded edge, and curve the pastries slightly into crescents.

• The half-moon-shaped "sambousak bi loz" of the Syrian and Iraqi communities is similar, but the filling is flavored with a drop of orange-blossom or rose water or with ground cardamom.

Babee bi Tamr

Iraqi Date-Filled Pies

MAKES ABOUT 20

These little pies are made of bread dough stuffed with date paste. The crust is thin and crisp, the inside creamy. It is best to use a soft variety of dried pitted dates.

    1 tablespoon dry yeast
    1 cup (250 ml) lukewarm water
    1 teaspoon sugar
    4 oz (125 g) butter
    3¼ cups (500 g) flour
    ½ teaspoon salt
    2 teaspoons ground fennel seeds

    2 tablespoons vegetable oil to grease the dough
    ¾ lb (375 g) pitted dates
    1 whole egg, lightly beaten, for glazing
    4 tablespoons sesame seeds

Mix the yeast in about ¾ cup (175 ml) of the water, add the sugar, and leave in a warm place for about 10 minutes, until it froths.

In the food processor, cream the butter, then add the flour, salt, and fennel seed and blend well. Gradually pour in the yeast-and-water mixture and process until well blended. Turn the mixture into a bowl and work with your hands to a soft ball, adding a little water if it is too dry or a little flour if it is too sticky. Knead by hand for 15–20 minutes (or more briefly in the food processor). Pour a little oil in the bowl, and turn the ball of dough in it to prevent a dry skin from forming. Cover with plastic wrap and leave to rest in a warm place for 2 hours, or until doubled in bulk.

Meanwhile, prepare the filling. If you have the soft variety of pitted dates, they can be turned into a creamy paste in the food processor with 4–5 tablespoons of water. If they are a dry variety, they should be chopped up and heated in a pan with the water until they soften, then mashed with a fork.

When the dough is well risen, knead it again for a few minutes. Take a lump the size of a walnut, roll into a ball, and flatten in your hand so that you have a round of about 3 inches (7½ cm) in diameter. Put a heaping teaspoon of filling in the middle, and lift the edges up over the filling to meet at the top, pinching them firmly together to close the dough into a ball. It does not matter if it looks messy—the good side will be the other, flat and smooth, side. Repeat with the rest of the dough and filling. Flatten the balls a little and arrange about 1½ inches (4 cm) apart on parchment paper on baking sheets, smooth side up. Brush the tops with the egg mixed with I teaspoon of water. Make a few holes in the tops with a fork to prevent the pies from puffing up, and sprinkle with sesame seeds. Bake in a preheated 350°F (180°C) oven for about 40 minutes, until golden. Let them cool.

VARIATIONS

- Adding 3 tablespoons of melted butter or oil to the date paste in the pan gives a more unctuous texture to the paste.
- You may brush the tops with egg whites alone (the seeds will not stick if you use the yolk alone).

Menena–Maamoul
Stuffed Tartlets

"Menena" is the Jewish name for the Arab "maamoul," and it is a little different from the Arab version—at least that is what I learned when I went back to Egypt and Muslim friends said they missed ours. Every Jewish family kept a boxful, and continued to do so for decades after they left. My mother always had a supply. For years she looked for the exact dented pincers with which we had made a little design on the top, and in the end she found somebody who made it for her—even though a fork could do just as well. The flour-and-butter pastry is perfumed with flower water and meltingly soft. The most common filling is with walnuts, the most prestigious with pistachios, and there is a lovely variation with a date paste. It is one of our greats.

For the dough

3⅓ cups (500 g) flour
2 tablespoons sugar
8 oz (250 g) unsalted butter
1 tablespoon rose or orange-blossom water
1 tablespoon milk or as required
Confectioners' sugar to sprinkle on

For the nut filling

1½ cups (200 g) walnuts or pistachios, finely chopped
4–6 tablespoons sugar
1 teaspoon cinnamon (only for the walnut filling)
2 tablespoons rose or orange-blossom water

For the date filling

10 oz (300 g) pitted dates, preferably a soft variety
4–6 tablespoons water or as required

For the dough, mix the flour and sugar and rub in the butter. (You may do this in the food processor, then turn into a bowl.) Add the flower water and just enough milk to bind the dough into a soft, malleable ball.

For the nut filling, mix all the ingredients together. For the date filling, blend the dates in the food processor with just enough water to make a soft paste.

Take walnut-sized lumps of dough. For each, make a hole in the center with your thumb and enlarge it by pinching the sides as if shaping a little pot, turning and pressing against your palm. The walls should be quite thin; any breaks are easily patched. Fill the hole with one of the fillings to three-quarters full, and bring the dough up over the opening to close into a ball. Flatten the filled balls slightly and arrange on a baking sheet with the smooth side on top. Make a design by pinching all over the top with dented pincers or by pricking with a fork. Bake in a preheated 325°F (160°C) oven for 20–30 minutes—no longer. Do not let them brown. The pastries will be very soft and still pale when they come out of the oven, but they will firm when they cool. Do not try to move them until they do. Sprinkle with confectioners' sugar.

Ataif

Pancakes in Syrup

MAKES 32 TINY OPEN ATAIF

There are two versions of this wonderful Syrian sweet. The pancakes can be tiny and topped with thick cream and a sprinkling of pistachios, or they can be large and stuffed with chopped walnuts or a soft bland cheese. Both kinds are soaked in a syrup that gives them a soft, spongy texture and a delicate perfume. Those topped with cream and the ones stuffed with cheese are specialties of Shavuot. You will find the stuffed ataif as variations.

For the batter

1 teaspoon active dry yeast
1 teaspoon sugar
1½ cups (350 ml) warm water
1⅓ cups (200 g) flour

For the syrup

1¼ cups (300 ml) water
2½ cups (500 g) sugar
Juice of ½ lemon
1 tablespoon orange-blossom or rose water

For the cream topping

½ lb (250 g) kaimak (see page 562),
    clotted cream, or mascarpone
1¼ cups (150 g) pistachios, finely chopped

For the batter, dissolve the yeast and sugar in ½ cup of the water and leave until it froths. Put the flour in a bowl, and add the yeast mixture and the rest of the water gradually, beating vigorously, to make a creamy, lump-free batter. Cover with plastic wrap and leave to rest for about an hour.

To make the syrup, bring to the boil the water with the sugar and lemon juice and simmer 10 minutes, then add the orange-blossom or rose water.

Make the tiny open ataif (pancakes), a few at a time, in a nonstick frying pan greased with a little oil. Pour the batter by the tablespoonful, making several little rounds that are not touching, in the pan at the same time. Cook over medium-low heat. As little holes form on top and the little pancakes come away from the pan and become golden on the bottom, turn and do the other side. Drop them into the syrup as they are done. To serve, arrange in one layer. Spread each with kaimak, clotted cream, or mascarpone. Sprinkle with chopped pistachios and pour the remaining syrup over them.

VARIATIONS

• To make about 12 (large) stuffed ataif with cheese (ataif bi jibn), pour the batter by the half-ladleful and cook on one side only (this is important), until the surface has lost its whiteness. Stuff the pancakes as you go along, while they are still warm and moist—otherwise they will not stick together easily. For the filling, use ¾ lb (375 g) half-and-half mixture of ricotta and mozzarella blended to a paste in the food processor. Put a heaping tablespoonful in the middle of each pancake, on the uncooked side, fold over the filling to make a half-moon shape, and close the pastries by pressing the edges firmly together. Deep-fry briefly in medium-hot oil until brown. Lift them out with a perforated spoon, drain on paper towels, and dip in the syrup. Serve preferably hot.

• For a walnut filling for ataif bi goz, mix 2 cups (250 g) finely chopped walnuts with 4 tablespoons sugar, I teaspoon cinnamon, and I tablespoon rose or orange-blossom water.

Bimuelos or Zalabia

Fritters in Syrup

SERVES 6

Fritters of all kinds fried in oil are the specialty of Hanukah, the Festival of Lights, when they recall the miracle of the oil (see page 33), and also a pastry of Purim, when they are shaped supposedly like Haman's ears (page 592). "Bimuelos" is the Judeo-Spanish name for the little flour-and-yeast fritters. In Egypt, where they were sold in the street, they were called "zalabia," and in Iraq, Persia, and India they were "zengoula." All over the Middle East they were eaten at Hanukah. After a day of trying and eating different versions, I felt that the Judeo-Spanish saying that Hanukah is *"el buen día a la tripa,"* which means "a good day for the stomach," is not at all true.

For the sugar syrup

> 5 cups (1 kg) sugar
> 2 cups (500 ml) water
> Juice of ½ lemon
> 1 tablespoon rose or orange-blossom water

For the batter

> 2 teaspoons active dry yeast
> 1 teaspoon sugar
> About 3 cups (750 ml) warm water
>   (1 part boiling to 2 parts cold)
> 3⅓ cups (500 g) flour
> ½ teaspoon salt

> Light vegetable oil for deep-frying

For the syrup, put the sugar, water, and lemon juice in a pan and simmer for 15 minutes, or until it is thick enough to coat a spoon. Add the rose or orange-blossom water and simmer a few seconds longer, then chill, covered.

For the batter, dissolve the yeast and sugar

in about ½ cup (125 ml) of the warm water, and let stand 10–15 minutes, until it froths. Put the flour in a large bowl, mix in the salt and the yeast mixture, then stir in the remaining water gradually and beat vigorously for about 10 minutes, until smooth and elastic. Cover with a damp cloth and leave to rise in a warm place for at least 1 hour, then beat the batter once more and let it rise again.

Make the fritters in batches. Pour little balls of batter by the teaspoon or tablespoon (they can be small or large) into 1½ inches (4 cm) sizzling but not too hot oil and fry until puffed up, crisp, and golden, turning them to brown them all over. You may find it easier if you dip the spoon in oil so that the batter rolls off easily. Lower the heat a little to give the fritters time to get done inside before they are too brown. The batter is light and produces irregular, rather than perfectly round, shapes. If the oil is not hot enough to begin with, the batter tends to flatten out.

Lift the fritters out with a slotted spoon, drain on paper towels, and dip them in the cold syrup for a few seconds, or let them soak up the syrup for longer. They are at their best hot, but are also good cold.

VARIATIONS

• Instead of dipping the fritters in the sugar syrup, you can pour over them a honey syrup made by heating honey with about half its volume of water.

• You can also sprinkle instead with confectioners' sugar and cinnamon.

Fazuelos–Figeolas–Mafis–Orecchie di Ammon

Fried Haman's Ears

Every Sephardi community has a sweet shaped like Haman's ears to celebrate Purim. This one—a pasta dough deep-fried in oil—is the most common. It is also a Hanukah specialty, because of the oil (see page 33). The recipe I have chosen is from Turkey. It is unusual in that brandy is added to the egg-pasta dough. It comes out crisp and light and keeps very well in a tin or other airtight container.

3 eggs
2 tablespoons brandy (optional)
A pinch of salt
About 2 cups (300 g) flour
Sunflower oil for deep-frying
Confectioners' sugar to sprinkle on
Cinnamon to sprinkle on

Beat the eggs lightly with the brandy and salt. Add as much flour as the eggs will absorb to make a soft dough. Start beating it in with a fork and continue working it in with your hands until the mass holds well together. Knead for 10 minutes, until the dough is smooth and elastic, adding a little more flour if it is too sticky. Wrap in plastic wrap and allow to rest for 15 minutes at room temperature before rolling out.

Divide the dough into 2 balls for easier handling. Roll each out as thin as possible on a lightly floured surface with a lightly floured rolling pin, working from the center outwards. Cut into strips 4 inches (10 cm) long and 1½ inches (4 cm) wide, and pinch each in the middle to form a butterfly (this is supposed to evoke the shape of Haman's ears). Deep-fry in batches in medium-hot oil, about 2 inches (5 cm) deep, till golden. Lift out and drain in a colander or on paper towels.

Serve cold, sprinkled with confectioners' sugar and cinnamon. They keep very well, for a long time, in a tin or other airtight container.

HOMMS DE PURIM

Honeyed Pastry Nuggets

THIS TUNISIAN PASTRY is like the Ashkenazi teiglach (page 193). The same pasta-type dough is rolled into thin ropelike rolls and cut diagonally into little nuggets, then deep-fried in moderately hot oil till golden. The drained pastry is then cooked in thick sugar syrup together with a good quantity of toasted and coarsely chopped pistachios, walnuts, hazelnuts, and pine nuts, until the syrup is brown and caramelized. The whole thing is poured onto an oiled surface and, while still warm, shaped into a sausage about 1¼ inches (3 cm) in diameter, cut in slices, and put in paper cases. It is too sweet for me.

VARIATIONS

• This type of fried dough is very common in many communities. In Bukhara, where it is the favorite Sabbath and festive pastry, the dough is cut into long ribbons like noodles.

• Georgians color the dough by adding a few drops of food coloring to the eggs. When I was preparing for a demonstration in a Jerusalem kitchen, my Georgian neighbor was making several batches of dough in different garish colors. She cut them into wide noodles, about 2 inches (5 cm) wide and 12–16 inches (30–40 cm) long, and rolled these around a broomstick handle held up horizontally, so that they were coiled when she dropped them in the oil. Georgians call them "burbushella."

• North African fazuelos or figeolas sometimes have a tablespoon of oil in the dough. The ribbons of dough (the same size as the Georgians') are pricked with a fork and coiled around it before deep-frying. The pastry is eaten with confectioners' sugar or bathed in a honey syrup: heat 1 cup (250 ml) honey with about ½ cup (125 ml) water to thin it a little, and add 2 teaspoons orange-blossom water.

• Italians use the same dough and the same honey syrup for their "orecchie di Ammon," but they shape their "ears" differently. Cut the dough into ribbons 1¼ inches (3 cm) wide and 6 inches (15 cm) long. Bring the 2 ends together in the shape of a pointed ear and stick them together with a little egg white.

Friteches–Sfereet–
Beignets de Pâques

Matzo Fritters in Syrup

MAKES ABOUT 20

Everyone has a Passover recipe for matzo-meal fritters. The North African version—called "friteches" in Tunisia and "sfereet" in Algeria—is particularly good if you like this kind of thing.

> 4 eggs, separated
> A pinch of salt
> Grated zest of 1 lemon
> 6 tablespoons matzo meal
> Oil for frying

For a honey syrup

> ¾ cup (175 g) sugar
> 1½ cups (350 ml) water
> ¾ cup (175 ml) honey
> Juice of ½ lemon

Make the syrup first. Put the sugar, water, honey, and lemon juice in a pan and bring to the boil.

For the fritters, beat the egg whites stiff. Lightly beat the yolks with the salt and lemon zest and fold into the whites. Then fold in the matzo meal, raining it on lightly. Drop by the heaping tablespoonful in moderately hot oil and deep-fry over medium heat, turning the fritters to brown them all over. Drain on paper towels and dip, while still hot, in the syrup. Let them soak for about 10 minutes and lift out with a slotted spoon. Serve hot or cold.

• For "beignets de Pâques à l'orange," dip the fritters in an orange syrup: bring to the boil 1½ cups (350 ml) freshly squeezed orange juice and ½ cup (100 g) sugar.

• You can serve them without syrup—simply sprinkled with sugar and cinnamon.

Sfenj

Orange Doughnut Rings

MAKES ABOUT 20

This was a Hanukah specialty in Morocco.

> 2 teaspoons dry yeast
> ½ cup (125 ml) or more freshly squeezed
>   orange juice, warmed
> 4 tablespoons sugar
> 3⅓ cups (500 g) flour
> Grated zest of 1 orange
> 2 eggs, lightly beaten
> 4½ tablespoons peanut or vegetable oil
> Oil for frying
> Confectioners' sugar to sprinkle on

Put the yeast in a bowl with about 4 tablespoons of the orange juice, 1 teaspoon of the sugar, and 2 tablespoons of the flour. Beat well, and leave for about 25 minutes, until it froths.

In a large bowl, mix the remaining flour with the orange zest, eggs, and 4 tablespoons of oil. Add the yeast mixture and mix well. Now add just enough orange juice to make a soft dough that holds together in a ball, adding it gradually, and working it in with your hand. Knead for about 15 minutes, till elastic and no longer sticky. Pour ½ tablespoon of oil in the bowl and turn the dough around to grease it all over. Cover the bowl with plastic wrap and leave in a warm place for about 1½ hours, until doubled in bulk.

Punch the dough down and roll out to about ⅓ inch (1 cm) thick. You do not need to flour the surface, for the dough is oily and will not stick. Cut into rounds about 3¼ inches (8 cm) in diameter. Make a hole in the middle with your finger and pull out the ring, enlarging the hole. Leave the dough rings on an oiled tray for another ½ hour to rise. Then deep-fry in batches in 2 inches (5 cm) of oil over medium-low heat (so that they do not brown too quickly), turning them over once to brown them all over. Drain on paper towels and serve dusted with confectioners' sugar or dipped in a syrup as in the recipe for bimuelos (page 591) or fritiches (page 594).

Pan d'Espanya
Sponge Cake

Serves 10

The Sephardi sponge cake, a Spanish legacy, was adopted by all Sephardi communities.

6 eggs, separated
6 tablespoons superfine sugar
Grated zest of 1 lemon or 1 orange
6 tablespoons self-rising flour

In a large bowl, beat the egg yolks and sugar to a thick, pale cream and add the lemon or orange zest. In another bowl, beat the egg whites until stiff, then fold them into the yolk mixture. Gradually fold in the flour. Pour into a well-oiled and -floured, preferably nonstick, 9-inch (23-cm) cake pan with a removable bottom, or a pan lined with baking parchment. Bake in a preheated 400°F (200°C) oven for 40 minutes. Turn out while still a little warm.

Bocca di Dama
Almond Sponge Cake

Serves 10

This is one of the popular Jewish cakes of Italy, traditionally served at the end of the meal that breaks the fast of Yom Kippur. It is Livornese, of Portuguese origin. You also find it in Tunis, where the Livornese formed an important community. It is deliciously light and moist.

5 eggs, separated
6 egg yolks
1¼ cups (250 g) sugar
1 cup (200 g) blanched almonds
Grated zest of 1 lemon
⅔ cup (100 g) flour
Confectioners' sugar to garnish
  (optional)

Beat the eleven egg yolks with the sugar in the food processor to a pale, light cream. Add the almonds and lemon zest and process to a smooth, soft paste. Then blend in the flour.

Beat the egg whites stiff in a large bowl. Pour in the egg-yolk-and-almond mixture and fold very gently. Pour into an oiled and floured 9-inch (23-cm) springform cake pan—preferably nonstick—with a detachable bottom and bake in a preheated 325°F (160°C) oven for ¾–1 hour, until firm. Turn the cake out when it has cooled and sprinkle with confectioners' sugar. I like it when it is still a little creamy in the center.

VARIATION

• The Tunisian version has 2 tablespoons of orange-blossom water instead of the lemon zest and 1 or 2 drops of almond extract to approximate the taste of bitter almonds, which are included in Tunisia.

PALLEBE

Moroccan Sponge

THE PALLEBE IS the pan d'Espanya (see page 595). When I visited a bakery in Fez once every surface, from the tops of tables and chairs to the floor, was covered by trays filled with little sponge cakes. The woman who was baking them explained that it was for a wedding and that she was going to turn them into a "paille" (this is the French spelling of the English word "pie"). These are "pièces montées de cérémonie," fantastically elaborate layered cakes, where the sponge is moistened with orange juice or rum or sugar syrup and orange-blossom water and filled with fresh fruit or fruit preserve and vanilla or caramel cream, or with chocolate mousse or coconut cream, or topped with mer-ingues. She said she had ten sons and they were all in Chicago, where they had joined the Lubavitch community.

Gato de Muez de Pesah
Walnut and Orange Passover Cake

SERVES 10

This is *the* Passover cake of Istanbul. Moist and aromatic, with a delicate orange flavor, it can well be served for dessert. The important thing is to find walnuts that do not taste stale. You must try them before you make the cake.

> *6 eggs, separated*
> *1¾ cups (375 g) sugar*
> *¾ cup (100 g) ground almonds*
> *Grated rind and juice of 1 orange*
> *1½ cups (200 g) walnuts, coarsely chopped*
> *Oil and matzo meal for the cake tin*

Beat the egg yolks with the sugar till light and pale. Add the ground almonds, then the orange juice and rind and the walnuts. Mix very well. In a separate large bowl, beat the egg whites stiff, and fold into the nut mixture. Oil a preferably nonstick springform 9-inch (23-cm) cake pan and dust with matzo meal. Pour in the cake mixture and bake for 1½ hours in a preheated 350°F (180°C) oven.

Tishpishti

Passover Walnut Cake with Syrup

SERVES 8–10

This famous Judeo-Spanish specialty of Turkey makes a rich and luscious dessert. It is best made at least a few hours before you are ready to serve, so that it has time to imbibe the syrup.

> *5 eggs, lightly beaten*
> *1¼ cups (150 g) walnuts, chopped*
> *¾ cup (100 g) ground almonds*
> *1 cup (200 g) sugar*
> *Juice and grated zest of 1 orange*
> *2 teaspoons cinnamon*

For the syrup

> *2¼ cups (500 g) sugar*
> *2 cups (500 ml) water*
> *1 tablespoon lemon juice*
> *1 tablespoon rose water*

Make the syrup first, so that it has time to chill. Boil the sugar and water with the lemon juice for 10–15 minutes. Stir in the rose water. Let it cool, then put in the refrigerator.

Mix all the cake ingredients thoroughly. Line the bottom of a cake pan with foil or greaseproof paper. Brush the foil and sides of the tin with oil and pour the cake mixture in. Bake in a preheated 350°F (180°C) oven for 1 hour, until browned. Turn the cake out upside down onto a deep serving dish as soon as it is out of the oven. Peel off the foil, cut into serving pieces, and pour the cold syrup all over the hot cake. After about ½ hour, turn the pieces over so that they can thoroughly imbibe the syrup.

VARIATION

- Use freshly squeezed orange juice instead of water for the syrup.

Gâteau au Sirop d'Orange

Almond Cake in Orange Syrup

SERVES 12–14

This most wonderful Judeo-Spanish cake, which is very like a "tarta de naranja" that I found in Spain, is one of my favorites. In the

PASSOVER CAKES

O NE OF THE gastronomic successes of Sephardi culture is the very wide range of Passover cakes made with almonds or nuts instead of flour, which are characteristic of the communities. Some, like the orange cakes, have a distinctly Iberian character. Chocolate cakes are a reminder of the early Marrano connection with the cocoa of the New World and with the first chocolate industries in Amsterdam and other Marrano centers.

ORANGES

ORANGE CAKES ARE typical of all the Mediterranean Jewish communities, even though they are not usually found in the local national cuisines. It is something these communities have in common with Spain. Jews have been associated with oranges since earliest times: they needed the citron—*etrog* in the Bible—as part of the religious ritual of the Feast of Tabernacles (Sukkot). The citron is a type of large lemon with a thick craggy skin and powerful scent (it is not edible raw, but its peel is made into a preserve and may be used as a flavoring). It was so important in Roman times that it was used as a Jewish symbol on coins and gravestones and in synagogue motifs. Silver boxes for the citron are objects of Jewish ritual art.

Because of their ritual requirements, Jews cultivated not only the citron but other citrus as well. After the fall of the Roman Empire, it was the Arabs who made the cultivation of oranges and lemons possible on a grand scale with their methods of irrigation, but the survival of citrus on the Mediterranean coasts is thought to be due to the agricultural activities of Jews. In a study on *The Influence of Religion in the Spread of Citrus Fruit* (1959), Erich Isaac finds that early centers of Jewish population coincide with the areas of citrus production in the Mediterranean today, and deduced that Jews were responsible for introducing citrus cultivation in antiquity.

Jews became known as specialists in citrus in Sicily and several other Mediterranean islands in the early Middle Ages and were invited to settle so that they could introduce the agriculture. In the twelfth century, King Roger of Sicily sent them to develop sericulture in Corfu. Jewish merchants from Northern and Eastern Europe who traveled to southern Italy and Spain, Sicily and Corfu, to purchase palm branches and citron, to celebrate the festival, were soon trading in oranges and lemons. In several North European cities, including London and Amsterdam, Jewish peddlers sold oranges and lemons from pushcarts until the beginning of this century. It is not surprising, then, that there are dozens of recipes for orange cakes and orange preserves in the Sephardi world.

Harvesting etrog, *or citron*

old Jewish quarter of Seville, the Barrio de Santa Cruz, I wandered around the squares packed with orange trees and the sinuous streets fragrant with the smell of oranges. I thought of the families who had brought the cake to Egypt—their names were the same as those of the barrio streets, and I imagined their ancestors making the cake with oranges picked in the square.

Make it at least a few hours before you are ready to serve, and preferably the day before, so that the orange juice has time to soak in. This is something you really must try.

8 eggs, separated
1 cup (200 g) sugar
Grated zest of 2 oranges
2 teaspoons cinnamon
1 cup (100 g) ground almonds
½ cup (100 g) blanched almonds, finely
    chopped

For the syrup

2½ cups (600 ml) freshly squeezed orange
    juice
1 cup (200 g) sugar

Mix well the egg yolks with the sugar, orange zest, cinnamon, and all the almonds. Beat the egg whites until stiff and fold them in. Pour into a greased and floured 10-inch (26-cm) cake pan and bake in a preheated 350°F (180°C) oven for about 1 hour.

Make a syrup by bringing to the boil the orange juice with the remaining sugar. Remove from the heat and stir to dissolve the sugar.

When the cake has cooled, make little holes on the top with a fork to allow the juice to be absorbed, and turn it out onto a deep pan or dish that will just contain it and the syrup. Pour the syrup on top and leave to soak for a few hours or overnight.

A nice way of serving this splendid cake is with orange slices in syrup (page 614).

Gâteau à l'Orange
Orange Cake

SERVES 12 OR MORE

I included this Judeo-Spanish cake, which is moist like a pudding, in my original *Book of Middle Eastern Food*, and it has been widely adopted (it is on the menu of several restaurants in Australia). But, like a few other recipes that I have already featured, it must be in this book too, because of its importance in Sephardi culture.

2 oranges
6 eggs
1¼ cups (250 g) sugar
2 tablespoons orange-blossom water
1 teaspoon baking powder
1½ cups (250 g) blanched almonds, coarsely
    ground

Wash the oranges and boil them whole for 1½ hours, or until they are very soft.

Beat the eggs with the sugar. Add the orange-blossom water, baking powder, and almonds and mix well. Cut open the oranges, remove the seeds, and puree in a food processor. Mix thoroughly with the egg-and-almond mix-

Orange Cake (cont.)

ture and pour into a 9-inch (23-cm) oiled cake pan dusted with matzo meal or flour—preferably nonstick and with a removable base. Bake in a preheated 375° (190°C) oven for an hour. Let it cool before turning out.

Torta di Mandorle e Cioccolata

Chocolate and Almond Cake

SERVES 10–12

Because Marrano Jews were involved in the early export of cocoa from Venezuela and were responsible for founding chocolate industries in Amsterdam in the mid-seventeenth century and later in France—in Bayonne and Bordeaux—Jewish chocolate cakes often have Marrano roots. I found this delightful one in a little book called *Dal 1880 ad Oggi: La Cucina Ebraica della Mia Famiglia* (1982). It is printed in the handwriting of the author, Donatella Limentani Pavoncello, and represents dishes once cooked in the Rome Ghetto. It is different in that it uses only the beaten egg whites and no yolks.

> *1½ cups (250 g) blanched almonds*
> *7 oz (200 g) dark, bittersweet chocolate*
> *1¼ cups (250 g) sugar*
> *7 egg whites*
> *Oil and flour or matzo meal for the cake pan*

Finely chop the almonds and chocolate together in a food processor, then add the sugar

and mix well. Beat the egg whites stiff and fold into the chocolate-and-almond mixture. Oil a preferably nonstick and springform 9-inch (23-cm) cake pan, then dust with flour or matzo meal. Bake in a preheated 300°F (150°C) oven for 1 hour, until firm.

Gâteau au Chocolat

Our Chocolate Cake

SERVES 10–12

I featured this chocolate cake in my first Middle Eastern book, and it has since gone into other people's books, so by now it has already had much exposure, but it is still our family favorite and an important recipe in the Passover cake collection. It was given to me by my mother's friend Lucie Ades-Schwartz. Years later she told me she forgot to put butter in the ingredients list. Although we have come to prefer the butterless cake, I will give her original, richer version and you can please yourself about adding it.

> *250 g (½ lb) dark, bittersweet chocolate*
> *4 oz (100 g) unsalted butter (optional)*
> *6 eggs, separated*
> *⅓ cup (75 g) sugar*
> *1 cup (100 g) ground almonds*
> *Flour or matzo meal for the cake pan*

Melt the chocolate and the butter together in a double boiler or a small pan placed in a larger pan with boiling water.

Beat the egg yolks with the sugar till pale. Add the ground almonds and the melted chocolate and butter and mix very well. In a separate large bowl, beat the egg whites stiff and fold them in. Grease a nonstick 9-inch (23-cm) cake pan and dust with flour or matzo meal. Pour the cake mixture in and bake in a preheated 350°F (180°C) oven for 45 minutes.

VARIATION

• Some people add the grated zest of an orange.

Torta di Datteri

Date Cake

SERVES 10

The Jewish community of the Italian port of Livorno has an ancient connection with Tunis, and there are many Livornese dishes with a Tunisian touch, like this cake. I have made it with moist California dates.

> *½ lb (250 g) dates, pitted and finely chopped*
> *1 cup (200 g) sugar*
> *1 cup (200 g) blanched almonds, finely chopped*
> *4 eggs, lightly beaten*
> *Oil and flour or matzo meal for the cake pan*

Thoroughly mix all the ingredients. Line a 9-inch (23-cm) cake pan with greaseproof paper or use a nonstick springform cake pan, rubbed with oil and dusted with flour or matzo meal. Pour in the cake mixture and bake in a preheated 350°F (180°C) oven for about 45 minutes.

Cochini Festive Cake

Spicy Semolina Cake

SERVES 8

This rather dense, thin cake has an exotic spicy flavor. The recipe came in a letter from Mrs. Queenie Halegua of Cochin, in southwestern India.

> *3 eggs*
> *⅔ cup (125 g) sugar*
> *1 cup (125 g) fine semolina*
> *1 cup (125 g) cashew nuts, finely chopped*
> *1 cup (125 g) currants, finely chopped*
> *¼ teaspoon ground nutmeg*
> *¾–1 teaspoon ground cardamom*
> *¼ teaspoon ground cloves*
> *2 tablespoons rum*
> *4½–5 oz (125–150 g) melted ghee (clarified butter) or unsalted butter*

Beat the eggs and sugar together to a pale, thick cream, then beat in the semolina. Add the nuts, currants (chopped if you like in a food processor), spices, rum, and finally the ghee or butter. Mix very thoroughly. Leave to rest for 2 hours, so that the semolina is properly soaked. Stir well before pouring into a small, 7-inch (18-cm) greased nonstick cake pan with a detachable bottom, or one lined at the bottom with greaseproof or baking paper. Bake in a preheated 350°F (180°C) oven for 45–60 minutes, till the top is brown and the cake feels firm. Turn out when it is cool.

Putizza di Noci

Trieste Yeast Roll

SERVES 15

This yeast-cake roll with a walnut-and-chocolate filling is a Slav specialty of Trieste. When the city was absorbed into the Austro-Hungarian Empire, the large Jewish community prospered enormously, to the point where a few of its members were given the title of "baron." Putizza became a Rosh Hashanah and holiday cake. The pastry is part of my childhood memories, because Maria, my Yugoslav-Italian nanny, who came from a village near Trieste, made it for us in Cairo. She made it with a poppy-seed filling. Like everything with yeast, it involves time and preparation.

> ¾ oz (20 g) fresh yeast or 1 tablespoon
>   dried yeast
> 4 tablespoons warm milk
> ½ cup (100 g) sugar
> 4⅓ cups (650 g) white bread flour
> 3 oz (80 g) butter, melted and slightly cooled
> 3 eggs
> 1 tablespoon rum
> Juice of 1 lemon
> 1 teaspoon salt
> 1 egg yolk for glazing

For the filling

> 1 cup (250 ml) wine or milk
> 1¼ cups (250 g) sugar
> 2½ cups (300 g) chopped walnuts

Grated zest of 1 lemon
7 oz (200 g) dark, bittersweet chocolate,
  grated or finely chopped in a food processor

Dissolve the yeast in the warm milk with ½ teaspoon of sugar in a large mixing bowl and leave, covered with plastic wrap, for about 10 minutes, until it froths. Add a little of the flour—enough to make a soft paste—and mix very well. Cover with plastic wrap and let it rise at room temperature for about 20 minutes, or until doubled in bulk.

Now work in the butter, eggs, rum, and lemon juice, then the salt, and the remaining sugar and flour (set some of the flour aside to add later if necessary) until everything is thoroughly blended and the dough forms a soft ball. Knead the dough for 15 minutes, until smooth and elastic and no longer sticky, adding a little more flour if necessary. Put a few drops of oil in the bowl and turn the dough in it to give it a light coating and prevent a dry crust from forming. Cover the bowl with plastic wrap and leave in a warm place for about 2–3 hours, until the dough has doubled in bulk.

For the filling, boil the wine or milk with the sugar, and add the chopped walnuts and lemon zest. Simmer, stirring often, for 10 minutes, then leave to cool.

When the dough has risen, knock it down and knead again for about 5 minutes. Roll out on a lightly floured surface into a sheet about ¼ inch (½ cm) thick. Spread the walnut mixture evenly all over it, leaving a border 1 inch (2½ cm) wide on the edges. Sprinkle the grated or chopped chocolate on top. Roll up the dough with the filling, starting from a long edge, and place the roll in a large well-buttered tray or baking dish that will contain it, seam side down, so that the dough does not open out during the baking.

Brush the top with egg yolk mixed with I tablespoon of water. Let the dough rise again for about 1½ hours, or until doubled in bulk. Bake in a preheated 375°F (190°C) oven for 45–55 minutes. Unmold the cake and tap the bottom. If it sounds hollow it is done. Leave it to cool on a wire rack.

VARIATIONS

• At Rosh Hashanah (the New Year), it is traditional to bake the roll in a 12-inch (30-cm) springform cake pan, coiled up like a snake.

• For another filling, mix ⅓ cup (60 g) pine nuts, ⅓ cup (60 g) chopped almonds, ¾ cup (100 g) chopped walnuts, ¾ cup (100 g) raisins or sultanas, and ⅓ cup (60 g) chopped candied citrus peels with I cup (250 ml) orange juice and I tablespoon bread crumbs. Bring to the boil and stir in 2 lightly beaten eggs. Remove from the heat almost at once, as soon as the eggs set to a light cream. Add sugar, if you like, to taste.

Gâteau au Coco

Moroccan Coconut Cake

SERVES 10

3 cups (250 g) dried grated coconut
1 cup (250 ml) fresh orange juice
1½ cups (300 g) sugar
4 tablespoons sunflower oil
6 eggs, separated

In a bowl, mix the dried coconut with the orange juice and leave about 20 minutes, until the coconut is soft. Add the sugar, oil, and egg yolks and mix well.

Beat the egg whites stiff and fold into the egg mixture. Then pour into a greased nonstick cake pan and bake in a preheated 350°F (180°C) oven for 45 minutes. Turn out upside down onto a plate while it is still warm. A creamy egg mixture, which will have sunk to the bottom, will come out on top.

LES FRIANDISES

Sweetmeats

WHEN ARMAND ELFERSI and his wife came to my house to talk to me about Jewish cooking in Morocco, and particularly in Essaouira, where Armand comes from, they brought a tray of mixed sweetmeats that had been sent by relatives in Israel. The Jews of North Africa, more than any, continue to make friandises— and the women from Essaouira, which used to be Mogador, are the mistresses of the art. They are famous for their ground-walnut meringues and caramelized nuts and sesame seeds, their little biscuits and coconut rocks, and for a variety of dried fruit and nuts stuffed with almond paste.

Semolina and Coconut Sabbath Cake of the Bene Israel

SERVES 12–14

This very soft and moist cardamom-scented cake is eaten for breakfast on Saturday morning by Jews in India. It derives its delicate flavor from coconut milk, which is obtained by blending fresh grated coconut with water, then straining the liquid. Solid creamed coconut or canned coconut milk or cream (see page 235) can be used instead. The cake—which is more like a pudding—reminds me (apart from the flavor) of what we called "basbousa" in Egypt.

> 14 oz (400 g) solid creamed coconut, cut in pieces
> 4 oz (100 g) butter
> 3⅓ cups (500 g) coarse semolina
> 1 cup (200 g) muscovado (unrefined brown) sugar or ordinary brown sugar
> ½ teaspoon salt
> ½ cup (100 g) whole blanched almonds
> 4 tablespoons raisins
> 4 teaspoons powdered cardamom

Bring to the boil 9 cups (2 liters) of water and put in the creamed coconut, stirring until it melts.

In a very large pot heat the butter, add the semolina, and stir over very low heat for 5–8 minutes, being careful not to let it burn. Add the sugar (muscovado is called "jaggery" in India and gives a distinctive flavor) and salt. Then pour in the coconut milk and cook, stirring until it is a thick dry paste.

Add almonds, raisins, and cardamom and stir very well. Pour into a buttered 12-inch (30-cm) baking dish and bake uncovered in a preheated 350°F (180°C) oven for ½ hour. Let it cool. Turn it out when you are ready to serve (it does not stick to the sides of the dish) and cut in slices.

Note

• To use canned coconut milk, mix 4 cups (900 ml) canned milk with 5 cups (1¼ liters) water.

Amandines

Almond Balls

MAKES 22–24 BALLS

This was our way of making marzipan. Amandines are extremely easy to make and keep for weeks. The proportions of sugar and ground almonds vary. In the past the same weight of each was used. Now people prefer to use less sugar. It used to be customary to have a few bitter almonds; now a tiny drop of almond extract intensifies the almond flavor while rose or orange-blossom water lends a delicate perfume.

MASSAPAN

ALMOND PASTE, or marzipan, is the basis of many sweetmeats and the jewel in the crown of Sephardi pastry-making and confectionery. It is served on such occasions as births, weddings, and bar mitzvahs, and it is also a specialty of Passover and Purim.

Spain is the largest commercial producer of marzipan in the world, and Toledo is the center of the trade. They have a marzipan museum, where the local delicacy is described as a product and symbol of the old Arab, Jewish, and Christian harmony in the city. Originally brought to Spain by the Arabs, it was adopted by Jews to celebrate their festivals—in particular Passover and Purim—and by Christians to celebrate Easter and Christmas. According to local tradition, the name "mazapan" came about because the Arabs in Toledo called their almond-and-sugar paste "maulhaban," meaning "sitting king"; pastries were imprinted with a coin showing a king sitting on a throne. Another conjecture is that the name comes from the jar that was used to store almonds; in Egypt we called it "martaban." The way they make marzipan in Toledo commercially is to grind and crush with rollers equal quantities of blanched almonds and sugar until the oil from the almonds binds them into a soft, smooth paste. The paste is pressed into traditional shapes, which are baked until they are slightly toasted on top.

It is interesting to note that marzipan owes its survival in Spain to its adoption as a craft by closed religious orders. Sicily is also famous for the marzipan confections made in convents. In Agrigento I visited a convent where the nuns grew their own different varieties of almond trees. Their story is that during the Arab occupation of the island this convent was for rich women who were sent there because they hadn't married. They brought with them their Arab maids, and it was they who introduced the marzipan, and also a sweet couscous with nuts, to the convents. Spanish and Italian convents go by centuries-old recipes. The lore is that the "secret" recipes are passed on by the mother superior on her deathbed.

Jewish communities have several ways of making their massapan and hundreds of pastries based on it. They have a different texture when you bite into them, and different regional flavorings, with orange-blossom water, rose water, grated orange rind, lemon juice, cinnamon, and cardamom. And there are refinements, such as fillings of chopped pistachios or egg-yolk cream, and the addition of grated chocolate and chopped citrus-peel preserve. In Iraq they mixed the almond-and-sugar paste with mastic (a kind of gum) and shaped it into little birds and pretty objects.

2 cups (200 g) ground almonds
½–¾ cup (100–150 g) confectioners' or
superfine sugar (plus a little more for
rolling the balls in at the end)
1 or 2 drops of almond extract (optional)
3 tablespoons rose or orange-blossom water
12 blanched almonds or pistachio nuts to
garnish (optional)

Mix the ground almonds and sugar in a bowl. Add the almond extract if you wish, and the rose or orange-blossom water, and work well with your hands. The mixture will seem dry at first, but the almonds will release enough oil to bind it. Knead to a soft dough.

Roll into 1-inch (2½-cm) balls (the size of large marbles). Roll in sugar and decorate each if you like with a split almond or pistachio nut stuck on top.

VARIATIONS

• Some people prefer to use blanched almonds and grind them very finely in the food processor with the sugar. In the past they used to mince and pound them.

• My aunt Régine, who prided herself on her refinements, used to make a hollow in the balls and would stuff them with ground pistachio nuts mixed with a little sugar and a drop of rose water.

• In Ferrara, in Italy, they bind the paste with a rose liqueur called "rosolio" and stuff it with a mixture of about ½ cup (75 g) finely chopped preserved (sugared) citrus peel or a mixture of peel with grated chocolate. The Italians call these sweetmeats "cedrini."

• In Turkey they mix the ground almonds and confectioners' sugar with a beaten egg, roll the paste into long thin rolls, cut them into pieces, and leave to dry for 1 or 2 days. The Turks call them "mogados de almendra."

Massapan–Pâte d'Amande

Judeo-Spanish Marzipan

MAKES ABOUT 44 LITTLE BALLS

This is the classic Judeo-Spanish way of making marzipan, starting with sugar syrup. The almond paste can be pressed into an oiled tray and cut into lozenges or rolled into balls. The usual way is to start with blanched almonds, but commercial ground almonds will also do well. A tiny drop of almond extract approximates the flavor once obtained by adding a few bitter almonds.

5⅓ cups (500 g) ground almonds
2 cups (400 g) sugar
1 cup (250 ml) water
Juice of ½ lemon
2 or 3 drops of almond extract
Superfine sugar to roll the balls in
Split almonds to decorate (optional)

Grind the almonds as finely as you can in the food processor, or use ground almonds.

Boil the sugar and water with the lemon juice in a pan for 5–10 minutes, until the syrup is thick enough to coat a spoon and sticky. Be careful not to let it caramelize. It must not color or it will be too hard.

Add the almonds and almond extract and stir vigorously over low heat for 2–3 minutes, until the paste no longer sticks to the pan. Let it cool.

Lightly oil your hands, take little lumps of paste, and roll into 1-inch (2½-cm) balls. Roll them in superfine sugar, and press a split almond on the top if you like.

Note

• If you overcook the paste, it will be too dry to shape. You can save it by blending it in the food processor with 1–2 tablespoons of water.

VARIATIONS

• The paste was sometimes shaped into little fruits and vegetables and tinted with food coloring.

• You may flavor with orange zest.

• In Turkey they roll the paste into long rolls ¾ inch (2 cm) thick, cut them diagonally into ¾-inch (2-cm) slices, and press a split almond on top.

• Moroccan and Iraqi versions use freshly squeezed orange or tangerine juice instead of water. In that case you don't need lemon juice.

• An Iraqi and Indian Baghdadi version called almond "lowzina" is flavored with 1–2 teaspoons cinnamon or with 1 teaspoon ground cardamom seeds. They pour the hot mixture onto a sheet of greaseproof paper on a tray and cut it into lozenge shapes with a sharp knife dipped in boiling water to prevent it from sticking.

• Italians call it "marzapane." Delightful versions emanating from the city of Ancona, which once had a large Jewish population (there were families called "Ancona" in Egypt), are Purim specialties. For these, mix the same basic marzipan with ¾ cup (100 g) finely chopped candied citrus peel, or with 4 oz (100 g) dark chocolate pulverized or grated in the food processor. At Purim the 3 versions are rolled out and layered together, then cut in the shape of a Star of David.

Macaroons

MAKES ABOUT 16

Macaroons are a Passover and Purim specialty in the entire Sephardi world. Although they are very easy to make, they are very tricky and can easily come out too hard or too chewy. Purists start with blanched almonds, but store-bought ground ones will also do. If you start with whole blanched almonds, grind them as fine as you can in the food processor.

2 cups (200 g) ground almonds
¾ cup (150 g) sugar
2 or 3 drops of almond or vanilla extract
Egg white of 1 small egg

Mix the ground almonds with the sugar and almond or vanilla extract.

Add the egg white and work the mixture very well with your hand, kneading vigorously, until the almonds exude their oil and hold together in a stiff paste. It is important not to have more egg white than you need. Take lumps the size of small walnuts, shape into round, flat cakes, and place on wax paper on a baking sheet—at a little distance from each other.

Bake very briefly in a preheated 425°F (220°C) oven for 8–10 minutes, until only slightly colored. They will be very soft, but they harden as they cool. Leave until firm before detaching from the paper.

VARIATIONS

• A blanched almond or pistachio is sometimes stuck on top for decoration.

• In Iran and Iraq, where they are called "haji badam"—a reference to the Turkish turban shape and to bitter almonds—I teaspoon ground cardamom is added, and sometimes also I tablespoon rose water.

• Many people have been telling me about a Jewish pastry shop on Via del Portico in the Roman Ghetto, a hole-in-the-wall type of place where there is always a giant queue. One of their pastries Romans rave about is amaretti, macaroons, crisp on the outside, meltingly soft inside. I appealed to Piera di Segni, who works for *Sorgente di Vita*, a television program on Jewish culture in Italy, for information about the pastry shop and their recipes. She answered with a fax. The *pasticceria* is called "Boccione," after the nickname of the late owner. There are four generations—mainly women—working there. She thought the ladies might not like to give away recipes, so she sent one that people make at home. The difference from the above is that I whole egg white is beaten stiff before mixing with the almonds.

Maronchinos
Almond Cookies

MAKES ABOUT 30

I know these little sweets were highly esteemed in Turkey and the Balkans, because one of my elitist grandmother's ironic remarks was *"A los asnos maronchinos,"* implying that you don't give

maronchinos to donkeys. They are perfect to serve with coffee—softer than macaroons, a little moist and not too sweet—and they never fail.

> 4 cups (400 g) ground almonds
> ⅔–1 cup (125–200 g) superfine sugar
> 2 or 3 drops of almond extract
> 2 tablespoons rose water
> 2 eggs, lightly beaten
> Confectioners' sugar to sprinkle on

Mix the almonds and sugar. Add the extract, rose water, and eggs and work to a smooth paste with your hand. Roll into walnut-sized balls, flatten them slightly, and place in little paper cases or on greaseproof or parchment paper on a baking sheet. Bake in a preheated 350°F (180°C) oven for 25 minutes. Let them cool before dusting with confectioners' sugar.

Guizadas
Pistachio or Almond Sweets

MAKES ABOUT 22

I love these little sweetmeats, which are a specialty of the "Livornese" community of Tunisia. They are soft and moist and delicately perfumed. You can find the almond version in the pastry shops of Lisbon.

> 2⅓ cups (300 g) shelled (unsalted) pistachios
> 1 cup (200 g) superfine sugar
> 1–2 tablespoons orange-blossom water
> 2 whole eggs
> 2 egg yolks

Coarsely grind the pistachios in the food processor (do not use store-bought ground ones, which are too fine for this). Add the rest of the ingredients and blend well. Drop by the heaping tablespoon into little paper cases and bake in a preheated 350°F (180°C) oven for 25 minutes, or until slightly firm.

VARIATIONS

• Use almonds instead of pistachios. In Tunisia they add a few bitter almonds; 2 or 3 drops of almond extract will approximate the flavor.

Mustacchioni

Almond and Chocolate Cupcakes

MAKES ABOUT 28

These little pastries are from Trieste. They are extremely easy to make, with no melting of chocolate or separating of eggs. You just blend everything together in a food processor.

> 7 oz (200 g) dark, bittersweet chocolate, broken into pieces
> 1 cup (200 g) lightly roasted blanched almonds
> 3 eggs
> ½ cup (90 g) sugar
> 2 tablespoons rum (optional)

Put everything in the food processor and blend to a soft, creamy paste. Drop into little paper cups by the heaping tablespoonful. Bake in

a preheated 350°F (180°C) oven for 25 minutes, or until slightly firm. They are meant to be soft and moist.

VARIATION

• For a version from Padua, use only 2 oz (50 g) of chocolate and add 2 oz (50 g) of chopped candied citrus peel.

Mustacudos de Muez

Walnut Pastries

MAKES ABOUT 16

This is a specialty of the Jews of Turkey.

> 2 cups (250 g) walnuts
> ½ cup (90 g) sugar
> 1 egg
> Zest of ¾ orange
> ¾ teaspoon cinnamon

Put everything in a food processor and blend to a firm paste with the walnuts still a little coarse. Moisten your hands with water or grease them with oil, so that the paste does not stick, and roll into walnut-sized balls. Arrange on oiled greaseproof paper on a baking sheet—a little apart, as they spread—and bake at 350°F (180°C) for 25 minutes.

Terfas aux Noix

Walnut and Almond Pastries

MAKES ABOUT 18

The recipe for these little Moroccan Passover pastries was sent, with a pile of others from Fez, by Dody Sabah. When I was there, Dody showed me around the Jewish old people's home, which has a little synagogue attached. The old people were wearing all kinds of different costumes from various Berber villages. Terfas are easy to make and lovely to serve with after-dinner coffee.

> 1 cup (150 g) blanched almonds
> 1 cup (125 g) walnut halves
> ⅔ cup (125 g) sugar
> 1 whole egg
> 1 egg yolk
> Confectioners' sugar

Finely chop or grind the almonds and walnuts in the food processor with the sugar. Add the egg and yolk and mix well. Leave the mixture to rest for 2 hours in the refrigerator, covered with plastic wrap. Grease your hands with oil so that the mixture does not stick, take lumps of paste the size of small walnuts and shape into balls. Dredge in confectioners' sugar and place in tiny paper cake cases. Arrange on a baking sheet and bake in a preheated 325°F (160°C) oven for 20 minutes, until they are lightly colored and cracks appear on the top. Turn off the oven, open the door, and let the pastries cool in the oven. Do not

be alarmed if they appear too soft and breakable. They will firm up after a while, when they cool.

Pizza Dolce Romana

Nut and Raisin Pastries

MAKES ABOUT 22

These meltingly soft pastries, full of almonds, pine nuts, raisins, and chopped candied citrus peel, are a very old specialty of Rome, where they are made for all the holidays and especially for Rosh Hashanah.

> 3⅓ cups (500 g) flour
> ½ cup (125 g) sugar
> 8 oz (250 g) unsalted butter, softened
> 5–8 tablespoons white wine, preferably sweet
> ⅓ cup (50 g) pine nuts
> ⅓ cup (50 g) slivered or coarsely chopped almonds
> ⅓ cup (50 g) raisins
> ⅓ cup (50 g) chopped candied citrus peel
> Confectioners' sugar to sprinkle on

In a large bowl, mix the flour and sugar and work into a soft dough with the butter. (You may use a food processor at this stage, then turn into a bowl.) Add just enough wine—a tablespoon at a time—to make the dough hold together. Then work in the almonds, raisins, and citrus peel. Shape into little round cakes, about 2½ inches (6 cm) in diameter, pressing the mixture firmly between your palms.

Place on oiled baking sheets or on waxed or parchment paper and bake in a preheated 325°F (160°C) oven for 25–30 minutes. They will still be soft and hardly colored, but they firm up when they cool. Do not try to remove them until they are firm. Sprinkle with confectioners' sugar.

VARIATION

• There is a version using oil instead of butter, but it is not half as good.

Ghorayebah

Butter Cookies

MAKES ABOUT 40

Everybody always had a tin of these and one of maamoul (page 589) in the house to offer with coffee. They are extremely easy to make and dangerously full of butter, and they melt in the mouth.

> *12 oz (350 g) unsalted butter, softened*
> *1 cup (200 g) superfine sugar*
> *3⅓ cups (500 g) flour*
> *Confectioners' sugar*

Cream the butter with the superfine sugar in the food processor. Add the flour and process until blended to a soft dough. Roll into walnut-sized balls and flatten slightly. Arrange on wax or baking paper on a baking sheet about 1 inch (2½ cm) apart—they spread.

Bake in a preheated 325°F (160°C) oven for about 25 minutes. They should still be white—not at all colored. They will be very soft and friable and seem uncooked, but they will firm up when they cool. Remove from the paper only when they have hardened, and dredge in confectioners' sugar.

VARIATIONS

• Add 1 teaspoon cinnamon to the dough.
• Iraqi Jews flavor with 1 teaspoon ground cardamom. They call it "shakar lemah."
• It is customary to press a blanched almond on the top of the pastry before baking, but in my view it is best without.
• Another traditional shape is to roll into a long thin sausage, form into a little bracelet, and press the ends together.
• Replace ½ cup (125 g) of the flour with ground almonds or ground hazelnuts.

Dattes Fourées

Dates Stuffed with Almond Paste

This little sweetmeat can be found all over the Sephardi world—even in Italy—but it is most visible in North Africa, at celebrations of every kind.

Use a soft variety of dried dates. Make a slit in each with a sharp-pointed knife and remove the pits. Use one of the basic almond pastes described in the recipe for amandines (page 604), which I use, or the one for massapan (page 606). Take small lumps of paste—about the size of a quail's egg—and press one into the opening of each date, so that the date remains a little open and the almond paste is visible. They keep a very long time.

Dates Stuffed with Almond Paste (cont.)

VARIATIONS

• Dip the filling side in superfine or confectioners' sugar.

• Dip the stuffed dates in a caramel syrup: make a sugar syrup (see page 591) and let it simmer until it turns a little brown.

• Tunisians color the almond paste with a few drops of green food coloring to simulate pistachio.

Noix Fourées

Walnuts Stuffed with Almond Paste

To stuff 2 cups (250 g) walnut halves, make an almond paste as in the recipe for amandines (page 604) or massapan (page 606). Take a heaping teaspoonful of paste, roll into a little ball, and press between 2 walnut halves. Some people dip in a sugar syrup (page 591) cooked until it begins to brown. When cool, it makes a thin caramel coat.

Bouchées aux Dattes

Date and Walnut Balls

MAKES 60

This is a specialty of North Africa and also found in Iraq. It is easy to make with commercially pitted dates, which now come in various qualities. It is best to use a soft, moist variety.

2½ cups (300 g) walnuts
1 lb (500 g) pitted dried dates of a
    soft moist variety

Coarsely chop about half the walnuts, and very finely chop or grind the rest. Turn the dates to a soft paste in the food processor, adding 4–5 tablespoons of water by the tablespoon, just enough to make a malleable paste. Work in the coarsely chopped walnuts with your hands.

Grease your hands with oil so that the paste does not stick. Take small lumps and roll into 1-inch (2½-cm) balls. Roll in the finely chopped or ground walnuts.

VARIATIONS

• A Tunisian way is to roll the date balls in pine nuts, pressing them in. These balls can also be dipped in sugar syrup cooked until it is brown and caramelized.

Abricotines

Apricot Balls

MAKES 56

Several years ago, I went to see Alan Mansoura, who has a Jewish bakery on Kings Highway in Brooklyn. He was making the same Syrian pastries, petits-fours, and fruit preserves that his father made in Egypt when I was a girl (he said King Farouk and Gamal Abdel Nasser both patronized the bakery in Cairo). There were trays of apricot balls, which are popular with the Brooklyn Syrian community.

These are my aunt Régine's. Make them with a natural—tart—variety of dried apricots, not the sweetened or honeyed ones. They must also be soft.

1 lb (500 g) dried apricots
½ cup (75 g) pistachios, coarsely chopped
Confectioners' sugar
A few whole pistachios to decorate

Do not soak or wash the apricots or you will produce a cream. Put them as they are in the food processor and blend them to a smooth paste, adding a very little water, by the teaspoon, if necessary. Then work the chopped pistachios in with your hands. Wash your hands and, wetting them or greasing them with a little oil so that the paste does not stick, take little lumps of paste and roll into marble-sized balls. Roll them in confectioners' sugar and press half a pistachio on top of each.

Friandises à la Noix de Coco

Coconut Rocks

MAKES ABOUT 12

Coconut, although considered the poor relative of almonds, is a common ingredient in pastry-making, especially among Jews from North Africa, Iraq, and India.

2 cups (200 g) dried unsweetened coconut
½ cup (100 g) sugar
2 eggs, lightly beaten

Mix the coconut, sugar, and eggs in a bowl and leave for an hour, until the coconut has soft-ened. Pour by the heaping tablespoon into little paper cases. Bake in a preheated 350°F (180°C) oven for 20 minutes, or until golden.

Candied Orange Peel

My mother used to peel all the oranges she and my father ate, in six sections, and kept the peels in plastic bags until she had collected a good amount; then she candied them. Other families made the same preserve with bitter-orange, grapefruit, and lemon peels. We called ours "naring," Spanish speakers called it "dulce de portokal." You need large oranges with thick peels. With a small, pointed knife, cut straight lines down the sides of the orange, from the point of the stem end, converging at the other end. Carefully peel off the segments formed, without breaking them. Weigh the peel, as you will need to use an equal weight of sugar.

2 lbs (1 kg) orange peels
5 cups (1 kg) sugar
4 cups (1 liter) water
Juice of ½ lemon

Soak the peels in water for a day, changing the water once. Drain and boil in water for about 20 minutes, until soft, and drain again. (All this is to remove some of the bitterness.) If the peel is too pithy, scrape some of the pith away with a soupspoon to make it less pasty. Roll up the strips of peel, one by one, and thread them onto a thick button thread with a needle, like beads in a necklace (this is so that they keep their rolled-up shape). Tie the ends of the thread together.

Make a syrup by boiling the sugar with the

FRUIT PRESERVES AND JAMS

I N MANY FAMILIES, the offering of preserves and jams to guests was something of a ritual ceremony. A selection was served in beautiful crystal bowls on silver trays with little silver spoons and glasses of iced water to accompany. People helped themselves to a spoonful, drank a little water, then dropped their spoons in a special glass. They were brought out especially on happy occasions such as births and circumcisions, so that the newborn and parents would be "surrounded by sweetness," and for all the festivals, most particularly on Rosh Hashanah, to augur a sweet New Year.

Preserves and jams were also eaten for breakfast with bread and kaimak, the thick buffalo-milk cream (see page 562). (Try them with heavy cream or mascarpone.)

Sometimes a spoonful was savored at the end of a meal in place of a dessert.

Many are common to all the Sephardi communities. The main fruits used are quinces, oranges, apricots, dates, and figs. Vegetables such as pumpkin, spaghetti squash, eggplant, and carrots are also used. Dulce de rozas—rose-petal jam—is a symbol of good luck in Turkey and the Balkan communities; in North Africa, orange blossom has the same symbolic association. When the jam is intended to last a long time, the fruit, vegetable, or petal is simmered in a syrup made with the same weight of sugar.

In the old days, large quantities were made during their season to last through the year. Women got together in each other's homes and spent the day pitting, peeling, stirring. It was a time for gossip and laughter, and they all went home with a bagful of jars.

Candied Orange Peel (cont.)

water and lemon juice. Drop the necklace in the syrup and simmer for about 1 hour. Lift out, remove the thread, and drop the rolls of peel in a glass jar. When slightly cooled, pour the syrup over them.

Alternatively, roll the orange peels in sugar and keep them as crystallized fruit in a box. They are so good.

Tranches d'Orange au Sirop

Orange Slices Cooked in Syrup

SERVES 6–8

This makes a most delicious and easy dessert to serve as an accompaniment to an orange cake or a plain rice pudding. It surprises everyone. I discovered it in Tunisia and Morocco, but it is also made by the Jews in Italy. You can serve the slices sprinkled with a little cinnamon and chopped pistachios and with a blob of cream. You need a lot of sugar for the syrup, but you can leave most of it behind.

4 large sweet oranges with thick skins
5 cups (1 kg) sugar
2 cups (500 ml) water
Juice of ½ lemon

Wash the oranges and leave them to soak in cold water for at least an hour. Then cut them into thick slices (about ⅓ inch [1 cm]) and remove the seeds. Put the sugar, water, and lemon juice in a large pan and bring to the boil. Put the orange slices in, pressing them down into the syrup. Put the lid on and simmer gently for 1–1½ hours, or until they are very soft. Lift out the slices and arrange on a serving dish. Reduce the syrup by simmering, uncovered, until it has thickened enough to coat a spoon, and pour a little over the slices. (Leftover syrup can be kept in a covered jar.)

VARIATIONS

• It is also very common to quarter the oranges instead of slicing them. Soak whole oranges in water for an hour (if using bitter oranges, for a whole day, changing the water a few times). Wash and boil 2 lbs (1 kg) whole oranges for about 20 minutes, or until they feel soft. Cut them into quarters and remove the seeds. Then put them in a pan with 5 cups (1 kg) sugar, the juice of ½ lemon, and enough water to cover them, and simmer for 1½ hours, or until they are very soft and the syrup is much reduced.

• The same thing can be done with grapefruit and lemons. These are usually soaked in water for 2 hours.

BIMBRIYO
Quince Paste

THE NAME IS a deformation of the Spanish word *membrillo*, meaning "quince." The Judeo-Spanish world inherited its love of quince from the Arabs in Andalusia. In her *Fruit Book*, Jane Grigson quotes a tenth-century love poem by the vizier of Córdoba, who describes quince as having the perfume of a loved woman and the same hardness of heart but the color of the impassioned and scrawny lover. He is afraid that the ardor of his breath could shrivel the fruit in his fingers. The Jews took the fruit to their heart, and quince paste, quince preserve, and quince jelly are part of their cultural identity.

Quince cannot be eaten raw. When it is cooked, the seeds and skin produce a rich and scented pink jelly. Varieties of the fruit vary in size, flavor, and perfume.

• A famous preserve in Baghdad was tiny tangerines in syrup. Use very small ones—with tight skins. Cut them in half across the segments and cook them in syrup.

• One tablespoon of orange-blossom water may be added at the end.

Bimbriyo
Quince Paste

Quince paste is one of the most characteristic features of Judeo-Spanish gastronomy.

4½ lb (2 kg) quinces
Juice of ½ lemon
5 cups (1 kg) sugar
More sugar to roll the pieces of paste in

Wash the quinces and rub off the down that usually covers them. Peel and quarter but do not core them. Put them in a heavy pan and cover with water. Add the lemon juice and cook for 2 hours. Then drain, keeping the precious liquid.

Remove the cores, seeds, and skins (they will already have given off their jelly-making pectin) and mash or process the fruit to a puree. Boil down the liquid to about ¾ cup (175 ml). Add the sugar and the puree, and cook, stirring often, with a wooden spoon, over very low heat, being careful not to let it burn, until it thickens and begins to splutter. Then stir constantly until it turns into a rich garnet-red paste that comes away from the sides of the pan.

Let it cool a little before pouring into a wide shallow pan or tray lined with plastic wrap or wax paper, spreading it out to a thickness of about ¾ inch (1½ cm).

Leave for a day or so to dry out in a warm, airy place, before turning out and cutting up the firmed paste with a sharp knife into ¾-inch (1½-cm) squares or lozenges. Roll the pieces in granulated sugar and pack them in a tin or other airtight container.

Loape de Bimbriyo
Quince Butter with Nuts

Make quince butter in exactly the same way as quince paste (preceding recipe), with the same quantities, but do not thicken the paste any further once it thickens and begins to splutter.

Add ¾ cup (100 g) each of pine nuts, blanched almonds, and pistachios and pour into jars or bowls. It forms a jelly when cool.

VARIATIONS

• An Iraqi version of quince butter and quince paste is flavored with ground cardamom and mixed with ground almonds.

• Another traditional flavoring is to add 6 cloves during the cooking.

Confiture de Courge
Pumpkin Jam

This jam is very widespread throughout the Sephardi communities. It is a special-occasion delicacy which appears at Rosh Hashanah. Its ritual significance on the New Year has to do with its golden color, which represents happiness and abundance for the year ahead.

Peel a piece of orange pumpkin and remove the seeds and stringy bits, then weigh it before grating or shredding it in a food processor. Put it in a bowl with half its weight in sugar and mix well. Leave it for at least an hour, so that its juices are drawn out by the sugar. Then put it all in a pan (including the juices) and cook for about 10 minutes, or until the shredded pumpkin is very soft. Add ½–1 tablespoon of orange-blossom water for each pound (500 g) of pumpkin. It is usual to mix in whole pistachios that have been blanched in boiling water to remove their skins (roll them gently with a rolling pin or bottle to loosen the skins further). Serve sprinkled with chopped pistachios and accompany with a bowl of thick kaimak (page 562), heavy cream, or mascarpone.

VARIATIONS

• To preserve the jam for a long time, add the same amount of sugar as pumpkin and cook until it is very thick.

• A common flavoring is with mastic (see page 571). Pound 2 grains of this resin to a powder and mix it in at the end of the cooking.

• Flavor if you like with cloves, added at the start of cooking, or sprinkle with cinnamon when serving.

• Baghdadi Jews of India add the seeds of 2 cardamom pods or 1 teaspoon of ground cardamom.

• For a Kurdish pumpkin preserve, cut the pumpkin into small cubes and simmer in a sugar syrup (see page 591). Serve sprinkled with chopped walnuts and, if you like, a few pinches of cinnamon.

Confiture de Cheveux d'Ange

Spaghetti Squash Jam

My father often asked me to make a jam with squash that he described as having a flesh like soft vermicelli. It was a Syrian specialty. When I made it with spaghetti squash, he said that that was it. It is lovely and fragrant and does have the thin vermicelli texture. Peel and cook as for pumpkin jam (preceding recipe), with the same weight of sugar as of squash. The flesh falls apart into threads.

Iraqi Apple Preserve

This is a New Year specialty.

> 2 lbs (1 kg) apples—Coxes, Golden
> Delicious, Granny Smiths
> Juice of 1 lemon
> 3⅓ cups (750 g) sugar
> 1 cup (250 ml) water
> 2 tablespoons rose water

Peel, cut in half, and core the apples and drop them in a bowl of water with three-quarters of the lemon juice to prevent them from browning.

Make a syrup by boiling the sugar and water with the remaining lemon juice, uncovered, for 10–15 minutes, or until very thick (this will prevent the apples from falling apart). Drain the apples and drop them into the syrup. Simmer for 20–30 minutes, or until they are tender and the syrup has become thick again (they produce quite a bit of juice). Add the rose water and cook, stirring, for a moment more. Lift out the apples and place them in a serving bowl or in jars. Pour the syrup over the apples. This is very sweet and is best eaten with heavy cream or yogurt.

Apricot Jam

> 2 lbs (1 kg) fresh apricots
> 2½ cups (500 g) sugar
> Juice of ½ lemon
> 2 tablespoons rose water or orange-blossom
>   water

Wash the apricots, cut them in half, and remove the pits. Put them in a bowl, cut side up, and sprinkle each layer with sugar. Let stand for a day, until the juices are drawn out. Turn them into a pan with the sugar and juices and the lemon. Simmer 15 minutes, or until the apricots are very soft and the juices thick enough to coat a spoon. Stir in the rose or orange-blossom water.

Let it cool before packing into a jar.

Date Preserve

This is a Syrian specialty. My aunt Régine made it for us on the New Year. It is very luscious.

> 1 lb (500 g) fresh dates
> About 30 blanched almonds
> 2½ cups (500 g) sugar
> 1 cup (250 ml) water
> Juice of ½ lemon

Skin and pit the dates. Try to pull out the pit from the stem end, so as not to make too big a hole. Replace the pit of each date with a blanched almond. Simmer the sugar and water with the lemon juice for 5 minutes. Add the stuffed dates and simmer 20 minutes. Let them cool, then lift them out and put them in a jar, covered by their syrup.

Raisins Confits

Grape Preserve

This simple Moroccan preserve, which was on the table the night of the Mimouna (page 554), was a surprise and a discovery for me. It is very easy to make. Serve it to accompany a pudding or cake.

> 4 cups (800 g) seedless grapes
> 2 cups (400 g) sugar
> 2 cups (500 ml) water
> ½–¾ teaspoon powdered ginger
> ½ cup (100 g) whole blanched almonds
>   (optional)

Wash the grapes well and drain them. Put the sugar in a pan with the water and ginger and simmer for 5 minutes. Cook the grapes and almonds in the syrup in 2 batches. Put in half the grapes and almonds and cook on low heat for 20–25 minutes, or until the grapes are soft. Lift out with a slotted spoon and transfer to a jar, leaving the syrup behind. Cook the remaining grapes and almonds in the syrup for 20–25 minutes and pour into the jar with the syrup.

Coconut Jam

This jam was made for Passover in Egypt. My mother would give each of us a pot to take home. We wondered every year why we never made it at other times, because we loved it.

> 500 g (1 lb) dried unsweetened coconut
> 2 tablespoons orange-blossom or rose water
> 2½ cups (500 g) sugar
> 2 tablespoons lemon juice
> ½ cup (100 g) blanched almonds or ¾ cup
> (100 g) pistachio nuts, chopped
> (optional)

Sprinkle the coconut with the orange-blossom or rose water and with enough fresh cold water so that it is just moist, fluffing it with your hands. Leave it overnight to swell and soften. Make a syrup by simmering the sugar with ⅔ cup (150 ml) of water and the lemon juice for a few minutes. Add the coconut and bring to the boil again slowly, stirring constantly. Remove from the heat as soon as it boils. Let it cool a little before pouring into a jar. Serve in a bowl, sprinkled, if you like, with chopped almonds or pistachios.

VARIATIONS

• An Indian version has cardamom seeds in the syrup.

• We used to eat the jam with whipped cream.

Haroset from Turkey

> 2 sweet apples weighing ½ lb (250 g),
> peeled and cut in small pieces
> ½ lb (250 g) dates, pitted
> 1 cup (150 g) raisins
> Juice and grated zest of 1 orange
> 1 cup (250 ml) sweet red Passover
> wine
> 2–4 tablespoons sugar or to taste
> (optional)
> 2 oz (60 g) walnuts, coarsely chopped

Put all the ingredients except the sugar and walnuts together in a saucepan and cook on very low heat until the mixture is soft and mushy and the liquid is reduced, stirring occasionally. Add sugar to taste. The amount will depend on the sweetness of the other ingredients. Blend to a paste in the food processor. Pour into a bowl and sprinkle with walnuts.

Haroset from Egypt

> ½ lb (250 g) pitted dates, chopped
> ½ lb (250 g) large yellow raisins or
> sultanas
> ½ cup (125 ml) sweet red Passover wine
> ½ cup (60 g) walnuts, coarsely chopped

Put the dates and sultanas with the wine in a pan. Add just a little water to cover. Cook on very low heat, stirring occasionally, until the dates fall apart into a mush. Cook until it thickens to a soft paste. Pour into a bowl and sprinkle with walnuts.

HAROSET

HAROSET IS the fruit paste that is part of the Passover ritual. It figures on the Passover tray, symbolizing by its color the mortar used by Hebrew slaves in Egypt to build the pyramids. There are infinite variations. John Cooper, in *Eat and Be Satisfied*, quotes a medieval sage, Rabbi Elijah of London, who thought that all the fruits mentioned in the Song of Songs should be used as ingredients for haroset, including "apples, dates, figs, pomegranates and nuts crushed together with almonds and moistened in vinegar." He also mentioned the use of valerian or nard (a seasoning favored by the Romans). John Cooper found among the archives of Bevis Marks, the oldest (Sephardi) synagogue in London, a recipe for haroset dated 1726 that contained raisins, almonds, cinnamon, pistachios, dates, ginger, hazelnuts, walnuts, apples, pears, and figs.

In Egypt we believed that the paste had to be the color of the Nile silt, which was used to make the mortar, and only a mixture of dates and raisins gave the right approximation. Since Egypt I have tried many versions, using all kinds of dried fruit and even one with bananas. In Algeria it is a blend of dates and dried figs with cinnamon, nutmeg, and sweet red wine. In Iraq it is simply date syrup mixed with plenty of chopped walnuts. A recipe from Surinam includes dried apples, pears, apricots, prunes, raisins, grated coconut, ground almonds, walnuts, and cherry jam. The following are traditional Sephardi classics, although proportions vary from one family to another and the texture can be coarse or smooth, thick or thin.

Haroset from Morocco

1 lb (500 g) dates, pitted and chopped
1½ cups sweet red Passover wine
1 teaspoon ground cinnamon
½ teaspoon ground cloves
1 cup (125 g) walnuts, coarsely chopped

Put the dates in a pan with the wine, cinnamon, and cloves and simmer, stirring occasionally, until you have a soft paste. Put through the food processor if you want a smoother texture. Let it cool and stir in the walnuts.

VARIATION

• A Libyan version is flavored with ground ginger, nutmeg, and cloves—¼ teaspoon of each.

Haroset from Italy

In Italy there are various regional versions of haroset. The haroset of Padua has prunes, raisins, dates, walnuts, apples, and chestnuts. In Milan they make it with apples, pears, dates, almonds, bananas, and orange juice. The following is a general version.

> *3 apples, sweet or tart*
> *2 pears*
> *2 cups sweet wine*
> *⅓ cup (50 g) pine nuts*
> *⅔ cup (50 g) ground almonds*
> *½ lb (250 g) dates, pitted and chopped*
> *¾ cup (100 g) yellow raisins or sultanas*
> *4 oz (100 g) prunes, pitted and chopped*
> *½ cup (100 g) sugar or ½ cup (125 ml)*
>   *honey or to taste*
> *1 teaspoon cinnamon*
> *½ teaspoon ground ginger*

Peel and core the apples and pears and cut them in small pieces. Put all the ingredients into a pan together and cook, stirring occasionally, for about 1 hour, until the fruits are very soft, adding a little water if it becomes too dry.

VARIATIONS

• Other possible additions: chopped lemon or candied orange peel, walnuts, pistachios, dried figs, orange or lemon juice, ginger, nutmeg, and cloves.

Piedmontese Haroset

This recipe is adapted from one sent by Nedelia Tedeschi, of Turin. She enclosed a little picture of a squirrel eating a chestnut, from the package of dried chestnuts she uses to make the paste. It was Passover, and the Italian store near my house had closed, so when I phoned around to try to find dried chestnuts and couldn't, I used cooked vacuum-packed ones instead. The result was very unusual and also delightful.

> *½ lb (250 g) cooked chestnuts*
> *⅔ cup (125 g) blanched almonds*
> *2 hard-boiled egg yolks*
> *Grated zest of 1 orange*
> *Juice of 1 orange*
> *About ¾ cup (175 ml) sweet red kosher*
>   *wine*
> *⅓ cup (75 g) sugar or more to taste*

Boil the chestnuts for a minute or two, and drain. Grind the almonds fine in the food processor, then add the rest of the ingredients, including the chestnuts, and blend to a paste.

THE LOST JEWS OF CHINA

IN ARTHUR MILLER'S PLAY *Broken Glass*, a protagonist tells the old joke about the Jew who goes to China and meets a Chinaman who claims he is Jewish. The Chinaman says, "It's funny, you don't look Jewish." Jews have always been tickled at the idea of Chinese Jews, and sightings of them have been part of Jewish travelers' tales over the centuries.

Rabbi David D'Beth Hillel, whose writings about his travels between 1824 and 1832 are edited by Walter Fischel (Ktav), recounts how a Cochin Black Jew told him he had visited a fair outside the walls of a large town in China and had met the people who lived in the town. They never allowed strangers through their gates, but on hearing that he was a Jew they said that they too were Jews and that the country on the other side of the river belonged to them. They did not allow him to go inside the gates but instead brought out food for him to eat. Among other things was meat cooked in milk. The Cochin Jew refused to eat this and asked his hosts how they could eat what was forbidden to Jews in India and other parts of the world. They replied that Moses only forbade the seething of a kid in its mother's milk. This meat, they explained, was not boiled in the mother's milk—they kept a rigorous check on the animals and made sure of that. The Cochin Jew insisted that according to the Talmud flesh must not be eaten with milk of any kind, and they replied with a question: "Who is greater, Moses or the Talmudists?"

A Chinese Jewish family, c.1920

In the city of Kaifeng in China, just south of the Yellow River in the Henan province, there is an ancient community of Jews—or, rather, its descendants. Their features are slightly different from those of the Chinese masses of this province. They once wore the blue yarmulka (skullcap), ate unleavened bread, eschewed pork, underwent circumcision, and observed the Sabbath, but since the communist revolution they no longer do. There is a street still known as Nan-Xuejing Hutong, meaning South Studying-the-Scriptures Lane.

The synagogue collapsed more than a hundred years ago, but several stone tablets with worn Chinese characters and fragile old Torahs are a clue to the Jewish past of those who were known as "the people who pluck the sinews."

No one knows how they got there and when. By one account, they came from Arab Jerusalem more than nine hundred years ago. A Chinese scholar of Jewish origin called Pan Guandan, who died more than forty years ago, thought that their community was descended originally from Jews who migrated to the Cochin area of India in the second century B.C. and sailed to China sometime in the eleventh century A.D. Others arrived through Persia. According to legend, they came to trade during the Song dynasty. They exchanged cotton cloth for silk and settled in Kaifeng, which was then the capital of China. Seven Chinese names were bestowed on their clans by the Song emperor. They prospered as merchants and bankers and rose to positions of influence. Over the centuries, they intermarried with the local Han majority, adopted its language and customs, and gradually lost their old traditions. They were called "blue-cap Muslims" because they didn't eat pork and wore blue yarmulkas. Smaller clusters of Jews settled in nine other cities, including Hangchow and Canton, and also became assimilated. For a time in the nineteenth century, when the Sassoons of Baghdad built a trading empire with branches in Shanghai, Canton, and Hong Kong, many of them were employed by Baghdadi and Syrian Jews and were brought into the Jewish fold. But now, they no longer have a distinct cultural identity. They say they are no different from other Chinese, though some still note their nationality as "Youtai" or Jewish.

A few years ago, I met Phyllis Horal, who had spent years looking for Jews in China and had prepared an exhibition on the Kaifeng Jews. She phoned and asked if I could identify a pastry that they made. A biscuity affair with honey, it might have been a version of teiglach or of homms.

Drinks

Sciroppo di Vino

Wine Syrup

Add 3–4 tablespoons of this Italian sweet-and-sour syrup to a glass of iced water.

> *2 cups (½ liter) red wine*
> *2½ cups (500 g) sugar*
> *Juice of 3 lemons*
> *A 2-inch (5-cm) cinnamon stick*
> *4 cloves*
> *Peel of ½ lemon*

Put all the ingredients together in a pan and simmer 20 minutes. Remove the cinnamon stick and lemon peel, and cool before pouring into a bottle.

Sharbat el Loz

Milk of Almonds

SERVES 8

This is expensive and an effort to make, but it is one of the great drinks—very delicate in flavor and quite seductive. It was one of the drinks served to break the fast of Yom Kippur.

> *1½ cups (250 g) blanched almonds*
> *9 cups (2 liters) water*
> *1 cup (200 g) sugar*
> *3 or 4 drops almond extract*
> *2 teaspoons rose or orange-blossom water or*
> *to taste*

INFUSIONS AND DILUTED SYRUPS

COOL REFRESHING DRINKS were made by diluting one or two tablespoons of concentrated syrup in a glass of iced water. There were all kinds of syrups. An orange syrup was prepared by boiling fresh orange juice with sugar; a pomegranate syrup, by adding sugar and lemon to the juice extracted from crushing pomegranate seeds; a tamarind syrup, by soaking tamarind pods in water and cooking the strained liquid with sugar. A lemon syrup, which was the first thing to pass the lips at the end of the Yom Kippur fast, was made by adding lemon juice and grated zest to a thick sugar syrup. Another Yom Kippur syrup was prepared by soaking apricot leather in water. Some also made scented waters by macerating dried melon seeds or petals, such as roses, violets, and orange blossoms, in boiling water for twenty-four hours, then draining and refrigerating the infusion.

Milk of Almonds (cont.)

Grind the almonds as finely as possible in the food processor or blender (do not buy them already ground). Add about 3 cups (750 ml) of the water and blend very thoroughly for several minutes. Pour into a saucepan, add the sugar, and bring to the boil. Simmer for a minute or two, then add the almond extract. Pour the rest of the water in and leave to macerate overnight. Strain through a fine sieve or muslin cloth and pour into a jug. Add orange-blossom water and chill, covered, in the refrigerator.

VARIATIONS

• In Morocco they stir in ¼ teaspoon pulverized mastic after boiling.

• In Iraq they flavor with ¼ teaspoon ground cardamom.

Laban
Yogurt Drink

Beat yogurt with a little less than its volume of water, carbonated mineral water, or soda water, adding a little salt to taste if you like.

Turkish Coffee

Coffee is the symbol of hospitality in the Levant, served at every possible occasion. Its making and serving are full of ceremony. Often this is the job of the men of the family. In ours my younger brother had the task. It was the custom, when the coffee was finished, to turn

LIQUORS AND SWEET WINES

Mahia

IN MOROCCO, once upon a time, the eau-de-vie mahia was distilled in every Jewish home (when I was there it was put out on the dinner table alongside whiskey and Coca-Cola). Now you have to have a license to make it. Then, it was a Jewish cottage industry, made from dried fruits such as dates, raisins, and especially figs, and flavored with aniseed and herbs. It was considered a digestive, a tonic, and a cure-all. You can buy it in Paris now, but it is hard to get in Morocco, since the Jews are no longer there to sell it.

This is how they made it: Figs or other fruit were covered with water, mixed with sugar and aniseed, fennel seed, or rosemary, and left to ferment for three weeks. A pinch of yeast was sometimes added to activate the fermentation. The mixture was boiled, and the cooled vapor distilled in an alembic.

Arak

MANY JEWISH FAMILIES made arak at home. In Syria and Lebanon it was made from grapes and flavored with aniseed. In Iraq, it was made from dates and flavored with mastic. In Iran, beet molasses and raisins or cherries were used, and it was flavored with mastic, fennel, or aniseed. Some people put lemon peel in the bottle for an additional aroma.

Sweet Wines

IN MOST ORIENTAL communities, especially in wine-making regions like North Africa, where the Muslim population hardly drank the produce and the wine was produced by French colonists, Jews made their own sweet wines. The usual way was to crush the grapes, add sugar, leave them to ferment for ten to twelve days, and strain the juice through muslin in a colander. Sometimes the sugar was caramelized first. Sacramental wine was made with raisins soaked in water. "Vin cuit" was the fermented juice boiled with sugar. "Vin à l'orange" had orange slices macerated in red wine with sugar for about 3 weeks, then filtered.

In Lebanon and Turkey they made a concentrated, boiled-down grape juice called "dibs" which they used as a sweetener and also ate mixed with diluted tahini.

the cups over, and someone would pretend to be good at reading the fortune in the grounds. A Judeo-Spanish exclamation is *"caves de alegría"* (coffee of joy), in the hope that the grounds would augur joy.

The Turkish way of making coffee is practiced in all the Oriental communities. Any kind of coffee can be used, as long as it is ground to the finest degree—that is, pulverized. Each country has its favorite blends. A high roast is popular but not general. The coffee is made in a small, long-handled brass pot and served in little cups. Everyone has his or her special tricks. My father at 94 suddenly discovered a new way of producing more of the precious froth—or *wesh* (face), as it is called—and told everybody who visited him about it.

To make 4 cups of medium-sweet coffee, put 2 cups (500 ml) water in a coffeepot and stir in 4 heaping teaspoons of pulverized coffee and 4 teaspoons sugar. Stir well and bring to the boil. Remove from the fire as soon as it begins to froth and rise (be careful—it boils over very quickly). Stir and put it on the fire once more until the surface trembles again.

Some people do not stir after the first boil, thinking that this will make them lose some of the froth. Serve in little cups, pouring a little froth in each—you may use a spoon to divide it evenly. (It was considered insulting to receive a cup of coffee without froth.)

Aromatics that go in coffee: The most usual flavoring added is 3 or 4 cardamom pods or ½ teaspoon or more ground cardamom. In Yemen and Aden they also added a pinch of ginger. Many communities had a special spice mixture to go in coffee, which they pounded to a fine

DIBIS—HALEK
Date Syrup

DIBIS IS AN IRAQI and Indian specialty (in India they call it "halek" or "sheera"). Mixed with chopped walnuts, it becomes their Passover haroset. In the old days, large quantities were made at home, to be used as a sweetener instead of sugar. Pitted dates were soaked for a few hours, then boiled, and the juice was pressed through thin muslin and left in trays on the roof, or boiled down to a thick syrup. Various qualities of commercial date syrup are available in cans.

powder and stored in jars. In Morocco it consisted of cinnamon, tiny pieces of mastic, aniseed, and coriander seed.

Thé à la Menthe
Moroccan Mint Tea

SERVES 4 WITH REFILLS

Mint tea can be made with fresh mint leaves alone or with a mixture of mint and green tea. In Morocco different types of green tea with a strong perfume are used, but Chinese gunpowder tea will do perfectly well.

Use a metal teapot, silver or aluminum (it has something to do with minimizing the heat loss). Moroccans commonly use ornately engraved Victorian ones. Wash the mint leaves. Warm the teapot. Pour a little boiling water in and swirl it around, then pour it out. Put in 1 tablespoon of a green tea like the Chinese gunpowder tea, a good bunch of fresh mint leaves, and 5–7 teaspoons of sugar or to to taste. Pour in about 4 cups (1 liter) of boiling water and leave to infuse a few minutes. Stir, and serve in small glasses, filled only half full. Put a mint leaf in each as garnish.

In Morocco they sometimes put a sprinkling of chopped walnuts in the glass, in Tunisia it is pine nuts. A drop of orange-blossom water can also be added.

INFUSIONS AND TEAS

VARIOUS AROMATIC leaves, herbs, and flowers are used to make delicate infusions. Among them are: vervaine, lavender, basil, marjoram, aniseed, sage, orange blossom, dried rose petals, and dried orange peel. In Tunisia, sweet strong tea is served in little glasses with pine kernels floating on top. In Yemen tea leaves are boiled with cardamom, cinnamon, and mint.

Shai Shaimoki
Bukharan Tea with Milk and Butter

SERVES 4

2 cups (500 ml) water
4 tablespoons tea
1 teaspoon salt
2 cups (500 ml) milk
1½ tablespoons butter
2 tablespoons chopped walnuts

Boil the water and tea in a pan for 1 minute and leave to infuse until it is quite strong. Add the rest of the ingredients and heat through. To serve, strain into glasses.

Shai Hamid
Dried Lime Tea

This is an Iraqi and Persian drink with a delightful tart musty flavor. You can buy dried limes in Oriental and Indian stores or you can make them yourself by letting limes dry out on a radiator, until they are brown and sound hollow. For 4: Break 2 dried limes open with a hammer. Put them in a pan with 4 cups (1 liter) of boiling water and simmer for 30 seconds. To serve, strain, and add sugar to taste.

Sahlab

Called "salep" in Israel as in Turkey, this thick, milky drink was and still is sold in the streets in various Middle Eastern countries, including Israel. It is made with a stone-colored powder—the ground bulb of a particular type of orchid called *Orchis mascula.* This is very expensive. I have often bought it in the Jerusalem market, Egypt, and the Istanbul bazaar only to find, when I got home, that I had got a fake or adulterated mix. A cheap and easy alternative is to use cornstarch as a thickener. Although you will not have the distinctive flavor of sahlab, the perfume of orange blossom and the trimmings—a dusting of cinnamon and a generous sprinkling of chopped pistachios—make it a very appealing winter drink.

To serve 4: Keeping a few tablespoons aside in a cup, bring to the boil 4 cups (1 liter) milk. Mix 2 teaspoons sahlab or 2 tablespoons cornstarch with the reserved cold milk to form a smooth creamy paste, and stir it into the hot milk. Simmer for about 10 minutes over very low heat, stirring often so that lumps do not form, until the mixture thickens. Stir in 4 tablespoons sugar, or to taste, and 2 teaspoons rose or orange-blossom water. Serve hot in cups, sprinkling each with cinnamon and plenty of finely chopped pistachios.

ETHIOPIAN JEWS

EVERYONE ASKS ME if I am including the cooking of the Ethiopian Jews. They are the most exotic in our eyes, because they were isolated for almost two thousand years and because they are black. They are now much in evidence in Israel, where you see tall, slim, fine-featured, stunning black soldiers—men and women—walking about in groups. They do not like the name "Falasha," which they were called in Ethiopia, because it means "alien." Little was known about them until recently.

They trace their descent from Israelite noblemen at the time of King Solomon. According to their tradition, their first Emperor Menelik was the son of the union between King Solomon and the queen of Sheba, who returned to Ethiopia on a flying carpet. Their first contact with white Jews was during the Renaissance period, when Italian Jews went to Abyssinia and discovered tribes with an imperfect knowledge of Judaism. In the middle of the nineteenth century, Italian Jews, because of their country's colonial interest in Abyssinia, started a movement to bring them into the fold of traditional Judaism.

Finding out about their cooking has not been easy. They have been very elusive. Several people, in Israel and elsewhere, said they would arrange meetings for me, but nothing ever materialized (there were problems with translators and intermediaries). I have eaten in Ethiopian restaurants. The first time I was taken by friends in New York, and I have glorious memories of sitting around a tray covered by a huge spongy pancakelike bread which fell over the edge like a tablecloth. On it were placed many little bowls of sauces, which we scooped up with ripped-off bits of the pancake bread. The sauces were very strong-tasting but interesting and enjoyable. There were lentil and bean dishes, meat stews, and chicken in a peppery sauce. In Israel I ate at a tiny restaurant called Teodros near the old Tel Aviv bus station, where I was taken by my friend the Israeli food writer and editor Dalia Lamdani. It was full of young Ethiopian soldiers with rifles and huge grins. We had the spongy bread, an Israeli mixed offal grill with a burning-hot spice mixture, and an equally peppery lentil dish. It was so hot that I could not stop crying.

Wine in the Jewish World

THE YIDDISH AUTHOR Isaac Leib Peretz famously commented, "We take a drink only for the sake of the benediction." Comedian Jackie Mason tells stories about liquor cabinets in Jewish homes gathering dust, and about gentiles at Jewish parties suffering a desperate need to have their glasses refilled while they are plied with food and their empty glasses are ignored. He says he hears Jews leaving the theater after a show ask, "Did you eat?" while gentiles ask, "Want to go have a drink?"

Jews have always been known for their moderation in drinking alcohol. By all accounts, even when they were involved in beer and alcohol production in Poland and Russia, they only drank in a moderate way. The authorities always complained that the Jews got Christians drunk while they themselves remained sober. Drunken-

ness was never a prevalent vice, although some old proverbs, like "The rabbi drains the bottle and tells the others to be gay," suggest that heavy drinking may not have been unknown. Yet Jews have a long association with wine, and wine has a special sacred place in Jewish life. It is used for Kiddush, the ceremonial blessing recited on the Sabbath and holy days, and for special celebratory occasions. Four glasses of wine are drunk at Passover, two at weddings, one at a circumcision, during which a baby boy gets his first taste of the drink on his tongue when he is eight days old. The Kiddush cup, in engraved silver or fine glass, symbolizes holiness and happiness in the family.

We know, from the constant mentions in the Bible and from the wine presses, vats, goblets, jugs, and amphorae unearthed in archeological digs, that the ancient Israelites made wine, treading the grapes by foot. The result was probably very potent, because it was often diluted by a third with water. It was made palatable by mixing in spices or honey (which may have been concentrated fruit-juice "honey") and rubbing the containers with resin, which was also a means of preservation. In addition, they made sweet wines with dried raisins, and sparkling wines, as well as wines from fermented date, fig, and pomegranate juices. Wine was considered the choicest of drinks and a symbol of happiness. It was used as payment of debts. Red wine was used in libations.

The wine used for sanctification is traditionally sweet red and usually fortified. Reasons

Wine-making in Petrovka, 1925

advanced are that it is for the whole family and children find it more palatable—almost like fruit juice; that an opened bottle will keep from one week to another; and that bad-quality wine can be masked with sugar. Another reason may be that in Orthodox communities it was common for families to make wine for their own ceremonial needs, and sweet wine from raisins is the easiest to make.

Because wine made by non-Jews could not be drunk, Jews have been involved in wine production when it was allowed. In early medieval times in Western Europe, especially in the Rhineland and France, vine-growing and wine-making were Jewish occupations. The famous rabbinical scholar Rashi earned his living from a vineyard in the eleventh century. He belonged to the community of Troyes, which was a major center of Jewish learning in northeastern France, and whose prosperity was founded on local fairs and wine-growing under the protection of the counts of Champagne. In the thirteenth century, Jews were noted for their vineyards in the south of France, where they held the market in wine in several cities. In Spain too they had vineyards. The medieval Jewish poetry of Spain is full of praise of wine, and wine songs, set to Arabian tunes, were introduced there in the grace after meals.

In Poland, Lithuania, and Russia, a traditional Jewish occupation was inn- and tavern-keeper—selling wine and liquor, which they distilled, to the local peasantry. In Jewish homes, though wine was seldom served during the meal, distilled alcoholic beverages such as vodka, schnapps, or slivovitz were drunk, and sweet fruit brandies and liqueurs were served after the meal with sponge cake and dry biscuits to dunk in. Morello cherries macerated in brandy were another special-occasion delicacy. Some of the first immigrants from Eastern Europe in London brought their old trades and opened pubs in Soho, which became legendary.

In Islamic countries like North Africa and Persia, where wine was forbidden to Muslims, Jews were involved in producing and selling wine and spirits, such as the anise-flavored arak and mahia. Persia had red and white wines made by Armenians, Nestorians, and Jews. The wines of Shiraz and Hamadan are said to have had a delicious flavor and bouquet. In Morocco there is still a wine called "Rabbi Jacob."

A famous passage in a letter written in 1488 by Obadiah of Bertinoro to his father in Italy, while Obadiah was in Alexandria on his way to Palestine, gives a vivid—and in my view probably exaggerated—description of Jewish Sabbath drinking rituals in the medieval Muslim world: "The following is the custom in all Muslim countries. They sit in a circle on the carpet, the cup bearer standing nearby. A small cloth is spread on the carpet and all kinds of fruit which are in season are brought and laid on it. The host now takes a glass of wine and pronounces the blessing of sanctification and empties the cup. The cup bearer then hands the cup to the whole company, always refilled, and each person empties it. Then the host eats two or three pieces of fruit and drinks a second glass and all the company say 'Health and life.' Whoever sits next to the host also takes some fruit, and the cup bearer fills a second glass for him and he says 'To your happiness' and the company responds. . . . Then a second type of fruit is partaken of and another glass is filled, and this is continued until each one has emptied six or seven glasses. . . . After all have drunk to their heart's content, a large dish of meat is brought and each one stretches forth his hand and eats quickly, for they are not very big eaters. . . . A glass of wine was drunk with each kind [of food]. Then followed raisin wine, which was very good; then malmsey wine from Candia; and again native wine. I drank with them and was exhilarated."

When waves of Jewish immigrants "returning to Zion" began to arrive in Palestine in the late nineteenth century, agriculture was seen as the best way of becoming self-sufficient. Vines were planted in the areas of settlement. The first vineyards were south of Tel Aviv, in Rishon Le-Zion (which means "the first to Zion"). Baron Edmond de Rothschild, who sponsored the early pioneer settlements, was the owner of Château Lafitte and believed that viticulture could be a good economic basis for Jewish villages. He brought grape varieties from the south of France, which had the same hot climate, and sent French viticulturists and enologists to advise. He built large wineries in Rishon Le-Zion and Zichron Yaacov. In 1906, the wineries were deeded to the growers, who formed their own cooperative. The company, known as Carmel, was the foundation of the modern Israeli wine industry. Most of the wine produced was sweet.

Today, since New World expertise from California has revolutionized wine-making and traditional grape varieties such as Cabernet Sauvignon, Sauvignon Blanc, Chardonnay, and Emerald Riesling have been introduced, and more propitious sites, like the Golan Heights, have been planted, the quality of Israeli wines has soared to a high international standard. Although the local consumption at four and a half liters per head per year remains very low (one must take into consideration that the Muslim population does not drink), the trend of the early years of the state, when 75 percent of the wine consumed locally was sweet, has been reversed; now 80 percent of wines consumed are dry or semi-dry.

ABOUT KOSHER WINES

KOSHER WINES are produced under rabbinical supervision in many wine-producing countries, including California, France, Italy, South Africa, and Australia, as well as in Israel. For a wine to be accepted as kosher, only kosher items may be used in the wine-making process, and from the time the grapes arrive at the winery, only religious Jews who observe the Sabbath may handle the product and touch the wine-making equipment.

The reason for the prohibition is that in the very ancient past wine was used in the worshipping of idols, and it was forbidden by the sages to use non-Jewish wine lest it could be the wine of idolatry. By extension, wine used in church could not be drunk. The prohibition against any wine touched by a non-Jew remained in effect by rabbinical decree for a further reason—to prevent social situations that lead to assimilation and to the formation of attachments leading to intermarriage. This means that even previously kosher wine becomes forbidden if handled by a non-Jew when unsealed. So kosher wine must be opened at the table, in front of the drinker, by a religious Jew.

The one type of wine that gets around this part of the prohibition and allows a nonobservant waiter to serve wine to a strictly religious person is "cooked wine," called *Yavin Meshuval.* It is not included in the prohibition because in the days of the Holy Temple boiling a wine made it unfit to be brought to the altar. It is not literally boiled but flash-pasteurized to 185°F (85°C) to limit the negative effect of such treatment.

Wine labeled "Kosher for Passover" is guaranteed not to have come in contact with bread, grain, or products made from leavened dough. Most kosher wines are also "Kosher for Passover."

Further regulations apply only to wineries in the Land of Israel, where agricultural laws date back to ancient times. For the first three years, fruit from a new vine must not be picked (the flower buds are removed to prevent fruit formation). Growing wheat between vines is prohibited. In accordance with Biblical law, every seventh year fields should be left fallow and allowed to rest, producing no crops. But because vineyards need to be nurtured and looked after, growers are allowed to "sell" their vineyards temporarily to a non-Jew for the duration of the seventh year. Finally, there is a symbolic ceremony in which 1 percent of the production is poured away in remembrance of the 10-percent tithe once paid to the Temple in Jerusalem.

Select Bibliography

I have used so many books and publications in my research that, by necessity, this list is very selective. The following were especially important to me. Some titles not on the list are mentioned in the text.

Ashtor, Eliyahu. *The Jews of Moslem Spain.* Translated by Aaron Klein and Jenny Machlowitz Klein. 3 vols. Philadelphia: Jewish Publication Society, 1979.

Baer, Yotzhak. *A History of the Jews in Christian Spain.* Philadelphia: Jewish Publication Society, 1992.

Cooper, John. *Eat and Be Satisfied: A Social History of Jewish Food.* London: Jason Aronson, 1993.

Elazar, Daniel. *The Other Jews.* New York: Basic Books, 1989.

Geller, Ruth Lilian. *Jewish Rome.* Translated by Desmond O'Grady. Rome: Viella, 1983.

Greenberg, Loui. *The History of the Jews in Russia.* New York: Schocken Books, 1976.

Haber, Barbara. "The Sephardi World: A Culinary Dispersal." Talk given at an Oldways International Food Symposium, Spain, 1992.

Israel, Steve. "The Story of the Jews in Spain: The Sephardi Diaspora." Part of the Educational Kit of *Exile 1492: The Expulsion of the Jews from Spain.* Jerusalem: Ben Zvi Institute, 1991.

Kirshenblatt-Gimblett, Barbara. "The Kosher Gourmet in the Nineteenth-Century Kitchen: Three Jewish Cookbooks in Historical Perspective." *Journal of Gastronomy* 2 (Winter 1986–87).

Lewis, Bernard. *The Jews of Islam.* London: Routledge and Kegan Paul, 1984.

Milano, Attilio. *Storia degli ebrei in Italia.* Turin: Giulio Einaudi, 1992.

Rejwan, Nissim. *The Jews of Iraq.* London: Weidenfeld and Nicholson, 1985.

Renard, Raymond. *Sepharad.* Mons, Belgium: Annales Universitaires de Mons, 1966.

Sacerdoti, Annie, and Luca Fiorentino. *Guida all'Italia ebraica.* Casale Monferrato: Marietti, 1986.

Schwartz, Oded. *In Search of Plenty: A History of Jewish Food.* London: Kyle Cathie, 1992.

Stiller, Freddie. "Israeli Wine." *International Wine and Spirits Review,* 1991.

Stillman, Norman. *The Jews of Arab Lands: A History and Source Book.* Philadelphia: Jewish Publication Society, 1979.

Sutton, Joseph. *Aleppo Chronicles.* Brooklyn, N.Y.: Thayer-Jacoby, 1988.

————. *Magic Carpet: Aleppo in Flatbush.* Brooklyn, N.Y.: Thayer-Jacoby, 1979.

Tas, Luciano. *Storia degli ebrei italiani.* Rome: Newton Compton, 1987.

Zafrani, Haim. *Mille ans de vie juive au Maroc.* Paris: Maisonneuve et Larose, 1983.

Cookbooks

A great number of Jewish cookbooks have appeared in recent years. Here I list a few that are important because they record lesser-known cuisines and break new ground.

Ascoli Vitali-Norsa, Giuliana, ed. *La cucina nella tradizione ebraica.* 2d ed. Padua: Edizione dell'Adei Wizo, 1979.

Badi, Meri. *250 recettes de cuisine juive espagnole.* Paris: Jacques Grancher Éditeur, 1984.

Benbassa, Esther. *Cuisine judeo-espagnole.* Paris: Éditions du Scribe, 1984.

Chiche-Yana, Martine. *La table juive: Recettes et traditions de fêtes.* Aix-en-Provence: Edisud, 1990.

Gubbay, Millie, Gaby Gubbay-Nemes, and Mozell Isaac, eds. *Awafi: Exotic Cuisine from the Middle and Far East.* Sydney: Ladies Auxiliary of the Sephardi Synagogue, 1990.

Hazan-Arama, Fortunée. *Saveurs de mon enfance: La cuisine juive du Maroc.* Paris: Robert Laffont, 1987.

Herbst-Krausz, Zorica. *Old Jewish Dishes.* Budapest: Corvina, 1988.

Hyman, Mavis. *Indian-Jewish Cooking.* London, 1992. Self-published.

Iny, Daisy. *The Best of Baghdad Cooking, with Treats from Teheran.* New York: Saturday Review Press/E. P. Dutton, 1976.

Jaffin, Leone. *150 recettes et mille et un souvenirs d'une juive d'Algérie.* Paris: Encre Éditions, 1980.

Kakon, Maguy. *La cuisine juive du Maroc de mère en fille.* Toulouse: Éditions Daniel Briand, 1994.

Karsenty, Irene, and Lucienne Karsenty. *Cuisine pied noir.* Paris: Éditions Denoel, 1974.

Levy-Mellul, Rivka. *La cuisine juive marocaine.* Paris: Albert Soussan Éditeur, 1983.

Limentani Pavoncello, Donatella. *Dal 1880 ad offi la cucina ebraica della mis famiglia.* Rome: Carucci Editore, 1982.

Machlin, Edda S. *The Classic Cuisine of the Italian Jews.* New York: Everest House, 1981.

Maffioli, Giuseppe. *La cucina veneziana.* Padua: Franco Muzzio Editore, 1982.

Marks, Copeland. *Sephardic Cooking.* New York: Donald I. Fine, 1992.

————. *The Varied Kitchens of India.* New York: M. Evans and Company, 1986.

Moryoussef, Viviane, and Nina Moryoussef. *La cuisine juive marocaine.* Paris and Casablanca: Taillandier/Sochepress, 1983.

Persian (Jewish) Cook Book. Compiled by the Sisterhood of the Persian Hebrew Congregation, Skokie, Ill.

Recipes from the Jewish Kitchens of Curaçao. Compiled by the Sisterhood of Mikve Israel–Emanuel. Drukkerij Scherpenheuvel N.V., 1982.

Roukhomovsky, Suzanne. *Gastronomie juive et pâtisserie de Russie, d'Alsace, de Roumanie et d'Orient.* Paris: Flammarion, 1968.

Sacerdoti, Mira. *Italian Jewish Cooking.* Melbourne: Hill of Content, 1992.

Sasson, Grace. *Kosher Syrian Cooking.* 1958. Self-published.

Sefarad Yemekleri. Compiled by Viki Koronyo and Sima Ovadia. Istanbul: Society of Assistance to Old People, 1985.

Stavroulakis, Nicholas. *Cookbook of the Jews of Greece.* New York: Cadmus Press, 1986.

Zeitun, Edmond. *250 recettes classiques de cuisine tunisienne.* Paris: Jacques Grancher Éditeur, 1977.

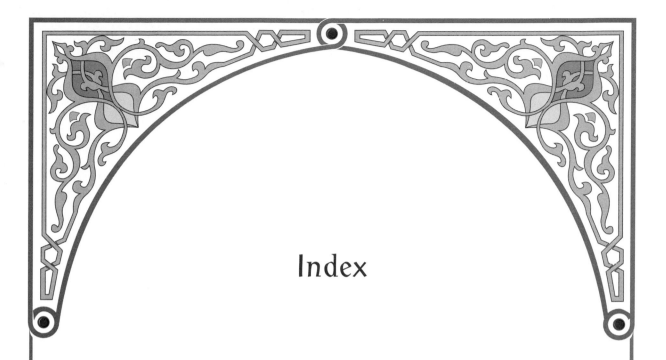

Index

almond(s) *(cont.)*
cream cheese mold with, 177–8
and egg cream, 577
lamb with
and fresh fava beans, 406
and raisins, 390–1
macaroons, 607–8
milk of, 624–5
paste, 605
dates stuffed with, 611–12
marzipan, 606–7
walnuts stuffed with, 612
pastries
crescents, 586–8
with egg threads, 577–8
filo triangles in syrup, 583–4
fingers, 584–5
marzipan coil in filo, 583
with raisins, 610–11
with walnuts, 610
and spinach dessert, 563
sweet breads with raisins and, 552
sweetmeats, 608–9
Almoravids, 221, 493
aloo makalla, 520
Alsace, 10, 65, 131–3
desserts in, 178
goose in, 70, 125, 127
Hanukah in, 33
kugelhopf, 99
noodles in, 154
meat in, 135, 137, 145, 149
rice in, 159
sauerkraut in, 163
Yom Kippur in, 30
Altman, Yochanan, 264
amande(s)
agneau aux, 390–1
aux fèves vertes, 406
beztels aux, 584
breik aux, 584
pâte d', 606–7
rose aux, 583
amandines, 604–6
amardine, crème d', 560
America, 12, 13, 41, 76–82, 184,
203, 206, 287, 288, 369
bagels in, 100
Bukharans in, 454
cheesecake in, 179
couscous in, 490
delicatessens in, 58, 61, 80

America *(cont.)*
discovery of, 481
drinks in, 200
Georgians in, 264
meat in, 136, 146
Persians, 449–50
smoked salmon in, 69
sweetmeats in, 612
Syrians in, 564–6
vegetables in, 507
wine in, 633, 634
Yemenites in, 322
anchovy sauce, pasta with, 475
anise bread, 551–2
anjuli, 328
Antiochus Epiphanes, King, 32
apam, 575
appetizers, 58–82, 245–77
calf's foot jelly, 72
celeriac and carrots in lemon
sauce, 249
celery cooked in oil, 251
cheese
cream cheese, 63
and egg, 272–3
fritters, 272
grilled, 272
chickpea and tahini dip, 275
cucumbers pickled in brine,
60–1
eggplant
fritters, 256
slices, fried, 255–6
and tahini puree, 275
eggs
cheese and, 272–3
chopped, with onions, 64
long-cooked hard-boiled, 246
scrambled, with onions, 64
fava bean fritters, 273–4
fish, cured, 276
fish roe
caviar, 68
cream, 276
dried, 276
gribenes, 58–9
herring, 66
chopped, 67–8
marinated, 67
horseradish sauce, 59–60
kidney beans with sour plum
sauce, 266

appetizers *(cont.)*
knishes, 73
pastry dough for, 74
potato dough for, 75–6
liver
chopped, 70–1
fried, with onions, 72
matzo brei, 76
mushrooms with cumin, 261
onions
sweet-and-sour caramel, 252–3
tart of, creamy, 65
piroshki, 73
cream cheese filling, 74
meat filling, 74–5
pastry dough for, 74
potato dough for, 75–6
potato filling, 75
potato latkes, 64–5
pumpkin puree, 261
ratatouille, 259–60
salmon, smoked, 69
tehina, 274–5
toast with beef marrow, 74
vine leaves, cold stuffed, 277
walnut and roast pepper paste,
267
zucchini, marinated, 260
see also salads
"appetizing" stores, 138
apple(s)
baked, 172
blintzes, 176
cabbage with
red, sweet-and-sour, 162
stuffed, 167
cake, 188
chutney, 241
compote, 171
latkes, 172–3
pastry, macaroon, 189–90
potato salad with herrings and, 68
pudding, 173–4
with bread and milk, 174
rice pudding, 179
rice with, 458
roast goose with, 125
sauce, 166
sautéed, 166
soup, 92
strudel, 180–2
stuffed cabbage with, 167

beef *(cont.)*
  eggplant roll stuffed with, 535–6
  goulash soup, 90–1
  kibbeh, 411–14
  kreplach, 86–8
  marrow, toast with, 74
  meat loaf, 142–3, 431
    with beans and tomatoes, 439
    in stew with beans and spinach, 438
    and stuffed chicken stew with chickpeas, 433
  meatballs
    couscous with, 498–500
    with leeks, 408–9
    pasta pie with chicken livers and, 486–7
    with spinach, 409
    sweet-and-sour, 143
    with sweet-and-sour beets, 410
    in tomato sauce, 406–8
  moussaka, 401–2
  with okra, 404
  onions stuffed with, 544
  patties, grilled, 387–8
  pies
    cigars, 304–6
    Greek, 289
    little triangles, 299
  pigeon stuffed with, 357–8
  pot roast, 140–1
  potato cutlets stuffed with, 546
  prune tzimmes, 140
  pumpkin stuffed with, 548
  rice with
    croquettes, 418–20
    and green herb sauce, 466–7
    ground rice dumplings in hamud sauce, 466
    and split pea sauce, 467–8
  salt, 135–6
  soup, 324
    with beans and vegetables, 320
    with melokheya, 316
  stew
    with beans and spinach, 438
    with cracked wheat, 441
    with haricot beans, 141, 402–3
    with quinces, 391–2
    with split peas and spinach, 403
  stuffed cabbage with, 167

beef *(cont.)*
  sweet-and-sour eggplant and, 400–1
  tomatoes stuffed with nuts, raisins, and, 541–2
  tongue, 135
    boiled, 137
    with sauerkraut, 145
    sweet-and-sour raisin sauce for, 137–8
  zucchini stuffed with, 542–3
beet(s)
  salad, with sour cream, 61
  soup, cold, 88–9
  sweet-and-sour, meatballs with, 410
Behmoaras, Lizi, 526
beid bi banadoura, 532
beiglach, 73
beignets
  de Pâques, 594
  de poissons, 351
  poulet en, 377
Belgian endive, cooked, 511
Belgium, 41
belila, 574–5
Belorussia, 46
Bendaoud, Raymonde, 586
Bene Israel, 365–70
  bread of, 550
  chicken dishes of, 371
  chutneys of, 241, 242
  desserts of, 573, 604
  fish dishes of, 345
  meat dishes of, 404
  pickles of, 240
  rice dishes of, 448, 462, 463
  salads of, 270
  vegetable dishes of, 518, 521, 536
Benjamin of Tudela, 366
Berbers, 219, 221, 384, 406, 434, 436, 490, 493–8, 610
berengena
  albdondigas de, 410
  almodrote de, 521–2
  assada, gayna kon, 376
  borekitas de, 283–4
  frita, 256
  rodanchas de, 301–2
  rulos de, 535
  tapada de, 284
berkoksh, 506

Bermant, Chaim, 66
Bernaldez, Andrés, 222
Bernstein-on-Essex (New York), 139
berry(ies)
  compote, 171
  in syrup, 171
bessara, 317–18
Beyazit II, Sultan, 224
beztels
  aux amandes, 584
  pastry for, 305
  aux pommes de terre, 306–7
bhakri, 550
Bible, 18, 21–27, 204, 214, 316, 321, 326, 379, 598, 631, 634
  see also Exodus
bimbriyo, 615, 616
  loape de, 616
  pojo con, 362
bimuelos, 591–2
biscuits, 194–5
bishak, 295
Blackburn, Tess Levy, 577
Black Death, 43, 482
black-eyed pea
  salad, 263
  stew, 402
Blanc, Raymond, 388
blé arricha, t'fina de, 441
blehat, 406
blintzes
  apple, 176
  cheese, 176
  cherry, 176–7
  meat, 144
bocca di dama, 595–6
boeuf aux haricots blancs, 403
boghatcha, 303–4
Bohemia, 42
Bolens, Lucie, 219, 220, 423, 440
Bolsheviks, 454, 455
bomba di riso al formaggio, 464–5
borekas(itas), 279
  basic dough for, 280
  de berengena, 283–4
  de espinaka, 283
  de handrajo, 284
  de keso, 281–2
  making, 281

cake *(cont.)*
    sponge, 187–8, 595
        almond, 595–6
caldero, 346–8
calf's foot, 423
    in dafina, 430
    jelly, 72
    soup, 425
    whole wheat casserole with, 441
calf's liver and onions, 145
calsones, rishta wa, 472
calves' brains and chicken cake,
    373–4
Canada, 12, 41, 76, 369, 495
    bagels in, 100
    delicatessens in, 58
capers, onion salad with, 252
caponata alla giudea, 258–9
capsicum chicken, 364–5
Carasso, Jean, 288–9
Carasso, Joe, 289
caraway, cream cheese with, 63
carciofi
    alla giudia, 509
    frittata di, 530
    ripieni, 545–6
    riso coi, 463–4
cardamom, 232
cardoons, meat stew with beans and,
    438
Carmel, Dalia, 267, 329
Carmel winery, 633
carne
    mina de, 309–10
    pasteles de, 289–90
Carnegie Deli (New York), 139
Caro, Joseph, 19, 278–9
carottes
    au carvi, 251
    salade de
        et pommes de terre, 251–2
        rapées, 248
carp
    jellied
        Polish style, 110–11
        Russian style, 112
    stuffed slices, 109–10
carpe à la Juive, 110–12
carrot(s)
    and celeriac in lemon sauce,
        249

carrot(s) *(cont.)*
    chicken with mint and, 371
    rice with chicken and, 457
    salad
        grated, 248
        sliced boiled, with caraway seeds,
        251
        with potatoes, 251–2
    tzimmes, 164
cassola, 575–6
cassoulet, 146
Catherine the Great, Tsarina of
    Russia, 46
Catholics, *see* Christians
caviar, fish roe, 68
caviare d'aubergines, 256
cedrini, 606
celeriac
    and carrots in lemon sauce, 249
    and fennel salad, 250
céleris raves et fenouils au citron,
    250
celery
    cooked in oil, 251
    rice with green vegetable sauce,
        465
chakla bakla, 238
Chaoua, Es Saad Fradj, 434
chapatis, 550
Charlemagne, 131
Charles VI, King of France, 482
cheese
    cracked wheat with, 469
    egg and, 272–3
        with fried peppers and
            tomatoes, 532–3
    eggplant halves with, 534–5
    flan
        with eggplant, 522
        with filo, 303–4
    fritters, 272
    grilled, 272
    labne, 269–70
    pancakes, 575–6
        in syrup, 591
    and peas curry, 513
    peppers stuffed with, 539–40
    pie
        basic dough for, 280–1
        coils, 300
        with eggplant, 283–4

cheese *(cont.)*
    filo triangles, 296
    Georgian, 295–6
    Syrian, 282
    tart, 302
    Turkish, 281–2
    ravioli, 472
    rice cake with, 464–5
    spinach and, 529
        cake, 527–8
    tomatoes stuffed with, 541
    white, 271–2
    zucchini and, gratin, 533
    see also cream cheese; curd cheese
cheesecake, 179–80
chermoula, 348
cherry(ies)
    in brandy, 199
    blintzes, 176–7
    compote, 171
    lamb with
        meatballs, 393–4
        roast, 392–3
    rice with
        and cranberries, 450–1
        pudding, 179
    soup, cold, 92
    stewed, on bread, 558–9
    strudel, 182
    varenikes, 156
chestnuts
    lamb with, 399
    with onions, 165
    and pumpkin accompaniment for
        couscous, 493
cheveux d'ange, confiture de, 617–18
chicken, 120–1, 353–4
    boiled, 122
    and calves' brains cake, 373–4
    capsicum, 364–5
    with chickpeas, 363–4
    with carrots and mint, 371
    in coconut sauce, 371–2
    couscous, 502
        with chicken balls, 502
    cracklings, 58–9
    croquettes
        Burmese style, 378
        with rice, 377–8
    with dates, 359
    with eggplant sauce, 376

egg(s) (cont.)
chicken soup with, 85
hard-boiled
chopped, with onions, 64
in dafina, 430
fava beans with, 533–4
long-cooked, 246
pasta salad with olives and, 471
lamb's trotters with chickpeas and, 425
and lemon sauce
cold, 247
fish with, 338–9
for pasta, 475–6
and lemon soup, 311
omelette
eggplant, 522
meat, 420–1
potato, 531–2
spinach, 528–9
meat pastries with, 306
poached, over spinach and cheese, 529
sauce, halibut with, 114–15
scrambled
with onions, 64
wurst and, 135
spinach and
cake with cheese, 527–8
omelette, 528–9
scrambled, 529
threads, almond pastry with, 577–8
and tomato, 532
cake, 531
with fried peppers, 532–3
egg cream, 200, 202
eggplant, 255
with cheese, 534–5
and cracked wheat, 469
pie, 283–4
chicken with, 376–7
coils, 301–2
flan, 521–2
fried, 255–6, 515
fritters, 256
with ground meat, 410
kobeba stew with, 417
layered dish, 521
omelette, 522
pickle, 240

eggplant (cont.)
pie
with cheese, 283–4
with tomato, 284
ratatouille, 259–60
rice with, 464
roll, stuffed with meat, 535–6
salad
boiled, 258
Italian, 258–9
mashed with oil and lemon, 256
with peppers, 257–8
stew, with meat dumplings, 417–18
stuffed
Indian, 536–7
with ground meat and pine nuts, 537–8
and tahini puree, 275
Egypt, 3–5, 7–9, 16, 81, 205, 215, 223, 229, 230, 287, 292, 396, 406, 461, 478, 480
ancient, Exodus from, see Exodus
cakes in, 599
cheese-making in, 271
chicken in, 353–4, 359–60
cooking oil in, 234
desserts in, 558, 562, 570, 572
drinks in, 629
falafel in, 274
fish in, 330, 335, 342, 343, 351–2
Hanukah in, 33
haroset in, 619, 620
jams in, 617, 619
Livornese in, 485
long-cooked hard-boiled eggs in, 246
meat in, 399, 401, 402, 404, 407, 412, 415, 416, 422, 425
medieval, 21, 26
Passover in, 35–6, 233, 388
pastries in, 279, 579, 580, 585, 589, 591
poultry in, 357–8, 379
rice in, 460, 465, 466
in Roman Empire, 493
Rosh Hoshanah in, 28–30
Sabbath pot in, 428, 429
salads in, 250, 262–3
savory pies in, 281, 282, 290, 299, 302, 304, 309
soups in, 311, 315, 316, 318
Spanish Jews in, 219, 220

Egypt (cont.)
spices used in, 232, 234
sugar refineries in, 580
sweetmeats in, 605, 612
Syrians in, 564–5, 569
vegetables in, 239, 516, 533–4, 541, 542, 544–5
wine in, 633
Yom Kippur in, 30–1
Eid el Kibir, 489
Elfersi, Armand, 603
Elias, Flower, 370
Elijah, 36
Elijah, Rabbi, 620
empanadas, 292
de pishkado, 293–4
endive, 511
Enlightenment, 49
épinards
pois chiches aux, 517
fila aux, 298
ragout aux, 403
tarte feuilletée aux, 302–3
erbe, torta di, 308–9
Esau, 316
escabèche, poisson en, 330–1
espinaka
albondigas de, 409
arroz kon, 462
avas kon, 403, 517
borekas de, 293
bulemas kon, 300–1
fritada de, 527–8
Essex Street Pickles (New York), 138
Este family, 223, 483
Esther, Queen, 33–4, 449, 524
Ethiopia, 21, 22, 549, 630
Eucalyptus Inn (Jerusalem), 94, 573
Exodus, 35–36, 97, 312, 317, 387, 389, 508
Ezra, Esmond David, 368

falafel, 273–4
farfel, 153
with mushrooms, 165
farka, 576
Farouk, King of Egypt, 612
Fascists, 477
fassoulia
bi zeit, 262–3
hadra, lahma bi, 404

mullet
  marinated, 332
  with raisins and pine nuts, 333–4
  in tomato sauce, 334
mumbar, 426
Murray's Sturgeon Shop (New York),
    138
mushroom(s)
  and barley, 158
    soup, 88
  chicken with, 123
  with cumin, Moroccan style, 261
  Hungarian style, 166
  kasha with, 157
  kreplach, 87–8
  saffron risotto with, 448
  soup, 94
  with sour cream, 165
  veal breast stuffed with kasha and,
    150–1
Muslims, 16, 26, 213–30, 232, 339,
    395, 507
  alcohol forbidden to, 626, 633
  in Bukhara, 454, 455
  in Egypt, 4, 589
  feasts of, 31, 320, 489
  in Greece, 286, 287
  in India, 367, 369, 370
  in Iraq, 397
  meat eaten by, 384
  in Morocco, 389, 493–4, 554
  pastries of, 580
  in Persia, 449
  on Sabbath, 27
  in Sicily, 478
  in Spain, 215–23
  in Syria, 567–9
  in Tunisia, 434, 436
  in Turkey, 408, 524–6
  vine leaves of, 277
  in Yemen, 321–2
mustacchioni, 609
mustacudos de muez, 609
mutton, 384
  cured, 386
  see also lamb

Nadel, Fanny, 105
nahit, 167
Nahoum and Sons (Calcutta), 370
Nahum, Rabbi, 8

nanaeya, 411
Napoleon, Emperor, 49, 479
Nasser, Gamal Abdel, 612
Nassis, 133
National Federation of Fish Friers,
    British, 113
Nazis, 51, 231, 287, 477
Nebuchadnezzar, 214, 394
Nehama, Joseph, 288
Nepal, 215
Nessim ben Nessim, 498
Nestorians, 633
New Year, see Rosh Hashanah
Nini, Yehuda, 321
noci, putizza di, 602–3
noix
  cigares aux, 584–5
  fourées, 612
  mounettes aux raisins et aux, 552
  pruneaux aux, 492
  terfas aux, 610
noodles
  dough for, 152–3
  kasha with, 157
  lentils with, 471
  pudding, 154
    with apple, 174–5
    with cheese, 155
    Hungarian, 175
  simple ways to serve, 154
Norman Conquest, 183
nougada, 330
nuez, peshe kon, 340–1
nut oils, 234
nuts
  couscous cake with dates and, 576
  dried fruit compote with, 559–60
  filo triangles filled with, in syrup,
    583–4
  haroset, 619–21
  konafa filled with, 581
  multi-layered pastry filled with,
    581–2
  quince butter with, 616
  whole wheat or barley in syrup
    with, 574
  see also almonds; hazelnuts; pista-
    chios; walnuts

Obadiah of Bertinoro, 16, 21, 26,
    633

oca, prosciutto e salame d', 383
oeufs, bouillon de poule aux, 312
offal, 14, 422–7
  brains
    and chicken cake, 373
    fritters, 424
    in tomato sauce, 424–5
    with egg-and-lemon sauce, 424
  calf's foot, 423
    in dafina, 430
    jelly, 72
    soup, 425
    whole wheat casserole with, 441
  intestine, stuffed, 150, 426
  lamb's trotter soup, 425
  tongue
    boiled, 137
    pickled, 135, 423
    sweet-and-sour raisin sauce for,
      137–8
  tripe stew, 426–7
  see also liver
Ohrnberg, Kaj, 216
oignons
  caramélisés, 252–3
  confits, et raisins secs, 492
  farcis, 544
  aux marrons, 165
  salade d', 252
  tarte aux, d'Alsace, 65
oils, 234
ojaldres, 296
okra
  meat with, 404
  stew, with meat dumplings,
    417–18
  with tamarind, 514
  in tomato sauce, 513–14
Oldways Preservation and Exchange
    Trust, 218
  International Symposium, 490
olio, vitello sott', 388–9
olive oil, 234, 526
  cold fish in, 327
  cold veal in, 388–9
  deep frying in, 351
olives
  chicken and, 363
  orange salad with, 249
  pasta salad with hard-boiled eggs
    and, 471

olives (*cont.*)
pommes de terre aux, 519
potatoes with, 519
salad, 250
poulet aux, 363
omelettes
artichoke, 530
eggplant, 522
meat, 420–1
potato, 531–2
spinach, 528–9
onion(s)
barley with, 158
caramelized
with raisins
sweet-and-sour, 252–3
chestnuts with, 165
and eggs
chopped, 64
scrambled, 64
liver with, 145, 172
pies, 294
rolls, stuffed with meat in
tamarind sauce, 544
salad, with capers, 252
sauce, 359
sweet-and-sour chicken in,
372–3
tart, creamy, 65
orange(s), 598
cake, 599–600
doughnut rings, 594–5
flan, 558
gâteau à l', 599–600
gâteau au sirop d', 597–9
granita, 558
peel, candied, 613–14
salad
dessert, 558
with olives, 249
slices, cooked in syrup, 614–15
syrup, almond cake in, 597–9
Passover cake with walnuts, 596
tranches d', au sirop, 614–15
zest, 232
orange-blossom water, 232, 234–5
orecchie di Ammon, 592–3
Orient Express, 287
osban, 426, 498, 499
meat stew with beans, spinach,
and, 438

oshee kifte, 325
Osherovich, M., 79
oshi tos kadu, 547–8
osmanlia, 581
Ottoman Empire, 211, 213, 220,
224–30, 338, 527
Balkans in, 160
Egypt in, 4
filo pastry in, 297
fruit compotes in, 559
Greece in, 285–6, 288
Hungary in, 50, 160
Iraq in, 395, 396
Passover in, 310
Syria in, 569
Tunisia in, 436, 437
vegetables in, 536
Yemen in, 323
Oxford Symposium on Food and
Cookery, 9, 525, 576

Pahlavi dynasty, 449
pain juif à l'anis, 551–2
palacsinken torte, 177
Pale of Settlement, 46
Palestine, 41, 203, 230, 287, 402
ancient, 214, 448
wine in, 633
Yemenites in, 322
pallebe, 596
pancakes
cream cheese, 176–7
layered, with apricot jam and
meringue topping, 177
matzo meal, 198
ricotta, 575–6
stuffed with meat, 144
in syrup, 590–1
pan d'Espanya, 595
Pan Guandan, 623
paprika, cream cheese with, 63
Pardo-Rokes, Louise, 278
pareve foods, 21
Parfitt, Tudor, 368
Parsees, 369
paschka, 177–8
Pasha, Sakakini, 572
passerini, spinaci con pinoli e, 516–17
Passover, 9, 10, 13, 23, 34–36, 59,
233, 406, 554, 565
in America, 81

Passover (*cont.*)
cakes for, 596–7, 600
dietary laws for, 21
during Inquisition, 222
eggs for, 246
fava beans for, 461, 508
fish for, 326
haroset for, 198, 619–21, 627
in India, 370
jams for, 619
matzo for, 76, 184
meat for, 384, 387, 389, 390,
411, 415, 416, 426, 500
pastries for, 188–90, 198, 594
rice for, 466
Sabbath during, 429
savory pies for, 309–10
soup for, 312–13, 317
in shtetl, 56
sweetmeats for, 605, 607, 610
turkey galantine for, 380
unleavened bread for, 550
vegetables for, 526, 527, 544
wine for, 631, 634
pasta, 470
with anchovy sauce, 475
chicken with, 359–60
roast, with raisins, and pine
nuts, 476
cold, with tomato sauce, 474–5
dough, 152–3
with egg-and-lemon sauce, 475–6
kasha with, 157
lentils with, 471
soup, 317
pie, with meatballs and chicken
livers, 486–7
pudding
with apples, 174–5
with cheese, 155
Hungarian, 175
savory, 154
rice with, 460
salad, with olives and hard-boiled
eggs, 471
simple ways to serve, 154
stuffed, *see* kreplach; ravioli
with spinach, 485–6
pasteles
basic dough for, 280
de carne, 289–90

pumpkin *(cont.)*
  pie
    Bukharan, 295
    Italian, 293
  puree, 511–12
    appetizer, 261
  ravioli, 473–4
  soup, 93
    with split peas, 319
  stew, with meat dumplings,
    417–18
  stuffed, 547–8
  tzimmes, 164
purdah pilau, 451-2
Purim, 9, 33–4, 98, 290, 406, 481,
  524
  couscous for, 506
  milk pudding for, 570
  pasta for, 470, 471
  pastries for, 186, 192, 578, 591–3
  sweetmeats for, 605, 607
putizza di noci, 602–3

Qaddafi, Muamar, 484
qouzi, 419–20
quadrucci coi spinaci, 485–2
quails, stuffed roast, 357, 358
quatre épices, 234
queijinhos, 577
quince(s)
  butter, with nuts, 616
  chicken with, 361–2
  in jelly, 560–1
  paste, 615, 616
  and pumpkin accompaniment for
    couscous, 493
  stew, 391–2
    kobeba, 417
  in wine, 561

Raban, Joseph, 366
radish salad, 62
  with oranges, 249
ragout
  aux épinards, 403
  de morue, 339–40
raisin(s)
  apples baked with, 172
  caramelized onions with, 492
  carrot tzimmes with, 164
  cheesecake with, 180

raisin(s) *(cont.)*
  chickpeas and, 492
  compote, 171
  couscous with pumpkin and, 503–4
  cream cheese mold with, 177–8
  hallah with, 97
  lamb with almonds and, 390–1
  meatballs with, 143
  noodle pudding with, 154
  and nut pastries, 610–11
  red mullet with pine nuts and,
    333–4
  rice with, 464
    and prunes, 159
  rice pudding with, 179
  sauce, sweet-and-sour, 137–8
  stuffed cabbage with, 167
  sultana, spinach with pine nuts
    and, 517
  sweet breads with nuts and, 552
  sweet-and-sour red cabbage with
    apples and, 162
  tomatoes stuffed with meat, nuts,
    and, 541–2
  and walnut crescents, 193
  yogurt and cucumber salad with,
    270
raisins confits, 618–19
raisins secs
  agneau aux, 390–1
  couscous à la courge rouge et aux,
    503–4
  mounettes aux noix et aux, 552
  oignons confits et, 492
  pois chiches et, 492
raita, 270
Ramadan, 31, 320
Rashi, 131, 632
Rashid, Harun al-, 215, 217
ratatouille, 259–60
Ratners Dairy Restaurant (New York),
  139
ravioli
  cheese, with tagliatelle, 472
  dough for, 152–3
  plum and apricot, 156
  pumpkin, 473–4
red mullet
  marinated, 332
  with raisins and pine nuts, 333–4
  in tomato sauce, 334

Reformation, 44
Reform Judaism, 78
reines claudes, hlou aux, 493
reizflomesa, 159
reiz kugel, 178–9
relish, chili, 243
relleno, 431
Renaissance, 482–3
Reuben, M., 345
rice, 445–6
  with artichokes, 463–4
  basic ways of cooking, 444,
    446
  boiled, 446
  cake, with cheese, 464–5
  chicken and, 364
    beef and rice stuffing, 356–7
    with carrots, 457
    croquettes, 377–8
    pie, 451–2
    Sabbath pot, 441–3
  coconut yellow, 448
  croquettes
    with chicken, 377–8
    meat filled, 418–20
  dumplings
    ground rice, in hamud sauce
      with, 466
    with meat filling, 415–17
  with eggplant, 464
  with fava beans, 461
  fried, 444
  with fruit, 458
  ginger garlic, 463
  green pea pulau, 462–3
  with green vegetable sauce, 465
  lamb stuffed with, with sour
    cherry sauce, 392–3
  and lentils
    brown, 460
    red, 459
  with meat, in bag, 456
  meat sauce for
    green herb sauce, 466–7
    yellow split pea, 467–8
  peppers stuffed with, 539
  with prunes and raisins, 159
  pudding, 178–9, 571–2
    baked, 572
    coconut creamed, 573
  reheating, 446

Illustration Credits

The illustrations reproduced in this book were provided with the permission and courtesy of the following:

Beth Hatefutsoth, Museum of the Jewish Diaspora, Tel Aviv: pages 35, 89, 224, 372 (Carmel Berkson), 374 (Carmel Berkson), 497, 524

Jacques Hassoun, Éditions du Scribe, from *Les Juifs d'Egypte:* page 9

The Jewish Museum, London: pages 228 (David Pearlman), 395 (Nain Dangoor), 568

Michael Riff's *The Face of Survival* (Valentine Mitchell, London): pages 50, 128, 182, 632

The Alfred Rubens Collection, London: pages 477, 587

Archive Gerard Sylvain (with thanks to Franck Landouch): pages 20, 32, 51, 52, 132, 133, 185, 205, 218, 233, 321, 337, 354, 432, 435, 450, 483, 496, 566, 598, 622

Roman Vishniac's *A Vanished World*, Farrar, Straus & Giroux, Inc., New York (© 1969, 1973, 1983): page 121

The Wiener Library, London: pages 27, 57 (State Ethnographic Museum, St. Petersburg), 98, 147 (Forward Art Section), 148 (Collection of Willy Puchner, Vienna), 189 (Eric Warburg, Hamburg)

The YIVO Institute for Jewish Research, New York: pages 46, 55 (Alter Kacyzne), 101, 199 (George Schwab), 201 (The Federation of Bessarabian Jews), 201 (Solomon Stedman), 453

Collection of Jean-Pierre Allali: page 436

Collection of Costis Copsidas, from *The Jews of Thessaloniki: Through the Postcards, 1886–1917* (self-published): pages 227, 286, 314

Collection of Naim Dangoor: pages 230, 349, 396, 419, 442

Collection of Sophie Jhirad: page 367

Collection of David Pearlman: pages 48, 71, 77, 154

Collection of the author: pages 5, 6, 523, 564

A NOTE ON THE TYPE

The text of this book was set in Centaur, the only typeface designed by Bruce Rogers (1870–1957), the well-known American book designer. A celebrated penman, Rogers based his design on the roman face cut by Nicolas Jenson in 1470 for his Eusebius. Jenson's roman surpassed all of its forerunners and even today, in modern recuttings, remains one of the most popular and attractive of all typefaces.

The italic used to accompany Centaur is Arrighi, designed by another American, Frederic Warde, and based on the chancery face used by Lodovico degli Arrighi in 1524.

Composed by North Market Street Graphics,
Lancaster, Pennsylvania
Printed and bound by Quebecor Printing,
Martinsburg, West Virginia
Designed by Cassandra J. Pappas

	DATE		